THE CAMBRIDGE WORLD HISTORY

*

VOLUME III

From the fourth millennium BCE to the early second millennium CE, the world became a world of cities. This volume explores this critical transformation, from the appearance of the earliest cities in Mesopotamia and Egypt to the rise of cities in Asia and the Mediterranean world, Africa, and the Americas. Through case studies and comparative accounts of key cities across the world, leading scholars chart the ways in which these cities grew as nodal points of pilgrimages and ceremonies, exchange, storage, and redistribution, and centers for defense and warfare. They show how in these cities, along with their associated and restructured countrysides, new rituals and ceremonies connected leaders with citizens and the gods, new identities as citizens were created, and new forms of power and sovereignty emerged. They also examine how this unprecedented concentration of people led to disease, violence, slavery, and subjugations of unprecedented kinds and scales.

NORMAN YOFFEE is Professor Emeritus in the Departments of Near Eastern Studies and Anthropology at the University of Michigan, and Senior Fellow at the Institute for the Study of the Ancient World at New York University, as well as editor of the Cambridge World Archaeology series.

THE CAMBRIDGE WORLD HISTORY

THE CAMBRIDGE WORLD HISTORY

The Cambridge World History is an authoritative new overview of the dynamic field of world history. It covers the whole of human history, not simply history since the development of written records, in an expanded time frame that represents the latest thinking in world and global history. With over 200 essays, it is the most comprehensive account yet of the human past, and it draws on a broad international pool of leading academics from a wide range of scholarly disciplines. Reflecting the increasing awareness that world history can be examined through many different approaches and at varying geographic and chronological scales, each volume offers regional, topical, and comparative essays alongside case studies that provide depth of coverage to go with the breadth of vision that is the distinguishing characteristic of world history.

Editor-In-Chief

MERRY E. WIESNER-HANKS, *Department of History, University of Wisconsin-Milwaukee*

Editorial Board

GRAEME BARKER, *Department of Archaeology, Cambridge University*
CRAIG BENJAMIN, *Department of History, Grand Valley State University*
JERRY BENTLEY, *Department of History, University of Hawaii*
DAVID CHRISTIAN, *Department of Modern History, Macquarie University*
ROSS DUNN, *Department of History, San Diego State University San Diego*
CANDICE GOUCHER, *Department of History, Washington State University*
MARNIE HUGHES-WARRINGTON, *Department of Modern History, Monash University*
ALAN KARRAS, *International and Area Studies Program, University of California, Berkeley*
BENJAMIN Z. KEDAR, *Department of History, Hebrew University*

THE CAMBRIDGE WORLD HISTORY

*

VOLUME III

Early Cities in Comparative Perspective, 4000 BCE–1200 CE

*

Edited by

NORMAN YOFFEE

CAMBRIDGE
UNIVERSITY PRESS

CAMBRIDGE
UNIVERSITY PRESS

University Printing House, Cambridge CB2 8BS, United Kingdom

One Liberty Plaza, 20th Floor, New York, NY 10006, USA

477 Williamstown Road, Port Melbourne, VIC 3207, Australia

314-321, 3rd Floor, Plot 3, Splendor Forum, Jasola District Centre, New Delhi - 110025, India

79 Anson Road, #06-04/06, Singapore 079906

Cambridge University Press is part of the University of Cambridge.

It furthers the University's mission by disseminating knowledge in the pursuit of education, learning and research at the highest international levels of excellence.

www.cambridge.org
Information on this title: www.cambridge.org/9781108407694

First published 2015
Paperback edition first published 2017

A catalogue record for this publication is available from the British Library

Library of Congress Cataloging in Publication data
The Cambridge world history / edited by Norman Yoffee, University of Michigan.
volumes cm
Includes bibliographical references and index.
Contents: v. 1. Introduction – v. 2. A world with agriculture, 12,000 BCE-400 CE – v. 3. Early cities and comparative history, 4000 BCE-1200 CE – v. 4. A world with states, empires, and networks, 1200 BCE-900 CE – v. 5. Expanding webs of exchange and conquest, 500 CE-1500 CE – v. 6, pt. 1. The construction of a global world, 1400–1800 CE: Foundations – v. 6, pt. 2. The construction of a global world, 1400–1800 CE: Patterns of change – v. 7, pt. 1. Production, destruction, and connection, 1750-present : Structures, spaces, and boundary making – v. 7, pt. 2. Production, destruction, and connection, 1750-present: Shared transformations.
ISBN 978-0-521-19008-4 (v. 3: Hardback : alk. Paper) 1. World history. I. Yoffee, Norman, editor.
D20.C195 2014
909–dc23 2014026364

ISBN 978-0-521-19008-4 Hardback
ISBN 978-1-108-40769-4 Paperback

Contents

Contents

Contents

Figures

Maps

Tables

Contributors

SUSAN M. ALT, Indiana University, Bloomington

JOHN BAINES, University of Oxford

SARAH C. CLAYTON, University of Wisconsin, Madison

GEOFF EMBERLING, University of Michigan

THOMAS G. GARRISON, University of Southern California

GERARDO GUTIÉRREZ, University of Colorado, Boulder

STEPHEN HOUSTON, Brown University

JOHN W. JANUSEK, Vanderbilt University

ANN E. KILLEBREW, Pennsylvania State University

ALEX R. KNODELL, Carleton College

JEFFERY D. KRUCHTEN, University of Illinois, Urbana-Champaign

DANNY LAW, University of Texas

RODERICK J. MCINTOSH, Yale University

FRANÇOISE MICHEAU, University of Paris I

IAN MORRIS, Stanford University

HANS J. NISSEN, Free University of Berlin

ADELHEID OTTO, Ludwig-Maximilians-University of Munich

TIMOTHY R. PAUKETAT, University of Illinois, Urbana-Champaign

CARLA M. SINOPOLI, University of Michigan

MIRIAM T. STARK, University of Hawaii, Mānoa

NICOLA TERRENATO, University of Michigan

GARY URTON, Harvard University

WANG HAICHENG, University of Washington

NORMAN YOFFEE, University of Michigan; Institute for the Study of the Ancient World, New York University

Preface

The Cambridge Histories have long presented authoritative multi-volume overviews of historical topics, with chapters written by specialists. The first of these, the *Cambridge Modern History*, planned by Lord Acton and appearing after his death from 1902 to 1912, had fourteen volumes and served as the model for those that followed, which included the seven-volume *Cambridge Medieval History* (1911–1936), the twelve-volume *Cambridge Ancient History* (1924–1939), the thirteen-volume *Cambridge History of China* (1978–2009), and more specialized multi-volume works on countries, religions, regions, events, themes, and genres. These works are designed, as the *Cambridge History of China* puts it, to be the "largest and most comprehensive" history in the English language of their topic, and, as the *Cambridge History of Political Thought* asserts, to cover "every major theme."

The *Cambridge World History* both follows and breaks with the model set by its august predecessors. Presenting the "largest and most comprehensive" history of the world would take at least 300 volumes – and a hundred years – as would covering "every major theme." Instead the series provides an overview of the dynamic field of world history in seven volumes over nine books. It covers all of human history, not simply that since the development of written records, in an expanded time frame that represents the newest thinking in world history. This broad time frame blurs the line between archaeology and history, and presents both as complementary approaches to the human past. The volume editors include archaeologists as well as historians, and have positions at universities in the United States, Britain, France, Australia, and Israel. The essays similarly draw on a broad author pool of historians, art historians, anthropologists, classicists, archaeologists, economists, sociologists, and area studies specialists, who come from universities in Australia, Britain, Canada, China, Estonia, France, Germany, India, Israel, Italy, Japan, the Netherlands, New Zealand, Poland, Portugal, Sweden, Switzerland, Singapore, and the United States. They include very senior scholars whose works have helped to form the field, and also mid-career and younger scholars whose research will continue to shape it in the future. Some of the authors are closely associated with the rise of world history as a distinct research and teaching field, while others describe what they do primarily as global history, transnational history, international history, or comparative history. (Several of the essays in Volume I trace the development of these overlapping, entangled, and at times competing fields.) Many authors are simply specialists on their topic who the editors thought could best explain this to a broader audience or reach beyond their comfort zones into territory that was new.

Reflecting the increasing awareness that world history can be examined through many different approaches and at varying geographic and chronological scales, each volume offers several types of essays, including regional, topical, and comparative ones, along with case studies that provide depth to go with the breadth of vision that is the distinguishing characteristic of world history. Volume I (*Introducing World History* [to 10,000 BCE]) introduces key frames of analysis that shape the making of world history across time periods, with essays on overarching approaches, methods, and themes. It then includes a group of essays on the Palaeolithic, covering the 95 percent of human history up to 10,000 BCE. From that point on, each volume covers a shorter time period than its predecessor, with slightly overlapping chronologies volume to volume to reflect the complex periodization of a truly global history. The editors chose the overlapping chronologies, and stayed away from traditional period titles (e.g. "classical" or "early modern") intentionally to challenge standard periodization to some degree. The overlapping chronologies also allow each volume to highlight geographic disjunctures and imbalances, and the ways in which various areas influenced one another. Each of the volumes centers on a key theme or cluster of themes that the editors view as central to the period covered in the volume and also as essential to an understanding of world history as a whole.

Volume II (*A World with Agriculture*, 12,000 BCE–500 CE) begins with the Neolithic, but continues into later periods to explore the origins of agriculture and agricultural communities in various regions of the world, as well as to discuss issues associated with pastoralism and hunter-fisher-gatherer economies. It traces common developments in the more complex social structures and cultural forms that agriculture enabled, and then presents a series of regional overviews accompanied by detailed case studies from many different parts of the world.

Volume III (*Early Cities in Comparative Perspective*, 4000 BCE–1200 CE) focuses on early cities as motors of change in human society. Through case studies of cities and comparative chapters that address common issues, it traces the creation and transmission of administrative and information technologies, the performance of rituals, the distribution of power, and the relationship of cities with their hinterlands. It has a broad and flexible chronology to capture the development of cities in various regions of the world and the transformation of some cities into imperial capitals.

Volume IV (*A World with States, Empires, and Networks*, 1200 BCE–900 CE) continues the analysis of processes associated with the creation of larger-scale political entities and networks of exchange, including those generally featured in accounts of the rise of "classical civilizations," but with an expanded time frame that allows the inclusion of more areas of the world. It analyzes common social, economic, cultural, political, and technological developments, and includes chapters on slavery, religion, science, art, and gender. It then presents a series of regional overviews, each accompanied by a case study or two examining one smaller geographic area or topic within that region in greater depth.

Volume V (*Expanding Webs of Exchange and Conquest*, 500 CE–1500 CE) highlights the growing networks of trade and cross-cultural interaction that were a hallmark of the millennium covered in the volume, including the expansion of text-based religions and the transmission of science, philosophy, and technology. It explores social structures, cultural institutions, and significant themes such as the environment, warfare, education, the family, and courtly cultures on both a global and Eurasian scale, and continues the examination of state formation begun in Volume IV with chapters on polities and empires in Asia, Africa, Europe, and the Americas.

The first five volumes each appear in a single book, but the last two are double volumes covering the periods conventionally known as the early modern and modern, an organization signaling the increasing complexity of an ever more globalized world in the last half-millennium, as well as the expanding base of source materials and existing historical analyses for these more recent eras. Volume VI (*The Construction of a Global World, 1400–1800 CE*) traces the increasing biological, commercial, and cultural exchanges of the period, and explores regional and transregional political, cultural, and intellectual developments. The first book within this volume, "Foundations," focuses on global matrices that allowed this increasingly interdependent world to be created, including the environment, technology, and disease; crossroads and macro-regions such as the Caribbean, the Indian Ocean, and Southeast Asia in which connections were especially intense; and large-scale political formations, particularly maritime and land-based empires such as Russia, the Islamic Empires, and the Iberian Empires that stretched across continents and seas. The second book within this volume, "Patterns of Change," examines global and regional migrations and encounters, and the economic, social, cultural, and institutional structures that both shaped and were shaped by these, including trade networks, law, commodity flows, production processes, and religious systems.

Volume VII (*Production, Destruction, and Connection, 1750–Present*) examines the uneven transition to a world with fossil fuels and an exploding human population that has grown ever more interactive through processes of globalization. The first book within this double volume, "Structures, Spaces, and Boundary Making," discusses the material situations within which our crowded world has developed, including the environment, agriculture, technology, energy, and disease; the political movements that have shaped it, such as nationalism, imperialism, decolonization, and communism; and some of its key regions. The second book, "Shared Transformations?", explores topics that have been considered in earlier volumes, including the family, urbanization, migration, religion, and science, along with some that only emerge as global phenomena in this era, such as sports, music, and the automobile, as well as specific moments of transition, including the Cold War and 1989.

Taken together, the volumes contain about 200 essays, which means the *Cambridge World History* is comprehensive, but certainly not exhaustive. Each volume editor has made difficult choices about what to include and what to leave out, a problem for all world histories since those of Herodotus and Sima Qian more than two millennia ago. Each volume is arranged in the way that the volume editor or editors have decided is most appropriate for the period, so that organizational schemata differ slightly from volume to volume. Given the overlapping chronologies, certain topics are covered in several different volumes because they are important for understanding the historical processes at the heart of each of these, and because we as editors decided that viewing key developments from multiple perspectives is particularly appropriate for world history. As with other *Cambridge Histories*, the essays are relatively lightly footnoted, and include a short list of further readings, the first step for readers who want to delve deeper into the field. In contrast to other *Cambridge Histories*, all volumes are being published at the same time, for the leisurely pace of the print world that allowed publication over several decades does not fit with twenty-first-century digital demands.

In other ways as well, the *Cambridge World History* reflects the time in which it has been conceptualized and produced, just as the *Cambridge Modern History* did. Lord Acton envisioned his work, and Cambridge University Press described it, as "a history of the world," although in only a handful of chapters out of several hundred were the principal actors individuals, groups, or polities outside of Europe and North America. This is not surprising, although the identical self-description of the *New Cambridge Modern History* (1957–1979), with a similar balance of topics, might be a bit more so. The fact that in 1957 – and even in 1979 – Europe would be understood as "the world" and as the source of all that was modern highlights the power and longevity of the perspective we have since come to call "Eurocentric." (In other languages, there are perspectives on world history that are similarly centered on the regions in which they have been produced.) The continued focus on Europe in the mid-twentieth century also highlights the youth of the fields of world and global history, in which the conferences, professional societies, journals, and other markers of an up-and-coming field have primarily emerged since the 1980s, and some only within the last decade. The *Journal of World History*, for example, was first published in 1990, the *Journal of Global History* in 2005, and *New Global Studies* in 2007.

World and global history have developed in an era of intense self-reflection in all academic disciplines, when no term can be used unself-consciously and every category must be complicated. Worries about inclusion and exclusion, about diversity and multi-vocality are standard practice in sub-fields of history and related disciplines that have grown up in this atmosphere. Thus as we editors sought topics that would give us a balance between the traditional focus in world history on large-scale political and economic processes carried out by governments and commercial elites and newer concerns with cultural forms, representation, and meaning, we also sought to include topics that have been important in different national historiographies. We also attempted to find authors who would provide geographic balance along with a balance between older and younger voices. Although the author pool is decidedly broader geographically – and more balanced in terms of gender – than it was in either of the Cambridge Modern Histories, it is not as global as we had hoped. Contemporary world and global history is overwhelmingly Anglophone, and, given the scholarly diaspora, disproportionately institutionally situated in the United States and the United Kingdom. Along with other disparities in our contemporary world, this disproportion is, of course, the result of the developments traced in this series, though the authors might disagree about which volume holds the key to its origins, or whether one should spend much time searching for origins at all.

My hopes for the series are not as sweeping as Lord Acton's were for his, but fit with those of Tapan Raychaudhuri and Irfan Habib, the editors of the two-volume *Cambridge Economic History of India* (1982). In the preface to their work, they comment: "We only dare to hope that our collaborative effort will stimulate discussion and help create new knowledge which may replace before many years the information and analysis offered in this volume." In a field as vibrant as world and global history, I have no doubts that such new transformative knowledge will emerge quickly, but hope this series will provide an entrée to the field, and a useful overview of its state in the early twenty-first century.

MERRY E. WIESNER-HANKS

Introduction: a history of
the study of early cities

NORMAN YOFFEE WITH NICOLA TERRENATO

M. I. Finley[1] provides the essential challenge to archaeologists studying ancient cities:

> It is difficult, perhaps impossible, to catch the 'feel' of an ancient city. What we see is either a ruin or a shadow overlain by centuries of subsequent habitation. Nothing can be deader than the models or reconstructions of ancient buildings and districts: they may serve to recreate the formal interactions of the architects but they mislead badly in recreating the living reality within a living community.

He could also have been talking about ancient historians whose data, in their own way, are as fragmentary as archaeological data, their reconstructions often elite-focused, formal, and drained of life. Texts shed dramatic points of light on ancient lifeways but give few clues as to how the points might be connected to form a picture of a vibrant community. And, if we have such urban textual lampposts and archaeological reconstructions of buildings and districts, how can we know why people came to live in cities, how cities flourished and/or collapsed, and how citizens understood their lives?

In the ancient world, from the fourth millennium BCE to the early second millennium CE (which is the timespan covered in this third volume of the *Cambridge World History*) the world was a world of cities. That is, the majority of the population lived in communities, not isolated farmsteads. Some of these communities were cities; and towns, villages, and the countryside, which was populated by pastoralists, were connected in various ways to cities.

But what is a "city"? The sages (some of whom are reviewed below) have replied: cities are permanent settlements that are rather large in area and

I thank Merry Wiesner-Hanks for inviting me to edit this volume. I also thank Roger Bagnall, Director of the Institute for the Study of the Ancient World, for hosting the conference of authors that led to this volume; Merry Wiesner-Hanks also contributed support for the conference. Finally, thanks to all contributors for their stimulating essays and goodwill for this project.
[1] Moses I. Finley, "The City," *Opus* 6–8 (1987–9), 309.

have quite a few people, several thousands of them, who live quite closely together and are socially diverse; there are leaders and their minions who keep track of people and things in the city and which leave and enter the city; cities have a center with impressive architecture that affords and/or restricts political, social, and/or ideological activity; cities depend on food-stuffs that are produced in the related countryside for the benefit of those in the cities; cities provide certain services and manufactured goods to people in the related countryside and acquire, through long-distance trade, luxury and utilitarian goods; cities provide a sense of civic identity to the people living in them (and related hinterlands), and they are the arenas in which rulers demonstrate their special connections to the high gods and the cosmos; and cities are containers of potential social drama and discontent among various competing/cooperating social groups and their local leaders; cities create and incubate significant environmental and health problems.

I won't be surprised if readers are not content with this smorgasbord-like "definition" of a city, whose parts are in fact gleaned from thinkers in many fields. Although I may be accused (rightly) of avoiding a simple and unam-biguous definition of the city, I submit that, together, these partial defin-itions are in fact variables that can structure research into ancient cities. There will be many exceptions and qualifications to the variables in my sprawling definition. This definition is really a kind of "ideal-typical" model (in the Weberian sense) that authors in this volume amend, emend, and liberally qualify. For the still discontented who would insist on a simple and tidy definition of cities, I refer you to the wisdom of G. F. Nietzsche, who said: "You can only define things that have no history."[2] In any case, the search for a definition of "the city," so that archaeologists can identify it, as opposed to other forms of settlement, is a relic of disco-age social theory. Modern archaeologists study how early cities are structured, what leaders in cities do and also what they do not do, how people in cities worked and worshipped, why many early cities are fragile, many resisting incorporation into territorial units, as well as a host of other activities and behaviors that can be studied in light of the variables of urban life that are posited above.

The justification for this volume is that early cities (that is, those cities that evolved after the time when there were no cities – see the previous

---

[2] Friedrich Nietzsche, "Definierbar ist nur Das, was keine Geschichte hat," in Friedrich Nietzsche, *Zur Geneologie der Moral: Eine Streitschrift. Zweite Abhandlung: "Schuld," "Schlechtes Gewissen," und Verwandtes*, O. Höffer (ed.) (Berlin: Akademie Verlag, 2004), p. 820.

volume in this series) were not rare. The earliest cities appeared in Mesopotamia and Egypt at the end of the fourth millennium BCE, in South Asia in the early–middle of the third millennium BCE, and in China not long after that. These cities developed independently in their regions. Subsequently, in Asia and in the Mediterranean world, numerous cities appeared and multiplied. In Africa outside the Nile Valley, cities were founded in the first millennium CE. In the New World, cities appeared early in the first millennium BCE in Middle America, slightly later in South America, and at least one city emerged at about 1000 CE in the Middle West of the USA. This volume attempts to "catch the feel" of these cities and to do so it advances some distinctive and new approaches.

Before describing these new approaches, however, it is necessary to review how and why cities evolved, although this is not the focus of this volume.[3] Cities evolved as "collecting basins" in which long-term trends toward social differentiation and stratification crystallized independently all over the planet. The earliest cities in many regions, like Mesopotamia, Egypt, South Asia, North China, in the Maya area, and in the Andean region, were competitors; indeed, the first "states" were usually "city-states" that did not encompass large, territorial expanses within a single political structure.

The many and often differentiated social groups that lived in the countryside in modest villages and small towns were drawn into and became recombined in cities. These cities grew as nodal points of pilgrimages and ceremonies, exchange, storage and redistribution, and as centers for defense and warfare. In these cities, along with their associated and restructured countrysides, new identities as citizens were created but did not entirely supplant existing identities as members of economic, kin, and ethnic groups. In the earliest cities, new rituals and ceremonies connected leaders with citizens and the gods. These displayed and justified the supremacy and legitimacy of the new rulers and reaffirmed their command over the social order. The social roles and practices of citizens were routinized within the urban layout of monumental constructions, streets and pathways, walls and courtyards. The built environment itself demonstrated the superior access to knowledge and planning and control held by the rulers, ostensibly on behalf of all. Statecraft in the earliest cities involved providing an order to the

---

[3] See Norman Yoffee, *Myths of the Archaic State: Evolution of the Earliest Cities, States, and Civilizations* (Cambridge: Cambridge University Press, 2005) from which this section is drawn.

present, which the rulers proclaimed in literature as timeless and the goal of history. Newly created urban landscapes overlay but did not eliminate the unruliness of a society composed of many groups, each with its own interests and orientations.

The growth of cities was often revolutionary, in the sense used by V. Gordon Childe (see below): early cities were not simply accretions on a stable rural base, nor were they simply the apex of a settlement pyramid. Settlements in the hinterlands now became "peripheries" of cities, and so in the evolution of cities, social life both in and outside of cities changed utterly, redefined in the process of urbanization and ruralization (as the countryside itself was recreated because of its new relation to cities).

A history of research, part one

If the above, generalized overview of the evolution of cities outlines import-ant commonalities in the evolution of cities around the world, it does not foreclose an investigation into significant divergences in the history of early cities nor critical distinctions in the nature of urban life. The chapters in this book speak precisely to these differences. Furthermore, the variations in urban life can only be identified and explained through a comparison of cities and social institutions.

Before describing how the following chapters will employ the compara-tive method, I present a brief history of the study of early cities. This will provide perspective on the definition of cities and their evolution presented above. (This digest of studies can be supplemented by reference to the "further readings" to this chapter.)

Today archaeologists have renewed interest in ancient cities, just as their geographer, sociologist, and historian colleagues and the public are con-cerned about the plight of cities in the modern world. Today, cities constitute 50 percent of the world's population, generate about 75 percent of the world's gross national product, consume 60 percent of the world's water, and emit 80 percent of global greenhouse gases.[4] The number of books about modern cities is legion, and there are valuable companions to the study of cities,[5]

---

[4] Thomas Gladwin, "Doomsday Alert: Megachallenges Confronting Urban Modernity," *Journal of the International Institute, University of Michigan* 16 (2008), 14–16.
[5] Gary Bridge and Sophie Watson (eds.), *A Companion to The City* (Oxford: Blackwell, 2000).

encyclopedias of cities,[6] evocative descriptions of modern cities,[7] and claims that cities are the "engines of innovation."[8] This last assertion is, of course, not new: to cite only studies by modern urbanologists, it was argued by Jane Jacobs[9] for the earliest cities, and she has been echoed by Edward Soja.[10]

The view of the city as locus of rational behavior and the good life harkens to the earliest works in the Western tradition on cities by Greek and Roman philosophers and historians, like Aristotle, Theophrastus, Pausanias, Strabo, and Vitruvius, and others. They contrasted urban life, which was ideally suited for political discourse, that is, as a place for self-government, and "civilized" behavior, and considered the countryside as backward, populated by simple rustics.[11] Of course, one can also find accounts of the city as the home of thieves, swindlers, tyrants, and malcontents. Mesopotamian literature, preceding the thoughts of Greeks and Romans by several thousand years, had much the same variety of views about cities and the countryside, as did early Chinese writers in the first millennium BCE. In the fourteenth century CE Ibn Khaldun wrote how urban life became corrupt and needed to be periodically cleansed by noble barbarians (nomads) from the countryside. There is not much new, it seems, in modern accounts of cities, only degrees of foregrounding social institutions and making moral judgments.

It is not necessary to review the history of evolutionary thought in the seventeenth and eighteenth centuries in which speculations of laws of society and laws of nature were propounded. Ideas of progress and of the great chain of being did not, of course, rely on archaeological evidence. Cain and his son Enoch were the first city-builders according to the writer of Genesis, and the antiquities of Greece and Rome had little prehistory except that speculated in classical literature. The evolution of cities played little or no part in the discussions in the West that focused on the distinctions

---

[6] Peter Clark, *Cities in World History* (Oxford: Oxford University Press, 2013); and Ray Hutchison, *The Encyclopedia of Urban Studies* (Thousand Oaks, CA: Sage, 2010).
[7] Mark Kurlansky, *The Big Oyster: History on the Half Shell* (New York: Random House, 2007); and Mark Mazower, *Salonika, City of Ghosts* (New York: Knopf, 2004); Gary Wills, *Venice: Lion City* (New York: Simon & Schuster, 2001).
[8] Edward Glaeser, *Triumph of the City: How Our Greatest Invention Makes Us Richer, Smarter, Greener, Healthier, and Happier* (New York: Penguin, 2011).
[9] Jane Jacobs, *The Economy of Cities* (New York: Random House, 1969) argued that the earliest cities (like Çatal Höyük in Neolithic Anatolia) evolved before farming, and domestication of plants and animals ensued to provide food for the cities.
[10] Edward Soja, *Postmetropolis* (Oxford: Blackwell, 2000).
[11] Moses I. Finley, "The Ancient City," *Comparative Studies in Society and History* 19 (1977), 305–27 presents a digest of classical accounts.

between "community" (Gemeinschaft) and "society" (Gesellschaft) by Tönnies or between "status" and "contract" by Maine. The evidence, such as it was, came from travelers and colonials observing "native" people, those thought to be in a "state of nature" and without history, which by implication meant non-urban. Consideration of the evolution of cities changed in the middle of the nineteenth century when the great geological and evolutionary time-depth of the world was established, and ancient Mesopotamian cities, known only from garbled references in classical sources and the Bible, were beginning to be excavated. Arguably, the first modern attempt to understand the ancient history of cities as living communities was developed by Fustel de Coulanges in 1864. Whereas scholars today cite his work in inevitable homage to a scholarly ancestor, it is due more careful consideration than that.

Fustel's ancient city

It is a long-established commonplace, when discussing ancient cities (especially in the Mediterranean context) at least to mention Fustel, or even to take his volume *La cité antique* as the point of departure for a chronological review of the relevant literature.[12] Ancient historians, anthropologists, and archaeologists, however, typically pay little more than lip service to his work, which is generally seen as outdated, quirky, and somewhat at odds with the later discourse on cities in these disciplines. Significantly, his legacy is instead much more influential in historical sociology and in urban studies, where his work is considered seminal and his influence on figures like Émile Durkheim, Werner Sombart, and Max Weber is carefully retraced and analyzed. Considering how in recent years the disparate threads of scholarship on pre-modern cities seem to be in the process of being tied together again in holistic approaches, it is arguable (as well as desirable) that Fustel's views be more seriously taken into account by all those who study ancient urbanism.

Numa Denis Fustel de Coulanges was trained in the 1840s and 1850s as a Greco-Roman historian at the École Normale in Paris.[13] His Latin dissertation was on the Roman hearth goddess Vesta as a powerful force in the emergence of political institutions. He expanded it and published it as his first major book in 1862, with the title *La cité antique. Étude sur le culte, le droit,*

---

[12] This section is written by Nicola Terrenato.
[13] François Hartog, *Le XIXe siècle et l'histoire: le cas Fustel de Coulanges* (Paris: Presses Universitaire de France, 1988).

les institutions de la Grèce et de Rome (Paris 1864). In the meantime, he had been appointed to a chair of general history at the University of Strasbourg, and he progressively devoted himself almost exclusively to medieval and modern French history, which he later taught at the Sorbonne and at his alma mater, the École Normale, till his death in 1889. This appeared to him a more urgent and patriotic undertaking than ancient history. *La cité antique* thus stands in splendid isolation in Fustel's personal intellectual trajectory, as well as in the context of late nineteenth-century historiography of the Greek and Roman world.

Fustel's main thesis is that family and other kin structures are fundamental elements and building blocks of ancient cities and that religion in general and the ancestor cult in particular provided the initial cement for the aggregation of population in cities. Extended family groups developed private property as a result of the need to place their dead on land they controlled, so that their worship as deified ancestors could be officiated by the elder male as a high priest of the group. Several family groups would then come together to form a wider lineage, again under the rule of a leader with priestly prerogatives. The city was a natural transposition of this basic structure on a larger scale, with the king as high priest of the wider lineage system represented by the citizens, and the city's territory was the private property of the polity. The state, in other words, was a new entity of a higher order but structurally similar to the families and lineages that continued their existence within the new organization.

A formation process of this kind would explain the emergence of political institutions in all Greek and Italian states in the early first millennium BCE (and resonates, with qualifications, for many other states, too, as will be noted below). While this in itself amounted to a daring comparative stance for classicists of his time, it is clear that Fustel believed that the model could be applied at least to all the cultures that shared what was then called Indo-European (or Indo-Aryan) religion and possibly beyond. In letters and unpublished papers, he explicitly considered Indian and even Phoenician, Chinese, and Native American cities as potential comparanda, although he never expressed this in print.

La cité antique is beautifully written, and it had considerable success with the educated public, not unlike a number of other pioneering books in the social studies that came out in the same decades and dealt with pre-modern culture, such as Maine's *Ancient Law*, Morgan's *Ancient Society*, or, slightly later, Frazer's *The Golden Bough*. While Fustel enjoyed high professional recognition – he was for a while the director of the prestigious École

Normale, and even taught history privately to the Empress Eugénie – his first book never really became a part of the ancient history curriculum, as it was considered too general and vague in its scope and too summary in its treatment of the primary and secondary literature. Fustel made no attempt at determining any chronological framework, nor did he detail the specifics of the process, an approach that was completely at odds with the dry philological historiography that was being codified at the time by the German school led by Mommsen (whom Fustel openly detested).

It was only in the second half of the twentieth century that some better-read classicists, such as Arnaldo Momigliano and Moses Finley, went back to Fustel in their search for a more interpretive ancient history, one closer to the social sciences than to the humanities. While they correctly reconstructed the intellectual milieu from which Fustel's vision had arisen, they generally failed to see much contemporary relevance for it. Meanwhile in Paris, academic filial piety had driven some *normaliens* to seek inspiration in his work, most notably Georges Glotz,[14] who explicitly tried to reimplant Fustel's ideas within the specialist discourse on ancient Greece.

At the same time as ancient historians were rethinking their discipline, social anthropologists were doing the same, developing evolutionary models to explain the emergence of states and cities. Like all revolutionary intellectual movements, they eagerly went back beyond the generation that had preceded them to look for early prophets of the new ideas. In doing this they were happy to recruit Morgan (who himself knew and referenced Fustel), as an early proponent of a stepwise succession of social organisms of increasing complexity. While some, like Clyde Kluckhohn, acknowledged the existence of Fustel, his scope seemed very narrow (mainly on ancient Greece and Rome) and its culture-historical approach too little concerned with the material conditions connected with the rise of political complexity. Fustel's insistence on religion and worldviews was enough to relegate him to a footnote in prefaces at best.

In sharp contrast with his reception among historians and anthropologists, Fustel was from the start hailed by the new discipline of sociology as one of its founding fathers. This was undoubtedly helped by Émile Durkheim, who was Fustel's star student at the École Normale – he dedicated his dissertation on Montesquieu to the memory of Fustel – but is also probably symptomatic of an intellectual bifurcation that happened

---

[14] Georges Glotz, *La cité grecque, evolution de l'humanité collective* (Paris: La Renaissance du Livre, 1928).

at that time and whose effects are still arguably current today.[15] Whereas theoretical reflections on urban life in all its cognitive aspects became a staple of sociological thought, archaeologists studying cities (see below) tended to ignore belief systems or regard them as epiphenomenal correlates of material conditions. Only occasionally cross-fertilization took place, as in the case of Max Weber (see below), who was originally trained as an ancient historian but who championed the new field of sociology and was also read by economists, anthropologists, and other social scientists. Weber certainly knew Fustel's work, to the point of paraphrasing extensive portions of *La cité antique*[16] in his *Wirtschaft und Gesellschaft* (1922). While Weber explained urban processes in materialist and institutional terms, which Fustel never did, it is interesting to note that Weber too did not ignore questions of ideology and its role in shaping the urban experience.

Another discipline that revered Fustel as one of its cherished ancestors was the history of religions. This is not surprising when one considers the critical role that Fustel assigned to religious beliefs in urban life. It is also clear that the study of non-monotheistic religions developed into one of the very few disciplines whose comparative approach included the classical world (which was marginalized in anthropological archaeology). Roman religion was and is studied in the context of other religions, and this is exactly what Fustel had been advocating ever since his doctoral dissertation. Indeed, it has been suggested that Georges Dumézil's lifelong commitment to explaining Roman religion in terms of Indo-European beliefs and culture was a direct extension of Fustel's original vision, in line with what happened in comparative linguistics.

Now that, as this volume asserts, the time has come for a comparative approach to pre-modern cities, it is relevant to assess what lasting value *La cité antique* may have. What is striking in reading the book today is how it locates itself in a peculiar space above history, as it were, but below pure political science (or structuralist timelessness). There is no chronology and not enough actual events in Fustel's study to be anything like an historical narrative, and yet it is not completely atemporal or abstract. Fustel's overriding concern is to understand where the very idea

---

[15] François Héran, "L'institution démotivée: De Fustel de Coulanges à Durkheim et au-delà," *Revue Française de Sociologie* 2 8 (1987), 67–97.
[16] Max Weber, *The City*, Don Martindale and Gertrud Neuwirth (trans.) (New York: Free Press, 1958).

of city originated and to reconstruct why participants in the process created cities in the form that they did, without relying on political abstractions. Fustel's city is made of actual people whose lives were structured by traditions and mentalities, but who also made decisions that led to social change.

There is much in *La cité antique* that is a harbinger of many current ideas. His insistence on the ideological sphere, for instance, certainly appears in many theories being applied to cities today. New discoveries about the central importance of religion in early and even pre-agricultural sites (like Göbekli Tepe in Turkey and Poverty Point in Louisiana) lend intriguing support to Fustel's theses about the importance of religion in early settled life.

Furthermore, Fustel's emphasis on religion as a way to shape relations between the natural world and the social world helps to frame the emergence of sociopolitical complexity in terms of the actual cognitive horizon of the actors involved. Fustel is also adamant that the *anciens* have nothing to do with the *modernes* and that any analogy with our time can only be grossly misleading. Such a perspective makes it impossible to think teleologically about political institutions.

Fustel arguably laid the groundwork for the concept of *mentalité* that would later be at the center of the historical and social thought of the Braudelian Annales school (ironically developed at his institution's arch-rival École des Hautes Études). He forces his readers to imagine what it would involve to be constrained by beliefs and behavioral norms that are very different from ours and still bring a city into existence. His most remarkable insight is that this is accomplished by taking an existing cultural element – the family – and recasting it on a different scale to create something that is new but still feels familiar and understandable to those who become a part of it for the first time. Moreover, he sees the family as the only *vrai corps* of ancient societies, rejecting any influence of modern individualism (a product of Christianity in his view).

Fustel's masterpiece is, like several other great essays of that glorious second half of the nineteenth century, a suggestive and engrossing read. It is certainly off the mark in many details – for instance, there is ample evidence against the notion that early Romans were buried on their private family land – but this does not detract from the fascinating cultural landscape it paints. *La cité antique* not only shaped modern thought about cities, but it also rings quite relevant in many modern studies of early cities.

A history of research, part two

Several strains of thought in the nineteenth century in Europe changed the way people thought about cities in the modern and ancient worlds. The first was in the new field of economic geography, which considered the formal spatial relation of the city (and cities) to the countryside. This led, indirectly, to a revolution in archaeological research, as we shall see. J. H. von Thünen in 1826 posited that rings of land use (the first ring being the production of fruits and vegetables, then rings of timber and grain farming, and finally ranching) surrounded a city. This analysis depended on an idealized landscape of no natural barriers and no roads or other means of transportation and the rational behavior of farmers, who seek cost-efficient ways to market goods and minimize expense. Von Thünen was himself a landlord, and his work was meant to be practically implemented. Alfred Weber in 1909 similarly studied the location of industrial processing plants in relation to sites of raw materials and markets in order to minimize costs for industrialists. These and other studies led to the later formulation of "central place theory" by Walter Christaller in 1933 and August Lösch in 1940. The translation of Christaller's book by English geographers in 1966 influenced American archaeologists in the late 1960s and early 1970s (to be reviewed below).

The second stream of ideas about cities that have impacted how archaeologists and ancient historians have oriented their studies of early cities is the philosophical and sociological concern with the nature of cities as spaces for new kinds of behavior. This is exemplified in Ferdinand Tönnies' typological distinction between "Gemeinschaft" (community) and "Gesellschaft" (society) in 1887, noted above. In considering the evolutionary difference between the two types, he specifically referred to the differences between rural-based and urban commerce, and drew on Marx's and Engels' analysis of class-based society in cities. This concern with life in cities and their associated hinterlands set him apart from Maine's typology of status and contract in 1861 and influenced Durkheim's distinctions between organic and mechanical solidarities.

Marx himself, though writing about the division of labor in cities, class distinctions in cities, and modes of production and industrialization that clearly had urban bases, did not specifically theorize, as it were, the city. Ancient cities were based on slavery and the ownership of agricultural land. Feudal cities and medieval European trade emphasized the division between cities and the hinterland and the distinction between modes of production. In modern times, however, both cities and the countryside were characterized by the capitalist mode of production, and the city qua city is of lesser interest. Engels did excoriate the nature of the capitalist metropolis, but this is the nature of economics not urbanism per se.

Georg Simmel in 1903 wrote specifically about the nature of "mental life" in cities. From his observation post in Berlin, Simmel noted the crush of people in cities, the noise and smell of cities, and how individuals encountered each other as consumers and producers, strangers essentially, not as people sharing common interests.

Simmel not only influenced Walter Benjamin, who studied with him, but also Robert Park and thus the University of Chicago school of urban sociology, to which I now briefly turn, because of the quite clear link between the Chicagoans and the economic geography school of urban studies, founded by Von Thünen and Alfred Weber.

The Chicago school of urban sociology strongly influenced scholars from the university's departments of anthropology, such as Robert Redfield and Milton Singer, who posited a folk–urban dichotomy, and Robert Adams in anthropology and the Oriental Institute. Adams' students (especially Henry Wright) and students of his students greatly influenced urban studies in archaeology. Paul Wheatley, who moved from London to Chicago, was a later addition to the Chicago school of urban studies tradition, and, as we shall see, an important heir to the tradition of Fustel.

In the fascinating annotated bibliography in the collection of articles on the city (in the book entitled, *The City*[17]), Robert Park refers to Simmel as having contributed "the most important article on the city from the sociological perspective." Members of the Department of Sociology of the university were engaged in a number of studies on the city of Chicago itself. Ernest Burgess, resuming earlier studies of German geographers, discussed concentric rings of urban life, with businesses in the center and various residential areas radiating out from it. Various groups resided with people of their own economic status or ethnic origin, and the process depended on a continuous flow of migrants into the city.

Louis Wirth in 1938 wrote perhaps the capstone article of the Chicago school, "Urbanism as a Way of Life," in which he defined the city as "a relatively large, dense, and permanent settlement of socially heterogeneous individuals."[18] In his discussions of the anomie of individuals and the

---

[17] Robert Park and Ernest W. Burgess (eds.), *The City: Suggestions for the Investigation of Human Behavior in the Urban Environment* (Chicago: University of Chicago Press, 1984).
[18] Louis Wirth, "Urbanism as a Way of Life," *American Journal of Sociology* 44 (1938), 1–24.

inequalities of city life, the competition for scarce resources among various social groups, the mix of ethnic relations and the breakdown of ethnic groups (and much else), Wirth attempted to produce "a theory of urbanism" and of "urbanism as a form of social organization."

For Wirth, Max Weber's long essay "The City" provided inspiration. It is well known that Weber's conception of society challenged Marxist tenets of economic infrastructure and the class analysis of society. For Weber, cities encompassed numerous constellations of political, economic, and social relations. These various groups – not only formed through economically determined kinds of stratification, but also through ethnicity, "race," occupation, and religion – interacted, negotiated, and struggled for dominance. For Weber, cities were loci of political struggle and social conflict. Through his studies of ancient China, India, Israel, Greece, and Rome, Weber placed value on the specific constellations of authority and conflict and coalition building that arose in different regions. Although some of Weber's larger-scale comparisons, of ancient cities as consumer cities, and medieval and modern cities as producer cities, have been overtaken by historical and archaeological research, his approach of identifying different modes of institutional control over different resources, including the production and distribution of information, has important dimensions in the studies of cities in this volume and the nature of sociopolitical change in ancient cities.

The beginnings of archaeological research on the nature of ancient cities

Although excavations of ancient cities have a relatively long history, at least as early as the mid-nineteenth-century work in Neo-Assyrian capitals (and of course explorations in classical cities), the first meaningful study of the development and nature of early cities by an archaeologist is acknowledged to be that of the Australian, V. Gordon Childe, in his article of 1950, which appeared in a non-archaeological journal but rocketed to archaeological fame.[19] Childe's work depended on significant new archaeological data on South Asian and Maya cities, and work at Mesopotamian sites, especially at Uruk. Although he vaguely notes Egyptian cities, he doesn't actually cite any such cities there.[20]

---

[19] Michael Smith, "V. Gordon Childe and the Urban Revolution: A Historical Perspective on a Revolution in Urban Studies," *Town Planning Review* 80 (2009), 3–29, with extensive bibliography.
[20] Most Egyptologists of Childe's time held that there were no cities in Egypt.

He forcefully and convincingly argued that one could compare and contrast the earliest cities; such a comparison revealed that the earliest cities represented "a new economic change in the evolution of society."

Childe called the generalized evolutionary trend an "urban revolution," by which he meant that the world of cities was dramatically different than the world of village life in a time before cities. Cities were many times larger than the largest such villages, and there was a different division of labor in cities than in any previous time. Childe does not specifically refer to the pace of the evolution of cities as being itself revolutionary, but recent research does give credence to the rapid development of cities from a time of modest village life.

Childe famously posited "ten rather abstract criteria, all deducible from archaeological data" that "serve to distinguish even the earliest cities from any older or contemporary village." One may arrange these "criteria" or, as they are usually described, traits, into groups. The *population* of cities was very large, and the neighborhoods of cities were not simply composed of kin groups but formed on economic or political grounds. The *economy* of cities depended on agricultural surplus so that some residents of cities were not occupied by subsistence pursuits but were supported by farmers. Foreign trade in luxuries and "vital materials" was of a different order than in villages. The *new division of labor* was the most important characteristic of early cities. The nature of the division of labor could differ among the earliest cities, but the great divide between the tiny number of rulers and all others held cross-culturally. In cities, *politics* was transformed by new leaders – kings – who instituted taxes, administered the economy and social structure through writing, mathematics, and the calendar, and erected large buildings. The kings were part of the ruling class, which included priests and "civil and military leaders." Thus, temples, it seemed reasonable to infer, were part of the political structure. Finally, in the earliest cities new *cultural forms* were invented. These included art, that is, sculpture and painting and seal-cutting. (Apparently Childe was greatly impressed by the work on Mesopotamian cylinder seals that appeared in the early levels of Uruk and other Mesopotamian cities.) Additionally, a new ideology was created to legitimize the control by the new ruling class in cities.

The importance of Childe was acknowledged by Robert Adams of the University of Chicago, who is the pioneering figure in the archaeological study of the evolution of cities. Indeed, it was Adams' citations of Childe's article that brought it to the attention of archaeologists. Influenced by the tradition of urban sociologists and social anthropologists of his university,

Adams launched surface survey projects[21] and with the use of aerial photography he was able to trace settlement systems and canals, how they changed over time, and further to specify the relation between cities and the countryside, other cities, and the development of such relations. Adams further demonstrated the effectiveness of controlled comparison (between Mesopotamian and Mesoamerican cities) in his book, *Evolution of Urban Society*, 1966.[22] Adams' magnum opus, *Heartland of Cities*, demonstrated how archaeologists could contribute original insights into the study of the development of cities and it has inspired archaeologists ever since.[23]

Walter Christaller's "central place theory" influenced archaeologists after his original work of 1933 was translated into English in 1966,[24] and a group of geographers from the University of Cambridge produced a volume of studies on the concept in 1967.[25] Christaller, a German geographer, constructed an idealized landscape of a system of cities in which consumers would visit those towns nearest to them that would supply needed goods and services, and in which progressively larger cities would offer those "functions" and additional rarer functions, too. The system of cities under ideal conditions (that is, with no barriers to transportation and an evenly distributed population) would be hexagonal in shape and multiple hexagonal systems would populate the entire landscape.

Archaeologists, using reconnaissance survey methods, could rank the sites by their areas (as Adams had done), construct histograms of site sizes and so detect hierarchies of villages, towns, and cities in a region. A four-tiered site-size hierarchy (three levels of decision-making, which doesn't include the lowest tier), in which the flow of goods and services was controlled by the major city, was – in the influential study of Henry Wright and Gregory Johnson in 1975 – a state.[26] Thus, archaeologists, relying on site-size hierarchies, sought to identify the first states in the archaeological record. Using rank-size distributions, furthermore, archaeologists like Gregory Johnson

---

[21] Gordon Willey is rightly credited as inventing regional settlement pattern survey in his work in Peru (published in 1953), which delineated the spatial distribution of cultural activities across a landscape.

[22] Robert McC. Adams, *The Evolution of Urban Society* (Chicago: Aldine, 1966).

[23] Robert McC. Adams, *Heartland of Cities* (Chicago: University of Chicago Press, 1981).

[24] Walter Christaller, *Central Places in Southern Germany*, Carlisle W. Baskin (trans.) (Englewood Cliffs, NJ: Prentice Hall, 1966).

[25] Richard Chorley and Peter Haggett (eds.), *Models in Geography* (London: Methuen, 1967). Less influential, but cited by some archaeologists, was August Lösch's work, translated into English in 1954.

[26] Henry T. Wright and Gregory A. Johnson, "Population, Exchange, and Early State Formation in Southwestern Iran," *American Anthropologist* 77 (1975), 267–89.

could graph the nature of a settlement system as economically "mature," dominated by the first-ranking city in the system, or as a non-regulated system.[27]

In sum, archaeologists by the 1980s employed their new data about cities in regions and new tools for understanding the settlement patterns of cities (which were debated among geographers) to trace in sophisticated ways the development of cities and urban settlement patterns. However, they tended to ignore the challenge of Finley with which I began this chapter: how can archaeologists "catch the feel" of a city (that is, how people lived in cities) from all these formalized and quantitative data? How could cities as members of states be understood? How are early cities different from each other, and if they are, why is this the case?

Comparing early cities: why and how?

In the last decades an enormous amount of archaeological field work in and around ancient cities has been conducted all over the world. On the one hand, we now know a great deal about the earliest cities in China, which were the largest of all the ancient cities (with the site of Anyang at 1200 BCE extending more than 30 square kilometers and with perhaps 200,000 people),[28] and new work in China indicates the earliest cities may date even earlier, to the late third millennium BCE. In regions where cities have been known longer there have been new projects, and there have been thoughtful appraisals and syntheses of research. It would be impossible to list all of these fruitful studies here (but see "further readings" for some examples).

On the other hand, there have been few comparative studies of early cities. One theme in comparative research, however, has been new perspectives on a venerable concept, that of city-states. In 1997 Deborah Nichols and Thomas Charlton published *The Archaeology of City-States: Cross-Cultural Approaches*.[29] The authors, writing on Mesopotamia, Egypt, South Asia, China, the Maya, Mexico, and the Andes region, explored how the first states were indeed rather small, micro-states or city-states.

---

[27] Gregory A. Johnson, "Aspects of Regional Analysis in Archaeology," *Annual Review of Anthropology* 6 (1977), 479–508.

[28] In the mid-first millennium BCE, Babylon had a similarly large population and size, and imperial Rome was even larger.

[29] Deborah Nichols and Thomas Charlton (eds.), *The Archaeology of City-States* (Washington, D.C.: Smithsonian Institution, 1997).

Authors pointed out that a city-state consisted not only of a city but a considerable amount of hinterland with resources and people that were tied to the social and political organization in cities as well. Many such city-states were "peer-polities," in that they were part of a larger cultural configuration, and battled each other with one city occasionally effecting hegemony over many others. Such hegemonic control, however, tended to be ephemeral, and "collapsed" into the autonomous city-states that preceded the larger territorial state. Using the term "city-state," of course, reflected (to classicists) on the ancient Greek concept of the *polis* and (to medieval European historians) on Renaissance city-states in Italy. This had previously been explored in *The City-State in Five Cultures* in 1981.[30] In 2000, Mogens Herman Hansen published *A Comparative Study of Thirty City-State Cultures: An Investigation Conducted by the Copenhagen Polis Center* and in 2002 *A Comparative Study of Six City-State Cultures*. Although there are a few scholars who are suspicious of comparing anything with the Greek *polis*, other archaeologists, like Henry Wright,[31] now pursue the concept of the "polycentric" evolution of early cities and states, that is, *mutatis mutandis*, of "city-state cultures" (in Hansen's terminology).

Modern archaeologists have also moved from a time when the dominant questions about cities had to do with the extraction of surplus from the countryside and the unquestioned control in cities of kings and political leaders. Today one reads about councils, assemblies, oligarchies, factions, middle-level elites. One significant direction in new archaeological research is to reconsider the role of religion as an organizational principle in early cities and indeed in sites that precede cities. In this volume, we shall read cases of the ritual centrality in cities, an argument made forcefully by Paul Wheatley in 1971.[32] The work of Fustel is not simply a footnote in the history of research on early cities but an early step in such research.

We can now take up the challenges of Finley about the lifeways in ancient cities and explore the Weberian (and Fustelian) questions of the constitution of cities: How many kin and what kinds of ethnic groups are recombined in cities? What is the relation between city and rural countryside? How does

---

[30] Robert Griffeth and Carol G. Thomas, (eds.), *The City-State in Five Cultures* (Santa Barbara: ABC-Clio, 1981).

[31] Henry Wright, "The Polycentricity of the Archaic Civilizations," in Vernon Scarborough (ed.), *A Catalyst for Ideas: Anthropological Archaeology and the Legacy of Douglas W. Schwartz* (Santa Fe, NM: School of American Research Press, 2005), pp. 149–68.

[32] Paul Wheatley, *Pivot of the Four Quarters* (Edinburgh: University of Edinburgh Press, 1971).

economic and political struggle exist in cities? And how is such struggle resolved (or not) by new ideological formations and new claims for legitimacy from sovereigns? How are ideologies created and challenged?

The most recent volumes devoted to the study of early cities are not conspicuously comparative.[33] Not only do they lack formal comparative studies, but also they make little use of modern urban studies by non-archaeologists. It is not necessary to hold that urbanism is a category that transcends time and space in order to concede that modern urban studies offer insights into and new questions about ancient urban life. The differences between modern cities and ancient ones – in industrialization, globalization, kinds of transportation and communication systems, and types of government, to name but a few of them – are clear. Still, there are similarities in such matters as the numbers of people and heterogeneity of social groups living in cities and the dependence of cities on their hinterlands.

The structure of this volume

The purpose of this volume is to delineate some distinctive features of ancient cities and then compare these features. The book is divided into six sections (apart from the introduction and conclusion), each section consisting of three or four case-study chapters. In presentations of new research and short discussions of why the evidence exists, who produced it, and for what purpose, each chapter discusses urban life in one or more ancient cities in a region and how the cities interacted. The section authors then co-write a chapter about how the features of their cities can be compared and why there are differences among them. This summary chapter in each section is an experiment in controlled comparison. That is, whereas the comparisons of each of the distinctive features of early cities cannot be artificially limited to the case studies presented (and references outside the case studies are occasionally mentioned), these restricted comparisons are the beginnings of larger-scale comparative research.

---

[33] Joyce Marcus and Jeremy A. Sabloff (eds.), *The Ancient City: New Perspectives on Ancient Urbanism* (Santa Fe, NM: School of Advanced Research Press, 2008); and Monica Smith (ed.), *The Social Construction of Cities* (Washington, D.C.: Smithsonian, 2003); Glenn Storey (ed.), *Urbanism in the Preindustrial World: Cross-Cultural Approaches* (Tuscaloosa: University of Alabama Press, 2006). See my review: Norman Yoffee, "Making Ancient Cities Plausible," *Reviews in Anthropology* 38 (2009), 264–89. Michael Smith offers important comparative perspectives on ancient cities in a series of essays that I list in "Further Readings."

The first section of studies concerns "early cities as arenas of perform-ance," which includes studies of Egyptian, Maya, and Southeast Asian cities. The chapters show that the landscape of cities provided for large-scale rituals and celebrations of the gods. There were also ceremonies of governance, with leaders depicting their essential and special connections to the gods. In many cities there were processional ways through the city leading to plazas where ceremonies were performed, and some cities, as Wheatley thought, were themselves planned as cosmograms, that is, as earthly representations of the cosmos. The chapters consider who performed the ceremonies, what is the nature of the audience, and how the cityscape itself is a performance space.

The second section analyzes "early cities and information technologies." The chapters in this section consider the invention and use of writing in early Mesopotamian cities, in particular in the city of Uruk toward the end of the fourth millennium BCE, in China toward the end of the second millennium BCE, and in Maya cities in the first millennium CE (with precur-sors in earlier periods). One chapter is on the use of quipus (or khipus), a sophisticated system of knotted-ropes that encoded information, in the Inka Empire in the fourteenth and fifteenth centuries CE. The focus of these chapters is on how leaders kept track of goods, services, and people in early cities. The media of writing include clay tablets, oracle bones, and stone stelae and pots. Who was responsible for record-keeping? How was the state made "legible," as James Scott has put it, in order for cities and states to be administered?[34] What sort of information was not encoded in writing systems or knotted-ropes?

Section three is titled, "Early Urban Landscapes." As noted above, when cities evolved they became the primary features, certainly in the visual sense, of their countrysides, which were restructured as the hinterlands of cities. The chapters in this section, on the Andean city of Tiwanaku in the late first millennium CE, Mesopotamian cities from the late fourth to the middle of the second millennium BCE, and the Mexican metropolis of Teotihuacan in the first centuries CE, discuss the process of "ruralization" (the restructuring of the countryside as an urban hinterland), as well as the structuring of the cityscape itself. The latter discussion pays particular attention to the construction of neighborhoods and their relation to admin-istrative and ceremonial districts. The routinization of daily life in urban

[34] James C. Scott, *Seeing Like a State: How Certain Schemes to Improve the Human Condition Have Failed* (New Haven, Yale University Press, 1998).

landscapes, as discussed by the archaeologist Adam T. Smith, and urban geographers and critics like Jane Jacobs and Edward Soja, is delineated.

In section four, "Early Cities and the Distribution of Power," chapters consider cities in the Harappan tradition (*c.* 2700–1900 BCE) and their successors in South Asia, Greek cities in the first millennium BCE, and Jenne-jeno and other early cities in Africa (excluding Egypt) mainly in the first millennium CE. There is a kind of "orientalist" argument (noted by Ian Morris and Alex Knodell) that cities and states before the Greeks were totalitarian monarchies, with palaces owning all the land and controlling all economic and political processes. Archaeologists and ancient historians have reassessed this view. These chapters discuss other forms of power and sovereignty in early cities.

In section five, "Early Cities as Creations," chapters consider the rise and fall of Cahokia, *c.* 1000–1300 CE, the great prehistoric city on the Mississippi, Jerusalem, which was created numerous times, including arguably the creation of the City of David around 1000 CE, and Baghdad, created as the Abbasid capital in the eighth century CE. The fates of these cities are related to the circumstances of their creation.

Section six concerns "early imperial cities" – Rome in the early centuries CE, the capital cities of imperial Assyria in the early to middle centuries BCE, and Tenochtitlan, the Aztec capital, in the fourteenth to early sixteenth centuries CE. These cities were centers of a military establishment, a state religion, massive constructions, and also a dependence on a far-flung empire for resources and labor. They were also population attractors, both voluntary and forced, and the new populations led to new problems in these cities. Clusters of people led to disease, violence, slavery, and subjugations of unprecedented kinds and scales.

These chapters offer new information on society, economy, and politics in early cities. They are not comprehensive reviews of the cities discussed, for which literature is provided in "further readings" (and which can take the reader to formidable amounts of references). The aim of this book is to introduce readers to the history of the world of early cities, to examine the interactions of cities in their regions and beyond, to explore similarities in early urban life, while delineating differences among cities, and to provide and plead for new kinds of comparative studies. It will not have escaped readers that comparisons of Rome to Tenochtitlan, Jerusalem to Cahokia, Athens to Jenne-jeno are not standard fare in the study of early cities. Discussions of the new research in the chapters and results of our comparative methods will be reviewed in the conclusion to this volume.

A history of the study of early cities

Archaeologists and ancient historians are confident that new data will constantly be produced and new models constructed to account for them. This volume reassesses old data in comparative perspective and provides room for new ideas, both of which can and will result in amendments, emendations, and utterly new views of the living past.

FURTHER READINGS

Adams, Robert McC., *The Evolution of Urban Society*, Chicago: Aldine, 1966.

Alter, Robert, *Imagined Cities*, New Haven, CT: Yale University Press, 2005.

Ampolo, Carminé, "Le origini di Roma e la "cité antique,"" *Mélanges de l'École Française de Rome* 92 (1980), 567–76.

Beard, Mary, *Pompeii: The Life of a Roman Town*, Cambridge: Profile, 2006.

Berry, Brian J. L., and James Wheeler (eds.), *Urban Geography in America: Paradigms and Personalities*, New York: Routledge, 2005.

Blanton, Richard, "Urban Beginnings: A View from Anthropological Archaeology," *Journal of Urban History* 8 (1982), 427–46.

Butzer, Karl, "Other Perspectives on Urbanism: Beyond the Disciplinary Boundaries," in Joyce Marcus and Jeremy A. Sabloff (eds.), *The Ancient City: New Perspectives on Urbanism in the Old and New World*, Santa Fe: School of Advanced Research Press, 2008, pp. 77–96.

Cantwell, Anne-Marie, and Diana diZerega Wall, *Unearthing Gotham: The Archaeology of New York City*, New Haven, CT: Yale University Press, 2001.

Chamboredon, Jean-Claude, "Émile Durkheim: le social objet de science: du moral au politique," *Crititique* (1984), 460–531.

Childe, V. Gordon, "The Urban Revolution," *Town Planning Review* 21 (1950), 3–17.

Clark, Peter (ed.), *The Oxford Handbook of Cities in World History*, Oxford: Oxford University Press, 2013.

Cowgill, George L., "Origins and Development of Urbanism," *Annual Review of Anthropology* 33 (2004), 525–42.

Duby, G., "Histoire des mentalités," in Charles Samaran (ed.), *L'histoire et ses méthodes, Encyclopédie de la Pléiade*, Paris: Gallimard, 1961, pp. 937–66.

Eisenstadt, Shmuel N., and Arie Schachar, "Theories of Urbanization," in Shmuel N. Eisenstadt and Arie Schacher (eds.), *Society, Culture, and Urbanization*, Newbury Park, CA: Sage, 1987, pp. 21–75.

Emberling, Geoff, "Urban Social Transformations and the Problem of the 'First City,'" in Monica Smith (ed.), *The Social Construction of Ancient Cities*, Washington, D.C.: Smithsonian Institution, 2003, pp. 254–68.

Fox, Robin, *Urban Anthropology: Cities in the Cultural Setting*, Englewood Cliffs, NJ: Prentice-Hall, 1977.

Fustel de Coulanges, Numa Denis, *La cité antique*, Paris: Libraire Hachette, 1864.

Hansen, Mogens Herman (ed.), *A Comparative Study of Six City-State Cultures*, Copenhagen: Royal Danish Academy of Sciences and Letters, 2002.

A Comparative Study of Thirty City-State Cultures, Copenhagen: Royal Danish Academy of Sciences and Letters, 2000.

Héran, François, "L'institution démotivée: De Fustel de Coulanges à Durkheim," *Revue Française de Sociologie* 28 (1987), 67–97.

Inomata, Taskeshi, and Lawrence S. Cobben (eds.), *The Archaeology of Performance*, Lanham, MD: Altamira, 2006.

Isin, Engin F., "Historical Sociology of the City," in Gerard Delanty (ed.), *Handbook of Historical Sociology*, London: Sage, 2003, pp. 312–25.

Janusek, John W., *Ancient Tiwanaku*, Cambridge: Cambridge University Press, 2008.

Keith, Kathryn, "Cities, Neighborhoods, and Houses: Urban Spatial Organization in Old Babylonian Mesopotamia," unpublished Ph.D. thesis, University of Michigan, 1999.

"The Spatial Patterns of Everyday Life in Old Babylonian Neighborhoods," in Monica Smith (ed.), *The Social Construction of Ancient Cities*, Washington, D.C.: Smithsonian Institution, 2003, pp. 56–80.

Kenoyer, J. Mark, *Ancient Cities of the Indus*, Oxford: Oxford University Press, 1998.

"Early City-States in South Asia: Comparing the Harappan Phase and the Early Historic Period," in Thomas Charlton and Deborah Nichols (eds.), *The Archaeology of City-States*, Washington, D.C.: Smithsonian Institution, 1997, pp. 51–70.

"Indus Urbanism: New Perspectives on its Origin and Character," in Joyce Marcus and Jeremy A. Sabloff (eds.), *The Ancient City: New Perspectives on Urbanism in the New and Old World*, Santa Fe, NM: School of Advanced Research Press, 2008, pp. 185–210.

Khaldun, Ibn, *The Muqaddimah: An Introduction to History*, Franz Rosenthal (trans.), Princeton, NJ: Princeton University Press, 1969.

Kraeling, Carl H., and Robert McC. Adams (eds.), *City Invincible*, Chicago: The University of Chicago Press, 1960.

Leick, Gwendolyn, *Mesopotamia: The Invention of the City*, London: Allen and Lane, 2001.

Liu Li and Chen Xingcan, *The Archaeology of China: From the Late Paleolithic to the Bronze Age*, Cambridge: Cambridge University Press, 2012.

Liverani, Mario, *Immaginare Babele: Due secoli di studi sulla città orientale antica*, Rome: Editori Laterza, 2013.

Uruk: The First City, London: Equinox, 2006.

Marcus, Joyce, and Jeremy A. Sabloff (eds.), *The Ancient City: New Perspectives on Urbanism in the Old and New World*, Santa Fe, NM: School of Advanced Research Press, 2008.

McIntosh, Roderick, and Susan Keech McIntosh, "Early Urban Configurations on the Middle Niger: Clustered Cities and Landscapes of Power," in Monica Smith (ed.), *The Social Construction of Ancient Cities*, Washington, D.C.: Smithsonian Institution, 2003, pp. 103–20.

McIntosh, Susan Keech, "Modeling Political Organization in Large-Scale Settlement Clusters: A Case Study from the Inland Niger Delta," in Susan Keech McIntosh (ed.), *Beyond Chiefdoms: Pathways to Complexity in Africa*, Cambridge: Cambridge University Press, 1999, pp. 66–79.

Momigliano, Arnaldo, "Foreword," in Arnaldo Momigliano, *Fustel de Coulanges, The Ancient City*, Baltimore, MD: Johns Hopkins Paperbacks, 1980, pp. ix–xiv.

Morris, Ian, "The Early Polis as City and State," in John Rich and Andrew Wallace-Hadrill (eds.), *City and Country in the Ancient World*, London: Routledge, 1991, pp. 25–57.

Mumford, Lewis, *The City in History*, New York: Harcourt, Brace, and World, 1960.

Nissen, Hans J., "Fruehe Stadtbildung im alten Vorderen Orient," in Mehmet Özdoğan, Harald Hauptmann, and Nezih Basgelen (eds.), *Köyden kente: Yakındoğu'da ilk yerleşimler (From Villages to Cities: Early Villages in the Near East- Festschrift Ufuk Esin)*, Istanbul: Arkeoloji ve Sanat Yayınları, 2003.

Raaflaub, Kurt, "City-State, Territory and Empire in Classical Antiquity," in Anthony Molho, Julia Emlen, and Kurt Raaflaub (eds.), *City-States in Classical Antiquity and Medieval Italy*, Ann Arbor: University of Michigan Press, 1990, pp. 565–88.

Redfield, Robert, and Milton Singer, "The Cultural Role of Cities," *Economic Development and Social Change* 3 (1954), 53–73.

Renfrew, Colin, "The City through Time and Space: Transformations of Centrality," in Joyce Marcus and Jeremy A. Sabloff (eds.), *The Ancient City: New Perspectives on Urbanism in the New and Old World*, Santa Fe, NM: School of Advanced Research Press, 2008, pp. 29–52.

Rothschild, Nan, "Colonial and Postcolonial New York: Issues of Size, Scale, and Structure," in Glenn Storey (ed.), *Urbanism in the Preindustrial World: Cross-cultural Approaches*, Tuscaloosa: University of Alabama Press, 2006.

Ryckwert, Joseph, *The Idea of a Town: The Anthropology of Urban Form in Rome, Italy and the Ancient World*, Princeton, NJ: Princeton University Press, 1976.

Scott, James C., *Seeing Like a State: How Certain Schemes to Improve the Human Condition Have Failed*, New Haven, CT: Yale University Press, 1998.

Sjoberg, Gideon, *The Pre-Industrial City*, New York: Free Press, 1960.

Smith, Adam, *The Political Landscape: Constellations of Authority in Early Complex Polities*, Berkeley: University of California Press, 2003.

Smith, Michael, "Ancient Cities," in Ray Hutchison (ed.), *The Encyclopedia of Urban Studies*, New York: Sage, 2009, pp. 24–8.

"The Archaeological Study of Neighborhoods and Districts in Ancient Cities," *Journal of Anthropological Archaeology* 29 (2010), 137–54.

"Editorial – Just How Comparative is Comparative Urban Geography? A Perspective from Archaeology," *Urban Geography* 30 (2009), 113–17.

"Empirical Urban Theory for Archaeologists," *Journal of Archaeological Method and Theory* 18 (2010), 167–92.

"Form and Meaning in the Earliest Cities: A New Approach to Ancient Urban Planning," *Journal of Planning History* 6 (2007), 3–47.

Smith, Monica (ed.), *The Social Construction of Ancient Cities*, Washington, D.C.: Smithsonian Institution, 2003.

Smith, P. D., *City: A Guidebook for the Urban Life*, London: Bloomsbury, 2012.

Soja, Edward, "Cities and States in Geohistory," *Theoretical Sociology* 39 (2011), 361–76.

Thirdspace: Journeys to Los Angeles and other Real-and-Imagined Places, Oxford: Blackwell, 1996.

Stone, Elizabeth, "City-States and their Centers," in Thomas Charlton and Deborah Nichols (eds.), *The Archaeology of City-States*, Washington, D.C.: Smithsonian Institution, 1997, pp. 15–26.

"The Constraints on State and Urban Form in Ancient Mesopotamia," in Michael Hudson and Baruch Levine (eds.), *Urbanism and the Economy in the Ancient Near East*, Cambridge, MA: Peabody Museum, 1999, pp. 326–80.

"The Development of Cities in Ancient Mesopotamia," in Jack Sasson (ed.), *Civilizations of the Ancient Near East*, New York: Scribner's, 1995, pp. 235–48.

"The Mesopotamian Urban Experience," in Elizabeth Stone (ed.), *Settlement and Society: Essays Dedicated to Robert McCormick Adams*, Los Angeles: Cotsen Institute of Archaeology, UCLA, 2007, pp. 213–34.

Terrenato, N., "The Versatile Clans: The Nature of Power in Early Rome," in Donald C. Haggis and Nicola Terrenato (eds.), *State Formation in Italy and Greece*, Oxford: Oxbow, 2011.

Trigger, Bruce, "Early Cities: Craft Workers, Kings, and Controlling the Supernatural," in Joyce Marcus and Jeremy A. Sabloff (eds.), *The Ancient City: New Approaches to Urbanism in the New and Old World*, Santa Fe, NM: School of Advanced Research Press, 2008, pp. 53–66.

"The Evolution of Pre-Industrial Cities: A Multilinear Perspective," in Francis Geus and Florence Thill (eds.), *Mélanges offerts à Jean Vercoutter*, Paris: Éditions Recherche sur les Civilisations, 1985, pp. 343–53.

Understanding Urban Civilizations, Cambridge: Cambridge University Press, 2003.

Tringham, Ruth, Peter Ucko, and George Dimbleby (eds.), *Man, Settlement and Urbanism*, London: Duckworth, 1970.

Van de Mieroop, Marc, *The Ancient Mesopotamian City*, Oxford: Clarendon, 1997.

Von Falkenhausen, Lothar, "Stages in the Development of 'Cities' in Pre-Imperial China," in Joyce Marcus and Jeremy A. Sabloff (eds.), *The Ancient City: New Approaches to Urbanism in the New and Old Worlds*, Santa Fe, NM: School of Advanced Research Press, 2008, pp. 211–30.

Wilhelm, Gernot (ed.), *Die orientalische Stadt*, Saarbrücken: Saarbrücken Drueckerei und Verlag, 1997.

Zeder, Melinda, *Feeding Cities*, Washington, D.C.: Smithsonian Institution, 1991.

"Food Provisioning in Urban Societies: A View from Northern Mesopotamia," in Monica Smith (ed.), *The Social Construction of Ancient Cities*, Washington, D.C.: Smithsonian Institution, 2003, pp. 156–83.

PART I

★

EARLY CITIES AS ARENAS OF PERFORMANCE

2

Ancient Egyptian cities: monumentality and performance

JOHN BAINES

By about 3100 BCE ancient Egypt formed a large state extending northward for a thousand kilometers from the First Cataract of the Nile to the Mediterranean Sea (see Table 2.1; dates are BCE unless otherwise noted). The state inherited several regional centers in the Nile Valley that may already have been cities. A couple of them had been the centers of polities that preceded the unified state (see Map 2.1). The other main component of the Egyptian settled landscape, the Nile Delta, possessed significant, probably urban centers by the same date.

During the period of state formation (c. 3200–3000), the area near Memphis, south of the apex of the Nile Delta and of modern Cairo, saw a great increase in density of settlement, as measured by the number and size of cemeteries in the low desert flanking the Nile Valley primarily on the west. At the beginning of the 1st dynasty and the "historical" period the city of Memphis itself, whose name is first attested from a couple of generations earlier,[1] was transformed into a monumental setting by the construction of the first colossal tomb on the western escarpment near to the core settlement. Ever since then, Egypt's largest urban center has remained in the same region, except during the Greco-Roman period, when Alexandria, the new capital founded by Alexander the Great on the coast at the northwest edge of the delta, emerged as one of the world's great cities, declining to relative unimportance after the Muslim conquest of 640 CE. Memphis was partly complemented by the sacred city of Heliopolis to the northeast, on the edge of the Nile Valley perhaps a day's journey away.

The regions of origin of founders of dynasties were significant in many periods. The most important of these, Thebes in the southern Nile Valley, was a primary or secondary capital throughout the second millennium, remaining

---

[1] Pierre Tallet and Damien Laisney, "Iry-Hor et Narmer au Sud-Sinaï (Ouadi ʿAmeyra): un complément à la chronologie des expéditions minières égyptiennes," *Bulletin de l'Institut Français d'Archéologie Orientale* 112 (2012), 385–7.

Table 2.1 *Chronological table of ancient Egypt*

Predynastic	*c.* 5000–3000
Naqada I (Nile Valley)	*c.* 4000
Ma'adi (delta and northern Nile Valley)	*c.* 3800
Naqada II (Nile Valley, later all Egypt)	*c.* 3500
Naqada III (late predynastic and dynasty o)	*c.* 3200
Early Dynastic period (1st–3rd dynasties)	*c.* 3000–2575
Old Kingdom (4th–8th dynasties)	*c.* 2575–2150
First Intermediate period (9th–11th dynasties)	*c.* 2150–1980
Middle Kingdom (11th–14th dynasties)	*c.* 1980–1630
Second Intermediate period (14th–17th dynasties)	*c.* 1630–1520
New Kingdom (18th–20th dynasties)	*c.* 1540–1070
Third Intermediate period (21st–25th dynasties)	*c.* 1070–715
Late period (25th–30th dynasties, Second Persian period)	715–332
Macedonian period	332–305
Ptolemaic period	305–30
Roman period	30 BCE–395 CE
Byzantine period	395–640 CE
Muslim conquest	640 CE

important long after. Over the millennia, however, the Nile Valley increasingly became a backwater. The majority of people lived in the delta, which contained numerous cities and was close to the Near Eastern and eastern Mediterranean world, into which Egypt became more and more closely integrated.

Possible forerunners to Memphis were the regional centers of Naqada and Abydos, which emerged in the southern Nile Valley from about 3700 onward. As is common in Egypt, evidence for these places comes primarily from necropolis and ritual areas in the desert, rather than from the settlements themselves; their size and character as urban places are little known. By contrast, a significant proportion of Hierakonpolis, the southernmost center, lay in the desert near to the valley. From the later fourth millennium onward, Hierakonpolis displayed clear features of nucleation, social differentiation, and large-scale production of food and craft goods, as well as major religious buildings and monumental tombs, all of which point to an urban character, though perhaps with a modest urban population. The settlements for which Naqada and Abydos formed cemeteries and ritual areas probably developed in similar ways. Memphis was therefore the urban successor of previous small cities, and was most probably expanded under rulers from Abydos who had become the kings of all Egypt.

The Nile Valley floodplain of the third millennium was not an easy location for cities. The main river channel moved, generally in an eastward

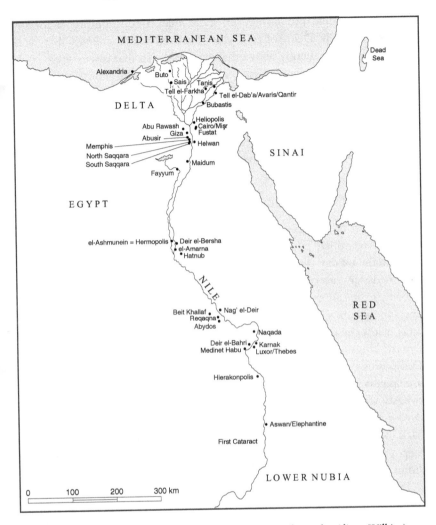

Map 2.1. Map of Egypt, with sites mentioned in the text (drawn by Alison Wilkins).

direction, destroying all trace of human activity in its path. The most favored sites for settlements were near the river, both for access to transport and because the banks were slightly elevated and could be protected more easily against the annual late-summer inundation, which submerged almost all the floodplain (in contrast to later periods, rainfall was also an appreciable climatic element). In the later second millennium largely successful efforts were made to create extensive cities on the floodplain. This new aspiration may have responded to changes in the natural regime of the Nile; water management could not have been more than a contributory factor. By contrast, the Nile Delta offered areas between water courses that were more or less permanently above the water table, so that towns there could have more secure settings. Some long-term stability of its environment is suggested by finds of Paleolithic flints at delta sites. A few very ancient places in the delta – such as Buto, Sais, Mendes, and Tell el-Farkha – almost certainly possessed urban character by the beginning of the third millennium, but no excavated large city there dates before the mid-second millennium, with the rise of Tell el-Dab'a / Avaris.

Third millennium Memphis and its setting

The location of the primary urban settlement of early Memphis has been plausibly identified by drill cores as a relatively modest-sized area well beneath the modern floodplain. The site, which is inaccessible to excavation, is immediately east of the desert escarpment at North Saqqara, on the crest of which are the earliest truly monumental tombs in the region, dating to the 1st and 2nd dynasties (c. 3000–2700); these probably belonged to people immediately below the king in status. The tombs and funerary ritual enclosures of 1st dynasty kings were at the traditional site of Abydos. The mid-1st dynasty king Den possessed a complementary commemorative space at Saqqara, and such arenas may have been created for other rulers. The first three kings of the 2nd dynasty were buried at Saqqara, a couple of kilometers south of the large 1st dynasty tombs, while their successors, in a politically troubled phase, moved back to Abydos. The first king of the 3rd dynasty, Djoser (c. 2650), built the Step Pyramid, which was his tomb complex and the oldest truly colossal stone monument in Egypt, next to the 2nd dynasty royal tombs.

From that time for half a millennium, all royal mortuary monuments and most tombs of the inner elite were constructed on the low desert west of the Nile Valley, in necropolis areas connected with the city of Memphis. These areas stretched over about 80 kilometers from Maidum in the south to Abu Rawash in the north, with the main groups in the 20 kilometers between South Saqqara and Giza (locations are given from south to north because the ancient Egyptians oriented toward the south). In addition, the largest single concentration, of more than 10,000 tombs ranging in date from late prehistory to around 2600, was at Helwan on the east side of the valley a little south of Memphis; mid-ranking elites seem to have been buried there.

This wide distribution of activities was no doubt rendered practicable by the relative ease of movement and transport on the Nile, supplemented by canals leading to places away from its main channel. The functions of royal

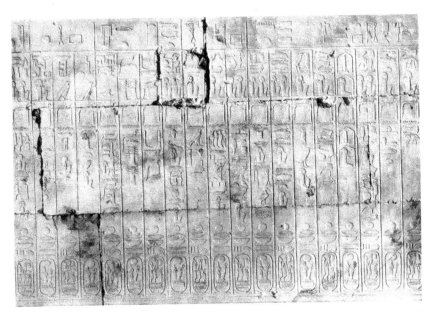

Figure 2.1 Section of a table of gods of Memphis, relief in the chapel of Sokar in the temple of Sety I (c. 1290–1279 BCE) at Abydos (courtesy Egypt Exploration Society).

residence, administration, and monument construction were distributed across the landscape, in configurations that changed from reign to reign, rather than being contained within the densely inhabited city itself. Administration and storage were probably sited close to the riverbank because they needed a dry location and access to transport.

The urban area of Memphis formed a dense religious landscape. A table of gods of Memphis, preserved in a 19th dynasty source but probably going back in part to the Early Dynastic period, is very suggestive here (Figure 2.1).[2] It includes sixty-three names, some repeated, divided into seven or perhaps eight sections corresponding to areas and local landmarks. The divisions may have related to individual shrines or to small temples where several deities were worshipped. As befits the country's most major city, a number of the names are learned and rather abstruse: two leading officials of the late 5th and early 6th dynasty used some of its content to display their special knowledge, in sets of probably artificial priestly titles.

What other functions were based within the city can only be suggested. Its original extent appears to have significantly been less than 1 square

---

[2] John Baines, *High Culture and Experience in Ancient Egypt* (Sheffield: Equinox, 2013), pp. 167–70.

kilometer,[3] suggesting that in addition to sacred precincts it acted as a node for activities conducted elsewhere and as a dwelling place for ordinary people. The list of gods is a witness to the cultural importance of the city, which may have contained institutions such as places for training administrators and priests, functions that were not fully distinct.

While members of the inner elite must have possessed local residences, they may have lived in rural settings near the city rather than within its confines. The values they and the king displayed on their monuments were rural rather than urban. The absence of a focus on the city can hardly reflect the reality of these people's lives, and the interest in rural matters, as well as the salience of mortuary monuments sited away from the main settlement, imparted a dispersed, mobile character to the display of power.

Display within the Memphite region

The third millennium state, especially its prime city and royal residence, was strongly oriented toward ceremonial, and ritual performances were often depicted or evoked in images. Five principal contexts of performance can be suggested.

First, the creation of monuments on a scale hitherto not seen anywhere in the world was itself a long-lasting performance that was celebrated at the end of construction, for example by the ceremonial transport of a pyramid's capstone,[4] while the finished monument was the setting for grandiose funerals as well as a continuing mortuary cult. Because materials for a monument were brought from many regions, construction and fitting-out were highly visible, as well as involving vast numbers of people. At work sites, short-lived urban settlements developed.[5]

Second, the king enacted his role as a perpetual performance that varied in intensity of ritualization. His activities centered around the royal residence while extending into the countryside. In the earliest dynasties he seems to have moved regularly around the country. For the Old Kingdom little specific evidence of royal travel is preserved; instead, the king is shown

[3] The estimates quoted by Norman Yoffee, *Myths of the Archaic State: Evolution of the Earliest Cities, States, and Civilizations* (Cambridge: Cambridge University Press, 2005), p. 43, relate to the region rather than the urban core.

[4] Zahi Hawass and Miroslav Verner, "Newly Discovered Blocks from the Causeway of Sahure," *Mitteilungen des Deutschen Archäologischen Instituts, Abteilung Kairo* 52 (1996), 177–86.

[5] AERA, *American Egypt Research Associates*, accessed November 12, 2013, www.aeraweb.org.

Figure 2.2 A ship's crew returning from an expedition abroad pays homage to the king, probably on arrival in Memphis. Relief from the mortuary temple of Sahure (*c.* 2450 BCE) at Abusir (after Ludwig Borchardt, Ernst Assmann, Alfred Bollacher, Oskar Heinroth, Max Hilzheimer, and Kurt Sethe, *Das Grabdenkmal Des Königs Sa3Hu-Re 'II: Die Wandbilder*, Ausgrabungen der Deutschen Orient-Gesellschaft in Abusir 1902–1908, 7 [Leipzig: J. C. Hinrichs, 1913], pl. 13).

receiving people at his residence and going to nearby places, for example to inspect building projects.

Third, the river provided a setting for performance and an organizing metaphor for crews working on monuments. The latter point exemplifies how significant the river was for ancient life. Elite groups who served the king and the gods were termed "watches" – Egyptologists use the Greek term *phyle* – performing duties in monthly rotation.[6] Two phyle names are nautical, meaning "starboard" and "port." Work teams on construction sites were also classified by phyles. The arrival of a fleet from abroad was treated as a celebration during which songs in praise of the king are depicted as being sung by the ships' crews (Figure 2.2). Images of the gods were carried on symbolic barques that would be visible during festival processions.

Fourth, worship of the gods in temples was highly developed, with regular daily service and numerous festivals. Elaborate recycling of offerings from gods to the dead and the living integrated the cult of the gods both with that of deceased kings and with the mortuary cult of the non-royal dead in the monumental necropoleis. That integration will have been highly visible, whereas the cult itself – and in principle the mortuary cult in tombs – was conducted in interior spaces to which access was severely restricted.

[6] Ann Macy Roth, *Egyptian Phyles in the Old Kingdom: The Evolution of a System of Social Organization* (Chicago: Oriental Institute, University of Chicago, 1991).

Fifth, outside the Memphite area, most kings of the 1st and 2nd dynasties were buried at Abydos, where they constructed tombs and separate cult enclosures, the latter being torn down reign by reign, with their mortuary cult probably being integrated with those of their successors. Within the same area, the necropolis sites of Nagʿ el-Deir, Beit Khallaf, and Reqaqna, where some members of the central elite had their tombs, show that for many centuries a significant center existed in the region. Kings are likely to have died near their Memphite residences or while traveling. Royal funerals, including the journey to Abydos, were surely among the most important performances of power, not least because they would affirm who had succeeded the deceased ruler.

Performance of power was articulated through these arenas of action and through patterns of display, of exclusion, and of display of exclusion. Only the king could have access to all contexts of performance. Display also extended to the central elite. The city and associated monuments were provisioned from estates scattered across the country. Visits by elites to and from their own country estates were depicted as parades of flotillas on the river. The arrival of deliveries from estates is shown in the form of processions of people, dressed for celebration, who carry goods and lead animals. While this would not have been a frequent practice, the manner of its representation fits with other evidence for display.

The region – and for royal funerals much of the country – was the stage for these performances, which required repeated, extensive movement in the Memphite area, both on the floodplain and into the surrounding desert. Major events and projects would be visible across the landscape; many people would participate, mostly in subordinate roles. Within the region, settlements and fixed points were scattered. The area's overall character was not strongly urbanized, except perhaps near the riverbank. Urban dwellers and elites relied on supplies brought from rural locations both within the region and at a distance. This visible interdependence of urban and rural, elite and others may have mitigated slightly the vast distinctions in wealth and power between the ruling group and the general population.

In this wider context, the urban core of Memphis was a limited setting. The list of gods suggests that it possessed an intense religious life, presumably conducted in small temples, typically hosting several deities, to the interiors of which few had access. Service in temple cults was a privilege and brought a small income. Most officials were pluralists who derived their livelihoods from several positions. Their associated movements no doubt exhibited their importance to others.

The king's life probably involved much movement while centering on the royal residence, which had a semi-urban character, possessing workshops, storehouses, and dwelling spaces for attendants and servants. Access to the king was controlled by layers of protection as well as ritual and ceremonial rules.

Thus, one should understand the third millennium ruling "city" of Egypt not as a single urban center but as a region, shifting in extent and configuration from reign to reign, which was circumscribed by its monuments on the escarpments bordering the Nile Valley and brought together by connections among them, as well as possibly extending to Heliopolis.

Later Old Kingdom changes

This admittedly hypothetical picture applies most strongly to the 3rd and 4th dynasties. More than half the kings of the 5th dynasty, whose monuments were much less grandiose than those of their predecessors, were buried at Abusir, a little north of the Saqqara necropolis, and at Saqqara itself. The second major king of the 6th dynasty, Pepy I, built his pyramid at South Saqqara. Associated with the pyramid was the royal residence *mn-nfr* "The enduring-of-perfection (monument of Pepy)," which is the ancestor of the later name Memphis. That residence was perhaps on a latitude with his pyramid, near to where the city grew in later periods, southeast of its former location. Later pyramids of the dynasty were in the same area.

Thus, toward the end of the Old Kingdom kings seem to have moved near to the urban center. The location of that center shifted, probably in response to changes in the river's course. Pepy I was an innovator in the country as a whole: material from his reign is known from many provincial sites, and he constructed a network of chapels for his mortuary cult next to local temple complexes. This greater emphasis on the core city was thus complemented by a dispersed royal presence across the provinces. These developments in display and in regional centers went together with a major reconfiguration of elite residence patterns. Important people now lived and were buried locally as well as in Memphite royal and elite cemeteries. How far these changes affected the display of power within the Memphite area is less clear. Distances traveled in major ceremonies probably reduced, and kings may have identified with the city more than before. Pepy I's successor Merenre named his residence *ḥ^c-nfr* "The arising-of-perfection (monument of Merenre)," and that name is used in relation to Memphis in a biographical text of the Ptolemaic period, 2,000 years later, suggesting that it too was remembered as being located very near the city.[7]

Middle Kingdom examples

Configurations of cities in the Middle Kingdom are poorly understood because the Memphite area has yielded little evidence. The nearby royal residence, which was named Itjtawy, an epithet of its founder Amenemhat I, acquired a paradigmatic status, perhaps chiefly because the Middle Kingdom was a "classical" period in the perspective of later times. As in the Old Kingdom, centers of power seem to have been relatively small and strongly associated with rural values and locations. Later 12th dynasty kings sited their monuments near to the newly developing lakeside region of the Fayyum, which was valued for its sporting and agricultural potential. Several "model" towns are known from the period, the majority constructed as fortresses in Lower Nubia, which Egypt conquered. Although these proclaim a peremptory image of power, they cannot well be termed cities, and I do not consider them here.

An important characteristic of the period was the prominence of regional elites, some of whom adopted royal modes of display. Striking among them is Djehutihotep, the nomarch (chief official) of the province of Hermopolis in the mid-12th dynasty. A composition in image and text in his tomb at Deir el-Bersha shows the transport of a colossal travertine statue of him extracted from the quarries of Hatnub in the desert to the southeast. The statue is said to have been 13 cubits high (almost 7 meters) and is shown being dragged by 172 men organized in paramilitary groups. The workforce is subdivided according to sectors of the province. They wear festive clothes, and captions give the chants the groups sing as they toil; a man standing on the statue's lap is beating time. Above the dragging lines are groups of men running and holding palm fronds, a sign of celebration still in use in the Middle East. The narrative states that the whole town – old and young and men and women – greeted the arrival of the statue, which was to be set up next to a weighing-station close to the river, where Djehutihotep was constructing a mortuary chapel alongside those of his ancestors (the wording is uncertain here). This was probably at the center

---

[7] Stela of Psherenptah, British Museum EA 886, line 11.

of a small city, perhaps named Djerty. The destination may be depicted at the end of the scene, but with little visual detail.[8]

In pictorial form this composition derives from Old Kingdom royal models or perhaps from lost Middle Kingdom successors. The colossal statue and its celebratory installation also adopt royal modes, while pointing toward display within towns, which is not directly attested for the earlier period. Djehutihotep, however, does not usurp the king's status: a refrain sung by those dragging the statue is "Djehutihotep, beloved of the king."

Another Middle Kingdom development can be seen at Karnak, the temple complex of Thebes, which later became one of the largest sacred sites anywhere. Karnak was founded, perhaps on an island in the river, during the First Intermediate period. By the 12th dynasty it was a center for cults that reached into the surrounding countryside. The ancient name of Thebes means simply "Settlement / Town (njwt)," which may suggest that it was not in origin a significant place; an anti-Theban inscription of the First Intermediate period even terms it "the mound that they forgot."[9] Thus, Karnak may not have been associated at first with much urban development, although a sizeable population must have lived in the area. Moreover, a late Middle Kingdom inscription (c. 1650) from Karnak narrates an episode during the inundation season when the king and his retinue had to wade through the flooded temple, while a 22nd dynasty text describes a comparable but more serious event in the Luxor Temple, Karnak's companion institution a couple of kilometers upstream.[10] These texts exemplify the risks involved in siting monuments on the Nile Valley floodplain.

In the late Middle Kingdom a large city developed in the Nile Delta at Tell el-Dab'a / Avaris, becoming the capital of the ethnically Levantine 15th (Hyksos) dynasty. The city was located next to two river channels. It is the first securely attested delta city among many from later periods,

---

[8] Harco Willems, Christoph Peeters, and Gert Verstraeten, "Where Did Djehutihotep Erect His Colossal Statue?", *Zeitschrift für Ägyptische Sprache und Altertumskunde* 132 (2005), 173–89.

[9] Jacques Vandier, *Mo'alla: la tombe d'Ankhtifi et la tombe de Sébekhotep* (Cairo: Institut Français d'Archéologie Orientale, 1950), p. 198, line 3 of text.

[10] John Baines, "The Sebekhotpe VIII Inundation Stela: An Additional Fragment," *Acta Orientalia* 37 (1976), 11–20 (more fragments of this text have now been identified); and Susanne Bickel, "The Inundation Inscription in Luxor Temple," in Gerard P. F. Broekman, R. J. Demarée, and Olaf E. Kaper (eds.), *The Libyan Period in Egypt: Historical and Cultural Studies into the 21th–24th Dynasties: Proceedings of a Conference at Leiden University, 25–27 October 2007* (Leiden: Nederlands Instituut voor het Nabije Oosten, 2009), pp. 51–5.

including places such as Bubastis, for which in the mid-first millennium Herodotus (2.60) described a festival attended by "700,000" people.

New Kingdom developments

The picture sketched so far is markedly different from that of the New Kingdom, when Thebes and Memphis became sizeable cities that were sited on the floodplain. How this change was achieved is uncertain, but the progradation of the Nile Valley, with some associated lowering of the water table, may have made it possible to protect larger areas from flooding than hitherto. Little points to major changes in water technology. The shaduf, a water-lifting device, was introduced from the Near East by the 18th dynasty, but it could not have had a role in lowering water levels or flood defense. Intensified contact with the Near East could have favored aspirations toward new forms of city planning, but it is not possible to draw precise parallels between regions.

During the New Kingdom Karnak developed progressively, forming the heart of the ritual and ceremonial setting of Thebes, in which the east and west banks were linked by processional ways using the river, canals, and roads on land (Map 2.2). One route ran parallel with the river from Karnak to Luxor, with some processions going by river and others by land. On a smaller scale than at Memphis, the Nile Valley and the west bank escarpment at Thebes constituted the arena of the city, within which a dense group of monumental temples developed, as well as a vast necropolis of elite tombs, with those of royalty concealed in a wadi a little way into the western desert (the Valley of the Kings). The eastern desert edge at Thebes is flat and seemingly devoid of monuments, so that the population center on the east bank was dominated by its temple complexes near the river and faced the landscape of the west bank, an area where mainly commemorative structures were scattered along the low desert for about 5 kilometers.

Egypt became an imperial power in this period. Kings were mobile, ranging in their travels and conquests from central Sudan to the Euphrates. Their principal residence was in the Memphite area, which was the state's administrative core. Memphis expanded on the floodplain, presumably near the riverbank. Thebes became famed as a place of fabulous wealth, for example in Book 9 of The Iliad, where Achilles says that it has "a hundred gates from each of which emerge two hundred warriors with horses and chariots." The city was the religious capital, receiving vast endowments for temple construction and acting as the stage for major rituals. Kings who

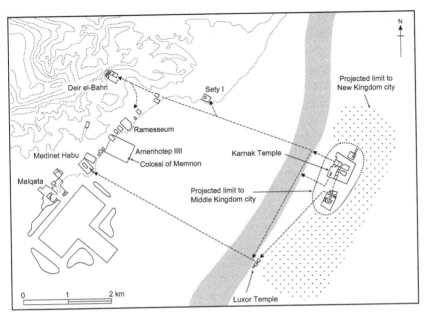

Map 2.2 Map of Thebes in the New Kingdom (*c.* 1100 BCE), showing routes of regular festivals and schematic plans of temples on the east and west banks of the Nile (adapted by Alison Wilkins, after Barry Kemp, *Ancient Egypt: Anatomy of a Civilization*, 2nd edn. [London and New York: Routledge, 2006], p. 266, fig. 97).

sought to bolster their legitimacy came to Thebes to participate in its largest annual festival, the Opet festival, which involved processions from Karnak to Luxor and back. They were confirmed or reaffirmed in their rule in a ritual within the Luxor Temple. While this would have been observed by just a few participants, the processions between the temples were depicted as involving vast numbers of participants on the river and on land. This tension between display and exclusion or concealment is a near universal expression of power and significance. The enormous scale of the temples contrasted strongly with the relatively small numbers of their personnel: temple spaces were crowded more with statues and stelae than with people.

In the Memphite area the future 18th dynasty kings Amenhotep II (*c.* 1428–1401) and Thutmose IV (*c.* 1401–1391) exploited travel from their residence to the already ancient site of the Giza pyramids and Great Sphinx to mark their aspirations. These journeys used the newish mode of transport by chariot, probably riding along the low desert, as is appreciated on horseback down to the present. Thutmose claimed to travel incognito, even though the Great Sphinx was by then the center of a cult, with a small temple constructed under his father. In his sphinx stela Amenhotep also described feats of rowing and shooting arrows from a moving chariot that were displayed before the army along the river somewhere in the Memphite area. He claimed to have rowed a large ship single-handed 2 Egyptian *iteru* – about 21 kilometers – roughly the distance from the city of Memphis to Giza. These two texts suggest that the New Kingdom Memphis stood in relation to its hinterland rather as its Old Kingdom forerunner had, but in a landscape already dominated by antiquity.

Patterns of display changed markedly with the reign of Amenhotep III (*c.* 1391–1353), when Thebes, Memphis, and probably other cities such as Hermopolis were remodeled on a colossal scale within the floodplain. Plans included construction or extension of large temples as well as, perhaps more significantly, setting up avenues of sphinxes to delineate ceremonial ways on the floodplain. What was done at Memphis is known only from inscriptions of high officials. Texts from Thebes are more informative and can be compared with remains in the city itself. The most remarkable project was the excavation of vast harbor basins near the desert edge on both sides of the river, a little upstream from the city. Just downstream from the western basin was a sprawling palace complex of the king, parallel with a range of ceremonial structures along the low desert. This whole area may have been constructed primarily for the king's *sed* festival, a ceremony held in principle to mark thirty years of reign and repeated every three years thereafter. A little north of the palace was the king's mortuary temple, the largest ever constructed, which was sited on the floodplain unlike those of his predecessors. This undertaking failed, presumably because it proved impossible to manage the water regime in the medium term; the temple was being used as a quarry and a source of monumental statuary within a generation of its construction. Significantly, an inscription extolling the king's projects dwells nearly as much on the god Amun's river barque as on some buildings: the river continued to bind the city together and provide the most important arena for movement and display.

Amenhotep III's partially successful design for Thebes documents a new aim to integrate a city and its monuments quite closely, in a different style from the dispersed older mode, and to create grand ceremonial routes. As had been the case throughout the 18th dynasty, the city focused around its temples, in contrast with the enormous royal tombs of earlier periods. Residential areas were probably concentrated to the east of Karnak.

While the enactment of wealth and power was fundamental to Amenhotep III's urban projects, cosmological aspects of the cities, comparable with those known in many societies, may have been equally important. Temples represented an ideal created world in their interiors; comparable associations were now projected into the wider environment, so that the king's presence in the city would replicate divine order, especially since he acquired a measure of deification late in his reign.

The projects of Amenhotep III preceded the still more extravagant undertaking of his revolutionary successor Amenhotep IV/Akhenaten (c. 1353–1335), to build a residence for his newly proclaimed god, Aten or Re-Aten, and for his own rule, in a bay on the low desert near the escarpment at el-Amarna, next to the east bank of the Nile at the exact mid-point of the country.[11] The city, which was occupied for just twenty years, may have housed up to 30,000 people. It stretched in a relatively narrow band for several kilometers, with a royal palace a little to the north of the urban area, a couple of small specialized settlements further into the desert, elite tombs in the escarpment facing the city, and royal tombs some distance up a wadi.

This distribution replicated the main features of earlier cities, but in a layout on only one side of the river. The site, whose ancient name was Akhetaten "(Morning) Horizon of the Aten," was probably chosen for its properties of landscape and cosmology. A conception of the broader area was displayed in the city's boundary stelae, of which more than a dozen were carved in the escarpments on both sides of the Nile Valley (at 20 km, untypically wide here). The texts of the stelae state that the whole area, including its agricultural land, was dedicated to the god, and its extent is named as 6 *iteru* (c. 675 km^2) plus fractions thereof (this cannot be reconciled with the data on the ground). Apart from el-Amarna itself, no settlement of Akhenaten's time has been identified within the demarcated area.

The spacious setting made it possible to lay out the city in a new way, while probably retaining echoes of residential patterns from its inhabitants' cities of origin. The center was devoted to temples, administrative buildings, and a palace that was not the king's main residence. To south and north were residential areas. Running through the city, roughly parallel to the river, were wide roads. Unlike the alleys of sphinxes at Thebes, these did not have monumental markers, and they did not separate ceremonial areas from

---

[11] Personal communications from David O'Connor and Claude Traunecker.

Figure 2.3 Relief in the tomb of Mahu at el-Amarna, perhaps showing the king's visit to the boundary stelae (after Norman de Garis Davies, *The Rock Tombs of el Amarna*, IV, Archaeological Survey of Egypt, 16 [London: Egypt Exploration Fund, 1906], pls. xxi–xxii).

residential ones in the same way as was done in that city. They nevertheless formed a grand setting for the royal display depicted in elite tombs at el-Amarna. The king is represented parading in his chariot, perhaps commuting from the North Palace to the city center. Tomb owners too are shown in chariots – for which there is also archaeological evidence – presumably using the same roads, if not at the same time. The king is accompanied by large military groups. One composition seems to show him visiting the principal boundary stelae, which are depicted as demarcated and linked by something like fences (Figure 2.3). Large public ceremonies are shown, some in which rewards are bestowed on high officials and one where he receives large numbers of foreign delegates. Cuneiform tablets recovered from the city, most of them in Akkadian, show that diplomats were indeed present, some of them staying for years at a time.

Many features of the pictorial record from el-Amarna, such as the military presence at peaceful ceremonies, have no close parallel from earlier periods. The city's layout, too, is not very similar to evidence from elsewhere. These differences can be accounted for in part by the desert location, which removed the constraints of flood protection, the exceptional circumstances of the king's religious revolution, and his evident desire to flout standard conventions. The basic functions of the city were probably similar to those of its predecessors, while the military had become salient over the previous couple of centuries. A significant factor in the layout seems to be the focus on wheeled vehicles, which brings requirements that are absent if only pack animals are used. The visual record may be misleading here, because the only vehicles that were regularly depicted were chariots, although other types are known to have existed. The chariot's introduction in the 16th century probably stimulated more open and linear configurations of cere-monial space, of which el-Amarna offers a sample.

Thus, el-Amarna can suggest some but not all features of an Egyptian ruling city. The site's abandonment and destruction after just twenty years, when the traditional religion was restored, show how closely it was identi-fied with its founder.

About a century after Akhenaten, Ramesses II (*c.* 1279–1213) constructed the new ruling city of Piramesse at Tell el-Dab'a–Qantir in the Nile Delta (Map 2.3), on the same site as the earlier Avaris and in a good position for contact with Asia and the Mediterranean. The detailed layout of this city is not well known, but literary "praise of the city" poems, addressed to scribes rather than to the ruling group, evoke significant characteristics. One passage runs:

> His Person ... has built for himself a fortress named "Great of victories."
> It is between Syria and Egypt,
> full of food and provisions.
>
> It is in the manner of Upper Egyptian Heliopolis (=Thebes),
> its lifespan like that of Memphis.
> The sun rises in its horizon
> and it sets within it.
>
> Everyone has abandoned their towns;
> they have settled in its districts.
>
> Its west is the estate of Amun ...[12]

This acknowledges the principal existing cities as models, while solar and cosmological aspects are explicit, and the whole is organized according to the temple complexes (estates) of deities. Something of the attraction of home is also implied: people must be encouraged to move to the new city. Dense urban settlement is not emphasized; rather, the city is a picture of semi-rural abundance. Archaeological evidence shows that it was also a diplomatic hub – as is implied by other stanzas of the poem quoted – as well as an industrial center, with manufacturing of weaponry and of glass. Royal tombs continued to be located in Thebes, which remained a religious

---

[12] My translation from the Egyptian in Alan H. Gardiner, *Late-Egyptian Miscellanies*, Bibliohteca Aegyptiaca 7 (Brussels: Fondation Égyptologique Reine Élisabeth, 1937), pp. 12–13.

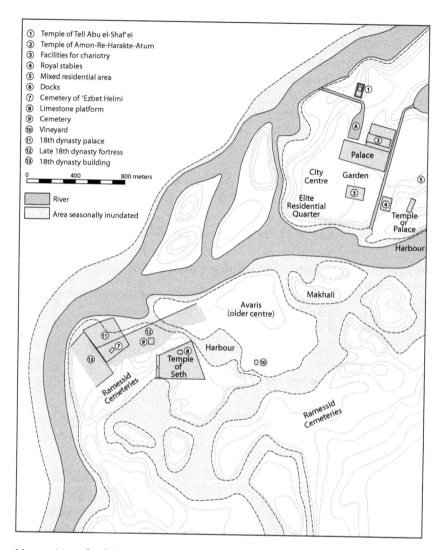

1. Temple of Tell Abu el-Shaf'ei
2. Temple of Amon-Re-Harakte-Atum
3. Facilities for chariotry
4. Royal stables
5. Mixed residential area
6. Docks
7. Cemetery of 'Ezbet Helmi
8. Limestone platform
9. Cemetery
10. Vineyard
11. 18th dynasty palace
12. Late 18th dynasty fortress
13. 18th dynasty building

0   400   800 meters

River

Area seasonally inundated

Map 2.3 Map of Tell el-Dab'a–Qantir in the late New Kingdom, when it was the capital of Ramesses II (c. 1279–1213 BCE) under the name Piramesse (drawn by Nicola Math, with kind permission of Manfred Bietak).

center, so that movement across the land continued to be a core mode of royal display.

Piramesse was short-lived. The adjacent Nile branch silted up, and the Third Intermediate period kings of the 21st dynasty (c. 1070–945) built a new residence at Tanis, further to the northeast, on another arm of the Nile. Tanis, which took over much large statuary from Piramesse, was constructed on a grand scale with major temple complexes, and was envisaged as a new Thebes in the north, as well as the burial place of kings of two dynasties. It was the first of several first millennium royal cities in the delta, culminating in the foundation of Alexandria on orders of Alexander the Great in around 332.

Conclusion

An essential aspect of the Egyptian performance of power was the creation of cities. From the development of Memphis at the beginning of the Dynastic period to that of Fustat, precursor of Cairo, after the Muslim conquest of 640–642 CE, rulers of Egypt have established cities to mark epochs, to initiate change, and to assert their dominance and power. Their prime cities possessed features found in many civilizations. From the New Kingdom onward, the cities also assumed a physical form closer to those known in other regions.

Early cities, by contrast, appear to have been highly distinctive in their layout, being constrained in part by their location on the Nile floodplain and in part by the dominance of dispersed mortuary monuments. The values of early rulers and elites seem not to have focused on cities, while cosmological representation may have inhered more in individual monuments and necropolis sites than in the configuration of complete settlements. Their presentation of power was not limited to the city narrowly defined, but was based on the distribution of elements across the landscape, on movement among those elements, and on the interplay of display of power and concealment of what was sacred and privileged in a wide range of contexts.

Egyptian cities changed fundamentally in character during the two millennia reviewed here. The society, whose population had probably risen significantly by the late New Kingdom, became more focused on cities, which came to resemble more those elsewhere in the Near East. Cities were the prime loci of display of power. They were associated with religion, king and court, and international relations, all of these being domains that can be documented especially from pictorial sources. Just two or three dominant cities were the state's principal arenas for the performance of power. Their relationships with their hinterlands and with the entire country were vital to the communication of their meaning to the wider society.

FURTHER READINGS

Arnold, Dieter, *Die Tempel Ägyptens: Götterwohnungen, Kultstätten, Baudenkmäler,* Zurich: Artemis & Winkler, 1992.

Baines, John, "Kingship before Literature: The World of the King in the Old Kingdom," in Rolf Gundlach and Christine Raedler (eds.), *Selbstverständnis und Realität: Akten des Symposiums zur ägyptischen Königsideologie Mainz 15–17.6.1995,* Wiesbaden: Harrassowitz, 1997, pp. 125–74.

"Modelling the Integration of Elite and Other Social Groups in Old Kingdom Egypt," in Juan Carlos Moreno García (ed.), *Élites et pouvoir en Égypte ancienne,* Lille: Université Charles-de-Gaulle, 2010, pp. 117–44.

"Public Ceremonial Performance in Ancient Egypt: Exclusion and Integration," in Takeshi Inomata and Lawrence Coben (eds.), *Archaeology of Performance: Theaters of Power, Community, and Politics,* Lanham, MD: AltaMira, 2006, pp. 261–302.

Bard, Kathryn, "Royal Cities and Cult Centers, Administrative Towns, and Workmen's Settlements in Ancient Egypt," in Joyce Marcus and Jeremy A. Sabloff (eds.), *The Ancient City: New Perspectives on Urbanism in the Old and New World,* Santa Fe, NM: School for Advanced Research Press, 2008, pp. 165–82.

Bietak, Manfred, "Houses, Palaces and Development of Social Structure in Avaris," in Manfred Bietak, Ernst Czerny, and Irene Forstner-Müller (eds.), *Cities and Urbanism in Ancient Egypt: Papers from a Workshop in November 2006 at the Austrian Academy of Sciences,* Vienna: Österreichische Akademie der Wissenschaften, 2010, pp. 11–68.

"Urban Archaeology and the 'Town' Problem in Ancient Egypt," in Kent R. Weeks (ed.), *Egyptology and the Social Sciences,* Cairo: American University in Cairo Press, 1979, pp. 97–144.

Bietak, Manfred, Ernst Czerny, and Irene Forstner-Müller (eds.), *Cities and Urbanism in Ancient Egypt: Papers from a Workshop in November 2006 at the Austrian Academy of Sciences,* Vienna: Österreichische Akademie der Wissenschaften, 2010.

Bietak, Manfred, and Irene Forstner-Müller, "The Topography of New Kingdom Thebes and Per-Ramesses," in Mark Collier and Steven Snape (eds.), *Ramesside Studies in Honour of K. A. Kitchen,* Bolton: Rutherford Press, 2011, pp. 23–50.

Bulliet, Richard W., *The Camel and the Wheel,* New York: Columbia University Press, 1990.

Campagno, Marcelo, "Kinship, Concentration of Population and the Emergence of the State in the Nile Valley," in Renée Friedman and Peter N. Fiske (eds.), *Egypt at Its Origins 3: Proceedings of the Third International Conference "Origin of the State: Predynastic and Early Dynastic Egypt," London, 27th July–1st August 2008,* Leuven: Departement Oosterse Studies, 2011, pp. 1229–42.

Cline, Eric H., and David O'Connor (eds.), *Amenhotep III: Perspectives on His Reign,* Ann Arbor: University of Michigan Press, 1998.

Graham, Angus, "Islands in the Nile: A Geoarchaeological Approach to Settlement Location in the Egyptian Nile Valley and the Case of Karnak," in Manfred Bietak, Ernst Czerny, and Irene Forstner-Müller (eds.), *Cities and Urbanism in Ancient Egypt: Papers from a Workshop in November 2006 at the Austrian Academy of Sciences,* Vienna: Österreichische Akademie der Wissenschaften, 2010, pp. 125–43.

Janssen, J. J., "El-Amarna as a Residential City," *Bibliotheca Orientalis* 40 (1983), 273–88.

Jeffreys, David J., and Ana Tavares, "The Historic Landscape of Early Dynastic Memphis," *Mitteilungen des Deutschen Archäologischen Instituts, Abteilung Kairo* 50 (1994), 143–73.

Kaiser, Werner, "Ein Kultbezirk des Königs Den in Sakkara," *Mitteilungen des Deutschen Archäologischen Instituts, Abteilung Kairo* 41 (1985), 47–60.

Kemp, Barry J., *Ancient Egypt: Anatomy of a Civilization*, 2nd edn. London: Routledge, 2006.

"The City of el-Amarna as a Source for the Study of Urban Society in Ancient Egypt," *World Archaeology* 9 (1977), 123–39.

"The Window of Appearance at el-Amarna and the Basic Structure of This City," *Journal of Egyptian Archaeology* 62 (1976), 81–99.

Kemp, Barry J., and Salvatore Garfi, *A Survey of the Ancient City of el-'Amarna*, London: Egypt Exploration Society, 1993.

Köhler, E. Christiana, "On the Origins of Memphis – the New Excavations in the Early Dynastic Necropolis at Helwan," in Stan Hendrickx, Renée Friedman, Krzysztof M. Ciałowicz, and Marek Chłodnicki (eds.), *Egypt at Its Origins: Studies in Memory of Barbara Adams, Proceedings of the International Conference "Origins of the State. Predynastic and Early Dynastic Egypt", Krakow, 28th August–1st September 2002*, Leuven: Leuven University Press, 2004, pp. 295–315.

Lacovara, Peter, *The New Kingdom Royal City*, London: Kegan Paul International, 1997.

Lehner, Mark E., *The Complete Pyramids*, London: Thames & Hudson, Ltd., 1997.

Luft, Ulrich, "The Ancient Town of el-Lâhûn," in Stephen Quirke (ed.), *Lahun Studies*, Reigate: Sia, 1998, pp. 1–41.

Martin, Geoffrey Thorndike, "Memphis: The Status of a Residence City in the Eighteenth Dynasty," in Miroslav Bárta and Jaromír Krejčí (eds.), *Abusir and Saqqara in the Year 2000*, Prague: Academy of Sciences of the Czech Republic, Oriental Institute, 2000, pp. 99–120.

Nims, Charles F., and Wim Swaan, *Thebes of the Pharaohs: Pattern for Every City*, London: Elek, 1965.

O'Connor, David, *Abydos: Egypt's First Pharaohs and the Cult of Osiris*, London: Thames & Hudson, 2009.

"City and Palace in New Kingdom Egypt," *Cahiers de Recherche de l'Institut de Papyrologie et Égyptologie de Lille* 11 (1989), 73–87.

"The City and the World: Worldview and Built Forms in the Reign of Amenhotep III," in Eric H. Cline and David O'Connor (eds.), *Amenhotep III: Perspectives on His Reign*, Ann Arbor: University of Michigan Press, 1998, pp. 125–72.

"Cosmological Structures of Ancient Egyptian City Planning," in Tony Atkin and Joseph Rykwert (eds.), *Structure and Meaning in Human Settlements*, Philadelphia: University Museum, University of Pennsylvania, 2005, pp. 55–66.

Ragazzoli, Chloé, *Éloges de la ville en Égypte ancienne: histoire et littérature*, Paris: PUPS, 2008.

Routledge, Carolyn, "Temple as Center in Ancient Egyptian Urbanism," in Walter Emanuel Aufrecht, Neil A. Mirau, and Steven W. Gauley (eds.), *Urbanism in Antiquity: From Mesopotamia to Crete*, Sheffield: Sheffield Academic Press, 1997, pp. 221–35.

Vleeming, S. P. (ed.), *Hundred-Gated Thebes: Acts of a Colloquium on Thebes and the Theban Area in the Graeco-Roman Period*, Leiden: E. J. Brill, 1995.

The dedicated city: meaning and morphology in Classic Maya urbanism

STEPHEN HOUSTON AND THOMAS G. GARRISON

Classic Maya cities were dynamic places constructed throughout the Yucatan Peninsula and adjacent zones during much of the first millennium CE (see Map 3.1). All contained elements that have become hallmarks of Maya architecture: pyramids, platforms, palaces, ballcourts, smaller settlements, and causeways. A special advantage of these constructions is their contextualization within numerous excavations and surveys. A further feature is their strong meshing with historical and textual information that can be rich yet variable. Copious at some sites, thin or non-existent at others, such messages convey indigenous perspectives on the meanings behind the shape or morphology of Maya settlements. This chapter examines how Maya cities were understood, used, and altered. Their dynamic growth and intermittent decline reflect an active relation between the concepts and ritual obligations that exercised an abiding effect on Maya cities and the ad hoc, short-term bursts of construction that reflected the will of kings and the courts around them.

At the outset, certain consensual understandings about Maya cities bear repeating. Few scholars would now dispute that, at their core, such settlements housed royal courts of varying size and influence. These had their origin in the final years of the Preclassic period, c. 400 BCE to 250 CE, when large settlements came into existence in the Maya region, within an area embracing most of what is now Guatemala, Belize, eastern Mexico, and parts of El Salvador and Honduras. Predicated on a novel, monumental scale of construction, the Preclassic settlements, some of vast size, such as El Mirador, in Guatemala, consisted of elevated platforms, possibly for residences, along with two distinct types of building.

The first is the "E-Group," so labeled because it was first discerned in a sector of that name at the ancient city of Uaxactun, Guatemala. The E-Group comprises a slightly elevated square plan with two buildings. On its western side looms a pyramid that, at most sites, especially in the final

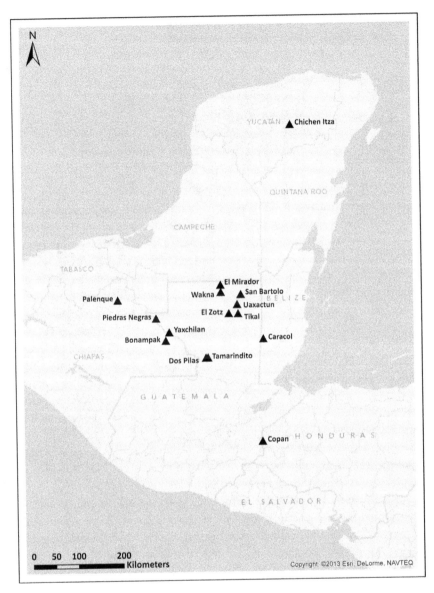

Map 3.1 Map of Maya sites.

years of the Preclassic, achieves a bulk unsurpassed in later times. The pyramid has another notable feature, stairways on its four sides, each corresponding to the quadrants of Maya directional symbolism. To the east is a low platform running north–south. The E-Group occurs at many sites

Table 3.1 Chronological table of the Pre-Hispanic Maya

Archaic	6000–2000 BCE
Preclassic	2000 BCE–250 CE
Early	2000–1000
Middle	1000–400
Late	400 BCE–250 CE
(Terminal Preclassic first two centuries CE)	
Classic	250–900
Postclassic	900–Spanish entrada

and appears to have been one of the first "civic" (monumental and community-wide) buildings of the Maya, materializing in many sites as early as *c.* 500 BCE. A common assumption is that it reflects solar orientations, especially with respect to the rising sun on the eastern horizon. But its motivation was doubtless more complex, growing out of a need to replicate sacred mountains at reduced scale under the control of certain communities.[1] In a sense, the Preclassic Maya introduced a timeless sacred mountain into a local, historically rooted setting.

The second kind of building, appearing some centuries after the E-Group, is the "Triadic" configuration. They are "triadic" because of their high platform, central pyramid, and two flanking buildings that define a courtyard on the summit. The Triadic Groups are among the largest structures erected by humans prior to the modern age. Clues from some sites, such as Wakna, Guatemala, which contains such a group with a major tomb, hint that they were, at least in part, mortuary in function, a pattern that prefigured some Classic buildings. That more tombs have not been found may result from the difficulty of excavating into such large constructions.

An immense concentration of Preclassic communities, some connected by elevated causeways, along with moated precincts at the center of sites, bespeak a level of planning and labor management without precedent in the Maya world. Yet scholars have tended to emphasize such monumental constructions, impressive as they are, at intellectual cost. Relatively little is known about the more modest residences in Preclassic cities. Large

[1] The most recent summation of E-Groups is in James Doyle, "Early Maya Geometric Planning Conventions at El Palmar, Guatemala," *Journal of Archaeological Science* 40 (2013), 793–8; and James Doyle, "Re-group on 'E-Groups': Monumentality and Early Centers in the Middle Preclassic Maya Lowlands," *Latin American Antiquity* 23(4) (2012), 355–79.

populations can be assumed to exist, but their living arrangements and means of support remain an important target for future research.

Equally puzzling are the linkages between the Preclassic cities and those of the Classic period, a time lasting from about 300 to 850 CE. Large Preclassic buildings served as the footings for Classic buildings, but their respective functions most likely diverged during the ruptures and demographic tumult at the end of Preclassic civilization. What can be affirmed is the continued focus, from the Preclassic into Classic times, on monumental symmetries, alignments, and rituals that accented cosmic centrality and processional engagement with multiple directions, including the sky, earth, and underworld supports. The causeways and elevated walkways, the emphasis on grandiose stairways, and the large plazas attest to an interest in channeling movement in formal ways. Certain plazas, patios, passageways, or landings punctuated these movements with places of interruption or momentary assembly. Yet these channeled spaces were as much about differentiating as joining groups of people. The summits of most monumental buildings were elevated but also difficult to access. The objective, pioneered in Preclassic cities yet expressed more fully in Late Classic Maya ones, was to reduce and modulate the flow of human traffic to a carefully monitored trickle of privileged people. The sight of bodies moving up and down stairways would remind those below of an experience that was, in all likelihood, restricted to the few.

Nonetheless, there are few secure records of rulers or elites in the Preclassic period, and the texts from that time are among the most opaque in the corpus of Maya glyphic writing. Most glyphs appear to extol gods. To take one example, the extraordinary Preclassic murals of San Bartolo, Guatemala, among the richest and most diverse known in the Maya region, do not clearly concern rulers, although the themes within them prefigure the later rituals of Classic dynasties. The existence of walls at sites like El Mirador, however, along with rare images of what may be war captives, hint at flesh-and-blood conflicts and human trophies from battle. But the historical texture that would deepen our understanding of the Preclassic has proved elusive.

Classic Maya cities are less mute in their motive and the identity of those who commissioned buildings. Scholars can often show that a certain king commissioned this expansion of a plaza or that construction of a pyramid or palace. The settlements can be described as courts in two senses, as social groups that focused on identifiable sacred kings, their consorts, and families, along with courtiers and servants, and as physical settings that housed the royal court within clustered buildings and palaces across the city. These patterns held particular force in the central part of the Yucatan Peninsula; other zones might have had more heterogeneous or diverse organization, without the same emphasis on spiritually charged leaders. Generally, with a few exceptions, the cities were highly variable in size, some with only a few hundred or thousand inhabitants, and others, depending on how boundaries are drawn, with considerably more. Size probably mattered: smaller communities, although equipped with sacred lords and attendant courts, would lend themselves to deeper relationships in which inhabitants had many opportunities for mutual recognition and dense interaction; larger ones would trend to more superficial knowledge of identities or personalities. Rulers and other elites probably fulfilled the role of the most recognizable people in such communities, and as logical focal points for collective action. In most regions, the settlements came to an end in the eighth and ninth centuries CE, with stronger continuity along the edges of the Yucatan Peninsula and in particular lake or river areas.

Another feature should be mentioned. A fundamental problem in looking at Maya cities is the temptation to engage in analytical anachronism. This is a process by which ideas are applied outside their time, often to jarring effect. For Maya cities, anachronism often arises from the use of typological labels. Presumed at times to be universal, these terms actually pertain to the periods or places in which they were formulated. A good illustration comes from the models of urban layout that issue from the Chicago school of sociology and its attention to industrial cities of the late nineteenth- and early twentieth-century United States or Europe.[2] On a vague level, the comparisons appear to be valid, but only in the sense that populations tend to centralize or to disperse at times into constituent clusters of varying function. The disadvantages of the labels are far stronger. For example, among the Classic Maya, no such groupings of population are industrial or capitalist; none are assisted by mass-transportation or automobiles, and, other than a small number of late cities such as Chichen Itza, Mexico – a city whose composition remains an enigma – few contain any evidence of

[2] For such views see, Joyce Marcus and Jeremy A. Sabloff, "Introduction," in Joyce Marcus and Jeremy A. Sabloff (eds.), *The Ancient City: New Perspectives on Urbanism in the Old and New World* (Santa Fe, NM: School for Advanced Research Press, 2008), pp. 3–26; views first espoused in Joyce Marcus, "On the Nature of the Mesoamerican City," in Evon Z. Vogt and Richard M. Leventhal (eds.), *Prehistoric Settlement Patterns: Essays in Honor of Gordon R. Willey* (Albuquerque: University of New Mexico Press, 1983), pp. 195–242.

distinct ethnic groups. Varied ethnicity is more a pattern beyond the Maya region, especially at Teotihuacan in central Mexico. A further implausibility, and another instance of anachronism, is the argument that Maya cities would house, as suggested for some cities such as Caracol, Belize, a set of "middle classes."[3] The site in question, nestled against the Maya mountains in Belize, is striking for its spider web of small causeways, most of limited investment in their construction, agricultural terraces, and relatively dense clustering of residential groups. The excavators see the city as exceptional for its size yet also an example for all Maya sites because of its internal organization. By definition, a "middle class" lies between "lower" and "upper classes." In its original formulation within political philosophy, it would include socially aspirant people that possess the voting franchise, newly disposable income from the industrial revolution, and a desire to live in more spacious areas, perhaps in emulation of social superiors. The attendant meanings are misleading and lie far from what can be construed of Maya cities.

The value of urban typology is that it furthers comparison. It affirms a view that sustained concentrations of humans in any one place might coincide with general patterns. But the implication that similar urban plans reveal similar motivations requires knowledge about the decisions and processes behind those plans. To offer one example, pedestrian cities without benefit of other forms of transportation would fail to configure space in the same way as a city with vehicles. Other evaluative terms like "sprawl" (described by Michael Smith as "low-density, scattered, urban development without systematic large-scale or regional public land-use planning") or "squatters" ("informal settlements and their associated poverty"), which are said to characterize Maya settlement, are equally suspect in that they imply knowledge, frequently unavailable to scholars, about land-holding and other influences on settlement.[4] The use of descriptive terms like "sprawl" and "squatters" encourages a general conversation about how to compare cities in different parts of the ancient world. But it must grapple in all seriousness with the historical and cultural contexts that generated those terms. At Maya sites, such low-density occupation probably results from the need to accommodate agricultural or horticultural production – hence

---

[3] Arlen F. Chase and Diane Z. Chase, "A Mighty Maya Nation: How Caracol Built Its Empire by Cultivating its 'Middle Class,'" *Archaeology* 49 (1996), 66–72.

[4] Michael E. Smith, "Sprawl, Squatters and Sustainable Cities: Can Archaeological Data Shed Light on Modern Urban Issues?", *Cambridge Archaeological Journal* 20 (2010), 229–53.

the plausible suggestion by some, such as Arlen and Diane Chase, along with Christian Isendahl, that the Classic Maya lived in "garden cities."[5] Yet, despite the suggestion that horticulture existed in Maya urbanism, virtually nothing is known of how land rights were apportioned. The key point is that morphology, the shape of a city, serves as only one means of understanding Maya clusters of population. There are other dimensions, too: (1) how the Maya labeled dense settlements, named the components within them, and bonded these to what the social constituents might have been; (2) how buildings and open areas functioned, and the linked question of the ways in which humans moved across spaces in daily and long-term patterns; and (3) how, over time, the varying wishes and commissions of royalty and other elites molded the layout of city design and use, especially with respect to that which could be seen and from where. These features open broader perspectives on the activities and meanings that informed Classic Maya cities.

Naming and social constituents

Any discussion of large settlements among the Classic Maya must begin with a paradox, that their inscriptions contain no known term for "city." A common misconception is that a title for lordship equates to a label for urban settlement, a problem in general with perspectives that apply much later evidence from the Maya to periods a millennium before. This is an imprecise reading. The title instead refers to dominion over places (Figure 3.1a). Called an "Emblem glyph" by scholars, the title describes a ruler as the "holy (k'uhul) + 'variable element' + lord (ajaw)." Where it can be understood, the variable element identifies a location, not a collection of people. In rare cases, rulers may claim sovereignty over two such locations, as in unusual examples of "twin Emblems" that occur in parts of the Usumacinta River drainage in Chiapas, Mexico, or at El Zotz, Guatemala. Even more unusual are instances in which rulers from different sites employ the same Emblem. This usage arises from the competing claims of quarreling lines in a single dynasty, as at Tikal and Dos Pilas, Guatemala, or from a linked process by which a cadet line "hives" off from its parent dynasty. As a label, "hiving" derives from the analogy of a new bee colony, flying away to a new home. In human terms, it could begin amicably, as a mechanism by

[5] Chase and Chase, "A Mighty Maya Nation"; Christian Isendahl, "Agro-urban Landscapes: The Example of Maya Lowland Cities," *Antiquity* 86 (2012), 1112–25.

Figure 3.1 Glyphic terms for rulers and components of cities: (a) *k'uhul ajaw* title from Dos Pilas Hieroglyphic Stairway 2 (photograph by David Stuart); (b) *ch'e'n* sign, Tikal Marcador (photograph by Stephen Houston); (c) *witz*, Río Azul; and (d) *ha'* from Río Azul Tomb 12 (photograph by George Mobley, courtesy George Stuart).

which potential competitors at royal courts left to represent dynastic interests elsewhere. These new settlements might extend the influence of the parent dynasty. But, at Tikal and Dos Pilas, the experiment went awry, and the cadet settlement became an ally of the traditional enemies of its family.

The contrast with later words and concepts for "city" is puzzling. Sources from after the Spanish Conquest do offer such terms, as in *chinam* or *noh kah* (in Yukatek Maya, spoken in the northern part of the Yucatan Peninsula). The first is a relatively late loanword from central Mexico, the second a reference to a large settlement or population. A cognate term, *tenamit* or *tinamit*, also of Mexican (Nahuatl) origin, occurs in Highland Maya languages. All such words carry the notion of a group of linked people, often living in close proximity, perhaps even as "territorial units." Other dictionaries from after the Spanish Conquest mention "big pieces of ground" (*muk'ta j-tek lum*, Tzotzil Maya, from Chiapas, Mexico) or "many neighbors" (*mucul ghculegh*, Tzeldal Maya, also from Chiapas). Not a few lists of words point to a term for a "community" of indeterminate size (for example, *popol*, Ch'olti' Maya, a language closely affiliated to that of most Maya inscriptions). Glyphic texts from the Classic period demonstrate a markedly different concern, with specific locations within such settlement. The notion of settlement as a gathering of large quantities of people seems to have been irrelevant.

Most such words highlight the tangible and the practical, but with nuances of deeper, often unexpected meaning. The basic locational term, from a reading by David Stuart that remains under discussion, is *ch'e'n*, "cave" or "rocky outcrop" (Figure 3.1b). In tropical conditions, where water is both a resource and a seasonal nuisance, exposed rock presents an attraction to settlement, and is more likely to appear in conditions of good drainage. Another view, that this essential concept of "place" relates to the ritual caves (*ch'e'n*) underlying settlement – such have indeed been found – is less an alternative than a supplemental perspective. Both views, the practical and symbolic, emphasize a place of stony fixity, prominence and permanence, along with subterranean labyrinths of some complexity, whether conceptual or real. The term for *ch'e'n* is sometimes coupled with the glyph for "earth," perhaps as an allusion to terrestrial firmament. Other texts appear to use *ch'e'n* in a poetic device, that of couplets, which juxtapose opposing elements so as to describe a greater totality. On one inscription from Tikal, Guatemala, a place is described as a "sky-*ch'e'n*, earth-*ch'e'n*," while other texts may abbreviate this expression to "sky-*ch'e'n*" only. At Palenque, Mexico, the exclusive use of this expression may, by another explanation, refer to an exalted or elevated place within a city.

A related term is *witz*, "hill" (Figure 3.1c). This, too, applies to many places of settlement, reflecting both a common Maya avoidance of ill-drained locations for settlement and a preference for settings that are breezy, dominant, and defensible. As with many place names, the term often carries a suffix read *nal*. The glyph comes from an apparent depiction of a maize cob, *nal* in certain Mayan languages, but its meaning is more diffuse. Possibly, the sign refers in some way to a place of cultivation or to some unrelated homophone. A central feature of the *witz* glyph is its evident blurring of the natural and human-made, a feature going back to Preclassic antecedents. The inscriptions make no real distinction between labels assigned to large hills and artificial constructions, such as the bases of pyramids. In Maya thought, they appear to have been equivalent. This was more than metaphor – a pattern known also in central Mexico, where the great pyramid of Cholula was labeled the Tlachihualtepetl (man-made mountain). One persuasive theory holds that, in a sense, Maya cities "captured" or replicated sacred features found in distant, undomesticated, notionally dangerous spaces – caves, hills – and brought them under central, elite control.[6] This replication cloaks a human act, one of commissioning and constructing a building or set of tiered platforms, within a magical claim that a product of human ingenuity is in fact both natural and eternal. A hill has always been there, and yet has just rematerialized by royal or elite command, simultaneously ancient and new. The inclusion of sacred wilds into communities recalls a larger proposition of both the Classic and later Maya – that distant forests, hills, and desolate zones are categorically distinct from the domesticated, civilized spaces of city centers. Yet, in seeming paradox, the heart of Maya cities consists precisely of those features that encapsulate danger. This sense of concentrated if controlled peril, a menacing unpredictability brought into the very core of settlement, is compounded by the "residents" of many Maya pyramids. Glyphic texts indicate that some of these buildings were *wahyib*, "sleeping places" for gods. In dormant, effigy form, these beings presumably occupied the pyramid summits until awakened by ritual. It is likely that their presence prompted awe from those who saw or approached such precincts. Visits to them would doubtless have been tightly regulated.

Another set of terms that refer to Maya settlements highlight a basic need, not for well-drained and defensible locations, but for water. Many place names refer to particular *ha'*, "body of water" (Figure 3.1d). Again, as with rocky outcrops or hills this involves more than mere convenience. Bodies of water were thought by the Classic Maya to contain snake-like spirits that were sometimes impersonated by Maya lords and ladies. The Maya clearly understood the relation of such sources of water to sustaining liquids deep underground and to expansive hydrological cycles that tied the ambient sea to storms overhead, and to run-off that entered the soil for eventual recycling. The glyph for plazas themselves may refer to a concept of a hollowed-out, watery space. What appears today as a flat surface might have been, to Maya eyes and symbolic understanding, a cavernous opening that connected subterranean locales to levels above. The intent seems less to facilitate

[6] Andrea Stone, "From Ritual in the Landscape to Capture in the Urban Center: The Recreation of Ritual Environments in Mesoamerica," *Journal of Ritual Studies* 6 (1992), 109–32.

movement between these zones than to acknowledge the complex, sometimes concealed layers of the city fabric, of things seen but remote or restricted in access, such as the top temple of a pyramid, along with features known to exist yet that remained invisible.

A notable attribute of many Maya cities is that later builders retained clear notions of what lay underneath, often in conditions of astonishing preservation. Few Maya buildings of monumental size were destroyed to enable new construction. Instead, sculptures were "de-activated," their nose, ears, mouths mutilated. The whole was covered carefully with sand, powdered limestone, and new fill. An effective illustration of this occurs at Copan, Honduras, where a succession of thematically linked buildings, most connected to solar aspects of a dynastic founder, occurs in and under Structure 10L-16, in a sequence of buildings that spans about four centuries, from c. 400 to 800 CE. In a sense, the same building was replicated over time, but in ever larger form and with new iconographic programs that emphasized different aspects of solar imagery.

Other named features of urban landscapes include pyramids and altars, neither, unfortunately, with fully accepted readings of their glyphic references. The pyramids emphasize frontal stairways, of the sort that occur in many examples of Maya graffiti. At the top are small summit buildings with what may be stylized incense burners. The stairways, some long and disposed into separate levels or sections, underscore a means of access and the steep and difficult ascent to a sacred space. The altars are often on stone pedestals, an arrangement that is in fact somewhat uncommon at Maya sites. What is striking is that the two signs combined, pyramid followed by altar, appear to serve as a Maya expression for settled, ritually observant locations, perhaps involving activities in sequence, a pyramid ascended, an offering made on an altar. A text at Copan ties their absence to the death, possibly in ambush, of a ruler of that site; the rather opaque inscription may, by one reading, refer to a wilderness where such an unthinkable act would take place. In much the same way, an interregnum at Palenque, Chiapas, employs a couplet, "lord" and "sacred lady," to suggest the core of governance and, in their loss or "disappearance" (*satayi* in the glyphs), the absence of royal rule.[7] Nonetheless, it is doubtful that the Classic Maya reduced their royal courts to king and queen alone. Dozens of other figures appear in the

---

[7] Nikolai Grube, "Palenque in the Maya World," in Martha J. Macri and Jan McHargue (eds.), *Eighth Palenque Round Table, 1993* (San Francisco, CA: Pre-Columbian Art Research Institute, 1996), pp. 1–13.

Figure 3.2 Building maquette, Mundo Perdido Complex, Tikal (Proyecto Nacional Tikal).

Bonampak murals, from the later ninth century CE, revealing a complex cast of persons that nonetheless lived in service and subordination to members of the royal family. It appears, from studies of bone isotopes, however, that the Maya could "vote with their feet," with higher rates of mobility than previously suspected – in their demographic composition, Maya cities, like many elsewhere, were relatively fluid.

Other buildings in the Maya texts correspond to stairways, known as *ehb*, and ballcourts recorded by glyphs that are not yet deciphered. Both are tied to ball games, often marked by the inclusion of a bouncing rubber ball, or, in the case of platforms, to renderings of tribute and captives in displays that could be seen by this expedient from some distance away. One of the few surviving depictions, a maquette, of a Maya city, from Tikal, shows a dense cluster of ballcourts, pyramids, and platforms, but, perhaps because of the compressed format, with surprisingly little space in between (Figure 3.2). The inscriptions also mention buildings, known as *naah*, "structure," or *otoot*, "dwelling." The former refers to the superstructure of buildings, the latter to a place of occupation. The sign itself shows a platform supporting a perishable building with thatch roof and vertical supports. That the building was of stone and mortar mattered less than the invocation of an ephemeral, organic archetype. The question arises as to whether these terms corresponded to the actual remains of houses in Maya cities. To a notable extent, settlement in Classic Maya cities expressed a pattern of formal if not functional replication. A square or rectangular space was delimited on all sides by buildings that faced inwards. A majority had a full complement of such constructions, yet some possessed only one detectable structure and a small platform at best. Contiguous blocks of patios proliferated in others. Regardless of scale and centrality, the patio defined in this way occurred in the most modest abodes all the way up to the central plazas of most cities.

The spaces accorded, too, with the many references in Maya texts to a field of peripheral vision, the *ichon*, that could be accommodated or framed in such enclosed areas.

A vexed question in Classic Maya cities is the social meaning of these patio groups (Figure 3.3). The likelihood is strong that they housed some discrete component of Classic society, whether of lineages or looser group-ings described by anthropologists as "houses" remains unclear.[8] One text, from the site of Tamarindito, Guatemala, suggests that, in the seventh century CE, certain families or lineages drew their identity from "structures" or *naah*. The mother was linked to a building with a floral name, the father with another related to maize, although the possibility remains that these were actual physical entities, not merely a set of social categories. Another proposal matches a title, "banner" or *lakam*, with tributaries at royal courts that have come from smaller collections of patio groups, yet this, too, continues more as an intriguing possibility than an established connection: no such titles have been found in explicit connection with these groups.[9]

Movement, obligation, and performance

A notable attribute of later Maya ideas about appropriate or correct behavior is that it conforms to movement and handed-ness. "Right" and "straight" correspond closely to concepts of "truth," "virtue," "cleansing," even "prophecy." The widespread nature of these notions today suggests their great antiquity, as does the emphasis in much indigenous ritual on visits to caves and high-points as necessary practices for the supplication of supernat-ural beings: that is, the movements constituted an obligation on the part of rulers and probably all other levels of society. Not surprisingly, Classic Maya evidence stresses the importance of this activity, in a variety of ways. Central to acts of dedication, most fire rituals involve a metaphor of "entering," as do expressions that describe the voyages of the dead by water or by road. Caves such as Naj Tunich in Guatemala are painted with texts that describe visits by youths of various royal houses, perhaps as parts of *rites*

---

[8] Susan D. Gillespie, "Maya 'Nested Houses': The Ritual Construction of Place," in Rosemary A. Joyce and Susan D. Gillespie (eds.), *Beyond Kinship: Social and Material Reproduction in House Societies* (Philadelphia: University of Pennsylvania Press), pp. 135–60.

[9] Alfonso Lacadena García-Gallo, "El título *Lakam*: evidencia epigráfica sobre la organi-zación tributaria y militar interna de los reinos mayas del clásico," *Mayab* 20 (2008), 23–43.

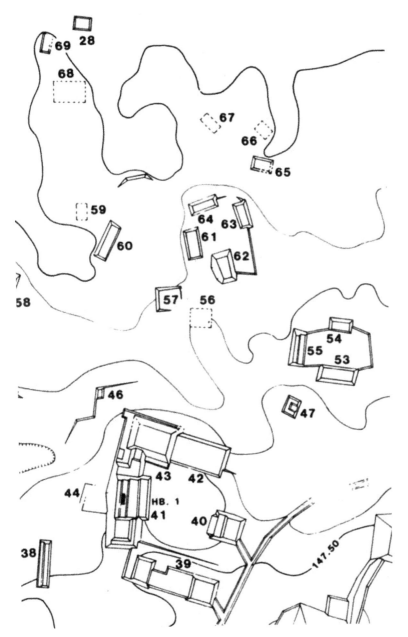

Figure 3.3 Patio Groups at Dos Pilas, Guatemala. Numbers represent designations of individual mounds within urban sectors (mapped and drawn by Stephen Houston).

Figure 3.4 Sakbih 2 from Ucí, Yucatan (photograph by Scott Hutson).

de passage; at least two other caves may refer to such visits as *ahni*, "running." An object that has been suggested to be a dynastic effigy, litter, sedan chair, or shrine of a portable sort played a large role in battle, was seized at times by enemies and transported to other sites. Such focus on movement is consistent with the presence of cleared, relatively straight causeways, elevated or stone-lined paths or walls that show an investment in directed movement or segregated spaces within some Maya sites (Figure 3.4). Yet not all were only about local linkages or leading to and from points of centrality. The largest causeway system of all, across the Yucatan, may have been about larger patterns involving the dominant movements of sun and rain across the peninsula. The glyphic terms for these connective spaces were *sakbih*, "white" or "artificial paths," so-named because of their prepared, stony, or plastered surfaces or possibly *bituun*, "road-stone," although the latter might also have been a word for a "patio" or more enclosed space.[10]

In the Mediterranean and elsewhere, connective facilities – roads, corridors, plazas, and less formal paths – have been described as "urban armatures" by William MacDonald, but they are, among the Maya, both constraining in the sense of affecting future movement and insecurely obedient to any central, coherent purpose.[11] There is no single design or package of intentions behind any one Maya city, and the attempts to find cosmological orderings behind the layout of elements have not met with

[10] David Stuart, "Hit the Road," *Maya Decipherment* (2007), accessed July 4, 2014, http://decipherment.wordpress.com/2007/12/07/hit-the-road/
[11] William L. MacDonald, *The Architecure of the Roman Empire: An Urban Appraisal* (New Haven: Yale University Press, 1986), p. x.

complete acceptance. But what the spaces do is both to channel how people move and to dictate by the space thus defined how many participants and viewers can be accommodated. Comparison between the postulated populations of certain sites and the number of people that could stand in such areas suggests a high degree of civic involvement. The impulse to move had its random or unmarked aspects, yet it likely included highly organized motions that corresponded to key moments in the Maya calendar. The later, Postclassic Maya were much concerned with placing wooden effigies in sequence, and by cardinal orientations. There are hints that the Classic Maya did the same by setting stones on the first dates of certain years. The marking of time and space served as a reinforcement and maintenance of order and, probably, a commemoration of primordial acts that established that configuration through offerings of blood, fire, and flesh. Directions corresponded to "world trees" in which supernatural eagles perched and spread their wings. Cluttering these now bare spaces could well have been a large number of perishable banners, parasols, and other objects whose existence is hinted at in Maya graffiti and stone supports at sites like Bonampak, Mexico.

What is more plain is that the large spaces of many Maya patios, the central nodes of causeways, were marked with sculptures designed to depict the rulers in eternal dance, and sometimes as impersonators of deities brought to earth. The majority of Maya stelae, and many other sculptures besides, show rulers, lords, and a few ladies in attitudes of dance. These movements must have been stately and decorous. The dances themselves often appear as little more than a slightly bowed body, a lifted heel, and, above all, a majestic stolidity that would contrast with more energetic dance elsewhere; for the Classic Maya, muscular dances were probably more appropriate for sacred clowns and non-elites. An essential property of royal dance, however, was that it brought deities to earth in active, palpable interaction with humans. This occurred when deities or other spirits took temporary residence in the dancer's body. The rich regalia of dance marked and facilitated such concurrent identities, so that one body could house multiple energies. Demographers count people to arrive at populations, but this enumeration would be complicated if, in Maya thought, denizens of a city could include spirits, a multitude of gods or ancestors with which one could communicate, or, in yet more surprising configurations, as noted by David Stuart, rulers becoming one with visible and concrete units of time. Much royal depiction would represent permanent embodiments of these acts of impersonation and calendrical celebration.

Commissions and viewsheds of kings

A final, remaining theme is that Maya cities accord with general concepts of landscape features yet also remain a malleable work-in-progress. The view of any such city today would contain a certain arrangement of buildings and spaces in "urban armatures." Archaeological excavations show time and again, however, that these views could change abruptly with new construction. Another conclusion is that the shifts are neither gradual nor arbitrary, but that they respond to royal or elite wishes when involving monumental or civic constructions. Classic Maya cities have no ultimate desired form and little evidence of firm, comprehensive planning; in some respects, Preclassic settlements seem more tightly organized in this regard. Without question, however, large Classic settlements have dominant orientations that appear to shift from city to city, but these are not the same as seamless, integrated wholes. The suggestion that cities were crafted in large part to capture water, as proposed by some researchers, may transform a necessity in a land of torrential, seasonal downpours into a design principle. The builders did, to be sure, respond to the inertia of preexisting buildings, which were difficult to remove. In fact, some structures, as at Piedras Negras, Guatemala, were probably left exposed and in advanced decay for centuries of otherwise robust activity around the site. Such decay must have been as meaningful as any program of periodic refurbishment.

If there is a characteristic of the final centuries of the Classic period, it is that buildings standing in distinct groups, not fully incorporated into flows of movement from one complex to the other, were enveloped by broader spaces. Cities like Palenque and Piedras Negras witnessed the construction of new temple sectors or the creation of large, connective spaces that buried earlier, less coherent groupings of buildings (Figure 3.5). Very likely, these occurred as ways to celebrate a crucial period ending in the Maya calendar, at 692 CE. Some of these new spaces, and courtyard compounds nearby, might have accommodated market facilities that become clearer. At Piedras Negras, this coincided with an attempt to create ever more restricted spaces in the royal palace – a process of closure that, on occasion, removed rulers, their families, and courtiers from general gaze.

Just as size mattered in Classic cities, so too did visual relations – the act of seeing and being seen. The operative concept here is that of a "visualscape," the means by which, in the martial world of the Classic Maya, threats could be perceived in time for ready response and buildings detected from areas far distant. The premise, amply confirmed by testing, is that such

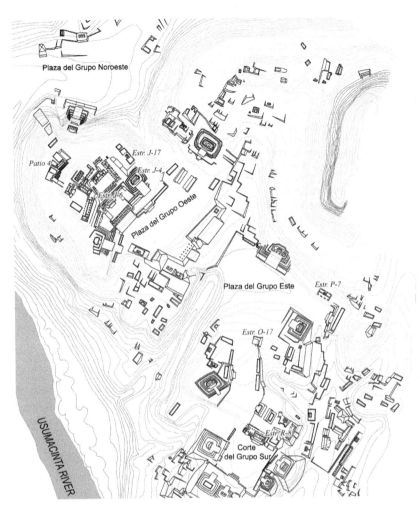

Figure 3.5 Plazas at Piedras Negras, Guatemala, north to top, 600 meters wide, showing massive leveled zone (generated by Zachary Nelson).

visualscapes were calculated and dedicated to the purposes of dominance. The analytical tool to study regional visibility is Geographical Information System (GIS) software packages. Although there are numerous problems associated with visibility analysis in GIS, many of these issues involved the distant ends of viewsheds (that is, edge effects and curvature of the earth). But, at such distances, people cannot be easily distinguished, nor can their intent.

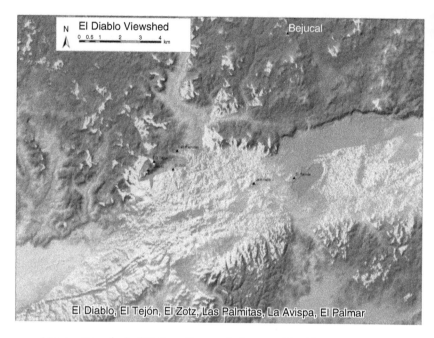

Map 3.2 Viewshed of El Zotz, Guatemala (generated by Thomas Garrison).

One such settlement is El Zotz, Guatemala, located along the foothills of the Buenavista Escarpment, which defines the northern side of the Buenavista Valley (Map 3.2).[12] This corridor represents a major geophysical connection between the northeast and northwest regions of northern Guatemala and beyond. El Zotz is also situated immediately to the west of the southern terminus of a drainage that splits the escarpment to the north; this valley leads up into the Mirador Basin and its Preclassic communities. Tikal, which was, at times an antagonist of El Zotz, lies about 21 kilometers to the east. The pyramids of Tikal are clearly visible from Structure F8-1 of the Diablo Group and slightly less visible from the main pyramid (Structure L7-11) adjacent to the El Zotz Acropolis.

The combination of a powerful aggressor nearby and a large natural travel corridor would have made visibility crucial at El Zotz. The city of

[12] These data came from Airsar and were subvented by R. Sharer and J. Quilter, SBE-BCS NSF Grant 0406472, "Archaeological Application of Airborne Synthetic Aperture Radar Technology in Southern Mexico and Central America," and R. Sharer and J. Quilter, NGS Grant 7575-04, "Archaeological Application of Airborne Synthetic Aperture Radar Technology in Southern Mexico and Central America."

El Zotz began to grow during the Early Classic period and its royal court was established, among other places, at the Diablo Group on top of the Buenavista Escarpment. In 2010, the tomb of the possible dynastic founder was discovered beneath a substructure of F8-1. The exterior facades and roofcomb of the adjacent structure, which faced the valley, were decorated with monumental architectural masks, painted in red with polychrome accents, and representing different guises of the Maya Sun God. This courtly structure would have been visible from the valley below. Distinguished yet further by its red surface, it was sure to stand out against the sky, catching sunlight at daybreak and sunset.

A viewshed generated from the highest elevations at El Diablo shows that the group would have been visible over great distances. Sentries had a commanding view of the Buenavista Valley, over a distance of *c.* 8 kilometers, from El Palmar in the east to a southern outcrop of the escarpment in the west. Any undetected passage by El Diablo would have been difficult other than by night or in conditions of heavy mist or rain. In contrast, the Late Classic pyramid L7-11 and the El Zotz Acropolis show a greatly reduced viewshed. This could reflect a false sense of security on the part of El Zotz following the defeat of Tikal by Calakmul, Campeche, Mexico, in 562 CE. Also, the Late Classic would have been the period of maximum deforestation in the region, perhaps requiring less elevation while observing the valley. Alternatively, the hilltop location at El Diablo may have still been used as a prominent lookout (along with other points along the escarpment), while the royal court was situated in a lower, more open area that allowed for expansion of the site core. Either way, it appears that control of the valley was still important, but the visibility of El Zotz's architecture, at the regional level at least, had reduced priority.

A very different viewshed characterizes the city of Piedras Negras, located on the eastern bank of a bend in the Usumacinta River as it flows northwest toward the Gulf of Mexico (Map 3.3). The river cuts a deep channel through the hilly karst landscape of the Sierra Lacandon. For some of its stretches – there are treacherous rapids that require portage and rope guides – the river represents the fastest way to travel through the region in both past and present. Piedras Negras lies some 43 kilometers northwest of its major antagonist, Yaxchilan, Mexico. With such a high-relief landscape, visibility along the river would have been crucial to anticipate attack and receive traders.

The South Group of Piedras Negras was an Early Classic seat of the royal court. A viewshed generated from the highest point in the South Group

Map 3.3 Viewshed of Piedras Negras, Guatemala (generated by Thomas Garrison).

shows a clear preference for visibility upriver in the direction of Yaxchilan, along with direct access to a side valley that would have been periodically replenished with agricultural nutrients from floodwaters. The viewshed covers 2 kilometers of the river, with 1.5 kilometers between the first visible point upriver and the South Group. During the Late Classic period the Piedras Negras royal court strongly focused in the West Group, located further downriver. The viewshed from the West Group covers 3 kilometers of the Usumacinta River and looks both up and downriver. Relocating the court inserted more distance between the heart of the city and possible attackers. The move may have been prompted by conflicts with Yaxchilan toward the end of the Early Classic. The acropolis in the West Group presented an intimidating sight as aggressors or merchants approached from upriver. The restricting nature of the geology appears to have made the river the focal point of local viewsheds. A viewshed from the highest point near Piedras Negras, on the hill behind Structure O-13, revealed that only an additional 100 meters of the river were visible compared to the viewshed from the South and West Groups.

Conclusions

For all the shared concepts and organizational principles, Maya cities showed the diversity that might be expected from complex, local histories. All had palaces and pyramids, most had ballcourts, none eschewed the massive leveling by which the subtle and sometimes dramatic gradations and declivities were flattened to provide spaces for civic movement, both casual and organized, individual and collective. What is notably lacking is any indigenous emphasis on demography as a determinant of labeling – the very term "city" had little bearing on their texts or representations. Rather, the Maya focused on places of worship, watered locations, prominent hilltops, individual structures and dwellings, and on blurred categories between the "natural" and the "artificial," and between surfaces and underground labyrinths. The diverse pattern of elevated or demarcated roads or causeways, the *sakbih*, points to a grappling with a wish to connect against the inertial reality of preexisting construction. If Maya cities were impressive, to travelers approaching from afar by channeled routes, then they also commanded increasing resources for maintenance in areas beset by seasonal rains, baking heat, and destructive molds. Tending such large establishments confronted later occupants with hard choices and the dilemmas of deferred maintenance. Still, the Maya cities were dedicated ones. They served the collective purposes of ritual and courtly service, at royal and elite levels; they framed the simplex and multiplex relations that made a city both grand and intimate; they sponsored the growth and harvesting of crops to feed the city, along with the making, trade, or distribution of goods to equip it. Underneath, in the waiting earth and masonry, they collected in final measure the bodies of those who came before, in a community of the quick and the dead, of ancestors in dialogue with the descendants who claimed them. The extent to which their social parts, their patio groups, the people who lived in them, articulated in smoothly functioning wholes remains a matter of debate. It is likely that the dedicated city was also, in most cases, a place like any another, torn by hope and tension, some needs met, but, in the main, most of them unfulfilled.

FURTHER READINGS

Ashmore, Wendy, "Some Issues of Method and Theory in Lowland Maya Settlement Archaeology," in Wendy Ashmore (ed.), *Lowland Maya Settlement Patterns*, Santa Fe, NM: School of American Research, 1981, pp. 47–54.

Ashmore, Wendy, and Jeremy Sabloff, "Spatial Orders in Maya Civic Plans," *Latin American Antiquity* 13 (2002), 201–15.

Barrera Vásquez, Alfredo (ed.), *Diccionario Maya Cordemex, Maya–Español, Español–Maya*, Mérida, Yucatan: Ediciones Cordemex, 1980.

Bruegmann, Robert, *Sprawl: A Compact History*, Chicago: The University of Chicago Press, 2005.

Chase, Arlen, Diane Z. Chase, and Michael E. Smith, "States and Empires in Ancient Mesoamerica," *Ancient Mesoamerica* 20 (2009), 175–82.

Conolly, James, and Mark Lake, *Geographical Information Systems in Archaeology*, Cambridge: Cambridge University Press, 2006.

Fash, Barbara W., and Richard Agurcia Fasquelle, "The Evolution of Structure 10L-16, Heart of the Copán Acropolis," in E. Wyllys Andrews and William L. Fash (eds.), *Copán: The History of an Ancient Maya Kingdom*, Santa Fe, NM: School of American Research Press, 2005, pp. 201–37.

Feldman, Lawrence H., *A Dictionary of Poqom Maya in the Colonial Era*, Lancaster, CA: Labyrinthos, 2004.

Graham, Ian, *Archaeological Explorations in El Peten, Guatemala*, New Orleans: Middle American Research Institute, Tulane University, 1967.

Houston, Stephen D., "Classic Maya Depictions of the Built Environment," in Stephen D. Houston (ed.), *Form and Meaning in Classic Maya Architecture*, Washington, D.C.: Dumbarton Oaks, 1998, pp. 333–72.

Hieroglyphs and History at Dos Pilas: Dynastic Politics of the Classic Maya, Austin: University of Texas Press, 1993.

"Living Waters and Wondrous Beasts," in Daniel Finamore and Stephen D. Houston (eds.), *Fiery Pool: The Maya and the Mythic Sea*, New Haven, CT: Yale University Press, 2010, pp. 66–79.

Houston, Stephen D., and Takeshi Inomata, *The Classic Maya*, Cambridge: Cambridge University Press, 2009.

Houston, Stephen D., and Patricia A. McAnany, "Bodies and Blood: Critiquing Social Construction in Maya Archaeology," *Journal of Anthropological Archaeology* 22 (2003), 26–41.

Houston, Stephen D., and David Stuart, "Of Gods, Glyphs, and Kings: Divinity and Rulership among the Classic Maya," *Antiquity* 70 (1996), 289–312.

Houston, Stephen D., David Stuart, and Karl Taube, *The Memory of Bones: Body, Being, and Experience among the Classic Maya*, Austin: University of Texas Press, 2006.

Inomata, Takeshi, "Plazas, Performers and Spectacles: Political Theaters of the Classic Maya," *Current Anthropology* 47 (2006), 805–42.

Inomata, Takeshi, and Stephen D. Houston (eds.), *Royal Courts of the Ancient Maya*, Boulder, CO: Westview Press, 2001.

Laporte, Juan Pedro, and Vilma Fialko, "Un reencuentro con Mundo Perdido, Tikal, Guatemala," *Ancient Mesoamerica* 6 (1995), 41–94.

Laughlin, Robert M., *The Great Tzotzil Dictionary of Santo Domingo Zinacantán*, Washington, D.C.: Smithsonian Institution Press, 1988.

Llobera, Marcos, "Extending GIS-based Visual Analysis: The Concept of Visualscapes," *International Journal of Geographical Information Science* 17 (2003), 25–48.

Looper, Matthew, *To Be Like Gods: Dance in Maya Civilization*, Austin: University of Texas Press, 2009.

MacDonald, William L., *The Architecture of the Roman Empire: An Urban Appraisal*, New Haven, CT: Yale University Press, 1986.

Martin, Simon, "Preguntas epigráficas acerca de los escalones de Dzibanché," in Enrique Nalda (ed.), *Los cautivos de Dzibanché*, México: Consejo Nacional para la Cultura y las Artes, Instituto Nacional de Antropología e Historia, 2004, pp. 105–15.

Martin, Simon, and Nikolai Grube, *Chronicle of the Maya Kings and Queens: Deciphering the Dynasties of the Ancient Maya*, London: Thames & Hudson, 2008.

Mathews, Peter, "Classic Maya Emblem Glyphs," in T. Patrick Culbert (ed.), *Classic Maya Political History: Hieroglyphic and Archaeological Evidence*, Cambridge: Cambridge University Press, pp. 19–29.

Maxwell, Judith M., and Robert M. Hill II, *Kaqchikel Chronicles: The Definitive Edition*, Austin: University of Texas Press, 2006.

Miller, Mary E., *The Murals of Bonampak*, Princeton, NJ: Princeton University Press, 1986.

Normark, Johan, "The Triadic Causeways of Ichmul: Virtual Highways Becoming Actual Roads," *Cambridge Archaeological Journal* 18 (2008), 215–38.

Plank, Shannon E., *Maya Dwellings in Hieroglyphs and Archaeology: An Integrative Approach to Ancient Architecture and Spatial Cognition*, Oxford: British Archaeological Reports, 2004.

Rice, Don, "Late Classic Maya Population: Characteristics and Implications," in Glenn R. Storey (ed.), *Urbanism in the Preindustrial World: Cross-Cultural Approaches*, Tuscaloosa: University of Alabama Press, 2006, pp. 252–76.

Robertson, John S., Danny Law, and Robbie A. Haertel, *Colonial Ch'olti': The Seventeenth-Century Morán Manuscript*, Norman: University of Oklahoma Press, 2010.

Ruz, Mario H., *Vocabulario de lengua tzeldal según el orden de Copanabastla de Fray Domingo de Ara*, México, DF: Universidad Nacional Autónoma de México, 1986.

Scarborough, Vernon L., "Reservoirs and Watersheds in the Central Maya Lowlands," in Scott L. Fedick (ed.), *The Managed Mosaic: Ancient Maya Agriculture and Resource Use*, Salt Lake City: University of Utah Press, 1996, pp. 304–14.

Sjoberg, Gideon, *The Preindustrial City: Past and Present*, New York: The Free Press, 1960.

Smith, Michael E., "The Archaeological Study of Neighborhoods and Districts in Ancient Cities," *Journal of Anthropological Archaeology* 29 (2010), 137–54.

"Can We Read Cosmology in Ancient Maya Cityplans? Comment on Ashmore and Sabloff," *Latin American Antiquity* 14 (2003), 221–8.

"Sprawl, Squatters and Sustainable Cities: Can Archaeological Data Shed Light on Modern Urban Issues?", *Cambridge Archaeological Journal* 20 (2010), 229–53.

Smith, Monica L., "Introduction: The Social Construction of Ancient Cities," in Monica L. Smith (ed.), *The Social Construction of Ancient Cities*, Washington, D.C.: Smithsonian Institution Press, 2003, pp. 1–36.

Spence, Michael W., "Tlailotlacan: A Zapotec Enclave in Teotihuacan," in Janet C. Berlo (ed.), *Art, Ideology, and the City of Teotihuacan*, Washington, D.C.: Dumbarton Oaks Research Library and Collection, 1992, pp. 19–88.

Stone, Andrea, *Images from the Underworld: Naj Tunich and the Tradition of Maya Cave Painting*, Austin: University of Texas Press, 1995.

Stone, Andrea, and Marc Zender, *Reading Maya Art: A Hieroglyphic Guide to Ancient Maya Painting and Sculpture*, London: Thames & Hudson, 2011.

Stuart, David, "'The Fire Enters His House': Architecture and Ritual in Classic Maya Texts," in Stephen D. Houston (ed.), *Function and Meaning in Classic Maya Architecture*, Washington, D.C.: Dumbarton Oaks, pp. 373–425.

"New Year Records in Classic Maya Inscriptions," *The PARI Journal* 5 (2004), 1–6.

"Reading the Water Serpent as *witz*," *Maya Decipherment* (2007), accessed August 9, 2014, http://decipherment.wordpress.com/2007/04/13/reading-the-water-serpent/.

Ten Phonetic Syllables, Washington, D.C.: Center for Maya Research, 1987.

Stuart, David, and Stephen D. Houston, *Classic Maya Place Names*, Washington, D.C.: Dumbarton Oaks Research Library and Collection, 1994.

Taube, Karl A., "Ancient and Contemporary Maya Conceptions of the Field and Forest," in A. Gómez-Pompa, Michael F. Allen, Scott L. Fedick, and Juan Jiménez-Moreno (eds.), *Lowland Maya Area: Three Millennia at the Human–Wildland Interface*, New York: Haworth Press, 2003, pp. 461–94.

Taube, Karl A., William A. Saturno, David Stuart, and Heather Hurst, *The Murals of San Bartolo, El Petén, Guatemala*, Barnardsville, NC: Boundary End Archaeology Research Center, 2010, Part 2.

Tokovinine, Alexandre, "The Power of Place: Political Landscape and Identity in Classic Maya Inscriptions, Imagery, and Architecture," unpublished Ph.D. thesis, Harvard University, 2008.

Tourtellot, Gair, "A View of Ancient Maya Settlements in the Eighth Century," in Jeremy A. Sabloff and John S. Henderson (eds.), *Lowland Maya Civilization in the Eighth Century A.D.*, Washington, D.C.: Dumbarton Oaks Research Library and Collection, 1992, pp. 219–41.

Vogt, Evon Z., and David Stuart, "Some Notes on Ritual Caves among the Ancient and Modern Maya," in James E. Brady and Keith M. Prufer (eds.), *In the Maw of the Earth*

Monster: Mesoamerican Ritual Cave Use, Austin: University of Texas Press, 2005, pp. 157–63.

Wheatley, David, and Mark Gillings, "Vision, Perception and GIS: Developing Enriched Approaches to the Study of Archaeological Visibility," in Gary R. Lock (ed.), *Beyond the Map: Archaeology and Spatial Technologies*, Amsterdam: IOS Press, 2000, pp. 1–27.

White, Christine D., Michael W. Spence, H. L. Q. Stuart-Williams, and Henry P. Schwarcz, "Oxygen Isotopes and the Identification of Geographical Origins: The Valley of Oaxaca versus the Valley of Mexico," *Journal of Archaeological Science* 25 (1998), 643–55.

4

Southeast Asian urbanism: from early city to Classical state

MIRIAM T. STARK

When the Portuguese admiral Alfonso de Albuquerque conquered the sultanate of Melaka (Malacca) on August 24, 1511, he brought under Portuguese control a Southeast Asian polity whose reach stretched across the Malay Peninsula. Melaka then housed an urban population of 100,000, in which eighty different languages were spoken by Malays, Chinese, Arabs, Indians, and other ethnicities. Melaka's urban form was not anomalous in sixteenth- and seventeenth-century Southeast Asia. Many of the region's coasts and river valleys housed port cities and capitals with populations of 50,000–100,000 people; population density/square kilometer varied from sparsely peopled hill country to lowland agrarian areas in northern Vietnam and Bali with higher densities than those in contemporary China.[1] The onset of European colonialism in the late eighteenth century reversed this seemingly inexorable trend toward Southeast Asian urbanism, whose roots lay two millennia deep.

It is this earlier heritage of Southeast Asian urbanism, and the role of the urban form in promoting and maintaining polity in first–second millennium Southeast Asia, that forms the focus of this chapter. Polity, power, and urbanism were linked in most regions of Southeast Asia, although the timing and nature of urbanization varied greatly across the region. While mainland Southeast Asians built large fortified urban centers, the densely populated island of Java remained largely free of cities until the thirteenth century CE. Disagreement over when the region's cities first appeared and the forms they took constitute the core of most debates on early Southeast Asian cities. Relatively few scholars, however, have queried the relationship

I thank Norman Yoffee for commissioning this chapter and including me in his NYU-ISAW conference.

[1] Laura Lee Junker, "Political Economy in the Historic Period Chiefdoms and States of Southeast Asia," in Gary M. Feinman and Linda M. Nicholas (eds.), *Archaeological Perspectives on Political Economies* (Salt Lake City: University of Utah Press, 2004), p. 230, Table 12.1.

between early Southeast Asian urbanism, ceremonial power, and performance. This lack of research is puzzling, given Chinese accounts of thirteenth-
century royal display and pageantry in Angkor, and nineteenth-century
accounts of royal collective suicide in response to Dutch militarism in the
Balinese states that we associate most closely with Geertz's model of the
theater state.[2]

This dearth is made more puzzling by the wealth of performance-oriented
iconography on Indic-influenced bas-reliefs that decorate ninth- through
fourteenth-century public architecture from Cambodia, Vietnam, and Java.
Documentary data (both internal and external) outline ways that early
Southeast Asia's leaders gained power through performance. Early Khmer
and Cham elites erected, dedicated, and sponsored shrines for particular
Hindu cults in early first millennium CE settlements that were the region's
first urban forms. Later Khmer and Cham elites built temples as funerary
monuments that anchored their capital cities; these temples honored putative royal ancestors and thereby legitimized their royal claims. Across
mainland Southeast Asia, rulers sponsored hermitages where ascetics practiced esoteric Hindu rituals, and engaged in public performances in rural and
urban shrines that cemented their roles as heads of state. Such performances
required an audience and a venue; the scale and nature of these venues
expanded through time in Southeast Asia's earliest urban centers.

My goal in this chapter is to review the timing and nature of Southeast
Asia's earliest urbanism, to trace changes in form from the first millennium
CE to the second millennium CE (and the Classical period from the ninth to
fourteenth centuries CE), and to examine some ways in which Southeast
Asia's early urban tradition was intimately tied to ritual practice and political
performance. Early Southeast Asian cities were exemplary centers that
shared key structural features, reflecting pan-regional systems that populations materialized through construction and ritual practice. Most mainland
Southeast Asian states had ceremonial centers[3] that also served political,
economic, and social functions (island Southeast Asian states urbanized
later, and in different forms). Central to the first millennium CE ideological
system was a kind of Sanskrit cosmopolitanism, but a growing body of
archaeological research identifies regionalization in urban form that

---

[2] Clifford Geertz, *Negara: The Theater State in Nineteenth-Century Bali* (Princeton, NJ:
Princeton University Press, 1980); and Zhou Daguan, *The Customs of Cambodia/Chen-la
feng tu chi'an*, P. Pelliot (trans.) (Bangkok, Thailand: The Siam Society, 1993).
[3] Paul Wheatley, *The Pivot of the Four Quarters* (Chicago: Aldine Publishing Company,
1971), pp. 477–8.

distinguished even the earliest Southeast Asian cities from their South Asian counterparts. That early Southeast Asian cities served as templates for the region's later Classical cities in organization, elite structure, and ideological underpinnings is clear in developments over a 1,500-year period in the Khmer region of the lower Mekong Basin.

The chapter begins by addressing methodological concerns and contextualizing urban trajectories in the first and second millennia CE by focusing on mainland Southeast Asia for the first millennium CE (where such settlement has been documented). General patterns in Southeast Asian urban morphology and function are reviewed. Discussion then turns to the lower Mekong Basin as a case study for investigating long-term patterns in urbanization and the performance of power.

Nature of data sources

Until quite recently, archaeologists have played a minor role in studying the gap between Southeast Asia's prehistoric and Classical past, in large part because most available information was epigraphic or documentary, and also because of a regional archaeological paradigm that privileged metal-age archaeological research. Yet it is precisely within this "gap" that the region's earliest centers developed, and sparse data sources are a problem. Han Chinese annals provide our earliest glimpses of Southeast Asians, as the Chinese conquered northern Vietnam in III BCE and converted the region into China's southernmost commandery. Their military campaigns south of the Hanoi region failed repeatedly; Chinese accounts of myriad diplomatic missions with various Southeast Asian polities describe a series of kingdoms and urban centers along coasts and river valleys. Most documentary-driven research on Chinese sources displays a bias toward China as catalyst for Southeast Asia's developments; counterbalancing this China bias is a South Asian bias in art historical research on associated statuary and architecture.

Research on the Early Modern period (that is, 1500–1850 CE) reveals that Southeast Asians nurtured a wide array of historical traditions, recorded in epics, court chronicles, music, and drama, and historical analysis of such indigenous sources sheds light on culture, society, and polity. That first millennium CE Southeast Asians were also literate is suggested by Chinese emissaries who describe libraries of texts. Yet the indigenous historical tradition that we can now access consists largely of inscribed stelae that record dedications and elite donations to local shrines and ritual monuments. Most archaeological research on first and second millennium

Southeast Asia views these sites as cultural patrimony and sources of tourism revenue. Today this work is published primarily in vernacular languages, concentrates on the second millennium (at the expense of the first millennium), and consists largely of technical reports on restoration/preservation rather than problem-driven research.

Early urbanism in Southeast Asia: *c.* 500 BCE–500 CE

In mainland Southeast Asia, urbanization began in the period associated with either the Iron Age or the Early Historic period; most scholars associate these changes with the embrace of Brahmanization or "Sanskritization"' from the Gangetic Plain of northeast India. By this time, Southeast Asians had established a tradition of what must be considered small urban states (Map 4.1): across the region, hydraulic works encircled large communities with thick earthen ramparts on whose exterior flanks were moats, connected to nearby waterways. Often constructed in more arid sections of the region's monsoon tropics, these moated settlements provided water during the annual dry season, and defense from outside elements. These early "urban" sites have been the focus of most work; recently, however, archaeologists have begun to document what are quite substantial hinterlands or countrysides that developed in concert with, and surrounded, these large settlements.

Within 500 years, such settlements grew exponentially in size. Ramparts surrounding the site of Co Loa (northern Vietnam), for example, encased an area of 600 hectares, or nearly 200 times the area of settlements associated with preceding Bronze Age settlements there.[4] The contemporary moated and walled site of Angkor Borei (southern Cambodia) encircles a 300-hectare area, and was linked to a series of settlements into the southern Mekong Delta to the site of Oc Eo; this delta-wide system moved goods into the South China Sea maritime trade network and into the lower Mekong Basin.

Form

Southeast Asian archaeologists describe these nucleated settlements as urban, and they appeared both on the coasts and in river networks; their inhabitants engaged in trade and agriculture. Regrettably the city-states of insular Southeast Asia have left a faint archaeological signature and offer little direct evidence of urban morphology. From the Dry Zone of Myanmar

---

[4] Charles F. W. Higham, *Early Cultures of Mainland Southeast Asia* (Chicago: Art Media Resources Ltd., 2003), p. 172.

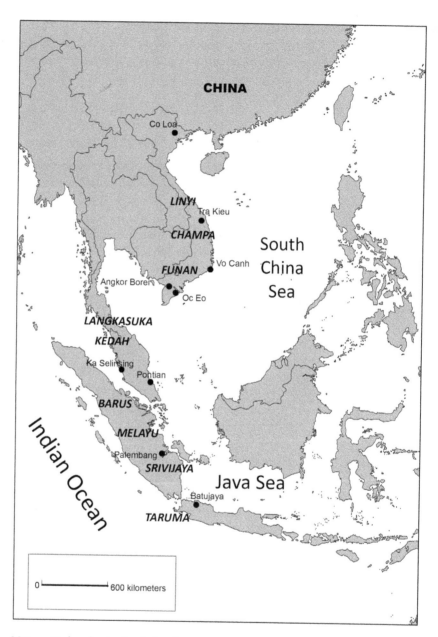

Map 4.1 Early urbanization in Southeast Asia: sites and Chinese toponyms
c. 500 BCE–500 CE (adapted from Pierre-Yves Manguin, "The Archaeology of the
Early Maritime Polities of Southeast Asia," in Peter Bellwood and Ian C. Glover (eds.),
Southeast Asia: From Prehistory to History [London: RoutledgeCurzon, 2004], pp. 282–313.).

to northern Vietnam, in contrast, mainland Southeast Asian urban centers have yielded architectural, sculptural, and artifactual remains that reflect a blend of social and religious concepts from neighboring cultures with an indigenous substrate.

Hermann Kulke's review[5] of first millennium epigraphic materials from insular Southeast Asian city-states offers a concentric urban model that shaped most Southeast Asian settlements.[6] Seventh- through eleventh-century Srivijaya, for example, had an inner core region under direct authority of the ruler, which included the ruler's residence (*kaduatan* or *kraton*), religious buildings, and a surrounding residential area of followers (*puri* or *bhumi*). Beyond that lay a ring of tributary states (*nusantara*) and then other countries (*desantara*) that later might be absorbed into the state.

The capital served as the political center and centripetal force of the early Southeast Asian state. First millennium settlements varied based on local topographic and hydrological features, and have been described previously; they shared the following structural traits:

1. Encircling wall and moat complex (earthen or brick wall; always outside [sometimes with additional interior moat]): moat generally linked to drainage system, and complex as single or multiple occurrence.
2. Brick ritual monuments (may be moat-mound complexes).
3. Central elite walled core (may be called "palace"), which housed the ruler and his retinue.
4. Mortuary areas.
5. Residential areas.

Figure 4.1 represents the southern Cambodian archaeological site of Angkor Borei (dated *c.* 500 BCE–500 CE). This large urban site is characteristic of the Early Historic period, with its encircling wall and moat complex, a scattering of collapsed brick monuments in its northeast and central sectors, a central elite core (labeled as Wat Komnou), and surrounding residential areas.

Function

That these urban centers served economic functions seems clear, although no archaeological work has yet focused on marketplaces or warehouses. And that they were political/administrative centers is also evident, based on

[5] Hermann Kulke, "Epigraphical References to the 'City' and the 'State' in Early Indonesia," *Indonesia* 3 (1991), 3–22.
[6] Pierre-Yves Manguin, "The Amorphous Nature of Coastal Polities in Insular Southeast Asia: Restricted Centres, Extended Peripheries," *Moussons* 5 (2002), 73–99.

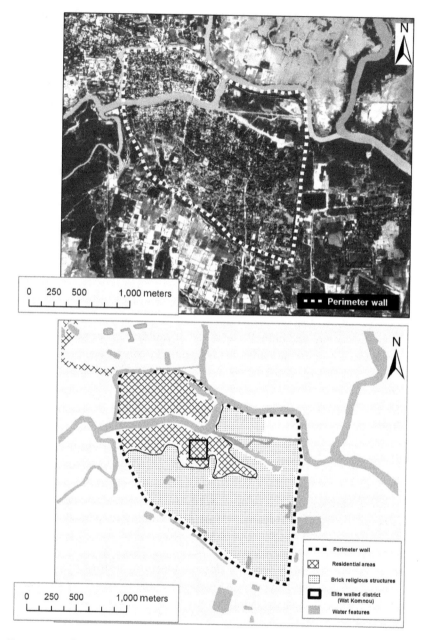

Figure 4.1 Archaeological site of Angkor Borei (Takeo Province, Cambodia) as example of early urban form.

settlement size, the co-occurrence of monumental architecture, and the range of non-utilitarian goods recovered through excavations. Most relevant here is their role as ritual centers. Few regional surveys have studied first millennium CE centers. Such work indicates that, within a broader ritual landscape, these centers housed higher densities of ritual architecture per unit area and larger numbers of religious statuary than that found in surrounding settlements. At least in some centers like Angkor Borei, evidence from the non-utilitarian ceramic assemblage suggests centralized public ritual rather than simply residence as at surrounding settlements. These urban centers thus housed religious complexes (temples and associated water features) and served as the locus of communal rituals. By the seventh and eighth centuries CE, rulers in these capitals consecrated monuments and held audiences with followers on a regular basis.[7]

Early Southeast Asian urban origins

Most early scholars working in mainland Southeast Asia wrote from an unavoidably regionalist bias that emphasized either the role of China or India in shaping early Southeast Asian cities, or the importance of Chinese documentary data. More recent approaches offer more regionally appropriate models to understand first millennium CE centers. Economic-based frameworks either contrast urban forms based on their role as redistribution centers (for example, Miksic's orthogenetic vs. heterogenetic paradigm[8]) or their emergence and operation as part of maritime trade networks.[9] The more materialist models of urbanism and of political organization emphasize economic functions over ideology, including iconographic practices and the construction of religious monuments.[10] Such approaches ignore a range of models that emphasize ideology and power as interlocked forces shaping early states at their own peril. First millennium elites across Southeast Asia

---

[7] Ma Touan-lin, *Ethnographie des peuples étrangers à la Chine: ouvrage composé au XIIIe siècle de notre ère*, Hervey de Saint-Denys (trans.) (Geneva, Switzerland: H. George, 1876–83).

[8] John N. Miksic, "Heterogenetic Cities in Premodern Southeast Asia," *World Archaeology* 32 (2000), 106–20.

[9] Pierre-Yves Manguin, "The Amorphous Nature of Coastal Polities."

[10] For economically driven interpretations of art styles, see Pierre-Yves Manguin and Nadine Dalsheimer, "Visnu mitrés et réseaux marchands en Asie du Sud-est: nouvelles données archéologiques sur le I millénaire apr. J.-C.," *Bulletin de l'École Française d'Extrême Orient* 85 (1998), 87–124. For economically driven interpretations of pre-Angkorian Cambodia, see Michael Vickery, *Society, Economics, and Politics in Pre-Angkor Cambodia* (Tokyo: The Tokyo Bunko, 1998); and Michael Vickery, "What and Where was Chenla?", in Francois Bizot (ed.), *Recherches nouvelles sur le Cambodia* (Paris: École Française d'Extrême-Orient, 1994), pp. 197–212.

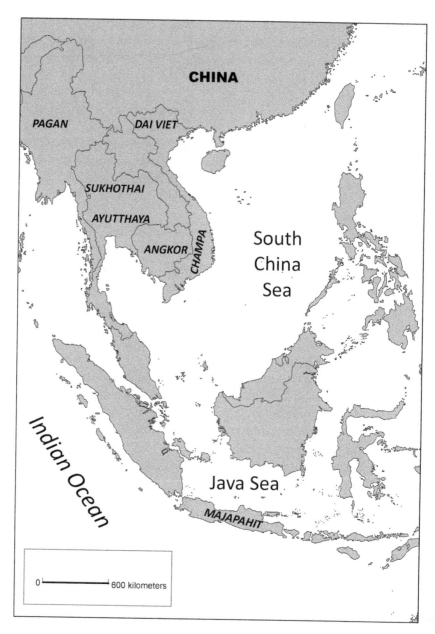

Map 4.2 Ninth- to fifteenth-century urbanized states in Southeast Asia.

Table 4.1 Early Southeast Asian states with large urban centers

Name	Location	Start date	End date
Angkor	Tonle Sap/Lower Mekong (Cambodia)	~ 802 CE	~ 1431 CE
Champa	Coastal Vietnam	~ 600 CE	1832 CE
Dai Viet	Northern Vietnam	939 CE	1407 CE
Sukhothai	Northern Thailand	1238 CE	1438 CE
Ayutthaya	Central Thailand	1350 CE	1767 CE
Pagan	Irawaddy Basin (Myanmar)	849 CE	1298 CE
Majapahit	East-central Java (Indonesia)	~ 1293	~1500

Note: Date ranges from Pamela Gutman and Bob Hudson, "The Archaeology of Burma (Myanmar) from the Neolithic to Pagan," in Peter Bellwood and Ian C. Glover (eds.), *Southeast Asia: From Prehistory to History* (New York: RoutledgeCurzon, 2004_, pp. 149–76; John N. Miksic, "The Classical Cultures of Indonesia," in Bellwood and Glover (eds.), *Southeast Asia*, pp. 234–56; and William A. Southworth, "The Coastal States of Champa," in Bellwood and Glover (eds.), *Southeast Asia*, pp. 209–33.

inscribed power through ritual performance that linked their actions and their spiritual essence to the Hindu gods they worshipped, and these gods lived in their urban centers.

Urbanism in Southeast Asia: *c.* 800–1400 CE

Southeast Asians did not abandon many of their first millennium CE centers, but they turned elsewhere to build their second millennium CE capitals (Map 4.2). Societies in what is now Thailand, Cambodia, and Myanmar moved their centers northward to found Tai, Khmer, and Burmese capitals at confluences of drainage and transportation systems; states associated with these urban centers are listed in Table 4.1. Dai Viet arose in the northern part of Vietnam, while Champa flourished in the country's center. And major states arose in the arable plains of Sumatra, Java, and Sulawesi; Java's Majapahit kingdom reigned supreme. I present here only a review of ninth- through fifteenth-century Southeast Asian cities; syntheses on this time period are available elsewhere.[11]

[11] See G. C. Bentley, "Indigenous States of Southeast Asia', *Annual Review of Anthropology* 15 (1996), 275–305; Jan Wisseman Christie, "State Formation in Early Maritime Southeast Asia: A Consideration of the Theories and the Data," *Bijdragen Tot De Taal-, Land-en Volkenkunde* 151 (1995), 235–88; Pierre-Yves Manguin, "Les cités-États de l'Asie du Sud-Est côtière: de l'ancienneté et de la permanence des formes urbaines," *Bulletin de l'École Française d'Extrême Orient* 87 (2000), 151–82; John N. Miksic, "The Classical Cultures of Indonesia," in Peter Bellwood and Ian C. Glover (eds.), *Southeast Asia: From Prehistory to History* (New York: RoutledgeCurzon, 2004), pp. 234–56.

Form

Each of these "Classical States" had an indigenous literary tradition, a penchant for monumentalism in either Hindu or Buddhist form, and a commitment to constructing large, walled urban centers with well-defined arteries stretching from the capital to secondary centers throughout each polity's realm. The orthogonal urban design of some Classical centers blended Indic cosmological principles and underlying animist beliefs, and many scholars argue that urban centers echoed ritual temples in form and structure.[12] Rulers lived in these urban centers, and change in rulers generally entailed a change in location of the polity center. Whether all cities were considered "royal" (and thus subject to dictates of geomancy) remains unclear, but some of the better-studied ninth- to fourteenth-century urban plans may reflect Indian cosmological (and modular) principles of urban planning that were articulated in the fourth-century *Arthasastra* (by Kautilya) and collectively as part of the *vastru shastas*.[13]

First and second millennium CE Chinese sources describe royal, elite, and common residences in wooden (and thus perishable) form whose as yet unexcavated middens offer the only hope for study. Most work has concentrated instead on mortuary and religious monuments of brick, stone, and laterite, which survived centuries of subsequent conquest and colonization and which are now the object of intensive historic preservation. Like their first millennium CE predecessors, these second millennium urban centers were walled and moated, contained well-defined administrative and religious districts, and served as ritual and political centers for an ever expanding rural elite. Not only does the proliferation of archaeological sites surrounding these centers suggest a well-developed core–hinterland system. Indigenous court chronicles like Java's mid-fourteenth-century CE *Nagarakertagama* poem enumerates towns in the Majapahit hinterland; scholars disagree over the nature of such regions vis-à-vis their urban centers.[14]

---

[12] Hans-Dieter Evers and Rüdiger Korff (eds.), *Southeast Asian Urbanism* (Münster–Hamburg–London: Lit Verlag, 2003); and Amita Sinha, "Design of Settlements in the Vaastu Shastras," *Journal of Cultural Geography* 17 (1998), 27–41.

[13] For example, Jacques Gaucher concludes that these Indian texts guided the construction of the nine-square-kilometer enclosed city of Angkor Thom, although its ultimate form reflects a mixture of Indian and Khmer ideas. See Jacques Gaucher, "Angkor Thom, une utopie réalisée? Structuration de l'espace et modèle indien d'urbanisme dans le Cambodge ancien," *Arts asiatiques* 59 (2004), 58–86.

[14] Pierre-Yves Manguin, "The Amorphous Nature of Coastal Polities," in contrast, argues that first millennium Southeast Asian states also had hinterlands. See Kulke, "Epigraphical References," p. 19, for reference to mid-fourteenth-century Java.

Function

Scholars vary in the functions that they assign to ninth- to fourteenth-century Southeast Asian cities. At one end of the continuum are those who call these ritual administrative centers, and at the other are scholars who emphasize instead their economic roles in broader world systems. This interpretive variability reflects the research emphasis of the scholar (for example, art history vs. economic history), the nature of the database under study (architecture, statuary and art, ceramics, settlement pattern), and the relative importance of international trade with China at any point in the sequence; for example, the Song and Yuan dynasties involved more active commerce with Southeast Asia than did portions of the succeeding Ming dynasty. An increasing research corpus suggests that these Southeast Asian cities varied in emphasis depending on location and access to foreign trade, but served the full range of economic, social, political, and religious functions as had their first millennium CE predecessors.

Interpretations

Some consensus exists not that most Classical cities in mainland Southeast Asia served multiple functions but that they formed the ritual/ceremonial core of their respective polities; a complementary pattern along island Southeast Asia's coasts were trade-based maritime polities whose size ranged from small chiefdoms to huge cities like Melaka and Makassar. Individual cities in these coastal regions rose and fell under successive raids and attacks, but the notion of "city" remained and inhabitants quickly rebuilt on ground where the razed cities once stood. In contrast, most Classical mainland cities dissolved by the late fifteenth century, the victims of shifting economic conditions as much as war. Some capitals moved south to take advantage of coastlines and the maritime trade relationships that coastal access afforded to the polities. Others fell under attack from neighboring polities. New urban centers that arose at this time, and the secondary centers whose linkages joined the capital to a broader system, were organized around most of the same principles. One substantial change lay in the addition of ethnic enclaves, often (but not always) to accommodate overseas Chinese, whose flight from the new Qing dynasty built widespread cultural and commercial networks that integrated Southeast Asia and South China into a single economic system. Sixteenth-century Europeans who came to Southeast Asia entered a world of commerce and urbanism that rivaled or exceeded parts of their home civilization in scale; what they couldn't see, and only understood centuries later, was how performance and power combined to build this urban tradition.

Performance and the Southeast Asian polity

From their earliest first millennium incarnations onward, the centripetal power of mainland Southeast Asian cities lay partly in their importance as venues for performance: ritual or secular, but public. Innumerable foreigners (Chinese, European, Arab) described pageantry and spectacle in the city capitals that involved rulers and their entourages and elite-sponsored events, from temple inaugurations and rededications to processionals and animal-fighting contests (particularly cock-fighting and pig-fighting), and from annual public prognostication events to state-sponsored funerals that memorialized fallen leaders and reinforced a sense of nationhood.

Ritual, performance, and power were intrinsic to most Southeast Asian cultures, writ small or large. Within the region's tribal societies, ritual specialists performed rites that allow them access to spirits who have the ability to right the situation. Sixteenth-century Spanish so feared the power of female *babaylan* or *catalonan* in the Philippines that they undertook wide-scale extermination.[15] Ritual specialists played yet more integral roles in the region's state-level societies, particularly the Saivite Brahmin priests. By the thirteenth century in Angkor and Majapahit, court-based Brahmins were key propagators of rituals of kingship; as royal advisors, they directed court rituals and administrated statewide religious observances necessary to maintain power and stability on annual and periodic cycles. In Theravada Buddhist Cambodia and Thailand today, Brahmins remain integral to royal administrative affairs.

Khmer rulers' power depended on their successful performance of secular and sacred ritual (for example, consecration ceremonies, annual festivals, and inauguration events), statecraft (audiences with subjects and judicial activities[16]) and – for many Southeast Asian rulers – through militarism. These intimate links between ritual performance and power in Southeast

---

[15] Grace Barretto-Tesoro, "Where are the Datu and Catalonan in Early Philippine Societies? Investigating Status in Calatagan," *Philippine Quarterly of Culture & Society* 36 (2008), 74–102; and William H. Scott, *Barangay: Sixteenth-Century Philippine Culture and Society* (Manila: Ateneo de Manila University Press, 1994), pp. 84–5.
[16] Merle Calvin Ricklefs describes the Khmer ruler's role as a "legal umpire" rather than ultimate arbiter in provincial-level disputes in Merle Calvin Ricklefs, "Land and the Law in the Epigraphy of Tenth-century Cambodia," *The Journal of Asian Studies* 26 (1967), 420. The mid-tenth-century Pre Rup inscription and Zhou Daguan's thirteenth-century account of the Khmer court both mention daily audiences.

Asia are forcefully illustrated in nineteenth- and early twentieth-century Bali, through suttee associated with royal cremation ceremonies and an analysis of *puputan* (ritualized, dynasty-ending defeat by Balinese royalty) as Balinese royalty capitulated their thrones to the Dutch colonizers. Clifford Geertz noted that rulers were both political actors and ritual objects, but emphasized the shallow power that such rulers held.[17] That intimate links have a deep history is clear in the following brief description of performance, power, and place in the history of the lower Mekong Basin, in what is now the kingdom of Cambodia. So too, however, is a close linkage between performance and genuine political power that Geertz, in his analysis of the nineteenth-century Balinese, minimized.

Power, place, and ritual in the lower Mekong Basin as case study

The lower Mekong Basin today includes Laos, Thailand, Cambodia, and southern Vietnam; at the peak of the Angkorian Empire in the thirteenth century, this entire region was under control of the Khmer center in the Tonle Sap region that we now gloss as "Angkor." Indigenous histories that Chinese emissaries recorded in the first millennium CE, supplemented by the eleventh-century Khmer *Sdok Kak Thom* inscription, suggest that the roots of the Khmer Empire lay in southern Cambodia and the Mekong Delta, that political power moved to central Cambodia by the sixth–eighth centuries CE, and that the Angkorian capital was first established in 802 CE on the banks of the Tonle Sap lake. As the tempo of historical archaeological research increases in Cambodia and its environs, this reconstruction may require revision to incorporate multiple "centers" of Khmer culture. Nevertheless, systematic research in these three regions offers some insights concerning how ritual and power combined to legitimize Cambodia's earliest rulers, and why the central places that they favored became the civilization's earliest urban centers.

The Lower Mekong from 500 BCE to 800 CE

The Mekong Delta

Archaeological research suggests that by the mid-first millennium CE, canals and waterways connected nodes in a Mekong delta settlement system that contained villages, religious-administrative centers, agricultural regions, and sacred hills. Settlements were located at the edges of the floodplain, where

---

[17] Geertz, *Negara*, p. 131.

inhabitants could maximize their farming yields through rain-fed and flood-water farming. Ancient settlement also surrounded each of the few hills in the region and each hill houses ritual structures, suggesting that Khmer cosmological beliefs concerning mountains have a pre-Angkorian basis. The modal archaeological signature is one or more mounds, surrounded by water features like moats or ponds. Some mounds contain fragmentary brick masonry and stone architectural elements that would have functioned as entryways or pedestals. Large settlements, signaled by dense and deep ceramic deposits, are much less common, and contain one or more areas with vestiges of brick ritual structures.

No indigenous records for this culture survive from its first five or more centuries; the first dated inscribed stela derives from the Angkor Borei site and dates to 611 CE. Third- and sixth-century Chinese emissaries who visited the delta, however, left extensive documentation of this polity they called "Funan." Their accounts not only record diplomatic missions and the goods that moved in both directions; such accounts also described the urban core, political-administrative structure, origins, and dynastic succession of this polity. This Chinese literary corpus combined with comparative analysis of seventh- and eighth-century Khmer and Sanskrit epigraphic data depicts a stratified society. At the top were rulers whom the Chinese described as "kings"; below them were one or more levels of indigenous elites, listed in the inscriptions using local terms, who may have been provincial- and district-level administrators (as prescribed by Indian texts).

Funan sovereigns allegedly built elite residences in urban centers to house their entourages and segregate space. They directed the construction of public works in and radiating out from the polity's center, including walls, reservoirs, ritual buildings, and canal and transportation systems that repre-sented the collective. Chinese annals describe Funan military expeditions as far west as the Malay Peninsula to found tributary or diplomatic relation-ships. They clearly monopolized control of economic resources and negoti-ated with visiting foreign traders and Brahmins who came on the monsoon winds from the Indian Ocean and East China Sea. Rulers practiced public rituals and embraced religious symbolism to bolster political action. Dense deposits of ritual vessels at Angkor Borei suggest the support of religious festivals to draw residents from surrounding areas to these centers to worship communally; whether populations observed the rulers' power through ritual performance cannot be proven.

Social stratification in this first millennium CE society reached below the ruler to provincial and district levels, where inscriptions indicate that local elites used ritual to establish their power. They merged Hindu statecraft ideologies with traditional animist beliefs to found their capitals in sacred locations as ritual administrative centers that they sanctified through the construction of ritual structures (shrines and temples). State capitals and ritual centers had deep histories of ancestral spirits, and involved key points in agrarian landscapes; some remain sacred to Khmers today. Shrines housed statuary that represented deities from the Saivite and Vaishnavite cults; each required resources to dedicate and maintain the structures, and at least the temples required ritual specialists who conducted ceremonies on a regular basis.

Chenla? c. 500–800 CE

No systematic survey-based archaeological work has yet been published on sixth- to eighth-century urbanism in its putative pre-Angkorian core (that is, central and northern Cambodia). Chinese emissaries trace the movement of the Khmer "Chenla" capital northward during this period, and multiple large centers have been documented in Kampong Thom and Stung Treng Province. Sites like Sambor Prei Kuk had dozens of brick temples whose statuary has long disappeared, but whose extant inscriptions describe a mélange of cults; statuary reflects these heterogeneous influences. These inscriptions, coupled with Chinese accounts, describe Khmer rulers who established large political-religious centers or "temple-cities" to accommodate competing cults that their followers practiced, sponsored the operation of these temples, and encouraged the development of state-level artistic traditions (particularly architectural) that have been found across the entire geographic domain that scholars associate with the pre-Angkorian world.

"Angkor" and northwestern Cambodia: c. 800–1432 CE

For more than a century of scholars have sought to understand the development and forms of the succeeding Khmer Empire, which its rulers made legible in the early ninth century CE. Yet this burden of architectural, art historical, and epigraphic data has prevented all but the hardiest scholars from investigating Angkorian urbanism through the archaeological record, and most have done so only recently. The earliest urban expression in the Angkorian period emerged in the ninth century CE through the construction of royal capitals and their increasingly large, associated hydraulic features. As the literature on Angkorian urbanism grows, so too grows the volume of disputation between key researchers. All scholars agree, however, that Angkorian urbanism was a case of "conurbation": at every point in the sequence, an Angkorian ritual-administrative core contained water features and temples, was ringed by an associated settlement zone, and may have been surrounded further by a periurban or suburban perimeter.

The urban organization of only one well-defined "city" in the Angkorian complex has been systematically studied thus far: that of Angkor Thom, created by the Khmer Empire's last great ruler, Jayavarman VII, in the twelfth and early thirteenth centuries. In sum, such work suggests that Angkor Thom followed Indian cosmological and urban precepts in its gridded form and spatial organization, that the city's four quarters included a religious center (the Bayon) and a royal quarter to the northeast, and that it was further organized through linear canals into smaller units, most of which contained what might be household clusters. That Indian cosmo-logical concepts guided Khmer (and Southeast Asian) construction at the architectural level is abundantly clear and the subject of innumerable art historical and architectural treatises; whether such concepts and Indian texts also guided urban planning also seems likely.

Performance, and particularly public performance, was fundamental to royal authority, but Angkorian rulers blended display with political, economic, and military acumen to succeed as heads of state. Each new Khmer ruler constructed a new capital around the Tonle Sap; each new capital required the erection and consecration of a central religious monument to memorialize a deceased royal relative through whose lineage the new ruler sought legitimation.

From their central location, Khmer rulers sponsored and institutionalized practices associated with state religion to merge "church" and state. Shared ideological traditions were materialized in state-level iconography in architec-tural decoration and statuary, whose redundant expression in provincial archi-tecture and statuary underscored the importance of the urban core. Temples in the core zone were adorned with bas-reliefs that celebrated military victories and recounted Hindu origins through scenes from the Ramayana epic.

Performing power required work within and beyond the urban state core. The strongest Khmer kings built road and transportation networks to link provincial areas to the Angkorian capital and economize the movement of tribute to the center. Rulers also awarded lands to provincial elite and for temple and ashram construction to accommodate a special class of religious elite whose practices were integral to the health of the polity. Jayavarman VII undergirded his claim to imperial power most vigorously in this regard: his temples, hospitals, resthouses, bridges, and roads knitted much of what are today northeastern Thailand, southern Laos, and southern Cambodia into an imperial system through which goods and people circulated.

The most successful of the Khmer kings practiced power through regular performance. They engaged in royal ceremonies and processions (which thirteenth-century Chinese visitors like Zhou Daguan described) and pilgrimages to heritage sites.[18] These events made full use of long promenades, causeways, and "avenues of approaches" in Angkorian period public architecture, and involved thousands of people. But participation in daily rituals, some originating in Vedic sacrifices, to essential deities were also integral aspects of rulership.[19] Khmer rulers inscribed their power into politico-religious monuments and made their settlements central through practice.

Conclusions

Urbanism has a deep history in Southeast Asia; from its inception, such Southeast Asian statecraft has been forged through a mixture of power, ceremonialism, and performance. Such a blend, while volatile, often carried real power (contra Geertz's [1980] example of colonial Bali) that sustained Southeast Asian states for generations and centuries. Urbanism in the ancient Khmer state exemplifies these relationships rather clearly: the Khmer state and its Angkorian urban forms exceeded its peers in geographic scale (if not also in administrative power), but emerging studies of the region's other Classical Hindu and Buddhist polities, like Bagan/Pagan (Myanmar) and Trowulan (Java) offer similar patterns.

As Gaucher and Miksic[20] note in their case studies of thirteenth- and fourteenth-century Cambodia and Java, Southeast Asians blended Indic and

---

[18] In 1296, Zhou Daguan in *Customs of Cambodia*, p. 72 described a royal procession with King Indravarman: "When the king leaves his palace, the procession is headed by the soldiery; then come the flags, the banners, the music. Girls of the palace, three or five hundred in number, gaily dressed, with flowers in their hair and tapers in their hands, are massed together in a separate column. The tapers are lighted even in broad daylight. Then come other girls carrying gold and silver vessels from the palace and a whole galaxy of ornaments, of very special design, the uses of which were strange to me. Then came still more girls, the bodyguard of the palace, holding shields and lances. These, too, were separately aligned. Following them came chariots drawn by goats and horses, all adorned with gold; ministers and princes, mounted on elephants, were preceded by bearers of scarlet parasols, without number. Close behind came the royal wives and concubines, in palanquins and chariots, or mounted on horses or elephants, to whom were assigned at least a hundred parasols mottled with gold. Finally the Sovereign appears, standing erect on an elephant and holding in his hand the Sacred Sword. This elephant, his tusks sheathed in gold, was accompanied by bearers of twenty white parasols with golden shafts. All around was a bodyguard of elephants, drawn close together, and still more soldiers for complete protection, marching in close order."

[19] Hiram W. Woodward, Jr., "Practice and Belief in Ancient Cambodia: Claude Jacques' Angkor and the Devarāja Question," *Journal of Southeast Asian Studies* 32 (2001), 249–61.

[20] Jacques Gaucher, "Angkor Thom," and John Miksic, "Nail of the World: Mandalas and Axes," *Arts Asiatiques* 64 (2010), 20–31.

indigenous ideas into their localized urban forms. Political power involved performance and entailed concrete results; cities formed the core for the centripetality that structured Southeast Asians' settlement systems. One might argue, further, that underlying the Classical Southeast Asian city was a "modular" notion of settlement (with a ritual epicenter with hydraulic features, a residential halo, and surrounding agrarian lands dotted with shrines) whose roots lay in a pre-Indic landscape peopled by ancestral spirits and their human-crafted homes that were objects of veneration. From northwestern Cambodia to central Java, ninth- through fourteenth-century Southeast Asian rulers forged and sustained their exemplary centers through practice at the court, capital, and cosmopolitan levels.

FURTHER READINGS

Bulbeck, David, and Ian Caldwell, "Oryza Sativa and the Origins of Kingdoms in South Sulawesi, Indonesia: Evidence from Rice Husk Phytoliths," *Indonesia and the Malay World* 36 (2008), 1–20.

Christie, Jan Wisseman, "State Formation in Early Maritime Southeast Asia: A Consideration of the Theories and the Data," *Bijdragen tot de Taal-, Land- en Volkenkunde* 151 (1995), 235–88.

"States without Cities: Demographic Trends in early Java," *Indonesia* 52 (1991), 23–40

Coedès, George, *The Indianized States of Southeast Asia*, W. F. Vella (ed.), S. B. Cowing, (trans.), Honolulu: University of Hawaii Press, 1968.

Cummings, Williams, "Historical Texts as Social Maps: *Lontaraq bilang* in Early Modern Makassar," *Bijdragen tot de Taal-, Land- en Volkenkunde* 161 (2005), 40–62.

Eisenstadt, S. N., "Religious Organizations and Political Process in Centralized Empires," *The Journal of Asian Studies* 21 (1962), 271–94.

Evans, Damian, Christophe Pottier, Roland Fletcher, Scott Hensley, Ian Tapley, Anthony Milne, and Michael Barbetti "A Comprehensive Archaeological Map of the World's Largest Preindustrial Settlement Complex at Angkor, Cambodia," *Proceedings of the National Academy of Science* 104 (2007), 14,277–82.

Hudson, Bob, "The Origins of Bagan: The Archaeological Landscape of Upper Burma to AD 1300," unpublished Ph.D. dissertation, University of Sydney, 2004.

Jacques, Claude, "Le pays Khmer avant Angkor," *Journal des Savants* 1 (1986), 59–95.

Jacques, Claude, and Pierre Lafond, *The Khmer Empire: Cities and Sanctuaries, Fifth to Thirteenth Centuries*, Bangkok: River Books, 2007.

Junker, Laura Lee, "Population Dynamics and Urbanism in Premodern Island Southeast Asia," in Glenn R. Storey (ed.), *Urbanism in the Preindustrial World: Cross-Cultural Approaches*, Tuscaloosa: University of Alabama Press, 2006, pp. 211–14.

Lavy, Paul A., "As in Heaven, So on Earth: The Politics of Visnu, Siva and Harihara Images in Preangkorian Khmer Civilisation," *Journal of Southeast Asian Studies* 34 (2003), 21–39.

Malleret, Louis, *L'Archéologie du Delta du Mekong*, Paris: Publication de l'École Française d'Extrême Orient, 1959–1963, Vols. I–III.

Manguin, Pierre-Yves, "The Archaeology of the Early Maritime Polities of Southeast Asia," in Peter Bellwood and Ian C. Glover (eds.), *Southeast Asia: From Prehistory to History*, London: RoutledgeCurzon, 2004, pp. 282–313.

"City-states and City-state Cultures in Pre-15th-century Southeast Asia," in Mogens H. Hansen (ed.), *A Comparative Study of Thirty City-State Cultures*, Copenhagen: Reitzels Forlag, 2000, pp. 409–16.

"Les cités-États de l'Asie du Sud-Est côtière: de l'ancienneté et de la permanence des formes urbaines," *Bulletin de l'École Française d'Extrême Orient* 87 (2000), 151–82.

"Southeast Sumatra in Protohistoric and Srivijaya Times: Upstream–Downstream Relations and the Settlement of the Peneplain," in Dominik Bonatz, John N. Miksic, J. David Neideland, and Mai Lin Tjoa-Bonatz (eds.), *From Distant Tales: Archaeology and Ethnohistory in the Highlands of Sumatra*, Newcastle-upon-Tyne: Cambridge Scholars Publishing, 2009, pp. 434–84.

Miksic, John N., "The Classical Cultures of Indonesia," in Peter Bellwood and Ian C. Glover (eds.), *Southeast Asia: From Prehistory to History*, New York: RoutledgeCurzon, 2004, pp. 234–56.

"Heterogenetic Cities in Premodern Southeast Asia," *World Archaeology* 32 (2000), 106–20.

Moore, Elizabeth, and San Win, "The Gold Coast: Suvannabhumi? Lower Myanmar Walled Sites of the First Millennium A.D.," *Asian Perspectives* 46 (2007), 202–32.

Mudar, Karen M., "How Many Dvaravati Kingdoms? Locational Analysis of First Millennium AD Moated Settlements in Central Thailand," *Journal of Anthropological Archaeology* 18 (1999), 1–28.

Pelliot, Paul, "Le Fou-nan," *Bulletin de l'École Française d'Extrême Orient* 3 (1903), 248–303.

Pollock, Sheldon, *The Language of the Gods in the World of Men: Sanskrit, Culture, and Power in Premodern India*, Berkeley: University of California Press, 2006.

Stargardt, Janice, *The Ancient Pyu of Burma, Vol. 1: Early Pyu Cities in a Man-made Landscape*, Cambridge: Publications on Ancient Civilization, Institute of Southeast Asian Studies, 1990.

Stark, Miriam T., "Pre-Angkorian and Angkorian Cambodia," in Peter Bellwood and Ian C. Glover (eds.), *Southeast Asia: From Prehistory to History*, New York: RoutledgeCurzon, 2004, pp. 89–119.

"Pre-Angkorian Settlement Trends in Cambodia's Mekong Delta and the Lower Mekong Archaeological Project," *Bulletin of the Indo-Pacific Prehistory Association* 26 (2006), 98–109.

"Southeast Asia Late Prehistoric: 2500–1500BP," in Peter Peregrine (ed.), *Encyclopedia of Prehistory*, New York: Plenum Press, 2001, Vol. III, pp. 160–205.

Vickery, Michael, "Funan Reviewed: Deconstructing the Ancients," *Bulletin de l'École Française d'Extrême-Orient* 90 (2003), 101–43.

Society, Economics, and Politics in Pre-Angkor Cambodia: The 7th–8th Centuries, Tokyo: The Centre for East Asian Cultural Studies for UNESCO, The Tokyo Bunko, 1998.

Wheatley, Paul, *Nāgara and Commandery: Origins of the Southeast Asian Urban Traditions*, Chicago: University of Chicago Press, 1983.

5

Cities as performance arenas

JOHN BAINES, MIRIAM T. STARK,
THOMAS G. GARRISON AND STEPHEN HOUSTON

The rapid development of early cities at different dates in many regions of the world affected their hinterlands profoundly. The cities became ceremonial and economic centers, appropriating functions that had previously been scattered, as well as serving as a stage for activities of new types, both in administration and, at least as importantly, in performances. In the late fourth millennium BCE, Uruk in southern Mesopotamia grew to cover more than 200 hectares, of which around nine were devoted to the Eanna precinct, a vast open area of uncertain but clearly ceremonial use. The construction of the city and of the sacred precinct, which required unprecedented amounts of labor, were themselves events and performances, creating arenas for repeated use in future performances. These new spaces were closely tied into the centers of population, unlike some great monuments of comparably early date, such as the third millennium megalithic circle of Stonehenge in southern England, which were constructed by dispersed Neolithic societies. The urban centers also drew population from hinterlands, which became "ruralized," depending on cities for most things apart from agricultural subsistence. In all of this elites played the primary role, while performances enhanced social solidarity and mitigated the societies' deep divisions in power and wealth. Performers could be seen as existentially distinct from non-performers, or even superior to them, but necessary to the collective existence.

In this chapter we explore themes that arise from comparison of our three case studies, while drawing some examples from societies treated elsewhere in this book. Our principal bodies of evidence vary in character. Ancient Egypt, in many periods a territorial state unlike the typical city-state configuration of the other regions in most periods, presents some of the largest monuments and the longest timespan for investigation, but its urbanism is imperfectly understood. Maya society, a world of city-states, is attested in a very rich archaeological record and much pictorial evidence, as well as significant ethnohistoric materials, but with textual information that is variable in scope and largely unconcerned with non-elites. Much of the development of the polities of Southeast Asia lies within the span of history known from written sources that runs down to the present, lending an immediacy to the archaeological evidence that cannot be matched in the other two regions. In their earlier period, those polities conformed to the city-state type, but some of them acquired an expansionist territorial character in the ninth–fifteenth centuries CE.

Types and characters of performance

In many cultures, the performance of power is closely associated with beliefs and practices that engage humans in supernatural frames of action and understanding. By no means all performances are religious in character or focus, but the secular is often inextricably bound up with the religious, making it meaningless to draw a distinction between them. For the Classic Maya, to cite one example, "production" could just as soon consist in an invocation of rain as the knapping of a flint blade, involving similar notions of acts and consequences. More broadly, the creation and maintenance of cities realize a vision of the cosmos and its constituent members that encompasses the entire society. Essential members of society are the spirit world of the gods and the dead, who dominate different societies in different patterns and may include divinized rulers among their number.

Among the societies we consider, the conceptual world of Egypt was very largely indigenous, and in most periods probably unquestioned. For the Maya, by contrast, many beliefs went back to precursors a millennium or so before their civilization coalesced, from areas at some distance in coastal and highland Mexico and groups speaking unrelated languages. The central element in traditional Southeast Asian societies was equally complex, with much elite culture derived ultimately from India, blending Brahmanism and Mahayana Buddhism with the indigenous local animism. The cities of all three regions cannot be comprehended without taking this full constitution of society into account.

Cities were the largest and most elaborate institutions of these divine–human societies. They dominated their landscapes visually to a greater degree than any previous constructions. For the Classic Maya, distinctions between "natural" and "cultural" worlds – one of them built, the other not – are countered by nomenclature: pyramids were known as "hills," and places were understood by reference to the rocky, cave-pocked stone underfoot.

The gods and the dead were present among the institutions of the living, and it was proper that, as the ultimate members of society, they should have the largest, longest-lasting, and most splendid dwellings, as well as being celebrated in the most elaborate ways.

The rulers partook in splendor in diverse ways. The monuments they inhabited in the city could be as grandiose as those of the gods, or more frequently they acted as the servants of the spirit world. In many societies the ruler resided outside the main inhabited area for reasons including amenity or security, in which case their journeys to the center constituted performances of power while also integrating the wider monumental and productive hinterland with the city.

Requirements for performance were realized by creating buildings, spaces, and urban configurations. Throughout the world, stages in the construction of important buildings are typically marked by ceremonies, from the identification, marking-out, and laying of foundations to completion of the roof and inauguration of full functioning. Comparable ceremonies commemorate refurbishments. The ceremonies often have apotropaic significance and may place buildings under the patronage of spirits or deities, whether or not what is built is a shrine or temple. Many ancient urban designs formed cosmograms, as did individual buildings within these cities, so that they were symbolically nested, as cosmograms within cosmograms. These contexts offer many opportunities for performances involving groups varying in size, from individual families to thousands of participants for events that concern a whole community. People from the hinterland and from other polities can be present, some coming from great distances, whether for pilgrimages or, for example, for state funerals. For the burial in 433 BCE of the marquis of the small state of Zeng on the Yangzi, dignitaries in chariots traveled from polities hundreds of kilometers away.

Most performances are repeated, in cycles ranging from daily through monthly and seasonal to annual and generational. Daily repetition sustains the order of things and is valued for continuity. Less frequent performances mark significant transitions and are attended by elites and rulers, for whose legitimacy they are essential. Performances enhance historical memory, which is guided by a sense of place that requires constant affirmation and is reinforced by the monumental environment. The most important locations in early cities, where major performances were typically held, were constructed of different materials from ordinary habitations – frequently of dressed stone in contrast with the perishable substances and loose masonry used for houses and royal residences – and they transcended other buildings in style and elaboration, as well as often being located beside large open spaces and at the end of approach routes, which were at a premium in dense-packed traditional settings.

This privileging of display and performance in the urban environment leaves a vast imprint on the archaeological record. Whereas habitations are constantly rebuilt or decay and the configuration of whole city quarters may change, monumental settings can remain fixed for long periods, reinforcing their salience in memory. New spatial configurations may signal major historical changes. In the monumental context, some performances are public, especially in processions and movement across the landscape, while others, often the most cosmologically significant, take place in interiors and are restricted to few participants and tiny audiences. Those who are excluded are conscious of their non-participant status and aware of the performances' importance. These discriminations, which are present in societies of any type and are essential to the exercise of power, reinforce social and symbolic hierarchies.

Performances in the public sphere require sumptuous pageantry and spectacle to constitute effective theatrics of social action. They may last for many days, even months. They address the senses of sound, smell, and taste in addition to sight, and they involve bodily discipline, indulgence, or both, frequently demanding stamina from participants as well as fasting and subsequent feasting. Spectators are drawn in not least by the length, elaboration, and attendant atmosphere, be it solemn or celebratory. Their organization, which is highly aesthetic, makes use of costly organic and ephemeral materials. These leave little or no archaeological trace, but they may be depicted or mentioned in texts. Comparable institutions in historical societies generally involve similar display using extravagant materials. One measure of the power of such display is that many ruling groups appropriate it or seek to curb it through sumptuary laws or other restrictions.

Performances: experience and connections among symbolic realms

Classic Maya performances were strongly sonic, with anticipation fortified by blasts of trumpet or conch, the pounding of large drums or tapping of smaller ones under the arm, whistles and maracas, singing, and the musical collisions of shells on the king's body. The burning of incense permeated the nostrils and eyes while the sounds of performance reverberated in the ears of those present. Archaeological evidence tends to emphasize the visual, but ancient performance yoked other sensations, which apprehended some events long before the eyes came into action. The spectacular murals at Bonampak, Mexico, depict the lively sensory environment in which such public performances took place.

Secular performances in Southeast Asia could involve hundreds or thousands of urban residents as participants and as spectators. A royal procession, depicted in relief on a twelfth-century Angkor Wat temple wall, includes 200 soldiers swearing a public oath to their king while large numbers of men blow horns, ring bells, and beat gongs; concurrently, Hindu ascetics with their head priest collectively carry a holy jewel and the sacred fire. Many ritualized performances fused entertainment, pedagogy, and propitiation. At the court and across the city, dances, dance-plays, recitations, and dramatic performances lasting many days involved shadow puppetry or human actors, drawing upon the great Hindu Ramayana and Mahabharata epics as well as the Buddhist Jataka tales. Most such events were state-sponsored and took place within the city's walls; benedictions and religious offerings preceded performances.

Ritualized secular performances in the same region – such as competitions in athletics, ball games, jousting, cock- and pig-fights, and chariot races – could also include markets, in which elite goods from Chinese porcelains to finely crafted bronze palanquin fittings were restricted to urban contexts, with their acquisition requiring formal protocol. All these organized and regulated features of public life reinforced the social order and demonstrated both the ruling group's control and its care for the whole community.

Ancient cities were the loci of spectacular display and conspicuous consumption but also of destruction or sequestration of valuable materials and manufactured objects. In Egyptian funeral processions, the garlanded shelters set up with wine and food beside the path taken by the cortège were torn down and the pots broken after the coffin had passed by. Sacrifices and dedications in temples had something of the same character of consumption, but they also disseminated some products among secondary elite groups. Most of the food and cloth that was used was later redistributed, the food to priests and their dependants, in a cycle that reaffirmed social hierarchies. Some fabrics that covered or clothed cult statues were reused to wrap the mummified bodies of the privileged dead, incorporating another essential sector of society into a web of connected performances. Such activities also linked domains of performance spatially: materials redistributed from temples, many of which were in city centers, were laid to rest in monumental burial spaces that were often outside the inhabited area but within sight of the wider city and forming part of it. This presence of the dead in society can set up performances that traverse whole polities. Salient examples are where leaders die away from the city or where they are buried in distant places that are hallowed by tradition or that become politically expedient after their deaths, as with the transport of the corpse of Alexander the Great from Babylon to Memphis in Egypt following his death.

All these practices had material and spatial correlates as well as implications for the maintenance and consumption of the artifacts used in performances. In the Maya world, the objects were stored in palaces, as at Aguateca, Guatemala. In tropical conditions they must have required frequent refurbishment or replacement: jaguar kilts and quetzal-bird feathers would be perishable, as would carved wooden headdresses or elements supported on royal backs. More secure storage was needed for regalia of office, including royal crowns, diadems, and scepters. Storage itself had performative and social dimensions. Some objects appear to have been tended by nobles, whose role was to dress the king, in an ensemble of objects brought together from different places in a Maya city. Evidence for the importance of these objects comes from texts and depictions as well as rare cases of exceptional preservation, as in some royal tombs at Copan, Honduras. The world of props for performance was much larger than can be attested directly, although Egyptian material in particular supplies valuable pointers.

Space, material culture, and practice

The typical alternation of dense settlement with just a few large open spaces and monuments in ancient cities was essential to the impact of performances. Exceptions are the dispersed urban centers like Angkor (Cambodia) and Anuradhapura (Sri Lanka), along with ruralized cities among the Maya, such as Caracol, Belize. The population of most cities was small compared to more recent times – Southeast Asia being the exception here – and the appropriation of space that would only be filled for occasional performances was a central expression of power and wealth. The more-than-human scale of such spaces and monuments, as well as their frequent emptiness, assert that normal human measures do not apply. In hot climates such spaces impose strains on performers, with attendants or temporary structures typically shading the principal actors from the sun.

The specialized material culture used in performances often comes from afar, displaying the connections of rulers, elites, and their cities with other regions within or beyond their own world. The artifacts may be created by craftspeople whose chief occupation is to service performances, such as those who make particular types of garments or musical instruments. Not only are these people supported economically by rulers and elites, but they may themselves be leading members of society, as in the Maya polity of Aguateca, where abandoned dwellings near the ceremonial center contained traces of manufacturing, including parts of a royal headdress, a prime display item in performances. The range of products and expertise employed is a measure of a polity's power that generally requires the specialization and complexity of a city and the royal court it houses. Acquisition of relevant materials is itself a subject for performance, as in third millennium Egypt, where the arrival of expeditions from abroad was depicted as being celebrated both in a public context and among the ruling group.

Such artifacts can be traced to some extent by archaeology, whereas the vital expertise in the conduct of performances is materially invisible, as well as being the subject of restricted knowledge in many societies. Cities are repositories of such expertise, and they sustain long periods of practice and rehearsal, which tend to be particularly elaborate in civilizations. The monumental scale of settings drives and is driven by cities, as is also true of the staging of performances.

In some cities, performance outweighed other functions. These cities might have small permanent populations. Royalty and elites traveled long distances to them for rituals and festivals, bringing the polity to the city through their movement. Monuments dwarfed ordinary habitations still more than in other places. Cities with this character are not economically self-sustaining unless they possess other significant functions, for example as pilgrimage centers. Their creation and maintenance – many of them were ancient sites that retained primarily symbolic significance – embodied the power of the deities to whom they were dedicated and the rulers who sustained them. Such cities are found in larger polities, with Thebes in Egypt offering a prime instance, or they have a supra-regional role in a city-state configuration, as with Nippur in ancient Mesopotamia. For the Classic Maya, cities focused strongly on such functions. At El Zotz, almost a third of the center was dedicated to public plaza spaces and causeways for ritual performances, with a further 7 percent made up of pyramids where rites could be observed from public gathering spaces.

Several of these aspects come together in the performance roles of rulers and their entourages. The actions of many rulers render the cosmos present in their persons and renew the world order ritually, and some of them play the parts of deities. In communicating this role to an audience, the ruler's body should visibly display associations of his role and should be as perfect as possible. His person assembles the materials that signify his qualities. In ancient Cambodia, the thirteenth-century king's diadem resembled that worn by Buddha images. In Egypt, where much in ideology favored rural values, the tunic of Tutankhamun was decorated with patterns derived from hunting motifs. By wearing such a garment, the king, many of whose public appearances were in an urban context, displayed his mastery of the natural world and of the enemies of established order symbolized by wild animals.

In a more physical mode, Classic Maya kings danced in core rituals that were incorporated into the structure of their cities. Almost all plazas were configured for dances, immortalized in the stelae that show rulers in such choreography. The rulers were caparisoned in costumes that seemed to infuse the lord with other identities, often of gods, or alternatively of ancestors. More than masking or mummery, these dances made the gods immanent and employed the ruler's body as their temporary host. Places for these performances required locations for dressing and storage of accouter-ments, where the king might be transformed into a god, an ancestor, or himself in a particular guise. When not in use, the plazas carried the memory of performances and their meaning, imprinting them on the landscape and constantly communicating such messages to inhabitants. To walk through a Maya city was to immerse oneself in a cross-flow of different times and to witness the presence of beings beyond the ordinary.

Until the mid-twelfth century CE, Angkorian rulers employed open spaces surrounding monumental architecture for their public events. By contrast, late twelfth-century temples included more interior space, perhaps for Tantric group ritual, and a 350-meter-long, 3.5-meter-high Elephant Terrace for use as a reviewing stand where the ruler and his court observed public ceremonies and greeted returning armies. These two developments exem-plify the tension between the display of performance and the requirement of seclusion for some types of sacred action. In altering the configuration of the temple and hence of the city, the space created for such performances influenced people's perceptions of authority, conveying a message both of exclusion and of the rituals' significance.

Exclusion was conveyed still more powerfully by the great temples that dominated Egyptian cities from the late second millennium BCE onward. Only those who were initiated and obeyed rules of purity could enter even intermediate areas of temple complexes. These vast areas, which dominated cities visually and divided them spatially, were sparsely peopled by priests and subordinate temple personnel. Others experienced the presence of deities only in festival processions outside temples, during which most cult images were kept within shrouded portable shrines. The cities were configured for such festivals with processional ways, some of which were enclosed by walls that separate these semi-sacred arenas from their surroundings, constraining everyday movement. Rulers attended the processions and entered temples, but temple institutions rather than royal ones came to dominate the physical form of cities.

It was necessary to provide for the presence of large numbers of people at major festivals and special events such as royal accessions and state funerals. These occasions connected cities – which could not be self-sufficient in subsistence – more strongly with their hinterlands, and in riverine Egypt also with more distant places. For exotic artifacts used in performances cities were connected with remote places that might have a mythical character. While interdependence between city and polity was a precondition for staging performances, their perceived necessity legitimized appropriations from the hinterland. Leaders of peripheral communities had to accept that the dues they contributed brought benefits to them and not just to the city, or at least to accept that the whole polity needed the performances. Splendor and the involvement of many people were essential to persuasive power.

Movement within a cosmic and temporal space

Movement is key to performance. Buildings and transit spaces were not only designed for performance and commemoration but also channeled people's movements and imparted specific meanings to them. Performance or awareness of it were imprinted on inhabitants. Another type of movement was of those who went to or came from beyond the body politic: royal visitors, ambassadors or tributaries, princesses brought to reinvigorate a bloodline or affirm an alliance, princelings sent to foreign courts for cultural polish and as hostages to their parents' good behavior. At Piedras Negras and elsewhere among the Classic Maya, texts relating to such visits stressed origins and endpoints and, for certain ritual items or founders of dynasties, places where a trip had come to a safe conclusion.

Movement was not only about shifting from one point to another: the process itself carried equal weight, as did the identities of those involved. For the Maya, palanquins carried kings and gods, presumably on days determined by festival calendars or by special needs; patron gods issued forth, carried on human backs, to celebrate war or combat drought. Ancient Southeast Asians traversed urban centers constructed according to axial plans that linked temples together. Cities condensed local understandings of existence and the requirements of ritual practice. The design of spaces to channel move-ment and host particular rituals integrated the rituals' substance and the beings they were intended to succor into the cities' very fabric.

Movement within cities was non-random. Everyday tasks, going back and forth from fields or the hunt, acquiring food and other goods from markets, visiting kin or serving royal courts, had their own rhythms, set by habit and necessity but also structured by the monumental setting and constrained by the power that it rendered palpable. Visits to specific places within a Maya city, across specific plazas or causeways, had both targets and zones of transit. A target could be a focal point, a temple, a carved rock showing captives or depicting celestial dancers, a palace or exit route from the city. An area of transit would channel movement without much pause. The most formal routes, the *sakbih* "white paths," crystallized movements toward various targets around a city. Of varying size and scale, some had parapets that might discourage viewing by onlookers; others were little more than straight, stone-lined paths that differed slightly from the informal paths that criss-crossed cities.

The Maya understood time as not just experienced but also materialized. In target areas, usually open plazas at the core of settlements, where movements would pause and rituals take place, the king would erect stelae that embodied units of time and claim them as parts of royal identity. People moved through space while seeing time before them, not as memorials or abstractions but as solid petrifications. Movements between such targets bonded space and community additionally by according with directional symbolism. Processions to the four cardinal directions, along with attention to cosmic centers, recalled the structure of the cosmos within which cities were embedded. By replicating primordial acts, they also sustained settle-ments through the royal effort of performing these acts. By moving and enacting such practices systematically, rulers ensured a smooth ordering of the communities for which they were responsible.

How ancient Southeast Asians moved through urban space depended on the time and place. Whereas Brahmanism emphasized ritual practice by and for the elite, Buddhism connected practitioner and followers through per-formance: monks taught the laity their religion through stories; actors animated the epic Ramayana and Mahabharata religious tales. Pilgrims to sacred, frequently urban places embodied their religion through circumam-bulation, which was associated with both Hindu *pradaksina* (delimitation of sacred space) and Buddhist practice. In central Java the early ninth-century CE ruling Sailendra family sponsored the construction of Borobudur. This world's largest Buddhist monument, whose urban setting remains largely unexplored, exemplifies performance through movement. Its visitors began at the monument's base, followed corridors and stairways up six stories of three Buddhist cosmological levels en route to nirvana, glimpsing 1,400 wall reliefs of Buddha's previous 700 lives (the Jataka tales) as they proceeded. Jataka tales also graced the walls of most ninth- to fourteenth-century Burmese cities: residents in the great city of Pagan circumambulated temple terraces to express their faith.

City and countryside

In many regions the emergence of cities generated a reorganization of their countryside; in others, these processes occurred at the same time. Hinterlands were physically linked to cities by roads, canals, and river systems; hinterlands contained sites of memory and worship. Rulers established temples beyond the formal city (sometimes along axes) and these served as the polity's "guardians"; they founded religious sanctuaries and ashrams; many places attracted urban and rural residents, commoners as well as elites.

Ancient Southeast Asian capitals were both models of heaven and *axes mundi*. Royal power radiated out throughout their domains in the form of donations to support religious institutions and costs of their ceremonies, as well as establishing religious retreats. Many rulers peregrinated through their realms each year. Power and resources flowed toward the center through market goods, taxes, and tribute. This movement was enacted by people (and, in the Khmer case, their stone gods), who journeyed to the capital for annual festivals to pay fealty to their universal monarch, to celebrate his court, acknowledging the capital's centrality for the society. Religious demands structured much of this movement, while codified ritual formalized its practice.

Maya cities similarly functioned as *axes mundi* within their polities. The city represented the taming of the wilderness by royal authorities. In the city the ruler performed rituals to convene with deities that would benefit those who toiled in hinterland fields. Sacrifices to sun and rain deities set the conditions necessary for a beneficial harvest. Through time cities also became places of physical sustenance for hinterland populations. Many Classic Maya capitals constructed large reservoirs that may have been the only sources of surface drinking water in particularly dry years. Elites living in the center relied on the hinterland for their food, but they controlled the water necessary for survival, both physically and spiritually.

Egyptian cities could draw upon extended hinterlands because river travel and transport were relatively easy. Cities were identified with their local areas, in a pattern that has parallels with the structure of city-states but rather different implications: the city represented its area, and some provincial centers were named simply "settlement/city" (the language did not have a developed vocabulary for settlement types). The largest extension of this idea is the identification of the principal city or royal residence with the country as a whole. The modern word "Egypt" derives ultimately from the Egyptian *ḥwt-k'-ptḥ* "estate of the vital force of (the god) Ptah," a name for the sacred quarter of Memphis, while the modern Arabic Miṣr – both "Cairo" and "Egypt" – derives from an ancient Semitic word for Egypt that was given to the Muslim conquerors' new city: to this day city and country have the same name (Cairo, the official name, was the word for the Fatimid period royal quarter).

Thus, in relation to the greatest Egyptian cities the entire country was the hinterland. Royal journeys through the country had the king's residence, normally in the Memphite area, as their point of reference. Foreign visitors accepted the Egyptian identification of city and country and were drawn into ceremonial enactments of power, in forms that were depicted in images of the city as well as being made visible in the decoration of palaces, where envoys would be received amid figures of their compatriots in poses of subjection. The whole country thus became a stage for enacting power, on which movement from provinces to the center marked their subordination, while the king's journeys through the land, which varied in frequency in different periods, asserted both his dominance and his concern for all parts of the realm.

In the tropical environments of Mesoamerica and Southeast Asia, movement outside cities involved risk of varying levels. To enter neighboring forested areas was to risk ambush and capture, injury from the supernatural denizens of wild and undomesticated places, or harm from dangerous animals. Yet for some people, non-urban space might allow freedom from elite control and supervision. In all our examples, the constraints of the city contrasted with different sorts of danger outside. The Egyptian rural and urban environment, by contrast, was profoundly altered by human action, but it too offered spaces that were used as refuges from urban concerns.

Participation: scale, actors, and distinctions among them

Public movement was generally toward a restricted space: ceremonies within a royal court could only ever have small numbers of participants and be observed by relatively few. Even large-scale celebrations might address only residents of the city or visitors, affecting the rural majority by hearsay.

While exclusion or restricted access is central to the efficacy of much ritual, cities make major events possible because a great range of specialists can be assembled there, because of the scale of their setting, or because the numbers who attend require a large infrastructure. The power of the city and of its rulers is displayed in the very existence of these performances.

Our three examples exhibit markedly different scales of performance. An Egyptian text perhaps originating in the mid-third millennium presents instructions for a funeral procession of someone of the highest status in which hundreds or thousands of people would be involved, on a scale fitting the vast size of the period's monuments. The biography of a widow from around 200 BCE states that "all Memphis" attended her funeral. Yet core ritual actions were hardly accessible. The contrast in number between those who saw some parts of ceremonies and the relatively tiny group of direct participants was itself a display of power, as is demonstrated by the most elaborate representation of a ritual, the festival of Opet in Thebes. This was depicted in the interior of Luxor Temple, where only royalty and institutional personnel could enter.

Southeast Asians performed individual rituals, temple-based rituals, and public rituals. The last of these could have potentially vast audiences, whom the spaces and buildings of some ninth- to fourteenth-century CE cities were in part designed to accommodate. The much smaller polities and cities of the Classic Maya were not suited to such large-scale events. The number of performers in and viewers of Maya ceremonies is difficult to quantify, but no more than several hundred, or in the largest communities one or two thousand, could have been involved, at rough estimate 1–2 percent of the population. The social configuration of Maya ceremonies was complex. The appointment or self-appointment of a principal performer assigned a role and necessarily denied it to others. Of the many involved in performances only a few stood on the proscenium or received any notice in images, which are notoriously inattentive to non-elites. By accepting an invitation to perform, people acquiesced in a precise social station. An array of captives brought to the ruler by his warriors, or a set of courtiers and ladies dressing a ruler, confirmed a pecking order. Those who sat displayed rank, and those closest to the ruler were highest of all, unless they were captives cowering at royal feet. Entitled to certain roles or objects, the participants in any tableau slotted into a relative scale that radiated outward from the king.

Similarities and differences

The centrality of performance in the creation and configuration of cities is common to our three cases and can be noted in other chapters of this book. Organizational functions and material developments are often seen as crucial to the emergence of cities and states. Some level of these elements must be preconditions for their existence, but they do not supply the initial motivation for their construction: ceremonial spaces and monuments are fundamental to the extra level of complexity and symbolic communication that cities exhibit. These features generally focus around deities and the dead – elements present in most societies, not just those with cities – as much as or more than on the presence and actions of rulers. Rulers exercise and display their power in ceremonies associated with the supernatural world or through their patronage of monuments dedicated to that world. Their palaces are very often less imposing than temples or tombs, for reasons of hierarchy, because monuments are not liveable, or because cities can be dangerous to rulers, who may fear disturbance or sedition there.

A striking instance of similarity and difference is in the realm of violence. Complex societies have need of adversaries as targets of their aggression, whether in single actions such as battles or military campaigns, in ideology and ritual, or in a mixture of these. Such aggression is a constant feature of the display of power, not confined to warfare. In frequently gruesome performances the cosmic order is maintained and the world of the gods and the dead is satisfied. Such performances are among the most eloquent expressions of power. Relevant practices, including human sacrifice, are found in our three principal cases, differing markedly in detail and less studied for Southeast Asia. They relate more to the cosmic realm of order than specifically to cities, but events were typically held in cities, especially in their temples, monumental tomb complexes, and in the construction or reconsecration of city walls.

In Egypt, the sacrifice of household members and retainers at burials of royalty and a few other people is known from the 1st dynasty (c. 3000–2800) but not later. For subsequent periods sacrifices are known mainly from frontier areas, where they were part of magical performances intended to ward off enemies. Rulers displayed the corpses of enemies killed in battles, from which the right hands of victims were also brought as trophies to the capital and ceremonially buried. Comparable practices are attested among the Classic Maya, with probable sacrifice of youths in certain royal burials, and the display and mutilation of captives as highlighted in the Bonampak murals of *c.* 800 CE. Some of the power of such performances can be seen in the burials of kings of the thirteenth–eleventh centuries BCE at Anyang in China, probably the largest known Bronze Age city site. There, rows of skulls of captured foreigners were displayed on ledges in royal tombs, while their bodies were buried in mass graves in the surrounding area.

Conclusion

The core expression of power in cities is through monuments, spaces that surround them, city designs focused around monuments, and performances that enliven them. These performances are both perpetual, in the regular form of religious cults and the ritual performance of rulers' lives, and infrequent or exceptional, marking major events. The former category is generally carried out in restricted spaces by small groups of personnel. It expresses power more by exclusion than by visible presence, and it claims to uphold the cosmic order through its regular enactment. The latter category is more inclusive and can involve large numbers of participants from several sectors of society, but seldom everyone.

In all these characteristics the cities in our three examples are similar, and in this respect they fit the pattern identified by Bruce Trigger, for whom the civilizations shared more in the character and role of their belief systems than in their economies and modes of subsistence.[1] As the salient innovation of early civilizations, cities were created in the interests of those belief systems, which they made physically manifest, as well as having other functions explored elsewhere in this book. Driving forces were more ideological and religious than simply material. In focusing around monuments, the physical remains of early cities provide vital evidence for this primacy of ideas that were expressed through performances and for the communication they fostered among participant groups, from deities and the dead, through rulers, elites, and foreign delegations, to wider populations.

If performance was so central to early civilizations with their core cities, should we see it as the dominant element in the societies, rather as Clifford Geertz wrote of an extreme case where polities under the stress of colonial dominance possessed relatively little substance outside the realm of pageantry?[2]

---

[1] Bruce Trigger, *Understanding Early Civilizations: A Comparative Study* (Cambridge: Cambridge University Press, 2003).
[2] Clifford Geertz, *Negara: The Theatre State in Nineteenth Century Bali* (Princeton, NJ: Princeton University Press, 1980).

The core factor here is power. Performance was essential to the assertion of power, but power was underpinned in other ways too. Nonetheless, in the actors' experience performance mattered enormously. Today people say that they live for performances of various types. Rulers of early states lived for, through, and by performances, which constrained their lives, circumscribed their relations with elites, and projected them to their societies. The most important location for the performance and exercise of power was the city.

PART II

★

EARLY CITIES AND
INFORMATION TECHNOLOGIES

6

Urbanization and the techniques of communication: the Mesopotamian city of Uruk during the fourth millennium BCE

HANS J. NISSEN

Urbanization in the Ancient Near East is inseparably tied to the name of the city of Uruk in southern Mesopotamia (Map 6.1). Like nowhere else, remains have been found there on a large scale and in great variety in the period that V. G. Childe once called the "Urban Revolution." In archaeological parlance this time around the middle of the fourth millennium BCE sails under the name of the "Late Uruk period." Since the earliest writing system appeared at the very end of this time, Uruk is best suited for a study of both the rise of this urban center and the invention of writing.

Although obviously no written information is available either on the trends toward writing or on the formation of cities before the existence of writing, enough material exists to reconstruct these developments by drawing on archaeological data and by deducing from the earliest textual information.

The latter first appear around 3300 BCE when we have a rich archaeological record, which is unmatched in other periods of the Ancient Near East. Indeed, the appearance of writing can only be understood in the context of the entire archaeological record. Also fortuitously, large areas of the central ceremonial district of Eanna, where the first tablets were found in Uruk, were only sparsely built over after the Late Uruk period, thus enabling excavations to reach layers of the end of the fourth millennium BCE easily. Remains of the so-called "Archaic Level IVa" in Eanna were uncovered extensively, and this layer has proven to be of particular importance for its large buildings and the oldest writing in Mesopotamia (or anywhere else). Unfortunately, however, there is very little information on the immediately preceding periods where only deep soundings revealed

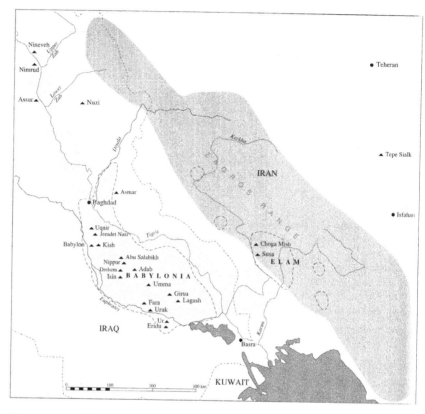

Map 6.1 Map of lower Mesopotamia with location of Uruk. Triangles represent site names and circles are modern cities.

earlier occupations at the site. Although giving exact dates is hazardous, a rough scale of the early development is provided in Table 6.1.[1]

After summarizing our knowledge of the time around 3300, I will discuss the earlier developments, focusing on the communication technologies, which can count as forerunners of writing. Finally, I present a picture of the interdependence between urbanization and the development of communication technologies.

---

[1] Henry Wright and Eric Rupley, "Calibrated Radiocarbon Age Determinations of Uruk-Related Assemblages," in Mitchell S. Rothman (ed.), *Uruk Mesopotamia and its Neighbors: Cross-cultural Interactions in the Era of State Formation* (Santa Fe, NM: School of American Research Press, 2001), pp. 85–122.

Table 6.1 Chronological table

BCE	Period	Levels in Uruk	Form of Settlement	Art/Writing
4300		XVIII		
	Late Ubaid			
4000		XV	Dispersed settlements	Stamp seals, clay figurines
		XIV		
3900	Early Uruk			
		IX		
3800				
		VIII	Massive increase in population and settlements	
3700			Multi-tiered settlement systems	
		VII	Emergence of urban centers. Massive numbers of beveled-rim bowls, first wave of "colonial" outposts; incorporation of Susiana (SW Iran) into the Mesopotamian sphere	Cylinder seals
3600		VI		
3500		V	second wave of outposts; contacts with Egypt; enhancement of the techniques of information storage and processing.	
	Late Uruk			
3400		IVc	Reorganization of foreign relations; abandonment of most outposts, loosening ties with Susiana. Uruk~250 hectares	Large-scale art
3300		IVa		Emergence of first writing (stage IV)
		IIIc		
3200				
	Jamdat Nasr	IIIb		Developed writing (stage III)

Uruk around 3300 BCE

During the time of Level IVa, around 3300 BCE, Uruk covered an area of at least 2.5 square kilometers and had a population of perhaps 50,000 inhabitants. On Map 6.2 the hatched area delineates the probable extent of the inhabited area. Presumably, Uruk was surrounded with a city wall built over during subsequent phases of city growth. Two distinct areas of the site seem

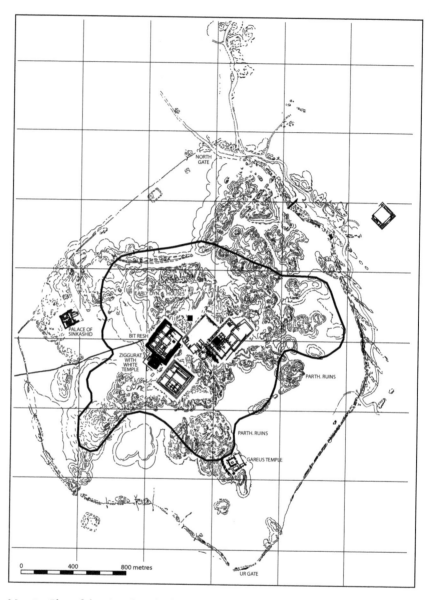

Map 6.2 Plan of the city of Uruk, the hatched area indicating the probable extent of the inhabited area around 3300 BCE.

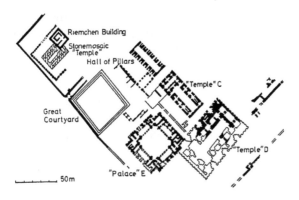

Figure 6.1 Uruk Level IVa (c. 3300 BCE) structures in the Eanna precinct (in J. N. Postgate [ed.], *Artefacts of Complexity: Tracking the Uruk in the Near East* [London: British School of Archaeology in Iraq, 2002], p. 3).

to be relics of once separate settlements that had faced each other on opposite sides of the Euphrates. Some time before 3300, the river shifted its course around the city rather than separating the two parts. No information is available on the time of this change.

The two parts of Uruk differ in various aspects: the west-central area, or "Anu" precinct, consists of an 11-meter-high terrace with a temple on top, while the eastern part, or Eanna, displays a number of large buildings on even ground without any sign of an architectural center (Figure 6.1). West and east again differ in their height above the plain by up to 6 meters. All the archaic tablets were found in Eanna; not a single one was recovered in the western part. Obviously, these differences – in particular the impressive difference in height – must have influenced both the behavior and the way of thinking of the inhabitants, and may be indicative of further dissimilarities in the social landscape of Uruk.

Since excavations have only rarely been carried out beyond the ceremonial areas, we are totally ignorant about the structure of the domestic quarters. On the basis of analogies, two situations seem possible: a dense coverage may be suggested by the contemporary site of Habuba Kabira,[2] or from later examples like Early Dynastic III Abu Salabikh.[3] A less dense

---

[2] Eva Strommenger, *Habuba Kabira, Eine Stadt vor 5000 Jahren* (Mainz: Philipp von Zabern, 1980).
[3] Nicholas Postgate, "How Many Sumerians per Hectare? Probing the Anatomy of an Early City," *Cambridge Archaeological Journal* 4 (1994), 47–65.

settlement may be inferred from a later literary text, the Epic of Gilgamesh, according to which Uruk consisted of one-third houses, one-third gardens, one-third open land, and the area of the Temple of Ishtar.[4] Only further excavations may provide us with an answer.

Around 3300 BCE the first written documents appear. The large majority of them consist of administrative records of a large economic unit. Since they all were found within the precinct of Eanna, which later is known as both the cultic and the economic center of Uruk, this may also be true of the early periods.

As will be argued later, these records are directly linked to the development of the enormous size of this unit. Although we do not have written information from smaller institutional units or from private activities, it is most probable that such units and activities also existed.

All of the oldest documents were found in rubbish layers. Hence, the exact date of the first writing and the context of the first writing remain unclear: there is no way to calculate the time elapsed between the writing of the tablets and their discard. A rough hint at the time of their final disposal, however, is given when the rubbish layer was built over by structures of Level IIIc, providing a *terminus ante quem* for the date of the deposition of the rubbish. In all probability then, the first appearance of writing falls into the time of the next lower (earlier) layer, Level IVa. It is certain that writing appeared only at the very end of the Late Uruk period.

No good information is available about the ethnicity of the population. All indications – particularly the continuity of the development of the script into later times – point to Sumerian being the main linguistic component.[5] However, as in later texts, there are presumably admixtures of different languages in the earliest texts. Since the names of many Mesopotamian cities cannot be etymologized as Sumerian, this has led some to posit a pre-Sumerian population with Sumerians as later immigrants. This anticipates an argument elaborated on below in which a Sumerian immigration may have been responsible for the enormous population increase in the first half of the fourth millennium BCE.

Nor can much be said about the social structure of the society in which the earliest texts occur. Some help comes from one of the so-called "lexical

---

[4] *The Epic of Gilgamesh*, Andrew George (ed. and trans.) (New York: Barnes and Noble, 1999).

[5] Claus Wilcke, "ED LU2 A und die Sprache(n) der archaischen Texte," in W. H. van Soldt (ed.), *Ethnicity in Ancient Mesopotamia* (Leiden: Netherlands Institute for the Near East, 2005), pp. 430–45.

Figure 6.2 Uruk tablet Level IV with the oldest version of the List of Professions (in Hans J. Nissen, Peter Damerow, and Robert K. Englund, *Archaic Bookkeeping: Early Writing and Techniques of Economic Administration in the Ancient Near East* [Chicago: The University of Chicago Press, 1993], p. 110).

lists," which enumerate words and concepts of a given semantic theme, like names of trees or of cities. One list (Figure 6.2) contains titles and designations of members of a hierarchically organized administration. It starts with a "master of the club" (NÁM:ESHDA), which in a dictionary of the twelfth century BCE is glossed as *sharru* (in Akkadian, which means "king"). It is followed by officers responsible for various areas like "law," "city(-administration)," "barley(-supplies)," and "plowmen," and other titles including the "head of the assembly." Later in the list certain professions are split up in two or three sub-levels, probably reminiscent of a master/journeyman/apprentice relation. Some of the titles turn up in economic documents where they receive large quantities of barley, which probably are meant to be distributed among the employees of their office, rather than for their personal use.

It is unclear what kind of administration is indicated: that of the central economic unit at Eanna or of the entire city. Worth mentioning is that not a single title seems to denote a religious office. Though most details remain unclear the list obviously is organized along a hierarchic principle, which most likely is the structuring principle of the society as a whole. This is underlined by archaeological observations. For instance, the manufacture of pottery in the Late Uruk period shows the extensive use of the potter's wheel and the output of mass-production, which points to an increased division of labor with differentiated tasks and responsibilities. The same applies for a presumed metal-working installation.

The "master of the club" may be the figure we encounter on pictorial representations, whom we identify as the ruler. On seals, but also on other pieces of art, we meet a figure who differs from other people in his attire and

Figure 6.3 Cylinder seal with prisoners being beaten in front of the ruler (in Postgate [ed.], *Artefacts of Complexity*, p. 10).

size: on a number of seals we see a tall figure with skirt and cap leaning on a spear (Figure 6.3). In front of him smaller naked figures use sticks to beat naked crouching and bound figures. Since no effort is made to identify the beaten figures as foreign by hairdo or other markers, it seems possible that the suppression of internal problems is meant. Again we meet the figure on the so-called cult vase from Uruk, where he leads a procession of gift bearers. Though broken except for some traces the ruler is depicted as larger in size and more splendidly attired than all other figures of the composition, including the high priestess standing in front of the symbolized temple of the goddess Inanna (patron deity of Uruk and the Eanna precinct). The ruler is shown as exercising physical power, as worshipping his city goddess, as hunting lions, or feeding animals, all of which in later times are the prerogatives of kings.

Pictorial representations never differentiate people other than the ruler on the one hand, and the rest of the people, on the other, but the actual situation must have been more complex, not only because of the evidence of many other official titles in the lexical list, but also because of other hints. Though of later date, a tale of Gilgamesh mentions two councils, one of the elders and the other of "battle-experienced young men," and these councils apparently formed a political counterweight to the ruler. (Such assemblies and councils are found throughout Mesopotamian history.) Still, in the poem, the ruler has the last say, and he rejects the decision of the council of the elders in preference to the advice of the council of "battle-experienced young men." Does the "leader of the assembly" of the lexical list of titles refer to such councils? And was it in the large halls in the Eanna precinct where they assembled? In any case, there was a large and differentiated urban elite and many other lower levels of people who lived in Uruk and in the countryside connected with the city.

With the exception of the lexical lists, the earliest documents contain records of economic transactions. Although these written texts are much more explicit than the earlier systems of information storage – which will be dealt with shortly – initially writing works along the same lines as those systems. That is, writing is used in the beginning to denote only those items that are deemed necessary to reconstruct a particular transaction, because a certain level of background knowledge was assumed. Since modern readers lack this knowledge, however, we often cannot even decide whether the goods recorded in a transaction were delivered to or were distributed from the central stores. Also, the writing did not reflect a spoken language with all its complex syntax; rather, the tablets were aides-memoires.

Large quantities of goods of all kinds recorded in the texts imply the existence of a complex economic institution. Tablets in which the items registered on one side are added up on the other side show us the main function of the records – that is, to record and control goods entering or leaving the central stores. The origin of the goods, however, is never mentioned. We are unable to reconstruct the chain between producer and consumer.

The complexity of economic life is further illustrated by the continued use of older systems of record-keeping, such as counting pieces (tokens), and various kinds of seals alongside the script. The complicated system of the script was apparently used only when unavoidable, whereas simpler methods continued to be used in less complex cases.

As in earlier times when stamp seals were employed, cylinder seals provide information by denoting the owner of the seal and person responsible for a transaction. Thus, seal decorations were differentiated to the extent that everyone who needed a seal could be furnished with an unmistakable design. The introduction of cylinder seals in the Late Uruk period offered a means for depicting figures and complex scenes and so made legible the growing number of people taking part in economic life. But these cylinder seals did not entirely displace the older stamp seals, which continued to be used. These stamp seals were less complex, and they were even joined by a new type of cylinder seal that used only a limited number of simple geometric patterns. Apparently these various types of seals were used for different purposes, in certain distinct areas of the economy. This explains why there are many impressions of the figurative seals, which were used repeatedly by bureaucrats, but almost no original seals were found. The contrary is true for the geometric and less differentiated seals. Although it is impossible to define the different areas of employment, they nevertheless show that various areas or departments existed in which different kinds of controlling devices were employed.

Although writing is restricted to the economic sphere, with the exception of lexical lists, it is probable that the other areas of administration mentioned in the titles' list were equally complex but did not require record-keeping with the precision needed to regulate economic affairs. This also applies to the area of conflict management, which must have been of major importance considering the large number of inhabitants confined within the city wall. This is reflected by the appearance of the title of someone responsible for legal affairs in the first lines of the title list.

Another largely unknown area is how the bulk of the population was provisioned. The accumulation of large quantities of food in the central stores of the main economic unit undoubtedly was meant to pay in kind large numbers of personnel. However, considering the number of inhabitants in Uruk, it is inconceivable that everybody was on the central payroll. As suggested earlier, we should reckon on the existence of smaller socioeconomic units of administration as well as of private and corporate groups with their own means of subsistence.

Undoubtedly, the sources of food originated in the hinterland of the city. The arable land directly outside the city wall would have been used by inhabitants of the city itself, as far as it was not already occupied by settlements very near Uruk. Since this land was certainly not sufficient to produce the needed surplus, we assume that the farther-flung hinterland was tied into a comprehensive network aimed at securing the necessary supplies for the central city. This hinterland was covered by settlements of all sizes that were organized as a "central place system" focused on the metropolis of Uruk.[6] In theory, settlements in the hinterland furnished supplies to the center in exchange for services provided by the city. However, as the written sources are silent on origins of food, we have no indication regarding how this provision was organized and exactly what services were provided. We may assume, however, that in order to meet the demands of the city, the hinterland had to be no less organized than the center.

The exact provenance of metals and precious stones also remains obscure. They all had to be imported since the alluvium provided little else other than reeds and mud. Mineral analyses of artifacts from Uruk show that most of the precious stones originated in the high Zagros Mountains of Iran,

---

[6] Robert McC. Adams and Hans J. Nissen, *The Uruk Countryside* (Chicago: The University of Chicago Press, 1972).

but nothing points to the areas of origin of the metals. All we know from the texts is that metals were in demand in considerable quantities.

Likewise both means and routes of transport of these imports are unknown. This has to be seen in the context of the so-called "Uruk Expansion."[7] Within the closer and wider vicinity of southern Mesopotamia, we find numerous settlements in Syria, southeast Anatolia, northern Mesopotamia, and Iran resembling the evidence from southern Mesopotamian sites in architecture and artifacts. The settlements were embedded in a sea of non-Mesopotamian cultures. Most probably, these "Urukian" settlements represent outposts that funneled supplies of raw materials to southern Mesopotamia. However interesting (and controversial), this topic does not fall within our discussion of the time of Level IVa, because – as will be seen later – with few exceptions, these settlements were abandoned before the time in which the first writing appeared.

The foundation of outposts (or in Guillermo Algaze's term, "colonies") far outside Mesopotamia points to southern Mesopotamia as the political and economic superpower in the Near East. This becomes even more obvious when we find items of undoubted Mesopotamian cultural affiliation in remote areas like central Anatolia or Egypt. The case of Egypt is especially significant, because the adoption of cylinder seals and particularly the application of Uruk-style niches to the outer facades of a large building indicate that Egyptians knew the Mesopotamian contexts of these features or, less likely, decontextualized them. This brings us to a long-debated question: Did Mesopotamian cuneiform writing and the Egyptian hieroglyphs, which appeared at roughly the same time, develop independently, or did one influence the other?

As I discuss below, the appearance of writing in southern Mesopotamia is preceded by a long development of various means of information storage and processing, related to the evolution of a stratified social system and highly differentiated economy. In Egypt, however, there seem not to have been forerunners to hieroglyphic writing. This lends credence to the direction of influence of the writing system of Mesopotamia on Egypt. If the idea of writing was a stimulus from Mesopotamia, migrating to Egypt along with the other cultural items, hieroglyphs – that is, the form of Egyptian writing – owed nothing to Mesopotamian cuneiform writing. In Mesopotamia, it should be noted, there is not a single item of Egyptian origin or affiliation

---

[7] Rothman (ed.), *Uruk Mesopotamia and its Neighbors.*

in the Late Uruk period. Clearly, the direction of influence is from southern Mesopotamia to Egypt.

Of the other Mesopotamian cities like Ur, Lagash, Nippur, or Kish little is known other than that they were occupied during the time of the final part of the Late Uruk period. In the next time periods (Jamdat Nasr and Early Dynastic – the end of the fourth millennium and start of the third – these and other cities are large, populous, highly stratified, and politically independent, and it seems reasonable to assume this for the older time as well. For the oldest phase of the script the only item outside of Uruk is a stone tablet from Kish. However, for the next writing stage there is ample evidence for the style of writing being almost identical throughout central and southern Mesopotamia. This indicates the existence of very close ties of a common cultural system, short of a unitary political structure.

Summarizing the preceding snapshot, it is evident that Uruk, at the end of the period named after it, together with other southern Mesopotamian cities, was a center of political and economic activity, exerting power into areas beyond its immediate hinterlands. In the next section I discuss how and why this happened.

Uruk before the advent of writing

Information on the time before 3300, including both the older part of the Late Uruk period, and the Early Uruk and Late Ubaid periods, is scarce. The best evidence comes from a deep sounding in Uruk itself, which reaches back into the fifth millennium BCE. However, the potsherds found in ever decreasing surface areas do not show more than that the site of Uruk was continuously inhabited for at least a millennium before the first writing appeared.

In addition to excavated material, we can draw on evidence provided by archaeological surface surveys. They show that the alluvium was only very sparsely settled during the Ubaid period (c. 5000–4000 BCE). Small settlements lay at such distance from each other that they were not part of a regulated or central system. However, they were part of an "Ubaid cultural network" that extended over large parts of the Near East. Common features of this network are temples on terraces; the so-called "house with a central hall" that is indicative of a certain common organization of daily life; and a new way of organizing the manufacture and decoration of pottery. The latter was due to the introduction of the "tournette" (or slow wheel) accompanied by the mass-production of certain types of ceramics and a new division of labor.

Central buildings with or without religious connotation suggest the existence of an elite, and of a social hierarchy. The use and storage of counting markers and of stamp seals as the means of information storage indicate a certain complexity in economic life. The introduction of the cubit, a standard unit in building construction, was part of the establishment of standards as a means of creating comparability and interregional exchange.

The transition to the next archaeological period, the Early Uruk (early fourth millennium), and the phase itself are not well attested, because hardly anything is known of them except for the sequence of pottery production. There was an almost total abandonment of painting along with a new composition of the paste, and the use of the potter's wheel. More we do not know.

Assuming that items present both in the Ubaid and the Late Uruk existed in the transition period as well, we infer the existence of the "house with a central hall" as well as the temple on a terrace. The impression of a stamp seal in Uruk Level XII (an Ubaid-to-Uruk transition period stratum) points to continuity also in this area. The size of settlements on the southern Mesopotamian plain does not differ significantly from the preceding Ubaid period, however, and settlements are still widely distributed.

This picture changes completely with the next archaeological phase: the earlier part of the Late Uruk period. To be sure, we still see continuity in the production of pottery, the "house with a central hall," and the temple on a terrace as well as in the use of counting markers and seals, but in addition we meet certain qualitative and quantitative changes that signal a total reorientation of the society.

Most visible are innovations in the sphere of economics. Already earlier, a decrease in the shapes of pottery vessels and changes in the process of manufacture pointed to an organization of workshops aiming at producing larger numbers of ceramics. This becomes supplemented by the output of the mold-made "beveled-rim bowls," an early form of mass-production, and indeed these were produced in the millions. Whether they were initially used for the distribution of food rations, as is claimed for their later use, or not, there must have been a mass-demand for these wares and the organizational ability to find an efficient solution for it. The almost equal capacity of the majority of the bowls implies a standard unit of measure.

Another response to the growing demands of the organization of a large and stratified population was the introduction of the cylinder seal.

Apparently, there was an increasing need to supply distinctive seals to denote differentiated responsibilities and lines of control that were harder to meet with the limited space of stamp seals.

An even greater change in social and political organization is reflected in settlement patterns. Already during the Early Uruk period the number of settlements had increased in the northern part of central Mesopotamia, but this only prefigured the dramatic changes in the Late Uruk period in the south. Instead of eleven Early Uruk sites we encounter more than 100 in the surveyed part of the hinterland of Uruk, many of which are larger than settlements of the previous phase. Apparently within a short period of time, the country is covered with settlements of all sizes, forming settlement systems around central places. At the top of this three-tiered system we find the city of Uruk.

At the same time as the increase in the number of settlements, the organization of the hinterland of the city must have undergone significant changes. Earlier, it was enough to produce sufficient supplies for themselves; now though rural settlements were drawn into a network that provisioned the city, and people in the countryside were forced to produce a considerable amount of surplus. However, we have no idea about the time and scope of this change.

The enormous growth in the number of settlements, and thus in population size, is more than can be accounted for by a natural population growth. Indeed, we see this development connected to a change to a slightly drier climate early in the fourth millennium BCE that rendered the alluvium habitable on a new and larger scale. This newly available land apparently attracted immigrants from neighboring areas. Possibly, some of these immigrants were Sumerian speakers. There is no indication of their area of origin, either archaeologically or linguistically (since Sumerian is a linguistic isolate). Here we are not so much interested in their putative ethnolinguistic affiliation as in the consequences of this extraordinary increase of settlements and population in southern Mesopotamia.

Although our dating of these changes is still dependent on pottery seriation from the deep sounding at Uruk, we are safe in assuming that the unprecedented density of settlements and concomitantly increased number of people required rapid transformations in political organization and information technology. The development of cylinder seals and beveled-rim bowls appeared quickly after the large-scale immigration to southern Mesopotamia. Furthermore, the increased volume of goods that were produced and distributed required more complex recording devices than the counters and stamp seals that each were able to store only one item of information. In the middle of the Late Uruk period (Uruk Level VI), we find artifacts that were able to increase the amount of information on the same medium.

In one case, the number of counters (or tokens), which represented the number of goods, was wrapped into a ball of clay (or bulla), the surface of which would be covered with seal impressions. At the same time or slightly later, we encounter flattened cakes of clay – resembling the later shape of written tablets – with indentations made using a reed stylus, representing numbers. The entire surface of the tablet would then be sealed. In both cases, numbers and information about an individual were stored together.

Since the Neolithic (c. 8000 BCE), counters/tokens worked on the principle that certain geometric shapes represented numbers of things. This system was now extended in two directions. On the one hand, some counters were given the shape of actual objects. The purpose of this eludes us since these complex counters have never been found in combination with simple counters that represented a number of counted items. On the other hand, both simple and complex counters could be incised and hatched, thus increasing the information to be conveyed. Although we are unable to "decipher" any of these early systems of counting and accountability, they are clearly part of the trajectory of new organizational techniques in an increasingly complex society.

For the new kind of administration other skills were also necessary and they were of no less complexity, such as the surveying of fields or solving of mathematical problems. No doubt, young people had to be trained in these techniques within an institutionalized frame. The curriculum in such "schools" may have included other fields as well, as can be inferred from the existence of the "lexical lists" found among the earliest written documents. Transferred from oral versions, they represent methods of teaching the cuneiform script as well as an early attempt to intellectually control the universe.

It was these "schools" where the inadequacy of controlling devices was recognized and where improvements were on the agenda. And it was most probably in these circles where the idea of a script was born, drawing on a number of codes like that of the counters, of pot marks, or elements of decoration used in pot, wall, or body painting. In this sense the appearance of writing, which in the first stage did not represent spoken language, was barely more than an extension of the techniques of accounting. Nevertheless, the invention of writing was an intellectual achievement of the highest order.[8]

The lists themselves offer a clue for understanding principles of social organization before the advent of writing. In particular, the existence of the list of titles implies that there was a structure of ranks that must have existed before it was put into writing. In later times, such lists were used as school texts, and this may have been their function already in the Late Uruk period. Their oral counterparts may even have been significant in the process of inventing the cuneiform writing system, as subsequently they acquired a quasi-sacrosanct position and were copied nearly exactly for more than 1,000 years, with only changes in the style of the written characters. The idea of the script and the entire system of its production and reproduction probably took little time, as in these "schools" its importance was immediately recognized and transmitted.[9]

Summary

After a long formative period ending with Early Uruk (c. 4100[?]–3800), in which a new division of labor, increased social stratification, and early forms of economic accountability were occurring, we may speak of a "proto-urban" phase of Mesopotamian civilization. However, in this period, settlement sizes seldom exceeded 20 hectares and simple counters and stamp seals were considered sufficient for the limited size of economic and political organization at this time.

Subsequently, at the beginning of what we call the Late Uruk period (3800–3300), as part of an exceptional increase of population and number of settlements, Uruk grew to a size of at least 250 hectares. We assume that the place started as an Ubaid settlement on the west bank of the Euphrates and during Late Ubaid was complemented by a settlement across the river. Both during Ubaid and Early Uruk the size of the site probably did not exceed the average size of Ubaid settlements. Consequently, the enormous increase

[8] Hans J. Nissen, "Schule vor der Schrift," in Gebhard J. Selz (ed.), *The Empirical Dimension of Ancient Near Eastern Studies* (Vienna: LIT Verlag, 2011), pp. 589–602.
[9] For other concepts of the development of writing, see Jean-Jacques Glassner, *The Invention of Cuneiform Writing in Sumer* (Baltimore, MD: Johns Hopkins University Press, 2003); and Denise Schmandt-Besserat, *Before Writing* (Austin: University of Texas Press, 1992).

from 20 to 250 hectares must have occurred during the approximately 500 years that we allot to the Late Uruk – probably during the earlier part.

This enormous scale of growth required new organizational means that we see mainly in areas of economic administration, such as the existence of economic texts, the mass-production of beveled-rim bowls, and the use of cylinder seals. The list of titles implies a new organization of the rules of social life.

Agriculture must have been intensified in order to feed the increasing population, and this was afforded by the great fertility of the alluvium and easy access to water. At the same time, the demand for raw materials of all kinds rose, for utilitarian uses and weapons as well as for cylinder seals and prestige items, especially for new objects of art (that I cannot discuss here). Presumably at a certain point, the traditional ways of procuring such materials proved to be insufficient, and this led to founding outposts like Shaikh Hassan on the Syrian Euphrates or at Tell Brak in the upper Habur. Administrative devices found at these distant places, such as beveled-rim bowls and cylinder seals, indicate that life there was organized according to similar rules as in the mother country. The continued demand for foreign goods necessitated the formation of a closer network of outposts, resulting in the additional foundation of such places as Habuba Kabira, Jebel Aruda, Nineveh, Tell i-Ghazir, and, even further, over the mountains, as shown by Hassek Höyük in Anatolia and Godin Tepe in Iran. Both internal necessities and the increase in goods flowing to southern Mesopotamia led to the need for new information storage systems. In the texts from Uruk there are many references to exotic stones and metals. Although most of the outposts were abandoned shortly before the time when writing was invented in southern Mesopotamia, the flow of goods to southern Mesopotamia did not decrease.

After a period of turbulent internal and external expansion, in the later part of the Late Uruk period, Uruk along with other early Mesopotamian cities became a center of immense economic and political power with far-reaching influence into the neighboring regions. This was not the end of rapid changes and adaptations, however, as is evidenced by the reorganization of the ceremonial precincts of Uruk at the end of the Late Uruk period, the twofold increase in size of Uruk over the following 300 years, and the gradual establishment of canal systems to meet the problem of the ongoing decrease of water supplies. But this is another story.

In comparison to the other cases of city–writing relations discussed in this section, Mesopotamia offers a clear example. Urbanization creates the economic, social, and intellectual hotbed for the emergence of writing.

But writing is not the first answer when demands grew for more efficient administrative devices, since for quite some time people tried to get along with minor enhancements to traditional technologies. The final solution in form of the script came only at the very end of the first round of urbanization.

The process of urbanization in Uruk was inextricably bound with changes in accounting and communication technologies and finally in the creation of the first writing system. Although the increase in population and the tightening of settlement networks have been named as the primary forces in these developments, none of the various strands dominated the others: the development of rules of economic and political life stimulated the development of communication technologies. At the same time the new "tool" of writing became a factor that led to new forms of politics and economics.

FURTHER READINGS

Algaze, Guillermo, *Ancient Mesopotamia at the Dawn of Civilization: The Evolution of an Urban Landscape*, Chicago: The University of Chicago Press, 2008.

Englund, Robert K., "Texts from the Late Uruk Period," in Pascal Attinger and Markus Wäfler (eds.), *Mesopotamien: Späturuk-Zeit und Frühdynastische Zeit*, Freiburg: Universitätsverlag, 1998, pp. 15–233.

Nissen, Hans J., *Alt-Vorderasien*, Munich: Oldenbourg, 2012.

　　The Early History of the Ancient Near East 9000–2000 BC, Chicago: The University of Chicago Press, 1988.

Nissen, Hans J., Peter Damerow, and Robert K. Englund, *Archaic Bookkeeping: Early Writing and Techniques of Economic Administration in the Ancient Near East*, Chicago: The University of Chicago Press, 1993.

Nissen, Hans J., and Peter Heine, *From Mesopotamia to Iraq: A Concise History*, Chicago: The University of Chicago Press, 2009.

Roaf, Michael, *Cultural Atlas of Mesopotamia and the Ancient Near East*, Oxford: Equinox 1990.

7

Writing and the city in early China

WANG HAICHENG

Chinese urbanism has a history of more than 5,000 years, and ever since the invention of the Chinese writing system more than 3,000 years ago, the process of urbanization and the uninterrupted transmission of literacy have gone hand in hand. Without the city, writing could not have come into being, nor could it have sustained itself. This chapter focuses on the second millennium BCE, the early Bronze Age. More specifically, it covers two consecutive episodes of that phase: the Huanbei period and the Yinxu period (see Table 7.1), mainly the latter. During the two periods, two large cities were built and abandoned in succession on opposite sides of a tributary of the Yellow River. Both sites are located in the modern city of Anyang in north China (Map 7.1). I will use them as my case studies for exploring the urbanization process in early China and the uses of writing that accompanied it. For each city I first review what archaeology can tell us about its urbanization, then writing's role in city administration.

Precursors of Anyang writing

Let me begin with a quick word about cities and writing in the two centuries before 1350 BCE. During the fifteenth and fourteenth centuries a great city flourished 200 kilometers south of Anyang, in today's Zhengzhou. The largest city of its time, it had two walls built of pounded earth. The inner wall, 22 meters thick at the base, has a perimeter of about 7,000 meters and

I would like to thank Norman Yoffee for inviting me to participate in this wonderful project. For penetrating comments on drafts of this chapter I am most grateful to Robert Bagley. I am greatly indebted to Kyle Steinke for redrawing several maps and figures. Cao Dazhi and Yan Shengdong generously sent me their own drawings; Shan Yueying, Song Guoding, Tang Jigen, and Wu Hsiao-yun were instrumental in obtaining photographs. The research was supported by a Royalty Research Fund Grant (project no. 65-3319) at the University of Washington.

Table 7.1 *Chronological table of early Bronze Age China*

Erlitou	1900–1500 BCE
Erligang	1500–1350 BCE
Huanbei	1350–1250 BCE
Yinxu	1250–1050 BCE
Western Zhou	1050–771 BCE

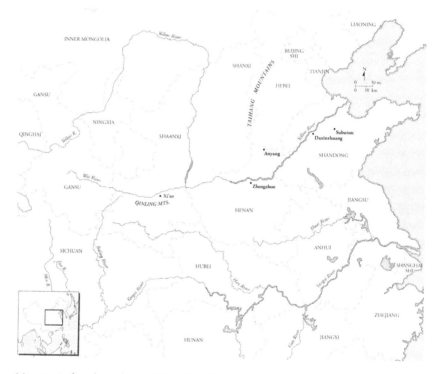

Map 7.1 Archaeological sites of the Early Bronze Age mentioned in this chapter (drawn by Kyle Steinke).

encloses an area of more than 400 hectares. The earliest examples of writing known from East Asia were found near Zhengzhou and belong probably to the fourteenth century. They are graphs written in vermilion on clay pots (Figure 7.1). Though few, they clearly belong to the writing system we know a century later from the so-called oracle bone inscriptions at Anyang. The Anyang inscriptions are the first substantial corpus of Chinese writing, but they are display inscriptions; neither at Anyang nor at Zhengzhou does

Figure 7.1 Corpus of Chinese writing from Xiaoshuangqiao, *c.* fourteenth century BCE. The corpus seems to include numerals, titles, kinship terms, and possibly a deity's name as shown on bottom right. The characters in the fourth and the eighth rows are from Xiaoshuangqiao, the second and the sixth rows from the oracle bone inscriptions a century or two later, the third and the seventh rows from bronze inscriptions a little later than the oracle bone inscriptions, the first and fifth rows are their transcriptions in modern Chinese (table after Song Guoding, "Zhengzhou Xiaoshuangqiao yizhi chutu taoqi shang de zhushu" *Wenwu* 5 [2003], p. 42, Table 1. Photographs courtesy of Song Guoding).

everyday writing survive. Everyday administrative documents were almost certainly written on perishable materials like wood and bamboo strips,[1] the

---

[1] Robert Bagley, "Anyang Writing and the Origin of the Chinese Writing System," in Stephen D. Houston (ed.), *The First Writing: Script Invention as History and Process* (Cambridge: Cambridge University Press, 2004), pp. 216–26.

standard materials of later times, and these do not begin to survive in the archaeological record until about the fifth century BCE. What we have from earlier periods is only inscriptions meant for display of some sort. The graphs in Figure 7.1, done in vermilion for some sort of ritual deposit, were clearly display writing. The polity based at Zhengzhou created an empire, building fortresses to secure new territories as far away as the middle Yangzi region 450 kilometers to the south, and it may well have used writing in the administration of its empire. But the empire was short-lived. Its fortresses were abandoned after a century or so, and eventually its capital too.

The Huanbei period

Material culture, especially elite material culture, strongly suggests that part of the Zhengzhou population, led by its elite, moved north across the Yellow River and settled at the Huanbei site at modern Anyang. The Huanbei site was discovered only recently, so survey and excavation data are very limited, but they do seem to represent a new city created by the organized migration of a population with prior urban experience. Creating the city had to begin with reconnaissance and migration. The next step was to erect temples to house ancestors and palaces to house the king and his family. At the same time, dwellings were built around the royal compound for the king's followers. Sometime later the royal palace and temple compound were enclosed by a wall to separate the royal precinct from the lesser dwellings. And finally another wall was built enclosing the royal precinct, the other houses, and some burials within a second rectangle of over 400 hectares, an area comparable to that inside the inner wall at Zhengzhou. Scattered over an area of about 800 square kilometers surrounding the Huanbei site, preliminary survey has found at least twenty small settlements that were probably controlled by the rulers of Huanbei. A site 400 kilometers to the east, at Daxinzhuang in Shandong province (Map 7.1), has the look of a Huanbei colony, suggesting that Huanbei's expansionism was directed eastward rather than southward.

Only two bits of writing datable to the Huanbei period have been found so far, both at the Huanbei site. One is a jade inscribed with three characters, perhaps an amulet; the other is a bone object bearing perhaps the name of a person or a lineage (Figure 7.2). No inscribed divination bones have been found. They may turn up in new excavations; but it is also possible that the decision to inscribe the bones used for divination was only made at the next stage, at the beginning of the Yinxu period around 1250 BCE. There are hints

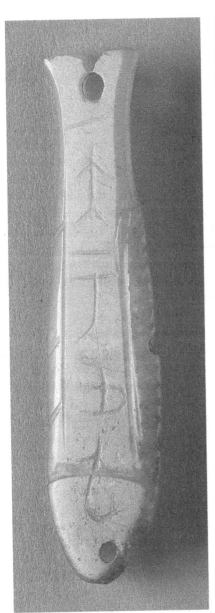
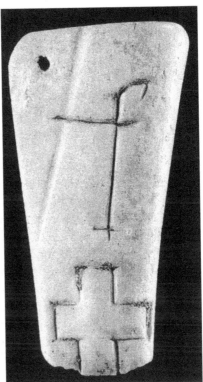

Figure 7.2 Two inscribed objects of the Huanbei period. Left: a jade pendant inscribed with three characters, from top to bottom read "great ancestors harm." From Xiaotun Tomb 331 at Anyang, length 6.7 cm, width 1.6 cm (photograph courtesy of History and Philology, Academia Sinica). Right: a bone fragment inscribed with two characters, perhaps a name. From Huanbei Huayuanzhuang, extant length 5.5 cm, width 1.8–2.8 cm (photograph courtesy of Tang Jigen).

that divinination practice changed at that time as the result of a royal decision taken in the midst of larger changes.

The Yinxu period

The founding and peopling of Yinxu

Around the middle of the thirteenth century the temple/palace compounds at Huanbei burned down. Whatever the cause of the fire, the buildings were never rebuilt. Construction work on the city wall, begun a short while before, seems to have stopped at the time of the fire. The site seems to have been abandoned in favor of a new one just across the Huan River, in an area today called Xiaotun, where a Huanbei period bronze foundry and settlement were already located. These earlier buildings seem to have been demolished to clear the ground for new royal temples and palaces.

We do not know the reasons for this relocation, but it was surely an act of will on the part of a governing elite, and the responsible agent seems to have been a king named Wu Ding. A number of notable changes may stem from Wu Ding's direct initiative. Here is a list, in descending order of our confidence in connecting them with him: (1) The construction of a royal cemetery outside the city, the earliest tomb probably being intended for Wu Ding himself (Map 7.2). (2) Certain rapid and dramatic changes of bronze style in Wu Ding's reign, changes that may have occurred simply as by-products of a tremendous expansion of the bronze casting industry (Figure 7.3). (3) The carving of divination records on the divination medium (bovine scapulae and turtle shells, for example Figure 7.4). (4) The addition of emblems and short dedicatory phrases to ritual bronzes (Figure 7.3). (5) The first attestation of horses in China and probably the earliest chariots, both of which were imported from the northwest and used as conspicuous symbols of elite power and status. (6) A distinct increase in the quantity of small carvings done in marble, a scarce material that from this time onward was used almost exclusively by royalty.

The new city that Wu Ding created is called Da Yi Shang (Great Settlement Shang) in his divination texts, so we will call its people the Shang people, but we will use the modern name Yinxu to distinguish it from Huanbei (Map 7.2). Unlike Huanbei, Yinxu had no city walls and no clearly demarcated perimeters other than those provided on the north and east by the riverbank. Allowing a riverbank to define city boundaries amounts to abandoning a tradition of orthogonal enclosing walls, a tradition that

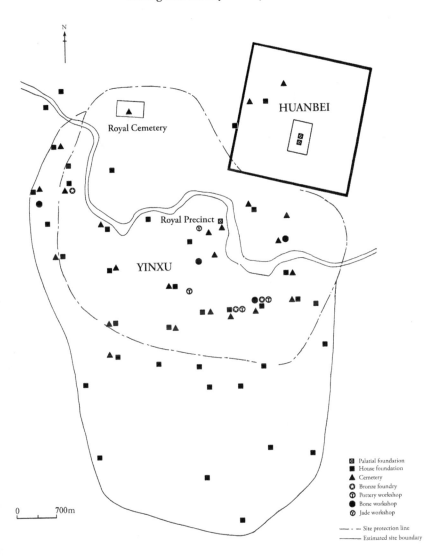

Map 7.2 Shang sites at Anyang (based on Niu Shishan, "Zhongguo gudai ducheng de guihua moshi chubu yanjiu," in Zhongguo shehui kexueyuan kaogu yanjiusuo [ed.], *Yinxu yu Shang wenhua: Yinxu kexue fajue 80 zhounian jinian wenji* [Beijing: Kexue chubanshe, 2011], p. 227, fig. 3; Meng Xianwu and Li Guichang, "Anyang Yinxu bianyuan quyu kaogu gaishu," in *ibid.*, p. 160, fig. 1; drawing by Cao Dazhi and Kyle Steinke).

Figure 7.3 Two bronze *he* vessels from the reign of Wu Ding, shown roughly to the same scale. Left: from a foundation deposit shown in Map 7.3 (lower right corner), with an inscription cast under the handle dedicating it to a certain "Father Yi," probably made by Wu Ding at the beginning of his reign for his father. Height 34 cm (photograph courtesy of Tang Jigen). Right: one of a set of three from Tomb 1001 at the royal cemetery shown in Map 7.2 (horizontal rectangle on upper left), generally believed to belong to Wu Ding; the vessel was therefore made at the end of his reign, and its architectural look makes it almost impossible to recognize its ancestry in the vessel on the left, made at most a few decades before. The set of three were inscribed under their handles "left," "middle," and "right," probably indicating their positions on the altar. Height 71.2 cm (courtesy of the Nezu Bijutsukan Tokyo).

extends back into the Neolithic. A change so significant must have been the king's conscious decision.

The current estimate of Yinxu's size is 30 square kilometers, but how much of that area was actually inhabited during the Yinxu period is unknown. Nevertheless, eighty years of mortuary and settlement archaeology tell us to visualize the city as an agglomeration of lineage settlements

Figure 7.4 Scapula inlaid with red pigment from the reign of Wu Ding. A series of divinations were recorded on this side and the other side, each beginning with a common question asking about the fortune of the coming week (as in text [7]), followed by the king's correct prognostication and what actually happened, including a death and a chariot accident involving the king. Why the king would display such disasters remains a mystery (after Zhongguo Guojia Bowuguan [ed.], *Zhonghua Wenming*. [Beijing: Zhongguo Shehui Kexue Chubanshe, 2010], p. 142, by permission of the National Museum of China)

and cemeteries that grew outward from the royal precinct in the northeast corner over a period of two centuries. Each lineage comprised perhaps twenty to fifty families. Each family, or several families together, lived in a courtyard compound. Several of these compounds, varied in size and sometimes just a meter apart, collected around a bigger compound that perhaps belonged to the lineage head or the lineage temple. Figure 7.5 shows a typical lineage settlement containing patio groups and such features of everyday life as wells.

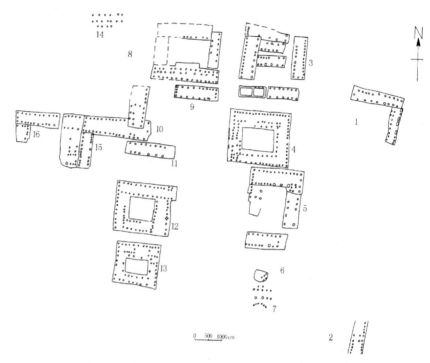

Figure 7.5 A lineage settlement at Xujiaqiao north, Yinxu. The excavated area of the house foundations (numbered 1–16) is approximately 2 hectares. About 400 tombs have been found inside and around the settlement, but to date none is published (from Meng Xianwu and Li Guichang, "Yinxu siheyuan shi jianzhu jizhi kaocha," *Zhongyuan wenwu* 5 [2004], p. 28, fig. 2. Redrawn by Kyle Steinke).

This spatial organization was mirrored in the lineage cemetery nearby, in which tombs clustered in three levels can be discerned, perhaps corresponding to nuclear family, extended family, and lineage. Each lineage had its own name and ancestors. Its name or emblem was often cast on the ritual vessels buried with lineage members (Figure 7.6). To date more than 15,000 burials have been excavated. Far fewer houses have been found, and houses were subject to continuous rebuilding, so how many lineages inhabited Yinxu at any one time cannot be reconstructed. It was probably fewer than the total number of lineage emblems known to us, about 150. But to get a very rough idea of the Yinxu population, let us suppose all 150 lineages coexisted; if we then assign 100–200 people to each lineage – a number that has some support from the mortuary data – we get a range of 15,000 to 30,000. This is lower than the

Figure 7.6 A selection of lineage emblems or names cast on Yinxu bronzes. Most of the components of these monograms are characters that stand for words, but they are not arranged in linear sequence of an ordinary text (for instance, the one shown in Figure 7.8), hence it is difficult to ascertain the meaning of each monogram. Many, but not all of these monograms are lineage emblems (from Zheng Ruokui, "Yinxu Dayi Shang zuyi buju chutan," *Zhongyuan wenwu* 3 [1995], p. 88, fig. 3).

commonly cited range of 70,000–120,000 but differs by an order of magnitude at most. Both ranges can accommodate references in divination texts to raising armies of 3,000 or 5,000 or even in one case 13,000 men:

[1] Crack-making on *dingyou* (day 34), Ke divined: "This season, (if) the king raises 5,000 men to campaign against the Tufang, he will receive assistance." (*HJ* 6409)[2]

---

[2] *HJ* is a standard abbreviation for *Jiaguwen heji* (Beijing: Zhongua Shuju, 1978–82), 13 vols.

Central planning and control of city layout are not much in evidence at Yinxu, but perhaps the recently exposed intersecting thoroughfares and long waterways along the major axes were designed from the first for wheeled traffic and water supply – the wheel ruts are very clear. The waterways passed through areas with heavy industry such as pottery workshops and bronze foundries (Map 7.2). The thoroughfares seem to have converged on the south side of the royal precinct.

The royal precinct and its divination texts

The royal precinct covers about 70 hectares, with over 100 building foundations found so far (Map 7.3). It is in storage pits associated with some of the buildings that most of the inscribed divination bones have been found. At least half of these texts can be dated to the time of relocation from Huanbei to Yinxu, in other words, to the reign of Wu Ding. The sudden appearance of so many divination texts suggests that the decision to inscribe the bones was somehow involved with the other changes taking place at this time. Most of these texts show the king anxiously divining about the fortune of the coming week or about the appropriateness of particular sacrifices to royal ancestors. Here are some examples:

> [2] Crack-making on *jimao* (day 16), Ke divined: "In performing an exorcism for [Lady] Hao to Father Yi, cleave a sheep, offer a pig, pledge ten penned sheep." (*HJ* 271)
>
> [3] Crack-making on *dingchou* (day 14), Xing divined: "The king hosts Father Ding, performs the *xie*-ritual, no fault." (*HJ* 23120)
>
> [4] On the eighth day, indeed decapitated 2,656 persons at Meng. Ninth month... (*HJ* 7771)

These texts, together with the sacrificial remains found in the precinct and in the royal cemetery, are gruesome testimony to the supreme importance of the royal ancestors in the institution of Shang kingship, and writing figured prominently in the rituals directed toward them.

Archaeological evidence suggests that during the rituals the ancestors were represented not by portraits but by small wooden tablets inscribed with their names. The ancestral cult, as reconstructed from divinations about sacrifices, included a cycle of five rituals performed on a fairly strict schedule. The schedule was complex, prescribing particular sacrifices to particular ancestors on dates determined by their positions in the Shang king list. For example:

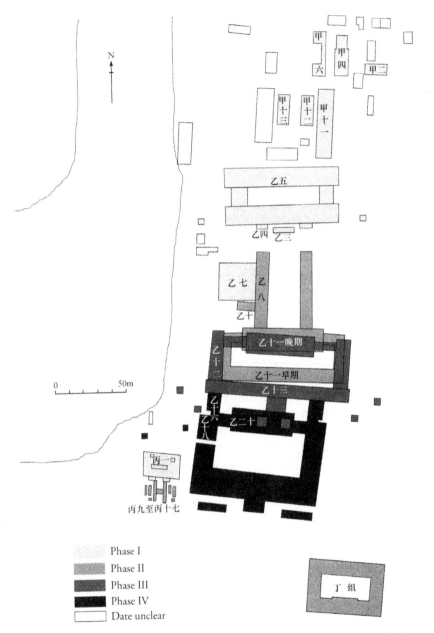

Map 7.3 The royal precinct of Yinxu, blocks showing the order in which major building foundations were constructed during the Shang period (Phase I here, perhaps includes a bronze foundry) and the Yinxu period (Phrases II–IV) (based on Du Jinpeng, *Yinxu gongdian qu jianzhu jizhi yanjiu* [Beijing: Kexue chubanshe, 2010], p. 407, fig. 11-2, redrawn by Kyle Steinke).

[5] *jiaxu* (day 11) the *yi* ritual [for] Shang Jia, *yihai* (day 12) the *yi* ritual [for] Bao Yi, *bingzi* (day 13) the *yi* ritual [for] Bao Bing, [*dingchou*] (day 14) the *yi* ritual for Bao Ding, *renwu* (day 19) the *yi* ritual for Shi Ren, *guiwei* (day 20) the *yi* ritual for Shi Gui ...   (*HJ* 35406)

Besides the continuing ritual cycle, there were many other occasions when sacrifices might be divined about and then offered:

[6] In praying (for rain) to (the ancestors) from Shang Jia (to) Da Yi, Da Ding, Da Jia, Da Geng, Da Wu, Zhong Ding, Grandfather Yi, Grandfather Xin, and Grandfather Ding, the ten ancestors, (we will) lead-in-sacrifice (?) a ram.   (*HJ* 32385)

Week by (ten-day) week, a sacrificial schedule was presented to the ancestors in writing.[3] The schedule probably included all the week's sacrifices, not just those of the cycle of five rituals but also others of such types as those seen above in texts [3], [4], and [6]. The ritual specialist had a duty to file a written report to the ancestors, but in substance his report was also a plan for the performance of the sacrifices, a document with an administrative function.

But further than this, the functions of writing in the Anyang ritual system are not well understood. Contrary to what is often stated in general books about Anyang writing or religion, writing was not essential to communication with the spirits. Most of the divination bones found at Anyang are uninscribed. The diviner first carved hollows on one side of the shell or scapula, then applied heat to the hollows in order to produce cracks on the other side. The cracks were then interpreted as the omen's response to a previously announced question. The vast majority of bones cracked for divination are not inscribed, and the bones that do have inscriptions were inscribed *after* the communication was finished. Some inscriptions were beautifully carved and even inlaid with red or black pigment (Figure 7.4); these clearly had a display function, but we do not know the audience for the display.

What seems likely is that a group of literate diviners interpreted most of the omens and kept records of them on documents made of bamboo or wood slips (a graph that depicts bundled slips actually occurs in the divination texts and in bronze inscriptions). These records, or a digest of them, would regularly be sent to the king to report on divine intentions. Perhaps

---

[3] Chang Yuzhi, *Shangdai zhouji zhidu* (Beijing: Xianzhuang Shuju, 2009), pp. 16–17.

only when grave matters were concerned would the king himself make the prognostication and record it on the bone, as in the following inscription:

> [7] Crack-making on *guisi* (day 40), Ke divined: "In the next ten days there will be no disasters." The king read the oracle and said: "There will be calamities; there may be someone bringing alarming news." When it came to the fifth day, *dingyou* (day 34), there indeed was someone bringing alarming news from the west. Guo of Zhi reported and said: "The Tufang have attacked in our eastern borders and have seized two settlements. The Gongfang likewise invaded the fields of our western borders." (*HJ* 6057)

In rare instances like this we glimpse another channel for gathering information: reports on earthly affairs made by subordinates. This inscription and others like it make it clear that Shang scribes were capable of writing not only reports of enemy attacks but also letters, royal decrees, almost anything the king might require. Guo of Zhi could have made his report in writing on perishable materials. He might even have been required to make his report in writing:

> [8] ... Junior Servitor Qiang assisted (the king) to attack. Mao [enemy leader] of the Wei [enemy state] was captured, (also captured), .. 20, captives 4, head trophies 1,570, captives of the Meifang 100, horses .., chariots 2, shields 183, quivers 50, arrows ... [the remaining text talks about making different kinds of human and animal sacrifice to various royal ancestors. It is broken at the point Junior Servitor Qiang was rewarded by the king]. (*HJ* 36481)[4]

> [9] On *renzi* (day 49) the king made cracks and divined: "Hunting at Zhi, going and coming back there will be no harm." The king read the oracle and said: "Prolonged auspiciousness." This was used (?). (We) caught foxes 41; *mi*-deer 8; rhinoceros 1. (*HJ* 37380)

The Shang king must have spent a great part of his time gathering two kinds of information, divine and human, comparing them, and only then making his final decision and giving his commands. All these activities are likely to have involved writing. The aforementioned practice of presenting the ancestors with written sacrificial schedules might well have been modeled on real-world administration. The divination texts make it clear that book-keeping had reached the realm of the ancestors:

> [10] Wo brought in 1,000 (shells); Lady Jing ritually prepared 40. (Recorded by the diviner) Bin. (*HJ* 116b)

---

[4] My translation follows a new reading by Liu Zhao; see Liu Zhao, "Xiaochen Qiang keci xinshi," *Fudan xuebao* 1 (2009), 4–11.

Considering that our sample of Shang writing, the divination texts, is limited to brief records of the king's questioning of his ancestors, it is remarkable how many traces of book-keeping we find in them, how much careful accounting of the flow of people and materials: 5,000 men, 2,656 human victims, 183 shields, 41 foxes, 1,000 shells . . . Communication with the spirits is the content of the first inscriptions that survive from ancient China, but communicating with the spirits was not the motive that inspired the invention of Chinese writing. The motive for invention was undoubtedly in the administrative sphere, where the overriding concern was to exert control, and the means of control was to make inventories and create accountability. The immense scale of Shang agriculture, metallurgy, and colonial enterprise, as revealed by inscriptions and archaeology, argue for heavy administrative use of writing. The inscriptions quoted here are the surviving tip of an administrative iceberg.

Agriculture and book-keeping

[11] "If the king orders the Many Yin (officers) to open up fields in the West, [we] will receive crops." (HJ 33209)

[12] Crack-making on *guihai* (day 60): "Should the king order the Many Yin (officers) to work on the field at Yu?" Crack-making on *yichou*: "Should the king order [the Many Yin] to work on the field at Jing? To work on the field at Xun?" (Kaizuka 1959–68, no. 2363)

[13] We will receive the harvest that Fu cultivates at Zi. (HJ 900)

[14] . . . if [we] greatly order the laborers, saying "Work together in the fields," [we] will receive harvest. (HJ 1)

Texts like these give us a general idea of Shang agriculture, especially the farming of the royal domain. The king sent officials to allocate fields, presumably to both royal and non-royal lineages, by ridging boundaries and making earth cairns.[5] This act presupposed a land survey, and surveyors are attested in the divination texts. An accompanying operation was to "build a settlement" in such-and-such a place, sometimes as many as thirty settlements in a single campaign. Royal crops were prefixed with qualifiers such as "the king's," "Shang's," "the great settlement's," or "our." Some of the farms had named locations; others were specified only by cardinal direction. Inscriptions [11]–[13] suggest that the Shang kings knew (at least roughly)

---

[5] Ge Yinghui, "Shi Yinxu jiagu de tutian fengjiang buci," in Song Zhenhao, *et al.* (eds.), *Jiaguwen yu yinshangshi (Xin yi ji)* (Beijing: Xianzhuang Shuju, 2009), pp. 69–78.

where the farms were located and what officers were responsible for them. Where did they obtain this knowledge? It seems likely that the royal house possessed lists of fields and officers. In the corpus of divination texts over a hundred toponyms occur in divinations that inquire about the harvest. Bone and bronze inscriptions mention an official inspection of fields that involved classifying them into four types. The character for field, *tian* 田, may depict a field divided into square parcels by a grid of pathways and/or drainage ditches. If land reclamation was organized by the royal house, as inscription [II] suggests, fields might have been laid out in a way that facilitated land survey, but there is no archaeological evidence for the shapes of Shang farms.

Regularly subdivided agricultural landscapes would help the state allocate land to discrete units of farmers.[6] Archaeological evidence suggests that labor gangs depended on the state for agricultural tools. Large numbers of stone sickles have twice been found in the royal precinct (one pit contained "a thousand" by the excavator's guess; the other had 444). These were most likely made by state workshops for distribution to harvesters. Efficient provision of tools depended on accurate knowledge of the users, their numbers, and their administrative units, information that would also have facilitated the distribution of rations. The king divined about sending officials to inspect granaries, some of which seem to have been located not far from the fields. Could it be that part of the stored grain was used for feeding the local laborers? In some early states the distribution of rations was managed with writing; the Inka state used khipus instead. In either case record-keeping was essential. The bone inscriptions have examples of "the counting of people" (*deng ren*) related to agriculture and warfare. As we have seen above, sometimes the numbers of persons and goods are specific enough to suggest that careful book-keeping was maintained. But the extant records do not tell us what kind of census information was collected beyond the number of persons, nor do they disclose whether there was any state-wide enumeration of the people. Nevertheless, the records suggest that accounting was a routine feature of state administration. Although the records we have were carved on bone, the sources for the numbers they contain must have been now-perished administrative documents written on wood or bamboo strips.

---

[6] See Introduction, this volume, for the concept of "ruralization" as a concomitant process of urbanization.

Book-keeping was not confined to religion, agriculture, war, and hunting. Animal husbandry must have been the main source for the meat consumed by the elite and the spirits. Skeletal remains together with countless divination records show that whole horses, cattle, sheep, dogs, and pigs were offered to the spirits in staggering numbers, and the living must have consumed equal or greater numbers both during rituals and in everyday life. Although it is possible that many domestic animals were acquired through long-distance trade or war, many more would surely have been raised locally, if not at Yinxu itself (where pens have not been found) then in some of the villages in the Huan River Valley. When we read an Early Dynastic Mesopotamian text recording the amount of fodder given to hogs, or an Assyrian shepherd's account of his sheep,[7] we cannot help wishing that Chinese administrators too had kept their records on durable clay. Yinxu archaeologists have given us many more bones than can be accounted for in the divination texts.

City industries and book-keeping

Map 7.2 shows some of the workshops excavated at Yinxu. Workshops for bone, jade, pottery, and bronze have been found, and there must be a workshop for chariot building somewhere too. At present four bone workshops are known. A waste pit at one of them contains about half a million fragments of cattle bones dumped there by wheeled vehicles. The fragments from another workshop weigh 32 metric tons. From wasters we can reconstruct the process of manufacturing a bone hairpin step by step, a process that may have involved minute division of labor. The Yinxu bone-working industry involved transferring materials from slaughterhouses to workshops in vast quantities. When we find receipts for quite small numbers of jades and turtle shells carved on a few jades and shells (for example, [10]), it is hard to imagine that scribes would not be regularly employed in tracking the vastly larger transactions in bone.

> [15] Crack-making on *dinghai* (day 24), Da [divined]: ". . . if (we) cast yellow ingots[8] . . . making *pan* basins, the auspicious day will be . . ." (*HJ 29687*)

---

[7] Bahijah Ismail and J. Nicholas Postgate, "A Middle-Assyrian Flock-master's Archive from Tell Ali," *Iraq* 70 (2008), 147–78; and Hans J. Nissen, Peter Damerow, and Robert K. Englund, *Archaic Bookkeeping: Writing and Techniques of Economic Administration in the Ancient Near East*, Paul Larsen (trans.) (Chicago: The University of Chicago Press, 1993), p. 103.

[8] On the reading of this character see Lin Yun (pen name Yan Yun), "Shangdai buci zhong de yezhu shiliao," *Kaogu* 5 (1973), 299.

Three bronze foundries of the Yinxu period have been partly excavated. The largest one, in the western part of the city (Map 7.2), is estimated to have covered an area of 5 hectares. There is no doubting the complex division of labor here. One pit contained raw clay for making molds and models. Four pits were floored with charcoal, upon which sat clay cores that had perhaps been covered by mats. These pits were probably used to dry clay models, molds, and cores in the shade. In two semi-subterranean rooms were found unbaked models for big tripod legs, clay molds for casting round vessels more than 1.5 meters in diameter (no bronze vessel of such colossal size has ever been found), and other foundry remains. The debris from this site includes numerous fragments of furnaces, along with molds and models for vessels, weapons, and tools. Many tools for carving the models and polishing the finished products were also recovered, along with tuyères and charcoal for melting the bronze in the furnaces.

Three groups of semi-subterranean houses were found surrounding the area with foundry debris. So far about ninety have been excavated. The number of rooms varies from one to five, with the one-room house being the most common (forty-five examples) and only one five-room house. The roofed area ranges from 5 to 25 square meters. The variation in size and number of rooms may reflect some sort of social hierarchy of the residents. Except for a small reception area in the multi-room houses, each room has a low earthen bench 0.8 to 1.4 meters wide, presumably a bed just large enough for one or two persons. Hearths and niches were found in both living rooms and bedrooms, with pottery, hairpins, divination bones, and sometimes animal bones from meat consumption.

The houses appear to have been built all at once, early in the Yinxu period, while the foundry debris is dated to a later phase. It is possible that the foundry was in operation from the beginning of the Yinxu period and that the people who lived in these simple houses were foundrymen under state control. Houses for ordinary lineage members in Yinxu were mainly above-ground courtyard houses (Figure 7.5), usually with many pits around them for storage or garbage disposal. Other adjacent features include wells and streets. But at the foundry site, the surroundings of the houses are strangely clean. The lack of storage facilities might signify the workmen's dependence on state rations (though they would have cooked the food themselves: the bread and other dry foods of many early state societies lend themselves to mass-production of the kind found in, say, Egyptian bakeries, but the Chinese prefer to boil cereals). The foundry's specialized and highly skilled workmen were a valuable resource and must have been under close bureaucratic supervision. Scribes presiding over the foundry's operations must have kept rosters and ration lists.

[16] Crack-making on *dingsi* (day 54), Gen divined: "Should we call upon (someone) to acquire (copper) ingots?" Divined: "Should we not call upon (someone) to acquire (copper) ingots?" The king read the oracle and said: "Auspicious. If . . ." (broken) (*HJ* 6567)

Records would also have needed to be kept of the tremendous quantities of copper, tin, lead, and fuel consumed by the foundry, at least the first three of which would have been obtained from long-distance trade. Smelting slags have not been found at Yinxu, so we can be sure that the extraction of metals from ores took place elsewhere (the logical place is at the mines, if fuel was available there, so that only metal, not ore, would have to be transported). But ore sources have not yet been pinpointed with certainty; provenance studies based on analyses of bronze artifacts face many difficulties of interpretation. Without documents like the Old Assyrian letters from Kanesh, little can be said about Shang trade other than that its scale must have been large and the geographic areas involved must have been great. Divination texts that mention "tribute" received by the Shang king might be interpreted as evidence of interregional trade. The tribute is sometimes large numbers of horse, cattle, sheep, jade, and cowry shells.

Colonial enterprise and writing

[17] On *renxu* (day 59) . . . order Jiang . . . to acquire salt . . . Second month. (*HJ* 7022)

Recent surveys and excavations in modern Shandong province tell us how the Shang procured one key commodity from a distant source. Ten to thirty kilometers inland from the modern coast of northern Shandong archaeologists have found over 200 seasonal camps for making salt from underground brine. The brine is distributed in a belt about 250 kilometers long that runs between salt water and fresh water further inland (Map 7.4). The camps range in size from 0.4 to 0.7 hectares, each including (1) a brine well; (2) a series of pits for percolation, sedimentation, and evaporation; (3) a closed kiln under a hut for evaporating brine in coarse helmet-shaped pots; (4) a workspace and pits containing brine,

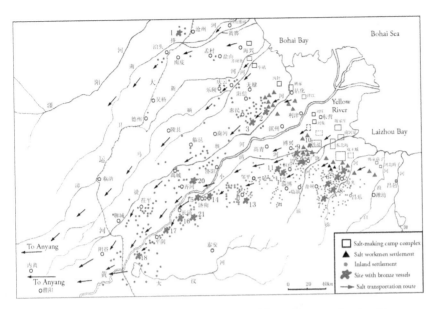

Map 7.4 Shang colonies in Shandong, showing possible traffic routes for the shipment of salt to Anyang, connected by sites yielding bronze ritual vessels. (1) Niyangtun; (2) Lanjia; (3) Daguo; (4) Gucheng; (5) Sangjiazhuang; (6) Yujia; (7) Laowa; (8) Subutun; (9) Zhaibian; (10) Huaguan; (11) Shijia; (12) Tangshan; (13) Jianxi; (14) Daxinzhuang; (15) Liujia; (16) Xiaotun; (17) Xiaoli; (18) Hongfan; (19) Xihua; (20) Haozhuang; (21) Gushan (drawn by Yan Shengdong and Kyle Steinke).

also under the hut (Figure 7.7). Ten men would be needed at each camp for one season of work, which would produce about 500 kilograms of salt. Several dozen such camps were clustered together in an area ranging from several square kilometers to several hundred (the little squares in Map 7.4).

During the off season the workmen lived in permanent settlements on the other side of the salt water–fresh water dividing line. These settlements, with a three-tier settlement pattern, were clustered at intervals of 2 to 3 kilometers. The settlements of the first tier housed about ten families in an area of 1 hectare; these were closest to the camps. Their inhabitants raised animals and made helmet-shaped pots for the camps, but they did not farm. Their grain, and perhaps timber for constructing huts as well, were imported from the second-tier settlements further removed from the camps. These ranged from 3 to 6 hectares; each was divided into zones for housing, storage, garbage disposal, cemetery, and

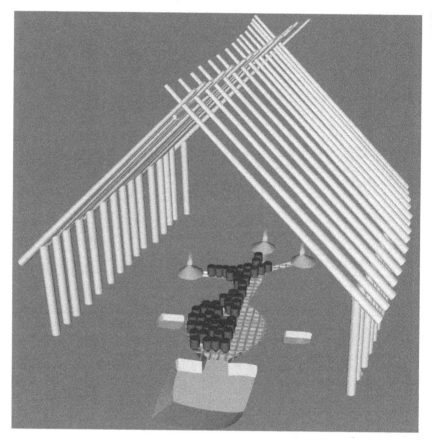

Figure 7.7 Reconstruction of a salt-making hut in Shandong, showing how the helmet-shaped pots are placed on a gridding frame (courtesy of Yan Shengdong).

sometimes crafts such as the making of pottery and lithic tools. Sickles, spades for tilling, and knives indicate that farming was a major occupation of the inhabitants. Ninety percent of the animal bones recovered were from domesticated species, suggesting that animal husbandry was another source of food. Minor elite tombs with bronzes were found in a few of these settlements. Two or three settlements located still further inland constituted the third tier. A cemetery near one of them (Subutum in Map 7.1 and Map 7.4, no. 8) had tombs comparable in form, size, and contents with the tombs in the royal cemetery at Yinxu. These are in fact the largest tombs of their time outside the Shang capital.

Few of these camps and settlements were established before the Yinxu period. Their abrupt appearance in northern Shandong was the result of population movement from somewhere else. The material culture of the sites, ranging from burial customs to utilitarian and elite objects, resembles that of Yinxu, and some of the lineage names inscribed on bronzes are attested also in divination texts and bronze inscriptions from Yinxu. It seems therefore that the Shang at Yinxu managed to colonize a region 1,000 kilometers away, at least in part to procure salt. Each year hundreds of metric tons of salt must have been made and shipped inland, while thousands of tons of grain, probably some meat or livestock, and large quantities of timber were transported to the salt-making bases. The archaeological findings that enable us to reconstruct the scale and traffic patterns of salt production here are remarkably clear and exact, and they immediately raise the question: how did the Shang organize this colonial enterprise?

Comparison with other early states suggests that effective control of regions at a distance depends on good communications, either by land, as exemplified by the famous road system of the Inka state,[9] or by water, as in the Ur III state's river-borne traffic in grains and bitumen,[10] or by a combination of the two, as in the Egyptian exploitation of Nubia, in which navigation on the Nile had to change to overland travel from time to time to bypass cataracts.[11] The divination records at Yinxu tell us that the Shang had a similar state-run system of communication.

[18] Crack-making on *guihai* (day 60), divined: "Is it today that the king should attack?" ... At night the king walked from the third fortress. (*HJ* 33149)

It appears that there were numbered relay stations and fortresses on major traffic routes terminating at Yinxu. The distribution of sites between Yinxu and Shandong where bronzes have been unearthed suggests two possible overland and two river-borne routes (Map 7.4). A group of divination texts found at Yinxu but made during a year-long military campaign in Shandong by a late Shang king suggests that Shang colonization was backed by military

[9] See Urton, Chapter 9, this volume. See also John Hyslop, *The Inka Road System* (New York: Academic Press, 1984).
[10] Wolfgang Heimpel, "The Location of Madga," *Journal of Cuneiform Studies* 61 (2009), 25–61; and Tonia Sharlach, *Provincial Taxation and the Ur III State* (Leiden: Brill, 2004).
[11] Barry Kemp, *Ancient Egypt: Anatomy of a Civilization* (London: Routledge, 2006), pp. 236–40.

power. Inscriptions in [1], [8], and [18] speak of campaigns against enemies; others speak of enemy attacks on borders or frontiers (for example, [7]), suggesting that Shang patrolled borders to its domain.

How did distant outposts communicate with Yinxu? Because the writing system in use at Yinxu had already developed the ability to record continuous speech, its administrative applications could have gone well beyond the making of ledgers for distributing rations. Did the frontier officials use written dispatches like the Semna reports in Egypt?[12] The content of inscription [7] is certainly comparable to the Semna dispatches.

David Keightley calls the administration of the Shang state "incipient bureaucracy" or "proto-bureaucracy."[13] It seems to me that his words "incipient" and "proto-" are too cautious. By the time of the divination texts the thinking behind administrative records had already permeated the realm of the supernatural and bureaucratized the form taken by communication between the living and the spirits. From near the end of the Shang dynasty we have a few lengthy commemorative bronze inscriptions cast by Shang noblemen (Figure 7.8). At this time awards from the king seem to have prompted nobles to make written reports of their achievements to be read by their ancestors. When we read in a bronze vessel that, on such-and-such a day, in reward for such-and-such a service, the king gave a nobleman gifts (carefully specified), whereupon the latter made the inscribed vessel for his ancestors, we may be reminded that in Mesopotamia and Egypt the commonest type of administrative document was the receipt. More importantly, the action of *reporting in writing* is the quintessence of developed bureaucracy. The two main functions of administrative documents in Mesopotamia and Egypt were to establish accountability and responsibility. Shang bronze inscriptions that list date, event, and participants seem to be performing just those functions in the particular context of the ancestor cult. This new genre of bureaucratized written display was adopted and developed further under the Zhou dynasty, which conquered the Shang shortly after the genre came into being.

---

[12] *Ibid.*, and Paul Smither, "The Semnah Despatches," *Journal of Egyptian Archaeology* 31 (1945), 3–10.

[13] David Keightley, "The Shang," in Michael Loewe and Edward L. Shaughnessy (eds.), *The Cambridge History of Ancient China: From the Origins of Civilization to 221 B.C.* (Cambridge: Cambridge University Press, 1999), pp. 286–7.

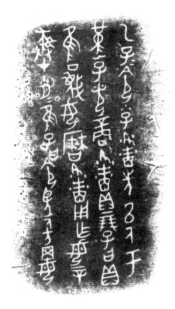

Figure 7.8 A late Shang inscribed bronze, the *Xiaozi X you* in the collection of the Hakutsuru Bijutsukan, Kobe. The rubbing reproduces an inscription cast in the lid. It reads vertically from top right to bottom left:

> On the day *yisi* [day 42], Zi ordered Xiaozi X to go in advance and deliver people [for sacrifice?] to Han. Zi awarded X two strings of cowries. Zi said: "The cowries are in recognition of your merits." X thereupon used them to make a vessel for Mother Xin. This was in the tenth month; it was when Zi issued the order to observe Mei [enemy leader] of Renfang [Shang enemy in Shandong].

Zi must have been a high-ranking commander serving one of the last two Shang kings. The latter led two (or even three) campaigns in Shangdong in his tenth and fifteenth year and left many divination records made en route, from which scholars have tentatively reconstructed campaign routes that by and large coincide with the suggested routes of shipping salt shown in Map 7.4. It has been convincingly argued that the generous spacing between the columns and tight stacking of characters within each column reflect a fair copy written on four bamboo slips laid side by side. Photograph after Umehara Sueji, *Hakutsuru kikkinshū* (Hyōgo, Japan: Hakutsuru Bijutsukan, 1934), no. 12 (rubbing after Zhongguo shehui kexueyuan kaogu yanjiusuo [ed.], *Yin Zhou jinwen jicheng* [Beijing: Zhonghua shuju, 1984], no. 5417-1).

Coda

The city of Yinxu was abandoned after the Zhou conquest around 1050 BCE. Modern cities decline and collapse for economic reasons, according to Jane Jacobs,[14] but in

---

[14] Jane Jacobs, *Cities and the Wealth of Nations: Principles of Economic Life* (New York: Vintage Books, 1985), pp. 156–232.

ancient China the death of major cities normally had political rather than economic causes. Dynastic change and the creation of empires propelled the cyclic renewal of urbanization. The renewals preserved some of the innovations of earlier cities, writing above all. The writing system and scribes of the Shang were adopted by the Zhou conquerors, who spread literacy to a wider area of China through their own process of urbanization. Writing permeated political, religious, administrative, military, and cultural life within and outside the cities. It was instrumental in constructing urban and rural identities. Yet its most persistent use seems to have been in the sphere of administration. The beliefs that held the moral community together could, it seems, change in an instant – think of the abrupt disappearance of the large-scale human sacrifice routinely practiced at Yinxu – but literate administration survived all political ups and downs.

FURTHER READINGS

Archaeology of early Chinese cities

Bagley, Robert, "Shang Archaeology," in Michael Loewe and Edward L. Shaughnessy (eds.), *The Cambridge History of Ancient China: From the Origins of Civilization to 221 B.C.*, Cambridge: Cambridge University Press, 1999, pp. 124–231.

Liu, Li, and Xingcan Chen, *The Archaeology of China*, Cambridge: Cambridge University Press, 2012.

Steinke, Kyle (ed.), *Art and Archaeology of the Erligang Civilization*, Princeton, NJ: Princeton University Press, 2014.

Early cities in comparative perspective

Houston, Stephen D., Hector Escobedo, Mark Child, Charles Golden, and René Muñoz, "The Moral Community: Maya Settlement Transformation at Piedras Negras, Guatemala," in Monica L. Smith (ed.), *The Social Construction of Ancient Cities*, Washington, D.C.: Smithsonian Books, 2003, pp. 212–53.

Kemp, Barry, *The City of Akhenaten and Nefertiti: Amarna and Its People*, London: Thames & Hudson, Ltd., 2012.

Chinese writing

Bagley, Robert, "Anyang Writing and the Origin of the Chinese Writing System," in Stephen D. Houston (ed.), *The First Writing: Script Invention as History and Process*, Cambridge: Cambridge University Press, 2004, pp. 190–249.

Keightley, David, "The Shang," in Michael Loewe and Edward L. Shaughnessy (eds.), *The Cambridge History of Ancient China: From the Origins of Civilization to 221 B.C.*, Cambridge: Cambridge University Press, 1999, pp. 232–91.

Wang, Haicheng, *Writing and the Ancient State: Early China in Comparative Perspective*, Cambridge: Cambridge University Press, 2014.

Writing in comparative perspective

Baines, John, John Bennet, and Stephen Houston (eds.), *The Disappearance of Writing Systems: Perspectives on Literacy and Communication*, London: Equinox Publishing Ltd., 2008.
Houston, Stephen D. (ed.), *The First Writing: Script Invention as History and Process*, Cambridge: Cambridge University Press, 2004.

8

Reading early Maya cities: interpreting the role of writing in urbanization

DANNY LAW

Ancient Maya cities have attracted the scholarly gaze of Westerners since at least the latter part of the eighteenth century (see map of Maya cities in Chapter 3, Map 3.1). The romanticism of the ancient crumbling structures surrounded by lush tropical rainforest was certainly not lost on early European and American explorers, nor on many archaeologists and amateur enthusiasts today. Massive stone pyramids, shrouded dramatically in jungle foliage, many covered in elegantly rounded and ornate hieroglyphics, inspired early claims that these structures "seem to have been old in the days of Pharaoh."[1] More considered (if less imaginative) assessments of time-depth, based on recent research in the lowlands of Guatemala, southern Mexico, Belize, and Honduras, place the emergence of large, densely populated urban centers in the Maya Lowlands during the "Late" Preclassic period, the final centuries BCE, and date most of the surface architecture visible to early explorers to the first millennium CE.

Parallel with the earliest evidence of cities, the Maya Lowlands also boast evidence, by the Late Preclassic, of a fully developed script tradition. Maya hieroglyphic writing, a complex system that combines logographic and phonetic signs to encode the complexity of language, has only recently been deciphered to the degree that it can be read with confidence. The earliest texts, however, continue to elude decipherment, in large part because of the small surviving corpus of texts. While the origins of Maya writing are perhaps lost in time, and the body of early texts is sparse indeed, what evidence does exist allows us to speculate about the role that writing had in the process

---

[1] Benjamin Moore Norman, *Rambles in Yucatan Including a Visit to the Remarkable Ruins of Chichen, Kabah, Zayi, Uxmal* (New York: Henry G. Langley, 1843), quoted in Michael D. Coe, *Breaking the Maya Code* (New York: Thames & Hudson, Ltd., 1999), p. 96.

of urbanization and in the implementation of the governmental apparatus in these ancient cities.

The subject of this study is what would appear to be straightforward empirical questions about writing in early Maya cities: Where do we find texts, who wrote them, and why? However, the answers to these questions are bound up in more complex theoretical ones: What does writing *do* in society (is saying that, "It encodes language in graphic form" an adequate answer?)? What social structures need to be in place for writing to be a viable practice? And how might the function of writing in society evolve over time? Thus, while one purpose of this paper is descriptive, simply reporting the "who," "what," and "why" of ancient Maya writing, that descriptive endeavor begs engagement with stickier questions about the nature of ancient cities and writing in general. The following sections will discuss the nature of texts in their social contexts, survey the earliest texts in the Maya Lowlands, and consider what these texts suggest about the relationship between the development of writing and the rapid rise of densely populated urban centers in the Lowland Maya Preclassic.

The development of writing – both its invention as a symbolic system of representation, and its extension to new and increased social, political, and economic spheres of use – seems in many places to have had a special relationship to the rise of ancient urban centers. Early Maya cities provide an interesting case study in the relationship of writing to processes of urbanization. The subject matter and presentation of texts in early cities, as well as the apparent trajectory of development of the semiotic system itself, appear to differ from what has been described for early urban centers of Mesopotamia and elsewhere. The importance of writing in early Maya urban centers is certainly evident in the remains of Classic Maya cities (approximately 200–900 CE), where the written word graces everything from massive structures to minuscule carved shells, ceramic vessels, and jades. Writing in earlier Maya cities (approximately 300 BCE to 200 CE) is generally less frequent and not so grand in scale, but was clearly integrated into the social and religious life of the city elite. A contextualized consideration of early Maya texts brings to the fore the intimate connection between writing and iconography, both in terms of form and function, as well as a disjunct between small, private texts, and large-scale public ones. The survey of early texts also begs careful attention to the accidental lacunae in the extant corpus of texts, and to how this unavoidably skewed sample has shaped our reading of text in early Maya cities.

Writing and culture

Before looking at the particulars of writing in early Maya cities, it is important to examine the relationship between writing and social and political structures. Scholars of writing systems often emphasize fundamental qualities of writing systems abstracted from social setting, that is: "writing encodes language in visual form"; or "writing provides a medium for creating durable messages." While writing as a technology is primarily semiotic, and amenable to such abstracted analyses, writing as a practice is much more than a code. It is institutions for learning to read and write, institutions to develop and enforce standardization of forms and meaning, and functions in society that legitimize its existence and perpetuation. Social norms and political structures constrain what is said and even what is "sayable" in writing, so that the idealized potential of language to express an infinite number of ideas is, in practice, much more circumscribed.

It is perhaps worth noting for this volume that writing, with its hallmark capacity to fix meaning in durable form, has many parallels with other common features noted for modern cities and states. James Scott, in his influential critical study of the modern state, notes that much of what we might call statecraft is engaged in the simplification and delimitation of subjects and spaces of the state. Scott uses a textual metaphor to describe this process: simplification makes subjects "legible" for the state.[2] Scholars of colonialism have noted that this process of "entextualization"[3] is not simply descriptive, as it is often represented, but profoundly creative. New selves and new meanings are constituted in the act of definition. When we look at material culture, the "inscription" of urbanity on the landscape, from the earliest cities to the present day, could scarcely look less metaphorical. Earth and rock are shifted and reshaped to make new spaces, a new "field," to use the concept developed by Bourdieu, with corresponding new subjects and new rules, or at least norms, of engagement.

Crucially, it is not just, and maybe not even primarily, the physical space that is reshaped in the definition of a new field: it is bodily dispositions, thoughts, beliefs, ways of speaking – the "habitus" of a people. William Hanks discusses this sort of reshaping with respect to the formation of a

---

[2] James C. Scott, *Seeing Like a State: How Certain Schemes to Improve the Human Condition have Failed* (New Haven, CT: Yale University Press, 1998).
[3] Richard Bauman and Charles L. Briggs, "Poetics and Performance as Critical Perspectives on Language and Social Life," *Annual Review of Anthropology* 19 (1990), 59–88.

Colonial variety of the Yukatek Maya language following the Spanish Conquest of the Yucatan Peninsula.[4] Hanks makes the case that this project, referred to by the Spaniards as *reducción*, extended far beyond settlement patterns and forced relocations to ramify on behavior, thought, and speech, ultimately creating a new form of language that Hanks calls *Maya Reducido*. It is easy to see in this case how the Spanish were pursuing what Scott called "legibility." Hanks observes, however, that Maya Reducido was not simply simplification. It involved a realignment of linguistic forms and meanings, what Hanks calls "commensuration," so that meanings could circulate more readily within the new social order imposed by the Spanish.

The ability to align and realign symbols and meanings is crucial for communication and exchange of any kind. Studies of face-to-face interaction have found that we have an extraordinary capacity to negotiate – to commensurate – symbols, linguistic and otherwise, on the fly. In the modern state, citizens yield some of that capacity for spontaneous negotiation of meaning to a government, which dictates, to a degree, what values or meanings are fixed (currency, codes of conduct, spelling conventions) or "entextualized," and which remain fluid. The historical particulars of these "regimes of truth," to use Foucault's language, vary from instance to instance, but at play is the erasure of variation and, consequently, the individuality of agents, thereby allowing a more contextually independent form to circulate. Scott provides a non-linguistic example of this in his discussion of the standardization of measurements and commodities to streamline production and trade. He notes that "Whereas artisanal products were typically made by a single producer according to the desires of a particular customer and carried a price specific to that object, the mass-produced commodity is made by no one in particular and is intended for any purchaser at all."[5]

Two themes, then, are significant in this discussion. First, we can understand the process of urbanization, more than just the concentration of inhabitants in a space, to be a radical restructuring of social practices, a redrawing of the field of engagement, which at the same time redefines and remakes the participants in that field, so to speak. Second, key in this process is the regimentation of meaning. Power is the space between signifier and signified, and states insert themselves in that space through various

---

[4] William Hanks, *Converting Words: Maya in the Age of the Cross* (Berkeley: University of California Press, 2010).

[5] Scott, *Seeing like a State*, p. 31.

hegemonic institutions with the aim to define not only what meanings circulate but what the limits of acceptable discourse might be, recalling Bourdieu's distinction between orthodoxy, the "universe of discourse" and doxa, the "universe of the undiscussed." This not only helps perpetuate the hegemonic status quo, but also allows for intercourse, as well as proper division, between the array of disparate groups that typically make up an urban center.

Writing in the state

From this perspective, the frequent association between the earliest cities and the development of writing takes on a slightly different hue. If writing requires regimentation of the type that states excel at providing, states can also benefit from the permanence of text: "To the extent that texts can move across contexts, they allow people to create the image of something durable and shared, independent of particular realizations such as readings, interpretations, or performances or their historical transformations."[6] A state can benefit from writing then, not only in terms of logistical considerations, but because it creates something that transcends particular contexts. It gives voice without allowing a response; the dictates and dictamen of a ruler transcend the immediacy of face-to-face interaction to become the will of the state.

Yet one can make the case that writing needs complex society more than complex societies need writing. After all writing requires just the types of control that complex political structures, like those in cities, excel at providing: it requires a revolution of social practice to create a space for scribes and for text, but more crucially it requires carefully prescribed uniformity of sign values to be intelligible, values capable of being extracted from the context of their creation. Spoken language also requires that participants in an exchange have reasonable confidence that they have a shared meaning for their utterances, but in spoken language, as in the case of artisanal production mentioned by Scott, that meaning can, and usually is, tailored to the context at hand. It is dynamic and negotiable. Meanings emerge and change in the course of interaction. This is not possible with writing, since, as Ricoeur noted, writing "has broken its mooring to the psychology of its author."[7] This

---

[6] Webb Keane, "Religious Language," *Annual Review of Anthropology* 26 (1997), 47–71.
[7] Paul Ricoeur, "The Model of the Text: Meaningful Action Considered as a Text," *New Literary History* 5 (1973), 91–117.

makes written languages uncontestable, a point developed by Walter Ong, who argued that, "like the oracle or the prophet, the book relays an utterance from a source, the one who really 'said' or wrote the book. The author might be challenged only if he or she could be reached, but the author cannot be reached in any book."[8]

Urbanization and writing in the Maya Lowlands

With these questions in mind, we will now look at the particulars of the emergence of writing and cities in the Maya Lowlands. The available data for the origins and early use of writing in the Maya region, though incomplete, are sufficient to allow us to explore both the implications of writing for the making of cities as well as the role of cities in the development of writing. I will first give an overview of Maya writing and a brief summary of current understanding of urbanization in the Maya Lowlands, followed by a discussion of how early writing and other modes of symbolic representation might have related to one another and to the project of ordering and maintaining order in ancient Maya cities.

The beginnings of Maya civilization are, not surprisingly, still shrouded in the mists of speculation, but an increased number of archaeological excavations, and improved techniques, are beginning to give form to some of its details. The conventional periodization of the Maya Lowlands is essentially a convenient relic from a much less advanced period of scholarship on the ancient Maya. Traditionally, pre-Columbian Maya history is divided into four major periods:

1. The Archaic period – around 6000 BCE (the earliest settled communities) until 2000 BCE
2. The Preclassic period – from 2000 BCE until 250 CE
3. The Classic period – from 250 until 900 CE
4. The Postclassic – from 900 CE until the arrival of the Spanish in the early sixteenth century.

The Preclassic, which is the focus of this chapter, is further subdivided into "Early" (2000–1000 BCE), "Middle" (1000–400 BCE), and "Late" (400 BCE–250 CE). In some cases, scholars also refer to a "Terminal Preclassic," which

---

[8] Walter Ong, *Orality and Literacy* (New York: Metheun, 1982), p. 77.

generally includes the first two centuries CE, a period during which several major Preclassic sites were abandoned.

Maya writing

The corpus of Maya hieroglyphic texts includes somewhere in the order of 15,000 texts, most of them fairly short, consisting of a dozen or two hieroglyphs, though some texts have well over a hundred glyphs. These texts can be found on everything from cave walls to ceramic vessels to hairpins to staircases, door lintels, wall panels, and massive stone stelae several meters in height. Iconography shows that hieroglyphs were even painted onto clothing, though none of these have survived in the material record. Four bark paper codices survive, in different degrees of preservation, all dating to around the time of the conquest. All earlier paper texts have succumbed to time and the humid tropical climate, though traces of codices, utterly illegible, have been found in Classic period tombs. There are also several depictions on Classic period ceramic vessels of scribes writing and reading from codices, so their use in the Classic period is indisputable. The corpus of available texts is heavily skewed toward the Late Classic. Of thousands of hieroglyphic texts, only 300 to 400 texts are known from the Early Classic and perhaps a dozen are known for the Preclassic. The reasons for this are probably multiple but include the fact that these texts are often buried meters under the surface, whereas Late Classic texts can be on or relatively near the surface. In addition, there have been several documented instances of intentional destruction of texts in ancient times, including a round of intentional destruction of texts near the end of the Early Classic.

Even allowing for this, however, the lack of texts is very likely due to a shift in the materials and contexts in which texts were used. In the Classic, and particularly the Late Classic, we see an enormous increase in texts that seem to be for public display, that is, large scale and positioned in highly visible areas within a site. This suggests an expansion of writing into a public sphere that it did not appear to occupy in the Preclassic, though this does not mean that writing was less important to Preclassic society than it was at the height of the Classic period. The increasingly public nature of inscriptions in the Classic suggests a shift from Preclassic to Classic in the processes of control at play through texts. Throughout the history of ancient Maya writing, we can see a high degree of control and uniformity, but with different orientations. In the Preclassic not only was knowledge of writing apparently highly circumscribed, access to texts themselves was also clearly controlled. By Classic times, hieroglyphic texts were tools for public consumption, to be seen and appreciated by many, even if mastery of the glyphic system, and the close control of the connections between glyphic signifiers and their significations, remained under the purview of the privileged few. One could argue that in the Preclassic, texts were exclusionary, secret almost, while in the Classic, they were subordinating: public but only truly accessible to the right kind of person.

Unequal access to writing is evident in the archaeological contexts in which texts are found. Throughout ancient Maya history, writing was primarily and almost exclusively associated with elite residences, burials, and ritual centers, though in the Late Classic, non-elite ceramics occasionally had decorative "pseudo-glyphs," usually a single sign or nonce glyph repeated over and over, which suggests a Late Classic fetishization of glyphic texts, perhaps deriving from increased public display of texts, not evident for earlier periods. Many Classic period inscriptions are signed by the author or engraver. The fact that many of the names in these signature statements include noble titles and epithets is consistent with iconographic evidence that writing itself was an elite specialization and highly valued in the royal court, though kings (*k'uhul ajaw*) themselves were not generally scribes. There is also some evidence that scribes and other artisans were exchanged and shared as tribute or to reinforce alliances with other cities.

Overview of urbanization in the Maya area

Our picture of the emergence of urban centers in the Maya Lowlands has been forced through several major revisions in recent decades, thanks primarily to the increase in high-quality excavations and the important discoveries these have generated. The received nomenclature for these periods clearly reflects the general sense of scholars of the day that the Maya Classic period was the apogee of Maya civilization. Following then current ideas about social evolution, the history of the Maya was decidedly linear: civilization in the region progressed slowly, scarcely achieving sedentary agriculturalism in the Preclassic, until suddenly, in the first centuries CE, progress accelerated rapidly, likely due to outside influence, perhaps from the Olmecs, giving rise to the flowering of Maya sophistication in the Classic period. The civilization then collapsed around 900 CE pulling the Maya Lowlands into the dark ages of the Postclassic.

This simple linear evolutionary narrative, as well as the abruptness of both the Preclassic to Classic and the Classic to Postclassic transitions have been called into question. New discoveries of the last fifty years have steadily revised our understanding of the Preclassic to the degree that, at present, the division between Classic and Preclassic is increasingly meaningless in terms of the development of complex societies. While there is ample evidence of societal upheaval at the end of the Preclassic, particularly in patterns of site abandonment at that time, virtually all of the material traits that were thought to define Classic civilization have been found to have developed much earlier than 250 CE. In addition, excavations, led by Richard Hansen, at several massive Preclassic sites in the Mirador Basin of Guatemala have confirmed that Preclassic sites were equal, and, in some cases, even larger (both in terms of estimated population and architectural works) than many Classic period centers.

From currently available data, it seems that Maya civilization begins to coalesce in the Middle Preclassic, and relatively large urban centers are in place within a few centuries. Middle Preclassic ceramics begin to share greater similarities across the Lowlands with the appearance of Mamom (600–300 BCE) and later Chicanel (300 BCE to 200 CE) horizon ceramics. Around the same time as the emergence of Mamom ceramics, we begin to see the construction of major monumental architecture, including ballcourts and a special grouping of structures consisting of a pyramid facing a platform topped with one or three structures aligned with the rise of the sun on key days of the solar year,[9] a configuration referred to as an E-Group. These E-Groups were important ritual complexes, as evidenced by the frequency of caches, and, in the Classic period, monumental stone stelae, associated with them, as well as their alignment relative to the zenith passage of the sun, a significant marker in the agricultural cycle. The agricultural cycle was the central theme of Maya ritual and cosmology through the Classic period.

---

[9] Anthony Aveni, Ann S. Dowd, and Benjamin Vining, "Maya Calendar Reform? Evidence from Orientations of Specialized Architectural Assemblages," *Latin American Antiquity* 14 (2003), 159–78, surveyed numerous Lowland Maya E-Groups and argue that each site seems to be aligned to track the sun on particular days, and those days were related in a consistent way to the zenith passage of the sun. Specifically, Lowland Maya E-Groups all marked points in twenty-day intervals from the day of the zenith passage of the sun for a particular location. A twenty-day interval is significant because this corresponds with the Maya month, or *Winik*, one of the main periods of time in both the 365-day *haab* calendar, as well as the so-called "long count." This correlation suggests that reckoning of time in twenty-day periods was as important in the Middle Preclassic as it was in the Classic period. The zenith passage in the Maya Lowlands is also significant for the agricultural cycle since the first zenith passage occurs around the beginning of the rainy season, and the second happens in early August, corresponding roughly with a short dry season, known as "canicula" before the rainy season resumes, during which another crop of Maize is generally planted. Thus the zenith passages provide a convenient point for determining optimal planting times for the two annual maize crops.

Around the same time that we begin to find the above-mentioned markers of increased regional unity and a shared regional ideology, we find evidence of a dramatic increase in population density at several sites, at levels that meet or even surpass peak population estimates for the major Classic period centers.[10] This time period, the Late Preclassic, is also when we see the earliest evidence of the institution of kingship, in a beautiful mural from San Bartolo showing a king seated on a scaffold accepting the accouterments of a *k'uhul ajaw* "Holy Lord."[11] The recent discovery of Preclassic elite burials in residential areas at San Bartolo and Holmul emphasizes the highly stratified nature of Late Preclassic Maya society.

The construction of these large E-Group plazas, rich with ritual and cosmological significance, the adoption of new ceramic forms, and even the gathering evidence of kingship are not simply a matter of new rituals or beliefs, however. Estrada-Belli, referring to the construction of an E-Group in the Middle Preclassic site Cival, argued that this major construction project "marked a threshold moment in the creation of these broad communities: the foundation of regional polities within bounded landscapes which, once established, were constantly recreated through ritual practices."[12] Like Spaniards relocating sixteenth-century Maya to carefully organized settlements around a central plaza and Christian church, the construction of E-Groups and related monumental architecture, the spread of new ceramic forms and technologies, and the portrayal of kings may only be the tip of much more dramatic changes in the social landscape of the time. Referring to the revolutionary nature of cities, Norman Yoffee noted that, "cities were not simply accretions on a stable rural base ... In the evolution of states and civilizations, the landscapes of social life changed utterly." "These new urban environments," he argued, "were supernovas that exploded from the environment of village life that preceded them."[13] The leveling and building up of plazas, platforms, and pyramids in E-Group patterns and the incorporation of imagery relating to kingship go beyond

[10] Richard Hansen, "Continuity and Disjunction: The Pre-Classic Antecedents of Classic Maya Architecture," in Stephen D. Houston (ed.), *Function and Meaning in Classic Maya Architecture* (Washington, D.C.: Dumbarton Oaks Research Library and Collection, 1998), pp. 49–122.
[11] Karl Taube William A. Saturno, David Stuart, and Heather Hurst, *The Murals of San Bartolo, El Peten, Guatemala* (Barnardsville, NC: Boundary End Archaeology Research Center, 2010), Part 2.
[12] Francisco Estrada Belli, *The First Maya Civilization: Ritual and Power before the Classic Period* (New York: Routledge, 2011), p. 77.
[13] Norman Yoffee, *Myths of the Archaic State* (Cambridge: Cambridge University Press, 2005), pp. 61–2.

Figure 8.1 San Bartolo Pinturas Sub-I depiction of king. San Bartolo, West Wall mural detail (drawn by Heather Hurst).

the simple mechanical and technological know-how required to build such shapes. In a very real way these plazas, and the rulers that commissioned them, shaped new communities, formed new spaces and new ways of coming together – a new field of interaction in which the rules of play might have differed drastically from what preceded it.

Development of writing

In the context of the revolution of kings and courtyards, we cannot miss the innovation of writing. In a convenient case of serendipity, the early depiction of kingship mentioned above at San Bartolo is further clarified with one of the earliest hieroglyphic texts for the Maya Lowlands (Figure 8.1). While most of the text is opaque – differences with readable glyphs from some 500 years later have frustrated attempts to decipher most of the text – one clear sign, at the very bottom of the column of hieroglyphs, is a logograph for "king" *ajaw*. If the pattern amply attested in Classic period texts is applicable here, the signs immediately above the *ajaw* hieroglyph would include names and titles for the individual acceding to the throne, a caption that disambiguates the image, giving it a very specific, and likely historical referent.

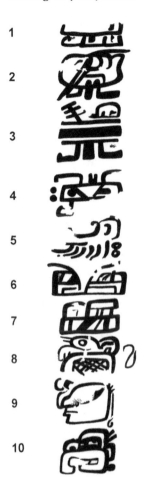

1
2
3
4
5
6
7
8
9
10

Figure 8.2 Earliest Lowland Maya writing. Pinturas Sub-V, San Bartolo (drawn by David S. Stuart).

The use of early text to refer to rulers was apparently not new at the time that the Pinturas Sub-I mural was painted. A fragment of text from a now mostly obliterated wall mural in an earlier phase of the same pyramid, designated Las Pinturas Sub-V, which dates to between 400 and 200 BCE, was discovered during excavations of the Las Pinturas pyramid, led by William Saturno in 2005. The text consists of ten hieroglyphs, one of which is clearly an early *ajaw* sign (Figure 8.2, glyph 7).

In addition to supporting the idea that the institution of kingship was in place at the beginning of the Late Preclassic, this text provides us with the earliest securely dated example of Lowland Maya writing. The find forced a reconsideration of previous ideas about the development of writing in Mesoamerica, since the San Bartolo text is roughly contemporaneous with the earliest texts from Highland Guatemala (El Portón Monument 1 – approximately 400 BCE), Oaxaca (Monte Alban Stelae 12 and 13 – 500–300 BCE), and the Gulf coast (the Olmec site of La Venta – 500–400 BCE based on stratigraphic context though a later date may be possible).

The fact that fully developed writing can be found in such geographically diverse locations by 300 BCE is evidence that the earliest writing must have been around already for at least several centuries before these early texts. A 2006 article in the journal *Science* by Rodríguez Martínez and colleagues reported the discovery of a small greenstone block with a lightly incised text consisting of sixty-two abstract symbols arranged roughly in horizontal rows.[14] The block was found near the Olmec site of San Lorenzo, in Veracruz, Mexico, and was dated, based on accompanying ceramics and stylistic considerations, to some time before 900 BCE. The form and execution of these symbols seems decidedly less masterful than the texts from 300 BCE, and, if authentic, likely represents a very early stage in script development. Formally, however, the Cascajal text has no clear parallels to Maya writing, or, indeed, to any other known script. If we are to think of it as a precursor to later script traditions, it seems that it would be in the order of the source of the concept of writing generally, rather than the mechanics of an individual writing system.

The picture that emerges of the earliest writing in Mesoamerica generally, then, is a single archaic script in the Olmec heartland in the Middle Preclassic, up until the rather abrupt Late Preclassic arrival of fully developed writing at roughly the same time in the Maya Lowlands (San Bartolo), Oaxaca (Monte Alban), the Olmec heartland (La Venta), and the Guatemalan Highlands (El Portón). In all of these cases, except, perhaps, La Venta, the writing system does not seem to be "proto" in any way, but each case represents what seems to be a well-developed script. In the Maya case,

---

[14] Rodríguez Martínez, Ma. del Carmen, Ponciano Ortíz Ceballos, Michael D. Coe, Richard A. Diehl, Stephen D. Houston, Karl A. Taube, and Alfredo Delgado Calderón, "Oldest Writing in the New World," *Science* 313 (2006), 1610–14

the San Bartolo texts are long enough to reflect grammar and syntax of an actual language, though this must remain speculative until more signs have been deciphered.

Icons indexing symbols: the relationship between writing and iconography

Throughout its use, Maya hieroglyphic writing was inextricably tied up with image. The iconic origins of most signs never faded away from the minds of scribes, and even abstract signs with no clear iconic form were often embellished and played with by scribal virtuosos as though they were depictions of actual objects, or animated by the addition of anthropo-morphic features. And the border between writing and iconography was equally porous in the other direction: iconography often integrated hiero-glyphic spellings into an image, particularly in the headdresses worn by rulers and their ancestors. A beautiful Early Classic example can be found on Stela 31 from Tikal (Figure 8.3), which depicts the ruler Siyaj Chan K'awiil, "K'awiil is born of the sky," identified not only in the accompanying texts, but also in the iconographic components of his headdress: an infant *k'awiil* (an important deity associated with kingship) emerging out of the hiero-glyph *chan* "sky" (Figure 8.3, B). Above him is a spectral depiction of his deceased father, Yax Nuun Ayiin "Green? Crocodile"; while the meaning of *nuun* is still being debated, its hieroglyph, a knotted cloth, can be seen in the headdress of the figure, along with the other elements of his name, the abstract symbol *yax* "green," and the curled snout of a crocodile (Figure 8.3, B).[15]

The hieroglyphic nature of Maya iconography can also be seen at Copan, in an Early Classic shrine to the Copan dynasty founder, K'inich Yax K'uk' Mo' "Lord Green Quetzal Macaw" (Figure 8.4). The shrine is decorated with a frieze of two birds with intertwined necks, one a quetzal, the other a macaw. Out of their beaks emerges the head of the sun god K'in, used frequently as a logograph for the royal title *k'inich*. On the birds' heads, like a feathered crest, is the abstract symbol for *yax* "green." Thus the

---

[15] See Stephen D. Houston, David Stuart, and Karl Taube, *The Memory of Bones: Body, Being and Experience among the Classic Maya* (Austin: University of Texas Press, 2006) for more discussion of the glyphic nature of headdresses and other adornment in Maya art.

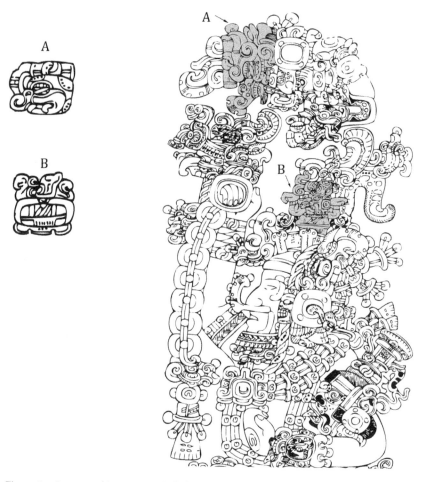

Figure 8.3 Iconographic names in Tikal Stela 31 (image by author based on drawings by William Coe [Christopher Jones and Linton Satterthwaite, *The Monuments and Inscriptions at Tikal: The Carved Monuments*, Tikal Report No. 33, Part A (Philadelphia: The University Museum, University of Pennsylvania, 1982), Fig. 51]; courtesy the University of Pennsylvania Museum of Archaeology and Anthropology).

components of the frieze provide all of the elements, in iconographic rather than glyphic form, for the name of the ruler, K'inich Yax K'uk' Mo'.

David Stuart has argued that this same mixture of art and writing can be seen in massive architectural masks found on many Preclassic structures. Often these masks seem to be portraying deities. In some cases, however, actual kings might be intended, with their names "spelled out," so to speak,

Figure 8.4 Copan Stucco frieze with ruler's name (drawn by Lucia R. Henderson).

by their adornments. While these masks do not have the benefit of accompanying texts that "prove" the connection with hieroglyphs, what is apparent is that Preclassic architectural masks and iconography clearly make use of a widespread and tightly structured repertoire of iconographic forms. The interplay between writing and iconography is possible because of this highly developed inventory of iconographic conventions, many connected with forms in other parts of Mesoamerica. In a very real sense, a "literate" elite would have needed to be as well versed in these iconographic conventions as they were in the logographs and syllabic signs that made up Maya writing.

The antiquity of this elite appreciation of symbols and iconography is evident on Pre-Mamom ceramics, dating to around 1000 BCE, well before the first writing in the Maya area, and before the emergence of the massive Late Preclassic centers. While ceramics from this time period in the Lowlands vary wildly in terms of form and style, they are often embellished with post-slip incised symbols that are abstract in nature, but have clear parallels to later

Maya hieroglyphic forms and to symbols found on ceramics and elsewhere throughout Mesoamerica. These forms are not hieroglyphs, but their meaning, where one can be reconstructed, is cosmological. They are elite symbols of power and authority. Francisco Estrada Belli argues that both knowledge of the meaning of these symbols and possession of the inscribed vessels would have been means of status distinctions in sedentary farming villages and, at around 1000 BCE, might represent the first indication of social ranking in the Lowlands and the first step toward state organization.

While it would be difficult, if not impossible, to prove that ancient Maya writing developed out of the highly conventionalized and widely dispersed inventory of abstract symbols found on Middle Preclassic ceramics throughout Mesoamerica, it is nonetheless unavoidable that knowledge of those esoteric symbols and the large inventory of iconographic conventions was part of the cultural and historical moment in which script was made, and would have effected its overall quality and perceived significance. While it is now widely accepted that script development can happen quite abruptly, or even be the invention of a single individual, the fact that this invention took place in the context of a longstanding tradition of highly valued cosmologically and ritually meaningful sign inventories must have shaped how writing was understood by its inventor and the rest of the society that adopted it. If such examples are indeed a functional as well as formal precursor to Maya writing, it suggests the primacy of such ethereal representation over the kinds of mundane referents that would have been primary in contexts of administration and accounting.

Early texts

Aside from the early mural texts at San Bartolo, and the large stucco masks that are only indirectly connected to writing, the corpus of texts that clearly date to the Preclassic is surprisingly small. In spite of its obvious preeminence in the Late Preclassic, El Mirador has only yielded one fragmentary text, on El Mirador Stela 2, in the form of a small incised caption accompanying a swirling Late Preclassic depiction of the Maya Principal Bird Deity, a common subject of Preclassic Maya art. While stylistically the stela is Late Preclassic, its exact date is unsure because its original context is unknown. In addition, due to the shallow incisions used to inscribe the text, all but the final three glyph blocks have long since eroded away and none of the surviving glyphs is readily recognizable.

Figure 8.5 Dumbarton Oaks jade pectoral incised image and text (drawn by Linda Schele, © David Schele, courtesy Foundation for the Advancement of Mesoamerican Studies, Inc.).

Several other Late Preclassic texts from the Maya Lowlands have been found, all on small portable objects with no documented contemporary archaeological context, and can only be dated to the Late Preclassic on stylistic grounds. These include, for example, texts incised on a small jaguar figurine (also known as the Grolier Figurine), a greenstone axe head and clamshell-shaped earflare, found in an Early Classic tomb at Kendal, Belize, and a (Middle Preclassic) Olmec flanged jade pectoral with a Late Preclassic incised text and accompanying image of a Maya ruler on the back (Figure 8.5). All of the Preclassic-style texts on portable objects share the fact that they are on elite goods, probably looted from tombs, and often heirloom objects, that appear to have been in use long before they were deposited. The jade pectoral, for example, would have been an ancient artifact at the time that it was inscribed with a text. The Kendal axe head also shows signs of wear from long use.

In addition, these portable objects, as well as the early mural texts from San Bartolo, show common themes and scale. The scale of these earliest texts contrasts with later monumental inscriptions, and with the symbolic-ally rich and clearly public architectural masks common at contemporary Preclassic sites. All of these Preclassic texts are small, bespeaking intimate rather than public access.[16] The size of texts on the portable objects was, of course, constrained by the small size of the objects themselves, but even the mural texts are only about 2 centimeters wide and visually very much subordinated to the iconography. Additionally, the placement of texts on the portable objects suggests that the texts were not for display. The jade pectoral currently at Dumbarton Oaks in Washington D.C. (Figure 8.5),

[16] See Stephen D. Houston, "Writing in Early Mesoamerica," in Stephen D. Houston (ed.), *The First Writing: Script Invention as History and Process* (Cambridge: Cambridge University Press, 2004), pp. 274–312.

which was inscribed with a text and image, would have been worn for display, but the text is on the back and would have been hidden when the pectoral was actually worn. The Kendal earflare and the jaguar figurine also have texts on the back, so that they would not have been the primary focus of attention. David Stuart argues that the intimate scale and placement of text is an important clue to the early function of these texts. Far from being tools of public display or "propaganda," the earliest texts were private, sacred, and powerful.

This does not mean, however, that these texts were unrelated to government and social complexity. Another commonality in these texts, though not universal, is the theme of kingship. In spite of the fact that these texts are mostly undeciphered, one recognizable glyph, *ajaw*, referring to kings and rulers, is mentioned twice in the San Bartolo Pinturas Sub-I mural, and a third time in the earlier Sub-V text dating to around 300 BCE. The same sign appears on the Dumbarton Oaks jade pectoral (Column B, Row 5), and the Kendal earflare, and possibly, in a different form, on the Kendal axe head. This suggests a recurrent theme of kingship in Preclassic texts, something that reinforces the connection between writing and the emergence of complex society, if not through public spectacle, then through its association with a particular segment of society. This theme is continued in Classic inscriptions, which have the lives and ritual acts of rulers as their primary subject matter.

Lacunae

More striking than their common features are the characteristics that are lacking, not only from these earliest texts, but also from the entire corpus of Maya hieroglyphic writing. Perhaps the most apparent, because of its prevalence in Mesopotamian texts and its place in theories on the evolution of writing, is the utter lack of administrative themes. We have no records of accounting, monitoring of production or tribute, communications with outlying centers, pedagogical materials, and other essentials of a burgeoning state.

We have reason to believe that this lacuna in the corpus is due more to problems of preservation than actual ancient practices. There is ample evidence, as mentioned above, that the ancient Maya, at least during the Classic period, made frequent use of bark paper books for writing and notations, all of which have long since decayed and disappeared. Indeed, the only texts that might be considered to be "logistical" are the Postclassic codices, the only surviving bark paper books, which provide a sort of ritual almanac that might have been used as a handbook by ritual specialists to keep track of significant calendrical and astronomical stations and their corresponding cosmological significance. Other evidence of text being used for logistical or administrative purposes comes primarily from painted scenes of courtly life on Classic period polychrome ceramics. Several of these depict a royal figure receiving bundles of tribute: folded cloth, cacao beans, perhaps even grain, beans, and other foodstuffs. Several of these scenes (K5453, K2924) show bundles labeled with quantities. For example, one vessel (K5453) shows kneeled supplicants in front of the figure of the king on his throne.[17] Next to him sits a large bundle of folded cloth and several long quetzal plumes. At the foot of the throne is a bag with a hieroglyphic label that reads *ox pik* "3 pik." A *pik* is a unit of 8,000, and this quantity is apparently tripled so that the bag must hold 24,000 of some tribute item, perhaps cacao beans. A similar label, indicating *5 pik kakaw* or 40,000 cacao beans, has also been found on the famous Late Classic murals of Bonampak.[18]

With such an obviously gaping hole in the available data, what can we say about how writing developed in the service of city government? To a degree we simply have the tautology of common sense to guide us: the Maya probably used writing for all of the administrative purposes we find in other literate early civilizations because it would have worked very well to do so. In the absence of anything like a representative sample of early Maya writing, we can scarcely hope to conclusively counter the prevalent idea that writing develops out of the basic accounting and logistical needs of an emerging state.[19] However, the cosmological and ritual significance of symbols from the Middle Preclassic on does seem to suggest that accounting as an impetus for writing in the Maya Lowlands does not seem very likely.

In the context of a pan-Mesoamerican tradition of highly structured iconographic conventions, the invention of writing – the binding of a set of abstract (or semi-abstract) graphic signs, to corresponding language forms

---

[17] Many Maya ceramics are identified by numbers preceded by K (referred to by Mayanists as Kerr numbers). These are unique identifiers for vase images available in Justin Kerr's extensive Maya Vase Database. Images for all artifacts with Kerr numbers can be found at www.mayavase.com.

[18] Stephen D. Houston, "A King Worth a Hill of Beans," *Archaeology* 50 (1997), 40.

[19] Nicholas Postgate, Tao Wang, and Toby Wilkinson, "The Evidence for Early Ceremonial Writing: Utilitarian or Ceremonial?", *Antiquity* 69 (1995), 459–80.

in a particular language – was, perhaps, no great leap. What was required was the institutional support to make and enforce that link between signifier and signified. In the end, the processes that help make texts legible in society are the very ones that inscribe citizens and subjects, and make them "legible" to the state. If the emerging administrative complexity of large city-states was not the principal motivation behind the development of Maya writing, however, then why did writing seem to burst on to the scene at essentially the same time as large urban centers with large-scale monumental architecture and the institution of kingship? One possibility, as mentioned earlier, is that, for all it does in the service of state organization, writing needs a state more than a state needs writing. In other words, it was the emerging control offered by a powerful social and political structure, its program of "legibility," that provided the kind of structured standardization that made writing possible. The benefits that Classic Maya rulers would have garnered from writing – its uncontestable solidity; its continuity across contexts – only seemed to be fully utilized in the Classic period. In the Preclassic, the control that allowed writing to emerge was also directed at controlling access to that potent and private technology.

FURTHER READINGS

Barth, Fredrik, "The Guru and the Conjurer: Transactions in Knowledge and the Shaping of Culture in Southeast Asia and Melanesia," *Man* 25 (1990), 640–53.

Bourdieu, Pierre, *The Field of Cultural Production*, New York: Columbia University Press, 1993.

Caso, Alfonso, *Calendario y escritura de las antiguas culturas de Monte Alban*, Mexico, D.F.: Talleres de la Nación, 1947.

Chafe, Wallace, and Deborah Tannen, "The Relation Between Written and Spoken Language," *Annual Review of Anthropology* 16 (1987), 383–407.

Chase, Arlen F., and Diane Z. Chase, "External Impetus, Internal Synthesis, and Standardization: E-Group Assemblages and the Cristallization of Classic Maya Society in the Southern Lowlands," in Nikolai Grube (ed.), *The Emergence of Lowland Maya Civilization: The Transition from the Preclassic to the Early Classic: A Conference at Hildesheim, November 1992*, Markt Schwaben: Verlag Anton Sarwein, 1995, pp. 87–102.

Cheetham, David, "Cunil: A Pre-Mamom Horizon in the Southern Maya Lowlands," in Terry G. Powis (ed.), *New Perspectives on Formative Mesoamerican Cultures*, Oxford: British Archaeological Reports, 2005, pp. 27–38.

Coe, William, *The Maya Scribe and His World*, New York: The Grolier Club, 1973.

Cooper, Jerrold, "Writing," in Eric Barnouw (ed.), *International Encyclopedia of Communications*, New York: Oxford University Press, 1989, Vol. IV, pp. 321–31.

Drucker, Philip, Robert F. Heizer, and Robert J. Squier, *Excavations at La Venta, 1955*, Washington, D.C.: Smithsonian Institution, 1959.

Errington, Joseph, "Colonial Linguistics," *Annual Review of Anthropology* 30 (2001), 19–39. *Linguistics in a Colonial World: A Story of Language, Meaning, and Power*, Malden, MA: Blackwell Publishing, 2008.

Estrada Belli, Francisco, *Investigaciones arqueologicas en la region de Holmul, Peten, Guatemala. Informe preliminar de la temporada 2008*, Boston: Boston University, 2009, accessed November 21, 2013, www.bu.edu/holmul/reports/informe_08_layout.pdf.

Estrada Belli, Francisco, Nikolai Grube, Marc Wolf, Kristen Gardella, and Claudio Lozano Guerra-Librero, "Preclassic Maya Monuments and Temples at Cival, Peten, Guatemala," *Antiquity* (2003), accessed November 21, 2013, http://antiquity.ac.uk/projgall/belli296/.

Freidel, David, and F. Kent Reilly III, "The Flesh of God, Cosmology, Food, and the Origins of Political Power in Southeastern Mesoamerica," in John E. Staller and Michael D. Carrasco (eds.), *Pre-Columbian Foodways: Interdisciplinary Approaches to Food, Culture, and Markets in Mesoamerica*, New York: Springer, 2010, pp. 635–80.

Hansen, Richard D., *An Early Maya Text from El Mirador, Guatemala*, Washington, D.C.: Research Reports on Ancient Maya Writing, 1991.

"The First Cities – The Beginnings of Urbanization and State Formation in the Maya Lowlands," in Nikolai Grube (ed.), *Maya: Divine Kings of the Rainforest*, Cologne: Koenneman, 2001, pp. 51–64.

Houston, Stephen D., "Writing in Early Mesoamerica," in Stephen D. Houston (ed.), *The First Writing: Script Invention as History and Process*, Cambridge: Cambridge University Press, 2004, pp. 274–312.

Houston, Stephen D., and Héctor Escobedo, "Descifrando la política Maya: Perspectivas arqueológicas y epigráficas sobre el concepto de los estados segmentarios," in Juan Pedro Laporte and Héctor L. Escobedo (eds.), *X Simposio de Investigaciones Arqueológicas en Guatemala*, Guatemala City: Ministerio de Cultura y Deportes, 1997, pp. 463–81.

Houston, Stephen D., and David Stuart, "The Ancient Maya Self: Personhood and Portraiture in the Classic Period," *RES: Anthropology and Aesthetics* 33 (1998), 73–101.

Justeson, John, "The Origin of Writing Systems: Preclassic Mesoamerica," *World Archaeology* 17 (1986), 437–58.

Law, Danny, "A Grammatical Description of the Early Classic Maya Hieroglyphic Inscriptions," unpublished MA thesis, Brigham Young University, 2006.

Marcus, Joyce, *Mesoamerican Writing Systems: Propaganda, Myth, and History in Four Ancient Civilizations*, Princeton, NJ: Princeton University Press, 1992.

"The Origins of Mesoamerican Writing," *Annual Review of Anthropology* 5 (1976), 35–67.

Pellecer Alecio, Mónica, "El Grupo Jabali: un complejo arquitectonico de patron triadico en San Bartolo, Peten," in B. Arroyo, J. P. Laporte, and H. E. Mejia (eds.), *XIX Simposio de Investigaciones Arqueológicas en Guatemala, 2005*, Guatemala: Ministerio de Cultura y Deportes, Asociacion Tikal, Fundacion Reinhart, 2006, pp. 937–48.

Restall, Matthew, "Heirs to the Hieroglyphs: Indigenous Writing in Colonial Mesoamerica," *Americas* 54 (1997), 239–67.

Rodríguez Martínez, Ma. del Carmen, Ponciano Ortíz Ceballos, Michael D. Coe, Richard A. Diehl, Stephen D. Houston, Karl A. Taube, and Alfredo Delgado Calderón, "Did the Olmec Know How to Write?", *Science* 9 (2007), 1365–6.

Schele, Linda, and Mary Miller, *The Blood of Kings*, Fort Worth, TX: Kimbell Art Museum, 1986.

Sharer, Robert James, and David W. Sedat, *Archaeological Investigations in the Northern Maya Highlands*, Philadelphia: University of Pennsylvania Press, 1987, pp. 49–73.

Stuart, David S., "Proper Names and the Origins of Literacy," Working Paper, Peabody Museum, Harvard University, 2001.

Taube, Karl, "The Rainmakers: The Olmec and their Contribution to Mesoamerican Belief and Ritual," in Michael D. Coe (ed.), *The Olmec World: Ritual and Rulership*, Princeton, NJ: The Art Museum, Princeton University, 1995, pp. 83–103.

Urban, Greg, *A Discourse-Centered Approach to Culture: Native South American Myths and Rituals*, Austin: University of Texas Press, 1991.

Metaphysical Community: The Interplay of the Senses and the Intellect, Austin: University of Texas Press, 1996.

Willey, Gordon R., T. Patrick Culbert, and Richard E. W. Adams, "Maya Lowland Ceramics: A Report from the 1965 Guatemala City Conference," *American Antiquity* 32 (1967), 289–315.

9

Inka administration in Tawantinsuyu by means of the knotted-cords

GARY URTON

In each provincial center they had accountants who were called "knot-keepers/orderers" [*quiposcamayos*], and by means of these knots they kept the record and account of what had been given in tribute by those [people] in that district, from the silver, gold, clothing, herd animals, to the wool and other things down to the smallest items, and by the same knots they commissioned a record of what was given over one year, or ten or twenty years and they kept the accounts so well that they did not lose a pair of sandals.[1]

To read Cieza de León's account, it would seem that the Inkas had devised a remarkably efficient system for overseeing the collection, management, and disposal of goods and resources in settlements throughout the provinces of their vast empire, which stretched some 5,000 kilometers along the spine of the Andes, from the border between present-day Ecuador and Colombia southward to central Chile (Map 9.1). What is interesting about Cieza's account is that he credits Inka administrative accomplishments to the information retained in the knotted-string recording device, the *khipu* (or *quipu*). While we have learned a good deal about the khipu's recording capacities in recent times,[2] nonetheless, there remain a number of questions concerning

Thanks to Helmut Schindler for his help and kind hospitality during my two-week visit to the Museum für Völkerkunde, Munich, in the summer, 2004. I also express my profound appreciation to Carrie Brezine, who provided me with the breakdown and initial structural analysis of khipu UR 28. Brezine was, at the time, administrator for the Khipu Database project. The further interpretation and analysis of that khipu in the form presented herein is the work of the author.
[1] Cieza de León, *El Señorío de los Incas*, Cieza de Leon (trans.) (Lima: Instituto de Estudios Peruanos, 1967), p. 36.
[2] Marcia Ascher and Robert Ascher, *Mathematics of the Incas: Code of the Quipus* (New York: Dover, 1997); William J. Conklin, "A Khipu Information String Theory," in Jeffery Quilter and Gary Urton (eds.), *Narrative Threads: Accounting and Recounting in Andean Khipu* (Austin: University of Texas Press, 2002), pp. 53–86; and Gary Urton, *Signs of the Inka Khipu: Binary Coding in the Andean Knotted-String Records* (Austin: University of Texas Press, 2003).

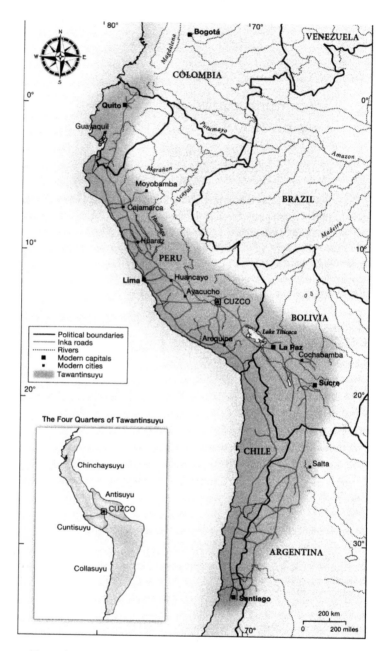

Map 9.1 Tawantinsuyu – approximate extent of the Inka Empire with inset map of the approximate boundaries of the four suyus (quadrants).

how these colorful knotted-cords could have encoded such a wide variety of information, and in as complex an array of forms, as is claimed for them by Cieza and a host of other Spanish commentators. The question, then, is not only whether we can document with Spanish testimony but demonstrate as well that Inka cord-keeping was highly efficient and effective. In order to attempt to address this basic challenge, we begin by acknowledging a few basic circumstances that limit our ability to identify and evaluate critically the characteristics of this accounting system.

Whatever its indigenous components and characteristics, as a functioning and effective set of institutions and practices of accounting and controls, the Inka administrative system had all but collapsed over the first few decades following the Spanish Conquest, which began in 1532. This period of desta-bilization, or what Wachtel called "de-structuration," occurred several decades before the first comprehensive descriptions of the administrative system were written down in the Spanish chronicles and administrative documents.[3] Although elements of the original system were in evidence in early and even mid-Colonial reports, nonetheless, major features of the administrative system and its recording apparatus had disappeared or become destabilized over the intervening years. Furthermore, the question arises of the degree to which native informants on Inka administration might have skewed or misrepre-sented the system in various ways out of political considerations.[4] And finally, I note that we do not possess colonial era meta-commentaries on the Inka administrative system provided by Inka administrative officials themselves. All we have are Spanish observations and the knotted-cords themselves, whose decipherment (assuming that such is even possible) continues to elude us.

The circumstances outlined above complicate the task before us. The question is: How shall we proceed? In the first place, we do have a number of excellent secondary sources on these matters.[5] These and other accounts

---

[3] Nathan Wachtel, *The Vision of the Vanquished: The Spanish Conquest of Peru through Indian Eyes*, Ben Reynolds and Sian Reynolds (trans.) (Hassocks, Sussex: The Harvester Press Limited, 1977).

[4] Gary Urton, *The History of a Myth: Pacariqtambo and the Origin of the Inkas* (Austin: University of Texas Press, 1990).

[5] Catherine J. Julien, "How Inca Decimal Administration Worked," *Ethnohistory* 35 (1988), 257–79; John V. Murra, "Las etno-categorías de un khipu estatal," in John V. Murra, *Formaciones económicas y políticas en el mundo andino* (Lima: Instituto de Estudios Peruanos, 1975), pp. 243–54; Martti Pärssinen, *Tawantinsuyu: The Inca State and its Political Organization* (Helsinki: Suomen Historiallinen Seura, 1992); and John Rowe, "Inca Policies and Institutions Relating to the Cultural Unification of the Empire," in George C. Collier, Renato I. Rosaldo, and John D. Wirth (eds.), *The Inca and Aztec States: 1400–1800: Anthropology and History* (New York: Academic Press, 1982), pp. 93–118.

inform us deeply with respect to the basic characteristics of Inka administration. While I will draw on material from these sources as a point of
departure for the present study, I will do so primarily as a way of moving as
quickly as possible to the aspect of that system I feel myself to be most
qualified to comment on – cord-keeping. Having myself spent almost
twenty years in close study of the corpus of extant khipus,[6] it is my intention
here to draw on data from the knotted-cord records in order to demonstrate
how khipu accounts were constructed, maintained, and manipulated by the
khipukamayuqs (knot-makers/organizers), the Inka record-keepers.[7] In this
way, I hope to produce an account of Inka administrative practice that is to
some degree grounded in what I would term "indigenous testimony" – that
is, native records produced in the course of Inka administrative practice.

In keeping with the desiderata and objectives outlined above, I will begin
by presenting an overview of the basic institutions and practices of Inka
administration. The intention in this initial section of the chapter will be to
indicate the central principles and features of the Inka administrative system,
as a basis for looking at the cord-records themselves. The discussion of the
latter will be divided into three sections: state, provincial, and local. An
illustration of cord-recording at each level will be presented. The principal
resource I will draw on in the cord-keeping sections is the Khipu Database, a
searchable, electronic database that I have been constructing and investigating, with the support of the National Science Foundation and the capable
assistance of computing consultants Carrie J. Brezine and Pavlo Kononenko,
at Harvard University, since 2002.

An overview of Inka administration

In early Colonial sources, the Inka Empire is referred to as Tawantinsuyu,
which we can gloss as "the four parts intimately bound together." The four
parts in question were Chinchaysuyu, Antisuyu, Collasuyu, and Cuntisuyu
(the suffix *-suyu* [part, turn] is often glossed as "quarter"). At the heart of this
quadripartite organization was the Inka capital city of Cuzco, located in the

---

[6] Gary Urton, "A New Twist in an Old Yarn: Variation in Knot Directionality in the Inka
Khipus," *Baessler-Archiv Neue Folge* 42 (1996), 271–305; Gary Urton, *Signs of the Inka Khipu*;
and Gary Urton and Carrie J. Brezine, "Khipu Typologies," in Elizabeth Hill Boone and
Gary Urton (eds.), *Their Way of Writing: Scripts, Signs and Pictographies in Pre-Columbian
America* (Washington, D.C.: Dumbarton Oaks Research Library, 2010), pp. 319–52.

[7] For additional descriptions, diagrams, and photos detailing khipu construction features,
see the website for my Khipu Database project: http://khipukamayuq.fas.harvard.
edu/.

southeastern highlands of present-day Peru. The overview of the administration of Tawantinsuyu that follows is constructed top-down, as it were, beginning with administrative officials, institutions and procedures in Cuzco, moving down (and outward) to provincial administrative centers, and, finally, to local settlements. My objective is not to be exhaustive and/or definitive, but rather to provide a reasonably accurate overview from which to look more closely at khipu administrative record-keeping.

State/imperial organization in Cuzco, the capital

As the capital, Cuzco was the center of supreme power and authority in the Inka Empire. It was here that the Inka king – the *Sapa Inka* (unique/sole Inka) – reigned at court along with his *Coya*, the queen (who in late imperial times was his sister as well). The administration within Cuzco was staffed by direct and collateral descendants of the ten to twelve Inka kings who had ruled the empire during its short history, which lasted only some 125–150 years. Given the rapidity of state formation, it is not surprising that, while the administrative structure was reasonably well consolidated in the capital city, things were more in flux, with considerable local variation, in the provinces.

At the top of the administrative hierarchy in Cuzco and the empire stood the Inka. The indigenous chronicler Guaman Poma de Ayala details a number of officials who saw to the everyday needs and interests of the king.[8] Most immediately, the Inka was attended to by a secretary (*Yncap cimin quipococ*, "he who carries the account of the words of the Inka"), a head accountant and treasurer (*Tawantin Suyo runa quipoc Yncap*, "he who carries the accounting of the people and goods of Tawantinsuyu"), as well as a counsel of four great lords, or *Apus*, each of whom was responsible to the Inka for the affairs in one or another of the four suyus of Tawantinsuyu. The Apus formed what Guaman Poma referred to as the *Consejo Real*, the "royal counsel," a body that was served by a secretary, the *Tawantin Suyo capac Yncacanap cimin quipococ* (he who carries the words of the Inka and the lords/Apus). These were the principal authorities at the heart of what we could term "civil governance" in the Inka capital. However, we should not lose sight of the fact that what we classify as civil affairs, on the one hand, and religious affairs, on the other, were never far apart in Inka statecraft. Thus, we must include the chief priest, the *Villac Umu*, as well as the hierarchy of priests he oversaw, as players in the civil administration.

---

[8] Guaman Poma de Ayala, *El Primer Nueva Corónica y Buen Gobierno*, John V. Murra and Rolena Adorno (eds.), 3 vols. (Mexico City: Siglo Veintiuno, 1980), pp. 1583–615.

We must take note of an institution, the so-called *ceque* system, which provided the framework for administrative activities, social organization, and ritual practices in the city. The forty-one ceques that composed this system were (invisible) alignments of sacred places – called *huacas* – located in and immediately around the city. The huacas were sites where important events had occurred in the mythical foundation of the ancient capital. Each huaca received sacrificial offerings on a particular day of the year. Cuzco and the ceque system were divided into moieties (Hanan/upper Cuzco and Hurin/lower Cuzco), each of which was further subdivided into two parts, forming the four parts or quarters of Tawantinsuyu. Within the quarters, the ceques were generally ranked in a repeating three-component hierarchical organization, the constituent elements of which were designated (from highest to lowest) *collana*, *payan*, and *cayao*. The order of these three categories, as they were repeated around the center of the system – that is, the Coricancha (the so-called "Temple of the Sun") – varied between the moieties. In lower/Hurin Cuzco, the ceque hierarchy proceeded counterclockwise, while in upper/Hanan Cuzco, the hierarchy ran clockwise (see Figure 9.1). I return to this point below.

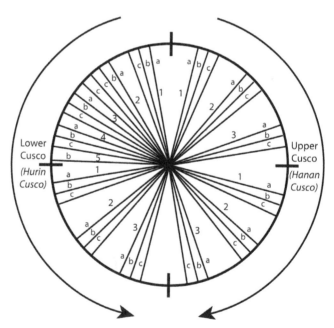

Figure 9.1 Schematic representation of the ceque system of Cuzco showing division into upper and lower Cuzco and the direction of hierarchical order of ceques in each half.

The performance of sacrifices at the some 328–350 huacas located along the forty-one ceques, plus an unnamed period of rest of thirty-seven days, structured the annual ritual calendar in the capital and empire as a whole. What made this ritual/calendrical system political, and, therefore, of relevance for a discussion of state administration, was the fact that specific royal and non-royal kin groups – called, respectively, *panacas* and *ayllus* – were responsible for making the sacrificial offerings at the huacas aligned along particular ceques. That is, specific sectors of the terrain in and around the city, as well as specific segments of time in the annual calendar, were related to one or another of the ten panacas or the ten ayllus into which the population was divided.[9] Information pertaining to the ceque system of the city of Cuzco is said to have been recorded on a khipu.

Khipu analog for a cord account in Cuzco

Without wishing to claim that we have identified anything so spectacular as a "ceque khipu," nonetheless, we can see in an extant pair of khipu samples a cord structure and organization that could have accommodated the segmentary and hierarchical features as outlined above.[10] As we see in Figure 9.1, the ceque system was a four-part arrangement with two quarters in the upper/Hanan moiety and two in the lower/Hurin moiety. Except for the quarter of Cuntisuyu (that is, which had fourteen ceques), the suyus generally contained (three x three =) nine ceques. We saw above that the hierarchical categories collana/payan/cayao proceeded clockwise in upper/Hanan Cuzco and counter-clockwise in lower/Hurin Cuzco. Now, we have identified a pair of khipus, currently in the Banco Central de la Reserva del Perú, in Lima, that reflects structural divisions and a hierarchical organization strikingly similar to the ceque system.

The two samples in question are part of a group of five khipus tied together in what I have termed a "linked set" (see Figure 9.2).[11] In the figure, the two samples we will focus on are labeled UR053B and UR053C. The samples in this linked set all share a particular organization of cords by color; that is, all five khipus display the repeating three-cord color pattern: white

---

[9] R. Tom Zuidema, "Bureaucracy and Systematic Knowledge in Andean Civilization," in Collier, Rosaldo, and Wirth (eds.), *The Inca and Aztec States*, pp. 419–58.

[10] Nathan Wachtel, *The Vision of the Vanquished*; and Pärsinnen, *Tawantinsuyu*; and R. Tom Zuidema, *The Ceque System of Cuzco: The Social Organization of the Capital of the Inca* (Leiden: Brill, 1964).

[11] Gary Urton, "Khipu Archives: Duplicate Accounts and Identity Labels in the Inka Knotted-String Records," *Latin American Antiquity* 16 (2005), 147–67.

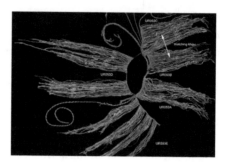

Figure 9.2 Khipu UR053 (ATE3517, Banco de la Reserva del Perú [photograph by Gary Urton]) showing the locations of the matching pair UR053B and 53C.

(W) / either light reddish-brown (RL) or moderate reddish-brown (RB) / light brown (AB). Note that RL and RB may replace each other (that is, some cords are light reddish-brown, while others are moderate reddish-brown; however, the two hues are assumed here to have equal value in the three-color schemes of khipus 53B and 53C). Table 9.1 juxtaposes the tabular data that we have recorded from samples 53C and 53B. In khipu 53C, the W/ RL or RB/AB color sequence is repeated across three-cord sets of pendant cords (the pendant cord numbers are given in the column on the far left) in the arrangement: 1–2–3 / 4–5–6 / etc.; however, in sample 53B, the W/RL or RB/AB sequence appears on sets composed of two pendant cords, the second of which carries a subsidiary cord (that is, 1–2–2s1 / 3–4–4s1). Thus, the likeness between these two samples in terms of the repeating color sequence belies a fundamental difference between them at the level of the number and arrangement of cords bearing those colors: pendant/pendant/ pendant vs. pendant/pendant/subsidiary. I suggest that what we see in these two samples is a three-term arrangement of categories that mimics the three-term collana/payan/cayao organization of hierarchical labels described above for the ceque system.

Next, as demonstrated by the arrangement of these two samples in Table 9.1, we see that, from pendant cord #11 of sample 53C and pendant cord #1 on sample 53B, the numerical values registered on respective cords shown across from each other are identical, or (generally) quite close in value. However, if these khipus were, in fact, meant to register the same (or similar) data, they must have done so in a way that classified that infor- mation in different structural terms, as we saw above that there is a basic difference between the two samples in terms of cord structure and the repetition of the three-color cord pattern. As we will see below, there is

Table 9.1 A pair of matching khipus (Banco Central de la Reserva del Perú)

KHIPU UR053C

Cord Number	Attch	Knots	Color	Value
1	V	1EE(24.0/Z)	AB	2
2	V	4S(7.5/S) 1EE(22.0/Z)	W	41
3	V	1S(7.0/S)	RB	10
4	V	6L(21.5/S)	AB	6
5	V	7S(8.0/S) 3L(21.5/S)	W	73
6	V	4L(21.5/S)	RB	4
7	V	5L(21.5/S)	AB	5
8	V	5S(8.0/S) 3L(22.5/S)	W	53
9	V	1S(9.0/S) 4L(21.5/S)	RL	14
10	V	2L(20.5/S)	AB	2
11	V	5S(7.0/S) 3L(21.5/S)	W	53
12	V	1S(7.0/S) 3L(20.5/S)	RL	13
13	V	3L(20.5/S)	AB	3
14	V	5S(8.0/Z) 3L(21.0/Z)	W	53
15	V	1S(7.5/Z) 5L(19.0/Z)	RB	15
16	V	5L(5.0/Z)	AB	5
17	V	6S(7.5/Z) 3L(21.0/Z)	W	63
18	V	1S(8.0/Z) 6L(21.0/Z)	RB	16
19	V	1S(8.0/Z) 6L(21.0/Z)	AB	16
20	V	6S(8.0/Z) 3L(21.0/Z)	W	63
21	V	1S(8.0/Z) 7L(21.0/Z)	RL	17
22	V	1S(7.5/Z) 7L(20.5/Z)	AB	17
23	V	7S(8.0/Z) 4L(20.5/Z)	W	74
24	V	1S(8.5/Z) 6L(20.0/Z)	RL	16

KHIPU UR053B

Cord Number	Attch	Knots	Color	Value
1	R	5S(1.5/S) 3L(14.0/S)	W	53
2	R	1S(6.0/S) 3L(16.0/S)	RL	13
2si	U	3L(15.0/S)	AB	3
3	R	5S(4.5/S) 3L(15.0/S)	W	53
4	R	1S(7.0/S) 5L(16.0/S)	RL	15
4si	U	5L(14.5/S)	AB	5
5	R	6S(6.0/S) 3L(15.5/S)	W	63
6	R	1S(6.5/S) 6L(15.0/S)	RL	16
6si	U	1S(5.5/S) 6L(14.5/S)	AB	16
7	R	6S(5.0/S) 3L(15.0/S)	W	63
8	R	1S(6.0/S) 7L(15.0/S)	RL	17
8si	U	1S(5.0/S) 9L(14.0/S)	AB	19
9	R	7S(6.0/S) 4L(14.5/S)	W	74
10	R	1S(6.5/S) 6L(14.5/S)	RL	16

Table 9.1 (cont.)

KHIPU URo53C

Cord Number	Attch	Knots	Color	Value	Value	Attch	Knots	Color	Value
25	V	8L(20.5/Z)	AB	8	10SI	U	8L(14.0/S)	AB	8
26	V	5S(8.0/Z) 3L(20.5/Z)	W	53	11	R	3S(6.0/S) 3L(13.0/S)	W	33
27	V	1S(8.0/Z) 3L(19.5/Z)	RB	13	12	R	1S(6.0/S) 3L(14.0/S)	RL	13
28	V	5L(21.0/Z)	AB	5	12SI	U	5L(13.0/S)	AB	5
29	V	5S(8.0/Z) 3L(20.0/Z)	W	53	13	R	5S(6.0/S) 3L(14.5/S)	W	53
30	V	1S(8.5/Z) 2L(20.5/Z)	RL	12	14	R	1S(6.5/S) 2L(15.5/S)	RL	12
31	V	1S(8.0/Z) 6L(19.5/Z)	AB	16	14SI	U	1S(5.5/S) 6L(14.0/S)	AB	16
32	V	5S(8.0/Z) 8L(20.0/Z)	W	58	15	R	5S(6.5/S) 8L(15.0/S)	W	58
33	V	1S(8.5/Z) 5L(20.5/Z)	RL	15	16	R	1S(7.5/S) 6L(14.0/S)	RL	16
34	V	1S(8.0/Z) 6L(19.5/Z)	AB	16	16SI	U	1S(7.0/S) 6L(14.0/S)	AB	16
35	V	5S(7.5/Z) 2L(19.5/Z)	W	52	17	R	5S(5.0/S) 2L(13.5/S)	W	52
36	V	1S(7.5/Z) 1E(21.0/Z)	RL	11	18	R	1S(6.0/S) 1E(13.0/S)	RL	11
37	V	1S(7.0/Z) 4L(20.5/Z)	AB	14	18SI	U	1S(5.0/S) 4L(13.0/S)	AB	14
38	V	3S(7.5/Z) 2L(21.5/Z)	W	32	19	R	3S(5.0/S) 2L(12.5/S)	W	32
39	V	1S(7.5/Z)	RL	10	20	R	1S(5.0/S)	RL	10
40	V	1S(7.5/Z) 4L(20.5/Z)	AB	14	20SI	U	1S(4.5/S) 7L(10.5/S)	AB	17
41	V	2S(6.0/S) 1S(19.0/S)	W	22	21	R	2S(4.5/S) 2L(11.0/S)	W	22
42	V	2S(6.0/S) 1S(19.0/S)	RB	26	22	R	2S(4.5/S) 7L(11.5/S)	RL	27
43	V	1S(16.0/S)	AB	5	22SI	U	6L(10.5/S)	AB	6
44	V	1S(6.0/S) 1S(17.0/S)	W	19	23	R	1S(4.0/S) 9L(11.0/S)	W	19
45	V	2S(5.0/S) 1S(17.5/S)	RB	25	24	R	2S(5.5/S)	RL	20
46	V	1S(17.0/S)	AB	9	24SI	U	9L(9.5/S)	AB	9
47	V	1S(5.0/S) 1S(18.5/S)	W	16	25	R	1S(5.5/S) 2L(11.5/S)	W	12
48	V	2S(5.5/S) 1S(19.5/S)	RL	26	26	R	1S(5.5/S) 5L(12.0/S)	RL	15

49	V	1S(6.5/S) 1E(17.5/Z)	AB	11	26SI
50	V	2S(5.0/S) 1E(14.5/Z)	W	21	27
51	V	2S(5.0/S) 7L(14.0/S)	RB	27	28
52	V	1S(4.0/S) 1E(14.0/Z)	AB	11	28SI
53	V	1S(5.0/S) 8L(16.0/S)	W	18	29
54	V	2S(4.5/S) TURNS?L(15.0/U)	RB	20	30
55	V	1S(4.5/S)	B	10	30SI
56	V	2S(4.5/S) 2L(14.0/S)	W	22	31
57	V	8L(11.0/S)	RB	8	32
58	V	9L(12.0/S)	AB	9	32SI
59	V	2S(6.0/S) 1E(14.0/Z)	W	21	33
60	V	1S(5.0/S) 6L(12.5/S)	RB	16	34
61	V	5S(10.5/S)	AB	50	34SI
					35
					36
				1408	36SI

U	1S(5.0/S) 7L(12.0/S)	AB	17
R	1S(4.5/S) 7L(12.5/S)	W	17
R	2S(4.5/S) 9L(11.5/S)	RL	29
U	1S(4.0/S) 3L(12.0/S)	AB	13
R	1S(5.0/S) 8L(12.5/S)	W	18
R	2S(5.5/S) 6L(11.0/S)	RL	26
U	1S(4.5/S)	AB	10
R	2S(5.0/S) 2L(10.0/S)	W	22
R	8L(11.5/S)	RL	8
U	9L(11.0/S)	AB	9
R	2S(4.5/S) 4L(11.0/S)	W	24
R	2S(4.5/S) 6L(12.0/S)	RB	26
U	1S(4.5/S) 1E(10.5/S)	AB	11
R	2S(5.0/S) 3L(11.0/S)	W	23
R	1S(5.0/S) 9L(11.0/S)	RL	19
U	6L(11.0/S) 3L(14.0/S)	AB	9
			1203

another feature by which we realize that these two samples are almost exact opposites of each other – we might say complementary opposites – precisely as the Hanan/Hurin moieties of Cuzco were complementary opposites (for example, clockwise vs. counter-clockwise hierarchical rankings).

If one looks at the second column in each set of data for khipus URo53C and 53B, one sees there the notation for how the pendant cords are attached to the main cord of the respective khipus. The two forms of attachment types (the details of which we do not need to go into here) are recorded as either "V" (= verso) or "R" (= recto). I would note that the direction of attaching subsidiary cords to pendant cords is not recorded on khipu URo53b (that is, the sample in which every third member of a three-member/cord group is a subsidiary). The subsidiaries are therefore labeled "U" (= Unrecorded). Now, the attachment types V and R are actually what we might call opposite sides of the same coin. That is, a cord attached V, as viewed from one side of a sample, will appear as an R attachment when the sample is viewed from the opposite side (and vice versa). What this means is that, while these two samples are, indeed, a "matching pair" in terms of numerical values knotted onto adjacent cords, the match is obtained only if one views sample URo53C from the V side of the khipu at the same time as one views sample URo53B from the R side. In fact, if one viewed the two samples from the same side (that is, either both in the V or the R position), the numerical values of adjacent cords would not align, or match, as they do when their attachment type is opposite, as shown in Table 9.1. Thus, the "pairing" of these samples, in terms of the sequencing of cord colors and values, is obtained only when the khipus are placed (and viewed) in opposing orientations.

My argument is that the difference just described between the orientation of cord attachments on these two samples is like that between the two halves (moieties) of the ceque system of Cuzco in which the hierarchical categories (collana/payan/cayao) of the three-ceque sets in one half run in a clockwise direction, while those in the other half run in a counter-clockwise direction. Given that it has often been suggested that the ceque system was recorded on a khipu,[12] the question has long been: How was such a complex organization of sections and categories recorded? My suggestion is that, in

<hr/>

[12] Brian S. Bauer, "The Original Ceque Manuscript," in Gary Urton (ed.), "Structure, Knowledge, and Representation in the Andes: Studies Presented to Reiner Tom Zuidema on the Occasion of his 70th Birthday," Special Edition of the *Journal of the Steward Anthropological Society* 23 (1997), 277–98.

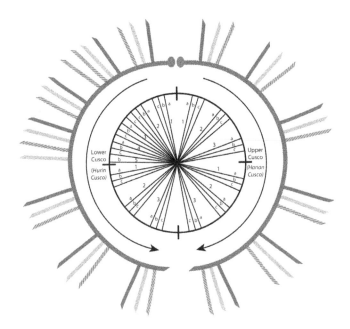

Figure 9.3 Hypothetical construction comparing the organization of the ceque system of Cuzco and the matching khipu pair URo53B and 53C.

fact, the ceque system most likely was not recorded on a single khipu; rather, I suggest that it was most likely recorded on a *pair* of khipus – one for Hanan/upper Cuzco, the other for Hurin/lower Cuzco (see Figure 9.3). A pair of samples like URo53B and 53C, shown in Figure 9.2, could have comfortably accommodated the recording of information in an arrangement of paired halves composed of three-term labels in which the terms repeat in a clockwise direction in one half and a counter-clockwise direction in the other half. A khipu pair of the type discussed here would have provided the instruments for recording and regulating – that is, administering – political and ritual positions and relations in the ceque system of the capital.

Provincial organization

As we move outward from Cuzco and down the administrative hierarchy, we come to the overseers of each of the eighty or so provinces that made up the empire. Each province was overseen by a *Tocricoc* ("he who sees/ watches"), who was attended by a khipukamayuq. This official recorded information, especially statistical data, that pertained to the province, such as census and tribute records. It is at the provincial level that we encounter the question of the degree to which decimal organization obtained in the hierarchy and oversight of state workers. The latter relates to the decimal-based system of corvée labor in which tribute was levied on subject populations in the form of a demand for labor time on state projects, such as the building and maintaining of roads, storehouses, bridges, etc.; the care and tending of lands belonging to the state and to the gods; and other tasks.[13]

Throughout much of the empire, corvée laborers were organized in decimal groupings according to the principles of dualism and five-part organization (see Figure 9.4). That is, five groupings of ten (*chunca*) workers at the local level made up groups of fifty workers, which were paired with another group of the same size to make a group of 100 (*pachaca*) workers. As we see in Figure 9.4, moving up the hierarchy, the principles of pairing and five-part organization worked together repeatedly to produce ever larger groupings of workers, up to the level of groups of 10,000 (*hunu*) tribute laborers. At each level, headmen (called *curacas*) oversaw the activities of the workers. Cord-keepers (khipukamayuqs) were assigned to record data concerning member attendance and participation in work tasks assigned to that group by the state.[14]

Recording data at the provincial level

A question that has been central to efforts to understand how Inka administration actually functioned, on the ground, concerns how information moved between adjacent levels of the decimal hierarchy. The gist of the problem is illustrated in Figure 9.4. In the decimal hierarchy, commands for labor, etc., from higher-level officials would be passed down the chain of command to lower-level officials. It is clear that such instructions – for example, send 100 workers to move the harvest into storehouses in Huánuco Pampa – would be transmitted via khipu accounts. This information would have been *partible* in nature; that is, assignments made to 100 tribute payers would be broken down between instructions to two groups of fifty, and, in turn, from there to on-the-ground instructions to the five groups of ten workers within a local community. In the reverse direction, accountants in local communities would pass data on tasks performed by decimally organized work groups upward through the hierarchical chain of officials. In the latter instance, information at

---

[13] John V. Murra, *The Economic Organization of the Inca State* (Greenwich, CT: JAI Press, 1980).

[14] Pärsinnen, *Tawantinsuyu*.

Inka Decimal Administration

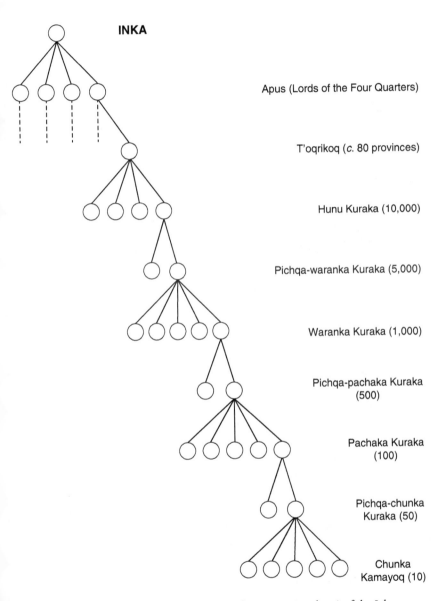

INKA

Apus (Lords of the Four Quarters)

T'oqrikoq (*c.* 80 provinces)

Hunu Kuraka (10,000)

Pichqa-waranka Kuraka (5,000)

Waranka Kuraka (1,000)

Pichqa-pachaka Kuraka (500)

Pachaka Kuraka (100)

Pichqa-chunka Kuraka (50)

Chunka Kamayoq (10)

Figure 9.4 Schematic hierarchial organization of one suyu (quadrant) of the Inka decimal administration.

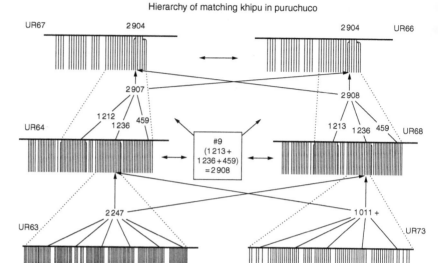

Figure 9.5 Schematic arrangement of the Puruchuco accounting hierarchy.

each level would represent the *summation* of accounts from the level immediately below. These accumulating data would eventually arrive in the hands of state accountants in Cuzco, where the highest level of accounting went on.

Only in very recent times have we identified a set of khipus linked hierarchically in the kind of reciprocal relationship of summation/partition that would have been characteristic of administrative accounting at the provincial level in the Inka Empire, as described above. As my colleague, Carrie Brezine, and I have shown, we see in a set of seven khipus from the site of Puruchuco, in the Rimac Valley, what we have termed an "accounting hierarchy" whose organization is strikingly similar to that outlined above (that is, summation upward; division downward). The Puruchuco accounting hierarchy (Figure 9.5) also contains elements of "checks and balances," whereby Inka accountants could ensure for themselves the veracity and trustworthiness of state records. The operation of this arrangement of khipus is too detailed to explain in full in the present context.[15]

[15] See discussion in Gary Urton and Carrie J. Brezine, "Information Control in the Palace of Puruchuco: An Accounting Hierarchy in a Khipu Archive from Coastal Peru," in

Basically, there are two principles at work in this accounting hierarchy: (a) khipus on the same level are "matching khipus" (that is, as we saw in Table 9.1); and (b) sums of groups of numerical values in different color-coded segments of khipus on lower levels are recorded on similarly color-coded segments of khipus on the next higher level. Thus, sums are being recorded "upward" (or, reciprocally, they are being sub-divided "down-ward") in the Puruchuco accounting hierarchy. Suffice it to say that this example provides us with a clear and convincing case study of the production of accounts in the territory of a local lord – a *señorío* – and the communication by means of khipus between the lord and the provincial center to which he reported (in the case at hand this probably referred to an Inka administrative site lower down in the Rimac).

Local administrative organization

When we consider the administration of public affairs within local settlements, the offices of greatest importance, both in terms of practices of local control as well as in the relationship between the community and the outside, were a hierarchy of local lords, the curacas. These were the heads of the local lineages that made up what were usually multiple ayllus (kin-based, land-holding, ritual/ceremonial groups). The principal officials within such local hierarchies were commonly referred to in Spanish documents as *cacique principal* (the head of the most powerful lineage in the local area) and a close subordinate, the *cacique*, or *segunda*. Now, we should note that the principle of dual organization, which takes the form, in social contexts, of moieties (halves), was pervasive in communities throughout the Andes in Inka times (we have already seen an expression in Cuzco, the capital). Local moieties, which were usually hierarchically related to each other, were commonly referred to (or classified) as *hanan* (upper; the one that takes precedence) and *hurin* (lower; the subordinate group). In most local socio-political organizations, the moieties were made up of multiple ayllus, each headed by a curaca. The cacique principal was often drawn from a lineage of the predominant ayllu of *Hanansaya*, while the segunda represented the ayllus of *Hurinsaya*. This pyramidal, hierarchical arrangement of local curaca officials was generally structured and organized as shown in Figure 9.6,

Richard Burger, Craig Morris, and Ramiro Matos (eds.), *Variations in the Expression of Inka Power* (Washington, D.C.: Dumbarton Oaks, 2007), pp. 357–84.

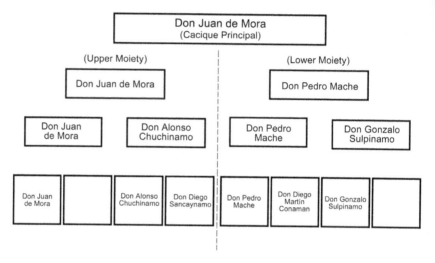

Figure 9.6 Dual, hierarchical organization of authorities in the Chicama Valley, 1565 (after P. Netherly, "The Management of Late Andean Irrigation Systems on the North Coast of Peru," *American Antiquity* 29 [1984], 234).

which is an example drawn from ethnohistorical documents from the Chicama Valley, on the north coast of Peru, after Spanish contact.

In terms of our interest here in administration and record-keeping, I should note that the head officials of the moieties were served by khipu-kamayuqs – that is, there was a pair of local cord-keepers, one for the Hanansaya ayllus, another for the Hurinsaya ayllus. We find suggestions in the early Spanish administrative documents to the effect that this pair of moiety-based local cord-keepers not only maintained the records of their constituent ayllus, but that each retained a copy of the information pertaining to the opposite moiety, as well (thus, each moiety cord-keeper would have retained a record of all information, especially demographic, pertaining to the community as a whole). As a result of this form of what I have characterized elsewhere as a system of checks and balances,[16] there were, at a minimum, at least two copies of all the records pertaining to any given local population. We now have solid evidence for such configurations of khipu samples in the extant corpus; one example, discussed in the previous section, is from Puruchuco, on the coast; the other example is from

[16] Gary Urton, and Carrie J. Brezine, "Khipu Accounting in Ancient Peru," *Science* 309 (2005), 1065–7.

Chachapoyas,[17] in the north-central highlands of Peru. We also see evidence of this organization in the account of a *visita* (census visitation) among the Lupaqa, who lived on the southwestern shores of Lake Titicaca, in early Colonial times. In testimony from a local cacique, don Martin Cusi, of the sector of Lurinsaya (= Hurinsaya), we read:

> It was asked if among the quipos, which in the other declaration it was said he had in his house, if he had found the quipo of the Indian tributaries they made in the time of the Inka in this province and that there were so many Indians, he said that he discovered the said quipo and then he exhibited certain cords of wool with some knots that was said to be the quipo and account of the tributary Indians that there had been in this province in the time of the Inka, the said quipo which the said don Martin Cusi and Lope Martin Ninara, who is the head quipocamayo of the said parcialidad [moiety] of Lurinsaya within the province, who is the person who has the account and explanation, as the accountant of the business [*negocios*] of the community they declared, and his declaration was made conferring part-by-part [in his reading] with the declaration made by don Martin Cari cacique principal of the moiety of Anansaya, the said person by his quipo, and it conforms in all sections and in the number of Indians of all the pueblos in both moieties *except* that in one part, that of the Canas Indians of the pueblo of Pomata, that [quipo] of don Martin Cari said they had 20 Indians and that [quipo] of don Martin Cusi and his quipocamayo by his quipo it appeared to be 22; in all other parts the declarations of the said caciques conformed.[18]

This account gives us a sense both of the hierarchical arrangement of record-keepers as well as indicating the importance of checks and balances in the administrative accounting of local, moiety-based cord-keepers.

A local khipu: numeration, rank, and value in a khipu from Nazca

The question that concerns us now is: How might khipu accounts have been organized to record information (on census, tribute, and so on) that was vital to the organization of local communities in Tawantinsuyu? Asking this question, we are indeed "on the ground," as it were, at the point where local information was collected, with all the messiness of political relations and

---

[17] Gary Urton, *The Khipus of Laguna de los Cóndores/Los Khipus de la Laguna de los Condóres* (Lima: Forma e Imágen, 2008).

[18] Garci Diez de San Miguel, *Visita hecha a la Provincia de Chucuito*, Palaeography and Bibliography by Waldemar Espinoza Soriano (Lima: Ediciones de la Casa de la Cultura del Peru, 1964), p. 74.

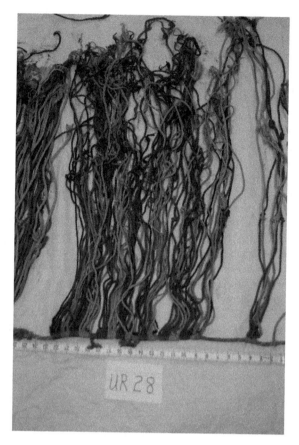

Figure 9.7 Khipu UR028 (Museum für Völkerkunde, Munich; s/n C; photograph by Gary Urton).

other factors local cord-keepers would have had to contend with. To address the question of how administrative information may have been gathered, synthesized, and recorded on cord accounts at a local level, I turn to the analysis of an important and highly complex sample, which is in the collections of the Museum für Völkerkunde, in Munich, Germany. The sample in question, which I will refer to here as UR28 (see Figure 9.7), is one of six samples tied together into what I term a "linked set." This set of samples was reportedly recovered from "grave robbers" (huaqueros) at Atarco, near Nazca, on the south coast of Peru. While some of the physical characteristics and organizational features that I will describe for UR28 are found in one or more of the other five samples in this linked set, I have space here only to discuss the one sample identified above.[19]

Sample UR28 is composed of seventy-four pendant cords made of final S-ply cotton threads. A dozen of the pendant cords bear one subsidiary cord each. The cords of UR28 are either light brown (AB) or medium brown (MB). At the most general level, this khipu is organized into three sections as defined by the following cord groupings: (1) cord #1, (2) cords #2–4, and (3) cords #5–74. The reader may follow my discussion of the organization of this khipu by viewing Figure 9.8.

Figure 9.8 is organized into three major *sets of columns*, as defined above, which are labeled (A), (B), (C). The left-most sub-column within each major set of columns shows the cord numbers, from #1 to #74 (the notation si that follows fourteen of the cords indicates a subsidiary attached to that cord). The next sub-column to the right (that is, within each major column set) shows the color of the cord, predominantly either AB or MB (several of the si cords in the lower part of the chart are color KB = "dark brown"). The next column to the right of the color notations displays the numerical values knotted into the respective cords. And finally, the right-most sub-column (appearing only in major column sets A and C) displays the sums of values recorded on groupings of cords in the sub-column(s) to the left.

What we find when we examine the organization of numerical and color values on sample UR28 is an arrangement that I would characterize as either the *summation* of set values from left to right and from bottom to top, or *repartition* (or subdivision) of set values from the top to the bottom and from right to left. That is, as we see, cord #1, an AB colored cord, carries the value 102; this same numerical value is the sum of the values knotted into cords #2–4 and their subsidiaries. The actual sums on the cord/subsidiary pairs of cords #2–4 are: 29/14, 13/10, and 12/24 (= 102). Note that the pendant cords are color AB, while the subsidiaries are color MB. What follows, in cords #5–74, is a complicated arrangement of various groupings of five-cord sets; some of these sets are what I would term "odd" five-cord sets, in that the cord number of the first cord of each of these five-cord sets is a value ending in 5 (that is, 5+15+25; 35+45; and 55+65). The cords of these "odd" type five-cord sets are all AB (light brown). In addition, there are what I term "even" five-cord sets; that is, ones the first cord of which has a cord number that is

[19] The full tabular descriptions for UR28 and the other samples in this linked set (that is, UR23, 24, 27, 28, 29, and 57) may be found in the Data Tables page of the Harvard University Khipu Database website.

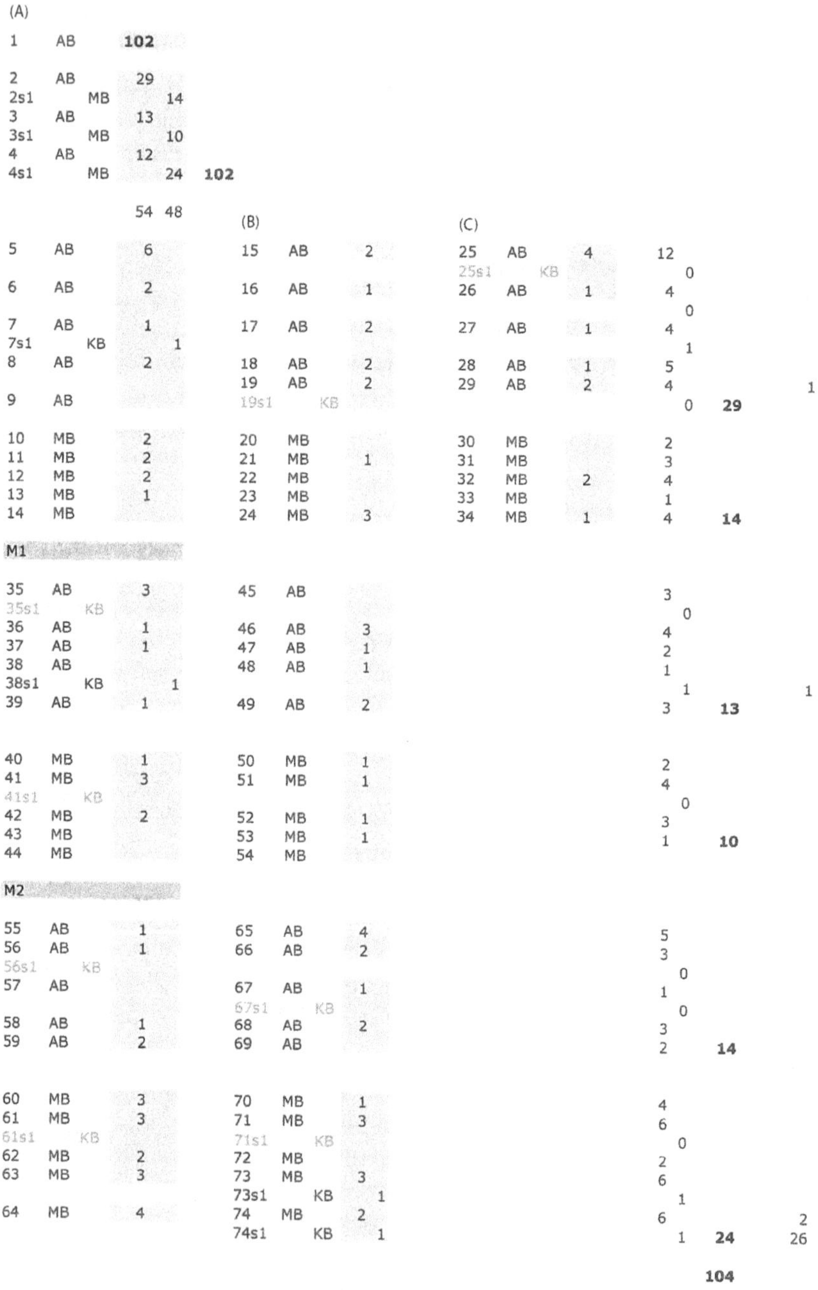
(A)
1 AB 102
2 AB 29
2s1 MB 14
3 AB 13
3s1 MB 10
4 AB 12
4s1 MB 24 102
54 48
(B)
(C)
5 AB 6
15 AB 2
25 AB 4 12
25s1 KB 0
6 AB 2
16 AB 1
26 AB 1 4
0
7 AB 1
17 AB 2
27 AB 1 4
7s1 KB 1
1
8 AB 2
18 AB 2
28 AB 1 5
19 AB 2
29 AB 2 4
1
9 AB
19s1 KB
0 29
10 MB 2
20 MB
30 MB 2
11 MB 2
21 MB 1
31 MB 3
12 MB 2
22 MB
32 MB 2 4
13 MB 1
23 MB
33 MB 1
14 MB
24 MB 3
34 MB 1 4 14
M1
35 AB 3
45 AB
3
35s1 KB
0
36 AB 1
46 AB 3
4
37 AB 1
47 AB 1
2
38 AB
48 AB 1
1
38s1 KB 1
1 1
39 AB 1
49 AB 2
3 13
40 MB 1
50 MB 1
2
41 MB 3
51 MB 1
4
41s1 KB
0
42 MB 2
52 MB 1
3
43 MB
53 MB 1
1 10
44 MB
54 MB
M2
55 AB 1
65 AB 4
5
56 AB 1
66 AB 2
3
56s1 KB
0
57 AB
67 AB 1
1
67s1 KB
0
58 AB 1
68 AB 2
3
59 AB 2
69 AB
2 14
60 MB 3
70 MB 1
4
61 MB 3
71 MB 3
6
61s1 KB
71s1 KB
0
62 MB 2
72 MB
2
63 MB 3
73 MB 3
6
73s1 KB 1
1
64 MB 4
74 MB 2
6 2
74s1 KB 1
1 24 26
104

Figure 9.8 Schematic diagram showing the organization of cords, colors, and numerical values in Khipu UR028.

an even decimal value, ending in 0 (that is, 10+20+30; 40+50; and 60+70). The cords of these "even" five-cord sets are all MB (medium brown).

Now, when we sum the values on the "odd" and "even" groupings of five-cord sets, as those groupings are defined above, we find that, with one exception (see below), the sums are equivalent to those appearing on either the pendant cords or the subsidiaries in cord positions #2–4. Specifically, the "odd"/AB five-cord set sums are equivalent to the values on pendant cords #2, 3, and 4, while the "even"/MB five-cord set sums are equivalent to the values on the subsidiaries of the above three cords (that is, #2s1, 3s1, and 4s1). It is clear that there is a recording error either on cord #4 (= 12) or on the two "odd" five-cord sets (55–9)+(65–9), which totals 14. I strongly suspect that the error is on the latter cord groupings, and that the intended sum of this latter pairing of "odd" five-cord sets should be 12 (as on cord #4), rather than 14. If we accept this explanation for where the error lies, we then note that the value 102, which is registered both on cord #1 and as the sum of values on cords #2–4, is replicated on the complex of "odd"/AB and "even"/MB five-cord groupings from cord #5 to cord #74.

In sum, khipu sample UR28 is a complex arrangement of bi-color (AB/MB) cords organized in different arrays of "odd"/"even" five-cord groupings whose numerical sum (102) is reproduced both on the cords and subsidiaries from cord #2–4, as well as on the first cord of this sample, #1. What can we surmise, or theorize, about what the use and significance of this khipu account might have been?

The first observation I would offer is that the numerical values registered on the five-cord sets strike me as similar in magnitude (that is, in the range 1–6, with an emphasis on the lower end of that range) to what I argued in an earlier paper[20] were census-type numerical values, particularly when what is displayed is not total household composition, but, rather, the number(s) of tributaries per household. In the case of khipu UR28, we could be looking at the count of tributaries within a number of ayllus, the clan-like social groupings. Specifically, I would interpret the six values on cords #2–4 and their subsidiaries (that is, the values 29/14, 13/10, and 12/24) as the tributary counts for six ayllu-like social groups in the area of Nazca. The total summary count, 102, is interesting in regard to census values, as well.

---

[20] Gary Urton, "Censos registrados de cordeles con 'Amarres': padrones problacionales pre-Hispánicos y colonials tempranos en los Khipus Inka," *Revista Andina* 42 (2006), 153–96.

Numerous Colonial Spanish sources[21] inform us that one of the principal groupings used to organize populations in the Inka state census was the pachaca (one-hundred), a group composed of 100 tributary (that is, corvée) laborers.

The above interpretation leaves us with the question of what could have been the meaning, or the sociopolitical organizational significance, of what appears to be a division of this (hypothetical) pachaca-sized census unit into two parts. This division is most apparent in the color difference between cords (that is, AB vs. MB) and in the distinction between odd and even five-cord sets. I would argue that here we are seeing the signing values used to identify a two-part moiety division of the pachaca. As we have seen, such dual groupings were exceedingly common in the Inka state. In most such instances, the two hierarchically related parts were referred to as Hanansaya (upper part) and Hurinsaya (lower part). I suggest that such a two-part sociopolitical moiety division was signed in khipu UR28 in three ways: (a) by color (AB/MB), (b) by the distinction between *pendant* cords vs. *subsidiary* cords, at cord positions #2–4, and (c) by the distinction between odd and even five-cord sets, at cord positions #5–74. In sum, I would argue that Figure 9.8 is a schematic representation of the moiety organization of six ayllus at Atarco, near Nazca, whose census was recorded on UR28.

It is interesting to note that the above interpretation may help explain why the summary cord (#1) in this sample is colored AB, rather than MB. That is, this would be explained on the principle of "encompassment,"[22] by which the dominant member of a ranked, asymmetrical pair stands for the two parts when they are represented as a single unit. Thus, when AB and MB are brought together within a single unit, the identity of that single unit is signed by the color identity of the dominant member of the pair – in this case, AB.

To the extent that the above interpretation of the numbers, colors, and odd/even distinctions among cord groups in sample UR28 might have combined to detail the organization and status relations among a group of six ayllus divided into moieties (as outlined in Figure 9.8), we could conclude that this khipu represents an instance of the organization of information by way of the linkage of signs for the numerical values and social

---

[21] Pärsinnen, *Tawantinsuyu*, pp. 381–9.
[22] Terence Turner, "Social Complexity and Recursive Hierarchy in Indigenous South American Societies," in Urton (ed.), "Structure, Knowledge, and Representation in the Andes," pp. 37–60.

types, or ethnocategories, making up a local population. Khipu UR28 represents the organization of local administrative information in an explicitly social register.

Summary and conclusions

We began this chapter by viewing a quotation from the chronicle of Cieza de León, in which he commented on the extraordinary efficiency and accuracy of the cord-recording system of the Inka Empire, the khipu. We asked the question at the beginning of this study of whether or not, in studying extant samples in collections around the world, we could find evidence that would confirm Cieza's observations on the accuracy and efficiency of Inka cord-keeping. I believe we have succeeded in demonstrating complexity in Inka administrative accounting from the level of state accounting (in the ceque system) in the capital, in provincial accounting (in the Puruchuco accounting hierarchy), and in local accounting (in the khipu sample from Atarco, Nazca).

The various examples discussed in this study suggest several features of khipu-based administrative accounting. First, khipu records employed the full range of structural and visual variability that characterizes these devices (for example, cord and knot construction, attachment, color, grouping of cords by spacing and color). Second, there is no particular form of encoding used in any one of our samples that seems to be beyond, or radically at odds with, that found on the other samples. This suggests that there was a relatively high degree of conventionality of cord manipulation from the bottom to the top of the administrative/recording hierarchy. And third, in its structural and organizational properties, the khipu appears to have been perfectly suited to recording information deriving from sociopolitical structures grounded in complementary dual organization and hierarchical segmentary organization. In short, the khipu was perfectly adapted to the encoding of administrative information in the Inka state.

It is to be hoped that future studies will direct additional light onto the practices, technologies, and systems of knowledge that sustained this extraordinary system of three-dimensional, cord-based accounting of ancient South America.

FURTHER READINGS

Bauer, Brian S., *Ancient Cuzco: Heartland of the Inca*, Austin: University of Texas Press, 2004.
Brundage, Burr Cartwright, *Lords of Cuzco: A History and Description of the Inca People in Their Final Days*, Norman: University of Oklahoma Press, 1967.

Covey, R. Alan, *How the Incas Built Their Heartland: State Formation and the Innovation of Imperial Strategies in the Sacred Valley, Peru*, Ann Arbor: University of Michigan Press, 2006.

"Inka Administration of the Far South Coast of Peru," *Latin American Antiquity* 11 (2000), 119–38.

D'Altroy, Terence N., *The Incas*, Malden, MA: Blackwell Publishers, 2002.

Provincial Power in the Inka Empire, Washington, D.C.: Smithsonian Institution Press, 1992.

Julien, Catherine J., "Inca Decimal Administration in the Lake Titicaca Region," in George C. Collier, Renato I. Rosaldo, and John D. Wirth (eds.), *The Inca and Aztec States, 1400–1800: Anthropology and History*, New York: Academic Press, 1982, pp. 119–51.

Malpass, Michael A., *Provincial Inca: Archaeological and Ethnohistorical Assessment of the Impact of the Inca State*, Iowa City: University of Iowa Press, 1993.

McEwan, Gordon, *The Incas: New Perspectives*, New York: W.W. Norton & Company, 2006.

Morris, Craig, and Adriana von Hagen, *The Incas*, London: Thames & Hudson, Ltd., 2011.

Silverblatt, Irene, "Imperial Dilemmas, the Politics of Kinship, and Inca Reconstructions of History," *Comparative Studies in Society and History* 30 (1988), 83–102.

Von Hagen, Adriana, and Craig Morris, *The Cities of the Ancient Andes*, New York: Thames & Hudson, Ltd., 1998.

Writing and record-keeping in early cities

DANNY LAW, WANG HAICHENG,
HANS J. NISSEN AND GARY URTON

Writing and other technologies for enhancing human memory and the reach of communication seem, in many instances in the ancient world, to have a special relationship with the rise of ancient urban centers. Early cities were large, socially stratified conglomerates of peoples, often with distinct and even competing histories, priorities, and ethnic affiliations, which nevertheless all formed parts of complex, hierarchical political systems. Craft specialization meant that people could do more with their labor than ever before but were also more dependent on a growing, varied set of other specialists. With such a diverse body, and an increasing reliance on collaboration, creating and maintaining common and consistent modes of measurement, behavior, and meaning were essential to the functioning of cities.

Ancient cities could not operate without some sort of common system of representation to connect and allow coordination among disparate groups, which they normally realized under the stewardship of an administrative bureaucracy. At some point in the gathering and ordering of people in cities, the logistical and administrative coordination required by the close proximity of so many interdependent people also must have outstripped the human mnemonic capacity, producing a demand for an additional specialization, record-keeping, to track and direct the flow of people and resources that made up and provisioned the city. With the emergence of cities, hierarchy and control had become fixed and elaborated. This required institutions responsible for marking distinctions and for surveillance. The greater size and density of urban populations (in comparison with those of villages), and, arguably, the increased technical specialization that cities made possible meant that more potential inventors were around to find solutions meeting these needs, while inter-city connections facilitated the diffusion of these solutions to other places with similar needs.

Writing, in the context of the emerging needs of major cities, was an invention of immediate value that seems to have originated independently in a relatively few places in the Old and New Worlds, all of which were urban centers, and then was adopted rapidly by many other contemporary and later cities. But not all major cities had writing and the precise way that writing evolved and was deployed across the ancient world differs greatly depending on where we look. In this chapter, we will compare the diverse instances, presented in the preceding chapters, in which writing and other forms of record-keeping developed apparently in close coordination with burgeoning cities. Cases from China, Mesopotamia, the Andes, and Mesoamerica show that responses to the challenges and possibilities that emerged because of urbanization are almost as numerous as the cases investigated. In spite of the variation, parallels do emerge. These similarities, across so many contexts, provide a better picture of some of the less visible changes to society through the urban revolution, as well as the social nature of writing and other systematic forms of representation and record-keeping.

Types of communicative technologies

The cases surveyed in the preceding chapters provide a rich sample of the diversity of technologies for recording and communicating in early cities. Before we can compare these ancient cities, however, it is important to establish exactly what the object of study is. How we define both writing and record-keeping more generally reflects our understanding not only of the material forms and symbolic meanings involved, but what those forms were used for. Written records, any kind that uses a tangible medium to register information, have two important qualities to bear in mind in our comparison of these technologies across the ancient world. Writing is not the only human solution to the need to store and communicate information. Humans innately have a finite, if large, capacity to store information and are wired for supple language to communicate that store of information to others. Early communicative technologies accomplished a sub-set of the work of both human memory and spoken languages. Unlike human memory, however, tangible records were external to the individual. They could be witnessed by multiple individuals simultaneously. They could be inspected and verified. Unlike spoken language, written records were also durable. They could move beyond their immediate place of production and, depending on the medium used, last far longer than the evanescent spoken word.

Writing and other forms of durable, external communication are not, however, independent of individual memory nor spoken language.

Portraying writing as language in visible form does not allow us to discuss the differences between diverse technologies, from Maya hieroglyphs, Inkan khipus, Late Uruk cuneiform writing, and earlier Mesopotamian seals. Recording technologies rely on the memory and shared understanding of both author and recipient, since in order to be effective, a record must make use of appropriate forms, and the recipient must know the proper interpretation of those forms. Ethnography and common sense tell us that the life of objects and the life of people are tightly entangled: a wedding ring, a stuffed animal, a picture of a family reunion … Each object is a memory aid, embodying a piece of memory to somebody. They become a sign, a representation of something else. But in many cases, these "aides-mémoires" are idiosyncratic. They only mean something to their maker because of that person's unique lived experience. While an object or sign might help that individual recall something that would otherwise be difficult to retrieve, anyone else confronted with these idiosyncratic signs would be unable to recover the original meaning assigned to them by their maker. In order for a sign to be communicative, that is, to express information not already known by the interpreter, it needs to have a shared, socially circulated value or meaning, one that anybody initiated into the use of that particular sign would recognize. In other words, the forms used to record information must be conventional within a certain group of people.

But the utility of a single sign is limited. The more signs with socially circulated values, the greater flexibility in communication and the less the need for contextual cues, as strings of signs provide context for one another. A set of signs that follows the same rules of use, modality, and social function produces a communicative system, one that can be used, among other things, to encode historical, logistical, administrative, or ritual messages in such a way that the information can be retrieved at a later point by anyone initiated into the rules of the system. The message does not need to be known in advance, only the system of representation. Spoken language is the universal example of this. But all of the ancient record-keeping and communicative technologies discussed here are also examples, though they differ substantially in their relationship to spoken language. Recording systems such as early cuneiform (Chapter 6) and khipu (Chapter 9) use conventionalized marks, or what we could term "markers" (in the case of the khipu), but are not necessarily bound to a particular language. The oracle bone inscriptions in Shang China (Chapter 7) and Maya hieroglyphs (Chapter 8) are capable of communicating exact graphical transcriptions of spoken language. A system that represents spoken language has the advantage of allowing people to communicate with that system anything that they are capable of talking about. However, that flexibility comes at a cost, as messages will often need to be quite lengthy and they will be unavailable to individuals who do not speak the language in question. Other forms of representing information, by restricting the semantic range of the system, are able to communicate certain types of information much more efficiently. Thus the color of a cord or a particular type of knot in the khipu system can communicate information to the initiated in a "semasiographic" modality in a manner that would likely require many words, if not paragraphs, to adequately describe in language. If a set of symbols can only indicate the name of an individual, as seems to be the case with seals in Uruk, the cost of interpreting that sign is greatly lessened, since use of that particular system itself provides us a great deal of interpretive information. The same is true for systems of numeration and quantification, both in Mesopotamia and in the Maya area. The latter case helps emphasize the fact that different types of communicative systems often coexist in a society, since each system is best suited for different functions within that society.

It is difficult to compare the communicative technologies that emerged in the context of ancient cities in different parts of the world. The comparison is hampered, in the first place, by the clear lacunae in the surviving corpus, particularly from China and Mesoamerica. These ancient writing systems seem, from the surviving record, to stride onto the scene fully formed with the purpose of recording the complexity of spoken language. In the chapter on Maya writing, Law suggests that the precursor to Maya writing, or at least a crucial element in the context of its initial innovation, was a rich and highly conventionalized iconographic tradition in which cosmological meanings were central.

In the Andean case, a wide range of technologies had for millennia been based on the construction of various configurations of spun and plied cords; therefore the ancient Andeans seem to have naturally turned to the possibilities offered by the cord medium (for example, construction variation, thickness, color, various topological configurations such as knots and attachments). Inkan khipus are not obviously connected to spoken language, and would only have been interpretable within certain carefully defined parameters, such as the management of tribute and corvée labor forces. Thus, we may say that when facing the need to devise a record-keeping system, a society will first turn to media that are readily available and familiar from existing technologies; later systems may innovate on the original medium and if existing media do not offer sufficient flexibility and variability to achieve the level of signing required, a new medium may be chosen.

A good example of the invention of a new medium for records is the invention of paper in early imperial China, which gradually replaced the use of wood and bamboo slips that had been the dominant writing surface during the Bronze Age. Like clay in Mesopotamia and cord in the Andes, wood and bamboo were cheap and readily available materials that had been used for various purposes (building, carpentry, basket-weaving, etc.) millennia before the rise of early cities; some early and middle Neolithic fragments have survived to this day under waterlogged conditions. The use of a brush in Neolithic times can likewise be ascertained by examining the exquisitely painted pottery; the calligraphic lines on bronze decorations suggest that the skillful wielding of the brush was continued into the Bronze Age. It is not surprising, therefore, that wood and bamboo were chosen as the media for record-keeping, not just used as a surface to convey brushed marks, but also made into calculi, comparable to the use of clay tokens and cotton or camelid fibers to count things in Mesopotamia and the Andes, respectively. Although the earliest extant bamboo slips are only dated to the fifth century BCE, their use at Anyang since the twelfth century is confirmed both by a character depicting an actual book (made of slips bundled together by cords), and by some bronze inscriptions, the peculiar columnar format of which strongly suggests that they were modeled on individual slips. One scholar[1] suggests that the characters for numerals in the oracle bone inscriptions originated from the different arrangement of bamboo calculi on a flat surface, echoing Schmandt-Besserat's[2] theory on the origin of cuneiform numerals in the shape of token impressions.

In Mesopotamia, on the other hand, surviving materials show that strategies of record-keeping run the range from counting tokens and owner seals with a very limited range of meaning to cuneiform texts clearly based on spoken language. The counters and stamp seals were only able to denote simple numbers of goods or a sealing individual. It isn't until the middle of the Late Uruk period (Uruk Level VI) that we begin to find artifacts that were able to store both pieces of information in the same mode. It has not been possible to identify the language behind the earliest texts. Yet even those clearly linguistically based writings were

---

[1] Ge Yinghui, "Shu Ben Miao Hu shuzheng," *Gudai wenming* 1 (2002), 284–9.
[2] Denise Schmandt-Besserat, *Before Writing: From Counting to Cuneiform* (Austin: University of Texas Press, 1992), Vol. 1, p. 193.

not used to directly capture speech, but instead employed a truncated style of expression, serving as aides-mémoires.

Each of these types of communication technology has strengths and weaknesses that have consequences for the kinds of functions to which they could be put in early cities. In the next section, we will turn to a comparison of these diverse functions, and how those functions appear to have changed over the centuries and millennia.

Functions

The functions to which information technologies were put in early cities run the gamut from economic administration to the performance and commemoration of ritual. A functional description of these different systems must necessarily attend to the trajectory of development: for what purpose was the technology originally developed, and to what purposes was the technology later applied? In truth, of the cases surveyed here, only the Mesopotamian context has direct data to support a reasonably complete sequence of development. To generate hypotheses about the purpose of the initial invention of writing or other information technologies in China, Mesoamerica, or the Andes, inferences must be made from other documented cases (Mesopotamia), or from the functional domains of use apparent in the surviving material record. Here we will focus on three salient functions, economic administration, accounting, and ritual, and what these case studies suggest about how these relate to the development of writing around the world.

Economic administration

By far the most widely proposed functional reason for developing writing or other information technologies was to facilitate the economic administration of large communities. When Uruk first grew to the size of a city, people could avail themselves only of seals to leave personal marks on the surface of clay fasteners, and clay tokens of different shapes used to denote numbers. These technologies allowed for the recording of quantity, type, and ownership of goods, but the limited number of types in the sign repertoire and the inefficiency of this method for dealing with large numbers of objects, as well as the growing demands of an ever increasing economic administration, led to attempts to increase the range of storeable information types. In Uruk, incremental advances in these technologies of accounting and administration are attested archaeologically: sealed clay bullae with tokens inside; sealed clay tablets with numerical indentations. Only after a considerable time did the first system of writing emerge as a tool. Cuneiform offered a relatively economical method to store as many pieces of information as were desired. However, as an extension of the former methods, it would be hard to make the case that writing was intended to represent language from the onset. That it did so to a degree was secondary to the quest for greater expressive range in records.

Because of a relatively complete sequence of development found at Uruk, and its clear administrative and accounting function, from the beginning, scholars often assume that economic administration, control and monitoring of flows of goods and services throughout a city would be the impetus for all of these advanced record-keeping technologies. Nevertheless, it is important to note that aside from Mesopotamia, there is precious little direct evidence for the actual trajectory of development. Early cuneiform at Uruk, as with Inkan khipus, was first and foremost a way to aid in accounting and economic administration, both of goods and of labor. They were records of the flow of goods and people involved in transactions. Writing is used in the beginning to denote only those items that are deemed necessary to reconstruct a certain transaction. The origin of the goods is never mentioned, presumably because it would have been obvious background knowledge. At the time, these inscriptions recorded and monitored goods entering or leaving the central store.

At Uruk some major administrative tasks that were covered by documents include land survey, calculating the amount of seed and distributing it to each field, and feeding the laborers. Animal husbandry was another important set of activities that needed to be controlled. The tablets gave a superior and clear sense of the amount and whereabouts of goods and manpower. This knowledge would allow the decision-makers to allocate them accordingly. In other words, the tablets served budgeting purposes. The contents of the tablets leave no doubt that redistribution played an important role in the city's economy – the provision of city dwellers has always been a real and day-to-day concern and it goes without saying that redistribution must have involved a certain degree of advance planning. At Uruk the building of monumental architecture and the production of elite objects would have been inconceivable without budgeting the city's resources.

The central institutions at both Uruk (in the Eanna precinct) and Cuzco seem to have had extensive control over the economic transactions within the city and its hinterland. They allocated large tracts of land to various officials and organized labor forces, presumably to work in the fields and for public projects such as digging canals and building roads. The khipu accounts generated at Cuzco must have served similar budgeting functions, enabling the Inka and his royal counsel to move goods and corvée labor along their famed highway system, which in itself was a superb example of central planning. The provincial governor (Tocricoc) gathered the summation of figures from the provincial level, which in turn were summations of data from the local level. The knowledge needed for the state budget had to be very abstract and drastically simplified, consisting mainly of numbers in various categories.

In China and the Maya Lowlands, however, there is virtually no direct evidence of surviving early texts that were explicitly used for accounting or economic administration. Palace scenes painted on polychrome ceramic vessels and wall murals from the Maya Late Classic period (600–900 CE) show bundles of goods with hieroglyphic labels of quantity and type (8,000 cacao beans, for example), suggesting that writing was used among the Classic Maya for economic administration of some degree, but no direct evidence of such uses in earlier periods exists. In the absence of direct data, we can only infer their existence, since the need in these early cities would have existed, and the technology would have certainly allowed for the production of such records; therefore, it is very likely that writing was used from early on in both China and the Maya Lowlands for economic administration.

Accountability

One important function of the khipu at Cuzco and other Inka cities and administrative centers is that the technology also served as proof of the official's fulfilment of his duty to execute and document the administrative task so ordered by his superior. Both actual khipu samples and early Colonial documents suggest that the khipu system was itself one of checks and balances. Under the principle of dual organization, the cord-keeper of one moiety could point to a khipu and declare it recorded the truth about his moiety, but his counterpart in the other moiety kept his own copy of statistics regarding the first moiety, and vice versa. If the two copies did not match, then something was wrong. It was a strategy of group surveillance, but it also guarded against individual administrators' mistakes or malfeasance.

Administration is a marked form of control. It creates accountability, which invites explicit accounting practices that record the administrative tasks generated by the system. Most of the early cuneiform administrative tablets and the khipus list the exact number of a certain material or labor, leaving no doubt that the liability for materials or labor involved in the task was of great concern to the central institutions. But whose liability was incurred: the institution's, a specific office's, or an individual's? In the Near East a time-honored way to record individual liability was with glyphic seals whose impressions on clay identify the individuals or the responsible parties involved in economic transactions. Some early cuneiform tablets were sealed, but they seem to have been exceptional. Some officials' names can be identified, but again they seem to have been rare. However, considering that the proto-cuneiform texts span a time of 200 to 300 years, and that some of these give evidence of daily account-making, the overall number of close to 6,000 is only a fraction of what once must have been written. It is very likely that we are missing entire thematic groups.

A similar concern with accountability can be seen in Shang China on some narrative inscriptions on the interior of ritual bronzes, inscriptions that would have been much easier for the ancestral spirits to access than for a living audience, especially when the vessels were filled with food or wine. These inscriptions usually state that a court official was rewarded for some deeds so he cast a bronze for his ancestor so-and-so: "On the day *guisi* the king awarded the Xiao Chen Yi ten strings of cowries, which he used to make this sacred vessel for Mu Gui. It was in the king's sixth *si*, during the *yong* cycle, in the fourth month."[3] This is a written report. It has a list consisting of numbers and names, reminiscent of the administrative lists at Uruk and the information recorded in khipus at Cuzco. But the narrative content of this report would be hard to derive from the highly circumscribed spreadsheet-like systems for describing quantities and categories used in those places. Oral narrations during the ancestral ritual would be one way to make this report, but these would be ephemeral. Full writing that was attached to language made possible communication across time and space.

The mate to a written report from the subordinate to the superior is a written authorization from above. The oracle bone inscriptions sometimes specify the source of authorization for certain actions (for example, plowing and harvesting) with a complete sentence: "The king orders/commands so-and-so to carry out such-and-such a task." The king might worry about the accuracy of oral transmissions, but his officials are perhaps more anxious to

[3] Most of the lengthy Shang bronze inscriptions, including the present one, are collected in Robert Bagley, *Shang Ritual Bronzes in the Arthur M. Sackler Collections* (Cambridge, MA: Harvard University Press, 1987), pp. 525–31.

have a written instruction in order to protect themselves in the future. In short, the pair of authorization and reporting in writing constituted another aspect of accountability. Unlike proto- and early cuneiform and khipu records, these texts from Anyang could be classified as letters of a sort, written to communicate without relying on the unreliability of oral commentaries. Because administrative documents were almost certainly written on perishable materials like wood and bamboo, we will probably never find them. Only after writing came to be used for display does archaeology begin to find traces of it.

Ritual activity

The straightforward logistical accounting that dominates khipus and early cuneiform inscriptions is essentially absent from both Chinese and Mesoamerican texts. Some of the divination texts at Anyang show characteristics of both display and administration. Likewise, while the subject matter of many Maya hieroglyphic texts is commemorating ritual activities, in another sense they are a statement of fulfilment of ritual obligations – a type of ritual accounting.[4] As John Baines has pointed out, display and administration are not mutually exclusive functions.[5] The manner in which a text is displayed is related to its anticipated and intended audience. Magistrates in many societies have been accountable to both human and divine interlocutors, and the need to provide an account, in these cases, through writing, unifies logistical administration and ritual activity.

Like the Preclassic Maya inscriptions, the size of the Chinese characters meant for display on the oracle bones is diminutive, visible only at close range. The audience for actual physical inspection of this display therefore must have been small, consisting of the inner elite around the royalty and the diviners. Though not public, the texts still constitute a report of activities, suggesting close monitoring and control, whether by man or deity. Although writing was not part of the divination process at Anyang, and hence not essential in communicating with the royal ancestors, royal ancestors were nevertheless part of the intended audience of the divination texts, as can be deduced from the fact that the bones were almost exclusively

---

[4] David Stuart and Danny Law, "Testimony, Oration and Dynastic Memory in the Monuments of Copan," paper presented at the 15th Annual European Maya Conference, Madrid, Spain, 2010.

[5] John Baines, "The Earliest Egyptian Writing: Development, Context, Purpose," in Stephen D. Houston (ed.), *The First Writing: Script Invention as History and Process* (Cambridge: Cambridge University Press, 2004), p. 151.

buried in the royal precinct, close to the ancestral temples. After a period of accumulation above ground these bones would be buried in large pits, reminiscent of the disposition of sacrificial animals and humans outside the ancestral temple. At Anyang one royal duty was to consult divine intentions on matters concerning the dynasty's rule. The display of the medium of divination, sometimes inscribed with the divined questions and outcomes, was possibly intended as a proof of the discharge of this royal duty. This suggests an administrative concern, namely accountability, especially toward the ancestors.

Most of the early Mesoamerican writings, including the dozen or so Preclassic Maya texts, seem to have used grammar and syntax of an actual language to express narrative contents, to judge from their length, linearity, and iconographic context. Some Preclassic texts perhaps include a mixture of logographs, syllables, and dates (including several concurrent calendar cycles, which in turn were composed of numbers and logographs for days/months). The carriers of these texts were of various types: wall murals, stone stelae, and portable objects usually made of precious stone. The latter two types have lost their original contexts, while wall murals seem to have existed mainly in temple buildings or pyramids, often as part of larger ritual architectural complexes constructed in accordance with Maya ritual and cosmology. These complexes arguably marked the creation of the city as a moral community, under the leadership of the king, whose duty was to perpetuate cosmological structures and operations.[6] Although the early texts on these murals remain mostly undeciphered, they do have a recognizable glyph for "king" *ajaw*, associated with depictions of ancient royalty. This, as well as the sacred setting of these murals, seems to suggest that their contents and purpose were closely related to Maya kingship and cosmology.

Since the setting for these texts was explicitly private, secret, and elite, public display does not seem to have been a major function of writing at this stage, in contrast with later, Classic period texts. The tiny scale of the Preclassic Maya texts, even on monumental murals, suggests an expectation of close and careful study of the text by a small and privileged audience. The absence of monumentalism in these Preclassic texts, in contrast with the large figural scenes that they accompany, indicates that the placement of glyphs on monuments was intended to caption pictures, a function

---

[6] David Stuart, "Ideology and Classic Maya Kingship," in Vernon L. Scarborough (ed.), *A Catalyst for Ideas: Anthropological Archaeology and the Legacy of Douglas Schwartz* (Santa Fe, NM: School of American Research Press, 2005), p. 269.

continued into the Classic period, by which time the scale of the glyphs had been enlarged to be proportional to the image. The glyphs could be names of gods and people, just as they are on inscribed objects of the Classic period. Some early texts on portable objects appear to be essentially lists of nouns, in a sense similar to the lists found in Uruk. Yet the nature of the recorded nouns is different. In early cuneiform it is the names of commodities that dominate, with only a few attested personal names. The reverse seems to be true in Preclassic Maya texts. Lists of deities occur on small portable objects with intrinsic value, perhaps as a means to identify their ownership, or to solicit godly invocations, or to provide incantatory cues for those reading the names. Names of real persons on small objects probably served as name-tags to label the owners or makers.[7]

The preoccupation with names of deities and powerful people in Maya writing, and their function as labels of images, betray an elite obsession with cosmological symbols and a fetishization of images and written names. This was the Maya's response to a human drive to represent the world around us and at the same time to create that world through representation. The act of naming is one manifestation of that impulse. Names have an intellectual or psychological importance that is well summed up by the Egyptologist Barry Kemp: "[T]o the ancients knowing the name of a thing made it familiar, gave it a place in one's mind, reduced it to something that was manageable and could be fitted into one's mental universe."[8] Graphical recording systems were devised to store and retrieve information across space and time very early on in human history. But it was not simply a desire to overcome bodily limitations of memory, time, and distance that prompted people to devise these systems. Through devising and using these systems people sought to capture the world. The compilation of lexical lists at Uruk, the veneration of a written king list at Anyang and the Maya Lowlands (as well as in Eygpt), and the census data at Cuzco were all attempts to represent elements of the universe. One main difference between them and the Maya case is that in the former the emphasis of representation seems to have been to attain intellectual control over man's immediate environment, the more mundane aspects of the universe, including both material and human resources, while in the latter the Maya seem to have been chiefly interested in the more spiritual aspect, seeking to connect the human world with cosmological power. Perhaps it is telling to recall that at

---

[7] Stuart, "Ideology and Classic Maya Kingship," p. 304.
[8] Barry Kemp, *Ancient Egypt: Anatomy of a Civilization* (London: Routledge, 2006), p. 71.

Uruk there was a list of professions in hierarchical order but no list of gods, in contrast to the situation in Maya cities.

Another difference between writing in Mesopotamia and Mesoamerica is that writing was not used to caption divine and royal figures on valuable objects from Uruk (though this did happen after the Uruk period), but for the Maya to write on a surface was to create objects of value in their own right. The content and the artistic quality of Maya writing, together with the expensive materials and the religious contexts, all made the inscribed objects into valued and powerful goods. In this respect inscribed Shang bronzes and jades from Anyang are comparable examples. But if an object's value is increased by the addition of an inscription, there has to be a commonly accepted recognition that writing, especially beautiful writing, is valuable. The only social mechanism to bring out this recognition is to create a script community, the members of which would accord great value to the thing that binds them together. Such communities must have existed in all cities employing graphical recording systems for communication, because communication depends on signs with shared meanings. Thinking in concrete terms, there must have been some sort of supporting infrastructure to perpetuate, mediate, and legitimize these systems of communication. This supporting infrastructure – schools, institutional supports, and the like – is the subject of our next section.

Supporting infrastructure

Training is indispensable if a record-keeping system is to be kept alive and functional. In Mesopotamia, pre-writing systems such as different kinds of seals, tokens, and their combinations were already complex enough to require established methods to transfer them, along with other skills, like measuring fields or performing mathematics. The literate civilizations in Mesopotamia, Egypt, China, and Mesoamerica all have a long history of script use – in the first three cases more than 3,000 years – so they clearly had effective means for teaching the scribal art. The Mesoamerican and Andean civilizations established schools to teach young students other ways of storing and communicating information. The training of scribes involves several interlocking key factors: a teaching place – a school in the physical sense; a curriculum – procedural and conceptual knowledge to be imparted; institutional or private sponsorship; sources of teachers and students; the logistics of running the school; and the occupations for which the students are being prepared. In many cases, the details of these important institutions and practices are not present in the surviving material record, though in all cases some inferences can be made.

Of particular interest for understanding scribal training at Uruk is the presence of so-called lexical lists: lists of words and phrases, arranged according to semantic groups. In certain erudite circles, attempts to control their universe had led to lists of names, which during the invention of writing served as guidelines for setting up the system. These lists were faithfully copied in large quantities over a period of more than a thousand years and held in high esteem because of their role in the initial process. Lists account for about 10 percent of the total extant archaic cuneiform tablets; the rest are administrative texts. There are no letters, legal documents, or literary works. This distribution of contents suggests that in the earliest phase of script development in Mesopotamia, the simple word lists used for scribal training were indispensable, in addition to learning the system of administrative control, and not other genres of writing featuring connected discourse.[9]

Another important point is that the curriculum of early schools would have involved training in a variety of other skills to be mastered by the scribes: the making of tablets, the layouts of the different tablet formats, book-keeping procedures, mathematics, history, mythology, and in some cases ritual practice. In early texts from Uruk, information about the relationships between entries and groups of entries in an administrative tablet is coded in a bewildering array of sub-cases, sub-columns, and varying column widths. Numbers make up a large part of the content in the archaic tablets. Unlike later Mesopotamian arithmetical practice, which principally employed the sexagesimal system regardless of the objects that were to be qualified, archaic book-keeping has several numerical systems that were used for different objects: the bisexagesimal system, the grain capacity system, the area system, and other systems that are still poorly understood. There were also derived systems for time-keeping and measurement.[10] The choice of a specific numerical system roughly corresponded to the bureaucratic division (land surveyor, tax collector, etc.). It is possible that individual scribes needed only to learn one system specific to their office. These non-grammatical and non-syntactical devices for encoding information were

[9] Robert Englund, "Texts from the Late Uruk Period," in Joseph Bauer, Robert Englund, and Manfred Krebernik (eds.), *Mesopotamien: Späturuk-Zeit und Frühdynastische Zeit* (Freiburg: Universitäts-Verlag, 1998), p. 90.
[10] Englund, "Texts from the Late Uruk Period," p. 111.

developed centuries before grammatical and syntactical elements appeared.[11] Connected discourse was not the stimulus for the invention of early cuneiform; ledgers then as now did not need complete sentences.

Several oracle bone inscriptions at Anyang contain a character that has been transcribed as *xue*, which in later classical Chinese has three basic meanings: (1) school; (2) to teach; (3) to learn. One fragment of an inscription mentions the approval of a proposal to build a *xue*, possibly within the Shang royal residence. Besides court schools there seem to have existed schools located outside the royal household. One inscription reads, "Crack-making on the day *bingzi*, divining: '[Should] the Many Children go to school? Will it not rain on their way home?'" A similar divination was made on the next day. Still another inscription seems to imply that noblemen or their children from other polities were "taught and admonished" in the Shang capital. Could these children be political hostages who nevertheless received education in court schools, like the ones in the Inka Empire (see below)?

The oracle bone inscriptions tell us little about what was taught in the schools. Some inscriptions mention learning ritual dance and music, but not necessarily in schools. No compelling evidence for literacy schooling at Anyang exists – apart from the conclusive evidence of literacy itself. A character written with brush and ink on a disused potsherd is at present one of the few direct witnesses of writing practice, and it is far too skillfully executed to have been done by a beginner. That Mesopotamian pupils spent much time practicing simple wedges and their combinations reminds us that Chinese beginners likewise have always had to start from basic strokes and then proceed to simple characters, adhering to a strict stroke order. Unfortunately no student exercise containing only basic strokes is extant from Shang times.

Ethnohistorical records provide more detail about education and training in the Inka Empire. Inka rulers certainly gave serious attention to the education of both the male and female members of the nobility. Lower-ranking women were trained to weave, cook, and brew for the state; higher-ranking women additionally were instructed in religious matters. Important provincial nobles were required to send their sons and close relatives to the court in Cuzco at the age of fourteen or fifteen years. Together with the

---

[11] The best introduction to the meta-script information contained in the archaic tablets is Margaret Green, "The Construction and Implementation of the Cuneiform Writing System," *Visible Language* 15 (1981), 345–72, esp. pp. 349–56. See also Margaret Green, "Early Cuneiform," in Wayne M. Senner (ed.), *The Origins of Writing* (Lincoln: University of Nebraska Press, 1989), pp. 52–4.

sons of Inka nobles they attended *yachawasi*, special schools run by learned men (*amautakuna*) who were also noblemen. Among the school children in the court schools were the eldest sons of the most important provincial nobles. They were hostages for their fathers' loyalty and second-generation nobles-in-training at the same time.

A later writer, Martín de Murúa,[12] informs us that the length of study at the court schools was four years. He gives us an outline of the curriculum organized by year. It included not only the chief subject – the court version of the Inka language – but also Inka rituals and calendrics, khipu record-keeping, Inka history, law, statecraft, military tactics, and behavior appropriate to the students' social class. Although Murúa's account is suspiciously Europeanized, the subjects taught do not conflict with those listed by earlier writers. However, it is not clear what kinds of khipu record-keeping were taught to what kinds of student at school. Other accounts seem to suggest that there was a specialist group of "khipu makers" (*khipukamayuq*). How they transmitted the knowledge of reading a khipu is not recorded by the Colonial chroniclers. A seventeenth-century friar, Antonio de la Calancha, left us the only general account about studying khipus. But we are not even sure whether the "khipu makers" actually made the khipus or simply read them.

> whether because of the privileges with which they honored the office, or because if they did not give a good accounting concerning that on which they were questioned they would be severely castigated, they [the khipu-kamayuq] continually studied the signs, ciphers, and relations, teaching them to those who would succeed them in office, and there were many of these Secretaries, each of whom was assigned his particular class of material, having to suit [or fit] the story, tale, or song to the knots of which they served as indices, and points of "site memory."[13]

In contrast to the sparse accounts of the learning of record-keeping, there are numerous reports that the Inka rulers ordered all their subordinates to learn the Inka lingua franca – Quechua. The order recognized the problem of heteroglossia in the vast empire and solved it in a way that was simple and consistent with the state ideology, making one language official and

---

[12] John Rowe, "Inca Policies and Institutions Relating to the Cultural Unification of the Empire," in George A. Collier, Renato I. Rosaldo, and John D. Wirth (eds.), *The Inca and Aztec States 1400–1800: Anthropology and History* (New York: Academic Press, 1982), p. 95.

[13] After Gary Urton, *Signs of the Inka Khipu* (Austin: University of Texas Press, 2003), p. 122.

requiring its use. To make such an order effective the Inka rulers must have required the establishment of local schools to educate the sub-elite. But we are ignorant of details, such as who had the right or obligation to go to the local schools. It is clear that the recruitment policy for the court schools recognized the authority of the local nobles. In the meantime by educating (and indoctrinating) the sons of the local and provincial nobility, the court sought to secure the loyalty of local and regional administrators, because it was the sons who attended the Inka court schools who would succeed to their fathers' offices, not their siblings who were not educated in the capital. Inka control of the provinces was further strengthened by the authority of governors appointed directly by the Inka rulers.

Little is known about scribal training in the ancient Maya tradition. There is a term "houses of writing" (ts'ibal na:h) in Classical Mayan, which, like the Sumerian "tablet house" or Egyptian "room of teaching" or "house of life," might refer to scribal schools. Several architectural structures, at Copan and elsewhere, have been identified as houses of writing, both because of texts and iconography on the structures themselves, and, more unusually, because of the discovery of remains of scribal paraphernalia (inkwells, mortar and pestle for grinding pigments), as identified by Takeshi Inomata at the Late Classic site of Aguateca.[14] There are only a few texts that can be compared to the pedagogical lists of Mesopotamia and Egypt. A glyph band carved on stone blocks on a "house of writing" at Chichén Itzá pairs glyphs that share a vowel but differ in their consonants. This is similar in some ways to the tu-ta-ti syllabic list from Mesopotamia, and, as Stephen Houston has suggested, may well represent a Maya syllabic primer.[15] A more recent discovery of astronomical tables painted on the walls of a structure at Xultun, Guatemala, may have been used for pedagogical purposes, as well as reference for experienced scribes responsible for performing complex astronomical calculations regarding the movement of the Moon, Venus, and Mars. Unlike the Mesopotamian list, which comes to us through student exercises on clay tablets, the Maya examples are permanent fixtures carved on stone or painted in a room. They perhaps functioned as a permanent and canonical model for students to copy on perishable bark and palm leaves. Alternatively it might just be a sort of display announcing

[14] Takeshi Inomata and Laura R. Stiver, "Floor Assemblages from Burned Structures at Aguateca, Guatemala: A Study of Classic Maya Households," *Journal of Field Archaeology* 25 (1998), 431–52.
[15] Stephen D. Houston, "Into the Minds of Ancients: Advances in Maya Glyph Studies,'" *Journal of World Prehistory* 14 (2000), 150.

the purpose of the building. The likely loss of writings on perishable materials, painful to acknowledge, unfortunately leaves much about the mechanisms for standardizing and transmitting the script to the vagaries of our imagination.

Scribal training in early cities seems to have had a mixed nature from the very beginning. City institutions (palaces, temples, and administrative offices) and private homes (teaching the teachers' own children or students from other families) complemented each other. In Mesopotamia and Egypt there seems to have been a standard pool of school texts for individual schools or teachers to choose from. This made it possible to achieve a measure of uniformity, especially in the sphere of administration. The mutual comprehensibility of scribes from different city-states in Mesopotamia or from different nomes in Egypt suggests that a more or less universal curriculum regulated at least at first by the state and by itinerant teachers helped to set standards. Training in numerical notation and mathematics was universal because of administrative requirements. Calendrical calculation, indispensable for ritual activities, was another significant subject.

Conclusions

The technologies for writing and record-keeping discussed here are diverse, both formally and functionally. Cuneiform, Chinese, and Maya hieroglyphs all developed a direct relationship with language. Inkan khipus are less tightly – or quite possibly not at all – related to language, but because of a more restricted communicative range were able to encode complex organizational information very efficiently. The shape of these technologies, in each instance, also reflects the history from which they emerged. The knotted-cords of khipus developed in the context of a highly valued and elaborated textile tradition in the Andes. Maya hieroglyphs developed in a rich Mesoamerican tradition of cosmological iconography. Cuneiform tablets were preceded and shaped by clay tokens and seals, and Chinese script was shaped by the bamboo strips on which it was written.

If we extend our comparison to the functions of these technologies, and how knowledge of them was maintained and transmitted to new generations, we are seriously hampered by the large gaps in the surviving historical record. The richness of data in the case of Uruk and Mesopotamia suggests that administrative and economic book-keeping was the central motivation for, and function of, writing. It is perhaps plausible to extend inferences about writing in Mesopotamia to its innovation and purpose in other parts of the world, but in the absence of direct evidence, we cannot be certain. Indeed, in the case of Maya writing, an early and abiding function was ritual and cosmological, not economic and administrative.

Regardless of the functions performed by writing and other record-keeping technologies, it is clear that in order to be effective tools, these systems needed to be conventionalized and rigidly maintained. In this sense, they are a very direct physical expression of control. Writing and other forms of record-keeping depended for their existence and perpetuation on the high degree of uniformity and control that cities made available. As with the earliest functional motivations for the emergence of writing, we are forced to make inferences about the institutional support for these technologies on the basis of incomplete data. Institutions for training scribes are apparent in the material remains for Uruk and are mentioned in ethnohistorical records for the Andes. The earliest records in China and Mesoamerica, however, offer very little direct evidence for schools and curricula. The uniformity of the systems, across time and space, makes it clear that institutions did exist, but we can only speculate about their exact nature.

Administering a city largely consists of managing taxonomies, and keeping records is an exercise in taxonomy. The aim of this chapter has been to investigate what early recording systems did and how they were perpetuated rather than just what they were. These technologies differed substantially in terms of their communicative capacities, their primary social or institutional functions, and their relationship to language. However, whether representing language or not, their lexicons and numerical systems gave these early recording systems a remarkable ability to *sort* and *quantify*. In an illuminating study of modern states, James Scott has stressed the state's need for what he calls "legibility," that is, for a clear and detailed knowledge of its population and resources. As Yoffee noted, ancient states, in the form of cities, had similar needs. With or without writing, legibility was achieved by simplification and classification. Indeed, the very act of writing and drawing is a human attempt "to reduce a complex and often chaotic reality to a comprehensible order."[16] Whether it is an aid in the process of urbanization, or a consequence of it, record-keeping goes hand in hand with striving for a rational ordering of the city.

---

[16] Kemp, *Ancient Egypt*, p. 182.

PART III

★

EARLY URBAN LANDSCAPES

Tiwanaku urban origins: distributed centers and animate landscapes

JOHN W. JANUSEK

Urban studies tend to emphasize either the centralizing or fluid dynamics of cities. Traditional urban studies, like those of the Chicago school of urban sociology, approached cities as spatially coherent, centralized phenomena or products. More recent urban studies, such as those of the Los Angeles school of urban sociology, focus on the fluid networks that constitute contemporary urbanism. In line with Abu-Lughod's[1] study of Islamic cities as "processes, not products," proponents of this approach study the evanescent relational networks that continually transform cities and create urban subjects. Yet cities at any moment are *products* that ground ongoing activity, just as ongoing activities – however quotidian, say getting to work – transform cities and create urban subjects. Like urban subjects, cities are processes *and* products.

Like all cities, Tiwanaku at any moment was process and product. A long history of incipient urbanism in the southern Andes produced Tiwanaku, and yet, in turn, urban centrality transformed the southern Andes. I tackle two critical aspects of Tiwanaku's emergent centrality. First, I suggest that its early development is best understood as part of a distributed network of Late Formative centers and settlements. Khonkho Wankane and Tiwanaku were sparsely inhabited centers of recurring periodic gathering and ritual activity. Cyclical mobility and regional transaction networks drove the increasing importance of the centers. Furthermore, in their early Late Formative histories, Khonkho and Tiwanaku formed something akin to paired centers on either side of the Kimsachata mountain range, a shared landscape of productive resources. Centers provided recurring gatherings for members of affiliated communities, and themselves comprised multiple

---

[1] Janet Abu-Lughod, "The Islamic City: Historic Myth, Islamic Essence, and Contemporary Relevance," *International Journal of Middle East Studies* 19 (1987), 155–76.

geographically separate nodes. I consider this manifestation of centrality a species of *distributed urbanism*.

Second, Andean urbanism animated and sanctified specific natural forces, cycles, and features. Centers indexed them spatially, materially, and iconographically, animating prominent landscape features and celestial bodies and rendering them critical to the constitution of human and non-human subjects. Political authority crystallized as the strategic mediation of these relations, particularly among those who tended emergent centers, lived near key ceremonial spaces, orchestrated periodic ritual-political events, and "kept time" by tracking complex celestial cycles. To term these foundations of authority "religious" renders them epiphenomenal. Epiphenomenal they were not. Communities and aspiring leaders fostered the animacy of particular forces, cycles, and features, and built them into – embodied them in – their centers precisely because they were considered to constitute the productive bases of life in a challenging high-altitude environment. Tiwanaku's emergence in the Andean altiplano was founded on an utterly pragmatic, if profoundly ritualized, *animistic ecology*.

In this chapter I explore the origins of southern Andean urbanism. I sidestep static definitions of what defines a city (minimum size, population, presence or absence of monumental architecture, palaces, corporate art, etc.) by focusing on urbanism as a long-term regional process consisting of multiplex incremental practices. In this perspective, urbanism consisted of the recurring practices that preceded and produced first cities. I begin by summarizing what we know about the city of Tiwanaku. Tiwanaku thrived as an urban center during the Andean Middle Horizon (500–1000 CE). I next explore Tiwanaku's urban origins by explicating the recently investigated Late Formative site of Khonkho Wankane, emphasizing its distributed proto-urbanism as Tiwanaku's precursor and producer. I then explore the reason people came to these centers to begin with, focusing on the importance of cyclical social gatherings at built landscapes that facilitated proximity to ancestral monolithic personages.

Tiwanaku: the city (500–1000 CE)

Tiwanaku emerged as a city between 500 and 600 CE in the Andean altiplano or high plateau. For some 500 years hence, it sprawled across the middle of a broad montane valley several kilometers from the southeastern shore of Lake Titicaca (Map 11.1). At its greatest extent, in 700–900 CE, Tiwanaku covered 4–6 square kilometers and housed 10,000–20,000 people. Like most

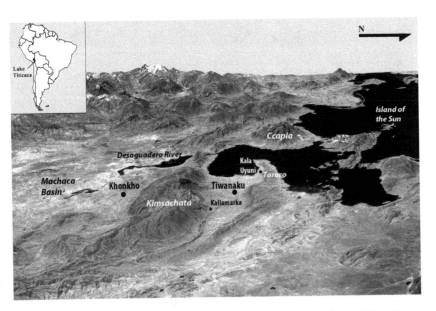

Map 11.1 View of the southern Lake Titicaca Basin showing Tiwanaku and Khonkho Wankane in relation to sites and landscape features mentioned in the text.

cities, Tiwanaku comprised built places dedicated to diverse social activities that spanned ritual, residential, and productive concerns. Though certain activities predominated in specific areas and places in Tiwanaku, different classes of activities overlapped in most areas of the city.

Two monumental campuses dominated Tiwanaku's urban core, affording the city a northeast (Kalasasaya-Akapana) to southwest (Pumapunku) ritual axis. Each was a monumental complex comprised of raised platforms, sunken courtyards, and extensive plazas (Figure 11.1).[2] The northeast campus consisted of two juxtaposed complexes that differ in chronology, spatial organization, and orientation. The Kalasasaya complex includes several structures that were built sequentially over generations: the Sunken Temple – Tiwanaku's earliest extant ceremonial structure – the Kalasasaya platform, and the Putuni complex (Figure 11.2). It manifests paradigmatic spatial patterns of built monumental ritual space, including

[2] John W. Janusek, *Ancient Tiwanaku* (Cambridge: Cambridge University Press, 2008); Alan L. Kolata, *Tiwanaku: Portrait of an Andean Civilization* (Cambridge: Blackwell Press, 1993); and Alexei Vranich, "The Development of the Ritual Core of Tiwanaku," in Margaret Young-Sanchez (ed.), *Tiwanaku* (Boulder, CO: Denver Art Museum, 2009), pp. 11–34.

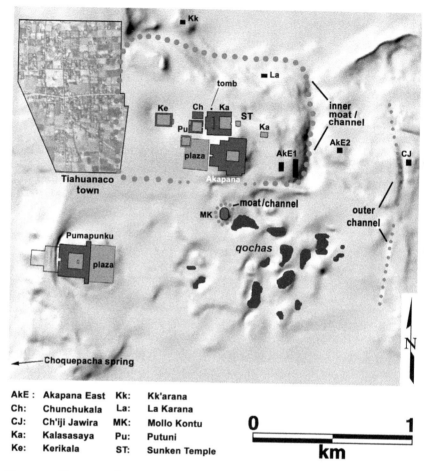

AkE : Akapana East Kk: Kk'arana
Ch: Chunchukala La: La Karana
CJ: Ch'iji Jawira MK: Mollo Kontu
Ka: Kalasasaya Pu: Putuni
Ke: Kerikala ST: Sunken Temple

Figure 11.1 Plan view of Tiwanaku demonstrating key architectural constructions in relation to key water channels and sunken basins (*qochas*).

raised platforms with built-in sunken courtyards. By 800 CE, the structures formed an integrated architectural complex that afforded movement leading from the early Sunken Temple, through the Kalasasaya, and into the Putuni courtyard. Structures with disparate histories, forms, and roles now provided a coherent proxemic narrative.

The Akapana and Pumapunku were built just when Tiwanaku was emerging as a primary urban center in the southern Lake Titicaca Basin (500–600 CE). The Akapana was built on the south edge of the Kalasasaya complex, appropriating and aggrandizing its historical legacy. Built in the

Figure 11.2 View of Tiwanaku's northeast monumental complex, facing south. The Kalasasaya complex occupies the foreground, shadowed by the Akapana and Mollo Kontu with its extensive *qocha* systems (productive sunken basins) further south.

form of a terraced mountain, the structure took the traditional platform-and-sunken-court complex to new heights. Though its upper central area has been gutted, it appears to have once incorporated a high sunken courtyard. Located several hundred meters to the southwest, the Puma-punku was built at approximately the same time. Pumapunku was a lower, more extensive platform that also contained a sunken courtyard. An exten-sive plaza abutted the west side of Akapana and another adjoined the west side of Pumapunku.[3] These plazas allude to the importance of large-scale social gatherings in association with the new platform structures.

Movement into and through built ritual spaces was critical for experi-encing Tiwanaku and maximizing its impact. Stone portals and portal iconography abound at Tiwanaku and its affiliated centers. The so-called "Gateway of the Sun" (here, the "Solar Portal") is the best known of numerous lithic portals that directed humans into and through Tiwanaku's monumental ritual spaces. Its elaborate frieze depicts a central ancestral deity standing atop a terraced platform or mountain surrounded by human and bird-headed attendants in procession. Numerous other portals stood in Tiwanaku, many decorated with similar friezes. Portals were key icons in Tiwanaku lithic architecture and iconography and they were clearly central elements of Tiwanaku's emergent cosmology.

Carved stone monoliths were focal objects of Tiwanaku monumental architecture. Portals bounded from sacral space while affording durable pathways that led toward small sunken courtyards featuring stone

---

[3] Vranich, "Development of the Ritual Core of Tiwanaku."

monoliths. The inner sancta of sunken courtyards afforded potent ritual experiences. Monoliths erected in these spaces depicted anthropomorphic personages wearing elaborate woven garments decorated with zoomorphic and anthropomorphic imagery. Some sunken courtyards housed single monoliths, while others – notably the Sunken Temple – housed monoliths of different carving styles and periods. Iconographic analysis indicates that the monoliths depicted – or more accurately, *embodied* – focal ancestors that objectified, and condensed in potent material forms, extensive community affiliations.

Tiwanaku's emergence also created productive "rural" landscapes within and outside of the city, in the form of extensive raised field systems on low lake shores and networks of sunken basins – or *qochas* – in relatively high, drier micro-environments.[4] Within the city, intricate water networks and productive systems surrounded monumental complexes. These included several channels and perimeter canal that isolated the urban core.[5] Alan Kolata suggests that this canal was a moat that defined the core as a sacred island. The canal and its water network also had productive roles. Mollo Kontu, a sector of the site linked into the network, incorporated multiple extensive *qochas* that served intra-urban agropastoral activities. The city showcased production and celebrated water. Neither the urban–rural nor the urban–nature dichotomies that characterize Western practical consciousness held for Tiwanaku.

The city incorporated several neighborhoods, each comprised of multiple walled compounds. Each compound, in turn, consisted of one or more household units, which I define (archaeologically) as a spatial cluster of one or more dwellings and their associated structures and activity spaces.[6] Compound groups developed specific relations to communities within and beyond Tiwanaku and engaged in particular productive activities. One bounded compound group produced specific types of ceremonial ceramic wares.

Nevertheless, relatively few excavated structures at Tiwanaku can be definitely termed "dwellings." Many of the structures built within bounded compounds housed temporary city dwellers (Figure 11.3).[7] Analogous to

[4] Alan L. Kolata, "The Agricultural Foundations of the Tiwanaku State: A View from the Heartland," *American Antiquity* 51 (1986), 748–62.
[5] Kolata, "Agricultural Foundations."
[6] John W. Janusek, *Identity and Power in the Ancient Andes: Tiwanaku Cities Through Time* (London: Routledge, 2004).
[7] Janusek, *Identity and Power.*

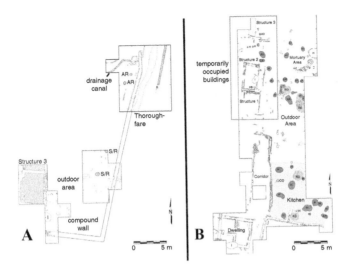

Figure 11.3 Plan views of two excavated residential compounds at Tiwanaku, Akapana East 1 M (A) and Akapana East 1 (B). Akapana East 1 incorporated several temporarily occupied structures.

contemporary structures constructed to house intimate visitors during key ceremonial occasions, these structures may have housed visiting family, friends, or business partners during important past ritual events. Furthermore, at any time, some 40–50 percent of Tiwanaku's urban periphery consisted of abandoned residential structures and secondary deposition.[8] The extent of refuse at Tiwanaku led the early twentieth-century Swedish archaeologist Stig Rydén to surmise that Tiwanaku archaeology was predominantly that of past "ritual meals." Secondary deposition included abundant "ash pits": amorphous, often immense pits filled with a distinctive bluish-gray ash, and containing abundant broken pottery, fragmented camelid remains, and lithic debitage. While some yield evidence for specialized production, most do not. The ubiquity of these pits supports Rydén's point that, at any time, many areas of Tiwanaku were sites of ritual engagement and, more specifically, ritualized commensality.

I argue that Tiwanaku was a cyclically pulsating "ceremonial urban center" to which people from multiple localities came for important ritual

---

[8] John W. Janusek, "Residence and Ritual in Tiwanaku," in Linda R. Manzanilla and Claude Chapdelaine (eds.), *Domestic Life in Prehispanic Capitals* (Ann Arbor, MI: Memoirs of the Museum of Anthropology, 2009), pp. 159–80.

events that centered on intensive commensality.[9] Tiwanaku became the center of a vast, distributed urban network that linked multiple centers and regions in the Lake Titicaca Basin and beyond. What else characterized Tiwanaku's social organization?[10] In particular, what were its sociospatial origins? Norman Yoffee argues that many early centers were spatio-material symbols for emergent pan-regional communities.[11] In the following section, I suggest that in its historical foundation, Tiwanaku was a center of social, political, and ceremonial convergence. I argue that key transformations in the materiality, spatiality, and lithic iconography of Khonkho Wankane and Tiwanaku jointly produced Middle Horizon Tiwanaka as a primary ritual-political center.

Proto-urbanism in the south-central Andes

Until recently we knew little regarding the generations of practices that produced Tiwanaku. Over the past ten years, research has targeted sites dating to the centuries that directly preceded Tiwanaku's emergence, what we term the Late Formative (200 BCE–500 CE). Late Formative ritual-political centers in the Lake Titicaca Basin, including Tiwanaku, manifest distinctive regional patterns. These patterns emphasize the importance of cyclical social convergence, landscape production, and specific transformations in spatial and material practices in the production of southern Andean urbanism.

The Late Formative was not the first time that centers had emerged in the region. During the preceding Early to Middle Formative (800–200 BCE), a cultural complex known as Chiripa predominated in the southern basin. Settlement clustered along lake shores and perennial streams. The site of Chiripa ultimately became (400–200 BCE) the most important center. Its primary temple was a sunken court within a raised platform on which a ring of structures were built. In light of evidence for ritual activities in and human burials under them, Hastorf interprets them as focal shrines for the multiple communities that affiliated with and periodically visited Chiripa for ritual and other activities.[12] Chiripa was a place of cyclical ritual convergence.

---

[9] Janusek, "Residence and Ritual in Tiwanaku."

[10] Edward Soja, *Postmetropolis: Critical Studies of Cities and Regions* (Oxford: Blackwell, 2005).

[11] Norman Yoffee, *Myths of the Archaic State: Evolution of the Earliest Cities, States, and Civilizations* (Cambridge: Cambridge University Press, 2005), p. 16.

[12] Christine A. Hastorf, "Community with the Ancestors: Ceremonies and Social Memory in the Middle Formative at Chiripa," *Journal of Anthropological Archaeology* 22 (2003), 305–32.

After 200 BCE, sociopolitical and environmental conditions shifted. During the early part of the Late Formative (LF 1: 200 BCE–250 CE), multiple new centers, each incorporating a distinct type of ceremonial complex, emerged in the southern basin. These include Kala Uyuni on the Taraco Peninsula, Kallamarka and Tiwanaku itself in the Tiwanaku Valley, and Khonkho Wankane in the Upper Desaguadero Basin (Map 11.1). While the ceremonial architecture of some centers comprised small ritual chambers – as at Kala Uyuni – others incorporated sunken courts and large open plazas – as at Khonkho Wankane and Tiwanaku.

In the following sections, I focus on Khonkho Wankane and Tiwanaku.

Khonkho Wankane in a multi-centered world

Khonkho Wankane is located in a high (3,900 masl), relatively dry area of the southern edge of the Lake Titicaca Basin. This is a particularly challenging portion of the Andean altiplano. Rather than intensive agriculture, the region lends itself to a greater reliance on camelid pastoralism via domesticated llamas and alpacas. There is evidence for (1) construction of nearby sunken basins (qochas) that served agropastoral practices; (2) exceedingly high frequencies of camelid remains at Khonkho; and (3) a predilection for camelid iconography on stone monoliths at the site.

Khonkho Wankane thrived during the Late Formative period as a ritual-political center. It occupies a portion of the Machaca Plain just below the foothills of the Kimsachata range (Map 11.1). It consists of two core mounds – Wankane and Putuni – surrounded by several smaller knolls. Both mounds were artificial platforms raised over natural hillocks during a few massive construction events. Wankane was the primary monumental platform.

Khonkho Wankane's construction demanded tectonic movement and monumental coordination. The platforms incorporated elaborate earthen stratigraphies that simultaneously captured rainfall (via sandy strata) and guided moisture off the mound to prevent erosion (via interlaced clay strata). The platform supported an elaborate ritual-residential complex centered on an extensive Main Plaza for large-scale gatherings. A smaller Sunken Temple on its southwest side provided an intimate space for ritual events, and adjacent ritual-residential compounds demarcated its east and southeast sides (Figure 11.4).

Constructing the two core platforms reciprocally created an anthropogenic productive landscape. Deep clay quarrying around them created a broad marshy channel fed by two springs in the nearby Kimsachata foothills.

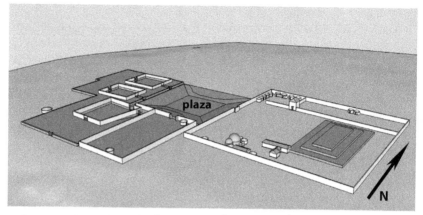

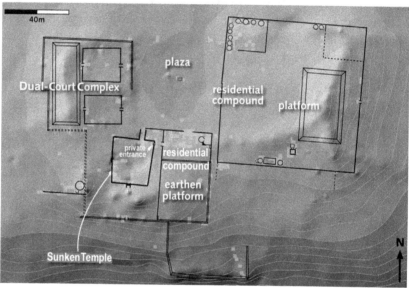

Figure 11.4 Oblique and plan views of Khonkho Wankane's central ritual complex. The image emphasizes key ritual structures, including the Main Plaza, Sunken Temple, and later Dual-Court Complex.

Additionally, activities in the ritual complex themselves supported the platform's surrounding marshy landscape. A centrally located basin in the Main Plaza drained run-off from all of the platform's structures into a massive, hypertrophic subterranean canal that carried water off the mound and into the marsh. The marsh afforded pasture for camelids. Khonkho Wankane incorporated a productive landscape and celebrated water, as did later Tiwanaku. Its encompassing, human-wrought marsh likely inspired the encompassing perimeter canal that surrounded the central portion of Tiwanaku.

Khonkho Wankane was predominantly a place for periodic regional gathering. Deep excavations in the Wankane mound revealed an early, thin occupation dating to 1–100 CE. Excavations in the Putuni fill indicated that it covered a contemporaneous occupation consisting of multiple superimposed, ephemeral surfaces, each covered with a thin layer of erosional sedimentation. Both incorporated short-term hearths and their carbonized cleanings as well as ceramic cookware sherds and splintered faunal remains. Before being covered by thick platforms, early mounds were locales for recurring, periodic gathering and commensality.

Research in the knolls outside of the marshy channel confirms this point. Survey yielded abundant artifacts dating to the Late Formative. We documented a classic two-tier network of inhabited settlements, what we would expect for an incipient ranked society or chiefdom: a multi-community polity. Yet, later excavations in several of the knolls yielded no evidence for permanent *in situ* occupation, offering suggestive evidence that the thin occupations have been deflated due to ongoing natural (rain, wind) and human (agropastoral) activities. That is, occupations on the peripheral knolls were, like those buried under and preserved by the Wankane and Putuni platforms, ephemeral and cyclical. Like the earliest occupations under Wankane and Putuni, their peripheral knolls housed recurring, temporary encampments.

This finding transforms our understanding of Khonkho in its regional setting and the sociospatial specificity of Tiwanaku urban origins. It indicates substantial cyclical mobility in the region. Foreshadowing later Tiwanaku, not all of those who affiliated with Khonkho or participated in its construction projects and recurring rituals lived at the center. Most did not. People came periodically, perhaps in seasonal or annual ritual cycles, to briefly inhabit the early core mounds and, later, the knolls that surrounded the two emergent platforms. Considering Khonkho was one of multiple centers in the region, Khonkho was less the center of a multi-community polity than it was one of many in a multi-centered macro-community. It was one in a distributed network of interlinked centers in the southern Lake Titicaca Basin.

Evident mobility during the Late Formative suggests some regional coordination among the communities affiliated with these centers. Perhaps each center offered particular times of ceremonial engagement that rotated over repeating temporal cycles and a ritual focus that served as a recurring matrix for communal social, economic, and political activity. Highly mobile networks linked centers in the southern Lake Titicaca Basin. These networks shaped succeeding generations of Tiwanaku urban hegemony.

Tiwanaku and Khonkho Wankane as paired centers during the Late Formative

Located just across the Kimsachata mountain range, Tiwanaku was an important Late Formative center. Little Late Formative research has been conducted at Tiwanaku, and most early occupations were buried or destroyed during the Middle Horizon. We know even less about local Late Formative regional settlement, except that it consisted of a number of smaller sites.[13] Whether they were temporary encampments like those that surrounded Khonkho is a task for future research. Still, the research that has been conducted in and around Tiwanaku indicates that it thrived as a ritual center parallel to Khonkho Wankane during the Late Formative.

There are remarkable parallels between the sites. First, Tiwanaku's earliest known ceremonial space was a Sunken Temple similar in size, form, and orientation to that at Khonkho. At each site, the court maintained a primary stairway entrance in its south wall prioritizing a primary north–south axis and a southward-facing visual path. The primary entrance to both sunken temples is offset from the center of the wall, at Khonkho to facilitate a southward view of Mount Sajama and at Tiwanaku to Mount Kimsachata. The parallel orientation may have simultaneously provided nighttime celestial observations. Each courtyard was relatively intimate and connected with an extensive plaza for larger-scale gatherings and events.

Second, stylistically similar monolithic sculptures were focal ritual objects at both centers during the Late Formative, and they collectively differ from those at other centers in the Lake Titicaca Basin. Four are known from Khonkho and four from Tiwanaku. Hewn of bright red sandstone, each monolith depicts an anthropomorphic being – I argue a mythical ancestral personage – with impassive face and arms placed over the chest. Though most were found *ex situ*, three *in situ* monoliths indicate that they originally occupied key sunken ceremonial spaces and plazas at each site.

Most telling is the precisely parallel location of the centers on either side of the Kimsachata range. The source of the springs that fed Khonkho

[13] Juan V. Albarracin-Jordan, *Tiwanaku: Arqueologia Regional y Dinamica Segmentaria* (La Paz: Plural, 2006).

Wankane, this range also produced springs and an extensive subterranean aquifer that sustained Tiwanaku. Kimsachata was the source of the red sandstone employed to craft temples and monolithic ancestral personages at both sites.[14] The shared range was a critical source of vitality for the two centers, a theme that was narrated on their personified monoliths (see below). Most remarkable, the two centers were settled on a nearly precise north–south alignment on either side of Kimsachata.[15] Their sunken temples share the same longitude (68° 40' 21", +/- 1"). Thus, the north–south geographical axis of the centers was mirrored in their ritual inner sancta.

Khonkho and Tiwanaku were paired centers during much of the Late Formative. This was another key element of their distributed character and of Tiwanaku's urban foundations. During Late Formative 2, 300–500 CE, that paired relation began to change.

Tiwanaku as emergent city in the south-central Andes

Tiwanaku's emergent urban centrality involved critical transformations in its spatiality, materiality, and iconography. These transformations created novel relations to landscape features and celestial – or "skyscape" – cycles. They were undoubtedly the work of new regimes. At Khonkho, a Dual-Court complex was built on the west side of the early Main Plaza (Figure 11.4). Marking a shift from the early Sunken Temple, which then deteriorated, the complex created a new axis of sight and movement oriented east–west. At Tiwanaku (Figure 11.2), the Kalasasaya was built on the west side of the early Sunken Temple and its adjacent plaza. Like Khonkho's new Dual-Court complex, Kalasasaya created a new axis of sight and movement oriented east–west. By the end of Late Formative 2, the Kalasasaya was an enormous platform construction with megalithic revetments. This was an important transformation that helped produce Tiwanaku as a primary urban center.

[14] John W. Janusek, "The Changing 'Nature' of Tiwanaku Religion and the Rise of an Andean State," *World Archaeology* 38 (2006), 469–92; and Carlos Ponce Sanginés, Arturo Castaños Echazu, W. Avila Salinas, and Fernando Urquidi Barrau, *Procedencia de las areniscas utilizadas en el Templo Precolombino de Pumapunku* (La Paz: Academia Nacional de Ciencias de Bolivia, 1971).

[15] Leonardo Benitez, "Mountains, Sunken Courts, and Dark Cloud Constellations: Archaeoastronomy at Khonkho Wankane and Tiwanaku," paper presented at the 72nd Annual meeting of the Society for American Archaeology, Austin, Texas, 2007.

Spatial transformations at Tiwanaku

In the later part of Late Formative 2 the Kalasasaya platform was expanded (Figure 11.5). Platform expansion aggrandized old walls, built predominantly of roughly hewn sandstone blocks, and created a westward "balcony wall" girded by eleven impeccably crafted volcanic stone (andesite) pillars. This wall, we now know, served as a celestial observatory. A central stone platform stands some 58 meters to the east. Standing on the platform and facing the wall in the evening, a person during the Middle Horizon witnessed the sun setting on the western horizon. From the platform, one could witness the sunset behind each of the pillars at critical times of the annual cycle. The two outer pillars demarcated the sunset on each of the two solstices: the north pillar demarcating the austral winter solstice and the south pillar the austral summer solstice.[16] Nearby stands the well-known Solar Portal. Its iconography mirrored a temporal sequence of visual paths from Kalasasaya's balcony observatory. Eleven rayed faces on the Portal's lowest band depict the eleven recurring sunset points on the western horizon as marked by Kalasasaya's pillars. The portal likely once stood over the viewing platform, serving as both an entrance into the observatory, perhaps limited to a priestly caste, and a ready guide for the specialists who produced Tiwanaku's calendars.

After 500 CE, Tiwanaku builders initiated Akapana, Pumapunku, and several other monumental constructions. Built near the older Kalasasaya complex,[17] Akapana blocked the southward visual path from the interior of the Sunken Temple toward the peak of Mount Kimsachata, resolutely directing visual attention toward the Akapana itself. The Akapana covered the plaza associated with the early Sunken Temple, and included the construction of a new one in front of its principal west stairway. Pumapunku, built at the west edge of Tiwanaku, may have served as a place where visitors, diplomats, and pilgrims first entered the center. In both Akapana and Pumapunku, a primary west stairway led ritual participants to the summit, where they were afforded an impressive glimpse of Mount Illimani, a glaciated peak east of the center in the Eastern Andean Cordillera, before being led into a sunken inner sanctum.

[16] Leonardo Benitez, "Descendants of the Sun: Calendars, Myth, and the Tiwanaku State," in Young-Sanchez (ed.), *Tiwanaku*, pp. 49–82.
[17] Kolata, *Tiwanaku*; Linda Manzanilla, *Akapana: una pirámide en el centro del mundo* (Mexico City: Universidad Nacional Autónoma de México, 1992); and Alexei Vranich, "La Piramide de Akapana: reconsiderando el centro monumental de Tiwanaku," *Boletin de Arqueologia PUCP* 5 (2001), 295–308.

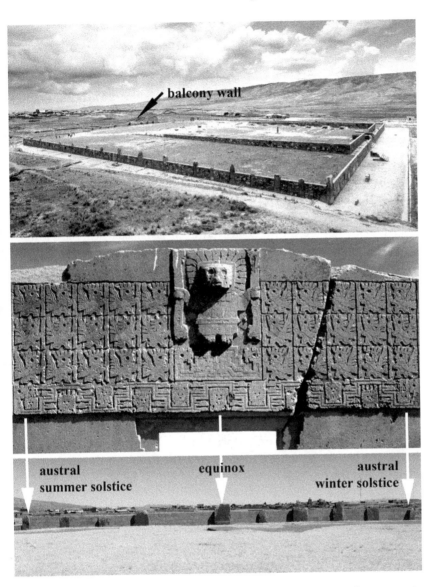

Figure 11.5 Kalasasaya, demonstrating the location of its west balcony wall (top image). The Sun Portal (middle image) occupies the west side of Kalasasaya. Its "serpent band" weaves together eleven solar faces, which match the eleven massive andesite pilasters (one has since been removed) that gird the west balcony. The northern and southern pilasters (lower image) establish solar setting places on the western horizon during austral winter and summer solstices. The central pilaster marks the sun's setting place on the horizon during each annual equinox.

The terraced platforms of Akapana and Pumapunku were human-wrought, "perfected" material icons of mountains.[18] Their terraced form figuratively domesticated natural mountains while ritual processions into and out of them made visual references to the powerful, ancestral, distant peaks that they manifested. Like the vital streams that flowed from mountain springs, Akapana and Pumapunku – like Khonkho Wankane before them – incorporated elaborate drainage canals. The drains carried seasonal rainwater from ceremonial spaces down onto and through lower terraces. Water movement was not only visible but also distinctly audible to ritual participants.

Stone portals like the Sun Portal led ritual specialists and participants into increasingly sacred, potent ritual spaces. A key innovation during the Tiwanaku period, they are known exclusively from Tiwanaku itself. Most formed narrow openings between rigorously bounded ritual spaces. Most also opened into narrow chambers,[19] instilling a sense of mystery, disorientation, and esoteric power as a person entered increasingly interior inner sancta.

The nested architectural plans of the Kalasasaya, Akapana, and Pumapunku platforms aggrandized the nested moldings of such portals. The temples themselves served as "portals" that facilitated rapport with powerful animate forces immanent in the environmental features and elements that human groups sought to appropriate to Tiwanaku. Ritual movement through the temples – entered via stairways that facilitated views of a majestic peak, punctuated by monolithic portals, and culminating in ritual performance within intimate inner sancta modeled on ancient Sunken Temples – facilitated ritual experience in a new key. Sprawled over massive landscapes like the mountains they indexed, the temples gathered the forces of earth and sky.

Material transformations at Tiwanaku: sandstone and andesite

Stone construction of monumental structures indexed potent natural features and embodied their sacral forces. The use of stone revetments, stairways, and pavements afforded ceremonial complexes mass and

---

[18] Kolata, *Tiwanaku*.

[19] Jean-Pierre Protzen and Stella Nair, "The Gateways of Tiwanaku: Symbols or Passages?", in Helaine Silverman and William H. Isbell (eds.), *Andean Archaeology II: Art, Landscape, and Society* (New York: Kluwer Academic, 2002), pp. 189–223.

permanence. Megalithic stones were quarried from nearby mountains, the very natural features the temples symbolically domesticated and whose immanent productive power they sought to appropriate. Temples were not simply icons of mountains; by incorporating the material essence of those mountains, they *embodied* them. In consecrating temples of stone, Tiwanaku builders sought to capture the generative forces of the earth. Yet stone quarrying, carving, and iconography changed significantly in relation to other monumental transformations. Most notable was a shift in emphasis from sedimentary sandstone to volcanic andesite, and throughout Tiwanaku's apogee, the strategic integration of these two lithic materials.[20]

During the Late Formative, monumental construction at Khonkho Wankane and Tiwanaku consisted of red sandstone and smaller quantities of other rock. Their early Sunken Temples are key examples. The structures and the monolithic personages housed within them consisted largely of sandstone. Red sandstone derives from nearby quarries in the Kimsachata range between Khonkho and Tiwanaku. The color indexed visible bedrock in the mountains, and may well have invoked blood, the fluid that affords life for llamas and humans. Red was also the primary decorative color for most Late Formative serving-ceremonial wares, potent material vehicles for the fermented liquids and foods that fueled recurring commensal events.

At Tiwanaku after 500 CE, craftsmen learned to quarry and hew massive blocks of andesite into exquisitely carved pilasters, portals, and monoliths. Quarrying and working andesite required an entirely new corpus of technical expertise. Andesite derived from distant quarries across the southern portion of Lake Titicaca, and largely from the foot of Mount Ccapia, a volcano west of Tiwanaku. Kalasasaya's andesite west balcony and Sun Portal were early Ccapia andesite constructions. If they manifested a critical new importance for solar observations, they also emphasized the increasing importance of volcanic stone for Tiwanaku's monumental construction. A visual path through Kalasasaya's east doorway offers a clear view of Mount Ccapia, the source of the massive pilasters that supported its west balcony.

Andesite's bluish-gray color likely indexed the color of Lake Titicaca, near the shores of which volcanic stone was quarried. "Titi Kaka" refers to the gray-haired local mountain feline frequently depicted on Tiwanaku drinking vessels. Just as sandstone indexed the bedrock of local sedimentary

---

[20] Janusek, "The Changing 'Nature' of Tiwanaku."

formations, andesite indexed more distant volcanic sources and invoked the complementary life-principle of Lake Titicaca's water. During the Tiwanaku period, vast lacustrine floodplains were transformed into anthropogenic landscapes focused on raised field farming systems, which depended on a critical range of lake and water table levels. In this light, andesite invoked and propagandized Tiwanaku's new political horizons and productive power.

Monoliths and monolithic iconography

Located at the ends of concatenated pathways that brought ritual participants to the centers and wove them through labyrinthine spaces, the stone sculptures punctuating Khonkho's and Tiwanaku's temple complexes provide an intimate perspective on the changes elemental to Tiwanaku's urban ascendance (Figure 11.6). Quarried pieces of mountains, stone personages constituted corporeal landscapes. Late Formative monolithic personages depict mythical ancestors or their living representatives (Figure 11.6a). They make a distinctive arm gesture in which one arm is placed above the other across the torso. Their bodies were decorated with terrestrial zoomorphic creatures. The monoliths themselves were considered "persons" much as were totem poles among many native North American societies. They idealized the corporeal forms, gestures, and iconography of didactically narrated and collectively remembered ancestral personages. In this sense they did not simply depict past persons or actions. They presented ideal persons and ritual attitudes that living people could strive for in their lives and after-lives. Furthermore, the monoliths did not just *represent* ancestral persons; crafted of sandstone quarried from Kimsachata, monoliths embodied those persons as metonymic instantiations of the powerful generative landscape that Khonkho and Tiwanaku shared.

Monolithic personages remained the focus of dramatic cyclical rituals during the early Tiwanaku period, but their forms, gestures, iconography, and overall meaning changed dramatically (Figure 11.6b). Perhaps by way of sumptuary law, large monolithic personages were now restricted to Tiwanaku itself. Many were now crafted of volcanic andesite. This may have occurred just as Tiwanaku monopolized the volcanic stone quarries of Ccapia. In place of crossed arms, each personage now made a dual presentation. In one hand it held a ceremonial drinking *kero* and in the other a tablet for ingesting psychotropic substances. These were vehicles for mind-altering substances that facilitated two dimensions of religious experience – one relatively communal and one relatively personal.

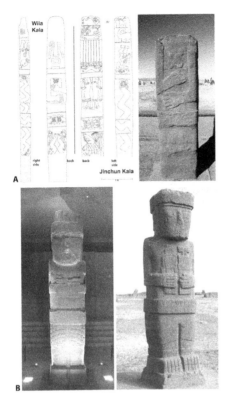

Figure 11.6 Monoliths. The top image, (A), presents three Late Formative monolithic stelae, the first two (drawn) from Khonkho and the third (decapitated monolith) from Tiwanaku. The bottom image, (B), depicts two representative Tiwanaku-style monoliths: the sandstone Bennett and andesite Ponce stelae.

They were, I argue, complementary ritual attitudes that came to constitute the ideal Tiwanaku subject.

Tiwanaku period monoliths differed from earlier personages in that they did not simply depict deified ancestors. The impassive faces still denote deified status, but bodily decoration now emphasized elaborate clothing; specifically the tunic, sash, and headgear of an elite person. These personages now depicted either ancestral deities bedecked as elite persons or elite persons dressed as ancestral deities, and it is likely that iconography deliberately promoted ambiguity. What these icons reveal is a lithic presentation of social status that, through recurring ritual practice and ongoing appeal to their didactic properties and telluric productive powers, legitimized the crystallization of class differences after 500 CE.

Unlike Late Formative monoliths, Tiwanaku monoliths depicted imagery that indexed the sky. Iconography included personages wearing headdresses with solar designs and a new emphasis on predatory avian imagery. For example, the braided tresses hanging from the back of the Bennett monolithic personage end in avian heads. The posterior iconography of the personage unfolds around a central figure standing on a terraced temple-mountain wearing a radiating solar headdress. Above the figure are disembodied portraits of the same face wearing solar headdresses, intermixed with attendants wearing the beaked masks of predatory birds and facing upward toward the sky.

Kalasasaya's Sun Portal, as noted above, indexed the sun and solar cycles. Partially covered in gold lamina, it dramatically performed this indexical relation by reflecting solar light across the space that it faced, capturing and aggrandizing the material power of the sun. Tiwanaku's emergent urban centrality was tied to a novel attention to the productive power of the sun and its recurring cycles, and an intensified attention to *skyscape* overall. Emphasis on solar cycles allowed emergent leaders to coordinate and integrate the multiple ritual cycles and productive rhythms of the diverse social and productive communities – fishers, farmers, and herders – they sought to integrate.[21] It was an astute strategy of cosmic integration.

Tiwanaku residential expansion and elite distinction

Transformations in cosmology and ritual practice were central to Tiwanaku's success. This is demonstrated in Tiwanaku's dramatic growth as a densely populated urban center after 600 CE. The Late Formative centers of Khonkho Wankane and Tiwanaku were lightly occupied relative to the size of their monumental cores. This is clearest at Khonkho, where occupants of the main platform were directly involved with the supervision and maintenance of its ceremonial spaces and the orchestration of rituals held therein. This appears to have been the case for Tiwanaku as well, at least until Late Formative 2. Both were centers dedicated to periodic rituals.

Tiwanaku's urban expansion began during late Formative 2, coincident with notable changes in its monumental spatiality and ritual practices. From this period through Tiwanaku collapse people lived in bounded residential compounds, yet most dwellings were now rectangular rather than circular.

---

[21] Janusek, *Ancient Tiwanaku*.

Clusters of adjacent compounds formed tightly connected barrios, some of which were dedicated to specialized activities such as the production of ceramic vessels. Others, in particular those located closest to the monumental core, supported ceremonial activities associated within Tiwanaku's increasingly extensive and complex temples. It is significant that all monumental and residential construction at Tiwanaku from Late Formative 2 through the Middle Horizon followed the axial orientation established during its early history, tied to proxemic and visual relations to specific celestial movements and terrestrial features.

Sociopolitical hierarchy crystallized just as Tiwanaku emerged as one of the most influential centers of the Middle Horizon Andes. At the Late Formative centers of Khonkho and Tiwanaku, status resided in proximity to key ceremonial spaces and in curating the ancestral monolithic personages that stood inside of them. It was tied to proximity with and purchase over these spaces and objects. Status continued to be spatially and materially linked to monumental space as Tiwanaku became a primary center. Elite activity was located adjacent to the Putuni and on top of the Kalasasaya and Akapana platforms. Human burials near the Putuni contained elaborate vessels and sumptuous bodily adornments crafted of rare materials such as coastal shell, sodalite, silver, and gold. Excavations in Kalasasaya recovered several diadems of hammered laminar gold encrusted with malachite and azurite. Thus, as Tiwanaku expanded, relative status, constituted as proximal relation to monumental places and practices, became more intensely polarized as elite "distinction."

What became of Khonkho Wankane? If Khonkho and Tiwanaku were closely interconnected during the Late Formative, it is odd that its monumental core was abandoned by 500 CE. I have suggested that the two centers had always been in competition and reached an inevitable showdown. Yet there is no evidence for violence or destruction at Khonkho. Rather, Khonkho's stylistically latest monolith appears to have stood within the main plaza for centuries. Although slumped over and eroded, it remains in its plaza today as one of the most powerful animate objects in the local region. Although speculative, I suggest that many of Khonkho's residents may have transferred to Tiwanaku. This idea meshes better with Tiwanaku's predominant incorporative political strategies. In one scenario, Khonkho's original inhabitants came to Tiwanaku and occupied the area that produced the Pumapunku campus. In fact, recent research indicates that Pumapunku was first occupied during Late Formative 2, when Khonkho was abandoned.

Kolata and Ponce[22] first suggested that Akapana and Pumapunku formed paired monumental ceremonial spaces in Tiwanaku. New evidence for the historical relation between Khonkho and Tiwanaku supports this idea. An early relation between powerful Late Formative centers on either side of the Kimsachata range, I hypothesize, may have been reconstituted as a paired relationship within Tiwanaku itself. This act would have recreated an enduring political aesthetic of dual centers within the emergent urban center of Tiwanaku. Resolving this hypothesis rests on the balance of future research.

Conclusions

Reciprocally process and product, Tiwanaku emerged over a long, complex history in the southern Lake Titicaca Basin. It originated as one in a network of interacting early Late Formative centers. Later, urban process found an axis in the pairing of Khonkho Wankane and Tiwanaku across the Kimsachata range. Khonkho and Tiwanaku formed paired centers of social gathering and cyclical commensal ritual for several generations. After 500 CE, Tiwanaku emerged as the primary center in the region. Urbanism was always distributed throughout the region, whether among multiple or between paired centers, but always focused in one or more centers that cyclically gathered distant populations for key ritual events. In each configuration, urbanism was distributed across a regional landscape of centers and settlements.

Astute agropastoral productive strategies allowed human groups and increasingly complex social institutions to thrive at one of the highest liveable altitudes on earth. Productive strategies, in turn, depended on pragmatic relations to the world that emphasized knowledge of the vitality inherent in terrestrial forces and recurring seasonal and celestial cycles. Political authority at Khonkho Wankane and Tiwanaku thrived not on shuttering attention to natural processes as in contemporary cities, but on rendering some of those processes central to the well-being of humans, their crops, and their herds. This was done by way of ritual practices linked to an ecology in which key landscape phenomena were deemed animate, ancestral forces that humans could tap into and influence for their own good. The

---

[22] Alan L. Kolata and Carlos Ponce Sanginés, *Tiwanaku: The City at the Center*, in *The Ancient Americas: Art from Sacred Landscapes*, R. F. Townsend (ed.) (Chicago: Art Institute of Chicago, 2002), pp. 317–34.

groups who successfully positioned themselves at the hub of social, spatial, and cosmic networks that linked humans with these forces accrued inordinate status. After 500 CE, these were the elites who lived on or near Tiwanaku's primary monumental campuses.

Urbanism in the southern Andes was an ongoing project that continually produced a highly ritualized yet profoundly pragmatic cosmology that I term an animistic ecology. Ancestral mountains, lakes and rivers, celestial bodies, and other key Andean landscape and celestial features were treated as animate persons who act in the world, ideally on behalf of self-identified descendants. Tiwanaku's terraced temples, laced with labyrinthine subterranean canals, were animate, human-wrought, life-affording mountains that, by way of ritual acts, people entreated to influence the greater ancestral mountains they indexed and, constructed of their lithic essence, embodied. Archaeologists have treated monuments and their personified monoliths as iconic representations of natural phenomena. Here, monuments and monoliths embodied and, thus, materially condensed and *manifested* those phenomena as agentive ancestral personages.

Emergent urbanism in the southern Andes has much to offer studies of past urbanism globally. Its sociospatial specificity was distributed and animating in its high-altitude landscape. It provides an alternative to many political economy models. According to the latter, past cities and political centralization were largely the work of a few naturally ambitious aggrandizers and their presumed lust for "wealth" – a laden term that flattens all kinds of practices and values to a single utilitarian function: profit. In the south-central Andes, emergent authority was at least as much about mediation as it was about aggrandizing. Further, it was made possible due to the production of intricate relations among diverse communities and built ritual-political centers, and of intimate relations between humans and worldly animate forces, which, together, through periodic ritual events, were rendered vital to human well-being.

FURTHER READINGS

Abercrombie, Thomas A., *Pathways of Memory and Power: Ethnography and History among an Andean People*, Madison: University of Wisconsin Press, 1998.
Albarracín-Jordán, Juan V., Carlos Lemuz Aguirre, and Jose Luis Paz Soria, "Investigaciones en Kallamarka: primer informe de prospeccion," *Textos Antropologicos* 6 (1993), 11–123.
Allen, Catherine, *The Hold Life Has: Coca and Cultural Identity in an Andean Community*, Washington, D.C.: Smithsonian Institution Press, 1986.

Couture, Nicole C., "Ritual, Monumentalism, and Residence at Mollo Kontu, Tiwanaku," in Alan L. Kolata (ed.), *Tiwanaku and Its Hinterland: Archaeology and Paleoecology of an Andean Civilization*, Washington, D.C.: Smithsonian Institution Press, 2003, Vol. ii, pp. 202–25.

Janusek, John Wayne, "El surgumiento del urbanismo en Tiwanaku y del poder politico en el altiplano andino," in Krzysztof Makowski (ed.), *Señores del Imperio del Sol*, Lima: Banco del Credito del Peru, 2010, pp. 39–56.

Janusek, John Wayne, and Victor Plaza Martinez, "Khonkho e Iruhito: tercer informe preliminar del Proyecto Arqueologico Jach'a Machaca," Research report submitted to the Bolivian Viceministerio de Cultura and the Unidad Nacional de Arqueologia, La Paz, Bolivia (2007).

"Khonkho Wankane: Segundo informe preliminar del Proyecto Arqueologico Jach'a Machaca," Research report submitted to the Bolivian Viceministerio de Cultura and the Unidad Nacional de Arqueología, La Paz, Bolivia (2006).

Kolata, Alan L., "Tiwanaku Ceremonial Architecture and Urban Organization," in Alan L. Kolata (ed.), *Tiwanaku and Its Hinterland: Archaeology and Paleoecology of an Andean Civilization*, Washington, D.C.: Smithsonian Institution Press, 2003, Vol. ii, pp. 175–201.

Ohnstad, Arik T., "La escultura de piedra de Khonkho Wankane," in John W. Janusek (ed.), "Khonkho Wankane: Primer Informe Preliminar del Proyecto Arqueológico Jach'a Machaca," Research Report submitted to the Bolivian Viceministerio de Cultura and the Unidad Nacional de Arqueología, La Paz, Bolivia (2005), pp. 52–68.

Ponce Sanginés, Carlos, *Descripción sumaria del templete semisubterraneo de Tiwanaku*, La Paz: Juventud, 1990.

Tiwanaku: Espacio, Tiempo, Cultura: Ensayo de síntesis arqueológica, La Paz: Los Amigos del Libro, 1981.

Portugal Ortíz, Max, and Maks Portugal Zamora, "Investigaciones arqueológicas en el valle de Tiwanaku," in Arqueología en Bolivia y Perú, La Paz: Instituto Nacional de Arqueología, 1975, Vol. ii, pp. 243–83.

Portugal Zamora, Maks, "Las ruinas de Jesus de Machaca," *Revista Geográfica Americana* 16 (1941), 291–300.

Posnansky, Arthur, *Tihuanacu: The Cradle of American Man*, New York: J. J. Augustin, 1945, Vols. i and ii.

Protzen, Jean-Pierre, and Stella Nair, "On Reconstructing Tiwanaku Architecture," *Journal of the Society of Architectural Historians* 59 (2000), 358–71.

Rivera Casanovas, Claudia S., "Ch'iji Jawira: A Case of Ceramic Specialization in the Tiwankau Urban Periphery," in Alan L. Kolata (ed.), *Tiwanaku and Its Hinterland: Archaeology and Paleoecology of an Andean Civilization*, Washington, D.C.: Smithsonian Institution Press, 2003, Vol. ii, pp. 296–315.

Smith, Scott Cameron, "Venerable Geographies: Spatial Dynamics, Religion, and Political Economy in the Prehistoric Lake Titicaca Basin, Bolivia" Ph.D. dissertation, University of California, Riverside, 2009.

Vranich, Alexei, "Interpreting the Meaning of Ritual Spaces: The Temple Complex of Pumapunku, Tiwanaku, Bolivia," unpublished Ph.D. dissertation, University of Pennsylvania, 1999.

12

Mesopotamian cities and urban process, 3500–1600 BCE

GEOFF EMBERLING

Mesopotamia is one of the world's oldest urban cultures. Its first cities, which may have housed 50,000 people or more, were built by 3500 BCE and many were continuously inhabited for as much as 3,000 years. During this long history, cities defined Mesopotamian culture.

According to Mesopotamian ideology, the gods selected rulers who exercised kingship over cities and in some cases over territories. In the Sumerian King List, composed just before 2000 BCE, kingship was said to have "descended from heaven" and then resided in different cities in turn. Kings were proclaimed to be the builders of cities, or at least of their symbolically important components, which included temples, palaces, city walls, and canals.

Confronting this literary ideology in which gods and kings were the central (indeed, the only) actors, the archaeological and documentary record shows that Mesopotamian urban communities were composed of a variety of identities, factions, and local authorities. Ancient Mesopotamian cities were built around kings and gods, but without slaves, workers, artisans, priests, bureaucrats, merchants, tribal leaders, and other intermediate political figures, they could not sustain themselves.

An extensive body of historical and archaeological research provides a starting point for a synthetic understanding of Mesopotamian cities. As built environments, Mesopotamian cities were focused on the temple of the major city god and the palace of the ruler. Narrow streets ran through urban neighborhoods that were densely packed with houses, shrines, craft workshops, and even taverns, and larger streets connected these to city gates. The community was surrounded by a monumental city wall, and the city gates and harbors located on canals or river branches served as market areas. Open spaces were also part of the city plan – the Epic of Gilgamesh describes the city of Uruk as comprising the city, date-groves, and clay pits for making mudbricks in equal area, along with the temple of Ishtar. Streets and canals could define neighborhoods or quarters in the city and along with larger spaces could also support public festivals and rituals like processions and feasts.

This familiar picture of Mesopotamian cities as physical places and communities, however, is a pastiche stitched together from different cities and different times. While it is understandable given the many gaps in our knowledge that we have assembled a static model of Mesopotamian cities, at the same time it deprives them of their dynamic, changing, and lived qualities. Cities are dynamic environments that themselves actively shape political, economic, and social relationships within their communities and across broader landscapes, and understandings of urbanism in Mesopotamia must take this into account.

Cities

Following V. Gordon Childe, we can broadly define cities as communities in which many households do not produce most of what they consume. It is difficult to specify the minimum population or density of occupation that defines a city, as the population of an urban center varies with local conditions of transportation and productivity of land. In practice, however, the threshold of population and productive specialization is often passed quickly and dramatically, leaving relatively little ambiguity in definition.

In newly developing cities, some people may have specialized in intensified agriculture or herding, and others – perhaps because of political or social position – worked to coordinate or control. Still others, using the surplus made available (or extracted), began to develop crafts or other technical knowledge and skill.[1] Economic specialization and social differentiation proceeded together. The crucial developments are concentration of people and specialization (or differentiation) of population, considered not as traits, but as ongoing processes. For provision of food and supply of population, cities also required and reshaped a rural hinterland.

People were moved into cities by political authority or military force or may have moved into them to seek economic opportunity or for protection. These varied processes could lead to the dissolution of old identities – for

---

[1] Guillermo Algaze, *Ancient Mesopotamia at the Dawn of Civilization: The Evolution of an Urban Landscape* (Chicago: The University of Chicago Press, 2008).

example, a breakdown of kinship ties[2] – as well as formation of new communities. Disease and nutrition in ancient cities probably led to decreased life expectancy, but whether cities required continual immigration to maintain their population remains an open question.

A dynamic view of the integration and disintegration of urban networks[3] from the rise of the first cities to the profound changes of the mid-second millennium BCE suggests that cities functioned to concentrate wealth and political authority in the hands of the elite, with economic processes that were increasingly differentiated and efficient. As people moved into cities and then back into an increasingly controlled rural landscape, old identities were modified and new urban identities were developed. The urban built environment also changed over the centuries, with development of new architectural forms as well as corresponding political practices and ideologies.

Mesopotamia, the land between the rivers

Mesopotamia, the area defined by the Tigris and Euphrates Rivers, is bounded by mountains to the north and east and by desert to the west (Map 12.1). It can be geographically and culturally divided into three zones. Upper Mesopotamia is an arc of foothills and plains that extends from southeastern Turkey and northeastern Syria through northern Iraq. Known in later times as Assyria, it received enough rain to grow barley and wheat without irrigation. The ecology of this dry farming landscape constrained cities to a size of roughly 100 hectares until the intensive irrigation projects of the Neo-Assyrian period.[4] Lower Mesopotamia, the alluvial plains of southern Iraq, was called Sumer and Akkad in early times and is known to historians and archaeologists as Babylonia after 2000 BCE. It receives little regular rainfall, and settlement depended on the construction and mainten-ance of irrigation canals, as it did in the adjacent Khuzistan Plain in south-western Iran, part of ancient Elam. Finally, the shifting marshes of southern Iraq were an important source of fish, birds, and reeds, as well as political

---

[2] Louis Wirth, "Urbanism as a Way of Life," *American Journal of Sociology* 44 (1938), 1–24. In Mesopotamia, kinship groups did not disappear in cities, but citizens had other social identities beyond their kin groups.

[3] Robert McC. Adams, *Heartland of Cities: Surveys of Ancient Settlement and Land Use on the Central Floodplain of the Euphrates* (Chicago: The University of Chicago Press, 1981).

[4] Tony Wilkinson, "The Structure and Dynamics of Dry-Farming States in Upper Mesopotamia," *Current Anthropology* 35 (1994), 483–520.

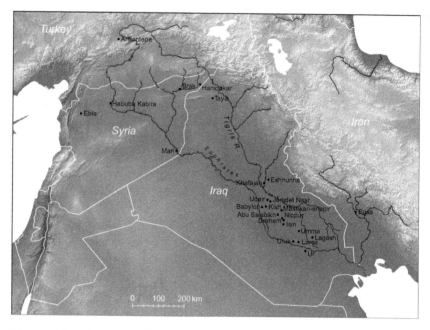

Map 12.1 Map of ancient Middle Eastern cities mentioned in the text (courtesy of Jason A. Ur).

refuge. Mesopotamia as a whole is relatively poor in natural resources other than fertile farmland, although Upper Mesopotamia possesses more stone and wood than the south. The entire area depended on trade from the mountains and sometimes from the Persian Gulf for many types of stone, copper, tin, large timbers for building, and valuable materials like silver, gold, and ornamental stones.

The first Mesopotamian cities formed during the Uruk period (4000–3100 BCE) in separate cultural traditions in Lower and Upper Mesopotamia. In the later part of this period, people from southern cities expanded throughout Mesopotamia and beyond.[5] While the nature and cause of this expansion are not agreed upon, it is clear that some local polities were conquered, and population in some areas decreased significantly. By the end of the Uruk

---

[5] Guillermo Algaze, *The Uruk World System* (Chicago: The University of Chicago Press, 1993); and Mitchell Rothman (ed.), *Uruk Mesopotamia and Its Neighbors: Cross-Cultural Interactions and their Consequences in the Era of State Formation* (Santa Fe, NM: School of American Research, 2002).

period, cuneiform writing had been invented (see Nissen, Chapter 6, this volume), and increasingly elaborate works of art marked the emergence of specialized artisans as well as new ideologies of authority.

During the Jamdat Nasr (3100–2900 BCE) and Early Dynastic (2900–2350 BCE) periods, Lower Mesopotamia, whose inhabitants largely spoke (or at least wrote in) Sumerian, was divided among cities that competed for power, with military conflict and the establishment of some brief regional hegemonies. Upper Mesopotamia, whose inhabitants spoke dialects of Semitic languages including Akkadian, as well as other languages, had been significantly deurbanized after the Uruk expansion but cities were rebuilt, borrowing cuneiform writing and other cultural forms from Lower Mesopotamia, beginning around 2600 BCE.

Much of Mesopotamia was conquered by the Akkadian Empire (2350–2200 BCE). After its collapse, the Ur III Empire (2100–2000 BCE) ruled Lower Mesopotamia and intensified administration as well as production while also extracting tribute from the Zagros Mountains to the east. Even before the Ur III period, tribal groups speaking Amorite (a West Semitic language) began settling in Lower Mesopotamian cities, and many rulers of the succeeding Isin–Larsa (2000–1800 BCE) and Old Babylonian (1800–1600 BCE) periods also claimed Amorite descent. During these centuries, kings from Susa in southwestern Iran to Yamkhad (centered on modern Aleppo) competed for political and economic dominance. Competing states were centered at Isin, Larsa, Babylon, Eshnunna, and Mari, among others, and they encompassed multiple urban centers. These periods also saw the first extensive use of cuneiform writing for non-palace, non-temple business, with letters and legal documents being written by and for private businesses and individuals as well as for palaces and temples. The collapse of this system, the arrival of Kassite rulers in Babylonia, and the rise of larger territorial states including Mitanni and Assyria in the years after 1600 BCE mark significant changes in the Mesopotamian political landscape.

There are three major sources of data for understanding Mesopotamian urbanism. The first comprises excavations and surface surveys of cities themselves – we have substantial areas of city and town plans apart from the monumental structures at a number of sites, including (Late Uruk) Habuba Kabira, (Early Dynastic III) Abu Salabikh, late third millennium Tell Taya (Figure 12.1), and Old Babylonian Ur (Figure 12.2), among others. The second source is the historical record – more than 100,000 cuneiform tablets for the periods under discussion here, the majority of which were purchased rather than excavated and so lack archaeological

Figure 12.1 Plan of surface remains at Tell Taya, *c.* 2300 BCE, suggesting houses and a radial pattern of streets (Julian E. Reade, "Tell Taya [1972–73]: Summary Report," *Iraq* 35 [1973], 155–87; courtesy of Julian Reade, map by George Farrant).

context. The number of cuneiform tablets known has recently been significantly increased by tablets looted in Iraq in the 1990s and early 2000s. Third are the fundamental regional archaeological surveys undertaken in Lower Mesopotamia by Robert McC. Adams and colleagues and more recent

Figure 12.2 A neighborhood in the city of Ur, *c.* 1800 BCE (C. Leonard Woolley and M. E. L. Mallowan, *The Old Babylonian Period*, Ur Excavations 7 [London: British Museum, 1976], fig. 124; courtesy of the Penn Museum).

Figure 12.3 Ancient clay tablet plan of the city of Nippur, *c.* 1300 BCE, with cuneiform captions naming gardens, a canal, the Euphrates River, city gates, and the temple and ziggurat of the god Enlil. The ancient city plan corresponds remarkably closely to the remaining ruins of the city (courtesy of the Hilprecht-Sammlung).

surveys across Upper Mesopotamia. Reanalysis of Adams' survey data has assessed and enhanced his results using models of site contemporaneity and satellite imagery.[6] A unique source is a clay tablet with a plan of the city of Nippur (Figure 12.3).

Each of these sources of data has well-known biases. Because of the focus of earlier excavations on monumental areas of sites, and because of the size and complex multi-component nature of most Mesopotamian settlements, our city plans are incomplete and chronologically uneven. There are no cases in which excavation has shown changes in city plan over any appreciable area because of the difficulty of working at the large scales this would require. The cuneiform texts record the perspective of the literate elite – palaces and temples in earlier periods, and private but still elite individuals beginning in about 2000 BCE. Although the number of available texts is large, they are also unevenly distributed. Discovery of a major palace archive from the mid-third millennium BCE, for example, might significantly alter our understanding of the relative role of palace and temple in the south. Finally, the available survey data for Lower Mesopotamia is hampered by alluviation that has covered an unknown but likely significant number of smaller and earlier sites, and the methods used by Adams, while

---

[6] Susan Pollock, *Ancient Mesopotamia: The Eden that Never Was* (Cambridge: Cambridge University Press, 1999); Jennifer Pournelle, "KLM to CORONA: A Bird's-Eye View of Cultural Ecology and Early Mesopotamian Urbanization," in Elizabeth C. Stone (ed.), *Settlement and Society: Essays Dedicated to Robert McCormick Adams* (Chicago: The Oriental Institute of the University of Chicago, 2007), pp. 29–62; and Carrie Hritz, "Tracing Settlement Patterns and Channel Systems in Southern Mesopotamia Using Remote Sensing," *Journal of Field Archaeology* 35 (2010), 184–203.

exemplary for the time, could be now improved by more comprehensive methods were it possible to work in Iraq. Neither of these problems applies to Upper Mesopotamia, where site visibility as well as survey methods have generally been excellent.

Political leaders and the rise of cities in Mesopotamia

Accounts of the origins of cities in Mesopotamia have focused on the city of Uruk since excavations there in the late 1920s and 1930s recovered abundant evidence of monumental structures of the late fourth millennium BCE at the center of a large city along with numerous early cuneiform texts (Nissen, Chapter 6, this volume).

There have been two significant comparative discussions of the origins of the city at Uruk. Adams focused on the city's location at an intersection of ecological zones in Lower Mesopotamia – irrigated farmland, pasture, and marsh – and suggested that the city arose as a center to coordinate exchange of these products in a redistributive system managed by an emergent urban elite.[7] In another study, Wheatley proposed that early cities were built around temples.[8] Accepting the existence of temples in pre-urban Mesopotamian settlements of the Ubaid period, he suggested that the religious authority of priests fostered the development of redistributive economy and that population subsequently grew around these ceremonial complexes, with temples being the dominant institution in the early cities. He based his argument in part on early studies of a temple archive from the city of Lagash (c. 2500 BCE) that had proposed that all the land and labor in the city was controlled by the temple.

It is not surprising forty or more years later that these explanations both require revision. First, the role of temples in the first cities of Mesopotamia was overstated. Forest has proposed that the so-called "temples" of the Ubaid period might relate to elite feasting instead.[9] These buildings all have relatively open access that is quite different from what we know of later Mesopotamian religious practice, in which the divine statue would be protected from view. Expanding on Forest's suggestion, is it possible that

---

[7] Robert McC. Adams, *The Evolution of Urban Society* (Chicago: Aldine, 1966).
[8] Paul Wheatley, *The Pivot of the Four Quarters: A Preliminary Enquiry into the Origins and Character of the Ancient Chinese City* (Chicago: Aldine, 1971).
[9] Jean-Daniel Forest, *Les premiers temples de Mésopotamie (4e et 3e millénaires)* (Oxford: Archaeopress, 1999).

these structures might have been meeting places for the assembly of elders that has been postulated as an important institution in early Mesopotamian cities? In addition, continuing study of the Lagash archive has shown that the "temple-city" model dramatically overstated the proportion of land owned by one temple, and that, moreover, the temple in question was supervised by the queens of Lagash.[10]

Furthermore, it is now clear that cities developed in Upper Mesopotamia at about the same time as the rise of Uruk. Recent work in northeastern Syria has shown that Tell Brak, some 750 kilometers north of Uruk, had developed into a large city before 3500 BCE. Brak encompassed about 130 hectares of settled area by that time (perhaps 10,000–20,000 inhabitants), with differentiated settlement areas that included a temple with large numbers of votive offerings known as the Eye Temple, as well as residential areas and areas of workshops for ceramics and lithics at the edges of the city.[11] Other northern sites of this date, including Tell Hamoukar and Arslantepe, also show signs of being part of complex urban systems.[12] We thus have to consider explanations for the rise of Mesopotamian cities that encompass both the dry farming north and the irrigated fields and marsh-land of the south.

Both Uruk and Brak developed from the small-scale polities of the Ubaid period and were initially organized by extended kin-based social units whose leaders retained a political role in the new and developing cities. Brak and Hamoukar appear to have developed from clusters of smaller earlier occupations, and Uruk itself may have developed from two settlements named Eanna and Kullab. A unique building at Brak that may have been a feasting hall associated with a relatively large concentration of wealth[13] may suggest the activities of these leaders. It is reasonable to suggest that these leaders may have been the members of the assemblies (of elders) that have various roles in Mesopotamian documents and literary texts into the early second millennium BCE, a proposal that

---

[10] Scott Beld, "The Queen of Lagash: Ritual Economy in a Sumerian State," Ph.D. dissertation, Department of Near Eastern Studies, University of Michigan, 2002.

[11] Joan Oates, Augusta McMahon, Philip Karsgaard, Salam Al Quntar, and Jason A. Ur, "Early Mesopotamian Urbanism: A View from the North," *Antiquity* 81 (2007), 585–600.

[12] Clemens Reichel, "Administrative Complexity in Syria during the 4th Millennium B.C. – the Seals and Sealings from Tell Hamoukar," *Akkadica* 123 (2002), 35–56; and Marcella Frangipane (ed.), *Economic Centralisation in Formative States: The Archaeological Reconstruction of the Economic System in 4th Millennium Arslantepe* (Rome: Sapienza Università di Roma, 2010).

[13] Geoff Emberling and Helen McDonald, "Excavations at Tell Brak 2000: Preliminary Report," *Iraq* 63 (2001), 22.

remains difficult to prove.[14] A similar notion of the preservation of pre-urban social forms in cities has recently been proposed for Tiwanaku (Janusek, Chapter 11, this volume), and represents a broader pattern in the formation of cities.

Most of the characteristics we associate with urban societies developed in Mesopotamia only after the first cities were built. This seems an obvious statement, perhaps, but it means that we cannot use later forms to explain the growth of the first cities. Thus, we cannot rely on the economic attraction of markets, the protection offered by city walls, or the pull of temple institutions to explain the rise of Mesopotamian cities, since these only developed fully in later historical times. A political explanation for the rise of cities would propose that leaders of kin-based corporate groups formed alliances (and assemblies) to manage conflict, and drew members of their groups into central places where these alliances were negotiated. Out of these political negotiations arose single leaders whose greater authority over greater numbers of people enabled them to organize agricultural intensification, construction projects, and military campaigns that brought captives as slaves into the cities. Temples may have had their origins in providing divine sanction to these new political realities.

Rule

Mesopotamian cities had rulers at least from the time of the first written records, and perhaps earlier. They were given a variety of titles in early Sumerian texts, including En, Ensi, and Lugal. Scholars continue to debate whether these differences were simply terminological or more substantive, perhaps reflecting different traditions of rule in different regions, cities, or ethnic groups, or functional differences between more military, administrative, or religious roles.[15]

In spite of the different terms used for kings, the range of functions they performed remained remarkably consistent through Mesopotamian history.

---

[14] Marc van de Mieroop, "Democracy and the Rule of Law, the Assembly and the First Law Code," in Harriet Crawford (ed.), *The Sumerian World* (London: Routledge, 2013), pp. 277–89; and Norman Yoffee, *Myths of the Archaic State: Evolution of the Earliest Cities, States, and Civilizations* (Cambridge: Cambridge University Press, 2005), pp. 109.

[15] Gebhard Selz, "'He Put in Order the Accounts ...' Remarks on the Early Dynastic Background of the Administrative Reorganizations in the Ur III State," in Leonid E. Kogan, N. Koslova, S. Loesov, and S. Tishchenko (eds.), *City Administration in the Ancient Near East* (Winona Lake, IN: Eisenbrauns, 2010), Vol. II, pp. 5–30.

As attested in representations beginning in the Late Uruk period, kings ruled on behalf of the gods and were held responsible for maintaining the gods' goodwill through rituals and by the construction and maintenance of temples. They were military leaders and skilled hunters as well as heads of their own palace household. The king was also the highest judicial authority in the state. What changed over time, in part because of the concentration of population into cities and the resulting availability of labor and wealth, was the scope of royal control and the scale of military and economic action it enabled.

One of the major physical manifestations of the ruler's authority in Mesopotamian cities was the palace, Sumerian "e-gal" or "big house." Early possibly palatial structures remain difficult to interpret. A fragment of an Ubaid period (c. 4500 BCE) monumental building with rooms more than 10 meters long found at Tell Uqair may have been an elite residence, but limited exposure makes it difficult to understand.[16] The functions of the monumental complex of buildings at Uruk remain unclear (Nissen, Chapter 6, this volume). And at Jamdat Nasr a large but fragmentary building contained tablets and seal impressions indicating the presence of scribes and administrators (c. 3100–2900 BCE). There was no direct evidence of a royal residence in the preserved portion of the building, but it may have been a palace.[17]

It is not until the later Early Dynastic period (c. 2600–2350 BCE) that excavations and palace archives converge to show similar practices of rule across much of Mesopotamia. Palace buildings were organized around a series of courtyards of increasingly controlled access, with reception rooms arranged around them. They contained residential areas for the king and a separate area for the women of the palace, as well as quarters for palace officials, attendants, slaves. Cooking, craft production, storage, and areas for ritual activity were also commonly part of these structures. The palace archives from Ebla (c. 2350 BCE) and Mari (c. 1800 BCE) (Figure 12.4) provide abundant information about the operation of these palaces.[18]

---

[16] Seton Lloyd and Fuad Safar, "Tell Uqair," *Journal of Near Eastern Studies* 2 (1943), 131–58.

[17] Roger Matthews, *Secrets of the Dark Mound: Jemdet Nasr 1926–1928* (London: British School of Archaeology in Iraq, 2002).

[18] Jean-Marie Durand, "L'organisation de l'espace dans le palais de Mari: le témoignage des textes," in Edmond Lévy (ed.), *Le système palatial en Orient, en Grèce et à Rome* (Leiden: E. J. Brill, 1987), pp. 39–110; and Paolo Matthiae, *Ebla, la città del trono: Archeologia e storia* (Turin: Piccola Biblioteca Einaudi, 2010).

Figure 12.4 The palace of king Zimri-Lim at Mari, *c.* 1750 BCE. Open spaces are in white, roofed spaces in gray, and letters designate functional areas of the palace; the throne room is at the bottom of Area M, room 65 (Jean-Claude Margueron, *Recherches sur les palais Mésopotamiens de l'Age du Bronze* [Paris: Guethner, 1982], fig. 437).

At Tell Brak, arguably the northern administrative center of the Akkadian Empire, three monumental buildings cover something like 10 percent of the occupied area of the city. These constructions are not residential palaces of the imperial household, but seem to serve broader interests of the empire, with administrative and storage areas along with small shrines and at least one larger courtyard with a throne base that was certainly a ceremonial area.[19]

Ritual and religion, temples and public spaces

Mesopotamian temples were the households of the gods. The deities were physically brought into their cult statues through rituals and the statues were clothed and fed. Major temples were not congregational spaces; rather, the divine statue was powerful and dangerous, and only those with ritual knowledge and preparation could be in its presence. In addition to their ritual function, however, temples were also significant economic institutions that held agricultural land, managed livestock, organized long-distance trade, and made loans.

The concentration of population into cities in early Mesopotamia led to the construction of the first temples and then to the increasing size of temple institutions, along with an increasing differentiation of size and location of temples and of the roles within them. Temples supported an ideology of rule in which kings were selected and supported by the gods and at the same time provided wealth and authority to priests and temple administrators who could resist royal authority.

Nissen (Chapter 6, this volume) discusses problems with the interpretation of the massive structures at the center of Uruk itself, the largest of which are more than 80 meters long and tripartite in form. Forest has proposed that only two quite different structures at Uruk be designated as temples: the so-called Steingebäude and the Riemchengebäude, each of which has a concentric plan with protective outer wall with a maximum dimension of 20–30 meters.[20] The plans of these buildings are more consistent with what we know of later Mesopotamian temples and cult practices than are the tripartite structures.

Mesopotamian cities contained temples dedicated to different deities. Beginning in the Early Dynastic period, massive temples within often curving enclosure walls were built at a number of sites. Of these "Temple Ovals" whose patron deities are known, most were devoted to the goddess Inanna rather than to the major deity of the city (Figure 12.5a).

[19] David Oates, Joan Oates, and Helen McDonald, *Excavations at Tell Brak* (Cambridge: McDonald Institute for Archaeological Research, 2001), Vol. II.
[20] Forest, *Premiers temples*.

(a)

(b)

Figure 12.5 Reconstructions of Mesopotamian temples: the Temple Oval at Khafajah (*c.* 2400 BCE; Delougaz, *The Temple Oval at Khafajah*, frontispiece; courtesy of the Oriental Institute of the University of Chicago) and the ziggurat at Ur (*c.* 2100 BCE; C. Leonard Woolley, *The Ziggurat and its Surroundings*, Ur Excavations 5 [Oxford: Oxford University Press, 1939], pl. 86; courtesy of the Penn Museum). As with most archaeological reconstructions, many features of these drawings remain conjectural.

The enclosure walls of these temples encompass a space more than 100 meters long. The most completely excavated of these structures, that of Khafajah,[21] provides some evidence of the temple's role as an economic institution, with kilns, and one storeroom containing stone-working debris and another containing agricultural implements including baskets and sickle blades set in bitumen. None of these temples is located in a particularly salient part of the city, neither elevated nor central. In some of these cases, what we would expect to be the Early Dynastic city god's temple is obscured by later construction. In those cases, then, these large temples would have existed alongside other temples at least as large. The notion that each city had a single patron deity thus appears from remaining architecture (as well as texts mentioning gods) to be an oversimplification.

Alongside these monumental temples, smaller temples or shrines appear within the neighborhood structure of Early Dynastic cities including Mari and Khafajah.[22] These smaller temples were built within existing neighborhoods and so were often irregular in plan and dedicated to relatively minor deities. While we know little from texts about the activities of these smaller temple institutions, they could have been the focus of significant wealth in

[21] Pinhas Delougaz, *The Temple Oval at Khafajah* (Chicago: The University of Chicago Press, 1940).
[22] Pinhas Delougaz and Seton Lloyd, *Pre-Sargonid Temples in the Diyala Region* (Chicago: University of Chicago Press, 1942).

the form of offerings. The plan of a residential neighborhood in Old Babylonian Ur contains a number of even smaller neighborhood shrines.[23]

The most visible form of Mesopotamian religious architecture, however, was the ziggurat – the stepped temple tower (Figure 12.5b). Although temples on platforms like the White Temple at Uruk were predecessors, and structures in Early Dynastic Kish may have been ziggurats, the first textual references to ziggurats date from the Ur III period (c. 2100–2000 BCE), relatively late in the historical sequence. The ziggurats of Lower Mesopotamia had stairways leading to a shrine at the top. Herodotus suggested that these shrines served as a location for the sacred marriage ritual in which the king impregnated a priestess representing the goddess Ishtar.[24] The cult statue of the deity did not reside in the ziggurat itself but rather in a temple at its base, and these temples were dedicated to the major deity of the city.

Ziggurats provided a ritual focus to the urban built landscape. They physically represented the huge labor force available to the state at the same time as they masked its power as service to the gods. It is intriguing that these structures would first be built when the imperial conquests of the Ur III kings led to the development of supra-urban political institutions. The Sumerian King List, which had a similar focus on cities as the proper locus of royal identity, was also composed during this time.

A comprehensive study of public ritual outside temples has not been written for Mesopotamia, but it is likely to have been a significant way that the urban community developed a communal identity. One form of public ritual would have been royal burials. At Ur, royal burials of the late Early Dynastic period (c. 2500 BCE) were located close to the center of the city. The burial ritual included a funerary procession, suggested by ramps leading down to the burial chamber as well as the presence of carts in the burials, and the burial of numerous retainers. While sacrificial burial was not a common practice in Mesopotamia, contemporary elite burials at Kish and Abu Salabikh also included carts, and although we know relatively little about other royal burials, it is reasonable to suppose that they also included public performances.

[23] Kathryn Keith, "The Spatial Patterns of Everyday Life in Old Babylonian Neighborhoods," in Monica L. Smith (ed.), *The Social Construction of Ancient Cities* (Washington, D.C.: Smithsonian, 2003), pp. 56–80.
[24] Jerrold S. Cooper, "Sacred Marriage and Popular Cult in Early Mesopotamia," in Eido Matsushima (ed.), *Official Cult and Popular Religion in the Ancient Near East* (Heidelberg: Universitätsverlag C. Winter, 1993), pp. 81–96.

It is also clear from ration texts and month names that the statues of gods were removed from temples and taken to visit other gods in their own temples, sometimes in boats. These processional rituals and associated public feasts would perhaps have focused on linear public spaces. The much later Processional Way of Babylon, with its molded glazed brick sculptures, was one such major public route.

Neighborhood and community

Cities, neighborhoods, and communities were formed and reformed by movements of people into and away from cities. Yet as difficult as it is to locate, survey, and perhaps excavate neighborhoods, it is even more difficult to investigate how urban community structure might change through time.

One of the most informative studies of Mesopotamian urban layout is the surface survey of the Isin–Larsa town at Mashkan-shapir (Figure 12.6).[25] Based on the traces of canals and walls, and based on the relatively even distribution of evidence for high status and for craft production in each zone of the city, Stone proposed that the city was arranged in roughly equivalent residential segments, with separate areas for palace, major temple, and the *kārum* (harbor).[26] Letters and legal documents of this period corroborate this idea of urban organization into wards or neighborhoods, which were known as *babtum*, and had their own authorities including local judges.

To what extent is this picture representative of other Mesopotamian cities of this or any other period? Is it possible that other cities might be organized by status, with elite families concentrated in one area? Pollock argues that houses excavated near the major temples in the Diyala region were relatively high status.[27] Is it possible that some cities might have been organized by profession? Studies of texts found in houses in Old Babylonian Ur suggest that people living close to the temple of Nanna were associated with the temple, and the city of Uruk may have been organized around craft guilds in the first millennium BCE.[28] The evidence, as sparse as it is, suggests

[25] Elizabeth C. Stone and Paul Zimansky, *The Anatomy of a Mesopotamian City: Survey and Soundings at Mashkan-shapir* (Winona Lake, IN: Eisenbrauns, 2004).

[26] Elizabeth C. Stone, "City-States and Their Centers: The Mesopotamian Example," in Deborah Nichols and Thomas Charlton (eds.), *The Archaeology of City-States: Cross-Cultural Approaches* (Washington, D.C.: Smithsonian, 1997), pp. 15–26.

[27] Pollock, *Ancient Mesopotamia*.

[28] Marc van de Mieroop, *The Ancient Mesopotamian City* (Oxford: Clarendon Press, 1997), p. 181.

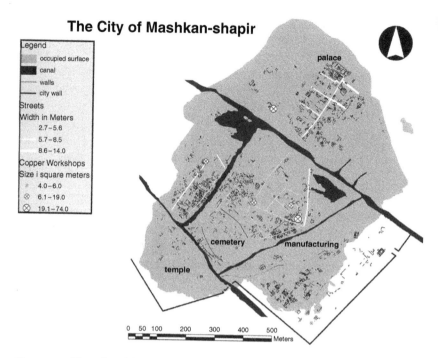

Figure 12.6 Plan of Mashkan-shapir based on surface survey and satellite imagery (Elizabeth C. Stone, "Surface Survey and Satellite Reconnaissance: Reconstructing the Urban Layout of Mashkan-shapir," *Iraq* 74 [2012], 65–74, fig. 1). Courtesy of Elizabeth C. Stone.

that there may have been varying forms of urban community organization through Mesopotamian history. Is it possible, for example, that the segmentary organization of Mashkan-shapir owes something to the increasing presence of Amorites in this region during the early second millennium BCE?

Another challenge in understanding Mesopotamian urban communities is the focus of the texts on palace and temple institutions, which makes it difficult to know what proportion of the population was not mentioned in these documents. Occasional mentions of groups like the *imru*, often translated as "clan," suggest that there were rural groups, and perhaps also people within the city, who were not recorded in these documents. During the Old Babylonian period, when textual production expanded considerably beyond the public institutions, texts mention a range of non-palace, non-temple authorities that include *rabiānum* (head-man) and the city elders and assembly.

Mesopotamian cities in their landscape

Mesopotamian cities depended on a countryside that urban institutions had a significant role in constructing. This process provides a basis for considering ways that Mesopotamian cities and urban institutions and residents shaped their rural landscape physically and ideologically.

Settlement

Survey data provide clear evidence for the way in which the process of urbanism altered the Mesopotamian landscape. In their initial formation, cities drew population from sometimes significant distances. This phenomenon is visible during the fourth millennium BCE around Uruk[29] and in the mid-third millennium BCE in Upper Mesopotamia.[30] It is possible that some of the population increase came from nomadic groups settling down, but in light of the decline in settlement on plains along the Zagros foothills, the evidence for violent conflict at some northern sites (Brak and Hamoukar), representations of conflict and prisoners on cylinder seals, and the appearance of terms for "slave" (written with signs meaning "man [or woman] from the mountain") in the earliest written texts that date to this period, it is also likely that some of the population represented prisoners of war.[31]

The proportion of people living in large settlements in Sumer increased in the early third millennium BCE and reached a peak at the end of the Early Dynastic period (c. 2400 BCE) in which Adams estimated that 78 percent of the population lived in sites larger than 40 hectares. The center of population moved away from Uruk and back to the Nippur area during the Akkadian period[32] and the population of Lower Mesopotamia increased as much as five times from the mid-fourth to the end of the third millennium BCE.[33] The population increase clearly expanded the labor force potentially available to the large institutions at the same time as it intensified the challenges of administration.

Steinkeller provides a different perspective on the proportion of rural settlement around Ur III Umma in the Ur III period (c. 2100–2000 BCE).[34]

---

[29] Adams, *Heartland of Cities*, p. 64; and Pollock, *Ancient Mesopotamia*, pp. 71–2.

[30] Jason A. Ur, "Cycles of Civilization in Northern Mesopotamia, 4400–2000 BC," *Journal of Archaeological Research* 18 (2010), 387–431.

[31] Robert K. Englund, "The Smell of the Cage," *Cuneiform Digital Library Journal* 4 (2009).

[32] Pollock, *Ancient Mesopotamia*, pp. 73–4.

[33] Adams, *Heartland of Cities*, pp. 69 and 142.

[34] Piotr Steinkeller, "City and Countryside in Third-Millennium Southern Babylonia," in Stone (ed.), *Settlement and Society*, pp. 185–211; and Robert McC. Adams, "An

According to his survey of place names, 70–80 percent of the population was settled outside Umma itself; Adams' survey data had estimated just 25 percent. This divergence is partially due to the different time scales of textual reference as opposed to archaeological survey, and partly a reminder of the proportion of rural settlements that survey may have missed in this alluvial environment.

The conquests of the Akkadian and Ur III Empires represented an extension of authority from an urban core across a broader territory. Ur III texts, in particular, describe a variety of specialized non-urban settlements that include rural estates (like Garshana, the estate of a general and a princess near Umma); massive centers for redistribution of imperial taxes (like Puzrish-Dagan [also known as Drehem]), and a variety of smaller sites including grain silos, threshing floors, and storehouses that enhanced production and distribution of agricultural products, as well as rural temples, weaving establishments, and stockyards.[35] The movement of people out of cities and into countrysides under imperial control and the increasingly specialized manipulations of the landscape are part of a development in which the large urban institutions extended control into the countryside.

In addition to drawing rural populations into cities, urban institutions also maintained political relationships with tribal groups that lived outside their direct control. This dynamic is known in detail for the Old Babylonian period, in which letters between kings and leaders of Amorite tribal groups, particularly at Mari, depict complex political and military interactions.[36]

Agriculture

Urban institutions increasingly involved themselves in agricultural production around Mesopotamian cities.[37] The concerns of temple and palace officials included construction of canals, demarcation of institutional land, management of agricultural labor (plowing, seeding, threshing), and receipt and storage of products including barley, wheat, and dates. The status of the

Interdisciplinary Overview of a Mesopotamian City and its Hinterlands," *Cuneiform Digital Library Journal* 1 (2008).
[35] See Walther Sallaberger, "Ur III-Zeit," in Walther Sallaberger and Aage Westenholz, *Mesopotamien: Akkade-Zeit und Ur III-Zeit* (Freiburg: Universitätsverlag and Göttingen: Vandenhoeck and Ruprecht, 1999), pp. 119–390.
[36] See Dominique Charpin, "Histoire politique du Proche-Orient Amorrite (2002–1595)," in Dominique Charpin, Otto Edzard, and Marten Stol, *Mesopotamien. Die altbabylonische Zeit* (Freiburg: Academic Press, 2004), pp. 25–480.
[37] Henry T. Wright, *The Administration of Rural Production in an Early Mesopotamian Town* (Ann Arbor: University of Michigan Museum of Anthropology, 1969).

people working for the palace and temple households ranged from slaves (prisoners of war and debtors) to semi-indentured laborers who were given rations of food (beer, bread, and oil) and wool for their labor. For the moment, these activities are known mostly from texts, although more detailed landscape archaeology with excavation of rural features and settlements will surely recover some evidence of land use.

When the first royal inscriptions proclaiming the activities of southern kings were written beginning in about 2500 BCE (although an earlier, unpublished inscription from Kish exists, according to P. Steinkeller), canal construction was among the first projects mentioned. In addition to providing water for irrigation and making efficient transportation of agricultural products possible, major canals were a visible symbol of the king's ideological role as provider. They also served as territorial boundaries that marked the extension of royal power. Inscriptions of Eannatum, ruler of Lagash, note that he defeated an alliance of enemies at a canal bordering the territory of Lagash, and in the Stela of the Vultures that records a conflict between Umma and Lagash over a field belonging to the god Ningirsu, canals form a part of the boundaries of the state.

Over the course of the third millennium BCE, the productive capacity of palace and temple households expanded dramatically. We do not know the extent to which this was the result of deliberate institutional policies of maximizing production or whether living conditions in and around the cities generated increasing numbers of people who needed food and work. Early texts record the dimensions of fields and the yield from them – at Jamdat Nasr, a town that was also the site of a large building that was likely a palace, the ruler ("en") held on the order of 300 hectares of agricultural land.[38] The estates of the Temple of Ba'u at Lagash – source of the "temple-city" debate – were by contrast nearly 4,500 hectares or 45 square kilometers.[39] During the Ur III Empire, the governor of Lagash was responsible for cultivating 858 square kilometers of land.[40]

---

[38] Robert K. Englund, "Texts from the Late Uruk Period," in Pascal Attinger and Markus Wäfler (eds.), Mesopotamien: Späturuk und frühdynastische Zeit (Freiburg: Universitätsverlag, 1998), pp. 15–233.

[39] Igor M. Diakonoff, "The Rise of the Despotic State in Ancient Mesopotamia," in Igor M. Diakonoff (ed.), Ancient Mesopotamia: Socio-Economic History (Moscow: Nauka, 1969), pp. 173–203.

[40] Kazuya Maekawa, "The 'Temples' and the 'Temple Personnel' of Ur III Girsu-Lagash," in Kazuko Watanabe (ed.), Priests and Officials in the Ancient Near East (Heidelberg: Universitätsverlag C. Winter, 1999), pp. 61–102.

Field measurements and proportions were standardized within regions, and by the end of the third millennium BCE, officials categorized types and sizes of available land in land surveys.[41] The overall impression of increasing control over the rural landscape is difficult to avoid, and at the same time, it remains difficult to estimate the proportion of the population that lived and worked beyond the regular labor requirements of urban institutions.

Herds and textiles

The concentration of population in cities also made possible the development of what would become the most important export from Lower Mesopotamia – woolen textiles. This extremely labor-intensive industry is mentioned in Late Uruk texts as well as being depicted on cylinder seals of that period, in which women (usually "pig-tailed") are shown working, most commonly on textile production.[42] Textiles were made in a variety of grades: some used for rations to workers, some for trade, and others to clothe the elite.

As with agricultural land, there is a clear trend through the fourth and third millennia BCE for intensification of institutional textile production. Some early texts mention shepherds and their flocks (the largest in the Jamdat Nasr period being about 1,400 animals).[43] These herds were also monitored for production of milk products and were used as offerings to the temple of Inanna. Early Dynastic texts from Lagash record rations to textile workshops of up to twenty-five female weavers.[44] By contrast, in provinces of the Ur III Empire, one text records 378 tons of wool, which would have come from something like 500,000 sheep and close to 15,000 weavers – mostly women, most dependent on rations from the temple – in a single textile factory.[45] Over 13,000 workers were employed by the "Wool Office" in the imperial capital of Ur, which also accounted for at least 2,000 tons of wool.[46] It is clear that not all these workers resided in the city and that

[41] Mario Liverani, "Reconstructing the Rural Landscape of the Ancient Near East," *Journal of the Economic and Social History of the Orient* 39 (1996), 1–41; and Maekawa, "'The "Temples."'"

[42] Susan Pollock and Reinhard Bernbeck, "And They Said, Let Us Make Gods in Our Image: Gendered Ideologies in Ancient Mesopotamia," in Alison E. Rautman (ed.), *Reading the Body: Representations and Remains in the Archaeological Record* (Philadelphia: University of Pennsylvania Press, 2000), pp. 150–64.

[43] Englund, "Texts from the Late Uruk Period," p. 147, fig. 50.

[44] M. Lambert, "Recherches sur la vie ouvrière. Les ateliers de tissage de Lagash au temps de Lugalanda et d'Urukagina," *Archív Orientální* 29 (1961), 422–43.

[45] Hartmut Waetzoldt, *Untersuchungen zur neusumerischen Textilindustrie* (Rome: Centro per le Antichità e la Storia dell'Arte del Vicino Oriente, 1972), p. 14.

[46] Thorkild Jacobsen, "On the Textile Industry at Ur under Ibbī-Sîn," in Fleming Hvidberg (ed.), *Studia Orientalia Ioanni Pedersen* (Munksgaard: Hauniae, 1953), pp. 172–87.

aspects of production took place in the countryside. Nevertheless, at a time when the city of Ur itself occupied not much more than 50 hectares in area, 13,000 people working in a single industry represents an extremely significant concentration of population.

It is not clear from these records where the 500,000 sheep were pastured, but this too represents a significant impact on the landscape. An innovation of the Ur III Empire was a series of centralized distribution centers that received taxes and tributes and redistributed them as necessary. The best-known of these was the livestock redistribution center at Puzrish-Dagan, and it is likely that some of the sheep and wool mentioned in the accounts of the Wool Office at Ur came from the broader imperial territory. In Old Babylonian times, palaces and temples conducted smaller-scale contracts with shepherds to produce wool.

Textiles produced in Mesopotamian cities were among the goods traded by Mesopotamian merchants. In the Early Dynastic period, these merchants were sent on trading expeditions by temple institutions. By the early second millennium BCE, trade was increasingly although not exclusively carried out by private family businesses, the best-known of which were the Assyrian traders who dealt in textiles from southern cities, along with tin, for copper and gold in the mountains of Anatolia. The clearest evidence for what we would recognize as modern economic behavior – fluctuating prices and profit motives – comes from the private businesses of the Old Assyrian period. Some scholars consider entrepreneurial behavior and most aspects of market economies to characterize Mesopotamia from the time of the earliest cities. However, others suggest that a market economy was itself a process that emerged in cities over the course of centuries, and particularly with the existence of huge productive capacity and the mechanisms for control and distribution at the end of the Ur III empire.

The economy of Upper Mesopotamian cities may also have focused on herds and textiles. The Early Dynastic palace archive at Ebla – Mesopotamian only in the broad sense of using cuneiform texts – suggests that the royal herds exceeded 600,000 animals.[47] Moreover, a distinctive urban form of Upper Mesopotamia known as *Kranzhügel*, with concentric walls enclosing empty space, may relate to the need to protect large flocks from attack.

[47] Lucio Milano, "Ebla: A Third-Millennium City-State in Ancient Syria," *Civilizations of the Ancient Near East* 2 (1995), 1219–30.

Conclusion: a landscape of cities

Mesopotamian cities have been extensively studied, and our view of these cities has ossified into a composite and static picture developed from all Mesopotamian cities. The account presented here proposes that ancient cities were dynamic and varied, and that they generated significant economic, political, and social change in Mesopotamian society. A potentially important step toward understanding these processes is the project begun by Tony Wilkinson and McGuire Gibson at the University of Chicago, Modeling Ancient Settlement Systems (MASS).[48] Mesopotamian cities were concentrations of population that were increasingly influenced by urban institutions of temple and palace. By concentrating people in cities, Mesopotamian rulers were able to increasingly produce and exchange agricultural products and textiles, which allowed them to build the central institutions of cities themselves. Urban merchants also contracted with temples and palaces, and were protected by rulers who negotiated treaties with their peers. The history of Mesopotamia cannot be told without reference to its cities, and an account of Mesopotamian cities resembles in some ways an account of Mesopotamian civilization itself.

FURTHER READINGS

Archi, Alfonso, "The City of Ebla and the Organization of the Rural Territory," in Erik Aerts and Horst Klengel (eds.), *The Town as Regional Economic Centre in the Ancient Near East*, Leuven: Leuven University Press, 1990, pp. 15–19.
Bernbeck, Reinhard, "Class Conflict in Ancient Mesopotamia: Between Knowledge of History and Historicizing Knowledge," *Anthropology of the Middle East* 4 (2009), 33–64.
Childe, V. Gordon, "The Urban Revolution," *Town Planning Review* 21 (1950), 3–17.
Cohen, Mark Nathan, *Health and the Rise of Civilization*, New Haven, CT: Yale University Press, 1989.
Cooper, Jerrold S., *Reconstructing History from Ancient Inscriptions: The Lagash–Umma Border Conflict*, Malibu: Undena, 1983.
Delougaz, Pinhas, Harold D. Hill, and Seton Lloyd, *Private Houses and Graves in the Diyala Region*, Chicago: The University of Chicago Press, 1967.
Durand, Jean-Marie, "L'assemblée en Syrie à l'époque pré-amorite," in Pelio Fronzaroli (ed.), *Miscellanea Eblaitica*, Firenze: Università di Firenze, Dipartimento di Linguistica, 1989, Vol. ii, pp. 27–44.

---

[48] T. J. Wilkinson, J. H. Christiansen, Jason A. Ur, M. Widell, and M. Altaweel, "Urbanization within a Dynamic Environment: Modeling Bronze Age Communities in Upper Mesopotamia," *American Anthropologist* 109 (2007), 52–68.

Emberling, Geoff, "Political Control in an Early State: The Eye Temple and the Uruk Expansion in Northern Mesopotamia," in Lamia al-Gailani Werr *et al.* (eds.), *Of Pots and Plans: Papers on the Archaeology and History of Mesopotamia and Syria Presented to David Oates in Honour of his 75th Birthday*, London: Nabu, 2002, pp. 82–90.

"Urban Social Transformations and the Problem of the 'First City': New Research from Mesopotamia," in Monica L. Smith (ed.), *The Social Construction of Ancient Cities*, Washington, D.C.: Smithsonian Institution Press, 2003, pp. 254–68.

Forest, Jean-Daniel, "La grande architecture obeidienne, sa forme et sa fonction," in Jean-Louis Huot (ed.), *Préhistoire de la Mésopotamie: La Mésopotamie préhistorique et l'exploration récente du Djebel Hamrin*, Paris: Éditions du Centre National de la Recherche Scientifique, 1987, pp. 385–423.

Gelb, I. J., "On the Alleged Temple and State Economies in Ancient Mesopotamia," in *Studi in Onore di Edoardo Volterra*, Milan: A. Giuffrè, 1969, pp. 137–54.

Kühne, Hartmut, "Šaiḫ Ḥamad, Tall (Dūr-Katlimmu). B. Archäologisch," *Reallexikon der Assyriologie* 11 (2008), 543–51.

Lebeau, Marc, "Les Temples de Tell Beydar et leur environnement immédiat à l'époque Early Jezirah IIIb," in Pascal Butterlin, Marc Lebeau, J. Y. Monchambert, J. L. Montero Fenollós, and B. Muller (eds.), *Les espaces syro-mésopotamiens: dimensions de l'expérience humaine au Proche-Orient ancien*, Turnhout: Brepols, 2006, pp. 101–40.

Liverani, Mario, "Ancient Near Eastern Cities and Modern Ideologies," in Gernot Wilhelm (ed.), *Die orientalische Stadt: Kontinuität, Wandel, Bruch*, Saarbrücken: Saarbrücker Druckerei und Verlag, 1997, pp. 85–107.

Margueron, Jean-Claude, *Recherches sur les palais Mésopotamiens de l'Age du Bronze*, Paris: Guethner, 1982.

Matney, Timothy, and Guillermo Algaze, "Urban Development at Mid–Late Early Bronze Age Titriş Höyük in Southeastern Anatolia," *Bulletin of the American Schools of Oriental Research* 299/300 (1995), 33–52.

McMahon, Augusta, "Mesopotamia," in Peter Clark (ed.), *The Oxford Handbook of Cities in World History*, Oxford: Oxford University Press, pp. 31–48.

Meyer, Jan-Waalke, "Town Planning in 3rd Millennium Tell Chuera," in J. Bretschneider, Jan Driessen, and K. Van Lerberghe (eds.), *Power and Architecture: Monumental Public Architecture in the Bronze Age Near East and Aegean*, Leuven: Peeters, 2007, pp. 129–42.

Postgate, J. N., *The West Mound Surface Clearance*, London: British School of Archaeology in Iraq, 1983.

Ristvet, Lauren, "Legal and Archaeological Territories of the Second Millennium BC in Northern Mesopotamia," *Antiquity* 82 (2008), 585–99.

"The Third Millennium City Wall at Tell Leilan, Syria: Identity, Authority, and Urbanism," in J. Bretschneider, J. Driessen, and K. Van Lerberghe (eds.), *Power and Architecture: Monumental Public Architecture in the Bronze Age Near East and Aegean*, Leuven: Peeters, 2007, pp. 183–211.

Seri, Andrea, *Local Power in Old Babylonian Mesopotamia*, London: Equinox, 2005.

Smith, Adam, *The Political Landscape: Constellations of Authority in Early Complex Polities*, Berkeley: University of California Press, 2003.

Smith, Michael, "The Archaeological Study of Neighborhoods and Districts in Ancient Cities," *Journal of Anthropological Archaeology* 29 (2010), 137–54.

Ur, Jason A., "Bronze Age Cities of the Plains and the Highlands: Southern Mesopotamia," in D. T. Potts (ed.), *A Companion to the Archaeology of the Ancient Near East*, Malden, MA: Wiley-Blackwell, 2012, Vol. I, pp. 533–55.

"Sennacherib's Northern Assyrian Canals: New Insights from Satellite Imagery and Aerial Photography," *Iraq* 67 (2005), 317–45.

Ur, Jason A., and Tony Wilkinson, "Settlement and Economic Landscapes of Tell Beydar and its Hinterland," in Marc Lebeau and Antoine Suleiman (eds.), *Beydar Studies*, Turnhout: Brepols, 2008, Vol. I, pp. 305–27.

Vallet, Régis, "Habuba Kebira ou la naissance de l'urbanisme," *Paléorient* 22 (1996), 45–76.

Weiss, Harvey, "The Origins of Tell Leilan and the Conquest of Space in Third Millennium Mesopotamia," in H. Weiss (ed.), *The Origins of Cities in Dry-Farming Syria and Mesopotamia in the Third Millennium B.C.*, Guilford, CT: Four Quarters, 1986, pp. 71–108.

Weiss, Harvey, M. A. Courty, W. Wetterstrom, F. Guichard, L. M. Senior, R. Meadow, and A. Curnow, "The Genesis and Collapse of Third Millennium North Mesopotamian Civilization," *Science* 261 (1993), 995–1004.

Westenholz, Aage, "The Sumerian City-State," in Mogens H. Hansen (ed.), *A Comparative Study of Six City-State Cultures*, Copenhagen: C. A. Reitzels, 2002, pp. 23–42.

Wright, Henry T., *The Administration of Rural Production in an Early Mesopotamian Town*, Ann Arbor: University of Michigan Museum of Anthropology, 1969.

Wright, Rita P., "Crafting Social Identity in Ur III Southern Mesopotamia," in Cathy Lynne Costin and Rita P. Wright (eds.), *Craft and Social Identity*, Arlington, VA: Archeological Papers of the American Anthropological Association, 1998, pp. 57–69.

Zeder, Melinda A., *Feeding Cities: Specialized Animal Economy in the Ancient Near East*, Washington, D.C.: Smithsonian Institution, 1993.

Zettler, Richard L., *The Ur III Temple of Inanna at Nippur: The Operation and Organisation of Urban Religious Institutions in Mesopotamia in the Late Third Millennium B.C.*, Berlin: Dietrich Reimer, 1992.

13

Teotihuacan: an early urban center in its regional context

SARAH C. CLAYTON

The first century BCE in the northeastern Basin of Mexico witnessed the emergence of Teotihuacan, a city that rapidly developed into the capital of a regional state of unprecedented size, monumentality, ethnic and social diversity, and political power in the Mexican Highlands (Map 13.1). Teotihuacan was a "primate" center, its peak population of more than 100,000 people dwarfing that of all contemporaneous settlements in the region. A varied mosaic of farmers, craft specialists, merchants, and immigrants resided in the 20-square-kilometer area identified as the urban zone of Teotihuacan. Teotihuacan's population was not limited, however, to the capital; it also extended to several rural settlements from which the state derived many resources necessary for sustaining the urban population. Teotihuacan extended its influence to such far-flung regions as the Gulf and Maya Lowlands, west Mexico, Oaxaca, and the Maya Highlands, engaging in interregional relations that likely ranged from occasional diplomatic interaction to political manipulation through acts of conquest. After flourishing for more than six centuries, Teotihuacan's political prominence and elite institutions had irrevocably dissolved by around 650 CE. Although its eminence was probably waning by the sixth century, Teotihuacan's eventual end was marked by calamitous events, as the city's central monuments and residences were violently attacked and burned. The city continued to be inhabited, supporting a relatively large population of perhaps 40,000, but it was never again to wield the degree of regional political power or interregional influence that it had previously achieved.[1]

---

[1] George L. Cowgill, "The Central Mexican Highlands from the Rise of Teotihuacan to the Decline of Tula," in Richard E. W. Adams and Murdo J. MacLeod (eds.), *The Cambridge History of the Native Peoples of the Americas* (Cambridge: Cambridge University Press, 2000), Vol. II, Part 1, pp. 250–317.

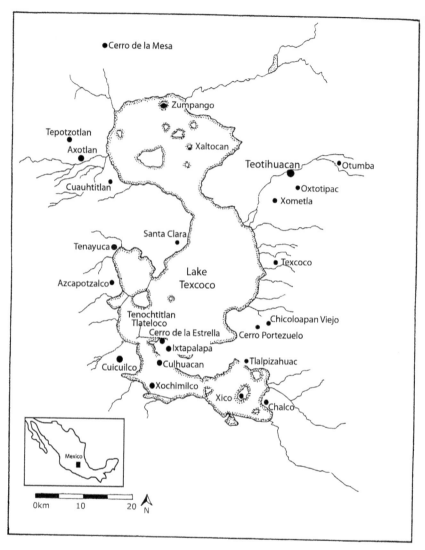

Map 13.1 Settlements in the Prehispanic Basin of Mexico (drawn by author).

To understand the structure and longevity of the Teotihuacan state as well as its eventual unraveling, archaeologists recognize the importance of investigating its social, economic, and political processes at multiple scales, from individual households to regional settlements. Individual members of complex societies like Teotihuacan do not experience their society in a monolithic way. Rather, they manage environmental and cultural circumstances in ways pursuant to their particular social positions and the resources and opportunities that those positions afford. Recent archaeological inquiry at Teotihuacan reflects a strong interest in the ways in which social heterogeneity impacted Teotihuacan's political and economic structures through time. Differences in economic activities, social organization and status, ritual and political ideologies, and expressions of identity among rural and urban sectors of the population were among the most significant dimensions of variation to shape Teotihuacan society.

Teotihuacan is often viewed as an impressive ancient city, but it must be understood as a regional phenomenon that included the city, its suburban periphery and surrounding countryside, as well as more distant rural settlements and populations as part of its sociospatial landscape. The urbanization of Teotihuacan was concurrently a process of *ruralization* of the surrounding region. In this chapter I explore Teotihuacan both internally (within the city) and regionally, in an attempt to consider the social terrain of this early state from a holistic perspective. I discuss current conceptualizations, based on archaeological research, of Teotihuacan's political development and the organization of its rural and urban communities and conclude with some suggestions regarding future research.

The growth of Teotihuacan

The reasons for Teotihuacan's rapid growth from marginal beginnings to a population on the order of 20,000 to 40,000[2] during the Patlachique phase, from 150 to 1 BCE (Table 13.1), remain enigmatic. Several factors have been suggested, including the desire for safety under conditions of persistent conflict and violence, promising economic opportunities, compelling religious ideas, and perhaps uncommonly capable and ambitious leaders. Teotihuacan's early growth is probably attributable to some combination of these factors, but further archaeological research is necessary in order to determine which were the most salient.

Until recently, many archaeologists believed that Teotihuacan's growth was due in large part to a catastrophic volcanic eruption that destroyed

[2] George L. Cowgill, "Quantitative Studies of Urbanization at Teotihuacan," in Norman Hammond (ed.), *Mesoamerican Archaeology: New Approaches* (London: Duckworth, 1974), pp. 363–96.

Table 13.1 *Chronological periods and corresponding Teotihuacan phases*

General Chronology	Teotihuacan Phases	Approximate Years
Early Postclassic period	Atlatongo	950–1150 CE
	Mazapan	850–950 CE
Epiclassic period	Coyotlatelco	650–850 CE
Teotihuacan period/Early Classic	Metepec	550–650 CE
	Xolalpan	450–550 CE
	Tlamimilolpa	200–350 CE
Teotihuacan period/Terminal	Miccaotli	125–200 CE
Formative	Tzacualli	1–125 CE
	Patlachique	150 BCE–1 CE

Cuicuilco, a center that developed earlier than Teotihuacan, in the shadow of the volcano Xitle, located in the southwestern Basin of Mexico. The rich soil surrounding the Cuicuilco settlement was superior to that of the Teotihuacan Valley and better suited for irrigation agriculture. Numerous monuments, including a circular pyramid standing more than 20 meters high, attest to Cuicuilco's sociopolitical importance within the region. Although the precise extent of the settlement is not known, Cuicuilco is believed to have covered at least 4 square kilometers. It hosted a population that Sanders and colleagues estimate to have been at least 20,000 during the Patlachique phase – similar to that of Teotihuacan.[3] This has led many researchers to view the two settlements as competitors, although more research is necessary to understand the nature of their relationship with each other and with their smaller contemporaries.

Recent studies of volcanic activity suggest that the eruption of Xitle occurred around 300 CE, when Teotihuacan was at its demographic height and already dominated the region.[4] Archaeological evidence indicates that ash and lava covered structures at Cuicuilco that were already in disrepair.[5]

[3] William T. Sanders, Jeffrey R. Parsons, and Robert S. Santley, *The Basin of Mexico: Ecological Processes in the Evolution of a Civilization* (New York: Academic Press, 1979).
[4] Claus Siebe, "Age and Archaeological Implications of Xitle Volcano, Southwestern Basin of Mexico City," *Journal of Volcanology and Geothermal Research* 104 (2000), 45–64.
[5] Carlos F. Cordova, Ana Lillian Martin de Pozzo, and Javier Lopez Camacho, "Paleo-landforms and Volcanic Impact on the Environment of Prehistoric Cuicuilco, Southern Mexico City," *Journal of Archaeological Science* 21 (1994), 585–96.

This information contradicts the traditional view that Teotihuacan's development was directly linked to the total destruction of Cuicuilco. It does not, however, negate the importance of volcanic activity in the decline of Cuicuilco and the growth of Teotihuacan; it is entirely plausible that the catastrophic eruption of Xitle was preceded by the occasional bursts of activity that often associate with active volcanoes. Perhaps such signs from Xitle were perceived as threatening enough for some people to relocate from the southwestern Basin to Teotihuacan, especially given the evident eruption of Popocatepetl during the first century CE. Popocatepetl remains active today, and its eruption may have prompted large-scale migrations from the southeastern Basin and western Puebla into the Teotihuacan Valley.[6] The events associated with the Popocatepetl disaster may not have directly impacted all parts of the Basin. However, they would have become part of the collective awareness and social memory of groups living across the central Highlands. Therefore, migration from the southeast should not be viewed in isolation, but as one process within a possible chain of events on a regional scale that contributed to the growth of Teotihuacan, the ideological concepts that undergirded its central institutions, and its political consolidation of the region.

Governance and the urban capital

Careful civic planning during the early stages of Teotihuacan's history is evident, although it is more likely that the ultimate configuration of the monumental core area evolved through time than that a coherent master plan was conceived in entirety from the beginning. Downtown Teotihuacan is characterized by striking monumentality and orderliness. Its major structures are aligned to 15.5 degrees east of north, neatly arranged around the 50-meter-wide path of the Avenue of the Dead, which follows the same canonical orientation. This avenue was the main artery of movement through the heart of Teotihuacan, gradually ascending northward for more than 5 kilometers from the southern margins of the city toward its termination at the Pyramid of the Moon. Teotihuacan's architectural monuments were within the daily viewshed of the entire urban population as well as those living in the suburban and rural fringes. They likely provided a constant reminder of both the power of the state and perhaps a broadly

---

[6] Patricia Plunket and Gabriela Uruñuela, "Recent Research in Puebla Prehistory," *Journal of Archaeological Research* 13 (2005), 89–127.

shared notion of Teotihuacano identity. The Avenue of the Dead also significantly shaped the Teotihuacano experience through the activities that it supported and by contouring movement through the urban space. It provided a key setting for political, religious, and economic action and would have been the ceremonial path for processions culminating at the Pyramid of the Moon, during which crowds of spectators may have gathered and watched from along the sides of the avenue. The Avenue of the Dead bisects the city into eastern and western halves, which are further divided into northern and southern quadrants by the narrower East–West Avenue. Whether these spatial divisions had symbolic significance when they were planned is not known, though they may gradually have come to represent or to cement sociospatial or economic differences among sectors of the urban population through time.

Researchers seeking to elucidate the structure of government at Teotihuacan have looked primarily to its most prominent monumental complexes for material evidence – the Pyramid of the Moon, the Pyramid of the Sun, and the Ciudadela, a large enclosure within which the Feathered Serpent Pyramid was situated. Governance at Teotihuacan remains enigmatic, and no buried ruler has ever been located within any of these monuments or elsewhere at Teotihuacan. Large-scale excavations at the Feathered Serpent Pyramid and the Pyramid of the Moon have uncovered the remains of elaborate rituals of offering and sacrifice. These offerings include predatory animals (Burial 2 in the Pyramid of the Moon, for example, includes pumas, birds of prey, rattlesnakes, and a wolf) as well as staggering numbers of human victims, many of whom appear to have been highly decorated warriors. These important projects have contributed to a clearer picture of the military might of the Teotihuacan state, but no individual inhumed in these monuments has ever been identified as a ruler. Moreover, there are no clear depictions of rulers in the large body of art and sculpture that has been recovered from the ancient city. The absence of depictions of glorified individuals suggests that rulership at Teotihuacan differed from that of other Mesoamerican states. The Maya, for example, were prolific in producing monuments commemorating the accomplishments of specific rulers.

Some have proposed that the Teotihuacan state began as a republic or had a collective political structure run by a governing council.[7] It may have

---

[7] See for example Linda Manzanilla, "The Economic Organization of the Teotihuacan Priesthood: Hypothesis and Considerations," in Janet C. Berlo (ed.), *Art, Ideology, and the City of Teotihuacan* (Washington, D.C.: Dumbarton Oaks, 1993), pp. 321–38.

originated through the deliberate convergence of several previously autonomous and politically equal groups. Such a synoikistic process was recently
argued on the basis of the Teotihuacan's earliest civic-ceremonial configuration, which comprised several architecturally distinct and spatially separate
complexes.[8] Cowgill has suggested, however, that if Teotihuacan's initial
institutions were relatively corporate in structure and the sanctioned ideology emphasized collectivity, they nonetheless seem to have been swiftly
subverted by strong rulers.[9] Powerful individuals, he argues, were likely
responsible for conceiving and executing the immense pyramids and other
ambitious buildings that were in place by 250 CE and represent the civic
configuration of Teotihuacan that is recognizable today.

Life in the city

More is known about the urban landscape of Teotihuacan than that of many
other ancient cities, due to the Teotihuacan Mapping Project (TMP), an
immense archaeological undertaking that began in 1962 under the direction
of René Millon.[10] Members of the TMP mapped the city in tremendous
detail (Map 13.2), made artifact collections from across its surface, and
carried out twenty-eight stratigraphic excavations that provided the basis
for developing a ceramic chronology for Teotihuacan. Among many other
things, the TMP revealed that urban Teotihuacan had covered about
20 square kilometers for several centuries and that at its height, most of
its population resided in some 2,300 large residential compounds.

Apartment compounds were not the only kind of dwelling present at
Teotihuacan, however, and it is increasingly clear that a significant proportion of the urban population resided in smaller, less substantial structures.[11]
These relatively ephemeral structures were located among apartment compounds and may have been prevalent in the immediate margins of the urban
capital, a "suburban" area that has, until recently, been largely overlooked in

---

[8] Tatsuya Murakami, "Power Relations and Urban Landscape Formation: A Study of
  Construction Labor and Resources at Teotihuacan," Ph.D. dissertation, Arizona State
  University, 2010.
[9] George L. Cowgill, "State and Society at Teotihuacan, Mexico," *Annual Review of
  Anthropology* 26 (1997), 129–61.
[10] René Millon, *The Teotihuacan Map* (Austin: University of Texas Press, 1973).
[11] M. Oralia Cabrera Cortés, "Craft Production and Socio-Economic Marginality: Living
  on the Periphery of Urban Teotihuacan," Ph.D. dissertation, Arizona State University,
  2011, and Ian G. Robertson, "'Insubstantial' Residential Structures at Teotihuacán,
  Mexico," report submitted to Foundation for the Advancement of Mesoamerican
  Studies (2008).

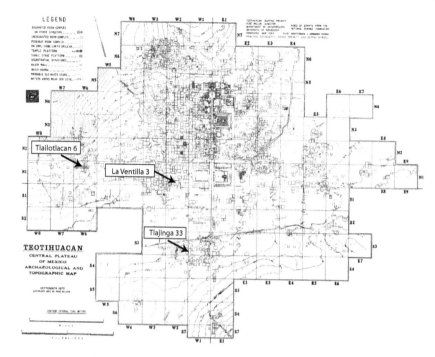

Map 13.2 Map of the city of Teotihuacan showing the locations of monuments and districts mentioned in the text (modified from the original 1:40,000 scale map by the Teotihuacan Mapping Project, René Millon, *The Teotihuacan Map* [Austin: University of Texas Press, 1973], Map 1).

archaeological research at Teotihuacan. Research focused on Teotihuacan's outer fringes is an important future direction that is crucial for understanding the socioeconomic make-up of the city, the dynamic nature of its boundaries, and the movement of people to and from the surrounding countryside.

The construction of apartment compounds across the city occurred as part of what Millon described as an urban renewal project.[12] Although the compounds vary considerably in size and layout, Millon argued that they conformed to sufficient criteria to imply the existence of a basic

---

[12] René Millon, "Teotihuacan: City, State, and Civilization, in Supplement to the *Handbook of Middle American Indians*," in Victoria A. Bricker and Jeremy A. Sabloff (eds.), *Handbook of Middle American Indians, Supplement* (Austin: University of Texas Press, 1981), Vol. 1, pp. 195–243.

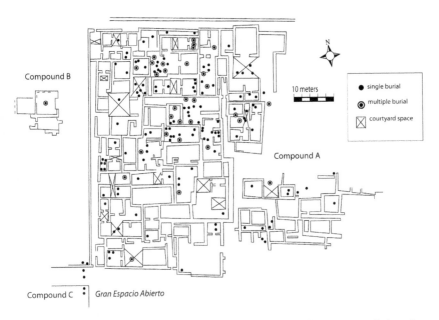

Figure 13.1 Layout of an apartment compound in the La Ventilla District, including the location of courtyards and burials (drawing after Sergio Gómez Chávez and Jaime Núñez Hernández, "Análisis preliminar del patrón y la distribución espacial de entierros en el Barrio de La Ventilla," in Linda Manzanilla and Carlos Serrano [eds.], *Prácticas funerarias en la Ciudad de los Dioses: los enterramientos humanos de la antigua Teotihuacan* [Mexico City: Instituto de Investigaciones Antropológicas, 1999], pp. 81–148).

model, which he proposed was designed by the state. This argument is based not only on the general adherence of compounds to certain architectural standards such as orientations consistent with those of major city streets and monuments, but also on the timing of their construction. These multi-room structures, which housed up to 60–100 people at a time, were built beginning in the Early Tlamimilolpa phase (200–275 CE), at the peak of Teotihuacan's regional dominance and its interregional expansion. They consistently contain several rooms arranged around open-air gathering spaces (Figure 13.1),[13] which are widely believed to have been loci

[13] Drawing after Sergio Gómez Chávez and Jaime Núñez Hernández, "Análisis preliminar del patrón y la distribución espacial de entierros en el Barrio de La Ventilla," in Linda Manzanilla and Carlos Serrano (eds.), *Prácticas funerarias en la Ciudad de los Dioses: los enterramientos humanos de la antigua Teotihuacan* (Mexico City: Instituto de Investigaciones Antropológicas, 1999), pp. 81–148.

for domestic rituals. Manzanilla argues that individual apartment suites within the compounds were associated with distinct households.[14] Compounds were generally enclosed by thick exterior walls, suggesting an inward focus and a degree of internal privacy shared by the compound residential group.

Although it is reasonable to posit that state rulers initiated a new mode of residential organization at Teotihuacan, there is evidence to suggest that the construction of individual compounds was not directed by the state. In addition to the variation in quality, size, and internal arrangement present among Teotihuacan's compounds, at least some compounds were expanded accretionally through time. Excavations at the compound Tlajinga 33, for example, demonstrate that it was remodeled no fewer than a dozen times, changing substantially through four centuries of occupation. Furthermore, its walls were never oriented to "Teotihuacan north" and its internal structures do not conform to conventions often thought to be typical of Teotihuacan domestic architecture.[15]

Apartment compounds and possibly neighborhoods containing clusters of compounds, often called *barrios*, may have formed an organizational level that articulated households and state administrative institutions. However, such residential clusters have proven elusive as social units, and the specific relationships among the individuals that co-resided within the compounds themselves are not fully understood. For example, some residential areas, such as the Oaxaca Enclave, are characterized primarily by their association with migrant groups, which were absorbed into these areas throughout Teotihuacan's history.[16] Residents of compounds that were inter-ethnic and

[14] Linda Manzanilla, "Houses and Ancestors, Altars and Relics: Mortuary Patterns at Teotihuacan, Central Mexico," in Helaine Silverman and David B. Small (eds.), *The Space and Place of Death* (Arlington, VA: American Anthropological Association, 2002), pp. 55–65; and Michael W. Spence, "Domestic Ritual in Tlailotlacan, Teotihuacan," in Patricia Plunket (ed.), *Domestic Ritual in Ancient Mesoamerica* (Los Angeles: Cotsen Institute of Archaeology, University of California, 2002), pp. 53–66.
[15] Rebecca Storey and Randolph J. Widmer, "Social Organization and Household Structure of a Teotihuacan Apartment Compound: S3W1:33 of the Tlajinga Barrio," in Robert S. Santley and Kenneth G. Hirth (eds.), *Prehispanic Domestic Units in Western Mesoamerica: Studies of the Household, Compound, and Residence* (Boca Raton: CRC Press, 1993), pp. 87–104.
[16] Michael W. Spence, Christine D. White, Evelyn C. Rattray, and Fred J. Longstaffe, "Past Lives in Different Places: The Origins and Relationships of Teotihuacan's Foreign Residents," in Richard E. Blanton (ed.), *Settlement, Subsistence, and Social Complexity: Essays Honoring the Legacy of Jeffrey R. Parsons* (Los Angeles: Cotsen Institute of Archaeology, 2005), pp. 155–97.

incorporated immigrants may have been distantly related or not related biologically at all. Such an initial arrangement may be expected, however, to develop through time into more kin-like social groups as individuals married into compounds and produced children.

Some compounds have been associated with specialized craft production activities on the scale of multiple households, and compounds are frequently discussed in terms of socioeconomic status. For example, Tetitla is often thought of as a "high-status" compound, Oztoyahualco is described as "middle class," and Tlajinga 33 has been described as both "typical"[17] and "impoverished."[18] The correlation between residence and status is further complicated by the fact that compounds were occupied by persons of varying status and likely had their own internal social hierarchies. Moreover, the economic and social structure of the compounds was not static. Economic activities sometimes shifted, as in the case of Tlajinga 33, where lapidary work as a specialization was ultimately replaced by pottery-making. Socioeconomic differences and a range of other notions of identity must have both impacted and been shaped by the social and architectural environment associated with compound residential organization.

Many compounds that were built in the Early Tlamimilolpa phase were occupied until the end of Teotihuacan's statehood, a period of around 400 years. Given the longevity of compound occupation, the "kin-like" relations among their occupants, and their joint participation in production activities, the concept of social "houses"[19] may provide a useful framework for linking social identity and residential affiliation in Teotihuacan society. The house model, which has been tentatively suggested by several Teotihuacan scholars,[20] foregrounds daily interaction, ritual practices, co-residence, and

---

[17] Storey and Widmer, "Social organization."

[18] Manzanilla, "Houses and Ancestors," p. 45; and Rebecca Storey, "Mortality through Time in an Impoverished Residence of the Precolumbian City of Teotihuacan," in Glenn R. Storey (ed.), *Urbanism in the Preindustrial World: Cross-Cultural Approaches* (Tuscaloosa: University of Alabama Press, 2006), pp. 277–94.

[19] Susan D. Gillespie, "Rethinking Ancient Maya Social Organization: Replacing 'Lineage' with 'House,'" *American Anthropologist* 102 (2000), 467–84.

[20] See for example Sarah C. Clayton, "Gender and Mortuary Ritual at Ancient Teotihuacan, Mexico: A Study of Intrasocietal Diversity," *Cambridge Archaeological Journal* 21 (2011), 31–52; George L. Cowgill, "The Urban Organization of Teotihuacan, Mexico," in Elizabeth C. Stone (ed.), *Settlement and Society: Essays Dedicated to Robert McCormick Adams* (Los Angeles: Cotsen Institute, 2007), pp. 261–95; Kristin de Lucia, "Looking Beyond Gender Hierarchy: Rethinking Gender at Teotihuacan, Mexico," in Cynthia Robin and Elizabeth M. Brumfiel (eds.), *Gender, Households, and Society: Unraveling the Threads of Past and Present* (Washington, D.C.: American Anthropological Association,

economic activities over blood ancestry. It does not preclude internal status variation within compound groups, but it does presuppose that the residents of these structures interacted with each other on a regular basis. This is a reasonable assessment, based on the presence of gathering spaces in compounds as well as the practice of burying the dead under compound floors and walls, which surely expressed a meaningful and lasting connection to these places.

Economic organization at Teotihuacan

Additional archaeological research at Teotihuacan period settlements across the Basin of Mexico is needed for fully comprehending the regional economic structure of this ancient state. Research focused on the materials produced and consumed by the urban population is plentiful, however, and indicates that individuals residing in the city engaged in a wide variety of economic activities and specializations. Households with access to or ownership of land and sources of water probably based their livelihoods on the exchange of products made from maize, maguey, and a wide variety of other cultivates. Households also practiced a variety of craft specializations, including pottery and stone tool production, lapidary work, and lime processing.

Some craft production at Teotihuacan required access to specific resources beyond the Teotihuacan Valley. These include, for example, obsidian from the Pachuca source in the Sierra de las Navajas and lime from sources near Chingú, in Hidalgo, as well as clay and other materials used in Thin Orange pottery, which was made in Puebla but imported to Teotihuacan, where it was widely consumed. The degree to which the importation, manufacture, and distribution of various resources and materials was controlled by the state, rather than by private groups, for example, is not completely clear. Specialized workshops for the production of lithic and ceramic objects have been identified in association with residential

2008), pp. 17–36; Annabeth Headrick, *The Teotihuacan Trinity: The Sociopolitical Structure of an Ancient Mesoamerican City* (Austin: University of Texas Press, 2007); Linda R. Manzanilla, "Corporate Life in Apartment and Barrio Compounds at Teotihuacan, Central Mexico," in Linda R. Manzanilla and Claude Chapdelaine (eds.), *Domestic Life in Prehispanic Capitals: A Study of Specialization, Hierarchy, and Ethnicity* (Ann Arbor: University of Michigan, 2009), pp. 21–42; and Gabriela Uruñuela and Patricia Plunket, "Tradition and Transformation: Village Ritual at Tetimpa as a Template for Early Teotihuacan," in Nancy Gonlin and Jon C. Lohse (eds.), *Commoner Ritual and Ideology in Ancient Mesoamerica* (Boulder: University Press of Colorado, 2007), pp. 33–54.

compounds as well as in close spatial proximity to major civic-ceremonial structures. Examples of the latter include a workshop adjacent to the north side of the Ciudadela, where ceramic censers and *adornos* were made,[21] and a workshop for the production of obsidian darts and other militaristic objects, located immediately west of the Moon Pyramid.[22]

Members of Teotihuacan's population were involved in diverse economic activities and the goods they produced likely circulated in a variety of ways, ranging from inter-household reciprocation to forms of state-managed redistribution. There is a distinct possibility, although it has not been thoroughly tested, that goods at Teotihuacan circulated through a market system. Teotihuacan scholars have identified a few locations where large marketplaces may have been situated, one being the central plaza of the Great Compound, located across the Avenue of the Dead from the Ciudadela. Here, large concentrations of serving vessels were unearthed by TMP excavations. Vendors may also have operated stands along the wide Avenue of the Dead itself, where food, goods, and services could be offered to passing customers on either a regular or cyclical basis. Market exchange at Teotihuacan would likely have operated on multiple scales, from neighborhood-level interaction to large, principal marketplaces like those known from the Postclassic Basin of Mexico. Systematic archaeological research focused on the identification of marketplaces, including the analysis of micro-artifacts and chemical residues in hypothesized marketplace locations, would contribute significantly to an improved understanding of Teotihuacan's economy.

Rural Teotihuacan

Archaeological investigations in the area that was once Teotihuacan's hinterland have become both increasingly difficult and increasingly urgent due to the rapid growth and extreme urban sprawl of modern Mexico City. This condition seriously impedes field work at smaller regional sites and in many cases has destroyed them altogether. Despite these challenges, a growing body of research focused on communities situated beyond the boundaries of

---

[21] L. Carlos Múnera Bermúdez, *Un taller de cerámica ritual en La Ciudadela, Teotihuacan* (Mexico City: Escuela Nacional de Antropología e Historia, 1985).
[22] David M. Carballo, "Implements of State Power: Weaponry and Martially Themed Obsidian Production near the Moon Pyramid, Teotihuacan," *Ancient Mesoamerica* 18 (2007), 173–90.

the ancient city represents a concern with regional inquiry that is vital for understanding how Teotihuacan the center related to the region that it dominated. This important work continues under the persistent strain of modern development.

The most significant project to explore diachronic settlement patterns throughout the region was the Basin of Mexico Settlement Survey, which covered 3,500 square kilometers through a series of separate surveys by William Sanders, Jeffrey Parsons, Robert Santley, and colleagues.[23] Given the dramatic changes that have shaped the Mexico City area in the decades following this project, archaeologists are tremendously fortunate to be able to consult and build upon the data that it generated. These data continue to be fundamental for examining demographic patterns of growth and decline among regional settlements as well as their particular environmental settings and access to resources. For many Prehispanic sites in the Basin, these surveys provide the only archaeological information we will ever have, since so many have been destroyed by modern development.

Only a few Teotihuacan period sites have been excavated since the regional survey project was conducted; most research concerning the Teotihuacan state has focused exclusively on the urban capital. However, some important exceptions to a generally urban-centric perspective have contributed to the issue of Teotihuacan's economic and political relationships with surrounding settlements. For example, Charlton's investigations of rural sites and trade routes in the Teotihuacan Valley and adjacent areas have led to a firmer grasp on exchange and the settlement organization of rural populations.[24] Recent field projects beyond the Teotihuacan Valley have also provided valuable data for examining differences and similarities among rural settlements and for comprehending how they related to Teotihuacan and its urban population. Large-scale excavations of the settlement of Axotlan present a noteworthy example.[25] The body of data and materials resulting from this project provide a useful source of

[23] Sanders, Parsons, and Santley, *Basin of Mexico*.
[24] Thomas H. Charlton, "The Influence and Legacy of Teotihuacán on Regional Routes and Urban Planning," in Charles D. Trombold (ed.), *Ancient Road Networks and Settlement Hierarchies in the New World* (Cambridge: Cambridge University Press, 1991), pp. 186–97.
[25] Raúl García Chávez, Luis Manuel Gamboa Cabezas, and Nadia V. Vélez Saldaña, "Excavaciones recientes en un sitio de la Fase Tlamimilolpa en Cuautitlán Izcalli, Estado de México," in María Elena Ruiz Gallut and Jesús Torres Peralta (eds.), *Arquitectura y urbanismo: pasado y presente de los espacios en Teotihuacan* (Mexico City: Instituto Nacional de Antropología e Historia, 2005), pp. 487–505.

information for examining the ways that life in a rural settlement differed from that of city dwellers.

Located 35 kilometers to the west of Teotihuacan in the Cuauhtitlan region, Axotlan was a large nucleated village of approximately 10 hectares with a population of around 800 people. The site does not appear to have had a significant occupation until the Tlamimilolpa phase, when Teotihuacan was at the height of its regional political dominance. Excavations at Axotlan revealed two large residential compounds as well as some poorly preserved stone architecture that may represent either a degraded compound or a cluster of less substantial structures. The use of apartment compounds like those of Teotihuacan lends a distinctively urban character to the settlement and expresses cultural likeness with the urban population. Compounds at Axotlan differed from each other in size, internal design, and quality of construction, echoing the variation present among compounds at Teotihuacan. They also share with many of Teotihuacan's compounds the directional orientation of 15.5 degrees east of north. Variation in the quality of construction among Axotlan's compounds suggests that residential groups in this community differed in terms of socioeconomic status.[26] Axotlan is unlikely to have hosted the members of the uppermost social echelons that resided at the urban center, but it is possible that its local households were integrated into the same general class structure that operated in the urban context.

In addition to similarities in residential architecture, residents of Axotlan produced and consumed many of the same kinds of material objects and engaged in ritual activities, such as funerary practices, which were highly congruent with many residential groups at Teotihuacan. These patterns are consistent with a relatively close social connection with urban communities as well as participation in the economic and political institutions connected to the Teotihuacan state. This does not mean, however, that there were not significant differences between Teotihuacan's rural and urban social groups. For example, there are marked differences in the mortuary treatment of males and females at Axotlan, a pattern that contrasts significantly with the relatively similar treatment of the sexes in most mortuary contexts at Teotihuacan. This suggests that principles of gender organization, including

[26] Raúl García Chávez, Luis Manuel Gamboa Cabezas, and Nadia V. Vélez Saldaña, "Excavaciones Recientes en un Sitio de la Fase Tlamimilolpa en Cuautitlán Izcalli, Estado de México," in María Elena Ruiz Gallut and Jesús Torres Peralta (eds.), *Arquitectura y Urbanismo: Pasado y Presente de los Espacios en Teotihuacan* (Mexico City: Instituto Nacional de Antropología e Historia, 2005), pp. 487–505.

the domestic and ritual roles of men and women, may have varied considerably across Teotihuacan society. This variation, which does not just speak to gendered experiences but also relates fundamentally to modes of household and community-level social organization, may have been most pronounced between rural and urban populations.

Beyond the rural–urban comparison, rural settlements may be compared along several dimensions, such as domestic organization and ritual life, to generate a more complete picture of diversity among communities in Teotihuacan's hinterland. Comparative analyses of archaeological assemblages and the behaviors that they represent help us to understand the economic and social connections between rural settlements and Teotihuacan. Equally important, however, is the information that archaeological research at a regional scale can provide regarding the relationships *among* rural settlements themselves. For example, how much direct control did the capital exercise over regional economic networks; or, conversely, to what degree were some rural settlements economically autonomous? How did they relate, socially and economically, to each other? Continued archaeological research at settlements in Teotihuacan's rural hinterland is necessary for answering these important questions.

In pursuit of Teotihuacan's changing social landscape

Ambitious archaeological projects such as the TMP and Basin of Mexico Settlement Survey made great strides toward conceptualizing the process of urban development and decline at Teotihuacan, its settlement density, the size of its population, and the extent of its regional political reach. Abundant research focused within the urban core continues to bring city life at Teotihuacan into focus, from its economic organization and socioeconomic disparities to the materialization of its governing institutions. Nevertheless, there is still much work to be done both within the city and beyond its margins in order to understand Teotihuacan society. Investigations of intrasocietal variation have demonstrated that Teotihuacan's compound groups and neighborhoods differed from each other in significant ways. Issues that require further attention include variation in domestic organization, the impact of immigration and processes of ethnogenesis, diverse ritual practices and the ideological differences that they reflect, and relative health and longevity, accessible through bioarchaeological studies. Significant contributions have been made in many of these areas through intensive excavations within select compounds and barrios. It is important to address these questions on a large scale, however, through the comparison of multiple compounds and neighborhoods, as well as from a diachronic perspective.

Perhaps the most significant issue that stands to benefit from diachronic archaeological research concerning Teotihuacan's social composition and diversity is that of its ultimate political collapse. That is, what processes and events culminated in the end of Teotihuacan, and why did they happen? Violent and destructive events associated with the end of the Metepec phase (550–650 CE) point to either internal rebellion or attack by external forces. These actions seem to have been selectively focused on the monuments and residences of the ruling elite and on elite individuals themselves. Members of the TMP survey identified 147 buildings concentrated around the Avenue of the Dead that exhibited unequivocal evidence of burning, mostly concentrated on staircases and the tops of temple platforms.[27] This burning as evidence for purposeful violence is bolstered by the discovery of smashed and scattered stone sculptures and dismembered skeletons with shattered crania found in the Palaces of the Ciudadela.[28] The numerous temples that were destroyed were never rebuilt and Teotihuacan never recovered, politically, indicating that the government had effectively been rendered impotent. There is evidence from one burned compound on the eastern side of the city to suggest that Teotihuacan was abandoned for a time,[29] but additional research in residences beyond the core is needed to fully explore this question. During the subsequent Coyotlatelco phase (650–850 CE), Teotihuacan supported a population in the tens of thousands. This was a large settlement, relative to its contemporaries in the region, though it was greatly diminished in comparison to the former metropolis.

Archaeologists do not know who was responsible for the violent acts associated with Teotihuacan's demise. Information from research focused on Teotihuacan's general population, however, suggests that increasing socioeconomic inequality, ideological difference, and mounting internal tensions factored in the eventual breakdown of a government that was

[27] René Millon, "The Last Years of Teotihuacan Dominance," in Norman Yoffee and George L. Cowgill (eds.), The Collapse of Ancient States and Civilizations (Tucson: University of Arizona Press, 1988), pp. 102–64.
[28] Ana María Jarquín Pacheco and Enrique Martínez Vargas, "Las excavaciones en el Conjunto 1D," in Rubén Cabrera Castro, Ignacio Rodríguez García, and Noel Morelos García (eds.), Memoria del Proyecto Arqueológico Teotihuacán 80–82 (Mexico City: Instituto Nacional de Antropología e Historia, 1982), pp. 89–126.
[29] Evelyn C. Rattray, "La industria obsidiana durante el periodo Coyotlatelco," Revista Mexicana de Estudios Antropológicos 27 (1981), 213–23.

unable to mitigate these challenges. Sempowski's[30] comparative analysis of status based on mortuary assemblages and Robertson's[31] investigation of Teotihuacan's internal socioeconomic landscape point, respectively, to growing status differentiation and increasing spatial segregation based on status and wealth. More recent analyses of mortuary practices among distinct urban and rural residential groups indicate that Teotihuacan was ideologically diverse, with segments of its population maintaining distinctive ritual traditions.[32] Bioarchaeological research at the Tlajinga 33 compound, a residence of commoners, indicates that quality of life may have been in a state of decline in Teotihuacan's later years, measured by increasing infant mortality and extreme nutritional deficiencies.[33] Additional research along these lines promises to enrich our understanding of the varied social composition of this early state, its possible sources of internal tension, and the dynamic circumstances that ultimately challenged the efficacy of its governing apparatus.

Finally, archaeologists seeking to understand Teotihuacan must strike a balance between research concentrated within its internal urban cityspace and investigations of its surrounding countryside. At stake is a fuller comprehension of the ways in which rural populations were politically integrated, the level of economic interdependence or autonomy among regional settlements, the degree to which rural communities subscribed to institutions of the state or identified socially with the urban population, and the role of rural populations in Teotihuacan's decline.

FURTHER READINGS

Andrews, Bradford W., "Stone Tool Production at Teotihuacan: What More Can We Learn from Surface Collections?", in Kenneth G. Hirth and Bradford W. Andrews (eds.), *Pathways to Prismatic Blades: A Study in Mesoamerican Obsidian Core-Blade Technology*, Los Angeles: The Cotsen Institute of Archaeology, University of California, 2002, pp. 47–60.

Barba, Luis A., and José Luis Córdova Frunz, "Estudios energeticos de la producción de cal en tiempos teotihuacanos y sus implicaciones," *Latin American Antiquity* 10 (1999), 168–79.

[30] Martha L. Sempowski, "Economic and Social Implications of Variations in Mortuary Practices at Teotihuacan," in Janet C. Berlo (ed.), *Art, Ideology, and the City of Teotihuacan* (Washington, D.C.: Dumbarton Oaks, 1992), pp. 27–58.

[31] Ian G. Robertson, "Mapping the Social Landscape of an Early Urban Center: Socio-Spatial Variation in Teotihuacan," Ph.D. dissertation, Arizona State University, 2001.

[32] Sarah C. Clayton, "Ritual Diversity and Social Identities: A Study of Mortuary Behaviors at Teotihuacan, Mexico," Ph.D. dissertation, Arizona State University, 2009.

[33] Storey, "Mortality Through Time."

Beramendi-Orosco, Laura E., Galia González-Hernández, Jaime Urrutia-Fucugauchi, Linda R. Manzanilla, Ana M. Soler-Arechalde, Avto Goguitchaishvili, and Nick Jarboe, "High-Resolution Chronology for the Mesoamerican Urban Center of Teotihuacan Derived from Bayesian Statistics of Radiocarbon and Archaeological Data," *Quaternary Research* 71 (2008), 99–107.

Blanton, Richard E., and Lane Fargher, *Collective Action in the Formation of Pre-modern States*, New York: Springer, 2008.

Cabrera Castro, Rubén, "La excavation de la Estructura 1B en el interior de la Ciudadela," in Rubén Cabrera Castro, Ignacio Rodríguez García, and Noel Morelos García (eds.), *Memoria del Proyecto Arqueologico Teotihuacan 80–82*, Mexico City: Instituto Nacional de Antropología e Historia, 1982, pp. 75–87.

Cabrera Castro, Rubén, and Sergio Gomez Chavez, "La Ventilla: A Model for a Barrio in the Urban Structure of Teotihuacan," in Alba Guadalupe Mastache, Robert H. Cobean, Ángel García Cook, and Kenneth G. Hirth (eds.), *Urbanism in Mesoamerica*, University Park: Pennsylvania State University, 2008, Vol. II, pp. 37–83.

Cap, Bernadette, "'Empty' Spaces and Public Places: A Microscopic View of a Late Classic Plaza at Chan, Belize," in Cynthia Robin (ed.), *Chan: An Ancient Maya Farming Community in Belize*, Gainesville: University of Florida Press, 2012.

Charlton, Thomas H., "Teotihuacan Non Urban Settlements: Functional and Evolutionary Implications," in Emily McClung de Tapia and Evelyn C. Rattray (eds.), *Teotihuacan: nuevos datos, nuevas síntesis, nuevos problemas*, Mexico City: Universidad Nacional Autónoma de México, 1987, pp. 473–88.

Cowgill, George L., "Origins and Development of Urbanism: Archaeological Perspectives," *Annual Review of Anthropology* 33 (2004), 525–49.

"Rulership and the Ciudadela: Political Inferences from Teotihuacan Architecture," in Richard M. Leventhal and Alan L. Kolata (eds.), *Civilization in the Ancient Americas: Essays in Honor of Gordon R. Willey*, Cambridge, MA: Peabody Museum of Archaeology and Ethnology, 1983, pp. 313–43.

"Teotihuacan as an Urban Place," in Alba Guadalupe Mastache, Robert H. Cobean, Ángel García Cook, and Kenneth G. Hirth (eds.), *Urbanism in Mesoamerica*, University Park: Pennsylvania State University, 2008, Vol. II, pp. 85–112.

"The Urban Organization of Teotihuacan, Mexico," in Elizabeth C. Stone (ed.), *Settlement and Society: Essays Dedicated to Robert McCormick Adams*, Los Angeles: Cotsen Institute, 2007, pp. 261–95.

Díaz Oyarzabal, Clara, "Chingú y la expansion teotihuacana," in Evelyn C. Rattray, Clara Díaz Oyarzabal, and Jaime Litvak King (eds.), *Interacción cultural en Mexico central*, Mexico City: Universidad Nacional Autónoma de Mexico, 1981, pp. 107–12.

García Cook, Ángel, "The Historical Importance of Tlaxcala in the Cultural Development of the Central Highlands," in Jeremy A. Sabloff (ed.), *Supplement to the Handbook of Middle American Indians*, Austin: University of Texas Press, 1981, pp. 244–76.

Gazzola, Julie, "La production lapidaria en Teotihuacan, estudio de las actividades productivas en los talleres de un conjunto habitacional," in María Elena Ruiz Gallut and Jesús Torres Peralta (eds.), *Arquitectura y urbanismo: pasado y presente de los espacios en Teotihuacan. Memoria de la Tercera Mesa Redonda de Teotihuacan*, Mexico City: INAH, 2005, pp. 841–78.

Gómez Chávez, Sergio, "La Ventilla: un barrio de la antigua ciudad de Teotihuacan," unpublished BA thesis, Escuela Nacional de Antropología e Historia, 2000.

Heizer, Robert F., and James A. Bennyhoff, "Archaeological Investigation of Cuicuilco, Valley of Mexico, 1957," *Science* 127 (1958), 232–3.

Longstaffe, Fred J., Michael W. Spence, Rebecca Storey, and Christine D. White, "Immigration, Assimilation, and Status in the Ancient City of Teotihuacan: Stable Isotopic Evidence from Tlajinga 33," *Latin American Antiquity* 15 (2004), 176–98.

McClung de Tapia, Emily, "Patrones de subsistencia urbana en Teotihuacan," in Emily McClung de Tapia and Evelyn C. Rattray (eds.), *Teotihuacan: nuevos datos, nuevas sintesis, nuevos problemas*, Mexico City: Universidad Nacional Autónoma de México, 1987, pp. 57–74.

Millon, René, "Social Relations in Ancient Teotihuacan," in Eric R. Wolf (ed.), *The Valley of Mexico*, Albuquerque: University of New Mexico Press, 1976, pp. 205–48.

Millon, René, Bruce Drewitt, and James A. Bennyhoff, *The Pyramid of the Sun at Teotihuacan: 1959 Investigations*, Philadelphia, PA: Transactions of the American Philosophical Society, 1965.

Plunket, Patricia, and Gabriela Uruñuela, "Tradition and Transformation: Village Ritual at Tetimpa as a Template for Early Teotihuacan," in Nancy Gonlin and Jon C. Lohse (eds.), *Commoner Ritual and Ideology in Ancient Mesoamerica*, Boulder: University Press of Colorado, 2007, pp. 33–54.

Rattray, Evelyn C., "Anaranjado Delgado: cerámica de comercio de Teotihuacán," in Evelyn C. Rattray, Clara Díaz Oyarzabal, and Jaime Litvak King (eds.), *Interacción cultural en México Central*, Mexico City: Universidad Nacional Autónoma de México, 1981, pp. 55–80.

Sanders, William T., and Larry J. Gorenflo, *Prehispanic Settlement Patterns in the Cuautitlan Region, Mexico*, University Park: The Pennsylvania State University, 2007.

Spence, Michael W., "Domestic Ritual in Tlailotlacan, Teotihuacan," in Patricia Plunket (ed.), *Domestic Ritual in Ancient Mesoamerica*, Los Angeles: Cotsen Institute of Archaeology, University of California, 2002, pp. 53–66.

"The Scale and Structure of Obsidian Production in Teotihuacan," in Emily McClung de Tapia and Evelyn C. Rattray (eds.), *Teotihuacan: nuevos datos, nuevos sintesis, nuevos problemas*, Mexico City: Universidad Nacional Autónoma de México, 1987, pp. 430–50.

Sugiyama, Saburo, *Human Sacrifice, Militarism, and Rulership: Materialization of State Ideology at the Feathered Serpent Pyramid, Teotihuacan*, Cambridge: Cambridge University Press, 2005.

Sugiyama, Saburo, and Ruben Cabrera Castro, "The Moon Pyramid Project and the Teotihuacan State Polity," *Ancient Mesoamerica* 18 (2007), 109–25.

Sullivan, Kristin S., "Commercialization in Early State Economies: Craft Production and Market Exchange in Classic Period Teotihuacan," Ph.D. dissertation, Arizona State University, 2007.

"Specialized Production of San Martin Orange Ware at Teotihuacan, Mexico," *Latin American Antiquity* 17 (2006), 23–53.

Widmer, Randolph J., "The Evolution of Form and Function in a Teotihuacan Apartment Compound: The Case of Tlajinga 33," in Emily McClung de Tapia and Evelyn C. Rattray (eds.), *Teotihuacan: Nuevos Datos, Nuevas Síntesis, Nuevos Problemas*, Mexico City: Universidad Nacional Autónoma de Mexico, 1987, pp. 317–68.

   "Lapidary Craft Specialization at Teotihuacan: Implications for Community Structure at 33:S3W1 and Economic Organization in the City," *Ancient Mesoamerica* 2 (1991), 131–47.

Yoffee, Norman, "Political Economy in Early Mesopotamian States," *Annual Review of Anthropology* 24 (1995), 281–311.

14

Urban landscapes: transforming spaces and reshaping communities

GEOFF EMBERLING, SARAH C. CLAYTON, AND
JOHN W. JANUSEK

The growth of cities fundamentally reorganizes economic, social, and political relationships, defines subjects, and reconfigures physical landscapes, although these effects vary in different cultural traditions and natural environments. In this chapter, we consider the social and physical environments of urban systems – both within cities themselves, and in the rural hinterlands they create and modify. Our comparison is based on urban systems in the ancient Middle East, Mesoamerica, and the Andes, and we have found areas of common ground and have also highlighted ways in which these cultural trajectories differ – Childe's classic model of urbanism was based largely on Mesopotamian cities, and it does not fit equally well the cultures of the New World.

In general, we see urbanism as a process that concentrates people and differentiates population into social categories. As political process, urbanism develops according to tensions and negotiations among a variety of factions and interests, including significantly the relationship between city rulers (and intermediate political leaders) and their subjects. As economic process, the large labor forces available in cities make possible new industries through technological innovation and economies of scale. And as social formation, cities erode some kinds of traditional kin-based relationships, subordinating them to higher authority and placing new demands of labor, tax, and decision-making on them, while also fostering the development of new urban identities. All these processes reshape the built environment of settlements and the landscapes that surround them in ways that structure urban life.

Reorganization of space in cities

The reorganization of space and of human relationships in cities begins with their initial settlement and construction. Like all beginnings, the earliest stages of urban development have often been difficult for archaeologists to discern, buried as they are beneath the large constructions of fully developed cities. Yet we can say something about the ways in which cities are founded based on the excavation of small exposures of these earliest urban layers, as well as later historical tradition, archaeological surveys of settlement and land use, and basic principles of anthropology and history according to which transformations must be explained by conditions existing at that time, rather than by later developments.

Initial settlement location

Existing explanations of urban origins consider cities to have developed in particular locations because they were on trade routes, or in environmentally advantageous locations, or in places that facilitated exchange among regions,[1] but there are often many locations that could have been so favored. The initial process of urban coalescence draws people in from a broad area to settle in a more concentrated area. An economic explanation of such developments proposes distributive relationships in which producers of agricultural or craft goods exchanged their goods in markets that were located in cities. In pre-market economies, however, production and exchange were significantly embedded in social and political relationships that constrained the movement of people into these postulated early markets. Arguably, then, political negotiations and authority were involved in the development of most cities.

Other factors are likely to have been salient in the initial growth of some cities, including the desire for safety and security under conditions of persistent conflict or during the anticipation or aftermath of a natural disaster. The growth of Teotihuacan, in the Basin of Mexico, for example, may have been catalyzed by volcanic events in what is now the state of Puebla, where the volcano Popocatepetl evidently erupted during the first century CE.[2] In the area closer to Teotihuacan itself, settlements in the southwestern Basin had long been threatened by the volcano Xitle, which blanketed the pre-Teotihuacan city of Cuicuilco under several meters of lava around 300 CE.[3] By the time this catastrophic eruption occurred, Cuicuilco had largely been abandoned and the city of Teotihuacan was at its height; nonetheless, the looming threat of disaster may have played a part in the

---

[1] Robert McC. Adams, *The Evolution of Urban Society* (Chicago: Aldine, 1966).
[2] Patricia Plunket and Gabriela Uruñuela, "Recent Research in Puebla Prehistory," *Journal of Archaeological Research* 13 (2005), 89–127.
[3] Claus Siebe, "Age and Archaeological Implications of Xitle Volcano, Southwestern Basin of Mexico City," *Journal of Volcanology and Geothermal Research* 104 (2000), 45–64.

spatial aggregation of populations in a new location and related processes of political, economic, and religious integration.

For some cities, at least, the choice of location was quite deliberate – a political decision that could be supported by readings of divine will. The Assyrian ruler Sargon II (ruled 721–705 BCE), for example, wrote that he proposed the location of a new capital city and that the great gods "commanded that the town be built and the canal dug."[4] And according to Aztec tradition, their capital city Tenochtitlan was located following the will of the god Huitzilopochtli where the Mexica would see an eagle perched on a nopal cactus and holding a snake.[5] Although these sites were supported by divine will, they clearly also responded to political realities. Sargon, as a usurper, was creating a new capital to disenfranchise an existing elite by moving away from their agricultural land and established political networks, and the Mexica, as recent arrivals in the Valley of Mexico, took what territory was available to them.

Primary urbanism – cities built in a region not otherwise in contact with urban populations – would have been built upon existing social and political structures and economies. In those cities, pre-urban forms of authority would not only have built the city but would have persisted in its earliest stages, at least. In Mesopotamian cities, for example, the existence of an assembly of elders very likely represents the persistence of pre-urban political forms.[6]

Polity

Cities may have been sited according to the political authority of pre-urban elites, and the ongoing concentration of an increasing population in urban communities created growing numbers of subjects who provided labor, agricultural and craft products, and the possibility of increasing use of military force. In short, cities could provide a basis for increasing political

---

[4] Daniel David Luckenbill, *Ancient Records of Assyria and Babylonia II* (Chicago: The University of Chicago Press, 1927), p. 64; and Otto, Chapter 23, this volume.
[5] Frederic Hicks, "Mexican Political History," in Elizabeth M. Brumfiel and Gary M. Feinman (eds.), *The Aztec World* (New York: Abrams, 2008), pp. 5–21; and Gutiérrez, Chapter 24, this volume.
[6] Gojko Barjamovic, "Civic Institutions and Self-Government in Southern Mesopotamia in the Mid-First Millennium BC," in J. G. Dercksen (ed.), *Assyria and Beyond: Studies Presented to Mogens Trolle Larsen* (Leiden: Nederlands Instituut voor het Nabije Osten, 2004), pp. 47–98; Robert McC. Adams, "Old Babylonian Networks of Urban Notables," *Cuneiform Digital Library Journal* 7 (2009); and Norman Yoffee, *Myths of the Archaic State: Evolution of the Earliest Cities, States, and Civilizations* (Cambridge: Cambridge University Press, 2005), p. 109.

authority, even as city rulers faced the possibility of opposition from other political factions that may have included priests and other temple personnel, non-ruling elite families, and distinct ethnic groups. The construction of cities represents not only the development of new forms of political authority, but also new kinds of subjects.[7]

Economy

Economies are transformed by the concentration of population in cities. Childe's definition of cities focuses on the growth of population beyond the point at which urban residents can provide their own food, whether through flocks or fields. Urban populations are thus relatively concentrated and specialized. This development also introduces an increased dependency – people cannot feed themselves, but must rely on redistributed or exchanged food. In general, urban processes of production are increasingly specialized, allowing for (and requiring) greater efficiency and employment.[8] The pace of technological innovation is increased by growing demand from a flourishing population and from urban institutions. These processes lead increasingly to concentrations of wealth in the hands of the urban elite. In Mesopotamia, the potter's wheel was developed as the first cities were being formed, production of textiles expanded greatly as cities grew, and early technological innovations developed in cities include first bronze-working and later glass-making as a related industry.

Despite the specialized economies and resulting interdependence of urban households for basic provisioning, it is increasingly clear that the food-producing capacity of urban spaces may have been much greater than traditional views of urban–rural interdependence afford. Current research concerning Mesoamerican urbanism, for example, includes studies of urban green space and the use of land surrounding residential structures. In an example from south-central Veracruz, Stark and Ossa argue that the dispersed urban form that characterized the Gulf lowlands was well-suited to intensive urban gardening and that land use around domiciles was symbolic as much as it was economically practical.[9] Although residential gardens were generally larger in more dispersed urban settings, they surely played

---

[7] Adam Smith, "Archaeologies of Sovereignty," *Annual Review of Anthropology* 40 (2011), 415–32.
[8] Guillermo Algaze, *Ancient Mesopotamia at the Dawn of Civilization: The Evolution of an Urban Landscape* (Chicago: The University of Chicago Press, 2008).
[9] Barbara L. Stark and Alanna Ossa, "Ancient Settlement, Urban Gardening, and Environment in the Gulf Lowlands of Mexico," *Latin American Antiquity* 18 (2007), 385–406.

a role in household provisioning and market exchange in densely aggregated cities as well. The Andean cities of Tiwanaku and Cuzco incorporated substantial agricultural fields and local gardens that were fed by intricate hydrological networks. Research in Mesoamerica and the Andes fits well with the well-known statement in the Mesopotamian Epic of Gilgamesh that characterizes the city of Uruk as comprising one-third city, one-third gardens, one-third clay pits (for sun-dried mudbricks), and an additional area for the main temple of the city.[10]

Society

The continuing concentration of population into cities begins a process of weakening pre-urban political and social ties, or at least subordinating them to more encompassing political relationships. The leaders of the extended kin units that would have structured communities and economies in towns were subjugated to the emerging urban rulers and their administration. At the same time, extended kin groups were, in many cases, gradually broken down into smaller family units. As urban spaces became more densely settled, it could become more difficult for extended families to remain in close proximity, as illustrated by Mesopotamian texts recording legal disputes over inheritance and division of property.[11]

At the same time, new and larger groups based in part on kinship could develop in cities, including in Mesopotamia of the Old Babylonian period (c. 1800 BCE) the *babtum*, or neighborhood, which had its own political hierarchy.[12] The breakdown of extended families and refashioning of kinship groupings may also reorient subjects in cities toward the urban authorities for resolution of disputes and for economic assistance.

In some cities, on the other hand, residential organization continued to be characterized by the cohabitation of large extended kin groups, including not only blood but also fictive kin, who participated collectively in the specialized production of goods as corporate economic groups. At Teotihuacan, more than 2,000 multi-room structures were built beginning in the third century CE as the primary form of housing within the city as well as within some coeval rural settlements. Housing up to 60–100 people at a time, many of these "apartment compounds" were evidently associated with

---

[10] See Emberling, Chapter 12, this volume.

[11] Elizabeth Stone, *Nippur Neighborhoods* (Chicago: The Oriental Institute of the University of Chicago, 1987).

[12] Andrea Seri, *Local Power in Old Babylonian Mesopotamia* (London: Equinox, 2005).

specialized craft production activities (for example, pottery-making, lapidary work, lime-processing, obsidian-working) on a supra-household scale. Beyond economic production, the inhabitants of compounds interacted socially through daily activities and various ritual practices, including the burial of their dead under the floors and walls of the compound. Residential affiliation was, no doubt, a key aspect of individual identity at Teotihuacan. Kin group or lineage-based identities may have been superseded by membership in the social groups associated with co-residence.

Cities are often divided into quarters, wards, or neighborhoods, and the organization thus produced and maintained may reflect preexisting social divisions, or may foster new ones. This appears to be true of Teotihuacan, where researchers have identified some areas as neighborhoods based on a combination of settlement patterns and the presence of architectural elements with complementary functions. For example, the 25,000-square-meter "La Ventilla" neighborhood included a temple, public buildings, a large open plaza, residential compounds, and water wells.[13] Some of Teotihuacan's neighborhoods (for example, "Tlailotlacan") were likely enclaves of foreign immigrants.[14] Studies of neighborhoods have been slower to develop in the Mesoamerican lowlands due to a history of scholarly disagreement over whether low-density settlements such as the sprawling Maya polity centers actually represent urban landscapes. Recently, however, the term "neighbourhood" has been explicitly applied in the Maya Lowlands to discrete clusters of houses; Smith argues that this sociospatial concept is relevant for other low-density cities in the world as well.[15] Stone and Zimansky proposed based on their surface survey at Mashkan-shapir that Mesopotamian cities were composed of functionally equivalent neighborhoods, each one of which had elite housing as well as evidence for local craft manufacture.[16]

[13] Sergio Gómez-Chávez, "Structure and Organization of Neighborhoods in the Ancient City of Teotihuacan," in M. Charlotte Arnauld, Linda R. Manzanilla, and Michael E. Smith (eds.), *The Neighborhood as a Social and Spatial Unit in Mesoamerican Cities* (Tucson: University of Arizona Press, 2012), pp. 74–101.
[14] Michael W. Spence, Christine D. White, Evelyn C. Rattray, and Fred J. Longstaffe, "Past Lives in Different Places: The Origins and Relationships of Teotihuacan's Foreign Residents," in Richard E. Blanton (ed.), *Settlement, Subsistence, and Social Complexity: Essays Honoring the Legacy of Jeffrey R. Parsons* (Los Angeles: Cotsen Institute of Archaeology, 2005), pp. 155–97.
[15] Michael E. Smith, "Classic Maya Settlement Clusters as Urban Neighborhoods: A Comparative Perspective on Low-Density Urbanism," *Journal de la Société des Américanistes* 97 (2011), 51–73.
[16] Elizabeth C. Stone and Paul Zimansky, *The Anatomy of a Mesopotamian City: Survey and Soundings at Mashkan-shapir* (Winona Lake, IN: Eisenbrauns, 2004).

In other periods of Mesopotamian history, residence may have been organized by craft, with areas of the city of Uruk seemingly inhabited by different guilds.[17]

There is evidence that the very existence of cities called a new form of identity into being – the "citizen." In Mesopotamia of the third millennium BCE, both members of the elite and workers named in institutional ration lists were known by their city of origin,[18] rather than by the ethnic terms in which we more commonly think of these societies. Archaeological research points to a similar process in the emergence of Tiwanaku in the Andean high plateau, or altiplano. The city expanded enormously between 500 and 700 CE. Residential sectors expanded beyond its monumental core in a highly organized manner, and similar to Teotihuacan, following a master spatial plan grounded in visual orientations to key mountain peaks and celestial cycles.[19] The basic unit of spatial organization was a walled compound, which incorporated several dwellings and their associated structures and outdoor spaces. Two or more contiguous compounds formed more encompassing barrios. Spatially divided compounds and barrios provided residence for kin-based or otherwise intimately linked urban communities in Tiwanaku. Artifact styles, architecture, and residential practices varied significantly among compounds, indicating that resident groups derived from different places and continued to produce their distinctive identities within the urban center. Some barrio communities practiced specialized trades.[20] Yet residents of Tiwanaku compounds and barrios all constructed their living spaces according to Tiwanaku's long-term spatial canon, and all adopted diacritical Tiwanaku practices, such as using Tiwanaku-style ceramics for commensal activities and digging massive subterranean "ash pits" for multiple purposes. Tiwanaku urbanism involved the transformation of local communities into urban subjects and citizens of an emergent political and cultural order.

Built environment

If our discussion of cities has begun with the ongoing transformations within urban communities, it is the physical environment of early cities that both constructs and represents these new relationships. The symbolic authority

[17] Marc van de Mieroop, *The Ancient Mesopotamian City* (Oxford: Clarendon Press, 1997).
[18] Geoff Emberling, "Urban Social Transformations and the Problem of the 'First City': New Research from Mesopotamia," in Monica L. Smith (ed.), *The Social Construction of Ancient Cities* (Washington, D.C.: Smithsonian, 2003), pp. 254–68.
[19] John W. Janusek, *Ancient Tiwanaku* (Cambridge: Cambridge University Press, 2008).
[20] John W. Janusek, *Identity and Power in the Ancient Andes: Tiwanaku Cities Through Time* (London: Routledge, 2004).

of the city ruler is often marked by representational art and in less personal-ized form by monumental architecture – palaces, temples, and city walls – and planned public spaces like processional ways or plazas that were the site of daily performance or urban identities as well as broader public rituals and ceremonies. Mesopotamian texts note regular public festivals, processions of cult statues, and occasional feasts commemorating (for example) the inaug-uration of cities, like the feast of the Assyrian king Ashurnasirpal (ruled 883–859 BCE) upon the completion of his new capital Kalhu.[21] Visual repre-sentations suggest the salience of banqueting at multiple scales up to the entire urban population.

Temples were critical as built forms and as the focal point of a range of cultural practices that included public ritual as well as production of agricul-tural and craft goods. Rulers of cities had a variety of relationships to temples, but in most cultures maintenance of these relationships was considered to be of crucial importance. In Early Dynastic Mesopotamia (*c.* 2500 BCE), temples owned fields and managed agricultural production, manufactured metals, textiles, and ceramic vessels, and organized long-distance trading expeditions to acquire valued raw materials. Kings took credit for the construction and maintenance of temples, making certain that both the gods and posterity knew of their role through foundation inscriptions and stamped bricks. Although ideologically it was kings who served temples, this relationship was increas-ingly reversed as the concentration of power in the hands of rulers grew.

Teotihuacan's built environment is extraordinarily monumental and pre-cisely ordered, its ultimate configuration culminating from early civic planning on a massive scale and subsequent enlargements and modifications made to its civic and residential architecture throughout the first half-millennium CE. The city has been aptly described as sacred,[22] with the blending of polity and religion visually manifested in more than 100 temple structures lining its central processional way, the Avenue of the Dead. A canonical orientation of 15.5 degrees east of north pervades the layout of Teotihuacan's civic and many of its residential architectural features; this standard orientation is exhibited even among some contemporaneous rural settlements in the region.[23]

---

[21] David Oates and Joan Oates, *Nimrud: An Assyrian Imperial City Revealed* (London: British School of Archaeology in Iraq, 2001).

[22] René Millon, "The Last Years of Teotihuacan Dominance," in Norman Yoffee and George L. Cowgill (eds.), *The Collapse of Ancient States and Civilizations* (Tucson: University of Arizona Press, 1988), pp. 102–64.

[23] Sarah C. Clayton, "Measuring the Long Arm of the State: Teotihuacan's Relations in the Basin of Mexico," *Ancient Mesoamerica* 24 (2013), 87–105.

The north end of the Avenue of the Dead terminates at the Moon Pyramid complex, the pyramid itself loosely echoing the shape of a prominent mountain, Cerro Gordo, located north of the city. It is highly unlikely that this arrangement is accidental. As Cowgill points out, Cerro Gordo is understood in recent traditions as a sacred, water-filled mountain; further, a personified mountain depicted in the mural art of Teotihuacan, as in the Tepinantitla complex, may be a reference to Cerro Gordo.[24] In addition to numerous architectural complexes, two other major pyramids mark Teotihuacan's sacred landscape. The Sun Pyramid, Teotihuacan's largest monument, is seated on the east side of the Avenue of the Dead, and the Feathered Serpent Pyramid is located inside the massive enclosure of the Ciudadela, a gathering space that would have accommodated 100,000 people. The environment that rulers created in the heart of this city was well suited to large-scale processions and public displays of sacred power and military might, including the practice of ritual human sacrifice in association with overt symbolic references to warfare.[25]

Andean cities differed remarkably in built form and in the way they produced urban subjects. Located in the Andean high plateau, Tiwanaku is reminiscent of Teotihuacan. Its spatiality was highly ordered and it was dominated by a dual monumental core consisting of ensembles of temples, plazas, and sunken courts featuring carved anthropomorphic monoliths. The northeast monumental sector centered on the Akapana–Kalasasaya complexes and the southeast sector, the Pumapunku complex. Ritualized commensalism was central to the ceremonies that took place in Tiwanaku's monumental complexes and residential compounds. Stone portals, including the well-known Sun Portal (Gate of the Sun), directed officiants, pilgrims, and ritual participants in carefully orchestrated routes that traversed extensive plazas, raised temple platforms, and ultimately led toward intimate sunken courts and their imposing stone sculptures. Though monumental spaces were not uniformly available to all ritual participants, Tiwanaku was built to be experienced and its ideological messages internalized by many.

Andean cities such as Wari and Chan Chan were far more enclosed and were designed to emphasize the sociospatial distinctions of their urban subjects. At its peak, the Peruvian coastal city of Chan Chan comprised

---

[24] George L. Cowgill, "Intentionality and Meaning in the Layout of Teotihuacan, Mexico," *Cambridge Archaeological Journal* 10 (2000), 358–61.

[25] Saburo Sugiyama, *Human Sacrifice, Militarism, and Rulership: Materialization of State Ideology at the Feathered Serpent Pyramid, Teotihuacan* (Cambridge: Cambridge University Press, 2005).

multiple palace enclosures, or *ciudadelas*, surrounded by increasingly larger swaths of lower-status and temporary urban housing. Some residential areas adjacent to enclosures housed palace retainers, while increasing portions of the south and west segments of the city incorporated differentiated urban barrios, many constituent communities conducting specialized trades such as metal, cloth, and ceramic vessel production.[26] The construction of the Laberinto palace enclosure in the latter part of Early Chimu (1100–1200 CE) institutionalized two enduring ciudadela patterns. First, a tripartite division into a northern entry court with surrounding rooms, a central court with an adjacent royal burial platform, and a southern sector with domestic housing and walk-in wells. Second, the increasing organization of internal palace space via ranked *audiencia* courts and their dependent storeroom clusters, which together manifest an increasingly intricate administrative structure. Burial platforms likely housed the mummified remains of the deceased ruler who had built and once inhabited the enclosure.[27] Intricate architectural annexes adjoined the outer edges of later enclosures, presumably housing later generations of family, retainers, or craft specialists who directly and officially tended a ciudadela's corporate community and ancestral mummy.

City walls have been the subject of a range of scholarly perspectives – were they for protection against enemies, to prevent citizens from leaving, to symbolize the power of rulers, to mark the city as a salient point in the landscape? It is of interest to note that the earliest Mesopotamian cities appear not to have been walled, and Egyptian city walls also developed centuries after the first cities were built.[28] Though most Andean cities were not walled, at Tiwanaku a water-filled "moat" surrounded most of its northeast monumental complex, effectively distinguishing a massive portion of its urban core as ritually significant space.[29] The moat was initiated very early in Tiwanaku's history and was expanded just as Tiwanaku developed into a sprawling urban center. Thus city walls and related boundaries manifest a further way in which urbanism is a process that develops and changes through time.

[26] John Topic, "Territorial Expansion and the Kingdom of Chimor," in Michael E. Moseley and Alana Cordy-Collins (eds.), *The Northern Dynasties: Kinship and Statecraft in Chimor* (Washington, D.C.: Dumbarton Oaks, 1990), pp. 107–44.

[27] Geoffrey Conrad, "The Burial Platforms of Chan Chan: Some Social and Political Implications," in Michael E. Moseley and Kent C. Day (eds.), *Chan Chan: Andean Desert City* (Albuquerque: University of New Mexico Press, 1982), pp. 87–118.

[28] Barry Kemp, Nadine Moeller, Kate Spence, and Alison L. Gascoigne, "Egypt's Invisible Walls," *Cambridge Archaeological Journal* 14 (2004), 259–88.

[29] Alan L. Kolata, *The Tiwanaku: Portrait of an Andean Civilization* (Cambridge: Blackwell, 1993).

Time and scale

Childe's notion of the "Urban Revolution" suggests that the construction of cities and the associated changes in political authority, economic organization, and identities was a rapid if not instantaneous change.[30] Yet clearly cities grew over time, and it is worth considering the length of time involved. For early Mesopotamia our best current information comes from Tell Brak in northeastern Syria, where the settled area expanded from 30 hectares to 130 hectares between about 3900 to 3500 BCE.[31] During those four centuries, several monumental structures that include an elite residence and a temple on a platform were built, and a feasting hall may represent the activities of an intermediate political elite, perhaps the leader of an extended kin group persisting from the pre-urban community.[32] While our evidence for assemblies of elders in Mesopotamia is discontinuous, they persisted in recognizable form until at least the Neo- Babylonian period some 4,000 years later. Urban transformations, while wide reaching, are best seen not as moments in time, but ongoing processes.

Andean cities were always under construction. Tiwanaku's temples manifest sections that were clearly being constructed even as they were abandoned, and the production of stone for monumental construction was an ongoing and eminently visible component of the urban landscape. Chan Chan expanded generationally with the establishment of each new ciudadela and its affiliated retainer and residential artisan sectors. Geoffrey Conrad draws on Inka historical accounts to argue that each new ruler had to establish a new palace and wealth-generating estate based on a royal kin-based principle of "split inheritance."[33] Cuzco expanded in this very manner. Located in the rugged central Andean sierra, the Inka capital was a relatively small city that, at the time of Spanish Conquest, housed a maximum of 20,000 persons.[34] It housed the palaces, temples, council halls, and *acllawasi* – monumental homes for the "chosen" women who wove elaborate clothing for Inka elites and produced feasts for elite-sponsored ceremonies – dedicated

[30] V. Gordon Childe, "The Urban Revolution," *Town Planning Review* 21 (1950), 3–17.
[31] Joan Oates, Augusta McMahon, Philip Karsgaard, Salam al Quntar, and Jason Ur, "Early Mesopotamian Urbanism: A New View from the North," *Antiquity* 81 (2007), 585–600.
[32] See Emberling, Chapter 12, this volume.
[33] Geoffrey Conrad, "Cultural Materialism, Split Inheritance, and the Expansion of Ancient Peruvian Empires," *American Antiquity* 46 (1981), 3–26.
[34] Brian S. Bauer, *Ancient Cuzco: Heartland of the Inca* (Austin: University of Texas Press, 2004).

to the noble factions that anchored political authority in the Cuzco heart-land. Cuzco housed more than ten royal factions, each centered on the kin-focused estate, or *panaca*, established by a new ruler, or *Sapa* (Unique) *Inca*, his primary wife (blood sister), and secondary wives and concubines. After a Sapa Inca's death, his panaca continued to thrive grounded in a core of his noble (*capac*) descendants as well as their affines, progeny, and retainers, all of whom collectively venerated his mummified remains and other sacred objects and places in Cuzco

Although the city of Teotihuacan certainly evolved through time, its early growth was remarkably rapid in terms of its expanding population and the sweeping changes in regional settlement that accompanied its development into the capital of an influential state. Teotihuacan was initially settled in the early centuries BCE. By 1 CE its population approached 20,000 and continued to expand, reaching a peak of 80,000 to 125,000 by 200 CE. A correspondingly precipitous decline in regional population numbers coincided with Teoti-huacan's explosive early growth. Sanders, Parsons, and Santley report a possible decrease of 80–90 percent of the population of the Basin of Mexico during the first century CE, presumably due to the movement, en masse, of regional populations into Teotihuacan.[35]

Rural hinterlands

In Mesopotamia, Mesoamerica, and the Andes, emergent urbanism gener-ated substantial transformations that transcended the production of urban cores. In each world region, urbanism simultaneously created particular forms of the rural hinterlands that were as much part of the process of emergent urbanization as cities themselves. Furthermore, the production of urban hinterlands was inextricably physical and symbolic. Examination of key elements of urban cores and hinterlands shows the preeminent role that productive concerns and hydrological engineering played in organizing urban space and linking urban core and hinterland.

Transformation of the rural landscape: production and ritual

The spatial order of cities and hinterlands is responsive to regional environ-mental conditions. In the Moche Valley of the northern Peruvian Pacific coast, Chan Chan coalesced and thrived as an autonomous city from 900 to

[35] William T. Sanders, Jeffrey R. Parsons, and Robert S. Santley, *The Basin of Mexico: Ecological Processes in the Evolution of a Civilization* (New York: Academic Press, 1979).

1450 CE, the Andean Late Intermediate period, as the political center of the expansive Chimu polity.

Located in extremely arid conditions, Chan Chan's urban growth was grounded in its regional hydrology. Chan Chan followed an oblique orientation aligned roughly perpendicular to the coast and parallel to the lower Moche River. Core elements of Chan Chan's hydrological regime included its canal systems, sunken gardens, and enclosed walk-in wells. Early urban growth depended on irrigating the vast, high plain of Pampa Esperanza that extended north of and above the city.[36] Throughout the city's history, Chimu hydraulic engineers constructed a series of primary canals from the Moche River that fed the pampa's farming systems and artificially raised Chan Chan's water table. These irrigation canals, including an ambitious, 70-kilometer inter-valley canal planned to import excess water from the neighboring Chicama Valley,[37] were successively stranded or extensively damaged by a massive El Nino event in 1100 CE and recurring tectonic uplift thereafter. Ongoing contraction of irrigation to the Pampa Esperanza and the consequent lowering of Chan Chan's water table generated two inner-city shifts. These included the intensification of sunken-garden farming, a coastal urban farming regime that required excavating fields in alluvial seashore bluffs to levels at which combined water table and ground moisture sustained crop growth.[38] These also included an increased reliance on deep wells for occupants of individual ciudadelas. In the late ciudadela Gran Chimu, such wells reached more than 15 meters deep.[39]

Some cities' hinterlands were organized as much to support ritual commensalism as to support daily subsistence. Tiwanaku's expansion after 500 CE and its increasing social and ritual catchment demanded a diversified productive base to both support permanent residents and recurring ritualized events. Massive floodplains around Tiwanaku and nearby valleys were converted into intensive raised field farming systems – most notably, a massive expanse of the adjacent Katari Valley. Raised fields transformed

---

[36] Michael E. Moseley and Eric Deeds, "The Land in Front of Chan Chan: Agrarian Expansion, Reform, and Collapse in the Moche Valley," in Moseley and Day (eds.), *Chan Chan*, pp. 25–33.

[37] Charles Ortloff, Michael E. Moseley, and Robert Feldman, "Hydraulic Engineering Aspects of the Chimu Chicama–Moche Intervalley Canal," *American Antiquity* 47 (1982), 572–95.

[38] Kent C. Day, "Ciudadelas: Their Form and Function," in Moseley and Day (eds.), *Chan Chan*, pp. 55–66.

[39] Alan L. Kolata, "The Urban Concept of Chan Chan," in Moseley and Cordy-Collins (eds.), *Northern Dynasties*, pp. 107–44.

low valley bottoms into productive field beds fed by the rise and fall of nearby Lake Titicaca and mountain-fed subterranean aquifers. Clusters of interlinked reservoirs – known as *qocha* systems – were excavated into higher, drier valley bottoms to facilitate local farming, pasturage, and small-scale lacustrine cultivation. Intensive raised field and qocha production came to coexist alongside more traditional rain-fed systems as innovative, high-stakes productive practices generated by and tending to Tiwanaku's urban expansion.

Tiwanaku's very urban constitution collapses clear distinctions between "urban" and "rural" processes. Kolata noted that Tiwanaku's massive platforms embodied metaphors for massive mountains that were rendered sources of water and vitality for agropastoral systems and the humans they supported.[40] Tiwanaku itself incorporated clusters of productive systems. The southeastern portion of the site consists of a cluster of large interlinked qochas, which likely served local agropastoral practices and to feed the large caravans of llamas and alpacas that periodically descended on the center. Clusters of raised fields occupied the low, northern edge of the site along the Tiwanaku River. In fact, these diverse systems were interlinked via a massive urban hydrological network. The qochas captured water from a subterranean aquifer and surface streams descending south from Mount Kimsachata. They helped to channel water into a massive "moat" or canal built around the monumental core, thereby directing water away from its susceptible floors and foundations. Water from the canal drained into the floodplain below the site that supported raised field systems.

Urban control of the hinterland

Both urban governments and elite extended families exerted control over rural spaces through a variety of political action, kin networks, and ritual practices. In Mesopotamia, this control focused on productive activities including notably the construction and maintenance of networks of canals that made agriculture possible – or intensified production, in the case of Assyria.[41] These canals also served to facilitate water-borne transportation of goods including grain from hinterlands to urban centers as well as among cities, and they could also be diverted in military operations to flood

---

[40] Kolata, *Tiwanaku*.

[41] Jason Ur, "Sennacherib's Northern Assyrian Canals: New Insights from Satellite Imagery and Aerial Photography," *Iraq* 67 (2005), 317–45.

resistance from defense of rebellious cities. Ritual control over the landscape was relatively underdeveloped in Mesopotamia.

In the highlands of Mexico, several lines of evidence attest to Teotihuacan's political dominance over its regional hinterland, including rapid changes to regional settlement patterns that accompanied its growth and the concentration of the population and major politico-religious monuments in the capital. Unlike some other regional urban landscapes that were dotted with large cities, Teotihuacan stands out as a singular capital many times larger than any other contemporary settlement in the Basin of Mexico. Its urban expansion closely corresponded to the development of a ruralized hinterland, which was a major source of demographic growth as well as food and a variety of necessary raw materials. Regional settlement surveys by Sanders and colleagues placed Teotihuacan within a 30-kilometer radius of a range of resources (for example, salt, reeds, basalt, and construction materials) from distinct ecological zones.[42] Teotihuacan exerted enduring and direct control beyond the Basin of Mexico into adjacent regions including parts of Hidalgo, Tlaxcala, and Morelos as well, which have been described as an "outer hinterland" from which particular resources were derived (for example, Pachuca obsidian from Hidalgo).[43] At its height, Teotihuacan's political reach appears to have been imperialistic, extending to distant polities in the Gulf Coast, West Mexico, and the Maya region. The nature of Teotihuacan's relationships with particular polities, including the degree to which they were direct or indirect, lasting or fleeting, historically accurate or fabricated by local elites, is a perennial topic of debate among Mesoamericanists.

Data from within the Basin of Mexico and beyond undeniably support a view of the Teotihuacan polity, with the capital city at its heart, as a highly centralized, militarily powerful, and profoundly influential ideological force across the Mesoamerican world. It is increasingly clear, however, that its regional and interregional involvements were also highly heterogeneous in terms of strategy, duration, success, and with regard to the economic and social implications of these relationships for local populations. There is a need to delineate in finer detail the area that represented Teotihuacan's hinterland at different points in its dynamic history, and to understand the kinds of interactions through which it was constituted. Research focused

[42] Sanders, Parsons, and Santley, *Basin of Mexico*.
[43] Kenneth Hirth, "Teotihuacan Regional Population Administration in Eastern Morelos," *World Archaeology* 9 (1978), 320–33.

within the Basin of Mexico, beyond the margins of the capital, is imperative for comprehending Teotihuacan's regional politics in fuller measure and for addressing basic questions concerning ancient cities in general, including how their institutions and populations were provisioned.[44]

By contrast, Inka incorporation of the Cuzco Basin and surrounding regions occurred over multiple generations, as narrated in an "official" history that telescopes the Inka rise to fame and power in the deeds of eleven successive rulers.[45] Early royal descent-groups (panacas) maintained lands and estates in the Cuzco Basin, while those of the ninth Sapa Inka, the "cosmic transformer" Pachacuti, and his imperializing successors established wealthy estates in the nearby Urubamba Valley and throughout the expanding empire. Pachacuti is credited with consolidating the Cuzco heartland and integrating it into an expanding urban core according to an innovative master plan that facilitated a flexible means of coordinating irrigation and production in the heartland.[46] Cuzco and its hinterland was divided into four radial (pie-slice shaped) quadrants, giving rise to the native name of the Inka Empire as Tawantinsuyu, "four lands joined" (see Urton, Chapter 9, this volume). Quadripartition mapped seamlessly onto an ancient dual sociospatial division into upper (Hanan) and lower (Hurin) Cuzco. Pachacuti integrated these organizing principles with an intricate system of radiating ritual paths, or ceques. The ceque system formed a network of forty-one paths leading radially from the primary Inka temple of Coricancha across the upper Cuzco Basin. Each ceque linked together multiple sacred places (waq'a), well over 300 in total and nearly a third of which consisted of water sources.[47] Ceques were grouped into clusters of three, and each ceque cluster integrated the lands and ancestral shrines of a particular panaca with one or more non-noble communities. Each ceque cluster also was associated with a particular time in the annual productive and ritual calendar. The ceque system wedded the spatial location of noble and non-noble communities to a rotating system of ritual and productive obligations tied to the

---

[44] Clayton, Chapter 13, this volume.

[45] Pedro Sarmiento de Gamboa, The History of the Incas, Brian S. Bauer and Vania Smith (trans. and eds.) (Austin: University of Texas Press, 2007).

[46] Juan de Betanzos, Narrative of the Incas, Roland Hamilton and Dana Buchanan (eds.) (Austin: University of Texas Press, 1996).

[47] Brian S. Bauer, The Sacred Landscape of the Inca: The Cuzco Ceque System (Austin: University of Texas Press, 1998), and Jeanette Sherbondy, "Water Ideology in Inca Ethnogenesis," in Robert V. H. Dover, Katharine E. Siebold, and John R. McDowell (eds.), Andean Cosmologies through Time: Persistence and Emergence (Bloomington: Indiana University Press, 1992), pp. 46–66.

local shrines that afforded their ancestral legitimacy and vitality. It codified a sociospatial, temporal, and productive order. Though each panaca maintained corporate ritual and political spaces in the urban center, and though all collectively worshipped at focal Inka shrines such as Coricancha, the gravity of panaca power, place, and activity resided outside of the city proper.

Limits of urban control

It is perhaps fitting to close with a note on the limits of the reach of cities and their transformations of landscapes. Certainly one limit of political control comes in the form of borderlands separating one city from the next, although arguably a landscape of cities is entirely transformed regardless of which city controls which plot of land. However, the margins of urban zones are often occupied by pastoral nomads – in the Zagros Mountains to the east of the Mesopotamian Plains, for example. Yet urban influence finally reaches even these regions, as the specialized production of pastoralists depends on urban markets, and the focus of their political resistance is essentially urban in origin. There is ultimately nearly no escape from the urban transformation.

PART IV

EARLY CITIES AND THE DISTRIBUTION OF POWER

15

Ancient South Asian cities in
their regions

CARLA M. SINOPOLI

In the autumn of 1924, the history of urbanism in South Asia was lengthened by 2,000 years.[1] Prior to this, scholars knew of the efflorescence of cities, states, and religious visionaries that had occurred in the Ganges Basin in the mid-first millennium BCE. However, little was known of what came before. This changed in September 1924 when Sir John Marshall, Director General of the Archaeological Survey of India, published a brief announcement in the *Illustrated London News* describing enigmatic objects – inscribed seals with an unknown script – that had been found at the abandoned cities of Harappa and Mohenjo Daro. These sites had been known for nearly a century and archaeological work in the early twentieth century by D. R. Bhandarkar, R. D. Banerji, M. S. Vats, D. R. Sahni, and other South Asian scholars had begun to point to their considerable antiquity. However, their precise dates and significance were unknown. Within a few weeks scholars had an answer, one that revolutionized understandings of the South Asian past and transformed the trajectory of South Asian archaeology. It was provided by three archaeologists working in Mesopotamia – A. H. Sayce, C. J. Gadd, and Sidney Smith – who responded that they had found identical objects in third millennium BCE deposits at several Mesopotamian cities, including Susa and Ur.

The discovery that cities had existed in South Asia in the third millennium BCE overthrew long-standing beliefs that history and "civilization" had come late to the region, and archaeological work immediately shifted from a focus on Early Buddhism to what came to be called the "Harappan" or "Indus

---

I dedicate this chapter to the late Gregory Possehl, friend, mentor, and dedicated Indus scholar. I expect that he would have disagreed with much of what is contained here; but I have no doubt that he also would have supported and encouraged this foray of a South Indian specialist into the archaeology of northern South Asia.

[1] Nayanjot Lahiri, *Finding Forgotten Cities: How the Indus Civilization Was Discovered* (New Delhi: Permanent Black, 2005).

Civilization." However, in one respect, things did not change. Colonial scholarship had long looked beyond South Asia's boundaries for sources of political and cultural innovation in the region. And the recognition of ancient contacts between Mesopotamia and the Indus region appeared to confirm foreign inspiration for Bronze Age South Asian urbanism: a view, I will suggest, that continues to trouble interpretations of Indus cities and polities.

Since 1924, thousands of archaeological sites containing Indus materials have been identified in Pakistan, India, and the Arabian Peninsula, and excavations have been conducted at large urban sites and countless smaller settlements. In this chapter I begin by reviewing current knowledge of this first period of South Asian urbanism, situating the Indus cities in their larger regional landscapes. I follow by briefly addressing the end of the Indus tradition and the cities that followed more than a millennium later. In so doing, I explore two very different urban trajectories and urban landscapes of ancient South Asia – the first characterized by a small number of massive widely spaced cities that existed as islands of urbanism in a vast sea of villages; the second characterized by closely packed urban places in a "landscape of cities" (*sensu* Adams).

Splendid isolation: Indus cities

The Bronze Age cities of Mohenjo Daro and Harappa (and the lesser known Dholavira, Ganweriwala Thar, and Rakhigarhi) are justly renowned for their scale, dense urban architecture, and distinctive material culture. Research on these sites and the numerous smaller settlements and specialized sites in the spaces between them has generated a vast literature on Indus chronologies, settlements, economies, long-distance interactions, and political structures.[2] It is not my purpose here to comprehensively review this literature. Instead, I focus on a single issue: the very small number of cities that existed within the enormous geographic region over which Indus tradition sites are found and the considerable distances that separated these few urban places (Map 15.1).

---

[2] See Jonathan M. Kenoyer, *Ancient Cities of the Indus Valley Civilization* (Oxford: Oxford University Press, 1998); Gregory L. Possehl, *The Indus Civilization: A Contemporary Perspective* (Lanham, MD: AltaMira Press, 2002); Shereen Ratnagar, *Understanding Harappan Civilization in the Greater Indus Valley* (New Delhi: Tulika, 2001); and Rita P. Wright, *The Ancient Indus: Urbanism, Economy, and Society* (Cambridge: Cambridge University Press, 2010).

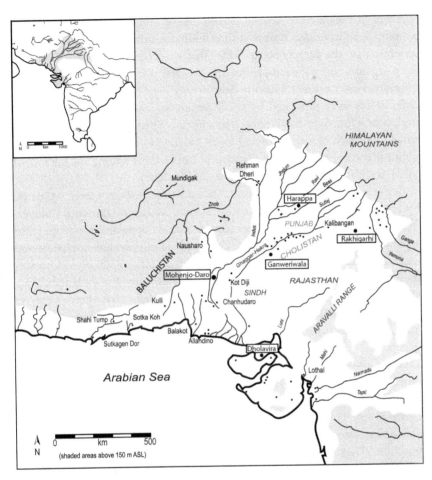

Map 15.1 Indus sites (after Thomas R. Trautmann and Carla M. Sinopoli, "In the beginning was the word," *Journal of the Economic and Social History of the Orient* 45 [2002], 492–523).

This is not a new observation, and has been discussed by Kenoyer, Shinde *et al.*, Wright, and others.[3] Both Wright and Kenoyer have argued that Indus political organization is best understood under the rubric "city-states" – multiple autonomous polities centered on cities and their hinterlands, which

---

[3] Also Jonathan M. Kenoyer, "Early City-states in South Asia," in Deborah Nichols and Thomas Charlton (eds.), *The Archaeology of City States: Cross Cultural Approaches* (Washington, D.C.: Smithsonian Institution Press, 1997), pp. 51–70; Vasant Shinde, Shweta Sinha Deshpande, Toshiki Osada, and Takao Uno, "Basic Issues in Harappan Archaeology: Some Thoughts," *Ancient Asia* 1 (2006), 63–72; and Wright, *Ancient Indus*, p. 333.

together participated in shared "civilizational" understandings and inter-actions. Both have also observed that the Indus urban landscape was quite different than the densely packed cities that we generally associate with city-state organization, for example in Early Dynastic Mesopotamia, the Aegean, Mesoamerica, or Early Historic South Asia (see below). In those cases, cities/states were separated by small distances – measured in tens of kilo-meters or a few days' travel time. The effective territory of such polities was small, and each city was able to exert (relatively) effective economic and political control over its hinterland; and interactions among inhabitants of these neighboring cities were intimate and frequent.

In the Indus region in contrast, the five documented cities were separated by enormous distances, with the closest two, Mohenjo Daro and Ganwer-iwala Thar, located 280 kilometers apart, and Harappa and Mohenjo Daro separated by 600 kilometers. These distances did not preclude exchange and other interactions, which are well documented archaeologically. However, their scale is striking. Indeed, if one were to assume that each Indus city effectively controlled its surrounding territories and that there were no Indus sites *not* under the authority of an urban center, Kenoyer has esti-mated the territories of Indus "city-states" as being between 100,000 and 170,000 square kilometers.

Given the vast scale of the Indus landscape and the remarkably small number of cities, it is challenging to understand the roles these cities played as loci of political, social, economic, and ideological order within the larger Indus world. This is not to imply that the Indus cities were not important places for Indus peoples and for scholars attempting to understand this tradition. They certainly were. Nonetheless, while the influence of urban centers on surrounding regions was no doubt significant, their effective political and economic control over surrounding territories and the majority of the population that did not live in or regularly encounter urban sites was likely more limited, and the political order of the Indus world was undoubt-edly more complex and more varied than can be accounted for by a single political model. Thus, while both cities and states were likely both import-ant actors in the Indus tradition, they existed in a shared civilizational nexus comprised of many differently constructed polities and societies.

Indus chronologies and the pre-urban setting

The urban phase of the Indus tradition spanned from 2600 to 1900 BCE and followed upon a millennium of increasing economic and material elabor-ation, manifest in multiple, geographically discontinuous, interacting, regional archaeological traditions (largely defined on the basis of distinctive styles of material culture, particularly painted pottery). Throughout this "Early Harappan" period (*c.* 3500–2600 BCE),[4] communities expanded into the rich alluvial plains along the Indus and Ghaggar-Hakra Rivers of modern Pakistan and northwest India.

It was during the pre-urban period that many practices that would come to characterize subsequent urban forms took shape. Population expansion into new environmental zones was accompanied by intensification and diversification in subsistence and craft production, with widespread evidence for increasingly sophisticated and specialized crafting technologies in a range of materials. And recent excavations at Harappa provide evidence for the beginnings of writing technologies – including the production of seals containing signs that appear to be related to later Indus scripts.[5] In each of the Early Harappan traditions (for example, Ravi, Amri, Hakra, Sothi-Siswal, and the widely distributed Kot Diji), we also see evidence for inter-settlement variability – in scale, productive activities, and settlement elaboration. Thus, in the Cholistan region along the ancient Ghaggar-Hakra Rivers, where arid conditions and low populations since the end of the Indus period have contributed to excellent site preservation, Mughal identified a diverse array of functionally differentiated "Pre-Harappan" sites, showing increasing elaboration and economic diversification over time – including small-scale craft production sites, camp sites, and settlements of diverse scales from 1 hectare to Ganweriwala at more than 25 hectares.[6]

Settlement layout became increasingly formalized throughout this period, with evidence for large-scale construction projects including major platforms, fortifications, and flood-control features. Recent excavations at

---

[4] Termed Pre-Harappan, Pre-Urban, "regionalization" phase by different scholars. Jim G. Shaffer, "The Indus Valley, Baluchistan, and Helmand Traditions: Neolithic through Bronze Age," in Robert W. Ehlrich (ed.), *Chronologies in Old World Archaeology*, 2 vols. (Chicago: The University of Chicago Press, 1992), Vol. I, pp. 441–64, and Vol. II, pp. 425–46; M. Rafique Mughal, "The Geographical Extent of the Indus Civilization during the Early, Mature, and Late Harappan Times," in Gregory L. Possehl (ed.), *South Asian Archaeological Studies* (Delhi: Oxford University Press, 1992), pp. 123–43; Gregory L. Possehl, *Indus Age: The Beginnings* (Philadelphia: University of Pennsylvania Press, 1999); and Wright, *Ancient Indus*, Chapter 4.
[5] Jonathan M. Kenoyer and Richard H. Meadow, "The Early Indus Script at Harappa: Origins and Development," in Richard H. Spoor and Eric Olijdam (eds.), *Intercultural Relations between South and Southwest Asia: Studies in Commemoration of E. C. L. During-Caspers (1934–1996)* (Oxford: Archaeopress, 2008), pp. 124–31.
[6] M. Rafique Mughal, *Ancient Cholistan: Archaeology and Architecture* (Lahore: Ferozsons [Pvt.] Ltd., 1997).

Harappa have documented the creation of massive enclosure walls and mudbrick platforms, evidence for functionally specialized neighborhoods, and an increasingly formal layout of space and routes of movement.

Constraints on regional survey due to intensive alluviation along the Indus and its tributaries do not allow for a good understanding of larger regional settlement patterns in many areas. Nonetheless, hundreds of Early Harappan sites have been recorded, and local settlement patterns are reasonably well documented in Cholistan and western India, with additional data from Baluchistan and around Harappa. Together with research on local material cultural traditions, these data point to a social and political landscape in the pre-Harappan period comprised of multiple polities of varying scales that were linked by complex relations and interactions, including trade and exchange, population movement and expansion, and conflict. The spaces between these polities and regional traditions were likely filled by variously organized small-scale communities (including pastoral communities) that may have played important roles in connecting dispersed regional centers.

Indus urbanism

Dramatic changes occurred across the larger Indus region beginning about 2600 BCE. These are evident in the creation of new distinctive material forms and styles, increases in the number and scale of settlements, and the formation of a small number of massive urban sites. While significant regional variants and ways of doing persisted, inhabitants of both urban and non-urban settlements shared (to variable extents) a common vocabulary in ceramic forms and decoration, iconography and representation (including writing), bodily ornamentation, weights, measures, construction technologies, and other categories of material culture. These widespread material similarities overlying a substratum of regional difference have led scholars to recognize the existence of an archaeological "civilization" or Indus tradition.

Sites containing this Mature Indus (or Urban Harappan) material assemblage occur over a vast area – with more than 1,000 known sites distributed over more than 1 million square kilometers. Within this territory, only five sites are considered "urban": Harappa, Mohenjo Daro, Ganweriwala Thar, Rakhigarhi, and Dholavira. These cities were large and highly structured places – ranging from 50 to more than 200 hectares in estimated extent. They have been variously documented. Harappa and Mohenjo Daro were first identified in the mid-nineteenth century and large-scale excavations began following recognition of their antiquity in the 1920s. The others were first identified in the 1960s – Ganweriwala in 1962, Rakhigarhi in 1964, and Dholavira in 1967. Because of its location near the contested Indian–Pakistan border, there has been little research at Ganweriwala, though some excavations have recently been initiated. Dholavira, in contrast, was excavated by the Archaeological Survey of India from 1989 through 2003; to date, publications are limited. Excavations have also occurred at Rakhigarhi, but only brief notes have been published and little information is currently available on its form or organization.

Mohenjo Daro, the most iconic of the Indus urban sites, is also its largest, at more than 200 hectares. It was excavated over many decades, with vast areas of well-preserved domestic and public architecture uncovered. High water tables and dangerous salinization have made the site vulnerable to erosion, and excavations have been banned for the last few decades. Non-destructive research and coring as part of conservation activities have, however, yielded important recent evidence, but much of our understandings of Mohenjo Daro derive from recent reanalyses of plans and excavation records and attempts to link material remains to excavated loci – a great challenge given the poor recording and gross stratigraphic units employed by early excavators.[7]

Like other urban sites, Mohenjo Daro is characterized by multiple spatial zones – here, a high western mound, some 400 x 200 meters in extent and rising more than 18 meters above the plain (often referred to as the "citadel" mound) and a more expansive eastern mound some 1,100 meters north–south and up to 650 meters east–west (the "lower town"). Recent surveys have revealed extensive occupational deposits between and beyond these mounded zones. Several distinctive monumental structures were excavated on the western mound (Figure 15.1). The names assigned by their original excavators remain attached to these structures: the Great Bath, the College, the Granary, the Stupa and Monastery. While the precise uses of these structures are uncertain, it is clear that they were sizeable, non-residential constructions, involving considerable labor investment and coordination. Also involving substantial labor were the massive mudbrick platforms and integrated hydraulic features constructed at various phases of the city's occupation. These platforms, which appear to have been constructed or

[7] Michael Jansen and Günter Urban (eds.), *Interim Reports* (Aachen: Forschungsprojekt "Mohenjo-Daro," 1984), Vols. I and II; and Giovanni Leonardi, *Interim Reports* (Rome: Forschungsprojekt "Mohenjo-Daro," 1988), Vol. III.

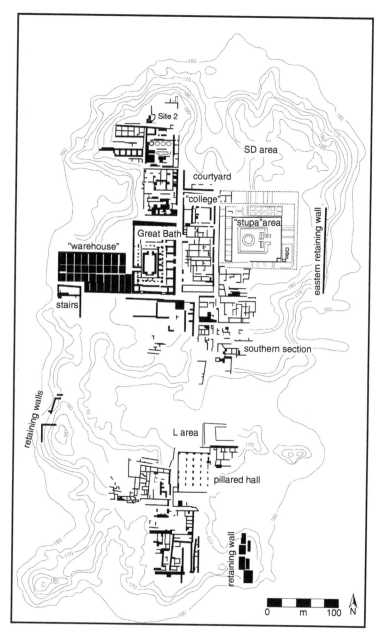

Figure 15.1 Mohenjo Daro citadel plan (after J. Marshall, *Mohenjo-Daro and the Indus Civilization*, 3 vols. [London: Arthur Probsthain, 1931]).

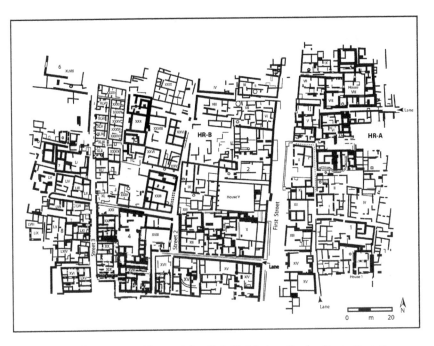

Figure 15.2 Mohenjo Daro HR area (after E. J. H. Mackay, *Further Excavations at Mohenjo-Daro*, 2 vols. [New Delhi: Government Press, 1937–8]).

augmented in discrete phases, were massive constructions that served as foundations for subsequent building phases – the largest are more than half a kilometer in length.

Platforms were also constructed on the eastern mound of Mohenjo Daro, the location of the city's densest residential architecture (Figure 15.2). Residences and workshops were organized in dense blocks bounded by large and small roads and footpaths. Houses varied in their interrelations, layout, and size, ranging from 90 to 183 square meters in floor plan. In addition, some very large residential structures have been documented; including HR 1, a structure of more than twenty-five rooms that also produced the famous "priest king" sculpture as well as fifteen seals and other elaborate artifacts of faience, steatite, alabaster, ivory, and semi-precious stone. Jansen and colleagues have documented two major patterns of household organization: clusters of residences oriented on a central space or courtyard and sharing a common well; and clusters consisting of large houses surrounded by smaller residences and, sometimes, associated workshops.[8] These data point to significant variability in household organization and scale, in the organization of urban spaces, and in social and economic statuses. In addition, several areas of specialized craft production have been documented in both of Mohenjo Daro's major mounds, with some suggestions that the production of certain categories of goods (for example, stoneware bangles) was under administrative control.

Harappa shares with Mohenjo Daro a spatial organization of a number of distinct mounds and/or walled zones. However, nineteenth-century brick-robbing associated with the construction of the Indian railroad resulted in considerable destruction of portions of the site, particularly in the western "citadel" mound (Mound AB). As a result, little is known of the architectural plan of this area or whether significant non-residential constructions, such as found at Mohenjo Daro, existed. There is evidence that an extensive enclosure wall or revetment enclosed the mound, but little can be said about what lay inside those walls.

What we lack in Harappa's Mound AB has been partly compensated by the important systematic excavations in other areas of the site by the Harappa Archaeological Research Project (1986–2001).[9] Rigorous excavations and regional survey efforts have resulted in a fine-scale chronology that has allowed the team to trace the history of the city from the late fourth millennium pre-urban periods through post-urban phases, which has put to rest any lingering arguments that the city appeared or disappeared abruptly. Excavations in the Mound E (lower town) area to the east of Mound AB have exposed a massive enclosure wall and elaborate gate systems, as well as domestic spaces, routes of movement, and craft production areas, and

---

[8] M. Jansen and F. Urban (eds.), *Interim Reports Vol. 1: Report on Fieldwork Carried out at Mohenjo-Daro Pakistan, 1982–83 by the IsMEO-Aachen University Mission* (Aachen: Forschungsprojekt "Mohenjo-Daro", 1984); and *Interim Reports Vol. 2: Report on Fieldwork Carried out at Mohenjo-Daro Pakistan, 1983–84 by the IsMEO-Aachen University Mission* (Aachen: Forschungsprojekt "Mohenjo-Daro", 1987).

[9] George F. Dales and Jonathan M. Kenoyer, "Harappa Excavations – 1988," *Pakistan Archaeology* 24 (1990), 68–176; Richard H. Meadow and Jonathan M. Kenoyer, "Harappa Excavations 1998–1999: New Evidence for the Development and Manifestation of the Harappan Phenomenon," in Ellen M. Raven (ed.), *South Asian Archaeology 1999: Proceedings of the Fifteenth International Conference of the European Association of South Asian Archaeologists, Held at the Universiteit Leiden, 5–9 July, 1999* (Groningen: Egbert Forsten, 2008), pp. 85–109; and Richard H. Meadow and Jonathan M. Kenoyer, "Excavations at Harappa 2000–2001: New Insights on Chronology and City Organization," in Catherine Jarrige and Vincent Lefèvre (eds.), *South Asian Archaeology 2001: Proceedings of the Sixteenth International Conference of the European Association of South Asian Archaeologists, Held in Collège de France, Paris, 2–6 July 2001* (Paris: Éditions Recherche sur les Civilisations, 2005), pp. 207–24.

evidence of efforts to monitor and control access and movement into the walled urban space. In the region around Harappa, Rita Wright and colleagues have developed methods to systematically document sites along water courses and drainages.[10] Although constrained by conditions affecting site preservation and visibility, they have successfully identified a number of sites that point to a complex regional infrastructure of various size settlements and agrarian landscapes in Harappa's immediate hinterland.

The third reasonably well-documented (though not yet fully published) Indus urban site is Dholavira, located on Kadir Island in the Great Rann (salt marsh) of Kutch in modern Gujarat, India. Fourteen seasons of excavation directed by R. S. Bisht of the Archaeological Survey of India beginning in 1989 yielded evidence of a complex and sophisticated urban space. Visually, the city of some 50 hectares (not including an extensive cemetery to its west) is quite different in plan and spatial organization than Harappa or Mohenjo Daro – though, like both, it contains multiple distinctive walled zones and elevational differences that distinguish segregated urban spaces. The excavators have defined seven major chronological phases, with Indus tradition occupations spanning from c. 2650 to 1900 BCE. Their data allow an assessment of changing urban organization over time – as the city grew from a small fortified settlement founded c. 2650 BCE – just on the cusp of the time of explosive urban growth at other urban centers. The city reached its greatest extent c. 2500 BCE, when the maximal enclosure walls and major water-control features were constructed. Assuring fresh water supplies to the city for consumption and subsistence production was essential to inhabiting the salt marshes of Kutch, and considerable labor was invested in channeling water into the city from the two seasonal monsoon-fed streams that flanked the city. This was accomplished through a sophisticated network of canals, elaborate interconnected reservoirs, and wells.

Within the city walls, walled enclosures bounded habitation areas and other specialized spaces. In the south-central area of the site was a heavily fortified and elevated enclosure containing residential and "public" architecture called "the citadel" by Bisht. This area came to be separated from

---

[10] R. P. Wright, M. Afzal Khan, and J. Schuldenrein, "The Emergence of Satellite Communities along the Beas Drainage: Preliminary Results from Lahoma Lal Tibba and Chak Purbane Syal," C. Jarrige and V. Lefevre (eds.), *South Asian Archaeology 2001* (Paris: Recherche sur les civilisations 2005), pp. 327–35; and R. P. Wright, J. Schuldenrein, M. Afzal Khan, and S. Malin-Boyce, "The Beas River Landscape and Settlement Survey: Preliminary Results from the Site of Vainiwal," in U. Frank-Vogt and H.-J. Weisshaar (eds.), *South Asian Archaeology 2003* (Aachen: Linden Soft, 2005), pp. 101–11.

"middle" and "lower" town residential zones to its north by an open space, which the excavators suggest was used for public or ceremonial gatherings. Other features excavated at Dholavira include monumental gate structures flanked by stone columns, stone sculptures of the kind previously only known from Mohenjo Daro, and evidence for a signboard at the North Gate, with an inscription of ten large signs (each more than 25 cm high) in Indus script, the first evidence that some Indus writing was meant to be read by public audiences. Future publication of the excavation report and detailed plans will no doubt allow much more to be said about this important site.

As noted, little information is available on the two other large Indus urban sites, Rakhigarhi and Ganweriwala Thar, though survey around the latter reveals that a complex and integrated hierarchical settlement system surrounded the city. More than a thousand other Indus sites are known from surface documentation, and excavations have occurred at dozens of sites. Several well-known sites, like Kalibangan, Lothal, and Chanhudaro, are relatively well documented. While these share complexly organized spaces and categories of material culture, they are small compared to the urban sites (about 5 hectares), though sites of intermediate scales have been recorded.

Conceptualizing the Indus

In conceptualizing the larger Indus phenomenon, questions of scale rise quickly to the fore. The geographic extent of sites containing Indus material culture assemblages is enormous. The major centers – the cities – were no doubt important and influential loci of cultural production and symbolic and economic power and wealth. Spaced at distances of hundreds of kilometers, each was likely the center of its own world in the day-to-day existence of its inhabitants. Yet each shared fundamental material connections and, presumably, associated values – as manifest in spatial logics, systems of weights, measures, and writing, and an array of shared quotidian and elite material forms. Many of these same material logics also played out in the numerous smaller settlements of the Indus tradition, though as an overlay superimposed on considerable local variability. The social, political, and economic actors and mechanisms that forged the relations that connected the disparate cities and the hundreds of communities that lay between them are, however, more elusive to identify. Certainly, the movement of craft products produced at an array of large and small sites, and likely individual artisans, artisan communities, and merchants were an important nexus of interconnections. Pastoral communities too likely filled the spaces between large centers and inter-acted in a variety of ways with rural and urban communities.

Political structures and relations and ideologies have been notoriously difficult to characterize for the Indus region, for reasons both evidentiary and historical. Part of the challenge, I believe, lies in the historical privileging of Mesopotamia alluded to earlier and to a trait list approach to the understanding of both ancient cities and ancient states. Thus, scholars have focused on what Indus cities are not, or are not in reference to idealized models of contemporary late Early Dynastic (ED) Mesopotamian cities (particularly the city of Ur), which flourished more than a millennium after Mesopotamia's first cities were created. These comparisons typically high-light what the Indus cities lacked (that ED cities had): royal burials, elite iconographies celebrating institutions of kingship and violence, and unam-biguous temples and palaces.

While not wishing to elide the very real differences in historical trajector-ies in Mesopotamia and the Indus, I would like to challenge this long-standing and by now rote comparison by suggesting that the more relevant and interesting juxtaposition is between these *first-generation* Indus cities and *first-generation* Mesopotamian cities of the fourth millennium BCE Uruk period. This comparison suggests that there may be more similarities in these regions during the early phases of urban creation than commonly acknowledged. Representations of leadership, power, and authority were indeed more prominent in Uruk iconography and texts (for example, the Warka Vase, seals, and sculptures) than in the Indus (where there are a number of representations of humans or deities battling fierce beasts or supernatural figures[11]). However, royal cemeteries were absent in both regions during the early centuries of urban formation, and distinctive palaces,[12] while perhaps present, have not been definitively documented in

---

[11] Kenoyer, *Ancient Cities*, pp. 114–15; and Wright, *The Ancient Indus*, pp. 290–3.
[12] The commentary on palaces, which presumes our ability to recognize such structures, is to me the weakest link of this critique. Palace structures can take many forms – from single massive structures to walled enclosures containing many structures (for example, in the medieval South Indian city of Vijayanagara, there is no single structure that could be identified as the king's palace but instead the palace area or "royal center" is a massive walled enclosure containing numerous elite residential structures, reception halls, administrative buildings, etc. John M. Fritz, George Michell, and M. S. Nagaraja Rao, *Where Kings and Gods Meet: The Royal Center of Vijayanagara* [Tucson: University of Arizona Press, 1985]). This is not to argue that there were necessarily "royal" palaces in the Indus cities; however, there clearly were very large residential structures and public architecture at the well-preserved Indus urban sites that provide evidence of significant social differentiation.

either. While it is always difficult to argue from the absence of evidence, it is tempting to suggest that during the periods when urban forms and new political orders were first being created in both regions (likely a time of considerable social, ideological, and economic stresses), social differences may have been materially veiled rather than celebrated. Again, this is not to suggest that the nature and trajectories of Indus cities and the polities that underlay them were not different than in Mesopotamian city-states. These differences may have included, as Kenoyer has suggested, a far wider distribution of power and authority among diverse Indus communities and elites, such that there was not a single "royal" administrative hierarchy (as did eventually develop in Mesopotamia).[13]

Early historic city-states

The Indus tradition, however we might best understand it, began to disintegrate around 1900 BCE. While settlement continued at some of the urban (and non-urban) sites, its scale and character changed dramatically – from highly organized urban centers to small non-urban communities. The widespread shared "civilizational" features of the Indus tradition – painted pottery forms and motifs, seals, writing systems, etc. – disappeared, as more localized regional traditions once again predominated across northern South Asia. Population, while not likely declining in overall numbers, was redistributed across the landscape, with the demographic center of gravity shifting eastward.

It was more than a millennium before urban places were again created in South Asia. This second urbanization encompassed portions of the greater Indus region, but its core was to the east in the alluvial plains between the Ganges and Yamuna Rivers. Scholars have debated how, or if, these later cities drew upon Indus tradition knowledge and memories or whether they were entirely new creations. While it is unlikely that all memories and knowledge of the Indus past were lost, this second period of South Asian urbanization followed unique trajectories and appears to have drawn on rather different and more diverse influences and populations.

Archaeologically, the prelude to Early Historic cities lay in the "Painted Grey Ware" (PGW) period from c. 1100 to 700 BCE. The distinctive wheel-made pottery after which the period is named is generally interpreted as an

---

[13] Kenoyer, *Ancient Cities*, pp. 99–102.

elite serving ware and is reported in low frequencies (never more than 10 percent of total ceramics) from nearly 700 archaeological sites over an extensive geographic area. Within the Ganges Basin, the PGW period was one of dramatic population growth and incipient social differentiation, fueled by *in situ* growth and, almost certainly, in-migration. Settlements grew in both number and diversity, spreading along tributaries and major rivers, as populations began to fill in the limited areas of relatively open land in this marshy and densely forested region.

This period of filling in and emergent and consolidating social and political differentiation was followed by the "Northern Black Polished Ware" (NBPW) period, from c. 700 to 200/100 BCE. It was during this span that enormous urban places were constructed and the emergent sociopolitical hierarchies of the PGW period were elaborated and cemented. The formation of these new cities and the states that governed them began in the core area between the Ganges and Yamuna Rivers, though similar and closely related "Early Historic" political formations and urban centers spread quickly across a broad expanse, extending east–west from the Gangetic Delta in eastern India and Bangladesh into what is today northwest Pakistan, and north–south from the Himalayan foothills of modern Nepal to central India.

Although there are no preserved written documents from the second and first millennia BCE, important sacred texts were composed throughout this timespan and are preserved in documents recorded centuries later. These texts – the Vedas and associated commentaries and exegeses, the Puranas and Shastras, and Buddhist and Jain literature – are foundational to today's Hindu, Buddhist, and Jain religious thought. The direct application of these (largely) proscriptive religious documents to the interpretation of political, social, economic, or even sacred orders or practices of the period is complex. Nonetheless, when critically analyzed, they provide key information about these early cities and an increasingly complex and hierarchical social and political landscape and its idealized social orders.[14]

Texts believed to have originated in the mid-first millennium BCE reference a landscape of great cities, the centers of variously organized states. These were the sixteen *mahajanapadas* (great states) (Map 15.2).[15] Both texts

[14] Brajadulal D. Chattopadhyaya, *Studying Early Indian: Archaeology, Texts, and Historical Issues* (New Delhi, Permanent Black, 2003); and Shonaleeka Kaul, *Imagining the Urban: Sanskrit and the City in Early India* (Delhi: Permanent Black, 2010).
[15] Upinder Singh, *A History of Ancient and Early Medieval India: From the Stone Age to the 12th Century* (Delhi: Pearson Longman, 2008).

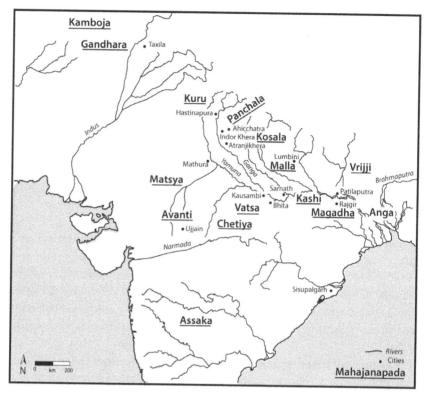

Map 15.2 Early Historic mahajanapadas (after F. R. Allchin,, *The Archaeology of Early Historic South Asia: The Emergence of Cities and States* [Cambridge: Cambridge University Press, 1995]., p. 116).

and archaeological survey data point to a complex hierarchy of places and people, including the cities on which these states were centered (*mahana-gara*), and subsidiary towns (*nagara*), markets and trading centers (*nigama/putabhedana*), agricultural villages (*gama*), as well as pastureland and forest. According to the texts, mahajanapadas took two forms: monarchies (*rajya*) and oligarchies (*gana*), the latter ruled by councils of elders elected for a limited term by members of the ruling lineage. The ganas appear to have been largely restricted to the Himalayan foothills and to have self-consciously differentiated themselves from monarchical states in the fertile Ganga–Yamuna heartland. Categories of people referenced in texts include the four *varnas* – Brahmanas, Kshatriyas, Vaishyas, and Sudras – the founda-tions of the later system of Hindu castes, and numerous distinct occupa-tional groups with specialized roles and ranked statuses.

By 600 BCE, a dense urban landscape existed over much of northern South Asia. In their core area, these city-states lay in close proximity, at most a few travel days apart, creating a landscape of cities far more familiar to comparanda in other regions of the world than was the Indus landscape discussed above. These Early Historic city-states engaged in a wide range of interactions – including economic exchange, elite intermarriages, and frequent warfare and competition. They shared a common elite and sacred material culture – evident in high-status NBPW serving vessels (known from more than 1,500 sites), terracotta figurines, a variety of ornaments and craft products of ivory, ceramic, glass, copper, iron, and stone, and aspects of urban architecture. Major polities issued coinage in silver and copper, and stone weights and seals and sealings indicate shared standards that were important in the long-distance and local exchange that bound the region together.

Many Early Historic cities also assumed significance as important sacred places, for Vedic deities, and as places in the lives of the Buddha and Mahavira, two religious leaders who lived during the tumultuous period of state formation and attracted a large number of followers both during and after their lives. The construction of sacred monuments likely occurred relatively early; however, additions by later rulers have obscured the earliest religious constructions while also likely contributing to the longevity of many early cities.

Archaeological research on Early Historic cities is difficult and, in general, our archaeological evidence is much less rich for the densely populated Ganges–Yamuna core region than for the larger Indus region. While dense human occupation and agrarian transformation of the swampy and densely forested Ganges–Yamuna Doab did not begin until the mid-second millennium BCE, once settled, populations expanded rapidly and dramatically along the tremendously fertile river plains. By Early Historic times, populations were already considerable and the largest cities were many times the size of the Indus cities. Today, this is the world's most densely inhabited region and three millennia of agriculture and settlement have destroyed or obscured countless archaeological sites. And unlike the Indus sites, few Early Historic cities were ever fully abandoned. Many continue to be occupied today, with their earliest levels lying beneath tens of meters of later deposition. As a result, only small areas associated with early phases of urban formation have been excavated and many sites known from texts remain unlocated. Only Taxila in northwest Pakistan and the small town of Bhita have had extensive horizontal excavations, both in the early twentieth century, before major archaeological attention shifted to the Indus period.

A further challenge in examining processes of urbanism is the discordance between the resolution of our long archaeological phases and the rapidity of sociopolitical transformations. Thus, the 500–600-year NBPW period encompassed momentous changes: beginning before the formation of Early Historic states and cities and encompassing their expansion and consolidation and the succeeding creation and collapse of South Asia's first imperial state – the Mauryan Empire. While efforts to refine the archaeological chronology are underway, we have few absolute dates or careful stratigraphic excavations to anchor the sequences, and the archaeological evidence is not yet up to the task of carefully documenting, much less allowing us to explain, the changes that we know were occurring. Nonetheless, in addition to the textual sources alluded to above, there are archaeological data from excavations and, in less densely populated areas further from today's river courses, from a small number of regional surveys, and there have been some important recent field projects by the Archaeological Survey of India and university researchers.[16]

Perhaps the most dramatic evidence preserved at several first millennium urban centers are the remains of the earthen ramparts that enclosed many Early Historic cities. The scale of these earthworks, which were sometimes faced with wood or burnt bricks, and the labor involved in their production, were enormous. For example, the ramparts of the city of Ujjain in central India, measured 75 meters wide at their base, are preserved to 14 meters high, and were over 5 kilometers in length. Comparable ramparts (though only 40 meters wide at the base!) were constructed at Kausambi, Rajgir, Ahicchatra, Atranjikhera, Hastinapura, and Mathura. Bastions, fortified gates, and watchtowers confirm the defensive roles of these walls. However, their height far exceeded any conceivable defensive needs. In addition to their defensive role, these walls would been visible from long distances on the flat expanses of surrounding plains, and no doubt signaled the power and importance of the places they protected to travelers and residents alike.

The areas enclosed by the ramparts reveal that these cities were sizeable – Kausambi, for example, is estimated to have covered about 50 hectares in 600 BCE and tripled in area, to more than 150 hectares, over the succeeding two centuries. Some cities were far larger. By the time of Mauryan

[16] Makkhan Lai, *Settlement History and the Rise of Civilization in the Ganga–Yamuna Doab from 1500 BC–300 AD* (Delhi: B. R. Publishing Corp., 1984); George Erdosy, *Urbanisaton in Early Historic India* (Oxford: Archaeopress, 1988); and Jaya Menon, Supriya Varma, Suchi Dayal, and Paru Bal Sidhu, "Indor Khera Revisited: Excavating a Site on the Upper Ganga Plains," *Man and Environment* 33 (2008), 88–98.

hegemony in the late fourth and early third centuries BCE, the total area of its capital Patilaputra (modern Patna) is estimated at more than 2,000 hectares.

Given the paucity of horizontal excavations, archaeological evidence tells us little about the internal organization of the cities. However, both texts and archaeological sources point to a high degree of economic specialization and social and spatial differentiation. Cities and towns were important loci of economic production and exchange, and traces of craft production workshops and crafting debris have been identified at a number of sites. Major roads led into the cities through large gates in the earthen and brick ramparts, with smaller roads and footpaths branching off from the major routes. Excavations suggest a considerable range in the size and layout of residences and in the formality of urban infrastructure. Where horizontal exposures exist, architecture is dense, further confirming that these cities were home to sizeable populations. Little is preserved of public or administrative architecture from the earliest phases of these cities, though textual sources suggest their existence.

Our information is somewhat better from the second half of the NBPW period. Historical knowledge is also richer for this period, with more sources and more concordances among them, allowing us to trace the rise of South Asia's first empire.[17] By the fourth century BCE, the long-standing conflicts among cities culminated in the ascendancy of one: the mahajanapada of Magadha, situated along the Ganges on the eastern edge of the core zone of early state formation. The names and regnal years of Magadha's kings are reported in a number of sources, allowing a reasonable outline of royal chronology from the sixth through third centuries BCE. Less is known about the state's political and economic organization, and how, or if, it differed from the peer polities that it eventually conquered. It is apparent that Magadha's Maurya rulers were effective both militarily and in forging political alliances, and, by the late fourth century, a series of military victories extended the territories of the kingdom over virtually all of northern South Asia. The most famous Mauryan king, Ashoka (268–232 BCE), is renowned for expanding the empire into the peninsula and as an important figure in the history of South Asian Buddhism. His inscriptions, found on columns and boulders over a wide region, are among the earliest preserved texts in South Asia. Today, Ashoka is also a national symbol

---

[17] Romila Thapar, *The Mauryas Revisted* (Calcutta: C. P. Bagchi and Co., 1984); and Romila Thapar, *Early India: From the Origins to AD 1300* (New Delhi: Penguin, 2002).

of an enlightened ruler of a united India, and sculptures from the period appear on India's currency.

Much has been written about this Mauryan period and Ashoka. Here I limit myself to a discussion of what we know about urban sites of the period. Here too, our evidence is limited by problematic chronologies and the prominence of the Mauryas in the historical imagination. Thus, archaeological phases and certain texts are argued to be "Mauryan" with only limited supporting evidence. The limited archaeological data do not provide evidence that dramatic changes in urban organization accompanied the formation of the imperial polity, though urban scales undoubtedly continued to increase. However, we do have somewhat richer evidence for city plans and constructions from the latter part of the NBPW period than are available from the first half (though how these specifically relate to any particular political dynasty is impossible to decipher).

Early excavations at Bhita and Taxila, mentioned earlier, and more recent work at Indor Khera,[18] provide the best horizontal exposures of the period. Information on the Mauryan capital Patilaputra comes from limited excavations conducted in the late nineteenth and early and mid-twentieth centuries and the fragmentary writings of Megasthenes, Seleucid ambassador to the Mauryan court during the reign of Candragupta (c. 324–297 BCE). Megasthenes described a vast and densely populated city some 12 kilometers long by 2.5 kilometers wide and enclosed by a wooden palisade flanked by a broad moat. Excavations have revealed traces of the palisade and the remains of a massive royal or administrative structure, with eighty massive stone columns arranged on a grid on a large platform. Other massive freestanding stone columns were transported long distances from their quarry site at Chunar[19] to several Early Historic cities, and bear inscriptions and "edicts" of the emperor Ashoka, which figure among the earliest preserved texts from South Asia. Elegant sculpted sacred images also date to this period and, with coins, may be among the few definitive material markers of Mauryan hegemony.

Mauryan rule did not long outlast the death of Ashoka in 232 BCE, and the empire collapsed some forty years later. However, as alluded to above, many of the cities of the period endured through this political

---

[18] Menon, Varma, Dayal, and Bal Sidhu, "Indor Khera Revisited."

[19] Vidula Jayaswal, *From Stone Quarrying to Sculptural Workshop: A Report on the Archaeological Investigations around Chunar, Varanasi, and Sarnath* (Delhi: Agam Kala Prakashan, 1998).

transformation and through the conquest, incorporation, and collapse of many successive states and empires over succeeding centuries and millennia. The resilience of these (always changing) urban forms and spaces is the result of the durability of a range of social, economic, and sacred institutions and mechanisms that were able to sustain urban life even in times of dramatic political upheaval. Understanding this durability will require us to separate the political from the urban to consider the broad range of social, economic, and sacred institutions and mechanisms that sustained and supported historic South Asian urban spaces.[20]

Discussion

In this chapter, I have briefly explored two urban trajectories in a single geographic region. Each was characterized by large, differentiated, and complexly organized urban places. They inhabited very different physical and cultural landscapes – from the widely dispersed largely rural landscape of the Indus region to the dense urban landscapes of the Ganges–Yamuna Basin. While often described as short-lived, the few cities and many more numerous smaller settlements of the Indus tradition thrived for some 700 years, before the Indus tradition declined and disappeared, until its rediscovery by archaeology millennia later. The duration of many Early Historic Indian cities continued much longer, many remaining vibrant centers of population long after the Mauryan Empire's fall and through numerous successive states and empires, and leaving a legacy that endures to the present.

FURTHER READINGS

Bisht, Ranvir S., "Dholavira: New Horizons of the Indus Civilization," *Puratattva* 20 (1991), 71–81.
"The Water Structures and Engineering of the Harappans at Dholavira (India)," in Catherine Jarrige and Vincent Lefèvre (eds.), *South Asian Archaeology 2001: Proceedings of the Sixteenth International Conference of the European Association of South Asian Archaeologists, Held in Collège de France, Paris, 2–6 July 2001*, Paris: CNRS, 2005, pp. 11–25.
Blackman, M. James, and Massimo Vidale, "The Production and Distribution of Stoneware Bangles at Mohenjo-Daro as Monitored by Chemical Characterization Studies," in Richard H. Meadow (ed.), *South Asian Archaeology 1989: Papers from the Tenth*

[20] Monica L. Smith, "The Archaeology of South Asian Cities," *Journal of Archaeological Research* 14 (2006), 97–142.

International Conference of South Asian Archaeologists in Western Europe, Musée National des Arts Asiatiques-Guimet, Paris, France, 3–7 July 1989, Madison, WI: Prehistory Press, 1992, pp. 37–43.

Chattopadhyaya, Brajadulal D., "The City in Early India: Perspectives from Texts," *Studies in History* 13 (1997), 181–208.

Erdosy, George, "City States of North India and Pakistan at the Time of the Buddha," in F. Raymond Allchin et al., *The Archaeology of Early Historic South Asia: The Emergence of Cities and States*, Cambridge: Cambridge University Press, 1995, pp. 123–52.

Urbanisation in Early Historic India, Oxford: British Archaeological Reports, 1988.

Fritz, John M., George Michell, and M. S. Nagaraja Rao, *Where Kings and Gods Meet: The Royal Center at Vijayanagara*, Tucson: University of Arizona Press, 1985.

Gaur, Ruby C., *The Excavations at Atranjikhera: Early Civilization in the Ganga Valley*, Delhi: Motilal Banarasi Das, 1983.

Ghosh, Amitav, "Taxila (Sirkap) 1944–45," *Ancient India* 4 (1948), 66–78.

Jansen, Michael, and Günter Urban (eds.), *Interim Reports*, Aachen: Forschungsprojekt "Mohenjo-Daro," 1984, Vols. I and II.

Jayaswal, Vidula, *From Stone Quarry to Sculpturing Workshop: A Report on the Archaeological Investigations around Chuna, Varanasi and Sarnath*, Delhi: Agam Kala Prakashan, 1998.

Kenoyer, Jonathan M., "The Indus Valley Tradition of Western India and Pakistan," *Journal of World Prehistory* 5 (1991), 331–85.

Kenoyer, Jonathan M., and Richard H. Meadow, "The Ravi Phase: A New Cultural Manifestation at Harappa, Pakistan," in Maurizio Taddei and Giuseppe de Marco (eds.), *South Asian Archaeology 1997: Proceedings of the Fourteenth International Conference of the European Association of South Asian Archaeologists, Held in the Istituto italiano per l'Africa e l'Oriente, Palazzo Brancaccio, Rome, 7–14 July 1997*, Rome: Istituto Italiano per l'Africa e l'Oriente and Istituto Universitario Orientale, 2002, pp. 55–76

Lal, B. B., "Excavations at Hastinapura and Other Explorations in the Upper Ganga and Sutlej Basins," *Ancient India* 11 (1955), 5–151.

Leonardi, Giovanni, *Interim Reports*, Rome: Forschungsprojekt "Mohenjo-Daro", 1988, Vol. III.

Marshall, John H., *A Guide to Taxila*, Delhi: Government of India Publications, 1936.

Taxila, 3 vols., Delhi: Motilal Banarsidas, 1951.

Meadow, Richard H., and Jonathan M. Kenoyer, "Excavations at Harappa 2000–2001: New Insights on Chronology and City Organization," in Catherine Jarrige and Vincent Lefèvre (eds.), *South Asian Archaeology 2001: Proceedings of the Sixteenth International Conference of the European Association of South Asian Archaeologists, Held in Collège de France, Paris, 2–6 July 2001*, Paris: CNRS, 2005, pp. 207–24.

"Harappa Excavations 1998–1999: New Evidence for the Development and Manifestation of the Harappan Phenomenon," in Ellen M. Raven (ed.), *South Asian Archaeology 1999: Proceedings of the Fifteenth International Conference of the European Association of South Asian Archaeologists, Held at the Universiteit Leiden, 5–9 July, 1999*, Groningen: Egbert Forsten, 2008, pp. 85–110.

Mughal, M. Rafique, "The Geographical Extent of the Indus Civilization During the Early, Mature, and Late Harappan Times," in Gregory L. Possehl (ed.), *South Asian Archaeological Studies*, Delhi: Oxford University Press, 1992, pp. 123–43.

"The Harappan Settlement Systems and Patterns in the Greater Indus Valley (circa 3500–1500 BC)," *Pakistan Archaeology* 25 (1990), 1–72.

Narain, Awadh Kishore, and T. N. Roy (eds.), *Excavations at Rajghat*, Varanasi: Banaras Hindu University, 1977.

Possehl, Gregory L., "The Date of Indus Urbanization: A Proposed Chronology for the Pre-urban and Urban Harappan Phases," in Catherine Jarrige (ed.), *South Asian Archaeology 1989: Papers from the Tenth International Conference of South Asian Archaeologists in Western Europe, Musée National des Arts Asiatiques-Guimet, Paris, France, 3–7 July 1989*, Madison, WI: Prehistory Press, 1993, pp. 237–44.

Indus Age: The Beginnings, Philadelphia: University of Pennsylvania Press, 1999.

Ratnagar, Shereen, *Enquiries into the Political Organization of Harappan Society*, Pune: Ravish Publishers, 1991.

Shaffer, J. G., "The Indus Valley, Baluchistan, and Helmand Traditions: Neolithic through Bronze Age," in Robert W. Ehlrich (ed.), *Chronologies in Old World Archaeology*, Chicago: The University of Chicago Press, 1992, Vols. I and II.

Sharma, Govardhan Raj, *The Excavations at Kausambi (1957–59)*, Allahabad: University of Allahabad, 1960.

Shinde, Vasant, Shweta Sinha Deshpande, Toshiki Osada, and Takao Uno, "Basic Issues in Harappan Archaeology: Some Thoughts," *Ancient Asia* I (2006), 63–72.

Sinha, Bindeshwari Prasad, and Lala Aditya Narain, *Patilaputra Excavation 1955–56*, Patna: Bihar Directorate of Archaeology and Museums, 1970.

Sinopoli, Carla M., "On the Edge of Empire: Form and Substance in the Satavahana Dynasty," in Susan E. Alcock, Terence N. D'Altroy, Kathleen D. Morrison, and Carla M. Sinopoli (eds.), *Empires: Perspectives from Archaeology and History*, Cambridge: Cambridge University Press, 2001, pp. 155–78.

Smith, Monica L., "The Archaeology of South Asian Cities," *Journal of Archaeological Research* 14 (2006), 97–142.

Spooner, David B., *Excavation at Shaji-ki-dheri: Annual Reports of the Archaeological Survey of India 1908–09*, Calcutta: Government Press, 1909.

Thapar, Romila, *Early India: From the Origins to AD 1300*, New Delhi: Penguin, 2002.

Tosi, Maurizio, Luca Bondioli, and Massimo Vidale, "Craft Activity Areas and Surface Survey at Moenjodaro: Complementary Procedures for the Reevaluation of a Restricted Site," in Michael Jansen and Günter Urban (eds.), *Interim Reports*, Aachen: Forschungsprojekt "Mohenjo-Daro," 1984, Vol. I, pp. 9–38.

Trautmann, Thomas R., and Carla M., Sinopoli, "In the Beginning was the Word: Excavating the Relations between History and Archaeology in South Asia," *Journal of the Economic and Social History of the Orient* 45 (2002), 492–523.

Verardi, G., "Preliminary Reports on the Stupa and Monastery of Mohenjo-daro," in Michael Jansen and Günter Urban (eds.), *Interim Reports*, Aachen: Forschungsprojekt "Mohenjo-Daro", 1984, Vol. II.

Vidale, Massimo, "Specialized Producers and Urban Elites: On the Role of Craft Production in Mature Indus Urban Contexts," in Jonathan M. Kenoyer (ed.), *Old Problems, New Perspectives in the Archaeology of South Asia*, Madison: University of Wisconsin, 1989, pp. 145–56.

Waddell, Austine L., *Report on the Excavations at Pataliputra (Patna)*, Calcutta: Bengal Secretariat Press, 1996.

Wright, Rita P., M. Afzal Khan, and Joe Schuldenrein, "The Emergence of Satellite Communities along the Beas Drainage: Preliminary Results from Lahoma Lal Tibba and Chak Purbane Syal," in Catherine Jarrige and Vincent Lefèvre (eds.), *South Asian Archaeology 2001: Proceedings of the Sixteenth International Conference of the European Association of South Asian Archaeologists, Held in Collège de France, Paris, 2–6 July 2001*, Paris: CNRS, 2005.

Wright, Rita P., Joe Schuldenrein, M. Afzal Khan, and S. Malin-Boyce, "The Beas River Landscape and Settlement Survey: Preliminary Results from the Site of Vainiwal," in Ute Frank-Vogt and H. J. Weisshaar (eds.), *South Asian Archaeology 2003: Proceedings of the Seventeenth International Conference of the European Association of South Asian Archaeologists, 7–11 July 2003*, Bonn, Aachen: Linden Soft, 2005, pp. 101–11.

16

Greek cities in the first millennium BCE

IAN MORRIS AND ALEX R. KNODELL

The Greek cities of the first millennium BCE were, by almost any definition, among the most successful episodes of urbanism in history. Around 1000 BCE there were about 500,000 Greeks, and their biggest town had perhaps 5,000 residents; a millennium later Greeks were ten times as numerous, with several cities of 100,000 or more. On average, per capita consumption rose more than 50 percent across the millennium, and Greek urban culture spread not just around the Mediterranean Sea but also as far afield as India.

This chapter begins with a brief description of the nature of historical and archaeological evidence concerning ancient Greek cities, and the environmental and agricultural context in which they were situated. The next sections discuss the diachronic development of the Greek city, from the Early Iron Age to the Hellenistic period and the beginning of the Roman Empire, focusing on issues of population, settlement size, and urban form, as well as political systems and the distribution of power.

During the first millennium BCE Greek settlement and political hierarchies steadily grew steeper. Both remained shallow (by the standards of complex pre-modern societies) until nearly 300 BCE, but after that the Greeks were incorporated into the Macedonian and Roman Empires, and took over the urban legacy of southwest Asia. After documenting these claims with a review of new archaeological evidence and recent reinterpretations of the texts, we suggest that it was their position on the fringe of expanding empires and economies in the eastern Mediterranean at a time of improving climate and increasing population, rather than any sort of a "Greek miracle," that accounts for their success. The Greeks were better placed than other

The original text of this chapter was written by Ian Morris for the March 2011 "A World of Cities" conference, on which this volume is based. Editorial work and additions were undertaken by Alex R. Knodell in May 2012.

groups to capture the benefits of these processes; thus, geography, environment, and the wider historical context of the eastern Mediterranean played major roles in the development of Greek culture, and must be considered together to understand the origins and expansion of Greek urbanism in the first millennium BCE.

Historical and archaeological evidence

Ancient Greece is best known for its amazing literary record, and the surviving sources (which begin around 750–700 BCE, shortly after the invention of the alphabetic script) often convey a vivid sense of what it felt like to live in Greek cities. Many thousands of pages of text survive, most of which were written in Athens, particularly in the fourth century BCE (most famously the political philosophy of Plato and Aristotle), or in the great cities of the Hellenistic kingdoms (especially Alexandria) in the third and second centuries.

From the late fifth century onward, growing numbers of public inscriptions on stone survive, which provide some balance to the geographical and class biases of the literary sources, and after roughly 330 BCE enormous numbers of documentary papyri and private letters survive from Ptolemaic Egypt.

The Aegean is also one of the most intensively explored archaeological regions in the world. Western European antiquarians greatly increased their collection of ancient art during the eighteenth century, and vaguely modern excavations began with Schliemann at Troy in 1870 (Map 16.1). This long tradition makes Greece home to some of the longest-running excavations of ancient cities in the world, for example, the excavations of the American School of Classical Studies at Ancient Corinth (1896–present) and the Athenian Agora (1931–present). However, in the mid- and late twentieth century the focus on art often led to delays in adopting methods pioneered in other parts of the world, but by the end of the century the best field work in Greece could bear comparison with any other regional tradition. Similarly, many Greek archaeologists were slow to grasp the value of the techniques of systematic, intensive survey, but since the late 1970s survey in Greece has been increasingly characterized by extremely detailed work and full integration of the natural sciences. The empirical richness of the Greek archaeological record is quite astonishing.[1]

---

[1] Anthony M. Snodgrass, *An Archaeology of Greece: The Present State and Future Scope of a Discipline* (Berkeley: University of California Press, 1987), and for a more recent

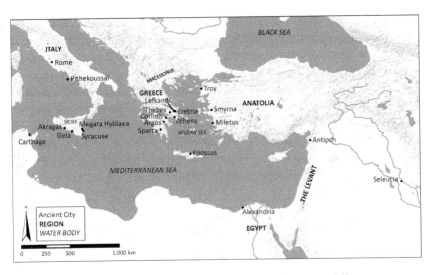

Map 16.1 Map of sites mentioned in the text (drawn by Alex R. Knodell).

The natural environment and agriculture

Mediterranean climates are defined as having (a) enough rain for regular dry farming, but not enough to support substantial forests; (b) cool, wet winters and hot, dry summers; and (c) a great deal of micro-regional variability. Greece generally meets this definition, though with the higher latitudes and elevations in the northwest, the climate is more Balkan. Rainfall varies significantly year by year, resulting in relatively high incidences of crop failure thus necessitating diversification.[2] This led Theophrastus to comment, "the year makes the crop, not the soil" (*History of Plants* 8.7.6).

The geography is also typical of the Mediterranean. Travel to and from the sea through small plains, foothills, and rough mountains is often over only a few kilometers, and farmland can be just a day's walk from higher pastures. Environment was also a factor as Greeks moved outside the

overview of sources of evidence and disciplinary history, see James Whitley, *The Archaeology of Ancient Greece* (Cambridge: Cambridge University Press, 2002).

[2] L. Jeftic, John D. Millman, and G. Sestini, "The Mediterranean Sea and Climate Change – An Overview," in L. Jeftic, John D. Millman, and G. Sestini (eds.), *Climatic Change and the Mediterranean* (London: Edward Arnold, 1992), pp. 1–14; and Peter Garnsey, *Famine and Food Supply in the Graeco-Roman World: Responses to Risk and Crisis* (Cambridge: Cambridge University Press, 1988), pp. 8–16.

Aegean, favoring zones like southern Italy and Sicily, ecologically like their homeland, but with more consistent rainfall and wider plains.[3]

For agriculture, dry-grain farming was most common. Irrigation was only occasional, but fertilization was common through the use of manuring: intensive surveys have revealed "halos" of low-density sherd scatters around higher-density "sites," which some scholars attribute directly to the spreading of manure and other waste as fertilizer.[4] Family farms in the Greek countryside would have produced only small surpluses to sell to cities, typically working only 5 or 6 hectares with little labor from outside the family. It would have also been sensible to store as much grain as possible in case of crop failure.[5]

It is difficult to quantify the cost of concentrating population. Some city dwellers would have walked out to their fields to work the land, but to feed some 20,000 non-farmers, urban markets would have needed surpluses from around 200,000 agriculturalists. Rural population density, transport technology, the nature of urban control over rural production, and farmers' assessments of the incentives for bringing grain to market would have all been important factors.

Textual and archaeological evidence indicates a strong preference for urban living, though the costs of this would have increased as urban populations grew. However, the nature of our evidence will always be skewed toward cities, due to the nature of the archaeological and textual record. The texts and architecture of city life are much more likely to last and be reproduced than the ephemera of country life, which was home to the people and practices that sustained Greek cities and allowed them to

[3] Walter Scheidel, "The Greek Demographic Expansion: Models and Comparisons," *Journal of Hellenic Studies* 123 (2003), 120–40; and Franco de Angelis, "Estimating the Agricultural Base of Greek Sicily," *Papers of the British School at Rome* 68 (2000), 111–48.
[4] On irrigation, see Victor D. Hanson, *The Other Greeks: The Family Farm and the Agrarian Roots of Western Civilization* (New York: Free Press, 1995), pp. 60–3; on manuring, see Anthony M. Snodgrass, "Survey Archaeology and the Rural Landscape of the Greek City," in Oswyn Murray and Simon Price (eds.), *The Greek City from Homer to Alexander* (Oxford: Clarendon Press, 1990), pp. 113–36; for an alternative view, see Susan E. Alcock, John F. Cherry, and Jack L. Davis, "Intensive Survey, Agricultural Practice and the Classical Landscape of Greece," in Ian Morris (ed.), *Classical Greece: Ancient Histories and Modern Archaeologies* (Cambridge: Cambridge University Press, 1994), pp. 137–70.
[5] Peter Garnsey, "The Yield of the Land in Ancient Greece,' in Berit Wells (ed.), *Agriculture in Ancient Greece* (Stockholm: The Institute, 1992), p. 148; Robert Sallares, *The Ecology of the Ancient Greek World* (Ithaca, NY: Cornell University Press, 1991), p. 79; and Thomas W. Gallant, *Risk and Survival in Ancient Greece: Reconstructing the Rural Domestic Economy* (Stanford, CA: Stanford University Press, 1991), pp. 60–112.

Table 16.1 Standard periodization of pre-Roman Greek history

Period	Dates
Late Bronze Age	*c.* 1600–1050 BCE (also known as Mycenaean period)
Early Iron Age	*c.* 1050–750 BCE (also known as Dark Age)
Archaic	*c.* 750–480 BCE
Classical	480–323 BCE
Hellenistic	323–30 BCE

exist. Moreover, Greek landscapes and culture were more suited to small-scale farming than the semi-industrial, irrigated agriculture that played such a major role in other early cities, which may be reflected in, or at least related to, political and social organization.

Greek cities: the Early Iron Age, *c.* 1050–750 BCE

Through most of the first millennium BCE, Greek cities were quite small. Around 1000 BCE, in the period often called the "Dark Age," the largest towns had probably just 1,000–5,000 residents. There is much controversy, however, over the precise numbers. Houses in this period were very light constructions, and little has survived: the most important Early Iron Age settlements tended to remain important throughout Greek antiquity, burying or destroying earlier remains. Moreover, compared to other periods, archaeologists have shown relatively little interest in Early Iron Age settlements.

Early Iron Age finds are often scattered across quite large areas – 50 hectares at Argos, 100 at Knossos, and 200 at Athens – but what evidence there is suggests small clusters of huts separated by spaces over 100 meters wide. Densities were probably rarely higher than 12.5–25 people/hectare, suggesting populations of 600–1,200 people at Argos, 1,250–2,500 at Knossos, and 2,500–5,000 at Athens. Lefkandi may have been somewhere around the same size as Athens, but despite the new excavations underway in the settlement, much remains obscure. It is likely that most Greeks lived in small hamlets of just a few dozen people throughout the Dark Age, yet there remains a remarkable amount of diversity in size and type of settlement.[6]

[6] James Whitley, *Style and Society in Dark Age Greece* (Cambridge: Cambridge University Press, 1991), pp. 84–90; and A. Mazarakis Ainian, *From Rulers' Dwellings to Temples: Architecture, Religion and Society in Early Iron Age Greece (1100–700 B.C.)* (Jonsered: P. Åströms Förlag, 1997).

Greek cities: the Archaic period, *c.* 750–480 BCE

There is a marked turning point in the history of Greek settlement in the middle of the eighth century BCE, often referred to in terms of "renaissance" or "revolution." At Eretria, one of the best-explored sites, a scattering of huts around 850 BCE turned into a group of interlinked villages covering 100 hectares by 700 BCE, with a population of perhaps 5,000. Corinth, Knossos, and Argos were surely at least as big as Eretria by 700 and there were probably dozens of communities like Smyrna, Thebes, and Miletus with populations over 1,000.[7]

The eighth and seventh centuries also saw the expansion of Greek settlement into the west Mediterranean and Black Sea. The total number of migrants was small – probably in the 30,000–50,000 range – but they founded some quite large settlements. Pithekoussai, the earliest (founded *c.* 775–750 BCE), probably had 4,000–5,000 residents in the late eighth century, although very probably not all were Greeks. Megara Hyblaea, founded in 728, probably began with just 240–320 settlers, growing to about 2,000 by 625 BCE.[8]

In the eighth century BCE the Greek world changed from one of villages to one of towns. Overall population grew very sharply – perhaps doubling between 800 and 700 – and the Greek world began developing its famous political landscape of several hundred tiny city-states, each with a territory (the *chora*) ranging from a few dozen to about 2,500 square kilometers centered on a small town (the *asty* or *polis*) with somewhere between a few hundred and 10,000 residents. By the sixth century there were at least 500 such *poleis*.[9]

In theory, each polis was an independent political unit, though in practice many were controlled by stronger neighbors. After 550, Sparta's Pelopon-nesian League (a name coined by modern historians) began incorporating

---

[7] Alexander Mazarakis Ainian, "Geometric Eretria," *Antike Kunst* 30 (1987), 3–24; and Ian Morris, "The Growth of Greek Cities in the First Millennium BCE," in Glenn Storey (ed.), *Urbanism in the Preindustrial World: Cross-cultural Approaches* (Tuscaloosa: University of Alabama Press, 2006), pp. 27–51.

[8] Scheidel, "The Greek Demographic Expansion'; on Pithekoussai, see Ian Morris, "The Absolute Chronology of the Greek Colonies in Sicily," *Acta Archaeologica* 67 (1996), 57; and on Megara Hyblaea, see Franco de Angelis, *Megara Hyblaea and Selinous* (Oxford: Oxbow, 2003), pp. 40–71.

[9] Ian Morris, "Early Iron Age Greece," in Walter Scheidel, Ian Morris, and Richard P. Saller (eds.), *The Cambridge Economic History of the Greco-Roman World* (Cambridge: Cambridge University Press, 2007), pp. 218–19; and Mogens Herman Hansen and Thomas Heine Nielsen (eds.), *An Inventory of Archaic and Classical Poleis* (Oxford: Oxford University Press, 2004).

other poleis into a loose alliance, in which allied cities provided troops for Sparta's wars and Sparta supported local oligarchies against rivals and coups (Herodotus, *Histories* 1.65–68). This turned Sparta into the greatest military power in Greece (Herodotus, *Histories* 1.69, 141, 152; 5.49).

The historical sociologist Charles Tilly laid out a very useful framework for thinking about European state formation since 1000 CE in terms of a spectrum of organizing principles, ranging from coercion-intensive to capital-intensive, with the former more typical of territorial states and the latter of city-states.[10] Sparta was extremely unusual in this regard: its power rested on the military domination of the neighboring region of Messenia, whose people labored as helots providing food so that Spartan citizens could concentrate on becoming full-time warriors.[11]

Most poleis, by contrast, seem to have pursued more capital-intensive paths toward state formation. Greek commerce developed rapidly: Greek goods (particularly wine) were traded widely across the Mediterranean, and almost as soon as the Lydians invented coined money in the late seventh or early sixth century, Greeks also began minting coins. By 500 BCE, small change was common. There has been much debate among historians over the exact causes of these developments, and whether early Greek coinage was in fact more a political statement than an economic tool. It now seems clear, though, that despite the fascinating ideological conflicts over the meanings of coined money, the introduction of coinage sharply lowered transaction costs.[12]

Across the eighth through sixth centuries, Greek cities began taking on their canonical "classical" form. Some villages were laid out on grid plans as early as 850 BCE, and in the late eighth century orthogonal grids seem to have been normal in the new colonies founded in Sicily and southern Italy. By 500, though, they were also common in cities in the old Aegean

---

[10] Charles Tilly, *Coercion, Capital, and European States, AD 990–1990* (Malden: Blackwell, 1992).

[11] At least, this is the traditional interpretation of the evidence: see, for example, Stephen Hodkinson, *Property and Wealth in Classical Sparta* (London: The Classical Press of Wales, 2000); but several revisionist accounts have suggested that in fact Sparta's labor regime was less peculiar than this: for example, Nino Luraghi and Susan E. Alcock (eds.), *Helots and Their Masters in Laconia and Messenia: Histories, Ideologies, Structures* (Cambridge, MA: Center for Hellenic Studies, 2003).

[12] Henry S. Kim, "Archaic Coinage as Evidence for the Use of Money," in Andrew Meadows and Kirsty Shipton (eds.), *Money and Its Uses in the Ancient Greek World* (Oxford: Oxford University Press, 2001), pp. 7–21; and Leslie Kurke, *Coins, Bodies, Games, and Gold: The Politics of Meaning in Archaic Greece* (Princeton, NJ: Princeton University Press, 1999).

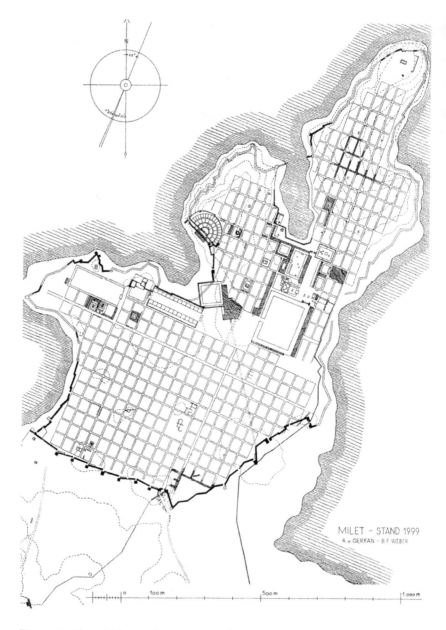

Figure 16.1 Plan of Miletus, showing a typical Hippodamian layout with gridded streets and public buildings in the center (A. Gerkan and B. F. Weber).

heartland. This type of urban planning was traditionally (though anachronistically) attributed to Hippodamus of Miletus (c. 498–408 BCE), who was most famous for his role in the design of Athens' harbor town, Piraeus, and the rebuilding of Miletus itself after its destruction by the Persians (Figure 16.1). The grid of streets divided Greek cities into blocks, and each block would be divided between several houses, typically organized around a courtyard, ringed by a wall with just one or two small doors.[13] The spatial arrangement of courtyard houses also became a central metaphor in Greek literature for the biological household.

By 700 cities were typically adorned with one or more large temples, where anyone was free to offer sacrifice or give gifts to the gods. The Doric and Ionic architectural canons stabilized across the seventh and sixth centuries and the Greek visual language began being widely imitated in the central Mediterranean. The height of temple building came in the sixth century, by which time the richer Greek cities also boasted fountain houses, stoas, and public sculpture. Such monuments were often concentrated in the civic and religious centers of cities, and in the Archaic and Classical periods typically were associated with the polis itself, rather than private individuals (a practice which did not become widespread until the Hellenistic and Roman periods).

It also became common after 700 BCE to ring cities with simple fortifications. As the Ionians (Greeks living along the west coast of modern Turkey) discovered after 600, these defenses could not deter large Near Eastern armies, but they were more than adequate to keep out the Greeks' own much smaller forces. Naval warfare became much more organized in the late sixth century, as Greek states' tax revenues reached the point that they could equip and maintain small fleets of triremes, the type of vessel that would become the dominant form of military machinery in the subsequent period.[14]

Greek cities: the Classical period, 480–323 BCE

Population growth accelerated in the fifth century. By the 430s there may have been as many as 5 or 6 million Greeks spread between the Black Sea and eastern Spain. Athens and Syracuse, the largest cities, grew to perhaps

---

[13] Lisa C. Nevett, *House and Society in the Ancient Greek World* (Cambridge: Cambridge University Press, 1999).

[14] Rune Frederiksen, *Greek City Walls of the Archaic Period, 900–480 BCE* (Oxford: Oxford University Press, 2011); and H. T. Wallinga, *Ships and Sea-Power before the Great Persian War: The Ancestry of the Ancient Trireme* (Brussels: Brill, 1993).

50,000 residents, and the total populations of these cities plus their hinter-lands were probably about 350,000 for Athens and 250,000 for Syracuse. Population densities rose extremely high in the fifth century, reaching about 139 people/square kilometer in the territory of Athens, while the carrying capacity of the region was around 35–42 people/square kilometer. Syracuse's density was more like 53–75 people/square kilometer, just one-third to one-half of Athens', but still high by pre-industrial standards.[15]

Because of this rapid growth, Greek cities came to depend on food imports. High levels of inter-annual variability in rainfall meant that Greek farmers had long needed ways to mobilize resources from outside their households in bad years, but by the fifth century Athens, Corinth, Aegina, and probably a dozen or more other poleis came to need imports every year. In the fifth and fourth centuries, much of the Mediterranean was drawn into a marketing network to feed Greece.

Greek cities were not large – at its peak in the early fourth century, Syracuse may have had 100,000 residents, and Athens probably never had more than 50,000 – but a remarkable proportion of Greeks lived in towns of 5,000-plus people.[16] The result was a highly nucleated culture with a very shallow settlement hierarchy. Greece's demographic success depended on its commercial success in creating and exploiting a Mediterranean food market, focused above all on Athens' great harbor of Piraeus. The import-ance of this harbor was emphasized by the construction, between 462 and 456 BCE, of the "long walls" that ran about 7 kilometers between Athens and Piraeus, making it impossible to besiege the city by land.

Remarkably, not only did the number of Greeks roughly double between 550 and 350 BCE (from perhaps 3 million to 6 million), but Greek standards of living also rose sharply across this same period. By 300 BCE, the typical Greek probably consumed about 50 percent more than his or her predecessors had done 500 years earlier. The combination of archaeological and real wage data suggests that Classical Greece had some of the highest standards of living known from pre-modern times.[17]

[15] Garnsey, *Famine and Food Supply*, p. 90; Sallares, *Ecology of the Greek World*, p. 72; and De Angelis, "Agricultural Base of Sicily."
[16] Mogens H. Hansen, *The Shotgun Method: The Demography of the Ancient Greek City-State Culture* (Columbia: University of Missouri, 2006).
[17] Ian Morris, "Economic Growth in Ancient Greece," *Journal of Institutional and Theoretical Economics* 160 (2004), 709–42; and Walter Scheidel, "Real Wages in Early Economies: Evidence for Living Standards from 1800 BCE to 1300 CE," *Journal of the Economic and Social History of the Orient* 53 (2010), 425–62.

On the face of it, this seems to fly against Malthusian orthodoxy, since we might expect rising numbers to have triggered declining marginal returns and a positive check on population. However, economic historians have recently recognized numerous examples of similar "efflorescences" in premodern times, and Scheidel has shown how a long wave of rising standards of living between 800 and 300 BCE can be reconciled with Malthusian cycles.[18]

The Classical period saw the peak of the canonical polis forms of social organization, focused on the relatively egalitarian male citizen community. Compared to most ancient societies, Greek cities strongly resisted class distinctions within the group of free, locally born male citizens. This sense of male egalitarianism developed gradually across the period 800–400 BCE, and underpinned the development of male democracy.[19] The first democracies appeared in the late sixth century (Athens' is usually dated to 508/507), and by the fourth century there were several hundred.

Greek cities rarely had kings or powerful priesthoods. The difficulties elites faced in convincing other Greeks that they were godlike (itself closely linked to the elites' financial and military weakness, relative to the strength of elites in other ancient societies) probably had much to do with the success of democracy as an answer to what Morris has elsewhere called "the Greek Question," of how a community can pursue the good life and make proper decisions in the absence of individuals who know what the gods want.[20]

Many poleis even went so far as to rotate important religious and political offices among male citizens by lot, without property qualifications. However, some Greek cities also practiced large-scale chattel slavery, importing slaves particularly from Anatolia and Ukraine. Some historians have seen chattel slavery as a logical concomitant of male citizen freedom, but others have emphasized the importance of free wage and slave price ratios in driving chattel slavery.[21]

---

[18] Jack A. Goldstone, "Efflorescences and Economic Growth in World History: Rethinking the 'Rise of the West' and the Industrial Revolution," *Journal of World History* 13 (2002), 323–89; and Walter Scheidel, "Demographic and Economic Development in the Ancient Mediterranean World," *Journal of Institutional and Theoretical Economics* 160 (2004), 743–57.

[19] Ian Morris, "The Strong Principle of Equality and the Archaic Origins of Greek Democracy," in Josiah Ober and Charles Hedrick (eds.), *Dêmokratia: A Historical and Theoretical Conversation on Ancient Greek Democracy and Its Contemporary Significance* (Princeton, NJ: Princeton University Press, 1996), pp. 19–48.

[20] Ian Morris and Barry B. Powell, *The Greeks: History, Culture, and Society* (Upper Saddle River, NJ: Prentice Hall, 2009).

[21] Moses I. Finley, *Ancient Slavery and Modern Ideology* (New York: Penguin, 1980); and Scheidel, "Real Wages in Early Economies."

Greek-style democracy was always a form of minority government. At Athens, the best-documented and also perhaps the most radical example, about two-thirds of the adult males were citizens, with the rest being slaves or resident aliens. So far as we know, no polis ever made women full citizens with political rights. Consequently, even in the most developed democracies, only one-third of the resident adults (or one-sixth of the total resident population) were enfranchised. However, compared to non-Greek ancient states, this was an extraordinarily high rate of political participation. Poor Athenians wielded quite astonishing power, and the openness of democratic institutions may explain much of the success of Classical Greek cities in solving collective action problems.[22]

Fifth-century Greece was highly nucleated, with perhaps as many as 75 percent of the population living in towns of 5,000-plus people. These towns were often laid out in very regimented ways, with equal-sized lots and repetitive "Typenhäuser" that may well reflect contemporary theories of egalitarian living like those developed by Hippodamus.[23]

In the fourth century, however, a partial shift away from nucleated settlement began. This is best documented in data from intensive surface survey, which suggest that a minority of the population – perhaps about 10 percent – shifted away from nucleated sites toward dispersed rural settlement. The significance of this has been much debated, but it may reflect a further intensification of farming and shift toward production for the market. Another much discussed class of evidence, off-site pottery scatters, may well reflect levels of manuring, which seem to have reached a pre-modern peak in the fourth and third centuries.[24]

The overall impression is that by about 350 BCE Greek cities were larger and richer than ever before, were involved in wider, denser, and more varied exchange systems, and were reaching levels of commercial development that have rarely been matched by pre-modern cities. In Athens, probably no more than half the population was engaged primarily in farming.

---

[22] Josiah Ober, "The Original Meaning of 'Democracy': Capacity to do Things, Not Majority Rule," *Constellations* 15 (2008), 3–9.

[23] Hansen, *The Shotgun Method*; and Wolfram Hoepfner and Ernst Ludwig Schwandner, *Haus und Stadt im klassischen Griechenland: Wohnen in der klassischen Polis* (Munich: Deutscher Kunstverlag, 1994).

[24] Compare Alcock, Cherry, and Davis, "Intensive Survey," and Anthony M. Snodgrass, "Response: The Archaeological Aspect," in Morris (ed.), *Classical Greece*, pp. 197–200.

But while the economic and cultural integration of Classical Greece reached impressive levels, its political integration did not. The Persian Empire's push into the Aegean under Darius I from 522 BCE onward eventually forced the Greek cities to cooperate on defense. When the Ionian Greeks rebelled against Persia in 499, Athens and Eretria decided to help them, with the consequence that Persia then tried to punish Athens and Eretria. A Persian army sacked Eretria in 490 but was defeated by Athens at Marathon – with the result that a much larger Persian army and navy returned in 480.

To avoid destruction, Athens and Sparta cooperated against Persia, but victory just confronted them with the new problem of how to keep Persia out of the Aegean. After a certain amount of jostling between the two cities, Athens organized the anti-Persian Delian League in 477, and rapidly began converting it into a kind of Greater Athenian State, with Athens functioning as the capital city. Several dozen formerly independent cities started paying taxes to Athens, using Athenian weights and measures, submitting cases to Athenian courts, sharing in Athenian rituals, surrendering foreign policy decisions to Athens, recognizing an Athenian monopoly on legitimate violence, and allowing Athenians to own real property within their territories.[25] Athens used the taxes acquired to finance the construction of the most powerful navy in the Aegean, and to embellish its city and territory with a variety of new projects, most famously with the Periclean building program that included the monuments of the Athenian Acropolis.

These developments terrified the Spartans, who fought two long wars (460–446 and 431–404) against Athens to disrupt them. The second ended in a decisive Spartan victory, thanks to massive financial and naval help from Persia. This effectively closed off the capital-intensive path of state formation that Athens had been following. Sparta, however, proved quite incapable of taking over and running the cities Athens had ruled, and after suffering catastrophic battlefield defeats in 371 and 362 BCE lost control of the Aegean.

The western Greek world followed a different but in the end equally fruitless path of political integration. For reasons that are now obscure, in the 490s the city of Gela defeated most of its rivals in eastern Sicily, but followed a much more patrimonial path of state formation. In 485 the tyrant Gelon shifted his base from Gela to the much larger city of Syracuse, and

---

[25] Ian Morris, "The Greater Athenian State," in Ian Morris and Walter Scheidel (eds.), *The Dynamics of Ancient Empires* (Oxford: Oxford University Press, 2009), pp. 99–177.

after defeating a Carthaginian invasion in 480 effectively divided most of Sicily between his own family and that of Theron of Akragas.

West Greek fiscal structures seem to have been much weaker than those developed by Athens, and in the 460s popular uprisings brought down the tyrannies all over the island and broke up the multi-city organizations. As early as the 440s Syracuse's demographic and economic weight began to swell again, though, and by the 420s the eastern part of Sicily was breaking into pro- and anti-Syracusan alliances. It took an Athenian intervention against Syracuse in 427–424 to scare the Sicilians sufficiently that they agreed to return to a situation of multiple independent city-states.

This balance was shattered by a major Athenian attack on Syracuse in 415–413 and then a Carthaginian invasion that destroyed most of the major Greek cities in Sicily between 409 and 405. The major outcome was that a new tyrant, Dionysius I, seized power in Syracuse and finally brought most of the island under his control. The ruinous wars that he and his son fought against Carthage and other Greeks, though, left Sicily in chaos, and by the 350s attempts to create multi-city organizations were no further forward in the west than they were in the Aegean.

Greek cities: the Hellenistic period, 323–30 BCE

The growth of Greek economic networks and the constantly expanding wars of the fifth and fourth centuries drew in many of the city-states' neighbors. In particular, the large, loose kingdom of Macedon became a major supplier of timber and silver. The Greek cities intervened regularly in its politics, playing factions off against each other; but at the same time, bold adventurers learned to make use of Greek financial, military, and political institutions in a Macedonian setting. Between 359 and 338 the boldest of these adventurers, Philip II, brilliantly exploited these techniques to make himself master of the Aegean.[26]

Philip probably wanted nothing more from the Greeks than to raise some cash and to secure his southern flank as a prelude to plundering Persia, and after his murder in 336 his son Alexander certainly focused entirely on Asia. Between 334 and 323 Alexander overran the entire Persian Empire, bringing Greek civilization into contact with a wider array of cultures than ever

---

[26] Nicholas Geoffrey Lemprière Hammond and Guy Thompson Griffith, *A History of Macedonia II* (Oxford: Clarendon Press, 1979).

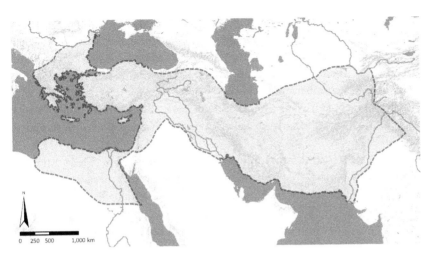

Map 16.2 Map of the Hellenistic expansion, showing the extent of Alexander's conquests (drawn by Alex R. Knodell).

before and founding cities throughout newly conquered territories. This, in combination with Macedonian hegemony in the Aegean, drastically changed the politics of power in the Greek world.[27]

Between Alexander's death in 323 and 301 his former generals carved the old empire up into a group of kingdoms, and tens of thousands of Macedonians and Greeks migrated to the new frontier (Map 16.2). In addition to new foundations, they took over much older and bigger cities than anything in the original Greek world, including Babylon, which probably had a population of 150,000 in the fourth century BCE. New cities, such as Alexandria, Antioch, and Seleucia, tapped into the taxable wealth of the Near East to grow even larger. By 100 BCE Alexandria may have had between 300,000 and 400,000 residents, dwarfing Classical cities like Athens and Syracuse.[28] The rapid expansion in the size of Greek political units after 334 BCE was paralleled by an equally rapid increase in the gradient of the settlement hierarchy.

[27] John F. Cherry, "The Personal and the Political: The Greek World," in Susan E. Alcock and Robin Osborne (eds.), *Classical Archaeology* (Cambridge: Cambridge University Press, 2007), pp. 288–306.
[28] On Babylon, see Tom Boiy, *Late Achaemenid and Hellenistic Babylon* (Leuven: Peeters, 2004); and on Alexandria, see Walter Scheidel, "Creating a Metropolis: A Comparative Demographic Perspective," in William V. Harris and Giovanni Ruffini (eds.), *Ancient Alexandria between Egypt and Greece* (Leiden: Brill, 2004), pp. 1–31.

By about 250 BCE, the great Greco-Macedonian migration to the Near East had slowed down, but it had already permanently transformed the situation of the Greek cities. The old Aegean and Sicilian worlds began turning into backwaters. Their populations shrank and trade routes shifted eastward.[29] After 264, Syracuse became a client of Rome; after a crushing defeat in 262, Athens reinvented itself as a kind of theme park, though maintaining its role as a cultural center; and by the 240s, Sparta was in the grip of a conservative revolution.

When nineteenth-century historians coined the term "Hellenistic" to describe this period, they meant to evoke a picture of decadence, as the once proud Hellenic culture became mixed with Oriental elements. In some ways, though, the third century has a good claim to have been the golden age of Greek civilization. The numbers of people speaking Greek and thinking of themselves as Greeks were larger than ever before. Greek explorers ventured into the Atlantic and Central Asia. Greek science and technology reached new heights. Greek cities were the biggest in the world, and the Museum at Alexandria was probably the most sophisticated cultural institution on the planet. It is not yet clear whether standards of living kept rising in the old Greek world after 300 BCE, but they certainly did so in the new world of Egypt and the Near East.

From 200 BCE onward, the Hellenistic Greek cities were increasingly swamped by Roman military intervention. The political narrative is complicated and messy, but by the 160s it was clear that none of the Hellenistic kingdoms would be able to stop Rome on the battlefield. Roman generals fought out many of their rivalries in the Greek world, with sometimes devastating results. In 167, the Romans enslaved 150,000 people in Epirus in a single day. In 146, they destroyed Corinth, by then the largest of the mainland Greek cities. Security was collapsing, piracy had become a major problem, and population was falling sharply. The old Seleucid kingdom, undermined by Roman assaults, was largely overrun by Parthian immigrants.

An anti-Roman revolt under Mithridates in 88 BCE led to the devastation of much of the Greek world, with Athens being brutally sacked in 83. In the Roman civil wars of the 40s–30s, competing generals treated the Greeks as a cash machine, and for propaganda purposes Octavian converted the final

---

[29] Susan E. Alcock, *Graecia Capta: The Landscapes of Roman Greece* (Cambridge: Cambridge University Press, 1993); and Susan E. Alcock, "Breaking up the Hellenistic World: Survey and Society," in Morris (ed.), *Classical Greece*, pp. 171–237.

phase of his civil war with Antony into a war between Rome and Ptolemaic Egypt, the last of the Hellenistic kingdoms. With the suicides of Antony and Cleopatra VII in 30 BCE, the last politically independent Greek state was absorbed into the Roman Empire.

The last two centuries BCE were a time of military, political, economic, and demographic disaster for the Greek cities, but in cultural terms this was an age of renewed success. Rome itself, like much of Italy, had been heavily influenced by Greek culture since the colonial expansion of the eighth century BCE. Rome's conquests in the third and second centuries brought in much plunder from the Greek world, including artwork and slaves educated in Greek literature, which set off intense debates over whether the Roman elite wanted to assimilate itself to the older, more prestigious Greek high culture. Meanwhile, Roman elites became active benefactors (yet at the same time oppressors) of cities in the Greek east, a trend that continued with Roman emperors in the following centuries. By 100 BCE a Roman reinterpretation of Hellenistic culture was emerging, with the cities that Rome founded around its west Mediterranean empire being, to a large extent, Hellenistic in form. By the end of the first millennium BCE Greek urbanism had, in a sense, conquered the entire Mediterranean Basin and been carried as far afield as the Danube, Rhine, and England.

Conclusion

The Greek cities of the first millennium BCE were remarkably successful. In 1000 BCE there was not really any such thing as a Greek city, with the largest site having probably fewer than 5,000 residents. By the third century Alexandria had probably more than 300,000 residents; by the first century, the Hellenized city of Rome had a million. With the Roman Empire acting as a conduit, the physical form of the Greek city could be found everywhere from England to Afghanistan.

This happened largely because the Greeks were particularly well placed to exploit larger social, material, and environmental changes during the first millennium BCE. The shift from the "Sub-Boreal" to the "Sub-Atlantic" climate regime that began in the ninth century BCE was probably particularly important. This generated stronger Westerlies off the Atlantic Ocean, bringing longer, cooler winters with more rainfall. In the Mediterranean Basin, the greatest challenge for farmers was lack of winter rain to fertilize their crops; the Sub-Atlantic regime must have been an economic blessing. The major causes of death in the pre-modern Mediterranean seem to have been intestinal complaints, with mortality concentrated in the summer months; cooler, wetter weather would have been a demographic boon. Although no one has systematically collected the evidence, it is clear that population started growing almost everywhere from Iberia to western Iran between 800 and 500 BCE, and by the end of the first millennium BCE the Mediterranean's total population had probably doubled.[30]

North of the Alps, by contrast, the major problems for farmers were wet, heavy soils and short growing seasons, and the major killers were pneumonic illnesses in winter months. By bringing colder, wetter weather, the Sub-Atlantic regime was a disaster, and population in temperate Europe generally shrank between 700 BCE and the onset of the "Roman Warm Period" 500 years later.[31]

Population grew particularly rapidly in the Aegean, in part because the region had seen an uncommonly severe contraction after 1200 BCE, but in part because Greece was unusually well placed to emerge as a commercial hub linking the reviving empires of the eastern Mediterranean to raw materials in the west.[32]

Across the eighth and seventh centuries the Phoenicians, on the fringe of the Assyrian Empire in modern Lebanon, initially seem to have benefited from these processes even more than the Greeks, but by 600 Greeks massively outnumbered Phoenicians in the west Mediterranean and Greek urban forms were having a much bigger impact on west Mediterranean populations. Whether this was simply a consequence of weight of numbers or whether Greek urban culture had a particular appeal that the Phoenician version lacked remains an open question.

In the Archaic period Greece was very much a periphery to the Near Eastern core, flourishing in a power vacuum that persisted from the fall of the Hittite Empire around 1200 to the expansion of Lydia after 600. This gave the Greeks space to pursue low-coercion, capital-intensive paths of

---

[30] On climate change, see Arie S. Issar, *Climate Changes During the Holocene and their Impact on Hydrological Systems* (Cambridge: Cambridge University Press, 2003); on seasonal mortality, see Walter Scheidel, *Death on the Nile: Disease and the Demography of Roman Egypt* (Leiden: Brill, 2001); and on population, see Walter Scheidel, "Demography," in Scheidel, Morris, and Saller (eds.), *Cambridge Economic History of the Greco-Roman World*, pp. 38–86.

[31] Jan Bouzek, "Climatic Changes and Central European Prehistory," in Anthony F. Harding (ed.), *Climatic Change in Later Prehistory* (Edinburgh: Edinburgh University Press, 1982), pp. 179–91.

[32] Morris, "Economic Growth in Ancient Greece"; "Early Iron Age Greece"; and Andrew Sherratt and Susan Sherratt, "The Growth of the Mediterranean Economy in the Early First Millennium BCE," *World Archaeology* 24 (1993), 361–78.

state formation, and by the time the Persians began seriously trying to draw the Aegean into an empire after 522, the Greek cities were in a position to convert their capital into impressive military power. After the victories of 480–479, the Aegean and Sicily began developing into cores in their own right, and in the 330s–320s the Macedonians were able to tap the Aegean core to overthrow the Persian Empire.

In this historical and geographical context, remarkable material changes took place as urbanism developed in the Greek world. Changes in the form and function of public spaces, monumental architecture, and urban planning occurred with remarkable uniformity across long distances and within relatively short periods of time. The general pattern was one of increasing homogeneity in the form of Greek cities as time progressed from the Early Iron Age to the Roman period, which can be attributed to intensifying trade networks and expanding political integration.

From a very early stage public monuments in Greek cities had a very different function than in other early urban centers. While often built under state sponsorship, they were not necessarily tied to a particular ruler, especially in the case of democratic Athens, which is a good example of the relationship between monumentality and public spaces. Relatively little is known about the urban form of Athens in the Early Iron Age, but by the Archaic period the agora (Figure 16.2) was home to various religious, economic, and political activities and was a clearly demarcated space, though only a few basic religious and administrative buildings were to be found. In the Classical period this changed significantly, with the addition of several buildings related specifically to the administration of the democracy (namely the tholos, the bouleuterion, and the mint). In contrast to palace- or temple-administered states, this made public the business of government, and emphasized accessibility, rather than exclusivity. Even in the Hellenistic period when we see particular rulers (and not Athenians) attaching their names to public monuments, these were meant to be seen as gifts, given to the city of Athens by Hellenistic kings who aimed to achieve cultural prestige, rather than assert political authority.

This chapter has suggested that the broad outlines of first millennium BCE Mediterranean history were driven by the interactions between geography and rising social development.[33] The extraordinary success of Greek urbanism is very much part of this pattern. However, the question has received very little attention in recent years.

---

[33] Ian Morris, *Why the West Rules – For Now* (New York: Farrar, Straus and Giroux, 2010), pp. 227–79.

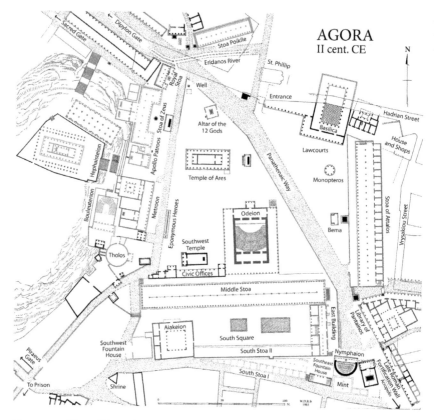

Figure 16.2 Plan of the Athenian Agora, showing buildings of the Archaic through Roman periods (Agora Excavations, American School of Classical Studies).

The historical theories of the nineteenth and much of the twentieth centuries tended to see Greek success as being a function of a superior culture. Since the 1980s many scholars influenced by postcolonial thought have tried to redress this picture by emphasizing the agency of indigenous populations, but as a result they often seem uncomfortable acknowledging the fact that Greek urbanism was spectacularly successful.[34] In this chapter

[34] For an influential view of Greek superiority, see John Boardman, *Greeks Overseas* (London: Pelican, 1964); for more nuanced and postcolonial views, see, for example, Robin Osborne, "Early Greek Colonization? The Nature of Greek Settlement in the West," in Nick Fisher and Hans van Wees (eds.), *Archaic Greece: New Approaches and New Evidence* (London: Duckworth, 1998), pp. 251–69; and Tamar Hodos, *Local Responses to Colonization in the Iron Age Mediterranean* (London: Routledge, 2006).

we have tried to show that Greek urbanism was in fact one of the greatest
success stories in pre-modern history; yet this depended on a complex set of
interactions between geography, history, and the numerous cultural traditions with which the Greeks came into contact as their civilization
developed and transformed over time.

FURTHER READINGS

Braudel, Fernand, *The Mediterranean and the Mediterranean World in the Age of Philip II*,
London: Harper & Row, 1972.

Cahill, Nicholas, *Household and City Organization at Olynthus*, New Haven, CT: Yale
University Press, 2002.

De Polignac, François, *Cults, Territory, and the Origins of the Greek City-State*, Janet Lloyd
(trans.), Chicago: The University of Chicago Press, 1995.

Hansen, Mogens H., *Polis: An Introduction to the Ancient Greek City State*, Oxford: Oxford
University Press, 2006.

Hölscher, T., "Urban Spaces and Central Places: The Greek World," in Susan E. Alcock
and Robin Osborne (eds.), *Classical Archaeology*, Malden, MA: Blackwell, 2007,
pp. 164–81.

Horden, Peregrine, and Nicholas Purcell, *The Corrupting Sea: A Study of Mediterranean
History*, Malden, MA: Blackwell, 2000.

Morris, Ian (ed.), *Classical Greece: Ancient Histories and Modern Archaeologies*, Cambridge:
Cambridge University Press, 1994.

Murray, Oswyn, and Simon Price (eds.), *The Greek City: From Homer to Alexander*, Oxford:
Oxford University Press, 1990.

Osborne, Robin, *Classical Landscape with Figures: The Ancient Greek City and Its Countryside*,
London: George Philip, 1987.

Osborne, Robin, and Barry Cunliffe (eds.), *Mediterranean Urbanization, 800–600 BCE*,
Oxford: Oxford University Press, 2005.

Snodgrass, Anthony M., *Archaeology and the Emergence of Greece*, Ithaca, NY: Cornell
University Press, 2006.

17

Different cities: Jenne-jeno and African urbanism

RODERICK J. MCINTOSH

Why study African cities?

If abundance of agricultural land, non-restrictive land ownership, lack of labor, and low population densities generally can be said to have characterized Africa before the last days of colonialism, life in cities has been the increasing to dominant experience of Africans since the mid-decades of the twentieth century. However, sub-Saharan Africa has also had a venerable urban history. The time-depth of this history is only recently becoming known through archaeology. And the variety of Africa's urban experience is also now becoming known through a reassessment of pre-colonial archival and oral sources.

Certainly, the continent has been at best an afterthought to most global urban social histories. Strange to say, it was sub-Saharan Africa's very variability of the city experience that rendered – at least to the early European visitors' perceptions – even some massive conurbations as merely "'a heap of huts' – clusters of scattered settlements interspersed with tracts of cultivation and pasture, seeming to lack order or formality to the visitor's unfamiliar eye."[1]

Why was African variability misunderstood and underappreciated? (And what does that tell us about how we have thought about the circumstances in which "exceptional" cities emerged elsewhere?) Why was sub-Saharan Africa for so long considered lacking in cities worthy of grand comparative theory? The answers to these questions are important to an understanding of how African variability will, in the future, influence how urban evolutionary theory may develop. In the first instance the answer is disciplinary: the

---

[1] David M. Anderson and Richard Rathbone, "Urban Africa: Histories in the Making," in David M. Anderson and Richard Rathbone (eds.), *Africa's Urban Past* (Oxford: James Currey, 2000), Note 4. The original is from Richard F. Burton, *The Lakes Regions of Central Africa* (New York: Harper & Brothers, 1961).

study of the African city has traditionally been the preserve of geographers, sociologists, and political scientists[2] and not, until recently, of urban social historians or archaeologists. (The continent, of course, suffers from the lowest density of archaeologists on earth, compounding the problem.) Contemporary cities are represented mainly as the sites of in-migration and family breakdown and products of cash economies, and of any number of modern "detribalization" processes. African cities have been viewed as a-historical; that is, modern African cities had no history.

We now recognize the shallowness and nonsense of this view. It is a legacy of a colonial period tradition of explanation that stripped Africans of their active agency. Dumped into the anomie of cities created by exotic, non-African interventions, as people poured into cities without an appreciable "indigenous" past, Africans became peoples without their own history, motivated by external politics and economies, and thus of marginal interest to the deep histories of cities.

A second reason for the late recognition of Africa's urban past has everything to do with scholars' (and nineteenth-century explorers') expectations of what cities should look like. African cities were, emphatically, not merely "a heap of huts." For our global understanding of the commonalities and differences in the urban experience in deep and in shallow time, African cities are pertinent examples, but also require new kinds of explanations.

Over and over, visitors to ancient African cities or to their ruins, whether Arab traders or European imperialists and mercantilists, saw organisms so different from those of their own experience, so alien from their expectations, that they were not even recognized as cities. Take this classic example from the late 1950s: a distinguished French historian-archaeologist, Raymond Mauny, walked over Jenne-jeno, a massive urban tell blanketed in potsherds in present-day Mali, and wrote of his bewilderment: "The archaeologist is utterly at a loss ... here we are in quicksand (*en terrain mouvant*), and we are left with the impression of being only at the very beginning of the pioneering stage of archaeology."[3] Lacking any prior mention of this town in the Arabic sources and lacking the expected urban signatures in its form and in monumental architecture, Mauny felt intellectually adrift and swallowed up – his own words[4] – by the enormity of the site and by his own

---

[2] Anderson and Rathbone, "Urban Africa," p. 10.
[3] Raymond Mauny, *Tableau géographique de l'Ouest Africain au Moyen Age, d'après les sources écrites, la tradition, et l'archéologie* (Dakar: I.F.A.N., 1961), p. 95.
[4] Roderick J. McIntosh, *Ancient Middle Niger: Urbanism and the Self-Organizing Landscape* (Cambridge: Cambridge University Press, 2005), pp. 9–10.

incomprehension due (as he himself acknowledged) to his expectations of what an early city should look like.

Clearly, the mere identification of an early African city presented scholars with a recognition problem and a comprehension problem. Pre-colonial urban forms in sub-Saharan Africa were different, one from another, and many from the scholarly expectation of what an ancient city should look like and how they functioned. It is a commonplace of Africanist historians and archaeologists to say that African cities defy attempts to classify and typologize them. That is to say that they don't fit normative urban models. But I will assert that (among many other causal factors) the expansive differences in African cities' form and function reflect the continent's "exuberance" in throwing up alternatives to the normative ideas of the distribution of power. I predict that the greatest contribution of the study of Africa's varied cities, when understood as the signature on the landscape of multiple expressions of power and authority, will be to encourage students of comparative early cities to take a more expansive view of power, its relations, its expressions, its abuses, and implications of resistance to it, in those urban landscapes.

African alternatives to the distribution of power in cities

I begin by posing the following question: Can we conceive of cities without citadels and palaces? In other words, is the expectation so engrained that there is a causal relationship between the appearance of cities and the emergence of new and areally expansive expressions of power, defined as the influence of a few over the many based on the threat of force, that it is impossible to think of cities as other than concentrations of political power? To be sure, as the archaeology of cities advances around the world, this simple causal equation of political power and urban form has been rethought and recast. However, it is fair to say that much of urban social thought is not commensurate with new prehistoric and early historic data. Cities *without* citadels and palaces – the imposing seat of power and unambiguous signposts of force – are still considered anomalous or the "exceptions that prove the rule" (unless they are just proof of archaeologists' incompetence, because surely the seat of power *must* be there, somewhere!). There has been, of course, much circularity of reasoning expressed in fieldwork: because citadels (or other architectural and monumental expressions of elites and their status) were thought to be causally key to urbanism, archaeologists tended to heap attention upon them, and large settlements without monumentality or palatial architecture tended to be ignored or not considered urban. In sub-Saharan Africa, however, the relationship between power and urbanism is decidedly complex.

As more early African cities are studied and as the archaeology of these sites develops and as the extreme subtlety of power and authority relations of the communities they sheltered is understood, the causal relationship of power and urbanism has been problematized. This is not to say that all cities lack citadels. Great Zimbabwe[5] or Aksum,[6] as we shall see, are examples of symbols of power in stone; Meroe[7] with over 200 pyramids is a place of monumentality. Yet, there is widespread consensus among Africanist archaeologists that a useful working definition – one that will guide field work and aid interpretation – must reflect what cities do and the role of the city within the evolving landscape in which they evolved. Understanding the function of the city within a larger and interconnected and always changing field of settlements is now understood as critical in the investigation of the several alternatives to distribution of power that characterizes the African landscape. One working definition of a city is "a large and heterogeneous unit of settlement that provides a variety of services and manufactures to a larger hinterland."[8]

Using this working definition, archaeologists can document the power relations (or alternatives to hierarchical power relations) that bind together the inhabitants within the city and with inhabitants of rural settlements in the served hinterland. Those power relations may be found in massive wealth or status asymmetries; power can be studied in a variety of expressions including, as we shall see, forms of great persuasive authority. Through time the urban landscape may shift back and forth between strong expressions of hierarchy (that is, vertical, centralized decision-making) and heterarchy (that is, horizontal social differentiation in which authority is vested in multiple hierarchies in which individual roles may differ in the various hierarchies[9]). Cities without citadels and/or palaces... is this a

[5] Innocent Pikirayi, *The Zimbabwe Culture: Origins and Decline of Southern Zambezian States* (Walnut Creek, CA: Altamira Press, 2001).
[6] David W. Phillipson, *Ancient Ethiopia: Aksum, Its Antecedents and Successors* (London: British Museum Press, 2000).
[7] Peter L. Shinnie, *Ancient Nubia* (London: Kegan Paul, 1996).
[8] Modified slightly from Bruce Trigger, "Determinants of Growth in Pre-industrial Societies," in Peter Ucko, Ruth Tringham, and G. W. Dimbleby (eds.), *Man, Settlement and Urbanism* (London: Duckworth, 1972), p. 577.
[9] Carole Crumley, "Three Locational Models: An Epistemological Assessment of Anthropology and Archaeology," in Michael B. Schiffer (ed.), *Advances in Archaeological Method and Theory* (New York: Academic Press, 1979), Vol. II, p. 144.

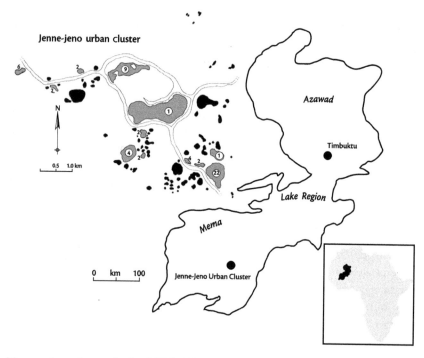

Map 17.1 Jenne-jeno and other Middle Niger cities and regions. The numbers refer to the number of excavation units sunk into each mound.

problem? Not at all, now that we have a working definition of urbanism that allows us to comprehend what is, arguably, the best-understood African city that is a case study of an alternative to the hierarchical distribution of power in an urban place.

The clustered city: Jenne-jeno

Over the marshes, winding streams, and rice fields of Mali's Middle Niger floodplain rises a tell that would not be out of place in Mesopotamia (see Map 17.1). Jenne-jeno's[10] descendant town, Jenne, lies 3 kilometers away; there its present-day inhabitants walk about on 9 meters of ancient city deposits. Within 4 kilometers are seventy tells in total, apparently all occupied contemporaneously with Jenne-jeno, and most abandoned at the

[10] Roderick J. McIntosh, *The Peoples of the Middle Niger* (Oxford: Blackwell, 1998); and McIntosh, *Ancient Middle Niger.*

same time, around 1400 CE. In fact, in the 55,000 square kilometers of the seasonally inundated Middle Niger floodplain there are many hundreds of similar mounds. In the roughly 170,000 square kilometers that were flooded yearly within the past four to five millennia (much now in the deepest Sahara) there are hundreds of tells more. Yet, as recently as the mid-1970s this was not recognized as an urban landscape.

When Raymond Mauny walked over Jenne-jeno in the late 1950s and cast a late-colonial eye over the jumble of potsherds, mudbrick houses, and eroding burials, he couldn't understand what he saw. Barely two decades later archaeologists came armed with new theory and excavation and survey methodologies that allowed them first to recognize and then to plumb the evolution, not just of the city of Jenne-jeno, but also of what we now call the "Jenne-jeno Urban Complex." As large and as heterogeneous as the principal site was, it was only a part of a seventy-site cluster that, together, provided urban services and manufactures to a hinterland of many thousands of square kilometers – and ultimately to the sister-city of Timbuktu over 400 kilometers downstream at the Saharan fringe. Ironically, it is the very laborious methodology that allowed archaeologists to ascertain the urban status of Jenne-jeno that makes modern investigations of the ancient city necessarily incomplete and frustrating.

In the era when a city was denoted by its citadel and palace, it was incumbent on the archaeologist to excavate the king's palatial domain, the associated residences of the elites, and the splendid temples in which kingship and its relation to the gods were celebrated, then to roughly gauge the area enclosed by the (obligatory) city wall. From such work the city could be delimited. Now, Jenne-jeno does have a city wall (curious, now that we think there was no warfare during its 1,500-year occupation; perhaps it was to prevent flooding), but no elite residences, no public architecture nor monuments, much less a king's palace. What the site does provide in ample volume is evidence of multiple occupations, multiple manufacturing areas and multiple "identity groups" as indicated by a great diversity of contemporaneous burial practices. After some thirty-five years of controlled stratigraphic excavations at some twenty-two units spread over the 33-hectare area of the site we have a plot of how that occupational and identity diversity burgeoned from the relatively simple (yet quite large at 20 hectares) community at its founding in the third century BCE. Note that sinking so many excavation units, some as large as 10 meters by 6 meters, into the 6-meter-(and more)-deep deposits is enormously time consuming, but absolutely necessary. One is, after all, investigating the emergence and evolution of complex society, that intricate mix and dynamics of interactions of multiple corporate groups (defined as self-identified groups that hold real or symbolic property in common).

A complication to the archaeologist's tasks is the tight clustering of nearby settlements in a density that roughly decreases with distance from the principal site. What does clustering mean? One way to answer that question is to surface collect artifacts and surface features (burials, house foundations, etc.) from all the sites in order to ask the question, are there anomalous concentrations of certain artifacts or features, compared to the range and relative proportions at Jenne-jeno that reveal special activities, concentrated at different locales? Take the case of iron smelting. This is a dirty, hot, and noisy activity, one that is today in Mande society associated with the production of highly dangerous occult power. Not something one wants next door. Through the Jenne-jeno sequence we see the migration of smelting from the focus site to multiple satellites. Adding to the tasks of sampling the activities at the main site, the urban archaeologist also must study the activities in each of the satellite sites. Already in the first season of surface collection in the Jenne-jeno Urban Complex we detected a pattern of mutual exclusivity, or near exclusivity, of activities at satellites.

Thus, as excavations began at Jenne-jeno, we began a randomized collection of sites within a larger 1,100-kilometer-square region – just to get a feel for how the distribution of artifacts and the pottery assemblages compared to those at Jenne-jeno. On the basis of that season's analysis, it was clear that site density dropped off radically after a c. 4-kilometer radius and that within that cluster some sites had an "overabundance" of certain classes (or of a single class) of features or artifacts. The next stage (simultaneous with expansion of the excavations at Jenne-jeno) was surface collection of 50 percent of the satellite sites and, ultimately, of 100 percent. The last stage has included the sinking of excavation units into a sample of satellite sites. A considerable degree of concentration of activities (especially, iron-working, various styles of fishing, hunting aquatic mammals and snakes, weaving) continues to be the best explanation for the non-uniform, non-random distribution of surface and stratified artifacts in the Jenne-jeno Urban Complex. What does this clustering mean and what does this landscape say, potentially, about the distribution of power and authority within the larger community?

Some three and a half decades of research in the Jenne region allow us to say two things, with considerable confidence, about how this society was structured. First, clustering appears to have been a solution to the problem of how different specialist corporations might maintain and display their distinct identities, while at the same time having immediate access to other providers of needed goods and services and access to those to whom they themselves provided materials. All well and good, but one needs at the same time to answer the question, who monitors or controls the exchange of those manufactures and services? An older theory of the nature of cities would have answered, "the king and his administration, backed up by force, of course." However, in the case of the Jenne-jeno Urban Cluster we appear to have an exchange system that functioned organically through the relations of reciprocity forged among corporate groups. If corporate groups as well as expectations and rules were defined unambiguously, including consequences if the rules were transgressed, the urban system would not have required a vertically hierarchical control structure – which in fact we do not see. Rather, corporate ownership of individual mounds by members of an occupationally defined/kin group is indicated by the archaeological data indicating near exclusivity of occupational debris at each of the satellite sites.

Second, we have no hard evidence of a state-like, top-down, elite-driven political engine powering this kind of urbanism through time. We find no indications of kings, citadels, palaces, or, indeed, any obvious elites. The political and economic organization of late first millennium BCE and later urbanism in the Middle Niger seems heterarchical. That is, one identifies separate, if sometimes overlapping, domains of authority, all functioning in an interactive field, not a vertical hierarchy of kings and subjects and unidirectional flows of information.

Emergent urbanism in the Middle Niger region

Recent research reveals cities even earlier than Jenne-jeno and especially a "pre-urban" landscape that was potentially several millennia in the making. This "pre-urban" landscape includes the creation of specialized sites and activities in a regional economy (a self-organizing landscape in the language of complex systems). This landscape displayed great resilience in a challenging environment as the Sahara transformed from a well-watered savannah (with vast lakes) as late as the fourth millennium BCE to its present condition by the late third or early second millennium.

Our search for antecedent settlements, and possibly causal conditions, starts in the then better-watered Sahara, some ten centuries or more before the founding of Jenne-jeno. In a curvilinear arc spanning hundreds of kilometers in the central Mauritanian wasteland are many score Late Stone Age stone-built ruins – urban in proportions. Just how urban were they? This is difficult to answer since decades after the first (and only) systematic survey and dating of hundreds of these distinctive stone ruins in the Dhar Tichitt region of Mauritania, we still speak of a generalized "sedentary pastoral" adaptation (see Figure 17.1). However, remote sensing reveals hundreds of multi-cellular Late Stone Age ruins (that is, multiple, essentially identical, enclosures with an exterior kraal walling, which we presume were cattle enclosures, with the residences in the interior). Unfortunately, the first systematic survey and test excavations of the 1960s have not been repeated since. Therefore, we are uncertain about the dating and contemporaneity of sites and whether there were smaller or less exotic settlements, which were observed in the initial survey. As we will see below, the same kinds of large stone enclosures are indeed associated slightly later with a variety of other sites in what we can begin to call an emerging urban landscape in which clustering is very much in evidence.

The Dhar Tichitt sequence occupies the latter half of a long, drawn-out movement of peoples beginning c. 4500 BCE as highly arid episodes increasingly disrupt the Sahara's second Holocene wet period. The instability of the climate intensifies after c. 2300 BCE, while the overall drying trend intensifies. These peoples, and those occupying the once inundated Azawad Basin of the ancient Middle Niger (stretching hundreds of kilometers north of Timbuktu), found refuge centuries later in the as yet inundated part of the southern Middle Niger. MacDonald hypothesizes that many peoples, with many emergent subsistence and perhaps even craft specializations, were thrown together in these more southerly refuges.[11]

One might imagine an initial situation of short contact and exchange among different groups of slightly different subsistence preferences, slightly different territorial ranges, which led to a seasonal, predictable co-occupation of a region. In this model of incipient complexity, "rules of engagement" for sustained interaction of a few communities of proto-specialists (some that favored fishing, some herding, and even some slightly differentiated as gatherers of various local grains) were developed. If regional exchange networks were successful, a movement toward true specialization ensued.

---

[11] Kevin C. MacDonald, "Dhar Néma: From Early Agriculture to Metallurgy in Southeastern Mauritania," *Azania* 46 (2011), 1 and 49–69.

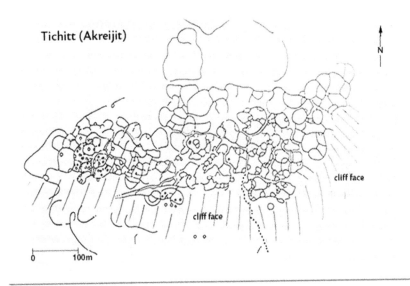

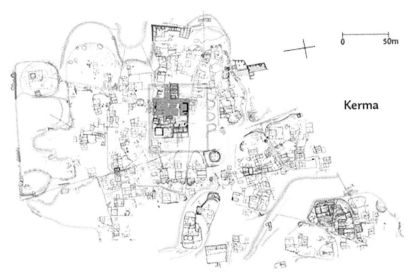

Figure 17.1 Top: Late Stone Age pastoral site of Akreijit of the Dhar Tichitt cliffs of central Mauritania (modified for publication with permission of Robert Vernet). Bottom: general plan of Kerma, Republic of Sudan (by permission of Ch. Bonnet).

Starting as early as perhaps 2000 BCE, we hypothesize a movement of some of the Tichitt herders and very likely the generalized, aquatic-oriented hunters/gatherers/fisherfolk of the great playalands to the south, attracted by the still-vibrant lakes and waterways of Timbuktu's hinterland and Lake Region further to the south. On present evidence, these peoples would have moved down palaeochannels, such as the Wadi El-Ahmar (visible just east of Timbuktu). On satellite imagery we see familiar-looking stone architectural sites on outcrops and escarpments of southeast Mauritania. Here, stone Tichitt-like sites lie near "tell" sites of varying size, some of stone, others of wattle-and-daub or dry mud walls. These are not yet urban in size, but clustering of apparently contemporaneous settlements of very different styles suggests intensive relations of very different peoples. Our corporate groups of Jenne-jeno would be their direct legacies.

The seasonal co-evolution in which increasing numbers and kinds of specialists spent more months of each year in proximity (in the early and middle first millennium BCE) would only work, of course, if the sites are contemporaneous. This we cannot yet verify for the Lake Region. But we do have initial evidence that this is the case for the Mema, on the basis of deep stratigraphic excavations at several mounds comprising the Akumbu Urban Cluster. Here streams and shallow lakes persisted into the first millennium CE, and aquatically oriented hunters/fisherfolk (present at least as early as 2000 BCE) lived with semi-specialized herders sharing lake-beach and levée localities. And, 400–500 years later, they were joined by proto-cultivators in clusters of sites on the landscape. This pattern implies that not only were the "rules of engagement" for peaceful interaction among these groups maturing, but also that the sense of security these networks of reciprocity provided encouraged certain communities to become even more specialized (with, perhaps, the appearance of specialist artisans, such as potters).

Our best evidence for the next step of the progression comes from extensive survey and excavation of several large and small tells of the Mema and, especially, of the Timbuktu region, dating to the Late Stone Age–Iron Age transition (or, about 2500 BCE).[12] Clustered sites in preferred locales of the Mema transmuted into clustered Iron Age mounds (including, eventually, several new satellites devoted predominantly to the craft of the iron smelters). If the inferred social contract is successful, then, the stage is set for

---

[12] Téréba Togola, "Iron Age Occupation in the Méma Region," *African Archaeological Review* 13 (1996), 91–110; and Douglas P. Park, "Prehistoric Timbuktu and its Hinterland," *Antiquity* 84 (2010), 1–13.

the appearance of cities. There is a contemporaneous explosion of site size in the Timbuktu region. Tells are of urban proportions (50–100 hectares) during the mid-first millennium BCE.

To bring the story full circle, as these cities were expanding, population also streamed into the previously unexploited far southern basins of the southern Middle Niger. In the last centuries before the Common Era, Jenne-jeno exploded on the scene, already large (>20 hectares) at its foundation. But, as opposed to the northern cities, the main tell remained at a "mere" 33 hectares throughout its maximal prosperity during the mid- to later first millennium CE. The urban population was dispersed among scores of specialist-oriented satellites of the Jenne-jeno Urban Cluster.

Although the evolution of urban centers in the region does not include the appearance of kings and urban elites, the trajectory to urbanism in other African cities is quite different (see Map 17.2).

Map 17.2 Cities and states mentioned in the text.

A spectrum of early African cities (outside Egypt)

The understanding of the evolution and nature of east African cities has similarly changed greatly in light of new archaeological field work.[13] For example, the early Nubian city of Kerma was once believed to have flourished during the Egyptian Middle Kingdom (c. 2000–1600 BCE) in the Nile's Dongola Reach, a product of trade with Egypt (see Figure 17.1). The city looked Egyptian, imitative in monuments (including huge brick "pyramids" that were religious structures called *defuffas*) and clearly derivative of Egyptian cities.

However, after thirty years of extensive excavation by the Swiss Archaeological Mission to the Sudan (Université de Neuchâtel), our knowledge of Kerma has changed the picture considerably. Although trade and cultural contacts down the Nile were important, the city's role as focus of a political and cultic capital owes much to local developments. The importance of manufactures and of crafts, especially of a spectacular ceramic production and perhaps even of the invention of faience, are clear. Also, from the earliest days, transhumant cattle-herding groups swelled the population seasonally. The symbolic importance of cattle is evident even in the tombs and tumuli of the kings and elite in a vast nearby cemetery. Anything but derivative, Kerma was urban by c. 3000 BCE and occupied a locale sacred to the worship of cattle that is traceable at least four millennia before that.

Kerma is one of the southern-most of a string of late fourth millennium "proto-towns," each with religious significance, which were part of an exchange-oriented and areally extensive Nilotic culture that only later coalesced in various forms, including the elite culture of ancient Egypt in which distinctive Egyptian cities developed (see Baines, Chapter 2, this volume). Kerma was eventually succeeded by Meroe, the southern capital of the Kingdom of Kush from approximately 800 to 350 BCE. Although Meroe was also once thought to be a derivative of Egypt, mainly because of the hundreds of distinctively Nubian pyramids nearby, we now appreciate the local jewelry, gold and iron industries, and the great importance of Red Sea trade (as opposed to north–south Nile trade) (see Figure 17.2).

Other African cities have formerly been regarded as secondary developments from more civilized corners of the ancient world. Such was the case with Aksum, long presumed to have begun as a Sabaean Arabian outpost,

---

[13] For more on the cities sketched in this section, see David W. Phillipson, *African Archaeology* (Cambridge: Cambridge University Press, 2005).

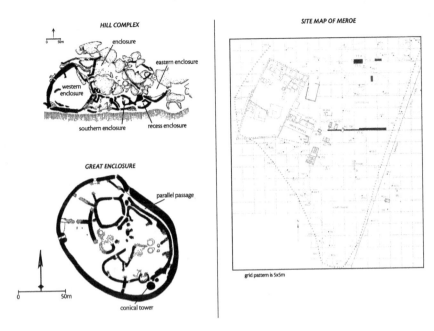

Figure 17.2 Right: Plan of Meroe (from P. L. Shinnie and J. R. Anderson, *The Capital of Kush 2: Meroë Excavations 1973–1984* [Wiesbaden: Harrassowitz Verlag, 2004], with permission). Left: Great Zimbabwe – Hill Complex above; Great Enclosure below (modified for publication with permission of Innocent Pikirayi).

but now understood as a purely African response to the potential of its location on the Horn of Africa. Indeed, Aksum participated in trading relations with lands as distant as India. Long controlling the lower Red Sea, and to a lesser extent the Persian Gulf from the first century CE until the latter half of the first millennium, the Aksumite Kingdom through its main port of Adulis was a major player in the pan-Indian Ocean trade linking Southeast Asia, India, the Gulf, and the Swahili coast of eastern Africa. Archaeology is only now revealing the extent to which the importance of this Indian Ocean network rivaled that of the Silk Route.

We know relatively little about the pre-Aksumite origins of urbanism on the eastern Horn (which made it far too easy to argue that cities were imported). Excavations have perhaps not surprisingly concentrated on the famous underground tombs of kings and nobles, on the foundations of the massive (some over 30 meters tall) commemorative stelae, and to a lesser extent upon the residences of the elite. Cosmopolitan and outward looking, Aksum welcomed traders from the Arabian Peninsula, Rome, Egypt, India,

and Nubia to its markets featuring goods from the African interior – ivory
and rhino horn, live wild animals, slaves, and grains. Aksum, the capital, was
also a classic primate city, much larger and more highly stratified than the
kingdom's other ports and interior towns.

Other classically primate capitals of African kingdoms, dating to later
times than this volume's cities, such as Njimi of eleventh–fifteenth-century
Kanem-Bornu (Chad and northeast Nigeria), and Kano (capital of the Hausa
state in central Nigeria, which may date as early as the tenth century), are
known more from ethnohistorical sources than from archaeology, and their
origins are obscure. New field work by African archaeologists will remedy
this lack of knowledge.

For hundreds of kilometers along the eastern coast of Africa one finds a
string of important city-states: the trading cities of the Swahili coast.[14] United
by a common language (Bantu at base), by belief in Islam, and by a long-
distance mercantile identity, many joined in temporary alliances, but none
achieved dominance over the others. Cities such as Kilwa, Sofala, Lamu,
Manda, Zanzibar, or Malindi varied as much by size and by elegance of their
mosques and elite residences, as by the advantages of their harbor or as by
the relations with affiliated villages and hamlets in the interior. Trade was in
slaves, gold, ivory, sandalwood, and spices. In a strange, but not uncommon, mismarriage of history and archaeology, the towns' origins were
thought not to have pre-dated the tenth century, the time of colonization
by Shirazi Persian immigrants – and, hence, archaeologists tended to stop
digging at places like Kilwa when "pre-Shirazi" levels were reached.

More recent excavations of towns and villages at Sanga, Pemba Island,
and the Comoros Islands, and coastal and other surveys outside of the
historically documented towns reveal a very different origin of "Swahili"
urbanism. The towns and cities were built upon layer upon layer of older
trade centers that were oriented to trade with China, Southeast Asia, and
South Asia. New research is just beginning to bring these urban origins
to light.

These long-distance interactions from the interior and then through
ocean-going trade are the backdrop for state formation and urbanism in
the interior. The best-known city is Great Zimbabwe (see Figure 17.2).[15]

[14] Mark C. Horton and John Middleton, *The Swahili: The Social Landscape of a Mercantile Society* (Oxford: Blackwell, 2000).
[15] Pikirayi, *Zimbabwe Culture*; and Peter S. Garlake, *Great Zimbabwe* (London: Thames & Hudson, Ltd., 1973).

Dominating the interior–coast ivory routes and set near important gold reefs, Great Zimbabwe was architecturally impressive (so much so that early European colonists refused to credit an indigenous origin) and symbolically highly charged. European mining interests despoiled gold artifacts and cult objects such that no undisturbed deposits remained for the first legitimate excavations in the 1920s. We rely mainly upon oral traditions of the descendant Shona peoples, and increasingly on excavations at other, earlier settlements (such as Mapungubwe, see below) to understand the trade, cultic, and political importance of Great Zimbabwe.

Conclusion

To summarize, some African cities developed in the context of interregional trade, others were politically dominant in their regions, and still others were "clustered cities," showing little political or economic hierarchy. African urbanism encompasses many kinds of cities and many kinds of power. There is much work, clearly, to be done to understand African cities. There is also a certain quest for African cities that can serve as the endpoint and prospective of this chapter.

There is first the pre-fourteenth-century capital of the Kongo Empire, which is known only from oral histories of Kongo people. In southern Mali and northern Guinea, archaeologists still search for the capital of the Mali Empire (Dakajalan, in the oral traditions), while respecting the warnings of traditionalists among the local Mande peoples of places not to go. Some cities are too dangerous for prying eyes. And in the highlands of Ethiopia, we know from oral accounts that there were wandering royal capitals that left no trace. All these cases, of course, have to be added to the calculus of what makes African urbanism so enthusiastically original.

Furthermore, extensive archaeological survey and excavation have failed to find undisputed urbanism at Mapungubwe on the banks of the Limpopo in South Africa. The eleventh-century site of that name did provide impressive elite burials as well as gold objects and glass beads from the Indian Ocean trade (dominance over which it relinquished to Great Zimbabwe in the mid-thirteenth century). But the site cannot be claimed to have been a city, however areally extensive the polity for which it served as political and ritual focus. What kind of power is this? Even more curious is the case of the Middle Senegal River Valley, on the other side of the continent. The very first state mentioned by the earliest of the Arabic Chronicles of West Africa is Takrur, which extended far north into the western Sahara and from the

Atlantic to the interior. Its gold workshops provided currencies for the Mediterranean world of late antiquity and medieval periods. To date, however, survey in the region of the Middle Senegal Valley, guided by oral traditions and the Arabic Chronicles, has yielded only clusters of hamlets or small village mounds that date to the early centuries of the Common Era. These clusters, however, cannot be called in any sense urban.

Early African cities and the distribution of power in them were neither cut to a normative pattern, nor did they develop from any single cause. Neither did every city need a state, nor every state a city.

FURTHER READINGS

Bonnet, Charles, *The Nubian Pharaohs*, New York: The American University in Cairo Press, 2003.

Connah, Graham, *African Civilizations*, Cambridge: Cambridge University Press, 1981.

Garlake, Peter, *Early Art and Architecture of Africa*, Oxford: Oxford University Press, 2002. *Great Zimbabwe*, London: Thames & Hudson, Ltd., 1973.

Insoll, Timothy, *The Archaeology of Islam in Sub-Saharan Africa*, Cambridge: Cambridge University Press, 2003.

Kusimba, Chapurukha M., "The Collapse of Coastal City-states of East Africa," in Akinwumi Ogundiran and Toyin Falola (eds.), *Archaeology of Atlantic Africa and the African Diaspora*, Bloomington: Indiana University Press, 2007, pp. 160–84.

"Early African Cities: Their Role in the Shaping of Urban and Rural Interaction Spheres," in Joyce Marcus and Jeremy A. Sabloff (eds.), *The Ancient City: New Perspectives on Urbanism in the Old and New World*, Santa Fe, NM: School of Advanced Research Press, 2008, pp. 229–46.

McIntosh, Susan Keech, ed., *Beyond Chiefdoms: Pathways to Complexity in Africa*, Cambridge: Cambridge University Press, 1999.

Shaw, Thurstan T., *Nigeria: Its Archaeology and Early History*, London: Thames & Hudson, Ltd., 1978.

18

The distribution of power: hierarchy and its discontents

CARLA M. SINOPOLI, RODERICK J. MCINTOSH,
IAN MORRIS, AND ALEX R. KNODELL

Over the last few decades, archaeological and historical research in many regions of the world has challenged long-standing ideas concerning the nature and organization of ancient states and cities. Scholars have come to recognize the limits of hierarchy and to acknowledge that ancient urban societies varied considerably in scale, physical form, social composition, and governance. Specifically, research has questioned the accepted wisdom that early cities were inevitably characterized by straightforward, linear hierarchies of control – with a mass of subjects on the bottom administered by a small number of elites at the top. They have also questioned whether the presence of a specific assemblage of architectural forms (for example, palace buildings, central temples, city walls) is required to make an urban place.[1] And as scholars have come to recognize that ancient communities had created very different kinds of urban forms in Africa, Southeast Asia, and elsewhere, this has called into question understandings of even the archetypal hierarchical early cities of Mesopotamia, where scholarship has expanded from a focus on palaces and temples to also consider the power and forms of authority exercised by various councils and assemblies, and/or diverse economic, kin, or other social groups (see Emberling, Chapter 14, this volume). The result has been both a broadening of perspectives on ancient urbanism and new understandings of the limits of hierarchy.

---

[1] Similar questions were also raised by earlier generations of Maya scholars, as they came to recognize that the dispersed settlement patterns of Maya households were part of the urban character of many Maya cities (for example, Richard E. W. Adams and T. Patrick Culbert, "The Origins of Civilization in the Maya Lowlands," in Richard E. W. Adams (ed.), *The Origins of Maya Civilization* (Albuquerque: University of New Mexico Press, 1977), pp. 3–24; Richard E. W. Adams and Richard C. Jones, "Spatial Patterns and Regional Growth Among Classic Maya Cities," *American Antiquity* 46 (1981), 301–22; and Joyce Marcus, "On the Nature of the Mesoamerican City," in Evon Z. Vogt and Richard M. Leventhal (eds.), *Prehistoric Settlement Patterns: Essays in Honor of Gordon R. Willey* (Albuquerque: University of New Mexico Press, 1983), pp. 195–242.

The three chapters in this section – on proto- and Early Historic cities of South Asia, Greek city-states, and West African cities – all address early urban formations that for various reasons have been viewed as lying outside of the normative structures of "typical" ancient cities (for example, in Mesopotamia).

For the first millennium BCE Greek city-states, discussed by Morris and Knodell, their exceptionalism has been seen to lie in their presumed position as the originators of Western democratic political thought: cities whose inhabitants consciously and creatively rejected hierarchical despotisms. However, as Morris and Knodell argue, numerous other factors, including geography, environment, and the larger geopolitical and economic contexts of the eastern Mediterranean region, may better explain the distinctive forms and long-lived success and expansion of Classical Greek cities. More-over, conceptions of exceptionalism concerning distributions of power in Greek cities are at least partly a product of Athenocentrism, as ancient Greece was home to a wide array of very different political systems. It seems as though the contrast between democratic and more centralized or palace-oriented societies is more applicable to the Classical period and preceding Bronze Age than to early Greek cities and their contemporaries (for example in Etruria or Phoenicia). These factors and the divergent disciplinary trajectories of classical and anthropological archaeology have made cross-cultural studies including cities rather rare.

In contrast, the West African cities discussed by McIntosh and the early South Asia Indus or Harappan cities discussed by Sinopoli, with their ambiguous or absent evidence of "expected" urban features, have often been viewed as both "other" and less than the ideal exemplars of ancient cities, such as Mesopotamian Ur with its monumental palace and ziggurats and elaborate royal burials. Indeed, lacking such features, both the Indus cities and West African cities such as Jenne-jeno have frequently been characterized as not quite cities and/or not quite states. Unlike the Greek cities, however, the African and South Asian communities who built and inhabited those urban places were presumed by earlier generations of scholars to have lacked the creativity to establish distinctive and original forms of urban life, leaving scholars without models to understand or explain their settlements.

In this chapter, we draw on our case studies and other recent research to consider alternate ways of being urban and to advocate for models of urbanism that recognize the existence of a broad range of organizational structures and institutions – both vertical and horizontal – through which power could be distributed in early cities. We begin by briefly reviewing how it is that the kinds of cities that we address came to be viewed as aberrant or somehow less than other more "typical" ancient cities. How is it that archaeological scholarship came to argue that (with the exception of the exceptional Greeks), ancient cities: (1) *must* have been ruled by kings who reside in elaborate palaces and belong to a restricted hereditary elite; (2) *must* have had central and powerful religious institutions (that is, state religions); and (3) *must* have been governed by rigid administrative hierarchies? Certainly, many ancient cities had all these features; but many others did not, and it is this latter category we explore in this chapter, with the larger goal of understanding why and how different urban forms developed and were sustained.

Shaping many early expectations of ancient civilization is the long legacy of Orientalist understandings of a despotic, totalitarian East – an "other" dominated by powerful, tyrannical, kings and priests. Orientalist thought had its origins in Classical Greek political and historical writings on Persia, authored by such historians and philosophers as Herodotus and Aristotle, among others. Their writings, composed at a time when Persia posed a significant military threat to the Aegean region, articulated the anxieties their authors felt about the enemy empire and also helped to mobilize independent Greek states to accumulate and deploy military and economic resources that could resist their powerful neighbor.

Through a long and complex genealogy,[2] Classical Greek views of tyrannical eastern kingdoms migrated to Rome and medieval Europe and were transformed into eighteenth- and nineteenth-century European understandings of the essential natures of the polities and peoples of Asia, Africa, and the Americas. These understandings are variously evident in the environmental determinism of Montesquieu,[3] the historical teleology of Hegel and Mill,[4] and, in a rather different vein, in Weber's construction of the patrimonial state.[5]

---

[2] Michael Curtis, *Orientalism and Islam: European Thinkers on Oriental Despotism in the Middle East and India* (Cambridge: Cambridge University Press, 2009); and M. Sawer, *Marxism and the Question of the Asiatic Mode of Production* (The Hague: Martinus Nijhoff, 1977).

[3] Charles de Secondat, Baron de Montesquieu, *The Spirit of the Laws*, Anne M. Cohler, Basia C. Miller, and Harold S. Stone (trans. and eds.) (Cambridge: Cambridge University Press, 1989).

[4] Georg W. F. Hegel, *The Philosophy of History*, John Sibree (trans.) (New York: Dover Publications, 1856); and James Mill, *The History of British India* (Chicago: The University of Chicago Press, 1975).

[5] Max Weber, *Economy and Society*, Guenther Roth and Claus Wittich (eds.) (Berkeley: University of California Press, 1978).

Within archaeology, Marx and Engel's writings on the "Asiatic Mode of Production,"[6] particularly as later utilized by Karl Wittfogel[7] and others are arguably among the most significant works. Imaginings of all-powerful Oriental tyrannies with their highly centralized economies and stagnant village communities came to frame the interpretations of those very regions where the world's earliest urban places had been first created. Early practitioners of archaeology brought these "truisms" to nineteenth- and early twentieth-century research on Mesopotamian cities, located as they were in the "cradle of civilization" at the site of the aboriginal Oriental kingdoms. These cities (problematically understood as they were), in turn, became the templates for understanding the ancient city writ large.

A second and related strand that has contributed to the long-standing views concerning the nature of early cities lies in the history of archaeology as a colonial enterprise. Numerous scholars have written of the development of archaeology in colonial contexts and of the deployment of archaeological knowledge in nineteenth- and twentieth-century colonial and postcolonial politics.[8] Understandings of South Asian and African cities and early civilizations in particular were shaped within colonial discourses that constructed and reified particular interpretations of historical change and social forms in these regions, in ways that explicitly or implicitly legitimized colonialism by constructing arguments for changeless and, indeed stagnant pasts. This is not to discount the tremendous amount of valuable archaeological research conducted by colonial era scholars in these areas, or even to say that all early archaeologists adhered to such views. We merely seek to make note of the problematic intellectual frameworks within which many early archaeologists worked and the intellectual legacies that

---

[6] See discussion in Carla M. Sinopoli, *The Political Economy of Craft Production: Crafting Empire in South India, c. 1350–1650* (Cambridge: Cambridge University Press, 2003), pp. 41–8; and Curtis, *Orientalism and Islam*.

[7] Karl Wittfogel, *Oriental Despotism: A Comparative Study of Total Power* (New Haven, CT: Yale University Press, 1967).

[8] See, for example Dipesh K. Chakrabarti, *Colonial Indology: Sociopolitics of the Ancient Indian Past* (New Delhi: Munshiram Manoharlal Publishers, 1997); Dipesh K. Chakrabarti, *A History of Indian Archaeology from the Beginning to 1947* (New Delhi: Munshiram Manoharlal Publishers, 2001); Jane Lydon and Uzma Rizvi (eds.), *Handbook of Postcolonial Archaeology* (Walnut Creek, CA: Left Coast Press, 2010); Claire L. Lyons and John K. Papadopoulos (eds.), *The Archaeology of Colonialism* (Los Angeles: Getty Research Institute, 2002); Himanshu P. Ray, *Colonial Archaeology in South Asia: The Legacy of Sir Mortimer Wheeler* (New Delhi: Oxford University Press, 2008); and Peter van Dommelen (ed.), *Postcolonial Archaeologies* (Abingdon: Routledge, 2011).

they passed on to later generations of scholars, which continue to influence popular and, to a lesser extent, scholarly writings.[9]

Turning specifically to archaeological research on early cities, Marxist archaeologist V. Gordon Childe certainly counts among the most influential voices shaping approaches to ancient urbanism in the mid-twentieth century. In his influential writings on the "urban revolution," also as viewed largely through the lens of Early Dynastic and later Mesopotamia, he was an inheritor of the two-millennia-long traditions of Orientalist thought. His writings (though often shorn of their nuance), and particularly his oft-quoted list of the ten criteria of urbanism, have influenced generations of subsequent work on early cities, both positively and negatively. And indeed, it was in part a rejection of what came to be critiqued as Childe's "trait list" approach that led archaeologists such as Henry Wright, Gregory Johnson, and others,[10] to shift their archaeological focus from cities to states during the 1960s and 1970s, defining states as systems of hierarchies of differentiated decision-making and administration rather than by a set of traits.

Ultimately, the three chapters in this section, as well as others in this volume, seek not to reargue old debates but instead to recontextualize and broaden our perspectives on early cities. We do this by addressing the limits of hierarchy and the existence, and indeed long-lived success, of other ways of being urban – and the specific times, places, scales, and forms in which some of those other urban places emerged, persisted, or failed.

Other ways of being urban: distributed power in early cities

Many of the cities discussed in this section were places where power was distributed in ways that worked to challenge or undercut straightforward linear hierarchies of authority and administrative

---

[9] See Stephen L. Dyson, *In Pursuit of Ancient Pasts: A History of Classical Archaeology in the Nineteenth and Twentieth Centuries* (New Haven, CT: Yale University Press, 2006); Nayanjot Lahiri, *Finding Forgotten Cities: How the Indus Civilization was Discovered* (New Delhi: Permanent Black, 2005); Ian Morris (ed.), *Classical Greece: Ancient Histories and Modern Archaeologies* (Cambridge: Cambridge University Press, 1994); Upinder Singh, *The Discovery of Ancient India: Early Archaeologists and the Beginnings of Archaeology* (New Delhi: Permanent Black, 2005).

[10] Henry T. Wright and Gregory A. Johnson, "Population, Exchange and Early State Formation in Southwestern Iran," *American Anthropologists* 77 (1975), 267–89; and Henry T. Wright, "Recent Research on the Origins of the State," *Annual Review of Anthropology* 6 (1977), 379–97.

control.[11] This is not to say that hierarchy was not recognized or did not exist in the Greek city-states, the Indus world, or the African clustered cities that are the focus of the chapters in this section. Various social, economic, and ideological hierarchies and inequalities most certainly were operative in all of these places and no doubt profoundly shaped and differentially affected the experiences of diverse urban residents (that is, non(male)-citizens, enslaved individuals and communities, gendered groups and other ranked social and/or economic groups) within each of these settings. Thus, it is not the *absence* of linear structures of authority or hierarchy that characterized these cities, but the existence of alternative and distinctive mechanisms that prevented or constrained hierarchical structures from becoming the sole or primary exercisers of diverse forms of power.[12]

In first millennium BCE Greece, for example, Morris and Knodell argue that the success of Classical period cities was fostered both by the ability of city dwellers to mobilize long-distance economic resources through extensive maritime market networks and by their citizens' philosophical commitment to male egalitarianism. The latter entailed the creation of mechanisms to assure that access to leadership appointments was circulated among the (relatively) large population of eligible male citizens. Governance of many Classical Greek cities was highly structured and institutionalized, with positions of leadership in both religious and political offices rotating among adult male citizens. Indeed, Morris and Knodell argue that such decentralized political systems and the high level of inter- and extra-cultural connectivity may help to explain the impressive versatility and success of the Classical Greek cities in addressing specific urban and regional problems, first independently, then as part of Athenian, Macedonian, and Roman imperial expansions.

While we know less about the formal political and social mechanisms through which African clustered cities were integrated and governed, McIntosh suggests that at Jenne-jeno, networks of horizontal relations among diverse, economically specialized, corporate groups created an urban

---

[11] Unlike the Indus cities discussed by Sinopoli, the Early Historic South Asian cities discussed in the same chapter more closely conform to more traditional models of ancient cities; similarly, not all of the ancient African cities reviewed by McIntosh had the same organization, and Greek cities too varied widely across their broad geographic and temporal distribution.

[12] *Sensu* M. Mann, *The Sources of Social Power* (Cambridge: Cambridge University Press, 1986).

system based on multiple and complex relations of reciprocity shaped within a widely understood "social contract." The result was an intricate network of dyadic relationships that contributed to the creation of a geographically dispersed "urban cluster" comprised of multiple zones of specialized residential and occupational areas. These clustered cities lacked a central core and distinctive administrative architecture, and looked and operated quite differently than more governmentally centralized urban forms. Even so, Jenne-jeno's expansive city wall reminds us that in such seemingly loosely integrated cities, considerable labor could be mobilized in a variety of ways without requiring recourse to central authorities. Such dyadic networks of inter-cluster links lent considerable fluidity and flexibility to clustered cities – allowing parts to break off or change while the whole endured.

Multiple corporate groups of merchants, artisans, and other urban residents may also have formed a distributed structure of power relations for the Bronze Age cities of South Asia, though here too we know little about the specific mechanisms or administrative structures through which these cities were governed. With their dense residential architecture, sophisticated urban infrastructure, and massive platforms and enclosures, the Indus cities, especially the well-known site of Mohenjo Daro, more closely resemble traditional expectations for early cities than do the dispersed West African places McIntosh describes. The elaborate and dense architecture and routes of movement and sophisticated hydraulic infrastructure that characterized these cities would certainly have required significant coordination for both their construction and long-term maintenance. Nonetheless, numerous scholars[13] have emphasized what Indus cities appear to have lacked: most often, unambiguous palaces and temples,[14] elaborate royal or elite burials and evidence for kingship, and warfare. If these traits are essential

[13] Stuart Piggot, *Prehistoric India* (London: Penguin Books, 1950); and Gregory Possehl, "Sociocultural Complexity Without the State," in Gary M. Feinman and Joyce Marcus (eds.), *The Archaic State* (Santa Fe, NM: School of American Research Press, 1998), pp. 261–91; Mortimer Wheeler, *The Indus Civilization* (Cambridge: Cambridge University Press, 1968).

[14] Though one wonders whether this is more a failure of imagination of archaeologists to recognize such features than an actual absence. In later South Asian cities, such as Vijayanagara, where Sinopoli has worked, there was no single palace structure. Rather, the "royal center" was a sizeable walled zone of several square kilometers that contained multiple large residences, administrative structures, temples, shrines, and an array of other features, and it was there that much of the life of the royal court occurred. This is not to suggest that the Indus cities were similarly organized, but merely to point out that the search for "a palace" can be problematic even in contexts where kingship is unambiguous.

characteristics of cities and states, the argument goes, then the Indus tradition cannot have had either. An alternative interpretation, however, might suggest that the particular forms that various Indus cities took – including the lack of evidence for elaborate material expressions of elite institutions and elite bodies – may be evidence for some very different political and urban dynamics. Specifically, current interpretations suggest that within Indus urban systems, power may have been variously distributed among competing and fluid social or economic groups rather than being highly centralized within a single ruling dynasty.[15]

These examples all point toward the multiple ways that ancient societies constructed and inhabited urban places, and they open the door to comparative archaeological and historical scholarship that seeks to understand the diverse routes and factors that led communities in various regions of the world to build large, complex, and economically, socially, and functionally differentiated residential centers – or cities. Each of the three chapters in this section discusses contexts in which power – economic, political, ideological, military – was variously distributed, such that no single kin or social group could effectively dominate the individual cities they resided in or the polities of which these cities were a part. Tensions and competition no doubt existed among the diverse kin groups and communities that constituted Greek, West African, and Indus cities, as they engaged in commerce, agricultural and craft production, diplomacy, sanctioned violence, and local, regional, and interregional interactions. In such urban places, a variety of social and ideological mechanisms would have been required to mitigate competition and limit the accumulation of wealth and resources that could have contributed to the increasing power of one or another corporate group, or the subjugation of others. Viewed from within this framework, we might point to the lack of evidence for elite burials in the Indus cities and the limited (but far from insignificant) range of material expressions of wealth and status differences as being the result of political and religious ideologies that discouraged the materialization of the hierarchies that did exist – part of an active and self-conscious political strategy that worked to maintain a non-hierarchical political structure (or – perhaps, more

---

[15] See especially, Jonathan M. Kenoyer, "Indus Urbanism: New Perspectives on its Origin and Character," in Joyce Marcus and Jeremy A. Sabloff (eds.), *The Ancient City: New Perspectives on Urbanism in the Old and New World* (Santa Fe, NM: School for Advanced Research Press, 2008), pp. 183–208.

accurately – a political structure that sought to ideologically render hierarchy less visible), rather than as evidence for the absence of political institutions.[16]

It is also important to point out that large-scale cooperation and coordinated urban activities were not precluded by the simultaneous coexistence of multiple loci of distributed power. We noted above the city walls of Jenne-jeno. In some Greek cities, citizens collaborated to form a government that built impressive urban monuments, created legal and juridical structures, launched major maritime expeditions, and went to war. The builders of Indus cities coordinated labor to construct and for centuries maintain massive public works, and were able to develop and agree upon large-scale standardized systems of weights and measures (and economic values) that allowed for economic interactions within and between Indus settlements, over enormous distances and involving numerous categories of commodities.

In sum, these urban places were successful and their residents developed organizational structures and accommodations that allowed them to endure for many centuries. Indeed, their success and resilience may well have been fostered by the *lack* of rigidity in their organizational structures and relations, which allowed individual households, neighborhoods, corporate units, and the city as a whole to respond to emerging situations and opportunities with greater ease than in highly bureaucratic administrative structures.

That said, it is not insignificant to note that early Roman emperors typically justified their efforts to dissolve republican institutions during times of crisis by arguing that democratic institutions such as the Roman senate were not sufficiently agile to respond rapidly enough to existential threats, and the slow, consensus-building, consultative democratic process endangered the Roman state and capital during times of political and economic crisis. In the millennia since, many similar claims have been made by many other powerful rulers seeking to centralize power and justify the dissolution of decision-making bodies. While such arguments clearly have a transparent

---

[16] It is perhaps worth noting that royal burials were not characteristic of Mesopotamia's earliest urban societies of the Uruk period, but did flourish a millennium or so after these earliest cities appeared; it is the Early Dynastic Mesopotamian city that has come to be the archetypal early city, *not* the first-generation cities of the Uruk period. A similar argument to the one we are making here was raised by Daniel Miller in the 1980s, who suggested that the lack of royal burials in Indus cites might be associated with renunciatory ideologies, such as were characteristic of Buddhist thought some two millennia later (Daniel Miller, "Ideology and the Harappan Civlization," *Journal of Anthropological Archaeology* 4 (1985), 34–71.

aggrandizing agenda, they do raise important questions about the limits of structures of distributed power that merit serious consideration. Below, we turn to a consideration of the constraints and limitations of cities organized around distributed power, addressing both internal and external challenges to the durability and success of these urban forms.

Can distributed power endure?

We take as our premise that the social, political, economic, etc. organization of *all* early cities entailed some degree of distributed power. Even in the most hierarchical and dictatorial of political systems, rulers cannot (and seldom try to) control all aspects of life, ceding (voluntarily or not) some degree of autonomy to various corporate groups and institutions. And urban residents will inevitably find ways to resist or subvert administrative, economic, or religious hierarchies – avoiding taxes, exchanging surplus food for extra pottery vessels a neighbor may have, worshipping family or household gods rather than at state temples. The distribution of power in urban centers may best be conceived as ranging along a continuum from more centralized to more distributed rather than as an either/or construction. Different realms of urban life may be situated at quite different locations along such a continuum (that is, military defense of urban boundaries may be organized hierarchically even as markets are not), and any city's overall position likely varied over both long and short time scales and in response to a variety of internal and external factors.

We take as a second premise that *not* generating hierarchies takes work, and that the long-term durability of distributed power relations requires both ideological commitments and material benefits to the actors involved. The Classical Greek city-states, Indus cities, and West African clustered cities all thrived for many centuries; as we have noted, they were by any measure large and successful cities. Until they were not. Below we consider the range of factors and conditions that may influence the durability of urban systems of distributed power. We focus on questions of scale, resource distribution, and long- and short-term temporal oscillations in production, consumption, and interregional interactions, as they played within the frame of local political histories and political actors. We begin by addressing how urban life itself may create conditions that foster the intensification and formalization of hierarchy, in ways that challenge the effectiveness of non-hierarchical modes of organizing residents and activities.

Urban life can offer many opportunities to city residents, and ancient cities were often magnets that drew dispersed rural populations and families and individuals to them in search of a better life. The presence of producers of craft and luxury goods, and the centrality of cities as centers of accumulation and commerce provided their residents with access to a broader array of goods than available in towns and villages. Cities provided (at least some of) their residents with opportunities for social and economic mobility and were sites for the creation of new kinds of social and kin affiliations. And they were centers for the construction and performance of elite (and non-elite) cultural values, and sites of religious worship. Early cities were likely also places of crime and violence, of scarcities and poverty, and of social alienation. As we have noted earlier, even in relatively non-hierarchical cities, it should not be forgotten that urban life was no doubt experienced very differently by citizens as compared to slaves, by women as compared to men, by land-owners as compared to the landless, and by the well-off as compared to the impoverished.

In considering the trajectories of early cities, we might also consider whether cities, as a consequence of being cities, intensify and generate inequalities and hierarchy. In the 1990s, at a conference on Asian cities attended by Sinopoli, Rita Wright – a specialist in Mesopotamian and Indus archaeology – astutely observed that once the inhabitants of the densely packed houses in Indus cities had invented and adopted indoor toilets, which fed to sewer drains that ran through the cities' streets, they also created the necessity for people to clean those sewers so that the urban infrastructure could continue to function. Sewer cleaners, trash collectors, tanners – one can easily identify numerous kinds of undesirable occupations that would be required to maintain dense urban places (though perhaps less so in the more dispersed clustered settlements of West Africa). Urban life, in other words, may generate its own social hierarchies, which then require new organizational and ideological responses. These hierarchies may be obscured in ideologies of democracy that exclude slaves, resident aliens, and women from participation, allowing for an urban structure that benefits a sizeable portion (but far from all) of their population. Or they may be regulated in non-hierarchical ways and/or by non-centralized self-regulating organizations; here we think of guilds or religiously sanctioned castes such as developed in Early Historic South Asia and which proved tremendously durable and effective in regulating both behavior and local and interregional political and economic interactions. The corporate kin and occupational groups that occupied the various groups of West African clustered cities may have operated in similar ways. Or the "winners" in ancient cities may regulate their emergent underclasses through the creation of new, more centralized and hierarchical administrative structures that undercut earlier distributed modes of organization. And, of course, cities may fail – and residents may, for a wide variety of reasons, "vote with their feet" and walk away from particular urban places or, in rare cases, like the Indus, from urban life entirely.

We have suggested above that cities characterized by distributed power may have greater resilience to some stresses than more hierarchically organized cities, though we have also noted that in other circumstances, they may be more vulnerable.[17] Comparative research on the long- and short-term histories and responses of early cities of diverse organizational forms to various kinds of stresses may allow us to better understand both individual urban trajectories and larger patterns of similarity and difference. Here, we only note a few of the larger themes around which such research might focus.

Most important among these are questions of scale and temporality: including both the frequency and intensity of temporal oscillations affecting a range of domains, from subsistence production to the social, economic, and political relations within and among any city's diverse communities. Internal challenges to the success of networks of distributed power may come from rapid demographic changes – population growth, reduction, or redistribution – that render unstable existing organizational modes. It is certainly the case that what constitutes "rapid" change may have been quite different in different historical contexts and environmental settings; and it is also likely the case that different urban organizational structures were likely better (and worse) able to respond to such change. These are questions for comparative empirical research.

Numerous external factors may also affect the durability of systems of distributed power. All early cities existed in larger networks of other urban (and non-urban) formations; and all these existed in larger worlds populated by numerous other cultures and societies with which they interacted. In their roles as centers of commerce, early cities were certainly affected by

---

[17] This is also the case of other systems best understood in terms of networks, as highly centralized systems are more susceptible to collapse than decentralized or distributed networks (see, for example, Alex Knodell, "Small-World Networks and Mediterranean Dynamics in the Euboean Gulf: An Archaeology of Complexity in Late Bronze Age and Early Iron Age Greece," unpublished Ph.D. dissertation, Joukowsky Institute for Archaeology and the Ancient World, Brown University, 2013.

larger regional and "global" networks through which material resources moved, such as the maritime exchange relations that allowed the Classical Greek cities discussed by Morris and Knodell to grow, thrive, and feed their subjects on crops imported from throughout the Mediterranean. And as we mentioned earlier, the Persian Empire initially gave common cause to fifth-century Greek cities and in the fourth century provided a reason and conduit for the conquests of Alexander; this, as Morris and Knodell report, "drastically changed the politics of power in the Greek world."

Large-scale threats and crises do of course pose challenges to all early cities – those organized hierarchically and those characterized by non-hierarchical structures of distributed power. And it is beyond our scope to address this topic. Here, we merely end where we began this chapter, arguing that the comparative study of early cities must take into account ancient cities that look different and were organized differently than our standard (and problematic) inherited model: cities that may have consisted of dispersed settlement mounds without a central core; cities that lacked kings, courts, palaces, and state religions; cities whose residents created systems and structures for leadership, administration, and international relations that were dispersed among diverse interlocking groups, rather than under singular linear systems of rule. Moreover, we must recognize that cities frequently grouped together as "Greek," "South Asian," or "African," for example, varied markedly in their scale and organization through time. We hope to show that this diversity (both within and between ancient societies) is precisely what makes the comparative study of ancient cities interesting and relevant. Scholarship on all ancient cities will benefit as a result.

PART V

★

EARLY CITIES AS CREATIONS

19

Baghdad, an imperial foundation
(762–836 CE)

FRANÇOISE MICHEAU

After the Visigoth armies captured Rome in 410, three cities dominated the Old World: Constantinople, capital of the Byzantine Empire founded by Constantine in 330; Xian, the distant capital of the Tang dynasty (618–907); and Baghdad, the capital of the Abbasid Caliphs. These capitals of empires, at the core of vast commercial networks, accommodating hundreds of thousands of inhabitants, were regarded as "world cities," not only because of their political importance, but also because of the place they occupy in the realms of the imagination. Baghdad was the city that medieval Arabic geographers put in the center of the world. It is said, according to an ancient Muslim tradition, that the man who has not seen Baghdad has not seen the world.

The history of Baghdad is divided into three phases: first, the prestigious capital of the Abbasid Caliphs from the time of its foundation in 762 by al-Mansûr up to its conquest by Mongol armies in 1258; then, for centuries, a simple provincial metropolis; and finally, since 1921, the capital of Iraq, whose dramatic present assails us with images of devastation. Here we are interested only in the beginning of the first of these periods that starts with the date of the foundation of the city and closes with the death of the Caliph al-Ma'mûn in 833 and the foundation of a new capital in 836 at Sâmarrâ'.

Why a new capital?

The Abbasid Caliphs took power in the aftermath of an important insurrection that overthrew the former Umayyad dynasty over the years 746–50. These Caliphs were at the head of a vast empire created during the Islamic conquests after Muhammad's death in 632. Under the last Umayyad Caliphs, the series of conquests ceased, and the empire was stabilized within its borders, which stretched from the Indus to the Atlantic Ocean and from the Sahara to the Caucasus (Map 19.1). There are many causes that led to the

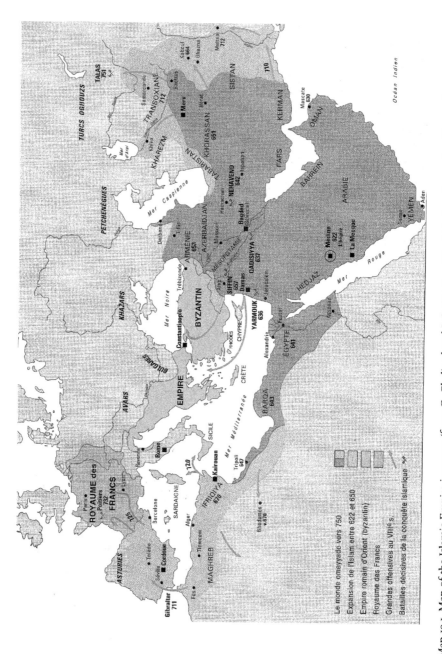

Map 19.1 Map of the Islamic Empire in 750 CE (from G. Chalinad and J.-P. Rageau, *Atlas historique du monde méditerranéen* [Paris: Payot, 1995], p. 23).

overthrow of the Umayyads. Among them, the following emerge as the most important: the end of the conquests, which resulted in a substantial reduction in spoils; the difficulties of administering a vast empire; the inability to integrate the different populations, in particular the non-Arabs newly converted to Islam; and the dispute over Umayyad legitimacy since the Umayyads had no family ties with Muhammad. The Umayyad Caliphs had their capital in Damascus in Syria, but they did not live there permanently. Rather, they tended to exercise their power increasingly in the several residences that they built in the regions of the steppe and the Euphrates; the most important of them was Rusâfa. Thereby, they initiated a shift toward the Mesopotamian regions.

The uprising against the Umayyad Caliphs, in which the Abbasids took power, is commonly referred to as "the Abbasid Revolution." It started in Khurâsân in eastern Iran, with the help of the soldiers of Kûfa and other cities of Iraq. Interestingly, it is in the city of Kûfa that al-Saffâh was proclaimed Caliph in 749. The legitimacy of this dynasty derives from the Hashimid clan, which was Muhammad's clan: Hâshim was the great-grandfather of Muhammad and the grandfather of al-'Abbâs, with whom al-Saffâh was in direct line of descendance. It would have been out of the question that al-Saffâh, and then his successor al-Mansûr, should settle in Damascus or in any other Umayyad city, since the Abbasids not only overthrew the Umayyads, who had suffered a military defeat, but they also quickly killed all the members of the Umayyad family during a banquet. They did everything they could to ensure that the Umayyad period would be regarded as a period of usurpation, injustice, and impiety.

A new capital, thus, for a new dynasty was called for, but where? From 750 to 762, al-Saffâh and al-Mansûr seemed to hesitate. Al-Saffâh, who first settled in Kûfa, where the insurgent army proclaimed him Caliph, swiftly built a new palace on the banks of the Euphrates, near the old Persian city of Anbâr. This palace was called Hâshimiyya to refer to the common ancestor Hâshim. It was in this palace that the first Abbasid Caliph died in 754. His brother al-Mansûr, shortly after succeeding to the throne, built another residence, also called Hâshimiyya, further in the south and near Kûfa (Map 19.2).

There are several reasons that explain why the Abbasids chose to reside in Mesopotamia: the fruitful area of the valleys of the Euphrates and Tigris; the communication facilities along the two rivers; the central position between Iran, Syria, and Egypt, just when the western regions of the empire (Maghreb and al-Andalus) started to free themselves from the Caliphs' direct

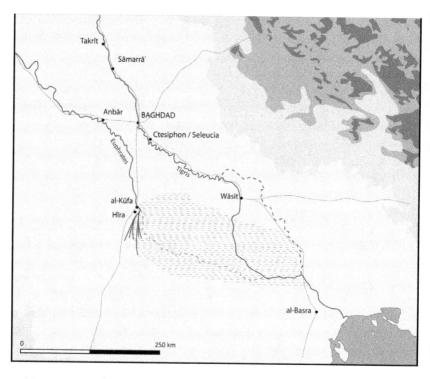

Map 19.2 Map of Lower Iraq. The hatched area corresponds to the swamp zone.

control; openness to Iranian and Iraqi people who had supported the insurgency and who would play a major role in the new empire.

In 757, al-Mansûr looked for a new site that would not be in the Euphrates Valley, but rather in the valley of the Tigris, and decided on the site of Baghdad. There are geographical reasons that can explain the choice for this place. It is at this exact place that the course of the Tigris is very close to that of the Euphrates, which allows the irrigation of the entire area on the basis of a system of canals bringing water from the Euphrates. Also, the new site had slight hillocks where houses could be sheltered from the periodic flooding of the Tigris.

A city known only through the texts

It is important to point out that no material remains from the time of the origin of Baghdad. The fragility of the buildings made out of unfired bricks, the recurring floods, the frequent fires, the destructions caused by wars and invasions (Hûlâgû's in 1258 and Tamerlane's in 1401), and the rapid decline of the city after the fall of the Abbasids in 1258 erased all traces of caliphal buildings.[1] From the fifteenth to the mid-twentieth century, Baghdad was only a small town, limited to the caliphal quarter, which was built in the late ninth century and located in the south on the eastern shore, and to a small area on the western shore. This extent was a fraction of the early city, which extended during the Abbasid period far in the north and west along both banks of the Tigris. The caliphal quarter, where the Abbasids resided from the tenth century on, was surrounded by a wall built in 1095 by the Caliph al-Mustazhir around the palace area. Although this great wall was demolished in 1870, the layout remains are still visible. The plan of early Baghdad cannot be discerned under the current topography. In addition, with the exception of few surveys, no archaeological excavation has been undertaken.

It follows that our knowledge of Abbasid Baghdad is based solely on written sources. For the first period we have no contemporary written sources, but there are systematic descriptions that belong to the following century. In particular, there is a work written by an Abbasid secretary named Ya'qûbî in 891: the *Kitâb al-buldân* or "Book of Countries,"[2] which gives a long account of the foundation of Baghdad by al-Mansûr. Although we shall often refer to Ya'qûbî's work, it is important to note that Ya'qûbî, like other writers who provided information on the Abbasid capital,[3] wrote at the time of the social and cultural splendor of the Caliphate. His perspective is therefore influenced by the Islamic and imperial ideology that makes him consider Baghdad as a "city-world." Baghdad was an imperial foundation, as is reflected in the Arabic sources and in the Arab and Islamic imagination. It is therefore essential not to follow the letter of the written texts, but rather to interpret these texts in the light of their historical context.

It can be difficult to figure out the architecture of the Abbasid capital on the basis of the descriptions made by the Arabic authors. The scholarly plans of Abbasid Baghdad are reconstructions based on the data provided by

---

[1] The oldest monumental remains date from the twelfth–thirteenth centuries and are extremely scarce. The most important is the Mustansiriyya madrasa founded in 1232; it was abandoned in the seventeenth century and very crudely restored in 1945 and 1960.

[2] Yâ'qûbî, *Kitâb al-Buldân*, M. J. de Goeje (ed.) (Leiden: Brill, 1892), and *Les pays*, Gaston Wiet (trans.) (Cairo: Institut Français d'Archéologie Orientale, 1937).

[3] The most important ones are the following: Ibn Sarâbiyûn, who for the early tenth century provided an accurate description of the canals in Baghdad; al-Tabarî (d. 923), whose chronicle is full of incidents that took place in Baghdad and provide us with information about the topography and the inhabitants of the city; al-Khatîb al-Baghdâdî (d. 1071), who introduced his biographical dictionary of Muslim elites with a description of the city.

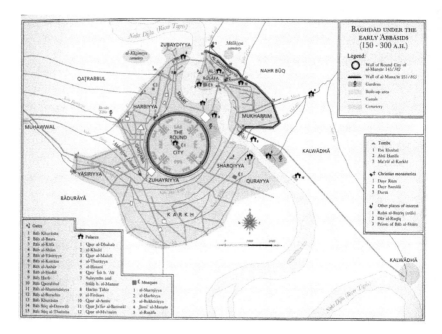

Map 19.3 Early Baghdad by Le Strange (from H. Kennedy, *An Historical Atlas of Islam*
[Leiden: Brill, 2002].

ancient Arabic sources. The pioneering work of reconstruction was that of
Le Strange. Relying on Ya'qûbî and Ibn Sarâbiyûn, he established plans by
period and by quarter, which he candidly presented as hypotheses: "my
plans of medieval Baghdad are, to a certain extent, tentative";[4] nevertheless,
they have often been cited. However, in the aftermath of field work in 1908,
Massignon criticized many of the places proposed by Le Strange.[5] Since the
1950s, significant research has been conducted by Iraqi scholars, including
Sûsa, Jawad, and Duri, who corrected Le Strange's work in many aspects.[6]
It follows that the plan drawn up by Le Strange for the city founded by
al-Mansûr (Map 19.3) should be revised in many ways: Le Strange overesti-
mated the dimensions of the Round City and also minimized the size of the
large districts; he did not know that the course of the Tigris runs differently

[4] Guy Le Strange, *Baghdad during the Abbasid Caliphate* (New York: Barnes & Noble, 1972;
   first edition 1900), p. xi.
[5] Louis Massignon, *Mission en Mésopotamie (1907–1908)*, 2 vols. (Cairo: Institut Français
   d'archéologie Orientale, 1910–1912).
[6] 'Abd al-'Azîz al-Dûrî, "Baghdâd," in *Encyclopedia of Islam*, 2nd edn., Vol. 1; Mustafa
   Jawâd and Ahmad Sûsah, *Dalîl mufassal li-kharîtat Baghdâd* (Baghdad: Iraqi Scientific
   Academy Press, 1958, in Arabic); Ahmad Sûsa, *Atlâs Baghdâd* (Baghdad 1952; in Arabic).

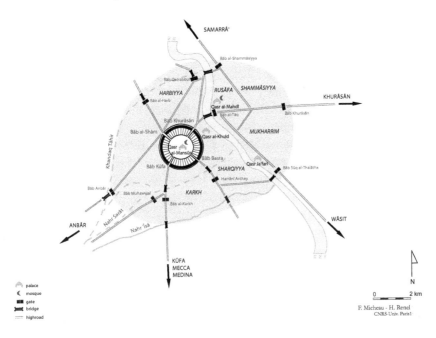

Map 19.4 Early Baghdad (762–836 CE) (copyright F. Micheau – H. Renel CNRS-Univ. Paris 1).

today; he drew a circular track for the canals as if they were running around the city. My map (Map 19.4) is based on new research, but more work that compares the written sources with hydrological and topographic data might result in modifications.

Foundation account

As with other foundation accounts, Ya'qûbî does not justify the choice of the site by reasons of geopolitical, strategic, or economic advantages, but rather because of its destiny. As he recounted, al-Mansûr stopped in a place whose name he asked for. "Baghdad" was the reply. At that time, Baghdad was only a small town that possessed Nestorian Christian monasteries and a weekly market known as the Tuesday Market. Nonetheless, the Caliph exclaimed:

> By God, this is the city that according to my father Muhammad ibn 'Alî I shall found, where I shall live and where my descendants will reign. Princes had lost track of it, before and after Islam, so that I shall fulfil the predictions and orders of God ... Praise be to God who reserved for me this capital and left it unknown by all my predecessors.[7]

[7] Ya'qûbî, *Kitâb al-Buldân*, p. 237, and *Les pays*, p. 10.

403

The historian al-Tabarî (d. 934) related that a prophecy was found in the ancient books of the Christian monks, foretelling of a great city to be built between the Sarât Canal and the Tigris, by a man bearing the name of Miqlâs. The Caliph al-Mansûr, hearing this prophecy, remembered that his nurse once called him by this name.[8]

The account of Baghdad's foundation is typically one of the foundation of an imperial city. It depicted a ruler accomplishing the divine plan by choosing a site already designated by God. In that respect, one should note that, according to some Arabic writers, the name of Baghdad would derive from the two ancient Persian words Bagh "God" and Dâdh "founded." Hence, Baghdad would mean "Founded by God."[9]

Once the site was chosen, Ya'qûbî wrote that the Caliph brought in engineers, architects, and skilful surveyors whom he asked to trace out the plan of the capital, as well as all kinds of workers, such as masons, carpenters, or blacksmiths. There is no doubt that the construction of the city required a large number of architects, artisans, and laborers. The text claims that these workers were summoned by the Caliph. They came from all parts of the empire and were paid. Their number – obviously symbolic – was 100,000. The new capital was born from the skill of the Caliph in rallying all the forces of the empire.

According to several accounts, Baghdad emerged as the heir of past empires. Reported by both al-Tabarî (d. 923) and al-Khatîb al-Baghdâdî (d. 1071), al-Mansûr is said to have ordered the demolition of the Palace of Chosroes in Ctesiphon in order to use its materials. Ctesiphon was the prestigious capital of the empire of the Sassanians, this great Persian dynasty in power since 224 CE, which was conquered by the Arabs in the seventh century. However, this demolition was soon stopped because it became too expensive.[10] This account should be regarded above all as symbolic. Since the Sassanian dynasty was defeated by the Arabs, its capital destroyed, and its vestiges erased, the new Abbasid capital could appropriate the material and cultural wealth of the conquered civilization. Thus the glory of the great Chosroes reflected on al-Mansûr.

---

[8] Al-Tabarî, *The History of al-Tabarî*, Jane D. McAuliffe (trans.) (New York: State University of New York Press, 1995), Vol. xxviii, p. 244.

[9] The name of Baghdad surely has a Persian origin, but its etymology is uncertain. I quote only the origin that seems the most interesting from a symbolic perspective.

[10] Al-Tabarî, *History of al-Tabarî*, Hugh Kennedy (trans.) (New York: State University of New York Press, 1990), Vol. xxix, pp. 4–5. For further details in this regard, see Jacob Lassner, *The Topography of Baghdad in the Early Middle Ages* (Detroit, MI: Wayne State University Press, 1970), pp. 128–31.

According to another tradition also reported by al-Tabarî, al-Mansûr ordered five iron gates to be carried from Wâsit. This city was established in southern Iraq, south of present-day Kut al-Amara in the early eighth century, by the governor al-Hajjâj, who took these gates from an old city in lower Mesopotamia called Zandaraward, which was already a ruin and whose foundation was attributed to Solomon. Four out of the five gates closed the four gateways of the main wall of the Round City, and the fifth was the gate of the Palace of Mansûr.[11] The meaning of this legend is clear: the Abbasids did not only gather the heritage of the Sassanians, but they also established themselves as the successors of the kings of the Bible by taking their symbols of power, namely the city gates of Solomon.

Casting the horoscope to ensure that the new foundation was under the best auspices is also part of the *topoi* of the foundation accounts. Ya'qûbî said that the plans were made during the month of Rabî' I (141 BCE/July–August 758 CE), when the foundations were built at the very moment chosen by Nawbakht and Mâshâ'allâh. The former was a Persian astrologer, while the latter was a Jewish scientist who became very famous in the Arabic and Latin Middle Ages. Fortunately, the horoscope of the founding of Baghdad was preserved in a book written by al-Bîrûnî in the eleventh century. My colleague Jean-Patrice Boudet carried out an analysis of this horoscope.[12] Accordingly, the astronomical positions of the chart actually corresponded exactly to July 30, 762 CE at 2 p.m. The conjunction of the stars was not exceptionally favorable, but it was still suitable to authorize the inaugural ceremony.

The Round City: a palatial city

The palatial city founded by al-Mansûr has often been called the "Round City" because of its circular form. Ya'qûbî affirms that it was the only round city known in the whole world. Although there were Mesopotamian oval

---

[11] Lassner, *Topography of Baghdad*, pp. 128–31.
[12] Muḥammad ibn Aḥmad Bīrūnī, *The Chronology of Ancient Nations: An English Version of the Arabic Text of the Athâr-ul-Bâkiya of Albîrûnî, Or "Vestiges of the Past,"* Eduard Sachau (ed.) (London: W. H. Allen and Co., 1879), pp. 270–1, trans., pp. 262–3. Jean-Patrice Boudet's analysis, "From Baghdad to *Civitas Solis*: Horoscopes of Foundations of Cities," in *From Masha'Allah to Kepler: The Theory and Practice of Astrology in the Middle Ages and the Renaissance, 13–15 November 2008* (London: Warburg Institute, forthcoming, see www.univ-orleans.fr/sites/default/files/CESFiMAdocuments/publications_jean-patrice_boudetmars2014.pdf).

constructions as possible antecedents,[13] this affirmation makes the Caliphate construction an exceptional one, unique in the world. The symbolism of a circular architecture with the Great Mosque and the Caliph's palace placed at the center is extremely strong. It refers to the Persian geographical tradition that considers that the earth is circular with Mesopotamia at the center. Thus Ya'qûbî starts his *Book of Countries* with the following words: "If I start with Iraq, it is simply because it is the center of this world, the core of the earth. I mention, in the first place, Baghdad, because it is the heart of Iraq, the most important city, with no equivalent in the East or West of the earth."[14] Also in the other civilizations, especially Chinese and Aztec, we find this same conception of a political city where the ruler lives, reflecting the cosmos, the pivot of the world by its central position. This concentric plan corresponds to the fundamental anthropological structure that Philippe Descola has called "analogism" and which can be found in a number of human societies before the modern era.[15]

The Round City was situated close to the right bank of the river Tigris, but its exact location remains uncertain since archaeological evidence is lacking, and the course of the river has changed over the centuries. The dimensions of the city, given in cubits by Arab geographers, have given rise to very different estimates that vary from 1,650 to 2,900 meters for its diameter, depending on the measurement of the ancient Arabic cubit and the purpose of the texts. As to the reconstruction of the plan, historians mostly agree on its general arrangement but remain divided over a number of more specific points, since written descriptions are often difficult to interpret.

The city was surrounded by double walls, with a deep ditch outside. The wall was topped by merlons and flanked by numerous towers. In the wall were four equidistant gateways: the southwest was the Kûfa Gate; the southeast was Basra Gate; the Khurâsân Gate extended to the northeast; and the Syrian Gate to the northwest. These four gateways faced the main provinces dominated by the Abbasid power. Each of the four gateways

[13] See the circular enclosures described in Keppel Archibald Cameron Creswell, *Early Muslim Architecture* (New York: Hacker Art Books, 1979), Vol. II, pp. 18–22. Two imitations of the Round City were built a few years later by which one can judge the descriptions of Baghdad: al-Râfiqa, which is a fortress founded by al-Mansûr himself near Raqqa, and al-Qâdisiyya, which is an octagon, geometrically related to a circle.

[14] Al-Ya'qûbî, *Kitâb al-buldân*, p. 233, and *Les pays*, p. 4.

[15] Philippe Descola, *Par-delà nature et culture* (Paris: Gallimard, 2005).

included a vaulted gate hall closed by iron doors;[16] a long thoroughfare with arcades; and the inner gate was also closed by iron doors with a large vaulted chamber overlooking the whole city. A third innermost wall surrounded the central area, at the center of which stood the palace of the Caliph and the Great Mosque. As a traditionalist of the ninth century pointed out,[17] the Caliph is placed at the center of the Round City, in the other words, at the center of the world, in equal distance from all countries and all peoples. Here we find the principle of *isonomia* formulated by the Greeks, according to which power must be located at the center of the civic space in order to maintain balance between all the elements composing the city.[18]

This palace is called the Palace of the Golden Gate or the Palace of the Green Dome, because it was crowned by a great, green dome – 35 meters above the ground and visible from all quarters of Baghdad. This dome was surmounted by a figure of a horseman, said to have been endowed with a magic power of pointing its lance in the direction from which the enemies of the Caliph were about to appear. There were also other buildings standing nearby: the Great Mosque, the guardhouse, the palaces of the younger children of the Caliph, the houses of his servants, and the principal public offices (Land Tax, Privy Seal, Army, etc.). Most houses in the palatial complex were located between the outer wall and the inner wall. They were distributed along streets and lanes, which linked the vaulted passage ways of the four gates without directly leading either outwards or inwards. These houses were totally under the control of the Caliph, and Ya'qûbî clearly says that their inhabitants were officers (probably including their soldiers), immediate followers, and other trustworthy persons likely to be called before the Caliph. In other words, al-Mansûr settled in the Round City all the elements of the state that were important to him, and these elements were separated from the public areas of the city by a fortification.

In 763 the buildings of Baghdad were sufficiently advanced to enable al-Mansûr to settle with his administration in this Round City, which was finished by the year 766. This Round City was an enormous palace complex combining the residence of the Caliph with the administrative agencies of the government. As Lassner writes, it was "the Caliph's personal domain,

---

[16] Those who according to a story came from Wâsit.
[17] Al-Wakî', a traditionalist of the ninth century, cited in *al-Khatîb al-Baghdâdî*; and Lassner, *Topography of Baghdad*, p. 52.
[18] See Jean-Pierre Vernant, *Entre mythe et politique* (Paris: Le Seuil, 1996), p. 260.

comprising the area, his residence, and the governmental machinery."[19] This monumental complex, with its moat, walls, and fortified gates, must, when seen from the outside, have aroused fear and respect. The sovereign lived far from his people, entrenched behind the walls of a fortress that was accessible only through its imposing gates. His prestige was based on remoteness, inaccessibility, and invisibility. This "empty centre," to quote the famous phrase of Roland Barthes,[20] was the space of sovereignty. It can be found in many Asian imperial cities, starting with Beijing's famous Forbidden City.

The city on the western side

The inhabitants of the new capital did not live in the Round City, with the exception of persons close to the Caliph. The texts clearly and thoroughly describe the entire city of al-Mansûr with the various quarters constructed around the Round City and the activities that took place in them. In that respect, it is interesting to note that, from the nineteenth century until today, those who have written about the foundation of Baghdad have been fascinated by this Round City, and they have restricted the dwelling districts to "suburbs,"[21] or even totally ignored these districts.

Al-Mansûr and his architects planned four major sectors around the Round City. Each of these areas was entrusted to a chief of the sector who was charged with determining the public space that should be reserved for shops and markets in each quarter. Avenues had a width of around 50 meters, streets a width of around 8 meters, as well as some passages. Mosques were built for the people of each sector, and finally, spacious locations were allotted for construction.

Furthermore, al-Mansûr made land concessions. The process was not new since it had been used at the founding of the first cities by the Arab conquerors, at Basra and Kûfa, which were established in 638 in lower Iraq, and Fustât founded in 642 in Egypt. In these cities the grants of lands were allotted to the tribal leaders who had led troops in the conquest. The description by Ya'qûbî shows that there was planned urbanism also in

[19] Lassner, *Topography of Baghdad*, p. 144.
[20] Roland Barthes, *L'empire des signes* (Paris: Flammarion, 1950), p. 50.
[21] The Arabic word that appears in the sources to describe the quarters of the city is *rabad*, because these quarters spread outside the walls of the Round City. However, the translation as suburb/*faubourg* suggests a misconception of what they actually were, namely the quarters of the city proper.

Baghdad: constructions were devoted to nobles, the members of the Caliph's military and civil entourage, who were charged to build their their own homes as well as the homes of their relatives, apartment houses, and also a mosque, a market, other service buildings, sometimes a garden. The quarters established in this way were named after the members of the Caliph's military and civilian entourage who were allocated an area in which to build. This is why Ya'qûbî devotes several pages to a list of these people. Although a detailed study of these names, amounting to hundreds, remains to be done, a first analysis, made by the Iraqi historian S. al-Alî, shows that the different quarters were populated by both civilians and military, Arab and Persian for the most part.[22] The majority of the Baghdad population comprised voluntary non-indigenous Arab and Persian migrants, and spontaneous immigration from the neighboring villages and rural zones was less significant. In the course of the following centuries, voluntary and forced migrations of scholars, officials, and tradesmen, bought or captured soldiers, slaves of various origins – black, Slav, Turkish, Berber — assured the cosmopolitan and multi-confessional character of a population for which the estimates of historians range from some hundreds of thousands to nearly 2 million people.

The vast quarter of al-Karkh with its important market unfolded in the south. It was crossed by two large navigable canals drawn from the Euphrates: the Nahr 'Îsâ and the Sarât. Ya'qûbî has affirmed that this densely inhabited quarter extended over a length of 2 farsakhs (about 10 km), with a width of approximately 1 farsakh. The importance of this area is attested by a sad anecdote reported by the historian al-Tabarî: 7,000 houses there were destroyed in a flood in 883. In the north another important area was the Harbiyya Quarter, named after a certain Harb, a native of Balkh in northern Afghanistan, who had become the chief of the Baghdad police.

The city had no wall, because there was no need for defense. But the numerous vaulted gateways, akin to triumphal arches, were built on the main highroads departing from the four gates of the Round City. Opposite to the Kûfa Gate, the highroad crossed the Sarât Canal on a bridge made of kiln-burnt bricks that was called the Old Bridge. Shortly after crossing this bridge the way bifurcated: to the left, the great Kûfa highroad leading south through the Bâb al-Karkh – this road was the Pilgrim Way leading to the

[22] S. al-'Alî, "The Foundation of Baghdad," in A. H. Hourani and S. M. Stern (eds.), *The Islamic City* (Oxford: Cassirer and University of Pennsylvania Press, 1970), pp. 87–103.

holy places of Mecca and Medina; to the right, the road, turning westward, was the first portion of the highroad to the town of Anbâr on the Euphrates, through the Bâb Muhawwal (named after a town located some kilometers southwest, whose exact location is unknown). Opposite the Basra Gate, the road crossed the Sarât Canal on another stone bridge, called the New Bridge, and went through the Harrânî Archway to the south; it led in the direction of the Tigris and crossed over the Lower Bridge[23] in front of the Sûq al-Thalâtha (or Tuesday Market). The Syrian Gate led out to the three principal highroads traversing the northern quarters of West Baghdad: on the right the road to the Upper Bridge passed through the Harbiyya Quarter diagonally; on the left the highroad went out by the Anbâr Gate to join the road coming from the Kûfa Gate at an undetermined point beyond Muhaw-wal town; it fronted the Syrian Gate into the Harbiyya Quarter and joined the Harb Gate, beyond which began the cemeteries afterwards known as the Kâzimayn. Finally, opposite the Khurâsân Gate, a road crossing the Tigris on the this gate there were three main roads: the northern road leading towards Sâmarrâ' and Mosul through the Bâb al-Shammâsiyya; a road going in the direction of Iran through the Bâb Khurâsân is mentioned by Ya'qûbî and formed the chief market of eastern Baghdad, where all kinds of goods and manufactured articles were gathered together; and the third road, named the Great Road, leading to the Lower Bridge and the Gate of Tuesday Market (Bâb Sûq al-Thalâtha). This description demonstrates that the city of Baghdad, from its foundation by al-Mansûr, had spread far beyond the Round City. Numerous quarters had grown up along these highroads, and many markets were installed along them.

Growth of the eastern side

The city founded by al-Mansûr was transformed quickly as the result of the displacement and multiplication of the Caliph's places of residence. Al-Mansûr himself built a new palace, outside the Khurâsân Gate, on the Tigris bank. This palace was called the Palace of al-Khuld, signifying the Palace of Eternity, for its gardens were regarded as competing with those of Paradise.

---

[23] Baghdad had three bridges on the Tigris: the first upstream, called the Upper Bridge; the second in the center opposite the Round City, considered as the Main Bridge; and the third downstream, called the Lower Bridge. These three bridges were bridges of boats.

Al-Mansûr moved there in 775, although the Palace of the Golden Gate remained his official residence.

After that al-Mansûr built another palace on the eastern shore for his son named al-Mahdî and nearby also a mosque. This palace was completed in 776. Although not as important as the Round City, it was surrounded by a wall and a moat. Chroniclers report that in 768 al-Mansûr and his entourage went out from the Round City to the eastern Tigris bank, in order to receive al-Mahdî, who was arriving victoriously from Khurâsân. All around the palace, grants of lands were given by al-Mahdî to his followers according to the same system as the one adopted at the west bank. Ya'qûbî again gives us the names of the beneficiaries. Thus developed the large quarter called Rusâfa. With the neighboring districts of al-Shammâsiyya and Mukharrim, the city on the east side of the Tigris quickly became as important as the city on the west side.

The Dâr al-Rûm, or the Christian Quarter of Baghdad, was situated in the neighborhood of the Shammâsiyya quarter, with the great monastery called Dayr al-Rûm where the Nestorian patriarch had his residence. During the Abbasid period, the Christians appear to have enjoyed complete tolerance in Baghdad under the government of the Caliphs, for besides this great monastery, they possessed many other churches and lesser monasteries in different quarters of the city.

Al-Mahdî mostly lived in his own palace, but sometimes also in the Palace of al-Khuld. Hârûn al-Rashîd, his son and successor, preferred the Palace of al-Khuld because of its gardens and its easy access. However, he did not like living in Baghdad. He therefore left for Râfiqa/Raqqa in the upper valley of the Euphrates, where he founded a vast city whose large foundations have recently been revealed by German excavations. He lived there until the end of his reign. After his death in 809, his two sons tore each other apart during a civil war lasting several years. On the one side there was al-Amîn, the eldest son, who lived in Baghdad and whom Hârûn had named the first in succession; on the other side there was al-Ma'mûn, the younger son, whom Hârûn had made the governor of the rich province of Khurâsân and the second in succession to the Caliphate. When al-Amîn appointed his own son as crown prince, al-Ma'mûn, now deprived of the succession, rebelled against his brother. After several years of conflict, he sent a powerful army to attack Baghdad and proved victorious. In 813 al-Amîn was killed and al-Ma'mûn took over his position as Caliph. The fighting had resulted in widespread destruction throughout the city, and in the end the quarter of Harbiyya was no more than a field of ruins. Al-Amîn had retired to the

Palace of the Golden Gate, which also had been bombarded and had suffered considerable damage. Even though the ruined areas were reconstructed, the Round City never fully recovered from this disaster. Furthermore, it soon was absorbed by new constructions. And no Caliph ever returned there. In 893 an important part of the Palace of the Golden Gate was pulled down in order to enlarge the neighboring mosque, and the green dome that still stood intact collapsed in a great storm in 941.

In this way the Round City of al-Mansûr disappeared forever from the urban landscape. Only the mosque survived until the late Middle Ages, but it was later abandoned. Travelers in the nineteenth century could see only fields and orchards in this area, which was once the Round City. In fact the city of Baghdad had both retracted and moved.

Al-Ma'mûn, when he arrived in Baghdad after the victory of his army, settled in the magnificent palace that the wazîr Ja'far the Barmecide had built for himself on the eastern Tigris bank below the Mukharrim Quarter and that carried the name Qasr Ja'farî. The Caliph al-Mu'tasim, who succeeded al-Ma'mûn in 833, decided to recruit Turks from Central Asia. But these Turkish mercenaries, freshly arrived in Baghdad, aroused hostility and caused riots in the city. Also al-Mu'tasim decided to leave the capital and founded a new city in 836 at Sâmarrâ', 125 kilometers to the north.

Since there are no remains of the Abbasid Baghdad, special attention should be given to Sâmarrâ', which provides a large field of ruins over more than 58 square kilometers, with visible remnants of palaces, mosques, and other constructions. The archaeologist Ernst Herzfeld conducted major investigations there in the early twentieth century.[24] Additionally, the entire site of Sâmarrâ' was recently examined by Alastair Northedge, mainly on the basis of aerial photos and textual data.[25] The topography of Sâmarrâ', the remains of the palace, and the fragments of decoration (including stuccoes, frescoes, and ceramics) give an insight into the splendor of the early Abbasid Baghdad. For example, the cantonment of al-Karkh in Sâmarrâ' should be very close to the first quarters of Baghdad. Al-Mu'tasim, when he settled in Sâmarrâ' in 836, allocated a vast area of more than 500 hectares to Ahnâs al-Turkî, where a mosque, his residence, and quarters for Turkish soldiers were built. Al-Harbiyya Quarter in Baghdad was most likely similar.

[24] Ernst Herzfeld, *Die Ausgrabungen von Samarra*, Vols. I–V (Berlin: Dietrich Reimer, 1923–1930), and *Geschichte der Stadt Samarra*, Vol. VI (Hamburg: Verlag von Eckardt & Messtorff, 1948).

[25] Alastair Northedge, *The Historical Topography of Samarra* (London: British School of Archaeology in Iraq – Fondation Max von Berchem, 2005).

With the death of al-Ma'mûn in 833 and the foundation of Sâmarrâ' in 836, the formative period of Baghdad came to an end. When the Abbasid Caliphs, following the revolts among their military troops, returned to Baghdad in the late ninth century, they settled once more on the east bank, but mainly to the south. First they took up residence in the palace of Qasr Ja'farî. However, they quickly built other palaces, such as the Qasr Firdaws and the Qasr al-Taj, further south on the east bank of the Tigris. These prestigious constructions were not the only ones. Inside the caliphal enclosure were numerous palaces, luxurious gardens, polo grounds, and racecourses. It is this district palace that was surrounded by a wall in 1095 on al-Mustazhir's orders. In the tenth century, the opposition between the two sides of the Tigris became highly marked: on the east bank lay the palaces, the sumptuous residences of great courtiers, high government employees, and emirs, while on the west bank there seems to have been a more popular and animated scene, with a large Shi'ite population. The chief quarter of modern Baghdad lies on the eastern bank of the Tigris, around the later palaces of the caliphs.

Conclusion

Until the tenth century in Baghdad there was not a fixed seat of caliphal power that was occupied by successive sovereigns. The continuity of the Abbasid dynasty was not expressed by the occupation of a single place, but rather by the ability of each family member to have his own residence demonstrating his personal power. Less than a symbol of power and continuity of the Abbasid dynasty, the palace was a manifestation of the power of each sovereign living there in isolation surrounded by his guards. In other words, Baghdad persisted for several centuries, a city with multiple nuclei.

Although the foundation of Baghdad obeyed a purely political logic, the prosperity of the city can be explained by its economic wealth, the importance of its elites, and its cultural vitality. The Caliph was far from being the sole architect of the urban fabric, as is proven by the growth of the city in the ninth century when the Caliphs resided in Sâmarrâ'. Baghdad got its resources above all from its rich hinterland – the black soil of Sawad – which provided the agricultural products necessary for consumption, raw materials, and income derived from crafts, export, and taxes. According to Ya'qûbî, al-Mansûr, when discovering the site of Baghdad, predicted: "This city will be the most prosperous in the world" because from all regions of the empire, there would be people and goods, ships and caravans streaming toward the area. This prediction, though obviously apocryphal, reflects the power and prosperity of the Abbasid capital. The main routes connecting Central Asia (the famous Silk Road) with the Indian Ocean, the Byzantine Empire and the Mediterranean coast converged on Baghdad. According to the ancient and medieval perception, the power of a city was related not to its role as a place of important production, but to its function as a center that attracted the wealth of the empire.

Baghdad not only displayed material prosperity, but also cultural wealth. Scientists and scholars flocked from everywhere, attracted by the material and intellectual conditions offered by the patronage of the Caliphs and the notables; students, who were drawn to the lessons of the greatest masters and came to Baghdad from far away, chose to settle there; translators, mostly Christians, collected and transmitted Greek knowledge. In essence, Baghdad was a unique place in the history of Arabic culture where the melting pot of peoples led to the emergence of new forms of thought and art.

This prestigious city gradually declined as the Caliphs' power was reduced by emirs and the sultans, and as political troubles and popular revolts multiplied. Even though new constructions were still enriching the urban landscape in the Seljuq period (1055–1194), and even though economic activity carried on, especially in the very active Karkh Quarter, in 1193 the traveler Ibn Jubayr describes a largely devastated city. From the late tenth century onwards, Cairo, another imperial creation that was founded in 969 by the Fatimids, who were rival Shi'ite caliphs aiming to overthrow the hated Sunni dynasty, would compete with Baghdad and finally eclipse it. The invasions of Hûlâgû in 1258, and of Tamerlane in 1401 were fatal blows to the city. Baghdad became a small country town, and it stayed so until the twentieth century. It remains nonetheless the symbol of the splendor of Islamic civilization, and it belongs as such to the realms of the collective imagination.

FURTHER READINGS

Arabica 9 (1962), special issue published on the occasion of the 1,200th anniversary of the foundation of Baghdad.

Archibald Cameron Creswell Keppel, *Early Muslim Architecture*, New York: Hacker Art Books, 1979.

Ghalib al-Hakkak, "Essai d'interpétation des textes relatifs à la ville ronde de Bagdad," *Revue des Études Islamiques* 51 (1983), 149–60.

Dimitri Gutas, *Greek Thought, Arabic Culture. The Graeco-Arabic Translation Movement in Baghdad and Early ʿAbbāsid Society, 2nd–4th/8th–10th Centuries*, London–New York: Routledge, 1998.

Al-Mawrid 8, 1979, special issue on Baghdad (in Arabic).

Françoise Micheau, "Bagdad in the Abbasid Era: A Cosmopolitan and Multi-Confessional Capital," S. K. Jayyusi, R. Holod, A. Petruccioli, and A. Raymond (eds.), *The City in the Islamic World*, Leiden–Boston: Brill, 2008, pp. 221–45.

20

Jerusalem: capital city created in stone and in imagination

ANN E. KILLEBREW

Jerusalem, in stone and imagination, is unique as a holy city of the world's three monotheistic religions – Judaism, Christianity, and Islam. The city's Late Bronze Age name in the Amarna Letters (URU *šalim* and variants) implies (for some, but not all, scholars) an association with (an obscure god) Shalim, perhaps an astral deity. This name may suggest a sanctity that long pre-dates monotheism and reflects the *raison d'être* of Jerusalem's initial foundation. Both past and present, Jerusalem is many cities, comprised of multiple layers of structures, peoples, and stories. According to biblical tradition, Jerusalem's creation as a capital and cultic center of the newly united Israelite tribes is attributed to David, the great warrior king who conquered this hill-country settlement inhabited by Jebusites. Solomon, David's son, subsequently built the first temple to Yahweh on Mt. Moriah, also the locale of the *Akedah*, or Abraham's binding of Isaac (Genesis 22:1–24). This first temple, along with the city of Jerusalem, was razed by Nebuchadnezzar in 586 BCE and much of its population exiled. The triumphal return of these exiles several decades later marks the initial construction of a second temple to Yahweh and the gradual recreation of the Jewish spiritual center. At the end of the First Jewish Revolt (66–70 CE), Titus with his four Roman legions devastated Jerusalem and set alight the second temple built by Herod, considered one of the architectural marvels of the Roman world. During later Roman times, early Christians revered Jerusalem as the location of the crucifixion and resurrection of Jesus. Following the visit of Empress Helena to Jerusalem in 326 CE and the rise of Byzantine Christianity in the east, Jerusalem was again reinvented, this time as the spiritual capital of Christendom and a locus of pilgrimage. A third layer of sanctity was added to this city by the tradition that associates Muhammad's night journey to Masjid al-Aqsa with an earthly Jerusalem (in Qur'an Surat al-'Isra [Q 17:1]). Early Islamic Umayyad period architects, who inherited Byzantine Jerusalem and its architectural traditions, created the city's most enduring and iconic image, which dominates Jerusalem's skyline still today – the Dome of the Rock. For many, both past and present, Jerusalem is imagined as an eternal future utopia, a vision that embodies national redemption, the reign of justice, peace, and religious fulfilment. At the same time, throughout Jerusalem's contested history, it has been at the center of fierce political, social, and religious conflict.

Though often envisioned in art and literature as the "center of the world," physical Jerusalem throughout much of its history was modest in territorial and demographic size (Figure 20.1). According to the modern "demographic definition" of a city, many of Jerusalem's cities would not qualify as an urban center. Estimating the size of Jerusalem's population through the ages is particularly challenging. This is due in part to the relatively limited excavated areas of most tell sites in general, and of Jerusalem's mound in particular, and damage by later building activities such as Herod's monumental structures, which often reached bedrock, destroying earlier occupation levels. Additionally, many Bronze and Iron Age Levantine cities tended to be administrative, political, and religious centers, lacking substantial domestic quarters, with most of the population residing in the countryside. Lastly, demographic coefficients (people per hectare) used to calculate ancient population size vary wildly, ranging from 100 to 1,000 people per hectare, which is complicated further by the inability to know with any certainty the percentage of the site that served as living quarters.[1]

At first glance, Jerusalem's location on the crest of the southern Levant's remote central hill country also defies conventional wisdom regarding the development of a city. Jerusalem is not situated on a major trade route nor did it ever serve as an important manufacturing or production center. Jerusalem is not surrounded by abundant arable land or natural resources. The historic Bronze and Iron Age core of the city is surrounded on all sides by the Kidron, Hinnom, and Central (Tyropoeon) Valleys, most likely

---

[1] Regarding a summary and critique of the various coefficients used to calculate population numbers, see for example Jeffrey R. Zorn, "Estimating the Population Size of Ancient Settlements: Methods, Problems, Solutions, and a Case Study," *Bulletin of the American Schools of Oriental Research* 295 (1994), 31–48. See Magen Broshi's estimates for Jerusalem (tenth century BCE: 2,000–5,000; seventh century BCE: 25,000; first century (pre-70 CE): 80,000; sixth century CE: 55,000–60,000): Magen Broshi, "Estimating the Population of Ancient Jerusalem," *Biblical Archaeology Review* 4/2 (June 1978), 10–15. More recently, see Avraham Faust, "The Settlement of Jerusalem's Western Hill and the City's Status in Iron Age II Revisited," *Zeitschrift des Deutschen Palästina-Vereins* 121 (2005), 97–118, and a response: Hillel Geva, "The Settlement on the Southwestern Hill of Jerusalem at the End of the Iron Age: A Reconstruction Based on the Archaeological Evidence," *Zeitschrift des Deutschen Palästina-Vereins* 122 (2006), 140–50.

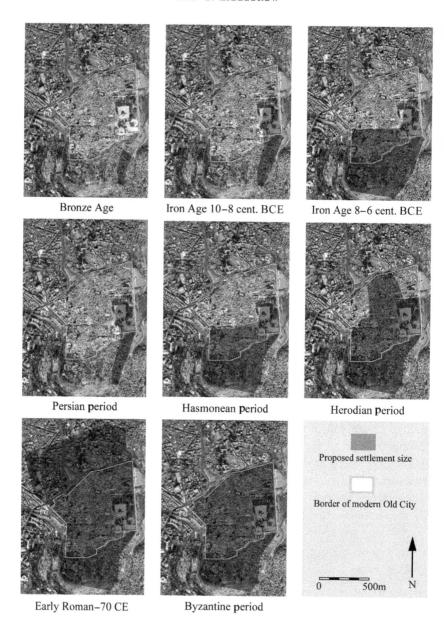

Bronze Age   Iron Age 10–8 cent. BCE   Iron Age 8–6 cent. BCE

Persian period   Hasmonean period   Herodian period

Early Roman–70 CE   Byzantine period

Proposed settlement size

Border of modern Old City

0   500m   N

Figure 20.1 Suggested settlement size of Jerusalem from the Bronze through Byzantine periods (graphics: Brandon Olson; copyright: Ann E. Killebrew).

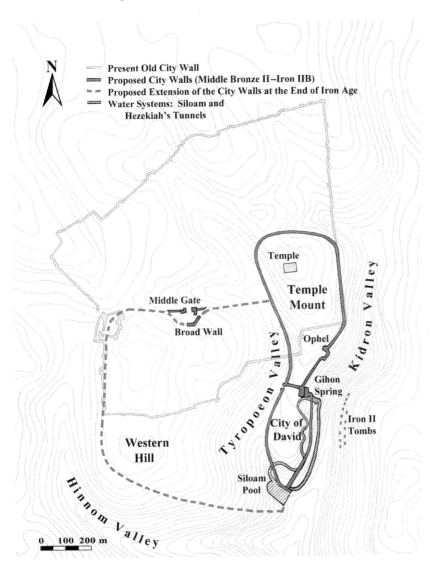

Figure 20.2 Topography and settlement size of Jerusalem during the Bronze and Iron Ages (graphics: Glynnis Fawkes; copyright: Ann E. Killebrew).

situated at this location due to its close proximity to Jerusalem's main water source, the Gihon Spring (Figure 20.2).

As part of the southern Levant, Jerusalem shared the general fate of this fragmented geographic region – located on the fringes of the great empires of the Old World, it never experienced full-blown independent state formation or the development of large, densely populated urban centers that characterize the great empires of the Near East. However, as a ritual focal point for millennia, location and function are key to Jerusalem's creation and continued significance today. Within this cultural, historical, and symbolic landscape, Jerusalem has emerged as one of the most revered and intensely examined cities in the world.

The many cities of Jerusalem

Primary sources

The most relevant primary texts describing the physical features of Jerusalem's cities discussed below include the Hebrew Bible, the New Testament, Roman and Late Antique Jewish sources (especially Josephus and, to a lesser degree, the Talmud), and Christian writings (especially Church Fathers, monks, and pilgrims). The sixth-century CE Madaba Mosaic Map that showcases Jerusalem at its center is particularly invaluable for reconstructing the basic city plan and location of key structures in Byzantine Jerusalem. In addition to descriptions based on a physical reality, there are also texts that portray an "idealized Jerusalem" town plan as in one of the Dead Sea Scrolls, referred to as the "New Jerusalem Scroll."[2]

Jerusalem is one of the most extensively explored ancient cities, and archaeology provides much of our most relevant primary information regarding the physical features of Jerusalem's cities in the past. The earliest remains of Jerusalem are located south of the Old City walls beneath the modern village of Silwan (the ancient "City of David"; Figures 20.1 and 20.2).

---

[2] Jerusalem is mentioned over 640 times in the Hebrew Bible. See for example Sara Japhet, "From the King's Sanctuary to the Chosen City," in Lee I. Levine (ed.), *Jerusalem: Its Sanctity and Centrality to Judaism, Christianity, and Islam* (New York: Continuum, 1999), pp. 3–15; and Avigdor Shinan, "The Many Names of Jerusalem," in Levine (ed.), *Jerusalem*, pp. 120–9. Jerusalem is mentioned over 140 times in the New Testament. See for example Peter W. L. Walker, *Jesus and the Holy City: New Testament Perspectives on Jerusalem* (Grand Rapids, MI: Eerdmans, 1996). Regarding Christian sources, see for example Yoram Tsafrir, "Byzantine Jerusalem: Configuration of a Christian City," in Levine (ed.), *Jerusalem*, pp. 133–50. For a discussion of Jerusalem in the Madaba Map, see for example Yoram Tsafrir, "The Holy City of Jerusalem in the Madaba Map," in Michele Piccirillo and Eugenio Alliata (eds.), *The Madaba Map Centenary, 1897–1997: Travelling through the Byzantine Umayyad Period. Proceedings of the International Conference Held in Amman, 7–9 April 1997* (Jerusalem: Studium Biblicum Franciscanum, 1999), pp. 155–63. Regarding Jerusalem as an idealized city, see for example Michael Chyutin, "The New Jerusalem: Ideal City," *Dead Sea Discoveries* 1 (1994), 71–97.

During the Iron Age and subsequent periods, Jerusalem expanded to the north and west, an area now covered by the present-day Old City and its immediate surroundings (Figure 20.1 and 20.2).[3]

Canaanite Jerusalem (Middle and Late Bronze periods)

Although Jerusalem was inhabited during the fourth and third millennia BCE, evidence for its first fortified settlement dates to the Middle Bronze II period and was significant enough to be mentioned in the Execration Texts as one of Egypt's enemies. During most of the second millennium BCE, independent city-states, each with its own local ruler, characterized Middle and Late Bronze Age urban society. Jerusalem is no exception and is typical of these second millennium BCE urban centers that served as regional administrative, political, economic, and/or cultic centers for a rural hinterland where the majority of the population resided.

Three separate archaeological expeditions, directed by Kathleen Kenyon, Yigal Shiloh, and Ronny Reich/Eli Shukron, have uncovered noteworthy segments of the Middle Bronze IIB fortification system in the City of David that were first constructed in the eighteenth century BCE. However, when this city wall went out of use is no less important and is key to our discussion of Jerusalem's cities. Excavations have revealed two city walls, one built on top of the other: an earlier Middle Bronze IIB wall and a second, but separate, Iron IIC (late eighth–seventh centuries) wall that often reused sections of the earlier fortifications. The excavators proposed that the Middle Bronze Age wall remained in use until it was rebuilt in the late eighth century BCE. Others have suggested that the Middle Bronze Age city wall fell into disrepair during the Late Bronze through much of the Iron Age (c. 1550–800 BCE). In this case, Jerusalem was fortified during the Middle Bronze IIB/C and then again only during the great expansion of the city in the later eighth century BCE when the city walls were rebuilt, utilizing the earlier remnants of the Middle Bronze wall as a solid foundation. Most recently, excavations have uncovered two monumental towers that were

---

[3] See for example multiple entries on Jerusalem in Ephraim Stern (ed.), *New Encyclopedia of Archaeological Excavations in the Holy Land* (Jerusalem: Israel Exploration Society, 1993), Vol. II, pp. 698–804, Vol. V, pp. 1,801–37, and bibliography there. For Bronze and Iron Age Jerusalem, see Jane M. Cahill, "Jerusalem at the Time of the United Monarchy: The Archaeological Evidence," in Andrew G. Vaughn and Ann E. Killebrew (eds.), *Jerusalem in Bible and Archaeology: The First Temple Period* (Atlanta: Society of Biblical Literature, 2003), pp. 13–80; and Ann E. Killebrew, "Biblical Jerusalem: An Archaeological Assessment," in Vaughn and Killebrew (eds.), *Jerusalem in Bible*, pp. 329–45; and for a summary of the various views and extensive bibliography.

part of the impressive Middle Bronze IIB/C fortification system. These towers, which testify to Jerusalem's importance during the Middle Bronze Age, were constructed to guard access to the Gihon Spring and its sophisticated public water system.[4]

Unlike the impressive and unambiguous archaeological evidence for Jerusalem in the Middle Bronze IIB–C periods, the excavated record for Jerusalem during the Late Bronze through Iron IIA periods is ambiguous and fraught with controversy. Our most important source of information regarding Jerusalem during the Late Bronze II period is a group of Amarna Letters documenting correspondence between the Egyptian pharaoh and Abdi-heba, the local ruler of Jerusalem, indicating that Jerusalem was significant to New Kingdom Egypt. Although Margareet Steiner has suggested that Jerusalem was modest in size, perhaps serving as a small Late Bronze Age fortress, Jane Cahill has argued that Jerusalem was a more significant settlement during the fourteenth and thirteenth centuries BCE. Regardless of the view one accepts, there is very little physical evidence for the Late Bronze Age Jerusalem ruled by Abdi-heba mentioned on numerous occasions in the fourteenth-century BCE Amarna archives.[5]

Jebusite and Davidic Jerusalem (Iron I and Iron IIA periods)

Debate surrounding twelfth- to ninth-century Jerusalem has only intensified during recent years. The demise of New Kingdom Egyptian imperialism in southern Canaan during the first half of the twelfth century, coinciding with the collapse of international trade networks at the end of the Late Bronze Age, marked the decline of the Canaanite city-state system. Due to the dearth of extra-biblical textual evidence for the Land of Israel during the first three centuries of the Iron Age (c. 1200–900 BCE) and contested ceramic typologies, Jerusalem is not alone in the chronological crisis facing archaeologists for the past decade.[6] In addition, many of the most promising areas

---

[4] For a recent summary and bibliographic references, see Yigal Shiloh, "The Early Period of the First Temple Period," in Stern (ed.), New Encyclopedia of Archaeological Excavations, Vol. II, pp. 701–2; and Ronny Reich and Eli Shukron, "The Gihon Spring and Eastern Slope of the City of David," in Stern (ed.), New Encyclopedia of Archaeological Excavations, Vol. V, pp. 1,801–5.

[5] For contrasting views, see Margreet L. Steiner, Excavations by Kathleen M. Kenyon in Jerusalem 1961–1967 (London: Sheffield Academic Press, 2001), Vol. III, pp. 24–41, and Cahill, "Jerusalem at the Time of the United Monarchy," pp. 27–33.

[6] For a recent overview of the debate and various interpretations of the evidence, see Amihai Mazar and Israel Finkelstein, The Quest for the Historical Israel: Debating Archaeology and the History of Early Israel. Invited Lectures Delivered at the Sixth Biennial Colloquium of the International Institute for Secular Humanistic Judaism, Detroit, October 2005 (Leiden: Brill, 2007), pp. 101–79 and bibliography there. In the discussion that

Figure 20.3 General view of the Stepped Stone Structure (photograph: Ann E. Killebrew; copyright: Ann E. Killebrew).

for excavation are below modern structures in the Silwan Village or located below Islamic monuments on the Haram al-Sharif, where tradition holds that King Solomon built the First Temple. Lastly, although Jerusalem has been extensively excavated, very few final excavation reports have been published.

Central to the debate surrounding the nature of twelfth- to ninth-century Jerusalem is the interpretation and dating of the Stepped Stone Structure, a large public structure that is a dominant feature of the Iron Age city of Jerusalem (Figure 20.3). The majority of excavators of the City of David, including Kenyon, Shiloh, Steiner, and Eliat Mazar, have dated its construction to the tenth (or tenth/ninth centuries) BCE. The only detailed documentation and final excavation report for the Stepped Stone Structure appears in Steiner's final report of Kenyon's excavations. She concludes that the terracing system, upon which the stone mantle of the Stepped Stone Structure rests, was constructed during an earlier period, possibly the Late Bronze Age. Based on this evidence, Steiner concludes that Jerusalem served as a regional administrative center during the tenth/ninth centuries BCE. Based on Shiloh's excavations of this massive rampart, Jane Cahill dates the Stepped Stone Structure several hundred years earlier, to the twelfth century BCE or to the "Jebusite" (Iron I) period. Cahill concludes that the terracing system and mantle were constructed together, and that this rampart went out of use in the tenth century when a four-room house was constructed

follows, I will use the conventional chronology for the twelfth–ninth centuries BCE. For an overview of the various interpretations, see Killebrew, "Biblical Jerusalem," pp. 339–43 and bibliography there.

into the mantle.[7] On the basis of remnants of domestic architecture, Cahill posits that tenth-century Jerusalem was larger than previously envisioned, though remarkable for its lack of public structures that one would expect based on the biblical account of Jerusalem during the United Monarchy. Although some of the most significant structures, including Solomon's Temple, theoretically could have existed on the archaeologically inaccessible Temple Mount/Haram al-Sharif compound, the missing strata dating to periods predating the ninth/eighth centuries BCE in the Southern Wall excavations seem to reinforce the view that Jerusalem was a relatively small administrative center during the tenth/ninth centuries BCE.

The most recent findings relevant to this discussion are the results of Mazar's excavations (2005–8) in the area directly behind, and above, the Stepped Stone Structure. These include the foundations of what appear to be a large public structure, which she termed the Large Stone Structure. According to Mazar, this structure dates to the tenth century, was constructed together with the Stepped Stone Structure, and may form part of a palace complex contemporary with the reigns of David and Solomon. Although several leading scholars have challenged Mazar's interpretation, if correct, her findings lend credence to the interpretation that tenth-century Jerusalem served as a regional, albeit modest, administrative center.[8]

Jerusalem – capital of the southern Kingdom of Judah (Iron IIB–C periods)

Jerusalem dramatically changed during the eighth century BCE, coinciding with abundant archaeological and textual evidence testifying to its significance as a major cultic and urban center with a large residential population, perhaps for the first time in the city's history. During this time, Jerusalem rapidly grew and expanded westward to include the western hill where today's Jewish Quarter is located (Figures 20.1 and 20.2). In the City of David, Kenyon's and Shiloh's excavations show that the eastern slope served

---

[7] See for example Steiner, *Excavations*, Vol. III, pp. 42–53; Cahill, "Jerusalem at the Time of the United Monarchy," pp. 33–66, but see Yigal Shiloh, *Excavations at the City of David I, 1978–1982: Interim Report of the First Five Seasons* (Jerusalem: Institute of Archaeology, The Hebrew University of Jerusalem, 1984), p. 17.

[8] Eilat Mazar, *The Palace of King David: Excavations at the Summit of the City of David. Preliminary Report of Seasons 2005–2007*, Ben Gordon (trans.) (Jerusalem: Shoham Academic Research, Jerusalem, 2009), pp. 43–65. Contra Mazar, see for example Israel Finkelstein, Ze'ev Herzog, Lily Singer-Avitz, and David Ussishkin, "Has King David's Palace in Jerusalem Been Found?", *Tel Aviv* 34 (2007), 142–64.

as a residential quarter of mixed neighborhoods of affluent and poorer families during the later eighth and seventh centuries BCE.[9]

Modest domestic structures dating to "before the eighth century" through the end of the Iron Age have been recently documented in the Giv'ati Parking Lot in Silwan Village, to the west of Mazar's excavations. Equally significant are the excavations by Reich and Shukron on the eastern slopes of the City of David, where they uncovered additional sections of the so-called extramural residential quarter that are in fact enclosed by previously unknown eighth- to seventh-century outer fortification walls. This lower wall, down slope from the main city wall, marks additional expansions of late Iron II Jerusalem. Continuing northward, excavations south of the Temple Mount have revealed that biblical Ophel flourished mainly during the eighth and seventh centuries BCE. A similar picture is emerging to the west of the Temple Mount. During recent excavations adjacent to the Western Wall Plaza, Shlomit Weksler-Bdolah and Alexander Onn have uncovered Late Iron Age remains including remnants of structures, probably four-room houses, and an alley constructed on top of the natural bedrock and remnants of a quarry. To the west of the Temple Mount, excavations in the Old City's Jewish Quarter provide indisputable evidence of Jerusalem's rapid expansion at the end of the eighth century BCE. They uncovered residential structures and discovered the western fortification system constructed in the late eighth century BCE that comprises a monumental city wall (the "Broad Wall") and tower. These excavations are evidence for a Late Iron Age Jerusalem that closely corresponds to the biblical account's portrayal of the city's centrality and importance during the period following the Assyrian destruction of Samaria and the northern Kingdom of Israel.[10]

---

[9] See for example Hendricus J. Franken and Margreet L. Steiner, *Excavations by Kathleen M. Kenyon in Jerusalem 1961–1967*, Vol. II (Oxford: Oxford University Press, 1990); Steiner, *Excavations*, Vol. III, pp. 54–111; and for example Donald T. Ariel and Alon De Groot, "The Iron Age Extramural Occupation at the City of David and Additional Observations on the Siloam Channel," in Donald T. Ariel (ed.), *Excavations at the City of David Directed by Yigal Shiloh* (Jerusalem: Institute of Archaeology, The Hebrew University of Jerusalem, 2000), Vol. V, pp. 155–64.

[10] For additional details regarding the expansion of Jerusalem, see for example Doron Ben-Ami and Yana Tchehanovetz, "Jerusalem, Giv'ati Parking Lot," *Hadashot Arkheologiyot: Excavations and Surveys in Israel* 120 (2008), accessed February 18, 2011, www.hadashot-esi.org.il/report_detail_eng.asp?id=873&mag_id=114; Ronny Reich and Eli Shukron, "The Urban Development of Jerusalem in the Late Eighth Century B.C.E.," in Vaughn and Killebrew (eds.), *Jerusalem in Bible*, pp. 209–18; Eliat Mazar and Benjamin Mazar, *Excavations in the South of the Temple Mount* (Jerusalem: Institute of Archaeology, The Hebrew University of Jerusalem, 1989); Shlomit Weksler-Bdolah,

The dramatic increase in the number of rock-cut family burial tombs dated to the eighth and seventh centuries BCE is an additional indicator of Jerusalem's importance, growth in population, and increased prosperity.[11] Archaeological surveys in Jerusalem's hinterland have documented an increase in the number of small settlements, including tells, fortified sites, villages, structures, agricultural installations, towers, and concentrations of sherds. This provides further evidence for the importance of Jerusalem during the Iron IIC period, which met its destruction at the hands of the Babylonians in 586 BCE.

Early Second Temple period Jerusalem
(Persian and early Hellenistic periods)

The reign of Cyrus the Great of Persia, conqueror of Babylon and the founder of the Achaemenid Empire, marks the beginning of the Persian period in the region. His edict, which allowed peoples, including the Judeans, exiled by the Babylonians to return to their homelands is celebrated in II Chronicles 36:22–33; Ezra 1:1–8; and Isaiah 44:28. According to the biblical account (Ezra 6:15–18), the second temple was built and rededicated in 515 BCE. In the mid-fifth century, Nehemiah initiated extensive building activities, including the restoration of Jerusalem's city walls (for example, Nehemiah 2:3; 12:27–43). Although the Bible provides a detailed description of the reconstruction of Jerusalem during the Persian period, few archaeological remains have been attributed to this period, giving rise to questions regarding the reliability of the biblical account. Although most scholars interpret the scant archaeological remains as an indication of a very modest Jerusalem, Mazar recently announced that she had found evidence for the building activities of Nehemiah. During her excavations in the City of David, she has proposed redating the Northern Tower and W. 27, previously interpreted as Hellenistic, to the Persian period based on artifacts

---

Alexander Onn, Briggite Ouahnouna, and Shua Kisilevitz, "Jerusalem, the Western Wall Plaza Excavations, 2005–2009: Preliminary Report," *Hadashot Arkheologiyot: Excavations and Surveys in Israel* 121 (2009), accessed February 11, 2012, www.hadashot-esi.org.il/report_detail_eng.asp?id=1219&mag_id=115; and Nahman Avigad, *Discovering Jerusalem* (Oxford: Blackwell, 1984), pp. 23–60.

[11] David Ussishkin, *The Village of Silwan: The Necropolis from the Period of the Judean Kingdom*, Inna Pommerantz (trans.) (Jerusalem: Israel Exploration Society, 1993); Itzhak Eshel and Kay Prag (eds.), *Excavations by Kathleen M. Kenyon in Jerusalem 1961–1967*, Vol. IV (Oxford: Oxford University Press, 1995), pp. 209–20; and Ronny Reich, "The Ancient Burial Ground in the Mamilla Neighbourhood, Jerusalem," in Hillel Geva (ed.), *Ancient Jerusalem Revealed: Excavations, 1993–1999* (Jerusalem: Israel Exploration Society, 2000), pp. 111–18.

below the tower, which Mazar dates to the late sixth/early fifth centuries BCE, contemporary with the reign of Nehemiah.[12]

King Herod's Jerusalem
(late Hellenistic–early Roman periods)

During the Hellenistic period, Jerusalem gradually expanded. Then, coinciding with the incorporation of Palestine within Rome's imperial sphere, the city quickly developed into a major urban center. Under King Herod (37 BCE–4 CE), the city underwent massive reconstruction and expansion. In the first century CE, Jerusalem reached its greatest territorial extent until modern times (Figures 20.1 and 20.4, lower image). Herod's monumental buildings have left their imprint on Jerusalem's landscape and topography; remnants are still visible today. Most noteworthy is Herod's renovation of the Second Temple, one of the "wonders" of the Roman world, serving as the religious, administrative, and economic focal point of his kingdom and a pilgrimage center for Jewish worship and sacrifice. Archaeological excavations and Josephus' descriptions of the first-century CE city allow for detailed reconstructions of Herod's Jerusalem (Figure 20.4, upper image).

Since 1967, large-scale archaeological projects, especially the multi-year southern and western wall excavations and Jewish Quarter excavations, as well as numerous smaller excavations in Jerusalem and its vicinity have transformed our understanding of Herod's Jerusalem. More recently, salvage excavations have uncovered additional impressive remains dating to the late Second Temple period. In the Giv'ati Parking Lot, a large architectural complex consisting of two main units including storerooms, living quarters, and *miqva'ot* indicates that this area of the City of David had an impressive residential quarter, containing a mansion that may have belonged to the family of Queen Helena of Adiabene. Other noteworthy discoveries include the remains of the Siloam Pool reservoir and a Herodian-period street and drain that connected the Temple Mount and Pool of Siloam (Figure 20.5).

---

[12] For a minimalist view of Persian period Jerusalem, see for example Israel Finkelstein, "Jerusalem in the Persian (and Early Hellenistic) Period and the Wall of Nehemiah," *Journal for the Study of the Old Testament* 32 (2008), 501–20. For a response to Finkelstein, see Oded Lipschits, "Persian Period Finds from Jerusalem: Facts and Interpretations," *Journal of Hebrew Scriptures* 9 (2009), accessed February 18, 2011, www.jhsonline.org/Articles/article_122.pdf. See also Finkelstein's rebuttal: Israel Finkelstein, "A Persian Period Jerusalem and Yehud: A Rejoinder," *Journal of Hebrew Scriptures* 9 (2009), accessed February 18, 2011, www.jhsonline.org/Articles/article_126.pdf. Regarding Mazar's recent discoveries, see Mazar, *The Palace of King David*, pp. 72–9. For an alternative view and critique, see for example Finkelstein, "Jerusalem in the Persian (and Early Hellenistic) Period," pp. 501–20.

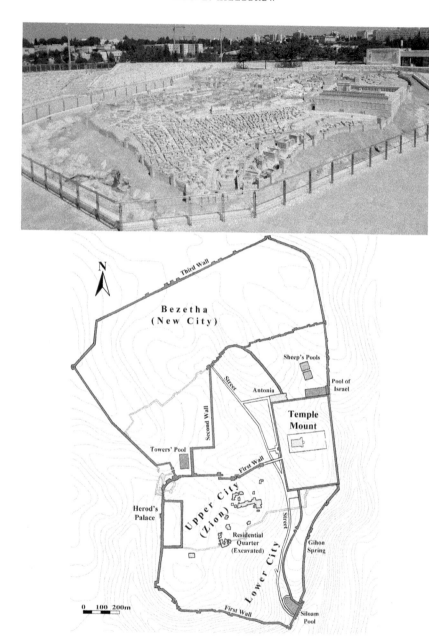

Figure 20.4 Suggested reconstruction of Jerusalem during the Second Temple period.
Upper: model of Jerusalem at the Israel Museum (photograph: Ann E. Killebrew).
Lower: plan of Jerusalem (graphics: Glynnis Fawkes; copyright: Ann E. Killebrew).

Figure 20.5 View of Herodian-period drain (photograph: Ann E. Killebrew;
copyright: Ann E. Killebrew).

This may be the type of drain, or actual drain, used by Jewish residents attempting to escape Jerusalem during the Roman conquest and destruction of Jerusalem in 70 CE as described by Josephus (*Jewish War* 7.215).[13]

Aelia Capitolina (late Roman period)

Following the destruction by Titus' legions, Josephus describes the devastation of Jerusalem as so total that "nothing was left that could ever persuade visitors that it had once been a place of habitation" (*Jewish War* 7.1.1). Over a half-century was to pass before the Emperor Hadrian declared his intention in 130 CE to reestablish a Roman colony, named Aelia Capitolina, on the ruins of Second Temple Jewish Jerusalem. Only after brutally subduing the Second Jewish Revolt in 135 CE and the expulsion of Jews from Judah did construction actually begin. The city plan was typical of Roman towns of the time with an urban grid centered on a north–south road (*cardo*) and east–west way (*decumanus*). A triple-arched gate, visible today under the present-day Damascus Gate, was located in the north of the city; however, the city was not fortified. Temples to Jupiter and Venus/Aphrodite were constructed in the newly planned city. Additional features included a forum, located at the junction of the main *cardo* and *decumanus*. The Tenth Legion was stationed in the Upper City (Western Hill), in the southwestern quadrant of the city. Recently a bathhouse has been discovered in the modern-day Jewish Quarter that is attributed to the activities of this Roman legion. Although few archaeological remains have been excavated from this period, Aelia Capitolina's typical Roman city plan formed the basic foundations for a city that shaped Jerusalem for centuries, outlines of which are still visible in Jerusalem's Old City today.[14]

---

[13] For overviews of Jerusalem during the Second Temple period, see Lee I. Levine, *Jerusalem: in the Second Temple Period (538 B.C.E.–70 C.E.)* (Philadelphia: Jewish Publication Society in cooperation with the Jewish Theological Seminary of America, 2002) and detailed bibliography. The large population of Jerusalem during the late Second Temple period is also indicated by the extensive cemeteries that have been documented, see for example Amos Kloner and Boaz Zissu, *The Necropolis of Jerusalem in the Second Temple Period* (Leuven: Peeters, 2007). For a summary of recent excavations in the Giv'ati Parking Lot, see Doron Ben-Ami and Yana Tchehanovetz, "The Lower City of Jerusalem on the Eve of Its Destruction, 70 C.E.: A View from Hanyon Givati," *Bulletin of the American Schools of Oriental Research* 364 (2011), 61–85. Regarding the Pool of Siloam, Ronny Reich and Eli Shukron, "The Pool of Siloam in Jerusalem of the Late Second Temple Period and Its Surroundings," in Katharina Galor and Gideon Avni (eds.), *Unearthing Jerusalem: 150 Years of Archaeological Research in the Holy City* (Winona Lake, IN: Eisenbrauns, 2011), pp. 241–55.

[14] See for example Yaron Z. Eliav, "The Urban Layout of Aelia Capitolina: A New View from the Perspective of the Temple Mount," in Peter Schäfer (ed.), *The Bar Kokhba*

Jerusalem – a city of Christian pilgrimage (Byzantine period)

Following the visit of the Empress Helena in the early fourth century CE, which heralded the beginning of Christian pilgrimage, Jerusalem (or Aelia as it continued to be referred to during the Byzantine period) regained its sacred status. Both contemporary texts and archaeology confirm that the general plan of Byzantine Jerusalem follows the architectural layout of Aelia Capitolina (Figure 20.6, lower image). One of the earliest accounts of the fourth-century city is recorded by the Bordeaux Pilgrim, who visited Jerusalem in *c.* 333 CE. He describes numerous Christian monuments, including the "basilica of the Lord" (Church of the Holy Sepulchre) that was being constructed by Constantine on the foundations of the Temple to Venus/Aphrodite. Prior to the arrival of Christianity in Jerusalem, the Tenth Legion had moved out of Jerusalem, providing a large area for the construction of churches, monasteries, hostels, and other religious structures. Although there is an abundance of Byzantine period writings on Jerusalem, the vast majority deal with the role of important individuals in the development of the Christian nature of the city. Secular matters and the daily life of Jerusalem's inhabitants were of little interest to these authors. Over 250 sites dating to the Byzantine period have been excavated or identified in Jerusalem. The vast majority of these remain unpublished thus greatly limiting our ability to reconstruct daily life in Byzantine Jerusalem.[15]

An indispensable source for Byzantine Jerusalem is the depiction of the city on the Madaba Map, a sixth-century CE mosaic that is located in the Church of St. George in Madaba, Jordan (Figure 20.6, upper image). This mosaic presents a detailed map of Christian sites in the Holy Land, which was apparently used by pilgrims as a guide. Jerusalem is located in the center of the map, indicating the city's centrality as the "omphalos" (navel) and most holy city of the world. The map depicts Jerusalem's city wall with twenty towers, four gates (including St. Stephen's/Damascus Gate), colonnaded roads, including the *cardo*, and forty buildings. Many of the

---

War Reconsidered: New Perspectives on the Second Jewish Revolt against Rome (Tübingen: Mohr, 2003), pp. 241–78; and Klaus Bieberstein, "Aelia Capitolina," in Zeidan Kafafi and Robert Schick (eds.), *Jerusalem before Islam* (Oxford: Archaeopress, 2007), pp. 134–68, and bibliography there. See most recently Jodi Magness, "Aelia Capitolina: A Review of Some Current Debates about Hadrianic Jerusalem," in Galor and Avni (eds.), *Unearthing Jerusalem*, pp. 313–24.

[15] For a brief summary, see for example Robert Schick, "Jerusalem in the Byzantine Period," in Kafafi and Schick, (eds.), *Jerusalem before Islam*, pp. 169–88, and bibliography there. See most recently Oren Gutfeld, "The Urban Layout of Byzantine-Period Jerusalem," in Galor and Avni (eds.), *Unearthing Jerusalem*, pp. 327–50.

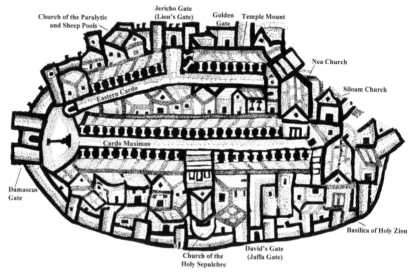

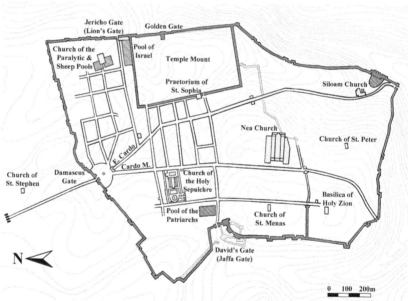

Figure 20.6 Suggested reconstruction of Jerusalem during the Byzantine period. Upper: Jerusalem as depicted on the Madaba Map (graphics: Glynnic Fawkes). Lower: plan of Jerusalem (graphics: Glynnis Fawkes; copyright: Ann E. Killebrew).

structures indicated on the map have been identified with buildings either described in contemporary sources or uncovered during archaeological excavations. Also noteworthy is what is not portrayed – the Jewish Temple Mount, which remained in ruins. There is a general consensus among scholars that this map does represent the physical reality of Jerusalem during the Byzantine period (Figure 20.6).

First and foremost Byzantine Jerusalem was a city of pilgrimage, whose main function was devoted to the "cult of holy places." As the center of Christendom, the city developed a very international character, hosting pilgrims from all over the world, both rich and poor, who stayed for varying amounts of time. Churches and monasteries and an infrastructure for accommodating the large numbers of Christian travelers seeking a religious experience dominated the city. Although greatly damaged during the short-lived Persian conquest of 614 CE, the city was renovated after the end of Sassanian occupation in 628. On the eve of the Islamic conquest, Jerusalem remained largely as it was depicted in the Madaba Map.

Bayt al-Maqdis/al-Quds (early Islamic period)

As a result of the Muslim conquest of Palestine, Jerusalem's administrative control was transferred to the Umayyad caliphs in 638 CE. The major transformation of the city from the spiritual capital of Christianity to an Islamic holy site renamed Bayt al-Maqdis (house of holiness), and later more commonly al-Quds, was the main focus of the renovation activities by the Caliphs Abd al-Malik and Walid of the Temple Mount, an area that had been in ruins for centuries. Their projects included the erection of the Dome of the Rock, the oldest standing Islamic structure in the world today, and the al-Aqsa Mosque. The Dome of the Rock, which forms the heart of the Haram al-Sharif (the Noble Sanctuary), was constructed over the rock (Sakhra) where later tradition holds that Muhammad ascended to heaven accompanied by the Archangel Gabriel. This area of bedrock is also believed by many to be the location of the Holy of Holies in the First and Second Temples. The function of the Dome of the Rock has been a topic of debate. It is noteworthy that its octagonal plan with a rotunda closely resembles commemorative Byzantine churches, most notably the Church of the Holy Sepulchre, suggesting that the Dome of the Rock may have been a commemorative structure. Others, such as Oleg Grabar, have proposed that the monument intentionally employed biblical connotations and a Christian-Byzantine architectural vocabulary to impose (or superimpose) Islam's presence in Jerusalem, a city holy to Jews and Christians. More recent interpretations have proposed that the construction of the Dome of the

Figure 20.7 View of the Umayyad-period administrative/palace structure as presented in the Jerusalem Archaeological Park (photograph: Ann E. Killebrew; copyright: Ann E. Killebrew).

Rock represented Abd al-Malik's attempts to model his sovereignty on the reigns of Kings David and Solomon, both esteemed in early Islam.[16]

The most important archaeological discovery dating to the Umayyad period is a complex of buildings situated to the west and south of the Haram al-Sharif. These include what appears to be a large administrative structure and/or palace built out of huge ashlar stones from destroyed Second Temple and Byzantine public structures (Figure 20.7). These monumental buildings probably stood several stories high and included many facilities such as a sophisticated sewerage system and bathhouse. With the exception of these structures, Umayyad building activities on the Temple Mount, and later texts dealing with the first centuries of Islam, little is known about Jerusalem during the early Arab period.[17]

---

[16] See for example Oleg Grabar, "The Meaning of the Dome of the Rock," in Marilyn J. Chiat and Kathryn L. Reyerson (eds.), *The Medieval Mediterranean: Cross-Cultural Contacts* (St. Cloud, MN: North Star Press of St. Cloud, 1988), pp. 1–10; Nasser Rabbat, "The Meaning of the Umayyad Dome of the Rock," *Muqarnas* 6 (1989), 12–21, and bibliography there; and Ofer Livne-Kafri, "On Muslim Jerusalem in the Period of Its Formation," *Liber Annuus* 55 (2005), 203–16.

[17] The excavation results for these structures have yet to be published. For a general overview, see Meir Ben-Dov, "Jerusalem," in Stern (ed.), *New Encyclopedia of Archaeological Excavations*, Vol. II, pp. 793–4. See most recently Donald Whitcomb, "Jerusalem and the Beginnings of the Islamic City," in Galor and Avni (eds.), *Unearthing Jerusalem*, pp. 399–416.

Under Umayyad rule, it is likely that Jerusalem's Christian institutions continued to flourish and the city's general plan and population remained largely unchanged as per the capitulation agreement, which prohibited the use of Christian buildings for Islamic purposes during this period.[18] What is clear is that the ambitious building projects on the former Temple Mount and the impressive administrative complex represent efforts to sanctify Jerusalem in Islamic tradition and to establish Umayyad political authority. Umayyad rule in Jerusalem left an indelible mark on the city – and still today the iconic Dome of the Rock symbolizes the multi-layered and enduring sanctity of Jerusalem.

Conclusions

For much of its contested 5,000-year history, Jerusalem has served as a central locale and crossroads for diverse populations and cultures. Biblical tradition holds that from its earliest history, this city was sacred, and it remains so today. As a result, Jerusalem has been created and recreated in stone and in imagination countless times throughout its existence. Jerusalem provides an excellent case study of multiple overlaid cities – each distinct in size, city plan, economic/political structure, and population, and each created in unique historical circumstances, cultural contexts, and ideological frameworks. Though lacking many of the criteria usually associated with the establishment of a city, what unifies these different Jerusalems over time is the belief in the sanctity of this specific geographic and physical location. In the case of Jerusalem, sanctity and ideology supersede more practical considerations that often determine a city's foundation, functioning, and development.

FURTHER READINGS

Bahat, Dan, *The Carta Jerusalem Atlas, Third Updated and Expanded Edition*, Jerusalem: Carta, 2011.
Barkay, Gabriel, and Amos Kloner, "Jerusalem Tombs from the Days of the First Temple," *Biblical Archaeology Review* 12/2 (March–April 1986), 22–39.
Benvenisti, Meron, *City of Stone: The Hidden History of Jerusalem*, Maxine Kaufman Nunn (trans.), Berkeley: University of California Press, 1996.

[18] See Gideon Avni, "From Hagia Polis to Al-Quds: The Byzantine–Islamic Transition in Jerusalem," in Galor and Avni (eds.), *Unearthing Jerusalem*, pp. 387–98.

Cahill, Jane M., "Jerusalem in David and Solomon's Time: It Really Was a Major City in the Tenth Century BCE," *Biblical Archaeology Review* 30/6 (November–December 2004), 20–31 and 62–3.

Galor, Katharina, and Gideon Avni (eds.), *Unearthing Jerusalem: 150 Years of Archaeological Research in the Holy City*, Winona Lake, IN: Eisenbrauns, 2011.

Geva, Hillel (ed.), *Jewish Quarter Excavations in the Old City of Jerusalem Conducted by Nahman Avigad, 1969–1982*, Jerusalem: Institute of Archaeology, The Hebrew University of Jerusalem, 2000, Vols. I–IV.

Gutfeld, Oren, *Jewish Quarter Excavation in the Old City of Jerusalem Conducted by Nahman Avigad, 1969–1982*, Jerusalem: Institute of Archaeology, The Hebrew University of Jerusalem, 2012, Vol. v.

Irshai, Oded, "The Christian Appropriation of Jerusalem in the Fourth Century: The Case of the Bordeaux Pilgrim," *Jewish Quarterly Review* 99 (2009), 465–86.

Kafafi, Zeidan, and Robert Schick (eds.), *Jerusalem Before Islam*, Oxford: Archaeopress, 2007.

Levine, Lee I. (ed.), *Jerusalem: Its Sanctity and Centrality to Judaism, Christianity, and Islam*, New York: Continuum, 1999.

Mayer, Tamar, and Suleiman Ali Mourad (eds.), *Jerusalem: Idea and Reality*, London: Routledge, 2008.

Mazar, Eilat, *Discovering the Solomonic City Wall in Jerusalem: A Remarkable Archaeological Adventure*, Jerusalem: Shoham Academic Research and Publication, 2011.

Reich, Ronny, *Excavating the City of David Where Jerusalem's History Begins*, Jerusalem: Israel Exploration Society, 2011.

Reich, Ronny, and Eli Shukron, "Light at the End of the Tunnel," *Biblical Archaeology Review* 25/1 (January–February 1999), 22–33 and 72.

Ritmeyer, Leen, *The Quest: Revealing the Temple Mount in Jerusalem*, Jerusalem: Carta, 2006.

Rosen-Ayalon, Miriam, *The Early Islamic Monuments of al-Haram al-Sharif: An Iconographic Study*, Jerusalem: Institute of Archaeology, The Hebrew University of Jerusalem, 1989.

Steiner, Margreet L., "The Evidence from Kenyon's Excavations in Jerusalem: A Response Essay," in Andrew G. Vaughn and Ann E. Killebrew (eds.), *Jerusalem in Bible and Archaeology: The First Temple Period*, Atlanta: Society of Biblical Literature, 2003, pp. 347–63.

"The 'Palace of David' Reconsidered in the Light of Earlier Excavations: Did Eilat Mazar Find King David's Palace? I Would Say Not," *The Bible and Interpretation* (2009), accessed February 18, 2011, www.bibleinterp.com/articles/palace_2468.shtml.

Ussishkin, David, "Big City, Few People: Jerusalem in the Persian Period," *Biblical Archaeology Review* 31/4 (July–August 2005), 26–35.

Vaughn, Andrew G., and Ann E. Killebrew (eds.), *Jerusalem in Bible and Archaeology: The First Temple Period*, Atlanta: Society of Biblical Literature, 2003.

Wasserstein, Bernard, *Divided Jerusalem: The Struggle for the Holy City*, New Haven, CT: Yale University Press, 2002.

21

City of earth and wood: New Cahokia and its material-historical implications

TIMOTHY R. PAUKETAT, SUSAN M. ALT, AND
JEFFERY D. KRUCHTEN

Imagine a continent with a vast open interior covered in prairie grasses and great temperate forests drained by an extensive river system. Imagine further that this continent had been peopled for 15 millennia, first by foragers and, later, by horticulturalists living along the interior rivers. They grew a host of starchy and oily seed crops, cucurbits, and, after 800 CE, maize, supplementing their diet with wild game. Finally, imagine that, one day, year, or decade near the beginning of the fifteenth millennium on that continent, one group of people designed and built a city – just one.

You have, of course, just imagined Cahokia, which was built midway through the eleventh century CE in the middle of North America only to be depopulated during the fourteenth century CE and, for all intents and purposes, forgotten by the time Europeans arrived (Map 21.1). Because of its seemingly historical isolation and its relationships to peoples and places that went before and came after, Cahokia may provide unique insights into the larger causal relationships between a city, its hinterlands, and its descendants. Much of what we know about this place revolves around the circumstances of its founding, which involve a convergence of diverse peoples, the formalization of religious practices, and a transformation of the rural landscape.

In this chapter, we examine these foundational circumstances in order to seek general answers to questions of cities (or at least this one city): What did this city do? What were its economic and social attributes? How did religious activity shape it and its hinterland relationships? Why was it abandoned? Our answers to such questions, we believe, point us toward a greater appreciation of the material and spatial dimensions of cities that were defined by and, in turn, defined movements of people and other things experienced. At Cahokia, in the beginning, the particular materiality of the place lent theatricality to everyday experience while, in the end, it ensured that the whole could be partitioned and forgotten. This chapter examines

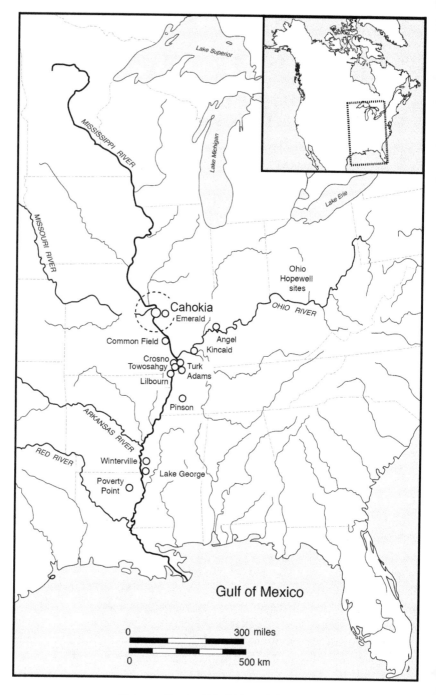

Map 21.1 Greater Cahokia's capital zone.

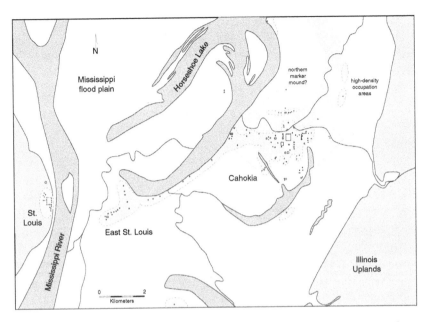

Map 21.2 Location of Greater Cahokia and other Mississippian towns mentioned.

the disposition of such features and the materiality of the process. But before examining the circumstances of its foundation, asking questions that follow from that foundation, and generalizations about materiality, we need to understand what Cahokia was.

What was Cahokia?

By 1100 CE, just fifty years into its existence as a city, Cahokia and the related complexes at East St. Louis and St. Louis sprawled irregularly across nearly 20 square kilometers of the Mississippi River floodplain and adjacent Missouri river bluffs, forming a "capital zone" (Map 21.2).[1] Site plans and excavations attest to key organizational differences between the big-three complexes, hinting that each was a distinct administrative or ritual-residential district. Within that whole, there were at least 191 earthen

---

[1] Compare B. L. Stark, "Formal Architectural Complexes in South-Central Veracruz, Mexico: A Capital Zone?," *Journal of Field Archaeology* 26 (1999), 197–226; and Michael E. Smith, "The Archaeological Study of Neighborhoods and Districts in Ancient Cities," *Journal of Anthropological Archaeology* 29 (2010), 137–54.

pyramids: 120 in Cahokia, 45 in East St. Louis, and 26 in St. Louis. There were also several major plazas and a series of apparent neighborhoods strung out archipelago-like between ancient oxbow lakes and the Mississippi River itself.

Based on counts of excavated houses and estimates of household size and building duration (calibrated by known numbers of rebuilds per fifty-year phase), estimates of maximum population sizes for the Cahokia and East St. Louis complexes range from 10,000 to 16,000 and 2,000 to 3,000, respectively.[2] St. Louis could have been comparable in size to East St. Louis. Combined, and taking into account several more small towns and a greater Cahokia region populated by farmers, 25,000 to 50,000 people may have routinely engaged or identified with the city during its early twelfth-century peak.

Up to the mid-twelfth century, Cahokia (and East St. Louis and, presumably, St. Louis) existed without one or more city walls. Rather, the cityscape was open, constructed using a close-to-cardinal orthogonal grid that provided the baselines for at least eleven major mound-and-plaza sub-groups or sub-communities, not counting East St. Louis and St. Louis. This Cahokian grid – an orthogonal configuration offset 5 degrees east of north – remained throughout the site's history once it was built into the cityscape at 1050 CE. Most of the mounds in the Cahokia and St. Louis districts were flat-topped packed-earth pyramids with rectangular outlines that were, in turn, aligned to the Cahokian grid. Another sixteen or so had rectangular shapes but "ridge-top" summits, denoting the location of a mortuary mound.[3] A few dozen more had circular perimeters, some or all with flat summits.

The Cahokia grid's north–south axis is visible today, beginning at the principal pyramid (Monks Mound) and continuing south of the primary or "Grand" plaza as a kilometer-long earthen causeway extending to a large ridge-top mound. A possible principal east–west axis was described in early historic accounts as an avenue that extended from city center eastward some 4 kilometers to a modified bluff platform, from there continuing to the

[2] Jeffrey D. Kruchten and Joseph M. Galloy, "Exploration of the Early Cahokian Residential Zone at East St. Louis," paper presented at the Midwest Archaeological Conference, Bloomington, Indiana (2010); and Timothy R. Pauketat and Neal H. Lopinot, "Cahokian Population Dynamics," in Timothy R. Pauketat and Thomas E. Emerson (eds.), Cahokia: Domination and Ideology in the Mississippian World (Lincoln: University of Nebraska Press, 1997), pp. 103–23.

[3] Melvin L. Fowler, The Cahokia Atlas: A Historical Atlas of Cahokia Archaeology (Urbana: Illinois Transportation Archaeological Research Program, University of Illinois, 1997).

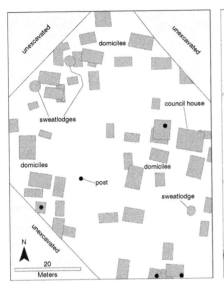

Figure 21.1 Plan views of Cahokian architecture at the East St. Louis (left) and Grossmann (right) sites, c. 1100 CE (East St. Louis image used with the permission of the Illinois State Archaeological Survey, University of Illinois at Urbana-Champaign).

outlying "Emerald" mound complex 20 more kilometers away. City boundaries may have been marked as well (shown by dashed lines in Map 21.2).

Cahokia's axial plan was likely adjusted at the sub-community or neighborhood level. Excavations in or near five of these mound-and-plaza subgroups revealed neighborhoods distinguished by subtle differences in the kinds and densities of craft production debris. Possibly, the histories, ritual duties, and kin or ethnic identities of people at Cahokia varied by neighborhood. But Cahokia's high-density residential neighborhoods, covering about 2.5 of the principal complex's 13 square kilometers, appear to have been standardized to a degree. Rectangular buildings, some with T- and L-shaped alcoves, and circular lodges or rotundas were built around small sub-community plazas and segregated from other domestic buildings. These patterns indicate a distinctly Cahokian architectural module repeated in specific locations into the countryside (Figure 21.1).[4]

[4] Susan M. Alt, "Cultural Pluralism and Complexity: Analyzing a Cahokian Ritual Outpost," unpublished Ph.D. dissertation, Department of Anthropology, University of Illinois, 2006; and Thomas E. Emerson, *Cahokia and the Archaeology of Power* (Tuscaloosa: University of Alabama Press, 1997).

All arrangements changed some over the course of 300 years, as evident when examining the alignments of pole-and-thatch buildings. Some buildings marked major astronomical happenings through their orientations, possibly indicating that certain residential sectors (or affiliated priestly surveyors) commemorated key celestial events, or the people associated with those events.[5] During the twelfth century, some of the largest public halls or great temples at Cahokia – covering up to 500 square meters with roofs supported by several large interior posts – were aligned to true cardinal directions. At the same time, the principal East St. Louis grid was different, offset *c*. 10 degrees west of north. So too were the long axes of at least five ridge-top mounds in Cahokia and East St. Louis (along with special pole-and-thatch buildings), which were aligned to extreme rising or setting positions of the moon over its long 18.6-year cycle.

Circumstances of foundation

The pre-Mississippian "Terminal Late Woodland period" (roughly pre- 1000 CE) occupation of what would become this sprawling capital zone was restricted to a small village at East St. Louis and a large one at Cahokia, home to a thousand or more residents (Table 21.1). Based on excavations in the old deposits beneath Cahokia and other villages in the region, it seems likely that public spaces within the pre-Mississippian village(s), here dubbed Old Cahokia, were yet geared toward small corporate-group aggregations. Non-local people from up to 300 kilometers away are identifiable at Old Cahokia through their locally made pottery wares. Presumably these were potters who married into prominent local families, but they might also have been entire families who relocated to Old Cahokia to enjoy its peaceful living conditions.[6]

Besides the facts of immigration and tranquility at Old Cahokia, there are two more circumstances surrounding Cahokia's "big bang" at *c*. 1050 worth mentioning. First, the decades on either side of 1050 were warmer and wetter than usual, ideal for growing bumper crops.[7] Second, the early–mid-eleventh

[5] Timothy R. Pauketat, *An Archaeology of the Cosmos: Rethinking Agency and Religion in Ancient America* (London: Routledge, 2013).

[6] Susan M. Alt, "Complexity in Action(s): Retelling the Cahokia Story," in Susan M. Alt (ed.), *Ancient Complexities: New Perspectives in Precolumbian North America* (Salt Lake City: University of Utah Press, 2010), pp. 119–37.

[7] Larry Benson, Timothy R. Pauketat, and Edward Cook, "Cahokia's Boom and Bust in the Context of Climate Change," *American Antiquity* 74 (2009), 467–83.

Table 21.1 *Chronology chart of the Pre-Columbian American Midwest*

Year CE/BCE	Era	Time period	Civic-ceremonial centers mentioned in text	Major development
1350 CE	Mississippian	Late Mississippian	southeast Missouri towns	Cahokia depopulated
1250 CE			Angel, Kincaid New Cahokia	Cahokia palisade built
1050 CE		Early Mississippian		
950 CE	pre-Mississippian	Terminal Late Woodland	Old Cahokia	Cahokia's "big bang" immigration into Cahokia region
850 CE		Late Woodland	none	
750 CE				
650 CE				
550 CE				
450 CE		Middle Woodland (aka Hopewell)	Hopewell (Ohio), Pinson (Tennessee) Great Hopewell enclosures in Ohio	
350 CE				
250 CE				
150 CE				
50 CE				
50 BCE				
150 BCE				

Figure 21.2 Downtown Cahokia showing principal pyramids and plaza (outlined by dashed line).

century was a period of great celestial activity: prominent comets, meteor showers, and supernovae made appearances. The Supernova of 1054 in particular might have incited politico-religious gatherings, constructions, or other sorts of commemorative activity. Whatever the combination of circumstances, Old Cahokia underwent a dramatic, fast-paced reconstruction at c. 1050. Around that date, a new public precinct – "Downtown Cahokia" – was constructed, comprised of a central 20-hectare Grand Plaza, large perimeter pyramids surmounted by pole-and-thatch architecture, and associated residential neighborhoods (Figure 21.2). Recent conservative estimates of the person-days involved in leveling and raising a third of that plaza exceed 10,000.[8] Off to one side, extensive sealed deposits beneath Mound 51 attest to great late eleventh-century politico-religious festivals. Here is a rich sequence of great autumnal feasts involving hundreds to thousands of butchered white-tailed deer, thousands of pots full of cooked pumpkin soups

[8] Susan M. Alt, Jeffrey D. Kruchten, and Timothy R. Pauketat, "The Construction and Use of Cahokia's Grand Plaza," *Journal of Field Archaeology* 35 (2010), 131–46.

and seed porridges, the smoking of much tobacco, the debarking of great cypress posts, and the making, using, and discarding of sumptuary goods and ritual objects.[9] The spatial extent of the Cahokia site expanded considerably as the population quickly reached 10,000 or more people.

What did this city do?

The result we dub "New Cahokia," and nothing like it had existed before 1050 north of Mexico. Indeed, nothing like it would exist again until the expansion of New York and Philadelphia after 1785. But Cahokia was heir to a millennia-old tradition of lightly populated ceremonial centers. Some of these were quite large. For instance, the central grounds of the great Archaic era site of Poverty Point covered more than 100 hectares at 1500 BCE, occupied by perhaps several hundred people at one point. Later in time, the great enclosure at the 2,000-year-old Hopewell site covered 49 hectares. The contemporary Middle Woodland complex at Pinson, Tennessee (c. 100 BCE–400 CE), covered 160 hectares, but had few long-term inhabitants. Other great embanked enclosures of the Middle Woodland Hopewell peoples in Ohio covered 8–20 hectares and were sometimes clustered together.[10]

All such places – and there were many hundreds down through the millennia in eastern North America – may have been emplaced religious movements: short-term reinventions of age-old religious practices centered on prophets or happenings. Cahokia was heir to this legacy, and one might reasonably look to religion to understand the circumstances of its beginnings. But Cahokia was also unlike these earlier places. It was the first center with a dense population that sprawled across a tripartite civic-ceremonial complex. It was the first with an integrated orthogonal plan and possible neighborhood or modular standardization, its baselines consisting of rows of quadrilateral packed-earth pyramids and avenues, plazas, and marker posts. And Cahokia was probably the first center to have its design extended into a hinterland.

It is in its hinterland that the history of New Cahokia may be more fully exposed. Much of the surrounding countryside was sparsely occupied before

[9] Timothy R. Pauketat, Lucretia S. Kelly, Gayle J. Fritz, Neal H. Lopinot, Scott Elias, and Eve Hargrave, "The Residues of Feasting and Public Ritual at Early Cahokia," *American Antiquity* 67 (2002), 257–79.
[10] Ephraim G. Squier and Edwin G. Davis, *Ancient Monuments of the Mississippi Valley* (Washington, D.C.: Smithsonian Institution Contributions to Knowledge, 1848), Vol. 1.

and after its 1050–1200 CE heyday, leaving patterns of development closer to the surface. Of these, there are four to be highlighted: (1) traditional floodplain-village farmlands 20 kilometers to the north and south of New Cahokia were reorganized; (2) upland forests and prairie-edge savannah lands east (and presumably west) of New Cahokia were brought under cultivation by relocated if not immigrant farmers; (3) at least two distinctive religious complexes, and a number of other minor towns or ceremonial centers, were constructed within a 50-kilometer radius of the city; and (4) Cahokian religious practices were emplaced across the region via architecture (within nodal farmsteads or villages) and the associated performance and production of religion and religious things, respectively, especially through theatrical mortuary rites. This kind of ruralization in the Cahokia region suggests to us an intensified economy of cosmic performance, procession, and pilgrimage.

The first two patterns have been discussed at length elsewhere. Suffice it to note here that the 1050 CE founding moment is readily identifiable near Cahokia as abandonments of pre-Mississippian hamlets and villages, usually replaced by single-family farmsteads.[11] In the uplands to the east, a host of villages, farmsteads, and special religious sites were built, some in locales that had been nearly devoid of inhabitants before 1050. Immigrants were among the relocated settlers as were higher-status Cahokians and their ritual architecture.[12] Presumably, Cahokian priests were on site and instrumental in the construction of many such places. Included among these, and the third hinterland pattern, are a series of suspected lunar temple complexes 20 to 25 kilometers east of the city. Two of three major complexes were founded at or slightly before 1050. The characteristics of all three contrast markedly with a "ritual-administrative" outpost just 8–12 kilometers to their southwest.[13] This outpost, the Grossmann site, highlights the fourth pattern, seen throughout the countryside and back at New Cahokia. The architecture of Cahokian religion or politico-religious administrators – oversized homes, medicine lodges, council buildings, ancestral temples, a charnel building, storage houses, a possible mortuary scaffold, and marker posts – crowded the hilltop site. Its readily identifiable T- and L-shaped buildings and the circular sweatlodges are known elsewhere in the uplands, but all

[11] Emerson, *Cahokia*.
[12] Susan M. Alt, "Identities, Traditions, and Diversity in Cahokia's Uplands," *Midcontinental Journal of Archaeology* 27 (2002), 217–36.
[13] Susan M. Alt, "Cultural Pluralism and Complexity."

such buildings were constructed in the greater Cahokia region only from 1050–1200 CE. At this site and elsewhere, such building complexes were associated with deposits of ritual objects derived from discrete events, perhaps like the festivals of Cahokia. As at Cahokia, craft debris at the hinterland sites is non-randomly distributed in concentrated deposits, as if production occurred as part of periodic religious gatherings.

Given their exceptional organizational characteristics, proximity, and suggestive indications of periodic processions, occupations, or craft production events, it is unlikely that any of these outlier complexes were simply towns or secondary centers that duplicated the administrative functions of the others (as in pre-state political-economic models). Rather, like the Cahokian capital zone itself, the outlier settlement districts betray organizational complementarities. As already described, such an ordered diversity – not present before 1050 CE and gone after 1200 – characterized the entire region.

Such a regional order might be attributed in large part to the great annual festivals that brought many thousands of worshippers into the Grand Plaza. But the most significant religious rite may not have been an annual affair but rather one scheduled every few years. It consisted of theatrical mortuary performances where multiple young adults, mostly women, were sacrificed. Such rites entailed the use of bodies, living and dead, and material props in the retelling of cosmic legends, likely including the stories of a female fertility deity. Importantly, in the only well-documented case (Mound 72), the sacrificial women were either born of immigrant families or were foreign captives.[14] Moreover, the mortuary sites and the subsequent ridge-top mounds were apparently public and open, the subject of repeated commemorations possibly attended by many from the region (Figure 21.3).

Thus, while the city of New Cahokia (like most later Mississippian towns) may be said to be a "diagram" of fundamental cosmic relationships,[15] that diagram was not a static template but a series of performed or lived relationships. And such relationships extended out into a hinterland. Indeed, we may conceive of the Cahokian landscape in relational terms such that human movement through it constructed the metaphors

---

[14] Susan M. Alt, "Unwilling Immigrants: Culture, Change, and the 'Other' in Mississippian Societies," in Catherine M. Cameron (ed.), *Invisible Citizens: Slavery in Ancient Pre-State Societies* (Salt Lake City: University of Utah Press, 2008), pp. 205–22; and Melvin L. Fowler, Jerome Rose, Barbara van der Leest, and Steven R. Ahler, *The Mound 72 Area: Dedicated and Sacred Space in Early Cahokia* (Springfield: Illinois State Museum, 1999).

[15] Spiro Kostof, *The City Shaped: Urban Patterns and Meanings through History* (Boston: Little, Brown, and Company, 1991).

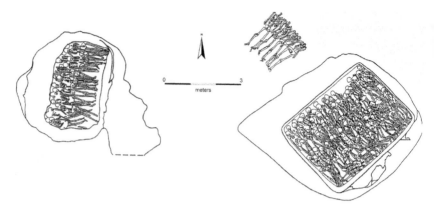

Figure 21.3 Select mortuary features in Mound 72: Left, pit containing twenty-two females buried atop former upright post. Right, four headless and handless males adjacent to pit containing fifty-three females (from Melvin L. Fowler *et al.* 1999, *The Mound 72 Area: Dedicated and Sacred Space in Early Cahokia* [Springfield: Illinois State Museum, 1999] used with permission of the Illinois State Museum).

of social life. In other words, it was by design the *axis mundi* of a complex cosmic order. No doubt, performances and movements were intended to lend an organic quality to the whole. (See Part I of this volume, "Cities as arenas of performance"). Likewise, performances of the regional order doubtless had an economic dimension. But New Cahokia was fundamentally about proffering the cosmos to its citizens, immigrants, and visitors. The cosmos in turn articulated identities, beliefs, and history and, to some extent, transformed people into a greater community.

Why was it abandoned?

The construction of a palisade wall shortly after 1150 CE was probably the harbinger of significant cultural change. More than likely, it was not designed strictly to protect economic resources. But its construction does indicate that, by 1200, Cahokian relationships proper were significantly reconfigured and downsized. In the following decades, the population of Cahokia proper would fall to between 1,000 to 3,500 people. At that time, the focus of Cahokian ceremonial life was the site's East Plaza.

As important as its diminution was the region-wide disappearance of New Cahokia's ritual architecture. After 1200 CE, the distinctive medicine lodges, circular sweatlodges, square council houses, and the oversized public buildings that characterized twelfth-century New Cahokia were not rebuilt. Among the last of these was a burned sweat lodge at an outlying rural "node" or shrine with a calibrated radiocarbon intercept of 1168 CE.[16] Instead of these buildings, only larger-than-average rectangular buildings were built for use as corporate meeting halls or temples. The largest such public or religious buildings – which date to the decades just after 1200 – cover no more than 90 square meters.

Such pervasive architectural changes might well have been related to an event at the East St. Louis site. Up to the 1160s, based on calibrated radiocarbon assays, East St. Louis seems to have been home to elite families living in overbuilt residential areas, including one walled compound, in association with council houses, medicine lodges, great open meeting halls or residences, storage buildings, oversized marker posts, and rotundas. However, some time around the 1160s, much of East St. Louis appears to have been burned down, likely an intentional if not ritually staged act. After that conflagration in the late twelfth century, large portions of the site were emptied. To the best of our knowledge, only two mounds and no off-mound buildings were constructed afterwards.[17]

There was occupational continuity during this critical phase at Cahokia and in the countryside, but a regional transformation of some sort had taken place, and its effects were felt at all levels of social life. For instance, mundane culinary and technological practices were simplified at about the same time and seemingly over a span of a few decades or less. By the end of it, c. 1275 CE, Cahokia had dwindled to a minor Mississippian capital town, albeit one that might have loomed large in its descendants' memories. The demise of Cahokia proceeded rapidly thereafter. By 1350, Cahokia was completely abandoned and, at European contact, forgotten. Proximate and ultimate reasons for the decline of Cahokia are difficult to sort out, but a loss of faith, a failure of leadership, destructive wars, factional competition, drought, and long-term climatic shifts remain in the mix.

If the answers to why Cahokia and its region were abandoned are, at present, unanswerable, understanding how it was abandoned may be within our reach. To wit, the region-wide conflagration event at East St. Louis

---

[16] Douglas K. Jackson and Philip G. Millhouse, *The Vaughn Branch and Old Edwardsville Road Sites* (Champaign-Urbana: Illinois Transportation Archaeological Research Program, 2003).

[17] Timothy R. Pauketat, *The Archaeology of the East St. Louis Mound Center* (Urbana: Illinois Transportation Archaeological Research Program, University of Illinois, 2005–7), Part 1; and Andrew C. Fortier, *The Archaeology of the East St. Louis Mound Center*, Part 2.

suggests something more than an inexorable slide into oblivion. There may have been a planned break-up of the tripartite capital zone, perhaps along the sub-community fault lines that existed throughout the region's history. Such a break-up might have entailed social or political segments emigrating at different moments out of the region, a possibility consistent with both regional demographic trends and the migration stories of possible offshoot populations. Intriguingly, after 1200, more than a dozen new Mississippian towns were founded to the south of the greater Cahokia region, and we might look to them for answers. These later towns, in southeast Missouri and western Kentucky, might have been founded by Cahokian émigrés. Each was home to hundreds of people between c. 1,200 and 1,400, and all possessed a common set of attributes: large pyramidal mounds fronted town plazas surrounded in turn by smaller platforms, orthogonally arranged houses, and a circumferential palisade wall.

It is plausible that some of these downriver town attributes were based on Cahokian practices. This is because orthogonally oriented rectangular buildings are not common to all Mississippian towns in the South. Moreover, the sizes of Mississippian towns across the South varied considerably. Large post-1100 contemporaries of Cahokia along the Ohio River – Angel and Kincaid – each cover more than 40 hectares and have two major plazas and impressive palisade walls. The largest capital towns in the Lower Mississippi Valley also have two plazas and circumferential walls enclosing impressive earthen pyramids, a double plaza complex, and residences. By comparison, the Missouri and western Kentucky towns cover from about 7 to 20 hectares, close to the same size as an average Cahokian mound-and-plaza sub-community.

Southeast Missouri towns also betray greater Cahokia's astronomical obsessions and, possibly at Common Field and Lilbourn, the celestial angles, with some obvious adjustments for landscape features or bodies of water, are evident at Adams, Turk, and Towosaghy, all possibly built using a common plan. Importantly, Cahokia-style circular sweatlodges are known from excavations at Lilbourn and Crosno to postdate the last in the greater Cahokia region. These may hint that the sodalities or priesthoods responsible for these ritual buildings had moved from Cahokia to southeast Missouri and western Kentucky.

Then again, free-standing marker posts, like those in Cahokia's capital zone or the outlying towns of greater Cahokia are not known from modest excavations in southeast Missouri or western Kentucky, whether singly, in rows, or in Woodhenge circles. Likewise, there were no ridge-top mounds or sacrificial ceremonies outside of greater Cahokia, with the possible exception of Mound C at the more distant Shiloh site (which also featured a carved Cahokian smoking pipe). Finally, Cahokia-style medicine lodges are not yet identified at any of the southern centers, although the houses of Mississippian leaders in the historic era Lower Mississippi Valley reportedly featured interior alcoves similar to Cahokia's medicine lodges.

Unfortunately, the excavated samples from the candidate downriver towns are inadequate for reaching any definitive conclusions about their relationships to the abandoned city of Cahokia. Suffice it to say that the later Missouri and western Kentucky towns are comparable in ways suggestive of historical linkages and at the same time a selective forgetting of key Cahokian ritual architecture and practices. Presumably, the commemoration of some Cahokian practices or ritual organizations among descendant communities could have been a function of either an intentional rejection of aspects of their Cahokian heritage or unintentional losses owing to the exigencies of emplacing traditional practices in new lands.

Why was it forgotten?

The demise of Cahokia was perhaps contingent in significant respects on the materiality of memory work. By this we mean to say that the production, enactment, performance, or erasure of social memories, which are at the root of all human cultures, political institutions, identities, city plans, etc., have a material dimension. But that materiality might vary in its experiential qualities, being more or less visible, audible, tangible, or durable, among other things. These differences may have been critical to the legacies of cities and towns in both ancient and contemporary times.

Given the earthen and wooden materials used in most Cahokian constructions, the great architecture, administrative buildings, and religious spaces of this precocious indigenous city were probably destined for obsolescence. Even if people attempted to transfer or re-place it elsewhere, as possibly in the downriver towns, it is unclear how they might have done so generation after generation. Presumably, pilgrims who might have made the trek back to the ancient city increasingly based their own memories of the place on stories of others and, thus, would have lacked the ability to reimagine and recommemorate the depopulated city, especially after 1200. Too much of it had moldered to dust, its pyramids eroding into mounds grown over with grass and saplings. Absent that ability, descendants were unavoidably and increasingly alienated from their own legacy.

Of course, it is also possible that this alienation and forgetting may have been part of a willful rejection of this particular indigenous experiment with urbanization. That experiment appears to have involved some extreme ritual practices, such as human sacrifice, that were hosted, planned, and carried out by someone with authority far in excess of that which existed in the pre-Mississippian era. Presumably, such authority was vested in a series of persons, ruling councils, or priestly elites and derived from the cosmic powers embodied by Cahokia, its monuments and outlier complexes, and its people. If that administration (whether comprised of political elites, influential families, or powerful priests) was ever perceived to have violated some sacred trust or to have lost their supernatural sanctions, pilgrims might have ceased coming to Cahokia. Farmers might have left the region. The entire experiment in indigenous urbanism could have been rejected, with descendants seeking to forget Cahokia.

Just such a willful rejection seems apparent in Cahokia's Puebloan contemporary, Chaco Canyon in northwestern New Mexico. Although not as populous as Cahokia, the Chacoan phenomenon (850–1150 CE) appears as a series of great politico-religious movements that transformed the Southwest. A network of monumental, masonry "Great Houses" were the focus of Chacoan public ceremony and were destinations for pilgrims from across the Southwest.[18] Intriguingly, oral traditions remain among contemporary Puebloan people that seem to tell of their rejection of the concentration of power in the hands of a few Chacoan leaders.[19] But Chacoan Great Houses were not completely forgotten, and there is evidence of later Puebloan shrines and visitors to the ruins of Chaco Canyon.[20] Given Chaco's durable materiality of stone, such visitors have been able to remember never to repeat Chaco.

---

[18] Stephen H. Lekson, *The Archaeology of Chaco Canyon: An Eleventh-Century Pueblo Regional Center* (Santa Fe, NM: School for Advanced Research Press, 2006); Barbara J. Mills, "Remembering While Forgetting: Depositional Practices and Social Memory at Chaco," in Barbara J. Mills and William H. Walker (eds.), *Memory Work: Archaeologies of Material Practices* (Santa Fe, NM: School for Advanced Research Press, 2008), pp. 81–108; and Ruth M. van Dyke, *The Chaco Experience: Landscape and Ideology at the Center Place* (Santa Fe, NM: School for Advanced Research Press, 2007).

[19] Stephen H. Lekson, "The Abandonment of Chaco Canyon, the Mesa Verde Migrations, and the Reorganization of the Pueblo World," *Journal of Anthropological Archaeology* 14 (1995), 184–202.

[20] William D. Lipe, "The Mesa Verde Region during Chaco Times," in David G. Noble (ed.), *The Mesa Verde World: Explorations in Ancestral Puebloan Archaeology* (Santa Fe, NM: School of American Research Press, 2006), pp. 29–37.

Conclusion

Similar sustained memory work was more difficult at Cahokia just decades after its depopulation. Yet, in its time, New Cahokia appears to have had profound cultural effects on eastern North America. Knowing what we do now, it would be difficult to imagine, for instance, the same historic configuration of Indian nations and tribes in the Midwest, Midsouth, and eastern Plains had Cahokia never coalesced. Similarly, various pan-tribal religious societies and widespread ceremonial practices were probably contingent on the rise and fall of Cahokia.

Not everyone agrees. Seemingly contradictory arguments have been made about New Cahokia by archaeologists seeking to explain its impacts on the Pre-Columbian history of eastern North America. On the one hand, some contend that Cahokia was simply a later and larger-than-normal expression of a millennia-old, pan-eastern pattern of large centers undergirded by mythic cultural continuities. On the other hand, in its foundations others see an historical disjuncture of sorts, involving the construction of something new in the form of Cahokia based on shadows of the past. Some of the shadows might even extend to Mesoamerica.

Advocates of the various points of view might agree that, regardless of the degree to which one sees continuity or change, New Cahokia was about the performance of religion. Intellectual disagreements reside in the historical implications attached to that religion. If Mississippian religion is understood as a relatively static belief system, then Cahokia may have little to tell us about that which similar cities did around the world. However, if we understand Cahokian religion as a dynamic component of urbanization, reinvented or reimagined during performances that ultimately altered the political, social, and economic lives of people in distant lands, then the extensive and immediate sub-continental effects of New Cahokia may argue for the need to more closely examine religion as the basis of governance and the reason for the rise and fall of cities.

Certainly, New Cahokia's foundational redesign, the organized diversity of its capital zone, its standardized yet shifting neighborhood alignments, and its mortuary theatrics are similar to other early cities around the world. Ultimately, Cahokia's history was contingent on the expansion of maize production by resettled and reorganized locals and immigrant families. But the legacy of Cahokia, or lack thereof, may be rooted in the materiality of its construction. Cahokia's earthen and wooden construction materials defined the field of memory work and constrained the futures of its descendants, which might have been quite different had only the Cahokians worked in stone rather than earth and wood.

FURTHER READINGS

Black, Glenn A., *Angel Site: An Archaeological, Historical, and Ethnological Study*, Indianapolis: Indiana Historical Society, 1967.

Cole, Fay-Cooper, Robert Bell, John Bennett, Joseph Caldwell, Norman Emerson, Richard MacNeish, Kenneth Orr, and Roger Willis, *Kincaid: A Prehistoric Illinois Metropolis*, Chicago: The University of Chicago Press, 1951.

Dalan, Rinita A., George R. Holley, William I. Woods, Harold W. Watters, Jr., and John A. Koepke, *Envisioning Cahokia: A Landscape Perspective*, DeKalb: Northern Illinois University Press, 2003.

Emerson, Thomas E., "An Introduction to Cahokia: Diversity, Complexity, and History," *Midcontinental Journal of Archaeology* 27 (2002), 127–48.

Emerson, Thomas E., Timothy R. Pauketat, and Susan M. Alt, "Locating American Indian Religion at Cahokia and Beyond," in Lars Fogelin (ed.), *Religion, Archaeology, and the Material World*, Carbondale: Center for Archaeological Investigations, Southern Illinois University, 2008, pp. 216–36.

Holley, George R., "Late Prehistoric Towns in the Southeast," in Jill E. Neitzel (ed.), *Great Towns and Regional Polities in the Prehistoric American Southwest and Southeast*, Albuquerque: University of New Mexico Press, 1999, pp. 22–38.

Milner, George R., *The Cahokia Chiefdom: The Archaeology of a Mississippian Society*, Washington, D.C.: Smithsonian Institution Press, 1998.

Pauketat, Timothy R., *Cahokia: Ancient America's Great City on the Mississippi*, New York: Penguin Press, 2009.

Chiefdoms and Other Archaeological Delusions, Walnut Creek, CA: AltaMira, 2007.

"Resettled Farmers and the Making of a Mississippian Polity," *American Antiquity* 68 (2003), 39–66.

22

Imagined cities

TIMOTHY R. PAUKETAT, ANN E. KILLEBREW,
AND FRANÇOISE MICHEAU

Some cities were imagined, designed, and created wholly or partially in ways that forever shaped their histories and the identities, governments, religions, and economies of their citizens. These include the great cities of Jerusalem, Baghdad, and Cahokia. They also include other imperial capitals (similar to Baghdad), lesser territorial centers, and religious complexes and pilgrimage centers (such as Jerusalem and Cahokia). Whatever they were and however they developed later in time, the details of their founding, along with the momentous and monumental constructions that redesigned or redefined various sectors within them make them case studies in the historical processes surrounding cities and their regional and continental effects.

Here, we seek to outline the commonalities, juxtaposed against the distinguishing features, of Jerusalem, Baghdad, and Cahokia in ways that draw out those processes. The multi-layered "eternal" city of Jerusalem, imperial Baghdad silenced for centuries before reemerging in the twentieth century, precocious Cahokia virtually evaporating in history: What was it about the creation of these places that transcended their histories? What was different in each case, such that their developmental outlines diverged? Comparisons with other cities will help us to focus on the reasons for such similar processes and divergent histories.

Foundational theories

To be clear, the extent that any city, city district, and city building, public space, or monument was designed and executed by people is the extent to which imagination and memory work need to be considered alongside the political, economic, and urban processes that produced the world's great places.[1]

---

[1] Barbara Bender (ed.), *Landscape: Politics and Perspectives* (London: Berg, 1983); Suzanne Küchler, "Landscape as Memory: The Mapping of Process and Its Representation in a

Great public and urban spaces may be designed with some greater social or cosmic order in mind.[2] They might inscribe the mythos or memories of a people, an event, or another place into their spaces.[3] But they also have experiential qualities that affect human emotions, knowledge, and institutions in unintended ways.[4] They might even be designed as imaginaries, which is to say as places where futures are actively reimagined or where people come to interact with their gods.[5]

Such imaginary potential might be purposive or not. It might also be realized by some but not all people, depending on their experiences of city spaces and monuments. Certainly, the sensuous dimensions of city spaces, including the things in them and the physical characteristics of them, can produce varying perceptions and understandings depending on who they were and why they were there.[6] In the same way, the experience of urban spaces might discipline the body, or clothe it with memories and sensibilities mundane and monumental.[7] Cities, that is, are the grounds for much embodied knowledge, that which is done because the body has learned to do it as second nature.[8] The merger of such embodied knowledge with governance becomes the basis of political authority.[9]

Indeed, we might consider these alternately commemorative or imagined qualities of city spaces in more purely political, social, and economic terms. The merger of embodied knowledge and governance, for instance, might be read as an intentional political strategy of city planners. The effect of life in

---

Melanesian Society," in Bender (ed.), *Landscape*, pp. 85–106; and Nick Shepherd and Christian Ernsten, "The World Below: Post-Apartheid Imaginaries and the Bones of the Prestwich Street Dead," in Noëleen Murray, Nick Shepherd, and Martin Hall (eds.), *Desire Lines: Space, Memory and Identity in the Post-Apartheid City* (London: Routledge, 2007), pp. 215–32.

[2] Paul Wheatley, *The Pivot of the Four Quarters* (Chicago: Aldine, 1971).

[3] Paul Connerton, *How Societies Remember* (Cambridge: Cambridge University Press, 1989).

[4] Gaston Bachelard, *The Poetics of Space: The Classic Look at How We Experience Intimate Places* (Boston: Beacon Press, 1994); and Henri Lefebvre, *The Production of Space*, Donald Nicholson-Smith (trans.) (Oxford: Blackwell, 1991).

[5] Shepherd and Ernsten, "The World Below," pp. 215–32.

[6] Susan Kus, "The Social Representation of Space: Dimensioning the Cosmological and the Quotidian," in James A. Moore and Arthur S. Keene (eds.), *Archaeological Hammers and Theories* (New York: Academic Press, 1983), pp. 277–98.

[7] Michel de Certeau, *The Practice of Everyday Life* (Berkeley: University of California Press, 1984).

[8] Rosemary A. Joyce and Lynn M. Meskell, *Embodied Lives: Figuring Ancient Maya and Egyptian Experience* (London: Routledge, 2003).

[9] Susan Kus, "Sensuous Human Activity and the State: Towards an Archaeology of Bread and Circuses," in Daniel Miller (ed.), *Domination and Resistance* (London: Unwin Hyman, 1989), pp. 140–54.

456

urban spaces, on the other hand, is a social process that might complicate the best-laid political intentions by introducing alternate motivations rooted in gender, class, ethnicity, and the like. So too would such complications have their own economy, with futures constrained by genealogies of social trans-actions, the relative success of exchanges in the marketplace, or even the biographies of specific things (precious stones, heirlooms, or magical objects).

Saying all of this is simply to caution against any simplistic reading of the foundations of cities, especially those such as Jerusalem, Baghdad, and Cahokia where the reasons for their initial establishment might seem apparent to us today. Simple measures of a city's historical developmental patterns might allow us to gauge the degree to which such cautions are warranted. In his study of Urartian cityscapes, Adam Smith focused on the relative uniformity or diversity of cities through a comparative-historical study of the symmetries and distributions of city plans.[10] We might approach Jerusalem, Baghdad, and Cahokia similarly.

However, we also will consider the legacy effect of the materials used to construct cities. We do this because the media through which people live their lives and, especially, build their cities are bound to constrain not only the immediate futures of cities, but also the long-term legacies of those cities. That is, if the histories of Jerusalem, Baghdad, and Cahokia were strongly influenced by the circumstances surrounding their foundations, then their legacies – how they were remembered or whether they might be forgotten – were based in part on their construction materials: stone, mudbrick, earth, or wood. In such ways, we may begin to ground the theories of our imagined cities in the hard realities of their foundations.

Foundational developments

In some ways, the foundations of Jerusalem, Baghdad, and Cahokia were very similar. All experienced intensive construction phases based to some extent on connections that people made between themselves and the cosmos. Although the foundations of these three cities are a result of different cultural imaginings in space and time, all three share a sense of cosmic order and destiny that is expressed tangibly and intangibly. In the case of Jerusalem and Cahokia, pilgrims traveled to these centers to engage the numinous in some way. The same is less true of Baghdad, although the

---

[10] Adam T. Smith, *The Political Landscape: Constellations of Authority in Early Complex Polities* (Berkeley: University of California Press, 2003).

city was said to have been founded in accordance with God's plan and its spatial order evinces a plan based on the cosmic principles that undergirded the Abbasid Caliphate.

Archaeological excavations reveal that Jerusalem was already inhabited by the fourth millennium BCE. Tradition holds that, long before Solomon erected his temple to early Israel's god on Mt. Moriah, Abraham (the father of three monotheistic religions: Judaism, Christianity, and Islam) offered up his son Isaac (or Ishmael according to Islamic belief) to God. This event, followed by the biblical account of the selection of Jerusalem by King David as his religious, administrative, and political capital, marks the beginning of Jerusalem's transformation into a spiritual center that remains a powerful symbol in the imagination of countless cultures and one of the world's most contested cities.

The physical development of Jerusalem has not always followed its imagined history. As is typical of many ancient sites in the region, Jerusalem emerged as a major urban and fortified center during the Middle Bronze Age (first half of the second millennium BCE). Though mentioned numerous times in the fourteenth-century BCE Amarna Letters, there is scant evidence for Late Bronze Age Jerusalem. The material remains and nature of Jerusalem during the tenth-century BCE United Monarchy, which is portrayed in the biblical account as a magnificent holy city built by Solomon, are ambiguous and remain a topic of heated debate.[11] Only several centuries later, during the late eighth and seventh centuries BCE, does the archaeological evidence correspond to the literary descriptions of Jerusalem as a major cultic, administrative, and political center.

The later ebbs and flows of Jerusalem's past reflect the region's tumultuous history and occupation by numerous empires and peoples, all of whom left their mark on the city. The city as the Judean spiritual and physical capital weathered several conquests, including its destruction at the hands of the Babylonians in 586. Herod the Great's magnificent city and temple, considered one of the architectural marvels of the Roman world, was razed to the ground by Titus in 70 CE. Beginning in 130 CE, Hadrian rebuilt the city, renamed it Aelia Capitolina, and expelled the remaining Jews from it. Several centuries later, Byzantine Jerusalem developed into the spiritual capital for all Christians. By the later seventh century CE, the city fell to Arab conquerors and evolved into one of Islam's holiest sites.

---

[11] See Killebrew, Chapter 20, this volume, for a detailed description and references.

Shortly thereafter, Baghdad was founded in 762 CE by the Abbasid caliph al-Mansûr after his regime had overthrown the Umayyad caliphs (all a result of an Islamic empire following Muhammad). Settling upon the site, the stars were consulted in its foundation, and the location – up to then just a small town – was deemed propitious. At that point, the caliph brought in engineers, architects, surveyors, and large numbers of workers to implement his vision. The population rapidly surged into the tens of thousands.

Being the seat of an imperial domain, the political administration physically defined Baghdad as the center of the world by importing pieces of that world and its history into the city center. The Caliph ripped down a palace elsewhere with the intent to use its pieces to build one in Baghdad. Iron gates thought to be connected to Solomon were imported from another city and used as entrances to inner Baghdad's "Round City."

The shape of this Round City itself referenced the shape of the world and the position of new Baghdad at that world's center. And at the center of this circular double-walled and ditched construction, some 2–3 kilometers in diameter, was the caliph's palace. Other buildings inside are palaces and administrative buildings. Outside were planned districts or quarters, mercantile areas, neighborhoods of Arabs and Persians, and slaves from Africa and Eastern and Central Europe, etc. There was no outer wall around Baghdad because there was no need. Baghdad was the all-powerful seat of an empire, with an unchallenged prosperity due to the economic wealth that its elites appropriated and concentrated from across its wider domain.[12]

A similar point might be made about Cahokia in its first century, although it was not the capital of an empire. Rather, between 1050 and 1150 CE, Cahokia was an unwalled seat of both religious and political authority comprised of at least three major precincts strung out in an irregular band some 10 kilometers in length. It was practically impossible to wall such a tripartite complex, which, in turn, is probably revealing of the organization(s) that crystallized as part of the founding.[13]

Cahokia's three precincts (St. Louis, East St. Louis, and Cahokia proper) each have their own distinct organizational symmetry, with some internal variation as well. Each precinct was composed by and large of thatched-roof wooden pole structures, large upright marker poles, and earthen pyramids. One precinct's architectural constructions and monuments were aligned to the cardinal directions and built around a single plaza. A second was built

---

[12] See Micheau, Chapter 19, this volume.
[13] See Pauketat et al., Chapter 21, this volume.

along an axis oriented 10 degrees west of north, with no clear central plaza. The third, and largest (aka, Cahokia proper), was configured along an axis that tilted 5 degrees east of north. This precinct, the largest, has one superordinate and several lesser plazas.

There are other known differences between at least two of these precincts. Special-status neighborhoods, those replete with public and ritual architecture, characterize all of East St. Louis. On the other hand, a mix of the public, ritual, and ordinary-status residential housing is well documented in the Cahokia precinct. A significant number of ordinary inhabitants in the latter area, as well as farmers in the countryside, appear to have been immigrants and resettled villagers who moved to the city in its early decades.

By the late twelfth century, bastioned palisade walls were added around the interior portions of East St. Louis and Cahokia. These construction projects mark the beginning of the end of Cahokia as a city and, some time in the late 1100s, a fire consumed most of the East St. Louis complex. A general emigration of citizens began. Many residents moved out of the city; many farmers left rural districts and went to points unknown outside of the region. Their departure meant that the city's pole-and-thatch architecture could not be rebuilt at the scale at which it had been for a century. And without reconstruction, the buildings that gave Cahokia its distinctive appearance and experiential potential ceased to exist.

Comparisons

In some ways, Jerusalem, Baghdad, and Cahokia all speak to the importance of founding moments. In other ways, the three occupy different positions along a politico-religious continuum. Jerusalem, with its centrality to three major religions, lies at one extreme. It is unique in its spiritual, physical, and political complexity, a continuously inhabited city of stone where construction and destruction events are yet remembered in detail. On the other hand, Cahokia was a short-term city built on a precarious balance of politics and religion. Once abandoned, few Native Americans returned, and it dropped out of oral histories. Baghdad occupies a position on the continuum between Cahokia and Jerusalem: a mudbrick city founded abruptly for clearly political reasons. It was abandoned for a long period before being resurrected in recent times.

To what extent are these differences a function of the variably religious, political, or administrative character of their foundations? Answers might be located in foundation stories, often imbued with heroic and religious underpinnings, which are a common feature of countless historic cities.[14] However, unlike Jerusalem, whose foundation stories remain meaningful to many, most traditions associated with ancient cities are considered little more than entertaining myths, which may or may not retain a kernel of historicity.

Indeed, few cities can boast a sacred tradition that can be traced back for millennia. Rome, the center of the Roman Empire, has kept its status as a Christian holy city over the centuries. Constantinople, the heart of Byzantine Christianity, was later conquered in 1453 by the Sultan Mehmed and transformed into a capital of the Islamic Ottoman Empire. Orthodox Greek Christianity continues to see this city as its spiritual center. Mecca, where tradition holds Ibrahim (Abraham) built the Kaaba, is the birthplace of Muhammad and the location where the Qur'an was composed. Today it continues to serve as Islam's most revered site and place of pilgrimage. The history of Varanasi, located on the River Ganges in India, is a city sacred to both Hinduism and Buddhism. Tradition holds that the city was founded by the Hindu deity Lord Shiva. Today, it serves as a major pilgrimage destination.

What distinguishes Jerusalem, in imagination and stone, from these sites and others is its sanctity for three major religions and resulting contested status, a reality that has shaped its history and continues to play a major role in Jerusalem today.[15] To some extent, that is, the density of the imaginings, and the ways in which (that is, the materials through which) these imaginings took shape, especially during their founding moments, may well have forever shaped the histories of these and other cities, along with the associated identities, governments, religions, and economies of their people.

Of particular concern here is what we might call the legacy effect of cities. Some last for millennia, as did Jerusalem. Stories, institutions, and religions grow up around them. Others had important historical effects, but their window of history was open for only a short period. Their brief histories might have been a function of the durability of their construction materials either by design or default.

---

[14] See for example Pedro Azara Nicholás, Ricardo Mar Medina, and Eva Subías Pascual (eds.), *Mites de fundació de ciutats al món antic: (Mesopotàmia, Grècia I Roma). Actes de Colloqui* (Barcelona: Museu d'Arqueologia de Catalunya, 2001) regarding cities in the ancient Near East and classical worlds.

[15] Tamar Mayer and Suleiman Ali Mourad (eds.), *Jerusalem: Idea and Reality* (London: Routledge, 2008).

Take for example Amarna in Egypt, which was built of mudbricks, allowing it to be established in a remote location in short order. Of course, this also made it easily abandoned and forgotten after the reign of Akhenaten. In this way it was like early Baghdad, which was also built of unfired mudbricks, giving it a degree of fragility. It could be deconstructed and abandoned as a world center, both physically and conceptually. Indeed, invasions, destructive floods, and fires led to a physical erasure of the spaces of Abbasid Baghdad after 1258.

The long-term effects of material differences between cities, whether they were built of stone, earth, wood, or mudbricks, are evident in other early cities around the world. For instance, Shang-period Chinese cities covered up to 30 square kilometers, featured inner enclosures, temples or palaces, and elite residences. But they were built entirely of earth and wood and, in some cases, occupied for just over a century.[16] Similarly, the proto-urban Olmec city of San Lorenzo Tenochtitlan, Mexico, covered 5 square kilometers atop a mesa.[17] The city's monuments are modest earthen and rubble constructions characterized by the episodic structured deposits of colored sediments.[18] The city survived for only 300 years.

The Olmec example is similar to Cahokia if not another proto-urban example, Tiwanaku in western Bolivia. Developing rapidly around 500 CE, Tiwanaku dominated the Titicaca Basin in Bolivia. It was a planned cosmic capital comprised of stone platforms, sunken temples, and plazas covering 4 to 6 square kilometers.[19] The central complex was surrounded by a moat, which was not built for defense but to define the city as an *axis mundi*.[20] Physical portals through which pilgrims passed and various commemorative offerings attest to the significance of the

[16] Lothar von Falkenhausen, "Stages in the Development of 'Cities' in Pre-Imperial China," in Joyce Marcus and Jeremy A. Sabloff (eds.), *The Ancient City: New Perspectives on Urbanism in the Old and New World* (Santa Fe, NM: School for Advanced Research, 2008), pp. 209–28.

[17] Michael D. Coe and Richard A. Diehl, *In the Land of the Olmec: The Archaeology of San Lorenzo Tenochtitlan* (Austin: University of Texas Press, 1980); Barbara L. Stark, "Out of Olmec," in Vernon L. Scarborough and John E. Clark (eds.), *The Political Economy of Ancient Mesoamerica: Transformations During the Formative and Classic Periods* (Albuquerque: University of New Mexico Press, 2007), pp. 47–63.

[18] John E. Clark, "Mesoamerica's First State," in Scarborough and Clark (eds.), *The Political Economy of Ancient Mesoamerica*, pp. 11–46.

[19] John W. Janusek, *Ancient Tiwanaku* (Cambridge: Cambridge University Press, 2008).

[20] Alan L. Kolata and Carlos Ponce Sangines, "Tiwanaku: The City at the Center," in Richard F. Townsend (ed.), *The Ancient Americas: Art from Sacred Landscapes* (Chicago: The Art Institute of Chicago, 1992), pp. 317–33.

city space enacting religion in a way that defined the city and its region for 600 years.[21]

The early Chinese and Mexican cities, like Cahokia, were relatively short-term affairs. The Chinese cities were impermanent constructions of earth and wood that afforded easy relocations of administrations and populations as necessary in early China's shifting political landscape.[22] So too could San Lorenzo be forgotten because its impermanent monumental symbolism "had 'escaped' into wide regional and social circulation."[23] Tiwanaku, on the other hand, was occupied for the longest amount of time, its highly visible stonework in its sunken temples, platforms, gates, and monoliths affording prolonged commemorations by residents and pilgrims. But even it did not have the dense overlay of sacred traditions, like Jerusalem, that might have seen it last beyond 1100 CE.

Conclusions

Jerusalem, Baghdad, and Cahokia are similar to the extent that cultural narratives, political institutions, and religious traditions were instantiated in their foundational imaginings and subsequent reimaginings. These were more than population aggregations with urban effects. They were more than commercial centers and trade hubs. And their histories were not simply defined by political cycles. The conditions surrounding their creation in each case gave them history-transcending qualities. They shaped and in some ways continue to shape collective identities and religious traditions.

They were, of course, very different in many ways. Jerusalem is the eternal city at the core of three major world religions. Imperial Baghdad's prominence was established by design but was silenced for centuries before reemerging again in the twentieth century. Precocious Cahokia burned brightly for three centuries before burning out. Yet their divergent histories – the facts of Jerusalem's enduring qualities, Baghdad's birth and rebirth, and Cahokia's disappearance – are due in some goodly measure to their imagined character.

Cities everywhere are to variable extent imaginaries. They enable people to experience and envision narratives, traditions, and institutions. But

---

[21] Deborah E. Blom and John W. Janusek, "Making Place: Humans as Dedications in Tiwanaku", *World Archaeology* 36 (2003), 123–41.
[22] Von Falkenhausen, "Stages in the Development of 'Cities,'" pp. 209–28.
[23] Stark, "Out of Olmec."

imagination is both an immaterial and a material process. People envision, experience, and imagine in spaces and through architectural constructions with things in hand.[24] That process might be variably dense, diverse, and complicated, like Jerusalem, or more uniform and centrally managed, like Baghdad or Cahokia. Either way, the process has clear historical implications. At its most basic level, a city's duration might be affected either by design, as in ancient Chinese cities if not to some extent Baghdad, or default, as with Olmec San Lorenzo, Amarna, or Cahokia. The point would seem to be that, even in their diversities and divergences, imagined cities share a common grounding in the processes of construction and the media of experience.

FURTHER READINGS

Azara Nicholás, Pedro, Ricardo Mar Medina, and Eva Subias Pascual (eds.), *Mites de fundació de ciutats al món antic: (Mesopotàmia, Grècia I Roma). Actes de Colloqui*, Barcelona: Museu d'Arqueologia de Catalunya, 2001.

Bachelard, Gaston, *The Poetics of Space: The Classic Look at How We Experience Intimate Places*, Boston: Beacon Press, 1994.

Bender, Barbara (ed.), *Landscape: Politics and Perspectives*, London: Berg, 1983.

Blom, Deborah E., and John W. Janusek, "Making Place: Humans as Dedications in Tiwanaku," *World Archaeology* 36 (2003), 123–41.

Clark, John E., "Mesoamerica's First State," in Vernon L. Scarborough and John E. Clark (eds.), *The Political Economy of Ancient Mesoamerica: Transformations During the Formative and Classic Periods*, Albuquerque: University of New Mexico Press, 2007, pp. 11–46.

Coe, Michael D., and Richard A. Diehl, *In the Land of the Olmec: The Archaeology of San Lorenzo Tenochtitlan*, Austin: University of Texas Press, 1980.

Connerton, Paul, *How Societies Remember*, Cambridge: Cambridge University Press, 1989.

de Certeau, Michel, *The Practice of Everyday Life*, Berkeley: University of California Press, 1984.

Janusek, John W., *Ancient Tiwanaku*, Cambridge: Cambridge University Press, 2008.

Joyce, Rosemary A., and Lynn M. Meskell, *Embodied Lives: Figuring Ancient Maya and Egyptian Experience*, London: Routledge, 2003.

Kolata, Alan L., and Carlos Ponce Sangines, "Tiwanaku: The City at the Center," in Richard F. Townsend (ed.), *The Ancient Americas: Art from Sacred Landscapes*, Chicago: The Art Institute of Chicago, 1992, pp. 317–33.

Küchler, Suzanne, "Landscape as Memory: The Mapping of Process and Its Representation in a Melanesian Society," in Barbara Bender (ed.), *Landscape: Politics and Perspectives*, London: Berg, 1983, pp. 85–106.

[24] Bachelard, *The Poetics of Space*.

Kus, Susan, "Sensuous Human Activity and the State: Towards an Archaeology of Bread and Circuses," in Daniel Miller(ed.), *Domination and Resistance*, London: Unwin & Hyman, 1989, pp. 140–54.

'The Social Representation of Space: Dimensioning the Cosmological and the Quotidian," in James A. Moore and Arthur S. Keene (eds.), *Archaeological Hammers and Theories*, New York: Academic Press, 1983, pp. 277–98.

Lefebvre, Henri, *The Production of Space*, Donald Nicholson-Smith (trans.), Oxford: Blackwell, 1991.

Mayer, Tamar, and Suleiman Ali Mourad (eds.), *Jerusalem: Idea and Reality*, London: Routledge, 2008.

Shepherd, Nick, and Christian Ernsten, "The World Below: Post-Apartheid Imaginaries and the Bones of the Prestwich Street Dead," in Noëleen Murray, Nick Shepherd, and Martin Hall (eds.), *Desire Lines: Space, Memory and Identity in the Post-Apartheid City*, London: Routledge, 2007, pp. 215–32.

Smith, Adam T., *The Political Landscape: Constellations of Authority in Early Complex Polities*, Berkeley: University of California Press, 2003.

Stark, Barbara L., "Out of Olmec," in Vernon L. Scarborough and John E. Clark (eds.), *The Political Economy of Ancient Mesoamerica: Transformations During the Formative and Classic Periods*, Albuquerque: University of New Mexico Press, 2007, pp. 47–63.

Von Falkenhausen, Lothar, "Stages in the Development of 'Cities' in Pre-Imperial China," in Joyce Marcus and Jeremy A. Sabloff (eds.), *The Ancient City: New Perspectives on Urbanism in the Old and New World*, Santa Fe, NM: School for Advanced Research, 2008, pp. 209–28.

Wheatley, Paul, *The Pivot of the Four Quarters*, Chicago: Aldine, 1971.

PART VI

★

EARLY IMPERIAL CITIES

23

Neo-Assyrian capital cities: from imperial headquarters to cosmopolitan cities

ADELHEID OTTO

The discovery of monumental sculptures of human-headed winged lions and bulls in the area of Mosul (today northern Iraq) around 1843 CE marks the beginning of the investigations of ancient Mesopotamia. The names of the Assyrian cities were known from a few Greek and Roman travelers and from references in the Old Testament. Nimrod, Aššur, and Nineveh stood for condemnable life, hubris, megalomania, and cruelty – features that seemed to be corroborated by the colossal beasts and the endless scenes of warfare on the stone panels, the vast palaces, which they decorated, and the incredibly large cities.[1] Today, although systematic archaeological research and the decipherment of tens of thousands of cuneiform texts provides more and more detailed information about the Assyrian Empire, it is still a challenge to define the characteristics of Assyrian cities and how people lived in them.

Historical and environmental background

The cities investigated here are all situated in the "Assyrian Heartland" in northern Mesopotamia, a fertile area within the rain-fed dry farming zone (see Table 23.1). Until 1500 BCE Assyrian cities did not exceed 100 hectares, because the hinterlands could not support larger cities. The Assyrians depended always on further income derived from trade, taxes, or tribute.

Assyria began as a modest city-state around the capital city Aššur (note that Aššur designates the highest god of the city and the empire, the city and the land). During the Old Assyrian period (c.. 2000–1700 BCE) Aššur was a

[1] The "sh" sound in Akkadian names and places is sometimes rendered š or Š in the chapter and figures and maps. The "h" sound in Akkadian is unmarked; the sound is an "Achlaut," like Scottish "loch" or Yiddish "chutzpah." The sound appears occasionally as "kh." The emphatic consonants (s and t, usually transliterated with dots under them) are not marked in the text.

Table 23.1 Chronological table of the Assyrian capital cities and the mentioned kings

	Assyrian kings mentioned	Capital city (*Ancient*/ modern name)
Old Assyrian period (*c.* 2000–1700 BCE)		*Aššur*/Qalat Šerqat
	Šamši-Adad I (1815–1776)	*Aššur*/Qalat Šerqat
Middle Assyrian period (*c.* 1700–1100 BCE)		*Aššur*/Qalat Šerqat
	Tukulti-Ninurta I (1233–1197)	*Kar-Tukulti-Ninurta*/ Tulul al-'Aqr
Neo-Assyrian Empire (*c.* 1100–612 BCE)		*Aššur*/Qalat Šerqat (until 864)
	Aššurnasirpal II (883–859)	*Kalhu*/Nimrud
	Šalmaneser III (858–824)	*Kalhu*/Nimrud
	Šalmaneser V (726–722)	*Kalhu*/Nimrud
	Sargon II (721–705)	*Dūr-Šarru-kēn*/Khorsabad
	Sennacherib (704–681)	*Nineveh*/Kuyunjik+Nebi Yunus
	Esarhaddon (680–669)	*Nineveh*/Kuyunjik+Nebi Yunus
	Aššurbanipal (668–631)	*Nineveh*/Kuyunjik+Nebi Yunus
	Sinšariškun (626–612)	*Nineveh*/Kuyunjik+Nebi Yunus
	Aššuruballit II (611–609)	*Harranu*/Harran

major trading center that flourished mainly due to its elaborate network of trading colonies in Anatolia. The expansionist efforts started during the fourteenth century, and in the following century Assyria was already an important military power, which subordinated Upper Mesopotamia and parts of Syria. After a period of weakness in the late second and early first millennium, the Assyrian Empire evolved into a "great power," dominating most of the Near East (ninth–seventh century): at the time of Sargon II and Sennacherib it extended from the Persian Gulf to the Taurus Mountains, and from Cyprus, Phoenicia, and Gaza until beyond the Zagros Mountains in Iran; even Egypt was occupied for some years during the reign of Esarhaddon and Aššurbanipal (Map 23.1).

Between 614 and 612 BCE the Assyrian capital cities of the heartland were besieged and sacked by an alliance of Medes and Babylonians. The destruction of Nineveh and of the Temple of Aššur marked the end of the Assyrian

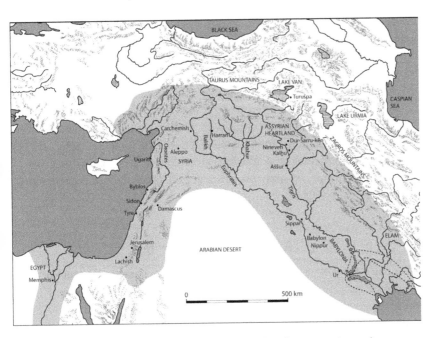

Map 23.1 Map of the Neo-Assyrian Empire at the height of its power (seventh century BCE) (drawn by M. Lerchl).

Empire. The last king, Aššuruballit II, briefly retained control over some western provinces and many provincial centers continued to exist, but Assyria as a state no longer existed.

Long-lasting internal problems made the empire collapse so quickly. They were rooted in the concentration of power in the hands of the king, struggles for the succession to the throne, the dependence of the enormous cities with a massive bureaucracy and a huge army that needed to be regularly supplied from the provinces and tributary states, the loyalty of which was seldom by choice. The huge capital cities in the Assyrian heartland were situated so close together that the agricultural output in their hinterlands was inadequate. Their provisions from distant regions required a sophisticated system of overland transport, shipping, and storage of large amounts of food.

The evolution to *the* superpower of the ancient Near East was accompanied by considerable population growth mainly due to mass deportations – it is supposed that up to 4 million people were deported between *c.* 850 and 614 BCE – and a certain voluntary influx of people. A large proportion of the conquered territory was steppe, which the Assyrians made arable with the help of deportees. This led to a restructuring of the provinces with a reformed administration and to a complete remodeling of the cities in the Assyrian heartland. The old capital city, Aššur, which had developed since the late third millennium, no longer met the social, economic, and political needs for the capital of a large empire, and several Assyrian kings felt the need to found new residence cities with distinctly differing structures (Kar-Tukulti-Ninurta, Kalhu, Dūr-Šarru-kēn, Nineveh). Even so Aššur always remained the religious and ideological center of the empire, because it was the seat of the city-god and national god Aššur, whose representative was the king.

Aššur, the eternal capital

The city of Aššur is situated at a strategically convenient position on a mountain spur high above the Tigris Valley. Best known is the city of the seventh century, from the end of the Assyrian Empire (Figure 23.1). At that time the overall area of the walled inner city measured c. 65 hectares, with the new city (southern extension) c. 73 hectares; the population is estimated between 30,000 and 50,000.

Mainly remains of sanctuaries are known from the late third millennium, and even at the Old Assyrian period the city is poorly known. The first floruit under the interloper king Šamši-Adad I didn't last long, but he gave the already existing main sanctuary, the temple of the god Aššur, its shape, which remained nearly unchanged for 1,200 years until the end of Assyria. He also erected the ziggurat, presumably after a Babylonian model. When

Figure 23.1 The city center of Aššur with the most important temples and palaces (from W. Andrae, *Das wiedererstandene Assur* [Leipzig, 1938], p. 44, Abb. 24).

Assyria came into power again in the thirteenth century, the city was enlarged by the southern extension. King Tukulti-Ninurta I, well aware that he had himself created enemies all over with his expansionist policy, fortified the strategic weak point of Aššur, the western flank. He was also the first king to leave the old, cramped city and founded Kar-Tukulti-Ninurta as his new capital (see below). With Aššurnasirpal II the Assyrian kings displaced the seat of the government definitively away from Aššur. However, the city's structure remained the same until 614 BCE. The official buildings were arranged, one beside the other, along the elevated northern edge. These are (from east to west) the Temple of Aššur and the ziggurat at the tip, the "Old Palace," and the Anu-Adad Temple. Opposite the main and processional road, which widens here to a plaza, were the temples of Ištar and Nabu, the Western Palace, the temple of Sin and Šamaš, and the Eastern Palace.

The temple of the god Aššur (Ešara) was a mighty complex, consisting of a main building and a large court surrounded by rooms. At special occasions such as ritual festivals the public had access to the large court. The holy abode was described by Esarhaddon: "I backed the cella of Aššur, my lord, with gold. Figures of *lahmu* und cherubs from shiny gold I put side by side. I plastered the walls with gold. . ." The temple held its own workshops (for example, of goldsmiths), a brewery, bakery, a butchery, and kitchens that prepared the daily meals for the god and his household. The coherence of the empire was performed there daily as the rations of meat were provided every day by a different province. In this way, the whole empire literally fed the god.

The existence of this temple contributed significantly to the enduring importance of the city, even when the governmental headquarters were displaced. The whole priesthood and temple personnel remained in Aššur with the god, and the Assyrian kings had to come there regularly for ritual purposes. But the temple also played a decisive role in the Assyrian royal and state ideology. The god Aššur was deemed the true king, who retained the cosmic order; his representative on earth was the king, who preserved the political order. Thus the legitimation of the Assyrian kings was immediately bound to the Temple of Aššur, which constituted the ideological center of the empire throughout its history.[2]

---

[2] Stefan Maul, "Der assyrische König – Hüter der Weltordnung," in Kazuko Watanabe (ed.), *Priests and Officials in the Ancient Near East* (Heidelberg: Universitätsverlag C. Winter, 1999), p. 214.

Close to it stood the "Old Palace," the main palace of the Assyrian kings
at least since the nineteenth century, when the complex of 110 meters by
98 meters with at least ten courtyards and 172 rooms had been erected. But
even after Aššurnasirpal II had deplaced the capital to Kalhu and inaugurated
his new palace there, almost every king seems to have altered this prestigious abode, as building inscriptions of at least twenty-one kings testify. One
reason for its continuous use were the royal tombs below the palace. At
least seven Assyrian kings of the eleventh–seventh centuries were buried
here. This indicates that many kings returned after death to this so-called
"Palace of the Fathers." Regular offerings and libations for the dead at the
ancestors' graves belonged to the fundamental duties of every mortal, the
king included.[3]

At least four other palaces are attested: one on the terrace of the "New
Palace" from the ninth century; the "Eastern Palace" of Šalmaneser III
100 meters southeast of the "Old Palace"; a palace or administrative
building between the Nabû-Temple and the Sin-Šamaš Temple; and the
palace of a crown prince of the early seventh century, which was the
only official building inside the housing quarters. In sum, the palaces
did not occupy a large proportion of the city area. Strikingly, and in
sharp contrast to the following Assyrian capitals, the area of the official
buildings merged smoothly into the residential zones. Although these
have been investigated only partially, their overall structure can be
discerned due to a systematic exploration with trenches. In the late
seventh century, tightly packed housing quarters extended that were
accessible through a regular street network. The houses of downtown
(*libbi āli*) are sizeable (surface area between 150 and 450 square meters)
and display quadrangular ground plans, while small houses with irregular
ground plans predominate in the places where new construction areas
were set out here in the seventh century. Apparently space had become
rare then.

The scheme of the larger houses consisted of a public sector near the
entrance (*bābānu*) and a private one (*bītānu*) in the rear sector – a pattern
similar to that of palaces. This was appropriate since the houses served not
only as dwelling places, but also as handicraft workshops or trade offices
with plenty of public audience spaces. The education of the intellectual elite
took place in the houses of "scribes" (not in schools). Underneath the

---

[3] Friedhelm Pedde and Steven Lundström, *Der Alte Palast in Assur: Architektur und
Baugeschichte* (Wiesbaden: Harrassowitz Verlag, 2008).

innermost chamber the deceased household members were buried in vaulted burial chambers and venerated regularly. Many houses contained private archives (real estate documents, marriage contracts, testaments, and business records) that give insight into daily life. The different urban districts seem to have accommodated a socially differentiated population. Many houses in the marginal zones of the city may be attributed to immigrants. Indeed, Aššur was a flourishing city with ethnically and socially highly differentiated inhabitants from all regions of the empire until the end in 614 BCE. Egyptians, Medes, Luwians, Arameans, and others are attested as house owners. Suburbs outside the city wall are attested by relevant sherd scatters.

Real estate affairs were under the responsibility of the urban administration. At least one civil servant had to be present during purchase and sale of houses and plots. The transactions were controlled by the "principal of the city" (ša muhhi āli), who was higher in rank than the mayor (hazannu), who had been appointed by the king. This hierarchy changed after the middle of the seventh century, when the mayor headed the urban administration. From 684 BCE onwards a council of three mayors is attested, who were responsible for three urban districts, from which the one for downtown (ša libbi āli) is the highest in rank.[4] The mayor and the principal acted also as judges, but their main duty consisted in linking the king and the city. No buildings devoted to the urban administration have been discovered so far. Perhaps there were none, or the administration acted in the office rooms of the temples, since at least one mayor of downtown is known to have been a goldsmith of the Aššur Temple.

The most remarkable features of the old capital city are the dominance of the temples compared to the palaces, and the fact that even the palaces and temples of prime importance for the state were not separated from the residential quarters. This contradicts the frequent assertion that Neo-Assyrian cities were characterized by a distinct segregation of royal and urban domains. But it may have been the main reason why numerous Assyrian kings made enormous efforts to transfer the administrative headquarters of the growing empire elsewhere.

---

[4] Karen Radner and Evelyn Klengel-Brandt, "Die Stadtbeamten von Assur und ihre Siegel," in Simo Parpola and R. M. Whiting (eds.), *Assyria 1995: Proceedings of the 10th Anniversary Symposium of the Neo-Assyrian Text Corpus Project, Helsinki, Sept. 7–11, 1995* (Helsinki: Neo-Assyrian Text Corpus Project, 1997), pp. 137–59.

Kar-Tukulti-Ninurta, the futile attempt to replace the capital at Aššur

Tukulti-Ninurta I, at the end of the Middle Assyrian period, was the first king to leave the venerable, but ramped city of Aššur and to found a new city 3 kilometers upstream on the other riverbank. The king claims to have created Kar-Tukulti-Ninurta (literally: the harbor of Tukulti-Ninurta) on virgin soil as "a city for cult and residence." This creation was an enormous undertaking: the new capital with an area of *c.* 240 hectares extended over at least 2.8 kilometers along the Tigris and was 900 meters wide.[5] A city wall with protruding towers fortified the rectangular urban area. A narrower inner wall enclosed the official area of the city (at least 35 hectares), which was situated at the edge toward the valley. In the middle of this area the "Temple of the Universe" was erected, which was dedicated mainly for the god Aššur. This was deemed pretentiousness, because Aššur resided in his age-old abode, and the temple was shut down after the assassination of Tukulti-Ninurta by his nobles. No later king ever tried to replace the seat of Aššur.

The only building that was erected on an elevated position, was the royal palace (The House of the Universe). An artificial mudbrick terrace, 15–18 meters high, supported the vast palace, which must have measured possibly 400 meters in length. With a total surface of *c.* 40,000 square meters this palace was at least four times larger than the "Palace of the Fathers" at Aššur. The lower city exhibits numerous settlement traces, including a small temple in the north. However, it is not clear how extensively the lower city was covered with buildings. A canal (Canal of Justice) supplied the urban area with water, and granaries for the storage of the grain tax are mentioned in texts. The building of a new capital city remained an episode, and the following kings continued to reign from the city of Aššur, until Aššurnasirpal II moved the capital to Kalhu.

Kalhu (or Calah) and the emergence of the military headquarters of the empire

Aššurnasirpal II built his new capital city at Kalhu, an already existing, fair-sized town, which he enlarged considerably to an area of 360 hectares (Figure 23.2). The citadel has the natural oval form of a tell site. Where it is included in the large mudbrick city wall, the city's contour is irregular; where the newly

---

[5] Reinhard Dittmann, "Ausgrabungen der Freien Universität Berlin in Assur und Kār-Tukultī-Ninurta in den Jahren 1986–89," *Mitteilungen der Deutschen Orient-Gesellschaft* 122 (1990), 157–71.

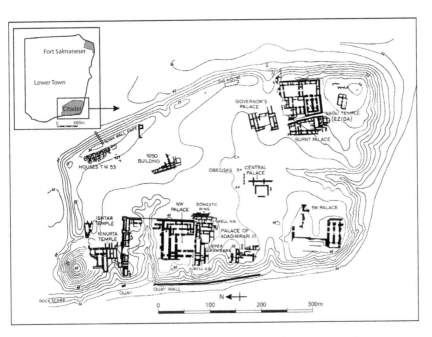

Figure 23.2 Plan of Kalhu with a multitude of palaces on the main mound (drawn by M. Lerchl after M. E. L. Mallowan, *Nimrud and its Remains* [New York: Dodd, Mead 1966], p. 32, fig. 1).

created Lower Town is enclosed, the contour is linear and forms a right angle. Extensive excavations have been carried out at the citadel and at "Fort Šalmaneser," while 90 percent of the city, the Lower Town, remains unexplored.

Aššurnasirpal II created a vast ensemble of official buildings high up the citadel mound. He claimed to have built nine temples for twelve gods at Kalhu. Further large buildings, usually called "palaces," served for administrative and residential purposes and were led by high-ranking officials. At least seven palaces were erected by Neo-Assyrian kings, but they were not all simultaneously in use. The Governor's Palace was probably not the seat of the governor of Kalhu, but rather of several high-ranking people in the administration of Kalhu. Some of the courtiers were allowed to reside on the citadel, such as an "entrance supervisor" and a eunuch and court official, who was also a merchant, landowner, and money lender: they lived in a group of densely packed houses, which were built against the inner face of the citadel's wall at the northeast side.[6]

---

[6] David Oates and Joan Oates, *Nimrud: An Assyrian Imperial City Revealed* (London: British School of Archaeology in Iraq, 2001).

The earliest and largest palace, the North-West Palace, was built by Aššurnasirpal as his main residence. On an area of at least 200 by 120 meters a large official part around the outer court was laid out, bordered by offices and storerooms, and several residential and provisioning arrays around smaller inner courtyards. Below the residential area the undisturbed tombs of the queens were found in 1989 (CE), the treasures of which display the enormous wealth of the royals. The extensive decoration with carved panels from Mosul alabaster, which was clearly influenced by similarly decorated buildings in the conquered Syro-Aramean kingdoms, was a novelty, which was to become the most typical decoration of Neo-Assyrian official buildings. The particular subjects of the narrative reliefs were chosen according to the function of the rooms: more private areas showed sporting scenes (for example, of hunts) of the king, while processions of people bringing tribute to the king decorated exterior facades. The throne room, as the virtual center of the empire, where major state ceremonies took place, was given the utmost care in decoration. The huge palace and its opulent decoration were "designed to impress, astonish, intimidate, to present an image of the Assyrian capital city as capital of the civilised world, of the royal palace as the centre of the universe, and of the Assyrian king as the most powerful man alive, deputy of Aššur, the most powerful god."[7]

At a safe distance from the citadel Šalmaneser III, the successor of Aššurnasirpal II, constructed the arsenal (*ekal mašarti*), nicknamed by the excavators "Fort Šalmaneser." The building, roughly 300 by 200 meters, is a novelty in Near Eastern architecture. It consisted in its southern part of rooms of state, which were used by the king and his courtiers. The northern part, where narrow rooms surround overly huge courtyards, was mainly used as barracks and workshops, housed troops, the military equipment from the soldiers and from the horses, chariots, and war machines. Later, the booty was stored here. This huge building, where the army was assembled and reviewed before the annual campaigns, reflects the growing importance of the Assyrian army in the ninth century.

We can only guess at the use of the Lower Town. The extensive building program was accomplished by deportees. Aššurnasirpal II reports: "When I consecrated the palace of Kalhu, 47,074 men and women, summoned from all the districts of my land, 5,000 dignitaries and envoys of the people of the lands Suhu, Hindanu . . . 16,000 people from Kalhu, and 1,500 palace officials,

---

[7] John E. Curtis and Julian E. Reade, *Art and Empire* (London: British Museum Press, 1995), p. 40.

all of them ... for ten days I gave them food, I gave them drink ..."[8] The 47,000 deportees, who worked for years to build his new palace in Kalhu, were brought to the job in addition to the 16,000 former inhabitants of Kalhu. It may be supposed that the deportees were the first to live in the Lower Town, and that the continuous supply of manpower, the population growth, and the military headquarters further contributed to the growing demands for housing space.

Dūr-Šarru-kēn: the politically motivated founding of a new capital

This city (modern Khorsabad) was created due to political reasons. King Šarru-kēn (Sargon) II (721–705 BCE) was not the legitimate heir to the throne. Due to internal struggles he felt the need to deplace the seat of the government. He chose a site in the hilly country along the Khosr River 16 kilometers northeast of Nineveh, which was unoccupied except for a small village, and created his capital named "Fort Sargon."

From the laying of the foundations in 717 BCE it took only ten years to raise a city, which was nearly square with sides measuring 1,760 x 1,830 x 1,620 x 1,850 meters, and was enclosed by a wall, 14 meters wide and allegedly 12 meters high. Seven gates, each protected by a pair of colossal human-headed winged bulls supporting an arch, controlled the access (Figure 23.3).

The temples must have been finished, when in 707 BCE the entrance of the gods was celebrated. A year later the city was inaugurated with pompous festivities to which all dignitaries of the empire and vassal rulers were invited. But Sargon enjoyed the splendors of this outrageous city for only one year; he died on a campaign in the Taurus Mountains in 705 BCE. The fact that his corpse was not found and could not be buried was a clear sign for his son Sennacherib, the heir to the throne, to transfer the seat of the government hastily, this time to Nineveh (see below). Dūr-Šarru-kēn continued to exist as the capital of a province.

Two citadels, distant from each other as far as possible, protrude from the rectilinear outline of the city. The smaller one, the *bīt kutalli* ("Review Palace," or Palace F), lay raised on a terrace above the lower city. It served as the royal arsenal comparable to Fort Šalmaneser at Kalhu. The larger one, measuring c. 20 hectares, was separated from the lower city by an interior

---

[8] A. Kirk Grayson, *Assyrian Rulers of the First Millennium B.C.* (Toronto: University of Toronto Press, 1991), Vol. 1, p. 293.

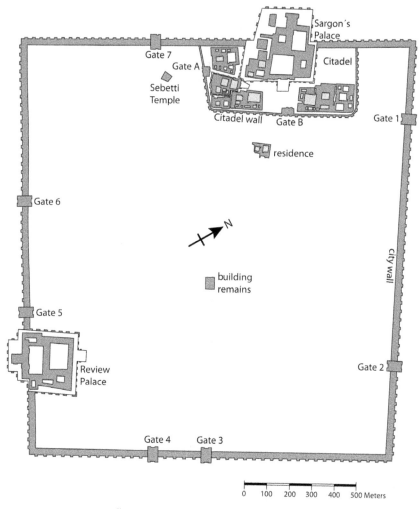

Figure 23.3 Plan of Dūr-Šarru-kēn, the newly founded capital city (drawn by M. Lerchl).

wall with protruding towers. Two chamber gates controlled the entrance to the citadel, inside of which were exclusively royal buildings, residences, and sacred buildings. Sargon's royal palace and the Nabû-Temple were further secluded by being laid on raised platforms. The palace was in every respect fabulous: it measured *c.* 250 by 190 meters and was lavishly decorated with colossal figures and hundreds of sculptured stone slabs. Immediately adjacent to the palace were built a ziggurrat and a temple complex, where six different gods were venerated. In this way, the shrines were under complete control of the royal apparatus, and the king could fulfil his religious duties without leaving his profoundly protected abode. The temples appear like small duplicates of the gods' main temples in the venerable city of Aššur. The remaining area of the citadel was densely covered with spacious subsidiary residences, where high state officials lived and administered.

The palace terrace projected into an artificial park and orchard area, which was created with great effort. Sargon claims that the park was "like the Amanus mountain, in which grows every tree of the Hatti-land and the fruit trees of every mountain." These royal gardens, where exotic plants from all the countries of the empire grew, underscored visibly the king's claim to universal power.

The most striking feature is the way in which the citadels were strongly fortified and carefully separated from the lower city. This has been ascribed to the fact that a motley collection of deportees from the whole empire were settled here under supervision of Assyrian officials. For lack of excavations it is difficult to figure out how much of the lower city was covered with buildings. However, earlier notions that this was no city, but a camping area of prisoners on a walled, empty space are no longer acceptable. The gates point to a regular road network, minor excavations in the center of the lower city brought to light a spacious elite house, and another residence and a temple were situated near the citadel.

Nineveh: the creation of the largest city in Mesopotamia by Sennacherib

From at least the mid-third millennium onwards Nineveh was known for its temple of the goddess Ištar – one of Mesopotamia's main sanctuaries. In the fourteenth century Nineveh served as a royal residence; at least three Middle Assyrian palaces are mentioned in texts. By the end of the second millennium BCE the city consisted of the citadel and a substantial lower town, extending from the Khosr River to the north, and probably already protected by a city wall. From that time it was the "second city" of Assyria, where the kings temporarily resided and received annual tributes. A multitude of palaces with adjacent gardens and several temples are mentioned as having existed at Kujunjik (the modern name for the main citadel of ancient Nineveh).[9]

---

[9] The most conclusive summary about Nineveh is given by J. E. Reade, "Ninive," *Reallexikon der Assyriologie* 9 (2001), 388–433. For the renewed excavations, which shed

It was king Sennacherib who first made Nineveh into the Assyrian administrative capital. He refurbished the city and enlarged it considerably (Figure 23.4). He states in his building accounts that the earlier city had a circumference of 9,300 great cubits (=5,115 meters; *c.* 150–200 hectares) and that he enlarged it to 21,815 great cubits (=12,000 meters), which fits well with the measured area of 750 hectares. An estimate of 15,000–20,000 inhabitants (100 per hectare) comes close to the number of people at Kalhu, before it was made the capital. New Nineveh was quadrangular, approximately 4 kilometers long and up to 2 kilometers wide and measured 750 hectares. It was by then ten times larger than Aššur. The population has been estimated (at an approximation of 100 persons per hectare) as 75,000, but this seems much too low. The number of "more than 120,000 persons and much cattle" mentioned in Jonah 4:11 is usually judged as exaggerated although it seems more in line with the 63,000 inhabitants of Kalhu, which had an area of 360 hectares.

Sennacherib described his buildings program: "I increased the site of Nineveh, my royal city, I widened its squares, made bright the avenues and streets and caused them to shine like the day . . . The wall and outer-wall I caused to be skillfully constructed and raised mountain-high. I widened its moat to 100 great cubits." Royal Assyrian building inscriptions are not objective sources, but describe an ideal city, not the real topography. Still, due to the fragmentary state of the archaeological remains, we have to take them into account.

The headquarters of the empire

The city enclosed several elevations. The two most prominent mounds both lay at the outer edge of the city and bordered the Tigris Valley, thus contributing to its protection. The smaller mound in the southern part (named Nebi Yunus after the prophet Jonah) was *c.* 15 hectares in area and 15 meters high. At least from the ninth century onwards the Neo-Assyrian Arsenal (*ekal mašarti/kutalli*) was located here. It served as a camp and provided ample space for stables and weapons. There is archaeological evidence that tribute and booty were stored there, for example, several

light on the development of the city and the diversity of its quarters, see David Stronach, "Village to Metropolis: Nineveh and the Beginnings of Urbanism in Northern Mesopotamia," in Stefania Mazzoni, (ed.), *Nuove fondazioni nel vicino oriente antico: realtà e ideologia* (Pisa: Giardini, 1994), pp. 85–114. The ancient texts are rendered after the timeless translation of Daniel David Luckenbill, *Sennacherib, King of Assyria, Annals* (Chicago: The University of Chicago, 1924).

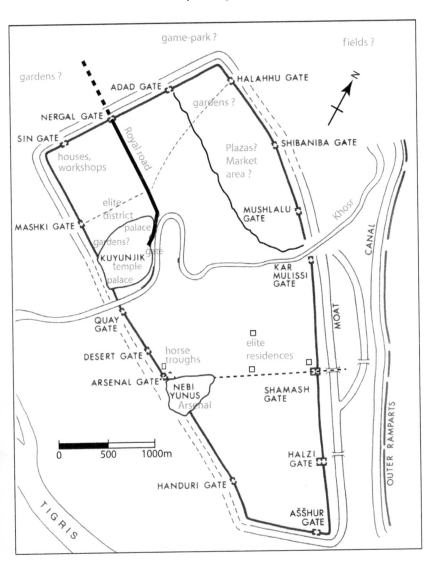

Figure 23.4 Nineveh, the largest city of its time; map showing the functions of the
urban area and its outskirts (drawn by A. Otto; adapted from David Stronach,
"Notes on the Fall of Nineveh," in Simo Parpola and R. M. Whiting [eds.], *Assyria 1995*
[Helsinki: The Neo-Assyrian Text Corpus Project, 1997], p. 312, fig. 2).

Figure 23.5 Depiction of the citadel mound of Nineveh "Kuyunjik" with its multiple fortification walls and Sennacherib's "Palace Without Rival" at the top; stone slab from Nineveh, North Palace, Room H (© Trustees of the British Museum).

statues of a defeated Egyptian king were prominently displayed in the entrance gates of the arsenal. Nebi Yunus was directly accessible from the west by a separate city gate named Marshalling everything: the Gate of the Arsenal, close to which stood horse troughs.

Kuyunjik is a steep-sided mound, c. 45 hectares in area and 25–30 meters high (Figure 23.5). It is a tell site, made up of continuous settlement layers since the seventh millennium. In Neo-Assyrian times it was fortified. A stone-paved ramp led up to the only entrance, the East Gate, flanked by colossal bulls. At least five temples must have occupied the center of the citadel. Private houses are mentioned in a text from 614 BCE but it is difficult to judge who inhabited the houses (high officials or royal servants?) and if Kuyunjik was a restricted area.

By far the largest buildings are the two palaces in the extreme southwest and northeast. Whereas little is known about the heavily eroded North Palace, where several crown princes and kings resided, much more is known about the SW Palace, the "Palace Without Rival." Sennacherib described extensively in his annals how he tore down the former palace and enlarged it. The palace must have measured approximately 12 hectares, but barely half of it has been excavated. It was the administrative center of the whole Assyrian Empire at its peak. It consisted of an outer court, probably surrounded by services and offices, giving access to the throne room. Beyond this lay the royal residential suite and the residence of the queen. Smaller units between them may have been the court eunuchs' apartments. A large part of the southern sector served various administrative purposes and probably replaced the free-standing palaces of high officials that are attested in earlier capitals. The walls of most of the rooms and courtyards were decorated with stone panels, which depict scenes of conquest during the military campaigns abroad and building projects in Assyria, often explained by captions.

At the southwestern edge, heading for the Tigris Valley, a terrace spread in front of a large facade. This may be depicted on a panel, which shows a two-tiered main city wall with protruding towers and a postern gate and a wall beyond a river; an inner wall with turrets and an outer wall, all topped by crenellations, probably depict the citadel wall of Kujunjik. The building above matches Sennacherib's descriptions of the palace fairly well with colossal winged bulls and bronze lion bases that supported cedar columns.

The city wall, streets, parks, and open spaces

Sennacherib's city wall (12 kilometers long) consisted of an inner mudbrick wall (The Wall whose Splendor Overwhelmes the Enemy) c. 15 meters thick and 25 meters high, and an outer stone wall (The Wall that Terrifies Evil), 11 meters thick and 4.5 meters high. At a distance of c. 80 meters there was a moat (dry or water-filled?), c. 55 meters wide, in places spanned by stone bridges. The city wall is reported as having fourteen to eighteen gates, which bear elaborate names such as "Adad who Gives Abundance to the Land: the Gate of Adad of the Game-park" (variant: "of the gardens"), describing what lay beyond the gate.

The Nergal Gate, approached by a stone paved ramp and flanked by colossal bulls, protected the entrance to the main or "royal road" that led straight to the empire's center on top of Kujunjik. Sennacherib claims: "62 great cubits I measured the width of the royal road, up to the park gate."[10] This 34-meter-wide boulevard was laid out straight between the Nergal Gate and the northeastern edge of Kujunjik, that is, on a 1,000-meter stretch. The road broke through the extant house quarters, and its construction works seem to have caused considerable trouble. Sennacherib feels obliged to add: "If ever (anyone of) the people who dwell in that city tears down his old house and builds a new one, and the foundations of his house encroach upon the royal road, they shall impale him upon a stake on his (own) house." This refers to the fact that not the king, but the urban administration was responsible for the real estate affairs in the lower town, and that the residents used to alter the dwelling zones and their lanes at convenience. Nineveh, besides being the administrative center of the whole empire, was also the capital of a province with a separate urban administration, the head of which was the governor.

The alleged "shining" of the road may refer to the paving of the streets with stone slabs, while the overland roads, even the famous royal road, *harrān šarri*, which was used on the annual military campaigns, and by traders and the post, were only earth tracks.

At least three extramural parks and game-parks, and several garden areas inside the city are attested. It has been argued that "Hanging Gardens," that is, artificially laid out parks, marvels of exotic fauna and flora, existed not only in Babylon, but also in Nineveh. It is unlikely that these were open to the public. However, private gardens, orchards, and fields existed outside and inside the city and were irrigated with the help of Sennacherib's sophisticated system of canals, dams, and aqueducts, which brought supplementary water from Jerwan, 40 kilometers north in the Zagros foothills.

The lower town

The city was divided by the Khosr River into a northern and a southern part. In the northern half, the raised mound extending about 400 meters north of Kuyunjik was occupied by a densely built elite district of the seventh century BCE with spacious, well-drained courtyard houses and two broad roads, one running eastwards on the axis of the Maški Gate. Adjacent to this area, in the northwestern corner of the city there is evidence for a densely populated urban district, where potters and other artisans worked and lived in small, tightly packed houses.

---

[10] See Luckenbill, *Sennacherib*.

Strangely, in the northeastern part of the city Sennacherib's wall included a high conglomerate river terrace, which – according to a survey – was only lightly settled. A part of this area may have been covered by gardens and orchards; another part may have had market functions. A city of that size must have had extended areas of daily barter and trade near the gates or within the city. Since Sennacherib boasted of his widening of the plazas, and since the two northeastern gates are named: "Always Possessing the Goodness of Grain and Cattle: Gate of the Town Šibaniba" and "Bringing the Produce of the Mountain(s): Gate of the Land of Halahhu," this area seems a likely candidate for daily economic activities.

Whereas the northern half of Nineveh clearly shows differentiated functions of neighborhoods, this is more difficult to discern in the southern half. Several remains of palatial buildings, belonging to military officials or members of the royal family, further indicate that throughout Nineveh the elite quarters seem to have been located along the main boulevards, which lead to the two citadels. There remains ample space inside the city, where the tens of thousands of inhabitants could have lived. We know from texts only that Nineveh was a cosmopolitan metropolis in the late seventh century, where deportees and other people from all over the empire worked and lived.

Conclusion

The development from a city-state (Aššur) to the vast Assyrian Empire led to a marked change in people's living conditions and to the concept of a city as a royal capital. The old, traditional capital Aššur lost its role as the seat of government, and several kings created new capital cities in the Assyrian heartland. These changes arose from population pressure, economic growth, security issues, and the increased desire for the visible representation of royal power. Equally desirable was the Assyrian kings' desire to outrank Babylon, the eternal rival, in size, splendor, and religious prominence. Since the Aššur Temple remained the religious and ideological center of the empire, the seat of the government could be transferred according to the requirements of the particular king.

The creation of the great cities, their thorough refurbishment or new planning belong to the most important programs of Assyrian kings. In the Assyrian self-concept a king's duty was to establish and maintain the order of the world. The regularity of the planned or remodeled cities, a dominant feature of all the cities, was therefore not only due to technical but also, to a considerable extent, to ideological reasons. The most visible expression of this are the king's building programs: he rebuilt ruined cities, regularize fortifications and streets, civilized nature by establishing botanical and zoological gardens, and even mastered the elements by means of a sophisticated water supply system. The previous assertion that the street network inside the cities was irregular has certainly to be abandoned. The king even breached already existing towns in order to create huge boulevards. Beyond this, the founding of "new" cities and the erection of "eternal" buildings were means to make their own names unforgettable and thus to achieve immortality – a fundamental aim of Near Eastern people.

Another prominent feature of the newly designed cities was the size. The dimensions of the cities, then among the largest in the world, the grandeur of the palaces, the massiveness of the fortifications, the width of the streets, the size of the statues and guardian-figures: everything was colossal. Also the effort and the expenses were enormous: tens of thousands of people worked for years in gigantic construction sites. The know-how and technical skills of countless inhabitants of the whole empire were needed for their completion. The center of government included a multitude of palaces; the palaces exhibit a confusingly large number of rooms; and the houses of the countless inhabitants must have sprung up like mushrooms.

The quality of the constructions was exceptional and illustrates visibly the infinite possibilities of the empire: exotic plants and animals from all the conquered territories, foreign stones, timber, and other imported materials such as ivory were employed lavishly. The desire to occupy the highest place is just another example of the royal quest for superlatives. The royal palace was always established on a citadel high above the lower city. Perhaps it is not by chance that the highest elevation of Kalhu and Dūr-Šarru-kēn, the ziggurat, was built as close as possible to the palace. In the last capital Nineveh/Kuyunjik the highest building must have been the royal palace itself. Size, number, quality, and height: every initiative of the king was colossal and excessive. The building projects were the elaborately staged signs of royal power and the king's privileged relation to the gods, and this was displayed to everyone.

The artfully designed imperial cities display a sharp division between elites and commoners. The supreme political and religious power in the administrative capitals was walled off from the rest of the city. This is understandable, since the huge royal palace served as the economic and administrative headquarters of a "worldwide" empire, where an immense amount of taxes, booty, and treasures were stored. This headquarters had to be segregated from the rest of the city, which disposed of its own administration, supplies, and complex network of public and private urban institutions and buildings. Enormous attention was paid to the military headquarters. Each capital of the ninth–seventh century includes a separate second citadel with arsenals that were carefully segregated from the lower city. The well-organized and equipped army was the major pillar on which rested the vast Assyrian Empire.

Millions of deportees and the additional voluntary influx of people caused tremendous demographic changes in the countryside and in the cities. For example, in Aššur the crowded housing quarters grew over the deteriorating city walls, and Egyptians, Medes, Babylonians, Luwians, and other ethnic groups from all over the empire lived there together. In order to avoid comparable shortages of living space, the lower cities of Nineveh and Kalhu were carefully designed. In Nineveh spacious elite residences lay in a preferred location close to the major citadel and along the main roads. But the entire area of the very large cities was not covered with buildings. We know of gardens, parks, and pasture land within the surrounding wall, and the existence of plazas for various economic and social purposes can be assumed. Extramural fields, gardens, and orchards belonging to the king and individuals were used for pleasure and contributed to the provisioning of the cities. Suburbs are so far only attested at Aššur, but may have existed elsewhere.

Even if royal construction work seems to have dominated the appearance of cities, in actual fact this is not entirely true. If we knew more about the lower cities with their neighborhoods, the image would probably be different. Urban affairs, real estate management, legal practice, and many other elements of daily life were in the hands of the urban administration.

The enormous cities with an estimated population of 30,000–120,000 were ethnically mixed and socially heterogeneous. Their welfare depended on an elaborate system of provisioning, communication, and transport. The water supply system at the highest technical level permitted the settling of tens of thousands of people. However, the cities of the heartland were too large to be maintained only by local resources and they depended on the exploitation of the provinces – a highly vulnerable system. The attack of the Medes and Babylonians was just the welcome opportunity for the people all over the empire to throw off the heavy burden of the Assyrian yoke.

FURTHER READINGS

Dalley, Stephanie, "Nineveh, Babylon and the Hanging Gardens: Cuneiform and Classical Sources Reconsidered," *Iraq* 56 (1994), 45–58.

Frahm, Eckart, *Einleitung in die Sanherib-Inschriften*, Vienna: Institut für Orientalistik, 1997

Fuchs, Andreas, *Die Inschriften Sargons II. aus Khorsabad*, Göttingen: Cuvillier, 1994.

Maul, Stefan M., "1903–1914: Assur, Das Herz eines Weltreiches," in Gernot Wilhelm (ed.), *Zwischen Tigris und Nil*, Mainz: Verlag Philipp von Zabern, 1998, pp. 47–65.

"Die altorientalische Hauptstadt-Abbild und Nabel der Welt," in Gernot Wilhelm (ed.), *Die altorientalische Stadt: Kontinuität, Wandel, Bruch*, Saarbrücken: SDV, 1997, pp. 109–24.

Postgate, J. N., and J. E. Reade, "Kalhu," in D. O. Edzard *et al.* (eds.), *Reallexikon der Assyriologie*, Berlin: de Gruyter, 1977–80, pp. 303–23.

Russell, John M., *Sennacherib's Palace Without a Rival at Nineveh*, Chicago: The University of Chicago Press, 1991.

Stronach, David, "Notes on the Fall of Nineveh," in Simo Parpola and R. M. Whiting (eds.), *Assyria 1995*, Helsinki: The Neo-Assyrian Text Corpus Project, 1997, pp. 307–24.

24

Mexico-Tenochtitlan: origin and transformations of the last Mesoamerican imperial city

GERARDO GUTIÉRREZ

On the eve of the Spanish Conquest, the city of Tenochtitlan was the largest human settlement and most densely built space in North America. It was a lacustrine city, founded on a conglomeration of small islands in western Lake Texcoco. Tenochtitlan was the metropolis of a native empire stretching over 300 kilometers of rugged mountains from the Gulf of Mexico to the Pacific Coast and some 500 kilometers across the arid plains of central Mexico to the exuberant forests of the Soconusco, Chiapas. Tenochtitlan became an imperial city in its own right, but its urban form and infrastructure were also shaped by enormous economic resources and human capital, which the Aztecs extracted from all over Mesoamerica. Originally founded by immigrants against the wishes of aggressive neighbors, the city struggled to survive under dire conditions during its first century only to rapidly emerge as a dominant polity through a combination of political shrewdness, military might, and serendipity. The urban form, function, and assemblage of Tenochtitlan had everything to do with its political and military successes; therefore, the analysis of this city cannot be disassociated from the history and archaeology of the Aztec Empire and its conquered provinces.

Tenochtitlan as a city represents the spirit of the Aztecs, as well as the most refined expression of Mesoamerican urbanism. It was the product of all the natives of central and southern Mexico, Aztec and non-Aztec, who voluntarily or through coercion financed the construction of its large temples, fine palaces, and maintenance of its warrior and commoner population through tribute and labor. In addition, Tenochtitlan was the beneficiary of more than 2,000 years of Mesoamerican experience in construction and urban dwelling. After its explosive growth, it was largely destroyed by Spanish conquistadors during the siege of 1521. Although the history of Tenochtitlan spans fewer than 200 years, there remains a large body of indigenous and European historical accounts of its former glory. In a similar way the damp clay of Lake Texcoco has unexpectedly preserved vast quantities of archaeological remains from the Aztec capital. These accidents of preservation provide the opportunity for dissecting the rise and fall, as well as the nature of urban life, in the last imperial society of Mesoamerica.

My objective here is to analyze the layout and culture of Tenochtitlan, along with its ideology as the capital of the dominant Mesoamerican polity during the Late Postclassic period. I begin with a brief theoretical discussion to frame the urban experience of the Aztec Empire within a larger political and territorial arrangement. Then, I summarize the history of the Mexica-Tenochca tribe and review its complex tributary system that siphoned wealth and resources from a large hinterland. Finally, I address the internal structure of the city, its urban history, and daily life. Tenochtitlan became the political hub, commercial emporium, and religious *axis mundi* of Mesoamerica, which was made possible by a change in the mentality and cultural practices on the part of the Mexica-Tenochca people, who regarded themselves as the "Lords of All Created Things." I conclude by analyzing how the mighty native city was torn apart by its Indian and European conquerors. It is noteworthy that Tenochtitlan was the first American city to be conquered by use of Old World siege craft, although the fall of Tenochtitlan cannot be reduced simply to the superiority of Spanish armaments.

Urban history of Postclassic central Mexico

Most approaches used by scholars of urbanism create models interpreting the urban experience from the Old World. Ancient, classic, medieval, mercantile, industrial, and modern cities are used and abused as models, consciously or unconsciously, to explain the origin, development, structures, morphology, and functions of non-Western settlements throughout the world. By doing so, we lose the full range of urban experiences worldwide.[1]

The urbanism of Postclassic central Mexico needs to be understood within the confines of a native political-territorial structure known as the *altepetl* in the Nahuatl language. Altepetl literally means "the waters, the

[1] Gerardo Gutiérrez, "Territorial Structure and Urbanism in Mesoamerica: The Huaxtec and Mixtec-Tlapanec-Nahua Cases," in William T. Sanders, Alba Guadalupe Mastache, and Robert Cobean (eds.), *Urbanism in Mesoamerica* (State College: Pennsylvania State University, 2003), pp. 85–95.

mountains," and it is what the Spaniards referred to as *señorío indio*, or "Indian kingdom." The Spaniards also translated altepetl as "city"; thus, for decades, archaeologists have referred to these political units as "city-states." These concepts are poor choices, since many altepetl[2] or native states were so complex they encompassed several cities under their domain. The Spaniards soon realized that Indian señoríos (kingdoms) had an intricate political organization. Most shocking for the Spaniards was the fact that an altepetl was governed by multiple rulers through councils, which formed loose confederations. Therefore, a critical element was how each segment of the altepetl was ruled by a particular *tlatocamecayotl* (ruling lineage). For tributary purposes, after the conquest, the Spaniards split the largest and most complex altepetl into individual segments, which they called *parcialidades* (parts), each governed by a single native ruler, who was referred to as a *cacique* (using the Caribbean term for "chief"). The dissolution of Prehispanic polities into modular segments has created significant confusion for generations of scholars who engage in convoluted debates on the nature of the native polity. The Colonial era practice of breaking apart native states into their minimal segments based on a single ruler needs to be set aside when evaluating Prehispanic sociopolitical organization. Instead, the entire community of the altepetl, with its multiple ruling lineages and council of rulers, is the more accurate Prehispanic form. This complex view of native sociopolitical entity allows for a better understanding of the confederate nature, multi-centrism, and, most importantly, the political and territorial organization in Mesoamerica.[3] The altepetl is composed of a network of settlements governed by a group of rulers tied together or bonded by kinship. The concept of altepetl *per se* does not recognize an urban–rural dichotomy, since it embodies all of the cities, smaller settlements, people, territories, and resources under the political control of the council of rulers.

The Mexica-Tenochca people

The people who founded Mexico-Tenochtitlan spoke the Nahuatl language, classified as part of the Uto-Aztecan family, which extended from the state of Utah to Central America. According to their mythology, these indigenous

[2] Altepetl is used here to refer to both the singular and plural.
[3] James Lockhart, *The Nahuas after the Conquest: A Social and Cultural History of the Indians of Central Mexico, Sixteenth through Eighteenth Centuries* (Stanford, CA: Stanford University Press, 1992), pp. 14–30.

people came from a place called Aztlan, supposedly located somewhere in northwestern Mexico or the southwestern United States. From this Aztlan comes the popular name of Aztecs. By order of their tribal god Huitzilopochtli (Hummingbird on the Left), they departed from Aztlan in the native year 1 Flint, corresponding to the European calendar year 1064 CE. Huitzilopochtli ordered them to seek a sacred land where they would be their own masters and "Lords of All Created Things." After wandering for many decades, they entered the Basin of Mexico and settled in the Chapultepec area c. 1299 CE.[4]

When the Mexica[5] arrived in the Basin of Mexico, there already was an urban network of more than forty cities located around an interconnected system of shallow lakes covering roughly 1,300 square kilometers. Powerful ruling houses resided in these cities, and through diplomacy, marriage alliances, and warfare they formed at least five fragile confederations. The Tepaneca confederation dominated the western shore of the lake with at least twelve cities. The eastern side of the lake was under the control of the Acolhua confederation with some fourteen cities under the leadership of Texcoco. The Culhua confederation controlled the Ixtapalapa Peninsula with three cities under the leadership of Culhuacan. The Xochimilca confederation also had three powerful cities including Xochimilco. Finally, the Chalca confederation controlled the rich hinterland of the western piedmont of the Popocatepetl volcano (Map 24.1). Each of these five confederations held vast quantities of resources, people, and strategic positions and they were constantly warring with each other. Alliances shifted continuously, which in practice generated stalemates.

When the Mexica tried to establish their own altepetl in Chapultepec, no one tolerated the newcomers. A combined force of Tepanecas and Culhuas attacked the Mexica position and overwhelmed them. The fleeing survivors were divided in two groups. The Mexica-Tenochca became captives of Culhuacan and were forced to settle in Tizapan located on the northern

---

[4] Domingo Francisco de San Antón Muñon Chimalpahin Cuauhtlehuanitzin, *Codex Chimalpahin: Society and Politics in Mexico Tenochtitlan, Tlatelolco, Texcoco, Culhuacan, and other Nahua Altepetl in Central Mexico*, Arthur J. O. Anderson and Susan Schroeder (eds. and trans.) (Norman: University of Oklahoma Press, 1997), p. 29.

[5] "Mexica" refers to the name adopted by the tribal group themselves who settled on the Island of Mexico. Their two principal sub-groups were the Tenochca and Tlatelolca. Primary sources in Nahuatl use the terms "Mexica" and "Tenochca" interchangeably to identify the Mexica-Tenochca sub-group, while Mexica-Tlatelolca are often referred to as "Tlatelolca." The term "Aztec" is used typically in English-language literature to refer to the imperial alliance of Tenochtitlan, Texcoco, and Tacuba, while Mexican authors refer to the "Triple Alliance" Empire.

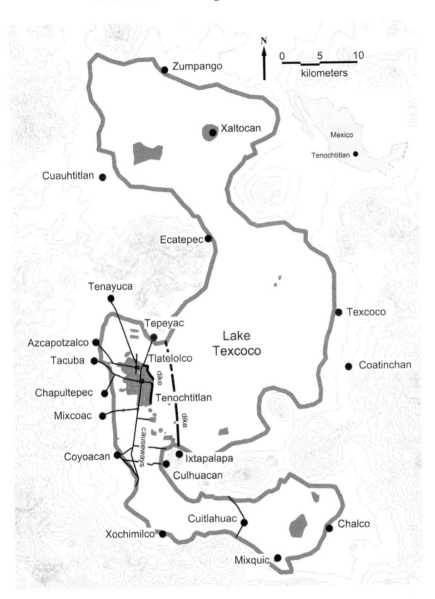

Map 24.1 Location of the cities of Tenochtitlan and Tlatelolco in the Basin of Mexico.

slope of the Ixtapalapa Peninsula. The other group, the Mexica-Tlatelolca escaped to a barren island in the lake where they became subjects of the ruler of Azcapotzalco. The Mexica-Tenochca and the Mexica-Tlatelolca were integrated into the political structures of their new masters. Primarily, they became tribute payers and provided military service in the wars of Culhuacan and Azcapotzalco.

In spite of having been accepted as subordinates of the Culhua confederation, the Mexica-Tenochca were expelled from Tizapan for having "married" a noblewoman of Culhuacan to their tribal god, Huitzilopochtli. Such a marriage involved the ritual flaying and killing of this unfortunate noblewoman. The Tenochca people took refuge in the low swampy island of Temazcaltitlan, just south of where the Mexica-Tlatelolca had been forced to settle earlier. While on the island, they allegedly saw a majestic eagle devouring a serpent atop a cactus (*tenochtli*). The Tenochca proclaimed that this was their promised land, and they won their altepetl in the native year of 2 House or 1325 CE. The island was renamed Tenochtitlan to reflect the portent of the eagle atop the cactus. Nonetheless, Tenochtitlan was located in a section of the lake claimed by the powerful city of Azcapotzalco, capital of the Tepanec confederation. Thus, the Mexica-Tenochca had to present themselves as supplicants to obtain the permission of Azcapotzalco to stay on the island.[6]

By the second half of the fourteenth century, the Mexica-Tenochca wanted their own *tlatoani* or ruler, in accordance with the altepetl political system of central Mexico. To attain this goal, they elected Acamapichtli as their first tlatoani, the grandson of a ruler of the prestigious Culhua confederation. When Acamapichtli died, his second son Huitzilihuitl was installed as ruler in 1391 CE. Huitzilihuitl was a great negotiator and managed to increase the status of Tenochtitlan within the Tepanec confederation by marrying the daughter of the ruler of Azcapotzalco. When Huitzilihuitl died his son Chimalpopoca became ruler of Tenochtitlan. In 1426 Tezozomoc, the old ruler of Azcapotzalco and leader of the Tepanec confederation, died and a war of succession ensued. Maxtlatl, the ruler of Coyoacan, seized power and implemented a policy of terror including systematic assassination of political rivals, including the Aztec ruler Chimalpopoca. Itzcoatl became the fourth tlatoani of Tenochtitlan in 1427, and, together with Texcoco and Tacuba, defeated Azcapotzalco in 1428. This is the beginning of the Triple Alliance or Aztec Empire. Tenochtitlan went from a humble settlement on the western side of the brackish Lake Texcoco to a city that surpassed all the former capitals of the old confederations in demographic size and political relevance.

[6] Bernardino de Sahagún, *General History of the Things of New Spain*, Charles E. Dibble and Arthur J. O. Anderson (eds. and trans.) (Santa Fe: School of American Research and University of New Mexico, 1961), Book 10, p. 196.

After his death, Itzcoatl was succeeded by his nephew Moctezuma Ilhuicamina (1440–68), then by his three grandsons Axayacatl (1468–81), Tizoc (1481–6), and Ahuitzotl (1486–1502). Moctezuma Xocoyotzin (1502–20), Itzcoatl's great-grandson was the last Aztec emperor, who extended the boundaries of the empire and beautified the imperial capital before the arrival of the Spanish conquistadors. He then became a key player in the fall of his own city and empire. The last two rulers of Tenochtitlan, Cuitlahuac (1520) and Cuauhtemoc (1520–5) were great grandsons of Itzcoatl too, but their role in history was to defend the city until it was impossible to resist the combined assault of Spaniards, Old World diseases, and not least the armies of its former native enemies.

The Aztec tributary system

Before the Aztecs coalesced into an empire, the typical tributary organization of the Postclassic period was structured at the local level, where each segment (*calpulli* or *tlaxilacalli*) of a political unit had at least one *tequitlato* who was a local officer in charge of organizing all things related to tribute. This tequitlato was responsible for allocating and collecting the tribute owed by each tributary unit, usually defined as a composite group of houses and co-residents. Tribute was paid in goods or in labor based on lists of tributaries. Once the Aztecs began a successful program of political expansion, they created a network of political operators and tribute collectors to oversee compliance by local lords to their demands. Imperial governors and native tribute collectors (*calpixque*) operated with autonomy, living in the provinces with their family and a few retainers.[7]

Based on Aztec tributary data as reported in the *Información de 1554*,[8] I have attempted to calculate an acceptable proxy for the total Aztec tributary revenue on the eve of the Spanish Conquest. The *Información de 1554* is the only tributary tally that provides exchange rates for tribute goods based on items of native cloth (*mantas*) at the time of the conquest. This provides the unique opportunity to standardize all the various types of tributary goods into one abstract unit based on mantas and capture a broad picture of the Aztec Empire. Thus, the total amount of tribute paid to the Aztecs is

[7] Diego Durán, *The History of the Indies of New Spain*, Doris Heyden (trans.) (Norman: University of Oklahoma Press, 1994), p. 181.
[8] Frances V. Scholes and Eleanor B. Adams, *Documentos para la historia del México Colonial IV: información sobre los tributos que los Indios pagaban a Moctezuma. Año de 1554* (Mexico: José Porrúa e Hijos, 1957).

estimated to be some 652,246 items of cloth per year (Table 24.1). When the data on the quantity of mantas paid by each province per year are grouped more broadly into classes with a range of 10,000 items of cloth (Table 24.2 and Figure 24.1), it is easier to distinguish that there were a few giant provinces paying considerable tribute, while there were many small provinces providing only a minor percentage of the total revenue.

The spatial distribution of tributary revenue is insightful as well (Map 24.2 and Table 24.1). Although there were twenty-six provinces within a distance of 200 kilometers from Tenochtitlan, contributing 54 percent of the tribute (351,981 mantas), another thirteen provinces located beyond the radius of 200 kilometers provided 46 percent of the total revenue (300,265 mantas). This indicates that provinces closer to Tenochtitlan were supporting its staple finance in grains and in bulky mantas to maintain the liquidity of the exchange system of the Aztec economy (Table 24.3).[9] In contrast, the primary wealth finance needed to support the sumptuous ideological and political life of the Aztecs was coming from exterior provinces located in the tropical coasts or in mountainous regions with abundant metamorphic rocks such as green serpentines. These tribute items were not as heavy or bulky, while offering great exchange value in the market system, as well as high desirability in the political and religious realms, specifically: gold, cacao, feathers, and precious stones.[10]

The cyclical concentration of tributary wealth and its subsequent ritual and political consumption had direct and indirect effects throughout Mesoamerica. A large tribute component was siphoned from a radius of 400 kilometers around Tenochtitlan, ending up in the Basin of Mexico. This constantly depleted the Aztec hinterland of staples and wealth, creating artificial scarcity. At the other end of the system, the flow of resources, as exemplified in enormous quantities and great diversity of goods, subsidized the urban population of the Basin of Mexico. Ideological practices were designated to absorb any excess supply of tribute, especially through destruction of vast quantities of goods in lavish rituals and feasting, in addition to calculated gift-giving and the assignment of war prizes to valiant warriors. In spite of these mechanisms and the supposed imposition of rigid etiquette prohibitions for the display of wealth, tributary goods were widely

[9] Elizabeth M. Brumfiel, "Specialization, Market Exchange, and the Aztec State," *Current Anthropology* 21 (1980), 459–78.
[10] See maps in Frances F. Berdan and Patricia Rieff Anawalt, *The Codex Mendoza* (Berkeley: University of California Press, 1992), Vol. x, pp. 67–77.

Table 24.1 Estimated value of the tribute paid annually by each province standardized in mantas.

Number in Map 24.2	Province	Tribute paid annually converted into mantas	Percentage of total tribute	Cumulative percentage
30	Tochtepec	99,715	15.3	15.3
37	Atlan	45,000	6.9	22.2
19	Tepecuacuilco	36,540	5.6	27.8
20	Cihuatlan	36,000	5.5	33.3
33	Cuetlaxtla	30,020	4.6	37.9
36	Tochpan	26,510	4.1	42.0
2	Petlacalco	24,725	3.8	45.8
3	Acolhuacan	24,513	3.8	49.5
39	Oxitipa	24,090	3.7	53.2
27	Coixtlahuaca	23,450	3.6	56.8
35	Tlatlauhquitepec	21,015	3.2	60.0
4	Quauhnauac	20,443	3.1	63.2
5	Huaxtepec	19,383	3.0	66.1
11	Xilotepec	15,297	2.3	68.5
18	Apan	14,844	2.3	70.8
10	Atotonilco de Pedraza	13,100	2.0	72.8
34	Tlapacoyan	12,900	2.0	74.7
31	Xoconochco	12,660	1.9	76.7
21	Tlapan	12,080	1.9	78.5
12	Quahuacan	11,115	1.7	80.2
38	Tzicoac	10,725	1.6	81.9
1	Tlatelolco	9,869	1.5	83.4
17	Tlachco	9,634	1.5	84.9
13	Tolocan	9,551	1.5	86.3
14	Ocuilan	8,643	1.3	87.7
32	Quauhtochco	8,600	1.3	89.0
29	Tlachquiauco	7,565	1.2	90.1
26	Tepeacac	7,501	1.2	91.3
9	Hueypochtlan	7,170	1.1	92.4
7	Axocopan	7,155	1.1	93.5
28	Coyolapan	6,825	1.0	94.5
8	Atotonilco el Grande	6,711	1.0	95.6
25	Chalco	6,625	1.0	96.6
22	Tlacozautitlan	6,465	1.0	97.6
6	Quauhtitlan	5,065	0.8	98.4
15	Malinalco	3,941	0.6	99.0
23	Quiauhteopan	2,440	0.4	99.3
16	Xocotitlan	2,339	0.4	99.7
24	Yoaltepec	2,025	0.3	100.0
	Total	652,246	100.0	

GERARDO GUTIÉRREZ

Table 24.2 *Percentage of annual tribute paid to Aztec Empire grouped by classes with a range of 10,000 mantas*

Classes (based on mantas)	Number of provinces in the class	Percentage of tribute by class
0–10,000	18	18.1
10,000–20,000	9	21.9
20,000–30,000	7	26.7
30,000 or more mantas	5	33.3
Totals	39	100

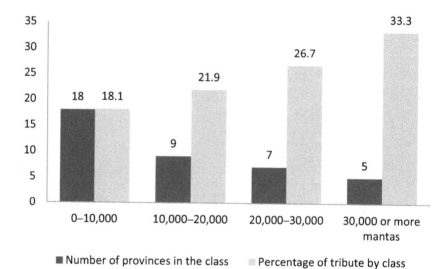

Figure 24.1 Percentage of annual tribute paid to Aztec Empire grouped by classes with a range of 10,000 mantas and the number of provinces in the class.

traded in the marketplaces and made Tenochtitlan, Texcoco, and Tacuba splendid and wealthy cities.

Mexico-Tenochtitlan and its ideological template

Tenochtitlan and Tlaltelolco began as entirely new settlements that did not have to adapt to previous urban forms. Since Tenochtitlan militarily subjugated Tlatelolco in 1473, the name of the former has achieved primacy;

Table 24.3 *Spatial distribution of the tributary revenue paid to Aztec Empire by distance from Tenochtitlan*

Distance from Tenochtitlan	Provinces within distance	Number of mantas	Percentage of mantas
0–100 km	17	20,3775	31
100–200 km	9	14,8206	22.7
200–300 km	9	14,5065	22
More than 300 km	4	15,5200	24
Totals	39	652246	100

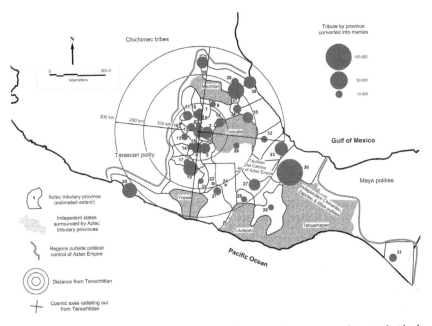

Map 24.2 Map showing the spatial distribution of Aztec tribute converted into individual items of cloth (mantas). The axes radiate out from Tenochtitlan, have as their center the juncture of the old Tacuba and Ixtapalapa causeways (the corner of Guatemala and Argentina Streets today), and are oriented approximately 8 degrees from true north, as is the general layout of Mexico City's downtown area.

nonetheless, the existence of Tlatelolco is important in any discussion of Tenochitlan. The urban space of both cities not only coalesced as they expanded over several small islets, creating a large semi-artificial island, but also the urban duality endured throughout the entire history of the

Mexica people. These twin cities were each planned with their own cosmological layout, and the organization of space responded primarily to negotiations between the two groups in the appropriation and allocation of scarce land in the swampy terrain and micro-topography.

According to their own lore, the founding of Tenochtitlan was embedded within an elaborate rituality that involved finding the "right place" for the future settlement and the performance of specific ceremonies for taking possession of the land. The Mexica practice of place-making began before the foundation of the altepetl of Tenochtitlan by invoking memories of an actual or mythical migration full of significant incidents. Elements in the landscape of their new home needed to fit within the narrative of ancient prophecies and previous foundation events, such as the "bent-shape" mountain, the cave, the V-shaped crag providing access to a mountain range, and clear spring waters had to be present to fulfil mythic parameters. In addition, the potential location for any new settlement also required a sense of sacredness. A place was perceived as sacred by the occurrence of extraordinary and supernatural events, which were interpreted as propitious omens. Many suitable locations were discarded if bad omens occurred, like the sudden falling of trees or a dispute between tribal factions. For the Mexica the portentous sight of the eagle atop the cactus marked the holiness of the place selected as the foundational node and cosmic axis of the new city. In Nahuatl this sacred place is referred as *altepeyolloco* or the "kidney" of the city, referencing its central religious district. The Mexica-Tenochca initially built three elements as part of the foundation of their city and to legitimize their taking possession of the land: (1) a ball court, (2) an earthen mound, and on top of it (3) an earthen altar. The mound was built at the edge of two natural caves, which were later buried under subsequent construction stages. Since many tribal gods were perhaps deified ancestors, the vertical axis created by the underworld cave and the main temple projecting into the sky was the ideal meeting point for the ancestor cult: the place where the living could communicate spiritually with ancient founding fathers. A cosmic axis was laid out with an azimuth of some 8 degrees, and the city was divided into four quarters: Moyotlan (southwest), Teopan (southeast), Atzacualco (northeast), and Cuepopan (northwest). On this humble first temple, each Mexica-Tenochca ruler committed to enlarging it, although that depended on the political fortunes of each ruler.

During the government of Ahuitzotl, the eighth tlatoani of Tenochtitlan (1486–1502), the Aztec capital acquired a more stable layout and operation. The Great Temple was expanded and the religious district became an enormous complex known as the sacred precinct. This was the symbolic heart of the Aztec Empire, grouping at least seventy-eight specialized buildings, temples, and shrines. Four walls surrounded the entire complex, embracing an area of some 14 hectares. The sacred area could only be entered through four gates oriented to the cardinal directions, as were the great causeways that led out of the city. Tenochtitlan was a symbolically planned city, following the template of the native cosmic map. Although Mexican archaeologists continue finding better information on the nature and organization of the sacred precinct,[11] we still have a sketchy plan of its former self. The main temple is the best-understood construction in this precinct. On February 21, 1978, workers from the Electric Light Company were digging at the corner of Guatemala and Argentina Streets and discovered a large stone carved with a series of reliefs. Excavations on the spot revealed an enormous monolith 3.25 meters in diameter, with a representation of a decapitated and dismembered female nude carved in relief. It was a depiction of the goddess Coyolxauhqui who, according to Aztec myth, had been killed by her brother, the war-god Huitzilopochtli. The discovery of the Coyolxauhqui stone led the authorities to order further work to expose this central area of Tenochtitlan.

Over a six-year period, Mexican archaeologists uncovered the material remains of seven construction phases of the Great Temple of Tenochtitlan.[12] Stage I was the sanctuary built by the Aztecs when they first founded Tenochtitlan in 1325. Stage II survived in excellent condition and has provided the best information on the religious ideology of the Mexica people. The temple of Stage II was more a platform than a pyramid. Nonetheless, it contains all the prototypical elements of the later stages. This temple was crowned by two shrines, each with its own stairway up the face of the pyramid, dedicated to the gods Tlaloc (north) and Huitzilopochtli (south). Each shrine faced west and had a sculpture associated with these deities. In front of the shrine of Tlaloc, there was a "chac-mool" (stone representation of a man lying on his back with a receptacle resting on his abdomen). Before the shrine of Huitzilopchtli, there was a blocky stone called a *techcatl*, upon which many were sacrificed in honor of that god. It is believed that Stage II

[11] Leonardo López Luján, *The Offerings of the Templo Mayor of Tenochtitlan* (Albuquerque: University of New Mexico, 2005).
[12] Eduardo Matos Moctezuma, "The Templo Mayor of Tenochtitlan: History and Interpretation," in Johanna Broda, David Carrasco, and Eduardo Matos Moctezuma, *The Great Temple of Tenochtitlan: Center and Periphery in the Aztec World* (Berkeley: University of California Press, 1987), pp. 30–5.

corresponds to the reigns of either Acamapichtli, Huitzilihuitl, or Chimal-popoca, that is, before 1428 (the year of Aztec independence from Azcapotzalco).

On the back wall of the Stage III pyramid of the Great Temple, at the base of the side devoted to Huitzilopochtli, there is a stone carved with the calendrical glyph 4 Reed. This probably references the date 1431, placing this construction stage in the reign of Itzcoatl (1427–40). The architecture and sculptures of Stage IV are the most spectacular of the Great Temple. The pyramidal base was enlarged and adorned with braziers and serpent heads on all four sides. Stage IVb is labeled as such because it designates a partial enlargement of the temple: the main facade, on the west side, was amplified and adorned with undulating serpent bodies wrapping around its corners and terminating in snake heads. In the middle of Huitzilopochtli's side, at the foot of the stairway, Coyolxauhqui's dismembered body is carved in low-relief on a huge stone. Little has survived from Stages V and VI. What has been uncovered is stucco plaster on the platform, and part of the floor of the ceremonial precinct, the latter formed by stone slabs joined by stucco. Stage VII of the Great Temple was seen by the Spaniards at the beginning of the sixteenth century. All that remains of this period is a section of stone flooring in the ceremonial precinct.

Mexico-Tenochtitlan and its urban infrastructure

At the founding of the city, Tenochtitlan and Tlatelolco had a total of twenty-nine calpulli, thus one can estimate an original population size of c. 3,000 people (assuming each migratory calpulli had a fluctuating population of some 100 people). Based on oral accounts of Spaniards who lived in Tenochtitlan from November of 1519, to June of 1520, Cervantes de Salazar reported the existence of 60,000 "houses" on the island. This figure has provoked debate on the definition of "house," leading to some estimates of 240,000–300,000 people (four to five persons per house).[13] Based on Calnek's work,[14] Sanders reanalyzed all the information available on the area occupied by Tenochtitlan and Tlatelolco, the size and nature of their households, and the possible land use of each sector of the city. He proposed a more

---

[13] Francisco Cervantes de Salazar, *Crónica de la Nueva España* (Madrid: Biblioteca de Autores Españoles, 1971), Vol. I, p. 324.
[14] Edward Calnek, "Tenochtitlan-Tlatelolco: The Natural History of a City," in Sanders, Mastache, and Cobean (eds.), *Urbanism in Mesoamerica*, pp. 149–202.

conservative figure ranging from 125,000 to 140,000 people[15] allocated among sixty-nine calpulli (forty-nine for Tenochtitlan and twenty for Tlatelolco). The final surface of the island would have reached some 13 square kilometers. If we take the figure of 3,000 individuals as the original founders and 140,000 people as the maximum population on the eve of the Spanish Conquest, the annual growth rate of the island's population is estimated at 2 percent – the city was doubling its population every thirty-five years. This growth is impressive given the high mortality rates usually associated with pre-industrial populations. What were the factors underlying this demographic growth? Natural growth does not explain this rate of increase, which must have included a significant and steady flow of immigrants from outside the island. Population movements were likely driven by factors associated with the expansion of the empire as well as from nearby settlements of the Basin of Mexico. Hernán Cortés relates how the Mexica forced the rulers of all subject polities to send and maintain permanently a son or close relative to live in Tenochtitlan.[16] This policy would have resulted in at least 400 small palaces representing conquered states, adding greatly to the urban layout of the city.

The Spaniards always referred to Tenochtitlan as "another Venice," due to the lacustrine nature of its urbanization, with some 20 kilometers of navigable water courses and a similar number of raised dry roads. The romantic character of the city, however, prevented Tenochtitlan from prospering initially due to lack of cultivable lands. The Tenochca were forced to trade with the people living along the shores of the lakes and in the piedmont. Originally the island's inhabitants specialized in the commerce of lacustrine resources, which were exchanged with their neighbors to acquire wood and stone. These materials were used by the inhabitants of Tenochtitlan to anchor a group of shallow islands in the lake for an artificial platform that achieved an area of some 13 square kilometers (Map 24.3). Millions of cubic meters of sediment were used to artificially raise this platform above the level of the lake. The chinampa system first developed in the lakes of Xochimilco and Chalco was used to create the raised fields connecting the islands. Lines of willow trees, brush, wooden stakes, and rocks consolidated the walls of these artificial blocks of the city. Deep canals were dug to allow canoe navigation; thus wooden bridges were necessary to

---

[15] William T. Sanders, "The Population of Tenochtitlan-Tlatelolco," in Sanders, Mastache, and Cobean (eds.), *Urbanism in Mesoamerica*, p. 213.
[16] Hernán Cortés, *Cartas de relación* (Mexico: Editorial Porrúa, 1988), p. 65.

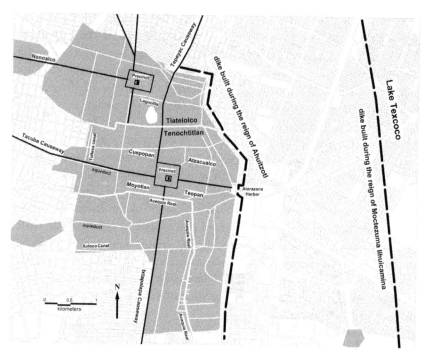

Map 24.3 GIS reconstruction of the island of Mexico based on the *Nuremberg Map* of 1524, *Mapa de Uppsala* of 1550, the *Plano Ignographico* of 1776–8 of Ignacio Castera, and *Plano de la Ciudad de México* by the Dirección de Catastro of 1929. This map shows the approximate shape of the island on the eve of the Spanish Conquest with the surviving network of primary canals in 1554. In the background in light gray is the layout of modern Mexico City in what used to be Lake Texcoco.

cross from one block to another. Moving through the city of Tenochtitlan would have involved a combination of canoes and walking through a complex network of streets and alleys connected by hundreds of bridges (Figure 24.2).

The most extraordinary projects, however, were the artificial causeways connecting the island to the main cities on shore, the aqueduct that brought fresh water to the city, and the dikes that regulated the level of Lake Texcoco. All these engineering projects were formidable tasks that would have been impossible without the forced labor of the conquered polities around the lake. The Xochimilcas were burdened with the construction of the first causeway during the rule of Itzcoatl. This causeway is known as Ixtapalapa Street and is some 10 kilometers long. Cortés reported that it was

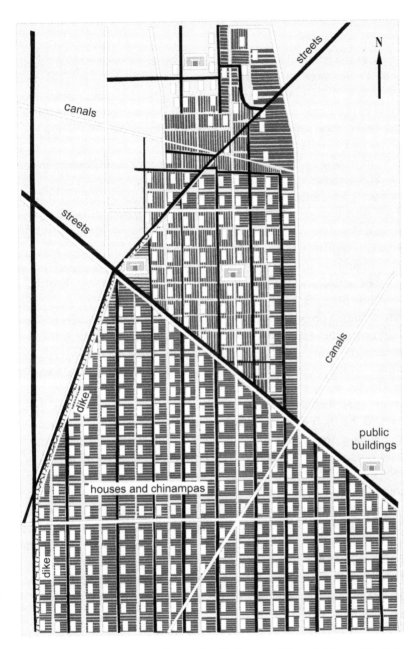

Figure 24.2 Schematic drawing of an unidentified sector of Tenochtitlan or Tlatelolco, based on the *Plano en Papel de Maguey*, which was painted *c.* 1557–62. Note the complex network of canals, dikes, streets, chinampa fields, and house plots in the margins of the artificial island at that time. Moving through the different neighborhoods of the city would have been an exciting experience involving the crossing of dozens of bridges and negotiating veritable labyrinths of narrow alleys often ending in deep canals or levees.

as wide as the width of eight horses.[17] Another three causeways were built, one to Tacuba (west), the other to Tepeyac (north), and a short one to the eastern side of the island. I would highlight that the four causeways converged in the sacred ceremonial precinct and were used for long religious processions, especially during the primary ceremonies when dozens of captives had to walk to their sacrifice.

The most famous hydraulic projects involved the construction of an aqueduct 5 kilometers in length connecting the springs of Chapultepec to the island. This was a great sanitary achievement for the city, and it would have helped to reduce mortality rates caused by gastrointestinal bacteria. Moctezuma Ilhuicamina ordered the construction of a 16-kilometer dike in the middle of Lake Texcoco to regulate tidal flooding. A second dike was built during the reign of Ahuitzotl on the eastern side of the island, but despite these efforts, the city was prone to floods and the Mexica people learned to cope by building houses with sturdy flat roofs, some with two stories where they could take refuge.

Moctezuma Xocoyotzin (1502–20), the last great emperor, proudly presented his city and all the other cities in the Basin of Mexico to Hernán Cortés from the summit of the Temple of Tlatelolco. Down in the marketplace, thousands from all over central Mexico were busily bartering, trading, and exchanging.[18] Tenochtitlan was a city in the broadest sense of the concept. Ideologically it was the most important center of native power in Mesoamerica. It also possessed the most elaborate religious precinct, the largest concentration of native nobility, the largest population, and the highest density of inhabitants per square kilometer. Tenochtitlan had become a cosmopolitan city, and all of its inhabitants likely felt the same pride in living in this important city and state. Lavish ceremonies accompanied by redistribution of resources, feasting, trade, as well as the large construction projects that directly and indirectly involved thousands of people from a radius of more than 300 kilometers would have provoked a mixture of emotions from all those subject to Tenochtitlan. Admiration, fear, and rancor are reported in multiple sources. Still, the Mexica people were slow to create a social and political identity embracing the entire empire or even the other states in the Basin of Mexico.[19] While the people of the

---

[17] Cortés, Cartas, p. 50.

[18] Bernal Díaz del Castillo, Historia de la Conquista de la Nueva España (Mexico: Editorial Porrúa, 1986).

[19] Friedrich Katz, "A Comparison of Some Aspects of the Evolution of Cuzco and Tenochtitlan," in Richard P. Schaedel, Jorge E. Hardoy, and Nora Scott Kinzer (eds.), Urbanization in the Americas from its Beginnings to the Present (The Hague: Mouton Publishers, 1978), pp. 212–13.

Triple Alliance seemed to have enjoyed special privileges for being part of this partnership, loyalties and identities created at the level of the altepetl were never broken, hence an imperial identity was never forged.

Both Tenochtitlan and Tlatelolco were destroyed during the Spanish siege of the island. Whatever was left standing, pyramids and stone monuments, was used as foundation stones in the houses later built for the European conquerors. Notably, the features that made Tenochtitlan an undefeatable city for their native enemies – its size, its location in the middle of a lake, its long streets with moveable bridges – ultimately became its major weaknesses during their battles with the Spaniards. In the fall of 1520, the Spanish conquistadors and their Indian allies began planning the assault on the city. This involved the latest siege craft techniques of the time. Cannons, firearms, lances, swords, cross-bows, and even a failed stone-thrower catapult were used. Special brigantines were built to be used in Lake Texcoco; this single action gave Cortés naval superiority on the lake. No longer was the lake a defense for the city, but instead allowed the Spanish brigantines to fire cannons at a city lacking defensive walls. The causeways in the lake became the roads of conquest for the Spanish–Tlaxcalan forces. The aqueduct was broken and food supplies were cut off by land and naval blockade. Suddenly the large population of Tenochtitlan was a liability. Starving people began to flee. Native lords from subject polities who had initially taken refuge on the island deserted the Mexica and became Spanish allies. Even the cities of Texcoco and Tacuba deserted the Mexica, ending a ninety-year-old alliance. Only the Tlatelolca remained with the Tenocha. Once again facing adversity, the people of Huitzilopochtli united to fight their last battle. At one point, even women and children took shields and swords and climbed to the roofs of their homes to simulate the appearance of a large army, when in reality there were not enough warriors left to stop the last assault.

Conclusion

The destruction of Tenochtitlan and Tlatelolco led to the creation of a new city that emerged on the same sacred locale where the Mexica immigrants first witnessed the signs to found their city and state. This new city, however, became the center for the Spanish colonization of Mexico, Central America, the southern half of the United States, and the Philippines. The Mexica, the Tlatelolca, the Tlaxcala, and all the rest of the Nahuatl-speaking people of central Mexico became foot soldiers for the Spanish expeditions throughout New Spain – another irony of history. The short lifespan and rapid emergence of Tenochtitlan and Tlatelolco provide the unique opportunity to analyze the rise of a Native American empire and the construction of its imperial capital. The ideology and symbolic elements of the Triple Alliance Empire were as important as the economic factors associated with its expansion. Tenochtitlan people endured difficult origins requiring them to adapt to a new ethos of warfare, diplomacy, and trade. They were very successful and solved the primary needs of the early city, including subsistence and construction materials – particularly the commoners who became the traders and merchants. The Tenocha exploited opportunities that other more established groups of Mesoamerica did not recognize. Ambitious elites were created from a combination of tribal leaders and prestigious Mesoamerican ruling lineages. Although over time they became more distanced from the commoners, they never completely separated themselves. Redistribution of tribute based on merit earned in battle helped to maintain social cohesion between elites and commoners. A state-run educational system helped to consolidate a Tenochca identity for those who lived in the imperial city at the calpulli level. The Tenocha relationship with their provinces, however, was exploitative, since they were interested in the appropriation of wealth produced by other Mesoamerican states. Nonetheless, they did respect regional ruling dynasties and thus minimized their impact on local affairs. Tenochtitlan became for other Mesoamericans a place with great power and wealth. "Culhua, Culhua, Mexico, Mexico" were the words the Spaniards heard when they asked the people of Tabasco for a place abundant in wealth.

Indeed, Mexico-Tenochtitlan was a place of power and wealth according to the Spaniards, but also for the Mexica people and their conquered subjects. Mexico was the place

> where the rock nopal stands, where the eagle reposes, where it rests; where the eagle screeches, where it whistles; where the eagle stretches, where it is joyful; where the eagle devours, where it gluts; where the serpent hisses, where the fishes swim; where the blue waters join with the yellow, where the waters are afire – there at the navel of the waters, where the waters go in; where the sedge and the reed whisper; where the white water snakes live, where the white frog lives; where the white cypress stands, where the most precious white willow stands.[20]

---

[20] Chimalpahin Cuauhtlehuanitzin, *Codex Chimalpahin*, Vol. 1, p. 27.

FURTHER READINGS

Armillas, Pedro, "Gardens on Swamps," *Science* 174 (1970), 653–61.

Brumfiel, Eizabeth M., "Specialization, Market Exchange, and the Aztec State," *Current Anthropology* 21 (1980), 459–78.

Calnek, Edward, "Tenochtitlan-Tlatelolco: The Natural History of a City," in William T. Sanders, Alba Guadalupe Mastache, and Robert Cobean (eds.), *Urbanism in Mesoamerica*, State College: The Pennsylvania State University, 2003, pp. 149–202.

Caso, Alfonso, "Los barrios antiguos de Tenochtitlan y Tlatelolco," *Memorias de la Academia Mexicana de la Historia, Tomo* 15 (1956), 7–62.

Chanfon Olmos, Carlos (ed.), *Historia de la arquitectura y el urbanismo mexicanos*, Mexico City: Universidad Nacional Autónoma de México and Fondo de la Cultura Económica, 1997, Vol. II.

Christaller, Walter, *Die Zentralen Orte in Süddeutschland*, Jena: Gustav Fischer, 1933.

Gibson, Charles, *The Aztecs under Spanish Rule: A History of the Valley of Mexico, 1519–1810*, Stanford, CA: Stanford University Press, 1964.

González Aparicio, Luis, *Plano reconstructivo de la región de Tenochtitlán*, Mexico City: Instituto Nacional de Antropología e Historia, 1973.

Gutiérrez, Gerardo, "Territorial Structure and Urbanism in Mesoamerica: The Huaxtec and Mixtec-Tlapanec-Nahua Cases," in William T. Sanders, Alba Guadalupe Mastache, and Robert Cobean (eds.), *Urbanism in Mesoamerica*, State College: The Pennsylvania State University, 2003, pp. 85–118.

Harris, Chauncy D., and Edward L. Ullman, "The Nature of Cities," *Annals of the American Academy of Political and Social Sciences* 242 (1945), 7–17.

Hassig, Ross, *Aztec Warfare: Imperial Expansion and Political Control*, Norman: University of Oklahoma Press, 1988.

Hicks, Frederick, "Cloth in the Political Economy of the Aztec State," in Mary G. Hodge and Michael E. Smith (eds.), *Economies and Polities in the Aztec Realm*, Albany: Institute for Mesoamerican Studies, State University of New York, 1994, pp. 88–111.

Hirth, Kenneth G., "The Altepetl and Urban Structure in Prehispanic Mesoamerica," in William T. Sanders, Alba Guadalupe Mastache, and Robert Cobean (eds.), *Urbanism in Mesoamerica*, State College: The Pennsylvania State University, 2003, pp. 57–84.

Hodge, Mary G., *Aztec City-States*, Ann Arbor: University of Michigan, 1984.

Katz, Friedrich, "A Comparison of Some Aspects of the Evolution of Cuzco and Tenochtitlan," in Richard P. Schaedel, Jorge E. Hardoy, and Nora Scott Kinzer (eds.), *Urbanization in the Americas from its Beginnings to the Present*, The Hague: Mouton Publishers, 1978, pp. 202–13.

Lockhart, James, *The Nahuas after the Conquest: A Social and Cultural History of the Indians of Central Mexico, Sixteenth Through Eighteenth Centuries*, Stanford, CA: Stanford University Press, 1992.

López Luján, Leonardo, *The Offerings of the Templo Mayor of Tenochtitlán*, Albuquerque: University of New Mexico Press, 2005.

Matos Moctezuma, Eduardo, "Buildings in the Sacred Precinct of Tenochtitlan," in William T. Sanders, Alba Guadalupe Mastache, and Robert Cobean (eds.), *Urbanism in Mesoamerica*, State College: The Pennsylvania State University, 2003, pp. 119–47.

"The Templo Mayor of Tenochtitlan History and Interpretation," in Johanna Broda, David Carrasco, and Eduardo Matos Moctezuma, *The Great Temple of Tenochtitlan: Center and Periphery in the Aztec World*, Berkeley: University of California Press, 1987, pp. 15–60.

Miranda, José, *El tributo indígena en Nueva España durante el siglo XVI*, Mexico City: Colegio de México, 1952.

Ouweneel, Arij, "Altepeme and Pueblos de Indios: Some Comparative Theoretical Perspectives on the Analysis of the Colonial Indian Communities," in Simon Miller and Arig Ouweneel (eds.), *The Indian Community of Colonial Mexico: Fifteen Essays on Land Tenure, Corporate Organizations, Ideology and Village Politics*, Amsterdam: Centro de Estudios y Documentación Latinoamericanos, 1990, pp. 1–37.

Reyes, Luis, "La visión cosmológica y la organización del imperio Mexica," in Barbara Dahlgren (ed.), *Mesoamérica, Homenaje al Doctor Paul Kirchoff*, Mexico City: Secretaria de Educación Pública and Instituto Nacional de Antropología e Historia, 1979, pp. 34–40.

Sanders, William T., "The Population of Tenochtitlan-Tlatelolco," in William T. Sanders, Alba Guadalupe Mastache, and Robert Cobean (eds.), *Urbanism in Mesoamerica*, State College: The Pennsylvania State University, 2003, pp. 203–16.

Smith, Michael E., *Aztec City-State Capitals*, Gainesville: University Press of Florida, 2008.

Wirth, Louis, "Urbanism as a Way of Life," *American Journal of Sociology* 44 (1938), 1–24.

25

The archetypal imperial city: the rise of Rome and the burdens of empire

NICOLA TERRENATO

The city of Rome was the center of a vast territorial empire for over five centuries. Not-too-dissimilar phenomena took place in different forms a number of times in human history, and yet it could be argued that the specific instance of Rome has often received far more than its share of attention, at least in the context of Eurocentric culture as it has developed in the last millennium and a half. Even before the actual collapse of the western Roman Empire, Rome at its heyday was unquestioningly taken for granted as an icon and as a role model by aspiring expansionists. From then on, the historiographic tradition in Europe and beyond grew inextricably linked with what was termed, with an absolute value judgment, "the classical period." As a consequence, no schooling was complete without a fairly extensive knowledge of Rome, its history, its laws, and its language. In no contemporary political conjuncture or challenge could the example of Rome be considered irrelevant. The larger-than-life presence of what was dubbed (with a revealing moniker) the Eternal City towered in the social sciences from their origin at least until the end of European colonialism and it is arguably still very central today.

It would be natural to consider such unparalleled name recognition as an enviable, if undeserved, privilege. Undoubtedly, the sheer quantity of books, movies, university chairs, and research funds devoted the world over to ancient Rome might be mouthwatering for other scholars. These did, however, come at a heavy intellectual price. From the court of Charlemagne to that of Mussolini, Rome has, more often than not, been brutally pressed into the service of the dominant discourse, or, worse, of blatant regime propaganda. While most today would agree that there cannot be an unbiased view of any past, it could be argued that the Roman one has been distorted further than most others and so many times that certain fictitious perceptions have become established facts that are still accepted today. A Google Image search on "Roman" will produce a screenful of reenacting legionaries with the occasional toga-clad senator, and little else. After centuries of political use and abuse of Rome, mostly in aid of various forms of militarism and dictatorship, it has become very hard not to assume, at least implicitly, that its empire was rooted almost exclusively in violence and threat.[1]

Another unwelcome consequence of the high visibility of Rome is its incomparability. Because the Roman Empire was so often painted as the most powerful, disciplined, and well organized of all, providing an example that should always be emulated but could never be attained, there has been a marked scholarly reluctance to put it on the same dissecting table along-side other empires. Roman historians have typically confined themselves to the "classical" world, naturally finding little in the Mediterranean that could equal the span and the durability of Rome's domination. The scholarly discourse has stayed very specialized and terminologically discrete, with extensive use of Latin and of Roman institutional concepts. The irony is of course that some of the most commonly used comparative terms in English, such as city or empire, are derived from Latin words that the Romans themselves used to describe political abstractions. On that basis, a wealth of cross-cultural state formation theories were produced over the last century, but they hardly ever included a consideration of Rome, where, arguably, the very concept of state had originated.

A victim to its own celebrity and fame, Rome cannot easily be considered separately from the intellectual concretions that have accumulated on it in the course of centuries of visibility in anything from blockbusters and documentaries to historical novels and theater plays. The embeddedness of Rome in Eurocentric culture has produced a delay in rethinking and updating our historical analysis of it. In the study of other periods, there is far less need to contend with strong assumptions and biases that were crystallized by Romantic scholars in the nineteenth century and are still floating around today. As a result, a pressing item in our agenda must be a realignment of Rome with current sociopolitical thinking as well as the restoration of this particular instance of empire within the broader fold of the history of complex societies anywhere.

From city to empire

Rome was first settled, like most other primary urban sites in Italy, in the late Bronze Age, at the end of the second millennium BCE, and it developed into a city-state during the first few centuries of the following millennium.

---

[1] R. Hingley (ed.) *Images of Rome* (Portsmouth, RI: Journal of Roman Archaeology, 2001).

Map 25.1 Italy in around 600 BCE.

Many similar centers emerged at the same time up and down the western coast of central Italy, while Greek and Carthaginian colonies were being founded further south and on the islands (Map 25.1).[2] Rome found itself within a particularly tight cluster of these polities, which often had their nearest neighbor only 20–40 kilometers away and ranged in walled size between 50 and 150 hectares. Located on the banks of the Tiber, the main river of the region, Rome was also straddling a deepening cultural boundary between Etruscan cities to the north and Latin and Greek ones to the south. From early on, the Romans probably cultivated a distinctive self-image of ethnic and cultural hybridity, explicitly acknowledging the contribution of a variety of elements that characterized their neighbors with more defined identities.[3] Also unusual for the region was the environmental setting of Rome, sprawled across several steep-sided hills separated by wide alluvial valleys that were seasonally flooded. Unlike other peer communities, which typically occupied vast and naturally defended volcanic plateaus, the Romans had to engage in massive land reclamation projects that involved

[2] H. D. Andersen (ed.) *Urbanization in the Mediterranean in the 9th to 6th Centuries BC* (Copenhagen: Museum Tusculanum Press, 1997).
[3] E. Dench, *Romulus' Asylum: Roman Identities from the Age of Alexander to the Age of Hadrian* (Oxford: Oxford University Press, 2005).

dumping soil over vast drains to create land bridges (one of which became the Forum) that could connect the hills and that kept being expanded for centuries.[4] It is significant that Rome acquired fortification walls only at a relatively late date, around the mid-sixth century BCE. Remarkably, the fortified area (c. 285 hectares) was much bigger than that of any other central Italian city, but it included vast amounts of unreclaimed floodlands as well as many unusable steep ravines around the individual hills.

In the late sixth–early fifth century BCE, the political systems in Rome and in neighboring city-states went through a phase of high instability, characterized by tyrannical coups and intense inter-city elite horizontal mobility. Great works were undertaken in the city, such as the creation of the first great state temple on the Capitoline and the drainage of the Forum Valley. Warfare was endemic, but mainly involved seasonal raids that had limited consequences and never led to the annexation or destruction of one of the major polities. Dominance spanning more than one city (typically achieved through the installation of friendly rulers) seems to have been unusual and short-lived. Similar phenomena occurred in Greek, Etruscan, and other states in peninsular Italy and Sicily. By the late fifth century, a republican system was certainly in place in Rome and in many other peer cities, in which elites competed for yearly elective military and civil commands, often, however, clearly furthering a factional and family agenda while in office.[5] This is when the global dynamics in the whole central Mediterranean underwent a radical change: Carthaginians and Syracusans in Sicily (quickly followed by some peninsular states) began engaging in a territorial expansionism that aimed at lumping together entire states and at the creation of directly controlled colonies (unlike the politically independent colonies they founded in the ninth–sixth centuries BCE).[6]

In this period, Rome attacked head on a major Etruscan state, Veii, which was its closest neighbor across the Tiber. Veii fell after years of war (in which Rome for the first time kept its army in the field year round and paid it a salary) and it was eliminated as an independent polity, an unprecedented act in central Italy. Many of its citizens were relocated to Rome, where they soon, however, received equal rights as the original Romans. This precipitated profound structural changes as the resulting new state needed to adapt

---

[4] A. J. Ammerman, "On the Origins of the Forum Romanum," *American Journal of Archaeology* 104 (1990), 627–45.

[5] T. J. Cornell, *The Beginnings of Rome* (London: Routledge, 1995).

[6] A. M. Eckstein, *Mediterranean Anarchy, Interstate War, and the Rise of Rome* (Berkeley: University of California Press, 2006).

quickly to a dramatic increase in its territory. Indeed, the archaeological record shows a sharp increase in the number and density of small farms in the period after the conquest, traditionally interpreted as those of Roman colonists. We now know, however, that the spread of small-scale farming is a broad central Mediterranean trend, not limited to the small areas of initial imperial expansion,[7] but rather connected with a sharp increase of specialized crafts and with the growth of urbanized areas everywhere, two processes that required a greater food surplus. It can even be posited that the high-energy transformation involved in imperial expansion was only made possible by the agricultural intensification that immediately preceded it.

From the start, Roman policy in the conquered human landscapes seems to have been an inclusive one, leaving existing local power structures in place and broadening the base that was subject to taxation and to the army draft. Rome's expansion quickly picked up its pace after Veii's destruction, a harsh treatment that was only repeated in strategic locations like Carthage or Corinth. At the other end of the spectrum is the policy toward Gabii, a Latin state as close to Rome as Veii, with which Rome struck an "equal" (that is, balanced) treaty that would later become a model informing hundreds of similar agreements with city-states around the Mediterranean. Essentially, during the fourth and third centuries BCE, the Roman Empire extended rapidly in peninsular Italy by means of a vast number of separate one-to-one treaties with the other cities, without the creation of an explicit confederation or of a clear imperial political infrastructure. Significantly, Romans kept referring to them as allies. They had been induced to enter into agreements through a combination of means such as negotiation, military threat, actual war, offers of protection against a common enemy and interference in their internal affairs. The Roman senate and the army commanders displayed a remarkable flexibility and flair for ad hoc diplomatic solutions with each separate polity, resulting in a highly complex mosaic of reciprocal obligations between Rome and each of its allied states. Therefore, the received idea of a mighty war machine making mincemeat of everything in its path is largely a Romantic-century fantasy that finds little confirmation in the ethnohistorical sources and even less in the archaeological record.

---

[7] P. A. R. van Dommelen and N. Terrenato (eds.), *Articulating Local Cultures: Power and Identity under the Expanding Roman Republic* (Portsmouth, RI: Journal of Roman Archaeology, 2007).

What is true instead is that all the main foci of expansion in the central Mediterranean at this time (Rome, Syracuse, Carthage, Macedonia) were benefiting from a snowball effect that made the next conquest more likely after each annexation, thanks to increased taxation, tribute, army draft, and to general economies of scale in the growing empires. However, expansion fed expansion in different ways, and the growing competition among empires played out in their efficiency in pooling imperial resources, much more than in pure military confrontations. Here, Rome had a distinctive advantage in its deeply rooted policy of admitting foreigners into its citizen body, as contemporary Greek rulers themselves had to concede. The population estimates for this period show an exponential growth that vastly exceeds the potential of fertility in pre-modern societies. Thus, rather than imagining ethnically pure Romans taking over Italy, it is clear that, with political nimbleness and no ethnic exclusiveness, urbanized communities were quickly co-opted and persuaded to identify with the conveniently vague and flexible concept of expanding Roman rule.

A consideration of Rome's expansion pattern in peninsular Italy is also revealing of the deep logic of the process. Far from concentrically expanding like an oil slick, Rome reached out to other major cities within 50 kilometers of the western coast, that is, the cradle of Iron Age Italian urbanism, along existing lines of communication. Its priority was clearly to have the other peer polities brought into its expansionistic bid as soon as possible. Non-urbanized, upland areas toward the spine of the peninsula were left to be dealt with later. As early as the fourth century BCE, Rome was far more worried with 1,000-kilometer-distant Carthage (with whom it had political and commercial treaties) than with the central Apennines, which were only 100 kilometers away but were mountainous and rural. Even the eastern coast of Italy, which was only very sporadically urbanized, although not far by way of sea (and only 200 kilometers away as the crow flies) figured much less prominently in the early narratives and in the archaeologically attested circulation or prestige goods than far-flung southeastern Spain or even the Nile Delta, which were important international commercial nodes.

In the rush to link together the main states of the central Mediterranean, Rome had a significant geographic advantage over its competitors. Being in a dense concentration of cities reduced the land surface costs in the early stages of the expansion, and meant that the empire did not have to rely exclusively on maritime routes like Carthage. For centuries, the core of the Roman state would be represented by a stretch of c. 300 kilometers of the western coast, extending 50 kilometers inland and with Rome at its center.

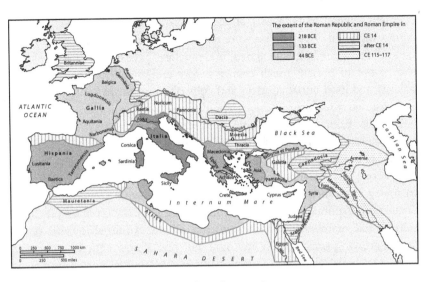

Map 25.2 Rome's expansion.

Other states scattered around the coasts of the Tyrrhenian Sea (bounded by Italy, Sicily, Sardinia, and southern France) would be progressively tied to that core in a relatively compact assemblage. Desert-bordered Carthage necessarily had to put together a much more disjointed and far-flung empire (albeit commercially a very productive one), while expanding Greek cities like Syracuse had never invested enough in the Italian hinterland and its inhabitants to be able to integrate it effectively (Map 25.2).

While Rome evidently prioritized existing cities, it also spread urbanism with the creation of colonies, which had the primary function of bringing into existence a new state that, from its birth and by definition, was a member of the alliance, rather than that of military outposts manned by ethnic Romans. A large number of Roman colonies of this period were founded in poorly urbanized areas of inland and eastern Italy. Quite a few, however, were placed inside existing urban systems (and even sometimes on top of existing cities), thus increasing even further the density of the urban network in western central Italy. Wherever they happened to be, they were also connected with a reorganization of the landscape around the new city. Each colonist family was connected with a parcel of land of a certain size to qualify for political rights, and cadastral systems were put in place to keep much better track of land ownership than before. Recent studies have shown that locals (as well as members of other allied communities) were routinely invited to be a part of the new polity and it is likely that land confiscation and dispossession were not as widespread as traditionally maintained.[8] Farm buildings and agricultural practices have been archaeologically shown not to present much change before and after the foundation of a colony, and local burial customs and cults often persist too.

A distinctive feature of Rome's colonies was that their inhabitants, besides being full citizens of the new city, also received some form of intermediate (or more rarely full) citizenship of Rome. Similar grants were also routinely made to allied communities to reward their continued loyalty to the federation. These rights typically included the ability to relocate to Rome, to marry and inherit from Romans, and to trade with Romans under the protection of Roman law. Voting rights were eventually given as a recognition of full membership in the budding empire. Unusually, freed slaves (a fast-growing social group in Rome and one almost entirely composed of non-Romans) were treated essentially in the same fashion. In this way, Rome's stakeholder base constantly expanded, offering to new allies tangible examples of the benefits of integration, which were much better than those offered by any competing Carthaginian or Greek imperialist. Another key trait of Rome's expansionist offer was that the political order it promoted was guaranteed to be slanted in favor of landed elites, whatever their ethnicity or background. Access to the senate was restricted to land-owners, and upward social mobility seems to have been much less common than horizontal elite mobility (a phenomenon that existed already from the early first millennium BCE). Non-Roman nobility from across the peninsula moved to (or had a foothold in) Rome with apparent ease and often reached the highest offices and the senatorial rank. The Roman army, led by the same people, was ready to come to the rescue of elites in allied communities and squelch social unrest and uprisings, which significantly happened more often than rebellions or secessions of entire incorporated cities against Rome.

In the late third and especially in the second century BCE, the expansion of Rome increasingly pushed up against other competing territorial empires. This prompted a series of prolonged wars that were different in their nature from the ones Rome had fought in Italy. They often escalated into desperate struggles for supremacy and always resulted, sooner or later, with the utter defeat of Rome's opponent. This was the fate of all the states that had arisen from the break-up of the empire of Alexander the Great, but also of

---

[8] G. Bradley and J. P. Wilson (eds.), *Parallels and Contrasts in Greek and Roman Colonisation: Origins, Ideologies and Interactions* (London: Duckworth, 2005).

emerging central Mediterranean powers like Syracuse or Carthage. By the 140s BCE, Rome controlled most Mediterranean coastal cities, whose political and economic structures were easier to integrate and win over with offers of citizenship and other benefits, resulting in a far-flung empire that had avoided and leapfrogged over the less digestible parts. At the same time, the reach of urbanism kept growing thanks to colonial foundations in areas like the Po Plain, which would become (and still are) among the most densely settled in Europe, paving their way for a fuller participation in the political life of the empire. Outside Italy too, once a city became part of the alliance it would typically maintain much of its local power arrangements and therefore adapt to the changed circumstances with relatively little turbulence, but it would be within a province. These administrative districts were assigned to yearly governors who were in charge of taxation, keeping the order, arbitrating between cities, and monitoring the frontier.

As earlier in Italy, for this phase too there is little archaeological evidence that the Roman conquest caused wholesale relocation of agricultural populations or land distribution to ethnic Romans. By far the most blatant symptom of the changed situation is represented by the vast infrastructural investment made by the central government (and to a lesser extent by provincial ones) in the countryside. An extensive network of roads was painstakingly built, not all going to Rome. The new lines of communication sometimes followed and improved existing routes but often cleared natural obstacles, such as the Apennines or the Alps, opening up brand-new opportunities for trade and contact. The magnitude of these projects contrasts sharply with the relative modesty of the public construction inside contemporary Rome. Other infrastructures included aqueducts (primarily to supply Rome, but also other cities), drainage channels, land reclamation, and much else. Piracy and brigandage were actively repressed and eventually eliminated, with the same goal as the road improvements. All these efforts characterizing the new Roman state from an early stage of its development clearly impacted a number of areas that were typically beyond the reach of individual cities, almost as if the aim was to offer a tangible proof of the advantages deriving from membership in the empire. As a general strategy, Rome let things be inside existing cities and in their immediate hinterland, and intervened instead at the interstices between city-states, connecting, integrating, facilitating, servicing, and arbitrating between them in exchange for the taxation that it extracted.

Moving toward a continental empire

Once the Mediterranean urban world had been almost completely unified under Rome (with the exception of Egypt and other bits of the African coast), it collectively turned its renewed attention to the vast continental expanses of western and central Europe and of western Asia. For centuries, Mediterranean traders and travelers had ventured up river valleys and across plains and plateaus to exchange finely crafted products and exotic delicacies such as wine with raw materials, slaves, and rare resources such as amber. It was a system that worked well, but it constrained the volume of trade and subjected it to outside variables. In addition to that, many pre-urban polities in these areas were finally moving toward statehood as a result of an endogenous process that had undoubtedly been helped along by the prolonged interaction with the Mediterranean. Fortified hilltop nucleated settlements in central France and Spain, for instance, were significantly growing in numbers, size, and internal stratification in the course of the late second and early first century BCE. These changes were long believed to have been directly produced by the Roman conquest, but finer chronological resolution now shows that they instead pre-dated the arrival of the Roman army, sometimes by just a few decades.[9] It appears that the Mediterranean urban alliance saw an opportunity for further expansion in the developments that were bringing new regions closer, making them "ripe" for a tighter form of integration. At the same time, there is no doubt that as they came in contact with these evolving polities, the Romans and their Mediterranean allies met more resistance and had to face much more post-annexation instability. Areas of central Spain (but also of France and even Liguria in Italy) had to be militarily dealt with again and again, suggesting strongly that for these people participation in a territorial empire was not the obvious option that it had been earlier on for the city-states.

In military terms, the push inland of the Roman Empire required a very different strategy from the ones used along the seaboard. Moving the army (and especially supplying it) could not be done by sea, thus slowing down the pace and the frequency of the campaigns. These tended to become multi-year affairs in distant parts of the world, where the yearly rotation of the elected military leaders (which usually involved a reorganization of the army and of its staff) was eminently impractical. Commands had therefore

[9] G. Woolf, *Becoming Roman: The Origins of Provincial Civilization in Gaul* (Cambridge: Cambridge University Press, 1998).

to be extended and provincial governors often played an important role, staying in the field with the same army for long periods, essentially free from senatorial supervision, at least until they returned to Rome. The very structure of the army was radically changed, eliminating the last vestiges of the original stratification of soldiers by social class, emphasizing instead veterancy and military rank acquired in the field. The conquest, which had proceeded along the coasts at a sustained and constant pace so that few years had seen no gains, now became much more unpredictable, alternating massive leaps and bounds with long periods of stable boundaries. Necessarily, expansion could only come from long expeditions that had to be planned well in advance and that, when successful, often led to the incorporation of areas many times the size of the whole of peninsular Italy (see Map 25.2).

Rome's administrative strategy in the continental regions always built, at least initially, on networks established earlier by other city-states. Thus they clearly benefited from the inroads that the Carthaginians had made in Andalusia along the Guadalquivir Valley and that the Greek city of Massalia (Marseilles) had made up the Rhone Valley. There too, the foundation of new cities and the reorganization of the rural landscapes had been fundamental tools to interact with the local communities and to make them more compatible with and interested in the Mediterranean world. The Roman effort, however, was much more sustained and, crucially, made space both for local agency (which was in a very dynamic phase anyway) and for the participation of individuals from all the cities around the empire. Again, infrastructural investments were not spared, and they sped up the process of integration and economic development. New provinces set up in this phase, like Provence or Hispania Citerior in eastern Spain, quickly became a full part of the global imperial machinery, effectively and permanently pushing out the boundaries of the Mediterranean world.

As the first century BCE progressed, the empire underwent even deeper changes in many areas. The political republican system collapsed, crushed by the emergence of large professional armies that were firmly loyal to the commanders under whom they had served for long periods. Clearly, the geographic and cultural mass of the alliance had become too big to be guided by officials elected every year in Rome, especially since there was a fast-expanding proportion of people around the empire that had voting rights but were de facto disenfranchised by their distance from the elections held in the capital. Rome's policy of political inclusiveness had reached its intrinsic spatial limitations. From then on, Rome was ruled by military dictators, called emperors, whose primary power base was within the army, and especially in the troops stationed near the capital. While military glory had certainly been instrumental in the ascent of the earliest of these condottieri, such as Marius, Pompey, or Caesar, from the first century CE onwards triumphs were no longer indispensable to obtain or maintain power, as the relevance of civilian public opinion declined. Military achievement did occasionally help usurpers, such as Vespasian or Septimius Severus, but as a powerful drive for new campaigns it lost much of its appeal. After 100 BCE, the Roman army and its generals were engaged in intestine and inglorious wars more often than they were deployed in external ones, and certainly with far greater casualties. Civil strife and factionalism had always featured in the history of the empire to a remarkable extent, but once these changes took place they largely dominated the political life (with the exception of some eighty years in the second century CE), often relegating foreign affairs to the distant background. Even the conquest of Egypt, the last incorporation of a major Mediterranean state, was merely a by-product of a protracted civil war between competing Roman dictators and their semi-private armies.

In spite of its status as the capital of the largest Mediterranean empire of its time, down to about 100 BCE the urban infrastructure of Rome remained relatively unchanged. The same city walls were maintained, the Forum was not yet monumentalized, and most of the investment seems to have gone in the foundation of a number of subsidiary temples around the city (Map 25.3). Individual prominent clans promoted these rivaling projects, in keeping with Rome's nature as a factionalized oligarchy at the time. It was only when power became concentrated in the hands of military commanders that massive urban amenities were undertaken. Piazzas, theaters, and even more temples arose at the expense of private quarters, eventually turning the whole center of the city into a mosaic of public spaces and monuments by the late first century CE.[10] The Palatine Hill emerged as the site of a vast imperial palace that served as a model for many royal residences in medieval and Renaissance Europe (Map 25.4).

Throughout the first and early second centuries CE, the imperialist machinery lurched into expansive action at irregular intervals and for different reasons. Early on, advances were made in the Rhineland, along the Danube, and in the northwestern Iberian Peninsula, ostensibly to

[10] J. C. Coulston and H. Dodge (eds.), *Ancient Rome: The Archaeology of the Eternal City* (Oxford: Oxford University School of Archaeology, 2000).

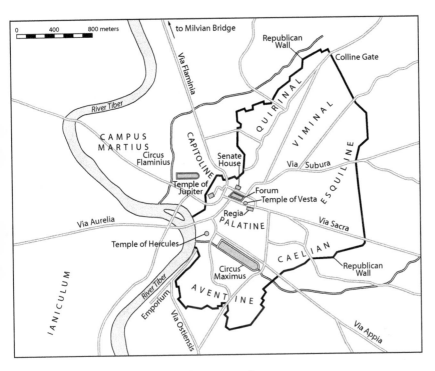

Map 25.3 Rome around 150 BCE.

reach more easily defensible frontiers. All these areas tended to be less compatible with the rest of the empire than any other previous province and offered much stronger resistance, occasionally causing heavy defeats. Decades later Rome suddenly invaded Britain, possibly as a result of developing political complexity in the southeast of the island as well as for its own internal political reasons. Again, areas that were culturally and structurally very different ended up within the empire and they showed a much greater propensity for instability and outright rebellion. Conquests of this kind were the exception rather than the rule: the empire would not have survived long if all the provinces had been as troublesome as Britain or Germany proved to be. The last great push took place around the 100s CE, with the rapid annexation of Romania and Mesopotamia. The former was culturally not unlike Germany and it was probably coveted mostly for its mineral resources, while the latter was fully urbanized and was wrested from the Parthians, a vast territorial empire that had grown out of Persia and whose western boundary with

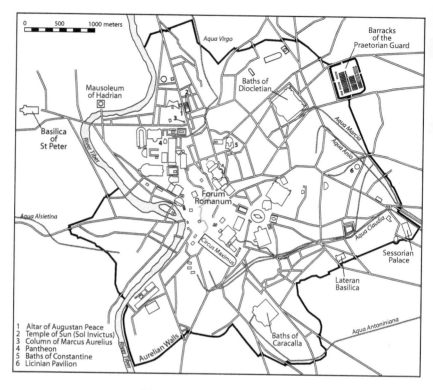

Map 25.4 Rome around 330 CE.

Rome moved back and forth many times. After this, there was no more expansion and Rome's foreign policy was almost exclusively limited to the defense of its frontiers and the repression of secession attempts, especially in the west. The city itself lost much of its centrality after about 200 CE, as alternative capitals were created by emperors who needed to be closer to the frontiers or to their competitors, and it was disastrously sacked in 410 CE.

Rome on the ground

Assessing the impact of the prolonged imperial expansion of Rome on the human landscapes it came to occupy has become harder in recent decades. For centuries, historians, politicians, schoolmasters, and Grand Tourists equated the diffusion of traits such as official inscriptions in stone, air-heated bathhouses, or legionary camps with a profoundly transformative experience. Idealists may have exalted Rome's civilizing mission, materialists measured a shift in the modes of production, and postcolonialists deploringly charted the demise of local traditions, but they all implicitly agreed that Rome had, for better or worse, effected a cultural revolution. In these reconstructions, the instances that were considered paradigmatic were the latter continental conquests (which often geographically overlapped with the modern nations where this scholarship was being created), rather than the more crucial Mediterranean ones. Now, mostly thanks to archaeological data of a finer quality, the picture has become much more nuanced, making it impossible to explain cases as disparate as those of central Italy, Morocco, and Austria with the same model. At the very least, a fundamental distinction must be drawn between the parts of the empire that were already urbanized before the conquest and those that became urbanized after it, or not at all. While they may show outward similarities, if one focuses on indicators like public architecture or inscriptions, the underlying cultural dynamics are profoundly different. Where cities already existed, they seamlessly continued to function as such, building on the commonalities that Mediterranean urban culture had developed throughout the first millennium BCE. In the rest of the empire, from the Apennine and Alpine ridges to the British Fens and Libya, cities or city-like local governments had to be founded, resulting in a much greater overall impact.[11]

Production and economy have been recently highlighted as an area where Roman expansion would have caused massive changes. In the agricultural sphere, for instance, large plantation estates called villas spread virtually everywhere across the empire, supposedly revolutionizing productive structures and agrarian power relationships by colonizing land seized from local small farmers. A closer examination of the villa phenomenon, however, shows that it originated in central Italy at the end of the second century BCE, centuries after the Roman conquest, and it was often linked to the status display of local aristocrats more than to investment cash-cropping. The latter appeared eventually and only in highly special areas connected with the supply of large cities, such as the immediate hinterland of Rome or the Mediterranean bread and oil baskets. Elsewhere, and especially in the outer

---

[11] S. J. Keay and N. Terrenato (eds.), *Italy and the West: Comparative Issues in Romanization* (Oxford: Oxbow, 2001); N. Terrenato, "The Cultural Implications of the Roman Conquest," in E. Bispham (ed.), *Roman Europe* (Oxford: Oxford University Press, 2008), pp. 234–64.

provinces, the existing peasant society was not replaced by gangs of chattel slaves, and data supporting agricultural intensification after the great expansion of the third century BCE are generally scarce. In terms of trade and mining, there is macroscopic evidence of economic development between the second century BCE and the second century CE. The frequency of Mediterranean shipwrecks peaked in this period and arctic ice cores indicate a vast increase in the smelting of lead-associated metals. Average height was apparently on the rise, suggesting better diet. Commercial hubs, such as Ostia at the mouth of the Tiber, reached a size and complexity that would not be seen again until the Industrial Revolution. These findings, however, need to be contrasted with the multitude of local contexts, which show little or no economic development. This is true of many continental areas but also of large parts of the urbanized East, such as continental Greece, where there is even a decline compared to the pre-conquest levels.[12]

The infrastructural network clearly continued to be a priority for the central government. Roads, bridges, aqueducts, drainage channels, dams, and water mills were built at a fast rate and with much improved engineering and building techniques. They certainly played the same role in the outer provinces as they did in Italy of offering tangible proof of the benefits of annexation. But their success naturally was a direct function of the need that the locals had for them, which was not everywhere as pronounced as in the Mediterranean. This was especially true where taxation was particularly unwelcome, for example, in areas that had no prior experience of it and that had little access to the coinage needed to pay it. Thus the same centrally instigated policies could have very different outcomes across the span of the empire. Another factor contributing to the heterogeneity of the empire is represented by its standing army. Once the constant expansion petered out, large contingents tended to be permanently stationed, typically along the frontier. The presence of thousands of people drawn from all over the empire and beyond, paid in cash, centrally housed, fed, and equipped obviously had a very significant local impact that would often exceed the one felt by less peripheral regions, away from the frontier.

To the spatial dishomogeneity of the empire, one must add the complex changes that took place once it had more or less stabilized, during the second through fourth centuries CE. After a long stint, the Italian Peninsula all but lost its centrality, along with treasured perks, such as its tax

---

[12] W. Scheidel, I. Morris, and R. P. Saller (eds.), *The Cambridge Economic History of the Greco-Roman World* (Cambridge: Cambridge University Press, 2007).

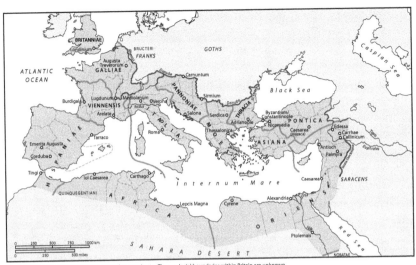

Many stretches of the boundaries shown are only approximate. The provincial boundaries within Britain are unknown.
Diocese of Britanniae comprises 4 provinces, Galliae 8, Viennensis 7, Hispaniae 6, Africa 7, Italia 12, Pannoniae 7, Moesiae 11, Thracia 6, Asiana 9, Pontica 7 and Oriens 16.

Map 25.5 The later Roman Empire.

exemption or demilitarization. Rome was only one of the many cities where short-lived emperors could set up their court. The eastern, Greek-speaking half of the empire, destined to outlive the western one by about a thousand years, experienced renewed development and went on improving its urban and extra-urban infrastructure, which elsewhere had started to decline. Italian wine and oil stopped being widely exported overseas, replaced by Spanish, African, and Oriental exports. Byzantium and Alexandria emerged as the new political, economic, and cultural hubs of the Mediterranean world. In short, the center of gravity slowly shifted back East, bringing the experience of Rome to a close and leaving continental Europe to its own distinctive historical trajectory (Map 25.5).

The distinctiveness and paradigmatic value of Rome

Stepping back to consider ancient Rome in its broader historical context and among other empires immediately reveals an apparent paradox. On the one hand, few political formations have had the same name recognition in our consciousness, or have figured so prominently in our political discourse, in our cultural imagery, and in the architecture of our cities. And yet, the scholarship on Rome has remained largely insulated from the

529

great intellectual syntheses on complex societies. For instance, state formation studies hardly ever consider Italy in its near universal comparisons, and the same is true for historical anthropology and sociology. Perhaps because of its exceptional value as a paradigm of imperial discipline and organization, the Roman Empire could not be analyzed with the help of general theories prevailing in the social sciences, nor brought to bear on them. The few times that this has happened, the results have made as little impression in the specialist literature as in the broader one. In light of this, it is essential to evaluate how unusual Rome actually was, once it is freed from its nineteenth-century encrustations and it is measured on the same scale as other comparable entities. To be sure, some defining elements appear to be rather common. Urban centrality, land-based taxation, army draft, provincial administration, specialized palace bureaucracy, performance of power, imperial cult, to name just a few, can all be found in many large territorial states. Other features, as it is to be expected, are less typical but far from unique, such as the primacy that was given, at least formally, to land-based wealth or the role that legal litigation had in elite transactions.

Surprisingly, one trait that is not a part of its stock image but may set Rome apart from many other empires is its ethnic and cultural inclusiveness. Having fashioned a very hazy concept of their own identity, the expanding Romans focused primarily on sociopolitical and citizenship status to determine who had a stake in the empire. Largely ignoring background, language, skin color (or other physical traits), religion or customs, the newcomers to the empire were only assessed in terms of their local rank, their land ownership, their urbaneness (*urbanus* meant civilized in Latin), and their willingness to participate in the imperial venture. By admitting millions of people into its citizenship over the course of five centuries, Rome ceased to exist as an ancient city in the proper sense of the word and became an exploded political entity whose local administration overlapped with the imperial one, whose electorate extended to the ends of the world, whose culture was conflated with a hybrid patchwork of ideas woven across millions of square kilometers. There is little doubt that those who were changed the most by the conquest were the Romans themselves.

FURTHER READINGS

Aldrete, G. S., *Floods of the Tiber in Ancient Rome* (Baltimore: Johns Hopkins University Press, 2007).

Ammerman, A. J., "Environmental Archaeology in the Velabrum, Rome: Interim Report," *Journal of Roman Archaeology* 11 (1998), 213–23.

Badian, E., *Foreign Clientelae, 264–70 B.C.* (Oxford: Clarendon Press, 1958).

Champion, C. B., *Roman Imperialism: Readings and Sources* (Malden, MA: Blackwell Pubblishers, 2004).

Coarelli, F., *Rome and Environs: An Archaeological Guide* (Berkeley: University of California Press, 2007).

Dyson, S. L., *The Roman Countryside* (London: Duckworth, 2003).

Giardina, A., and A. Vauchez, *Rome, l'idée et le mythe: du Moyen Age à nos jours* (Paris: Fayard, 2000).

Harris, W. V., *War and Imperialism in Republican Rome, 327–70 B.C.* (Oxford: Oxford University Press, 1979).

Laurence, R., *The Roads of Roman Italy: Mobility and Cultural Change* (London: Routledge, 1999).

Millett, M., *The Romanization of Britain: An Essay in Archaeological Interpretation* (Cambridge: Cambridge University Press, 1990).

Osborne, R., and B. Cunliffe (eds.), *Mediterranean Urbanization 800–600 BC* (Oxford: Oxford University Press, 2005).

Potter, D. S., *The Roman Empire at Bay: AD 180–395* (New York: Routledge, 2004).

Schiavone, A., *The End of the Past: Ancient Rome and the Modern West* (Cambridge, MA: Harvard University Press, 2000).

Torelli, M., *Studies in the Romanization of Italy* (Edmonton: University of Alberta Press, 1995).

Wallace-Hadrill, A., *Rome's Cultural Revolution* (Cambridge: Cambridge University Press, 2008).

26

Imperial cities

GERARDO GUTIÉRREZ, NICOLA TERRENATO,
AND ADELHEID OTTO

Looking at cities that were at the center of empires necessarily involves paying particular attention to issues such as political structures, expansionism, state formation, economic interdependencies, ideological hegemonies, and much else. In other words, imperial cities necessarily represent intricate intersections of power, cultures, and landscapes, and can only be understood within their broader geopolitical and human context. The present chapter aims at doing precisely that by drawing primarily on the cases provided by great imperial cities in three different cultures: Rome, Tenochtitlan, and the various Assyrian capital cities. As is well known, empires have been far less clearly and explicitly theorized than states in comparative terms, but they are generally understood as resulting from the aggregation of existing states (with the possible addition of other simpler polities). As a result, it seems reasonable to treat cities in empires as a special case in the general relationship that cities have with states – an issue, however, which is still actively debated and remains somewhat controversial in different theoretical frameworks. While, in fact, in some areas and periods urbanization has been equated with the emergence of states, to the point of treating them as the same phenomenon (this is the case in much of the Mediterranean, for instance), most comparativists have tended to disassociate the two processes.[1] This was based on the observation that there are instances of states in which there are no recognizable cities[2] and of cities that do not belong to or precede early states.[3]

---

[1] See, for instance, Linda R. Manzanilla, "Early Urban Societies: Challenges and Perspectives," in Linda R. Manzanilla (ed.), *Emergence and Change in Early Urban Societies* (New York: Plenum Press, 1997), pp. 3–39.

[2] For instance, in some cases of sub-Saharan African states: Daryll Forde and Phyllis M. Kaberry (eds.), *West African Kingdoms in the Nineteenth Century* (London: Oxford University Press, 1967).

[3] A claim that has been made for some large Old World pre-Bronze Age sites such as Tell Brak or Hamoukar; see Mitchell S. Rothman, "The Local and the Regional," in Mitchell

While in theory empires may not necessarily involve cities, few states and even fewer, if any, empires have existed without the presence of large and powerful cities. Even the complex, nomadic conquering societies that emerged from the vast steppes of Central Asia ultimately appropriated large existing cities as the focus of their horse-driven empires (for example, Beijing and Baghdad), or created their own imperial cities (for example, Moscow). Therefore, it is on this basis that the category of imperial cities is analyzed here, with specific reference to the interactions between these entities and the human landscapes in their hinterlands and, more generally, with the empire that is controlled by them.

The empire in this perspective is a higher-order, "superlative" state formed by the aggregation, incorporation, or integration of other states, frequently but not exclusively by military means. In their historical development, empires display common traits, such as their frequently becoming the largest political organizations within their regions and time periods, with some of them reaching continental or sub-continental scale. When empires are considered comparatively, however, it appears clearly that there is a strong degree of variability among them. The expanding polity that incorporated other groups can end up being politically organized in a myriad of different forms, and this of course impacts the subordinate polities as well, as will be discussed below. There is also strong diversity in the role that technological or organizational superiority can have in affecting the balance of power within an empire. There have been cases of conquest driven by mobile or sedentary groups with lesser technologies and simpler forms of organization at the expense of more politically "advanced" state formations. At the other end of the spectrum, more sophisticated imperial cores have often exploited dominions characterized by lesser complexity.

Why these imperial societies have emerged and how they have managed to impose their domination over many different peoples and over vast extensions of the globe are fascinating problems that have caused much ink to be spilled from antiquity to the present. As a first step toward exploring the rich spectrum of empires across time and space, many scholars have tried to create typologies based on supposedly diagnostic traits. For instance, Edward Luttwak[4]

S. Rothman (ed.), *Uruk Mesopotamia and Its Neighbors* (Santa Fe, NM: School of American Research Press, 2001), pp. 3–26.

[4] Edward N. Luttwak, *The Grand Strategy of the Roman Empire from the First Century A.D. to the Third* (Baltimore, MD: Johns Hopkins University Press, 1976). See also Terence N. D'Altroy, *Provincial Power in the Inka Empire* (Washington, D.C.: Smithsonian Institution Press, 1992).

proposed a few decades ago to distinguish between territorial and hege-monic empires. Territorial empires would focus their expansion and dom-ination on the conquest of lands and the resources contained in those lands, imposing a tight administrative control. Hegemonic empires, on the other hand, would impose their dominance over other groups without taking over the administration of the conquered territories in a significant way, and would simply extract tribute and resources with the assistance of local elites. Along similar lines, Michael Doyle[5] characterized empires on the basis of their formal or informal forms of control.

Theories of this kind, with their polar oppositions, were clearly influenced by Cold War era attitudes and expectations, and have tended to be replaced by more context-sensitive approaches. In the practice of controlling subor-dinated states, ancient empires would have had to resort to more flexible and varied strategies in different areas and times of their domains than any simple dichotomy can depict. Indeed, in the last decade or two, innovative scholars of early modern European empires have tended to advocate for more sophisticated analyses that could do justice to the staggering variety of the different cultural and political circumstances.[6] In parallel, archaeologists have been moving in a similar direction in their work on ancient empires, emphasizing local adaptations and complex interactions, especially between neighboring or competing empires.[7] A growing consensus is emerging that each empire needs to be studied within its own historical moment and particularities. Still, even in this changed perspective, there seem to be good intellectual reasons in favor of wide-ranging comparisons between empires. First, they are numerically far fewer than the thousands of states known in the history of humanity, arguably below one hundred. Then, they often tend to cluster in a limited number of core regions where they aggregate, fission, and succeed each other over very long periods of time. Because of this contiguity in space and time, imperial ideologies and ideas are often circulated and passed on, producing significant recurrences in different contexts. Indeed, sometimes ethnohistorical and semi-mythical narratives of empires of old can still affect the behavior of much later polities.

---

[5] Michael W. Doyle, *Empires* (Ithaca, NY: Cornell University Press, 1986).

[6] For instance, Anthony Pagden, *Lords of all the World: Ideologies of Empire in Spain, Britain and France c.1500–c.1800* (New Haven, CT: Yale University Press, 1995); and David Cannadine, *Empire, the Sea and Global History: Britain's Maritime World, c. 1760–c. 1840* (New York: Palgrave Macmillan, 2007).

[7] Susan E. Alcock, Terence N. D'Altroy, Kathleen D. Morrison, and Carla M. Sinopoli (eds.), *Empires: Perspectives from Archaeology and History* (Cambridge: Cambridge University Press, 2001).

Imperial cities

Since empires are unique, "superlative" kinds of political organization, imperial cities too should be seen as a special kind of urban form, having distinctive traits and markers in comparison with non-imperial settlements. This explains why, even if empires normally comprise many cities, the focus here is on the role of the primary imperial city, which is often referred to as the imperial capital, a central place where political, economic, and symbolic power take a material form in urban structures that represent the administrative and ideological institutions of the empire. It is crucial in particular to examine the connection between actual built environments and the material and ideal forces that generated them.

When the origins of imperial capitals are considered, it is immediately apparent that their emergence is frequently the result of a successful expansionist bid. Indeed, in many pre-modern cases, the imperial capital is simply a normal city[8] that manages to impose its control over its peers (as well as over less complex polities). Such was the case for Rome, for Tenochtitlan, and for Aššur, to stay within our examples, as well as many others, such as Venice, Carthage, or Cuzco. In these cases, the political institutions of these cities often have to be stretched and adapted to serve as administrative centers for a much larger group of peoples. They also have to grow at a dramatic pace, incorporating population from the dominions, a process that, as it has been argued in the chapter on Rome, can lead to an effective power sharing that provides a much broader and stable base for the emerging empire. Alternatively, imperial capitals can be founded once the empire has already reached a considerable size, either from scratch (as is the case for some Assyrian capitals, as well as many other ones, from Alexandria to Moscow) or by refounding existing regular cities and promoting them to a new and exalted role (for example, Constantinople) or finally by taking over capitals of empires that have been supplanted (for example, Ottoman Istanbul or Mongol Beijing).

Whatever their formation process, these capitals almost always tended to concentrate vast amounts of wealth from conquered regions far and close into relatively small areas. Such movements of resources typically enhanced and reinforced their status as the largest and the most sophisticated focal

---

[8] In some cultural contexts defined as city-states: Mogens Herman Hansen (ed.), *A Comparative Study of Thirty City-state Cultures: An Investigation* (Copenhagen: Kongelige Danske Videnskabernes Selskab, 2000).

points within complex networks and hierarchies of subordinated settlements over short periods of time. In the case of Tenochtitlan the acceptance and assimilation of external groups into the city played an important role in maintaining an effective program of imperial expansion, since demographically Tenochtitlan had several times more inhabitants than the average rival states around it. Rome's population too grew exponentially to reach a million as a result of similar processes. In material terms, this typically translated into a display of the newly acquired power by means of ambitious construction programs. Large palaces, lavish temples, impressive boulevards and plazas, complex networks of canals, and other sophisticated urban amenities are found densely packed within imperial capitals. These building projects are not only excessive in terms of their individual size and of their number, but also in terms of their quality relative to other forms of architecture. Enormous investments and efforts are made to achieve monumentality and excellence in every respect. All three of the cases of study presented in this section exemplify this unequivocally. The Great Temple and the pyramids of Tenochtitlan, just as the temples, fortifications, and palaces of Assyrian capitals, had no rivals in their world: The Assyrian king proudly named his palace at Nineveh, a miracle made up from more than 100 rooms, the "Palace Without Rival." The case of Rome, on the other hand, presents an interesting latency, as its nature of imperial capital did not manifest itself in monumental construction until a relatively late stage of its ascending parabola, essentially only when most of the expansion was complete and the power shifted to dynastic emperors.

A common trait to most imperial cities, in any case, was the pressing of art and architecture into the service of the dominant political ideology. The monumental structures themselves were often explicit in this sense, even simply in terms of the sheer scale of their displays. Colossal architecture and stone sculpture automatically proclaimed greatness and invincibility to the ruling group, to their subjects, and to their enemies at the same time. These projects in the capital attest to the ability of the empire to command the enormous labor required for the quarrying, the transport over long distances, and the erection of colossal stones. The topmost level of the carving and sculpting, typically done by the best artists within the confines of the empire, serves the same purpose in qualitative rather than quantitative terms. The imperial message is further reinforced and articulated through the visual arts. Very frequently, narratives of minor and major military successes are conveyed in sculpture and painting. Artists and patrons select and use iconography, motifs, styles, and public inscriptions as a medium to

celebrate past achievements of the empire and announce its future ambi-
tions. Monumentality is further complemented by the crafting and acquisition of fine transportable art that conveys symbolic power through the use
of abundant precious and exotic materials. The success or failure of individual emperors were displayed by the rate of continuous additions to the main
temple together with the burial of rich offerings coming from the newly
conquered regions. Here again, the imperial city further emphasizes its
exceptionalism by attracting the best craftsmen who master unique and
often secret technologies. The display of portable art in the imperial city (or
in a distant province) immediately signals the status of the settlement that
hosts it in the hierarchy of the empire. Imperial seals and insignia are carried
by imperial officers on objects and clothing. The display of such symbols
provokes respect and fear, thus facilitating the business of imperial administrators in the conquered provinces.

Imperial cities also often stand out because of the amount of urban
planning that is invested in them, when compared to ordinary cities. Piazzas,
marketplaces, avenues, gardens, game-parks, gates, and arches serve functional purposes as well as symbolic and propaganda ones, as they can
accommodate vast numbers of participants in religious and political ceremonies, business transactions, feasting, or recreational activities. Empires
tend to concentrate commercial and social exchange in the capitals and must
provide appropriate spaces for it. The primacy of the city, already signaled
by the monumental construction and the refined art, is further reinforced by
exceptionally spacious, impressive, and well-laid-out common areas.
Monumentality and planning are of course typically coordinated, with
broader and better-constructed thoroughfares leading to and showcasing
palaces, temples, pyramids, and gateways. These often are the setting for
processional routes, such as the Roman triumphal one along the Sacred
Way or the march of the captives to be sacrificed along the Ixtapalapa Street.
At Nineveh, the 34-meter-wide royal road led straight to the seat of the
emperor and the temples on top of the citadel. Long and wide causeways,
following ritually or politically significant alignments, might connect the
expansive open spaces, adding a sense of grandiose urban scenery. This
armature imposes an imperial order on the urban form and effectively
directs transit and movement along key vital points of the capital. Straight
lines converging in the distance on focal points, usually temples, palaces,
gardens, or sacred landmarks, create perspectives that capture the gazes of
the inhabitants of the city as well as those of its visitors. Pilgrims from all
over imperial domains can converge into capitals to experience veritable

hierophanies produced by the political and religious might embodied in their monumentality. More practical purposes can be found in vast engineering projects to supply the growing population of imperial cities. For instance, in the case of Tenochtitlan, its causeways functioned not only as streets, but also as dikes that collected vast amounts of fresh water in large collection ponds. This supply of water was regulated and used to irrigate the chinampa gardens and maintain an acceptable water level in the navigable canals. A sophisticated system of dams, canals, and aqueducts brought water from a distance of more than 40 kilometers to Nineveh, and Roman aqueducts are obvious examples.

The urban arrangements take different forms depending on whether the imperial capital was founded *ex novo*, grew slowly from simpler origins, was built on an existing city, or was taken over from a previous empire. In the first case, the planners had a free hand in designing a symmetrical, aesthetically pleasing, and harmonious complex. The tabula rasa offered by the virgin site is engraved with significant geometries – orthogonal, gridded, star-shaped – that celebrate the new political order without being impeded or clouded by other, older meanings and geographies. Such was the case of Tenochtitlan, Kar-Tukulti-Ninurta, and Dūr-Šarru-kēn in our cases of study. Other capitals, such as Aššur and Rome, instead grew slowly and organically as they established dominance over peer polities around them. Here the exceptional urban form is the end result of many smaller improvement projects carried out over many generations. Roads and piazzas are progressively widened, straightened, and redecorated, layouts realigned and regularized until the material city is considered to be worthy of its massively increased importance. In some such cases meaningful landmarks of the older city, as represented by ancient shrines, tombs, earlier fortification, palaces, sacred or natural features, cannot be moved or altered. There, the new urban layout must be arranged around such previous relics or they are completely subsumed within new buildings and precincts. This happened very frequently in the urban history of Rome;[9] at Tenochtitlan, the original foundational temple was covered by at least seven imposing superstructures. The temple of the god Aššur remained the religious and ideological center of the Assyrian empire for centuries.

[9] See for instance the case of the Black Rock in the Forum: Albert J. Ammerman, "The Comitium in Rome from the Beginning," *American Journal of Archaeology* 100 (1996), 121–36.

Ordinary cities that become capitals by imperial fiat often present similar processes except with an increased tempo, since the redesigning does not happen organically over long periods but rather as a sudden consequence of the promotion to capital status. In these cases the reorganization can be more structured and symmetric but the preexisting city still necessarily has a role in shaping the aspect of the new center of the empire. In seized capitals, finally, there is generally already a planned monumentality that needs to be reshaped to fit the political and ideological needs of its new owners. In the two last cases, urban planners and architects are often faced with a difficult balance between the conservation of existing landmarks and armatures and the exaltation of the present and future dominant ideology.

Imperial urban people

It is not only their physical form that sets aside the imperial cities from all other ones. The people who live there often represent an even more exceptional assemblage than the townscape surrounding them, in terms of resource accumulation, socioeconomic differentiation, functional specialization, cultural sophistication, ethnic composition, multilingualism, and much else. Precondition to the monumentality is of course the heavy flow of all kinds of wealth from all over the empire to the city at the center of it. Although most often remarked on by scholars, war loot, tribute, and taxes arguably are but the visible tip of the iceberg. Economic, human, and symbolic capital move to the center in massive quantities as a result, among many other factors, of elite and commoner migration, of group migration, of external investment and of internal growth. Successful imperial cities persuade elites everywhere that they cannot afford not to have a presence there without jeopardizing their status, merchants that they will find in the imperial capitals an insatiable market for their goods, ranging from slaves to exquisite fragrances and spices, prophets of exotic cults that they can find the audience that ignores them in their own land. Trade networks create another layer of centrality around the imperial capitals with exchange routes that can extend beyond the imperial frontiers. The wealth is as much in the imperial people themselves and in what they bring with them as it is in the literal coffers of the empire.

The convergence of the highest elites and the lowest beggars and enslaved prisoners in the same place necessarily produces a broader vertical socioeconomic range than anywhere else in the empire, which is often reflected in archaeologically visible private architecture. An equal if not greater variability is displayed horizontally in terms of functional and craft specialization. The state machine itself hires and trains special military forces, specific bureaucrats, and other expert civil servants. Hyperspecialized workshops, particular trades, unique productions can all be supported only at the intersection of elite demand for competing display. Complex religious and intellectual professions also tend to emerge, as high priests, seers, magicians, doctors, lawyers, engineers, astronomers, philosophers, artists, musicians, dancers, actors, chefs all find the discerning customer base without which they cannot exist at a high level of refinement.

The imperial kaleidoscope is particularly rich when it comes to identity, ethnicity, and language. Capitals are typically cosmopolitan, characterized by a veritable Babel of tongues, peoples, attires, rituals, mentalities, and mores. This further dimension of diversity can intersect in very complex ways with the hierarchies and specializations recalled above. Language and background can for instance be used to differentiate between social groups and ranks and be expressed through elements such as clothing, jewelry, or body markers. Moreover, it is generally assumed that the ethnic group that is responsible for the expansion automatically enjoys some privileges over those who were brought by force under the control of the empire. Recent studies that have been looking more closely at individual agents in this process often reveal more cultural permeability and power distribution than one would imagine, with subordinated elites often finding a way to mitigate (or even completely nullify) the disadvantage of having been conquered, for instance by infiltrating the dominant ethnic group in a variety of ways, from intermarriage to emulation.[10] At the commoner level, additionally, the size of imperial capitals typically balloons as a result of the constant inflow of people from the conquered provinces as prisoners, slaves, servants, laborers, or conscripts, and this automatically changes its demographic and cultural nature. Some version of the original idiom of the conquerors often becomes the official government language, as well as the lingua franca of the vast domains. But local communities often display a surprising attachment to their traditional tongues and dialects, especially at the commoner level, while the local elites can adopt bilingualism as a strategy that allows them to act as power and cultural brokers for their subordinates.

---

[10] For example, Martin Millett, *The Romanization of Britain: An Essay in Archaeological Interpretation* (Cambridge: Cambridge University Press, 1990); and Serge Gruzinski, *The Conquest of Mexico: The Incorporation of Indian Societies into the Western World, 16th–18th Centuries* (Cambridge: Polity Press, 1993).

Keeping together such disparate constituencies is probably the single biggest challenge that empires have to face. Coercion and threat may have had a critical role at the time of the conquest, but no empire can survive long without some additional cohesive force, typically found in the realm of ideology and religion. Legitimizing and justifying beliefs are constantly propounded by the center of power to all the participants in the empire. This "battle for hearts and minds" can take many different forms depending on the context, but it almost always includes the idealization of the imperial machinery, with a particular emphasis on its leadership. Positive moral attributes, such as bravery, nobility, wisdom, piety, fairness, are attributed in general to the victorious group and are unrivaled in the top echelon of the state, typically represented by monarchs. A monarch is often seen, appropriately for a "superlative" state that controls other states, as "king of kings." This is a title possibly first used for Tukulti-Ninurta I and then used in many other empires, from Persia to Ethiopia. In the Aztec Empire the *huey tlatoani* (the great speaker), who presides over many lesser *tlatoque* (those who speak) conveys a similar meaning. Rome (in spite of having coined the term "emperor") presents an anomaly in that it transitions to an absolute monarchy at a relatively late stage in its trajectory and the emperor acquires royal and divine status only in the third century CE, a couple of hundred years before the collapse.

The head of the state sits at the very top of the political hierarchy, very far from the next rung on the ladder. He is usually the highest magistrate of the empire and rules in matters of life and death. As a leader of his people, he is the apex of a complex network of followers. Among them are retainers who are in charge of the administration, the cult, and the military structure that maintains the imperial program. These imperial followers, who can be members of the ruling lineage, satraps, petty or puppet kings, oligarchs, bureaucrats, or elected officials, become more diverse and cosmopolitan as the empire grows and expands. The emperor takes precedence over everybody, with the possible exception of the highest god of the empire, unless of course he is himself a divine incarnation. In any case, thanks to his transcendent investiture, he is venerated and embodies all ritual and political powers. The emperor continuously displays his divinity (or his unique link to the major god) and earthly powers through complex ritual performances that recreate and confirm his covenant with the divine realm.[11] He highlights

---

[11] Nicole Brisch (ed.), *Religion and Power: Divine Kingship in the Ancient World and Beyond* (Ann Arbor, MI: Edwards Brothers, 2008).

his position by performing the primary ceremonies of the religious calendar, and the main sanctuary of the empire becomes the most sacred place in the empire, where all the major civic and religious festivals take place.

In the capital, the religious and political supremacy of the emperor (or in any case of the prime source of power) is materialized in space with the construction of palaces, senate chambers, tombs, and high courts. Temples are almost always associated with these compounds, clearly signaling the indivisibility of religion and rulership. The palaces in particular subsume and embody many of the higher functions that are at the core of the imperial administration. They are often clearly and tightly segregated from the rest of the city, for instance, walled off or physically placed in an elevated and dominant position. They contain the residence of the royal family, the treasury, headquarters of the administrative apparatus and of the military organization. The "Old Palace" of Aššur is a perfect example of the role that these built environments can have over hundreds of years, since even after other palaces had been built and the capital had been moved elsewhere, the Assyrian kings would return to be buried there. The regularity of the buildings and the order of the Assyrian cities may have also been due to ideological reasons, because in the Assyrian self-concept the king's duty was to establish and maintain the order of the world. In the case of the Aztec capital, the later emperors began the tradition of building their own palace and reusing those of their predecessors for different purposes. The main palace of the last emperor, Moctezuma, was located close to the main ritual precinct. Even though it was vast and multi-functional, it did not suffice to cover the new demands of the growing court and empire; thus Moctezuma created more specialized palaces outside the central area of the city as well as recreational gardens, hunting parks, and a zoo to display animals coming from all over Mesoamerica. In Rome (in spite of having originated the term "palace" from the name of the Palatine Hill, where the later emperors resided), it is only after the great fire of 64 CE that space is made in the center of the city for a palace of similar scale to those of other Mediterranean rulers. Until then, the primary materialization of imperial ideology was represented by the main city temple, in line with the original oligarchic nature of the political system.

The imperial hinterlands

Just as the capital city in many ways mirrors the imperial structure that generated or appropriated it, so the city itself transforms the hinterland around itself but also the furthermost countryside of the empire. The

administrative policies implemented by the leaders of course have reper-
cussions wherever they are applied. But, almost more importantly, all that
the city is in terms of its demography, economics, culture, technology, and
religion has an important effect on the rest of the empire. People, commodities, goods, and wealth converge there and this apparently bottomless
demand can stimulate growth, deplete resources, or change productions.
Improved (and often cheaper) trade routes change the nature and the size
of long-distance trade. Information, beliefs, and propaganda circulated by
the capital affect decision-making everywhere. Reviewing all these complex
interconnections is impossible, but some of the main patterns can be
outlined.

Highly visible, especially through the archaeological record, are the
infrastructural investments that are usually associated with the establishment and growth of the capital city. These include road networks that can
encompass the whole empire, as well exemplified by the Roman or Persian
Empires. Water supply, canals, dikes, river walls, and drainage systems are
also almost invariably required as the city's needs exceed the local resources.
The monumental remains of the Chapultepec or Claudian aqueducts are
eloquent mementoes of such a significant component in the process that
scholars like Karl Wittfogel even saw it as a prime mover for the process of
state formation that is a precondition to the emergence of empires.[12] More
generally, landscape modifications in the hinterland and further afield are
often undertaken, as happened with the lacustrine or lagoon environments
of Tenochtitlan or Venice, which became completely humanized with a
network of causeways and dikes to create artificial islands and water farms.
A similar process can be observed for the floodplains of Mesopotamia and
central Italy.

At the political and administrative level, on the other hand, empires tend
to reorganize the regions they conquer into provinces with their own
administrative centers, frequently recycling the former capital of a local
state for this purpose. The extraction of tribute in labor, kind, and taxes
from the rest of the empire is of course an important source of income for
the capital, but also has deep effects on the local taxpayers. The power
relationships between core and periphery are obviously asymmetrical, but
their economic consequences can range from exploitation and impoverish-
ment to an increase in the production of goods in demand or to the spread

---

[12] Karl A. Wittfogel, *Oriental Despotism: A Comparative Study of Total Power* (New Haven,
CT: Yale University Press, 1957). This view, however, has long been rejected.

of currency and more advanced exchange systems. Empires may vary widely in terms of their actual administrative practices (hence the recalled dichotomy of territorial versus hegemonic). The differences begin already in the immediate aftermath of the military conquest, with some empires entirely replacing the local power structure and looting and confiscating a large proportion of the resources, while others are content with imposing heavy tributes, payments, and levies but otherwise leaving the incorporated community to its own devices. Similarly, some empires are keen on imposing administrative overseers, like the Mexican *calpixque*, and on having governors sent in from the center, as happened for the later Roman provinces.

Most empires, in any case, rely heavily on ideological propaganda (as well as on actual consensus-building measures). The main message is that domination is beneficial over the long term for all the imperial subjects. This is not necessarily and not always completely false. The large-scale reorganization can actually prevent or mitigate regional competition and violence, which in turn can stimulate more production and trade. A similar effect can be produced by the increased demand, the central investments, and the improved lines of communication. There are also of course intended or unintended consequences for the rulers, from incorporating conquered people into the imperial network. The convergence of resources, information, and people to the core of the empire and to its capital city necessarily changes by degrees its original nature. Gods and other sources of symbolic power are appropriated from the defeated people, while culturally their very identity, mentality, and ethos are incorporated and blended into a newly emerging common worldview.

Epilogue

A trait that is common to many mature empires is the creation of additional capital cities as an answer to the growth of bureaucracy or to highlight the sacredness of the original capital, which then can become a purely ceremonial city. This delicate decision requires consensus and negotiation among the different relevant constituencies and can result in overt factionalism. It also requires the reallocation and expenditure of vast amounts of wealth that can easily test the economy and organizational limits of the empire. It is not a coincidence that, as exemplified by the case of Assyria or Egypt, these momentous actions are usually undertaken by powerful and charismatic emperors. In spite of that, in some situations the emergence of a second capital, typically at the opposite end of the dominions, is a clear sign of imperial weakness. It can mark the beginning of the end for the original capital, at least in its present form, but it can also be a harbinger of civil strife and of imminent fission (or even dissolution) of the empire. Described more generally by human geographers and spatial archaeologists as the transition from a concave to a convex rank-size curve,[13] the loss of primacy of the main city is often a trait of empire maturity, and it illustrates well the significance and diagnosis value of the capital for the overall health of the state around it.

What happens to empires after they peak has attracted at least as much historiographic attention as the first half of their parabola, from Gibbon onwards. As they become larger and more complex, empires seem to become more vulnerable. Once the zenith of expansion has been reached, the gradual and perhaps unintended assimilation of subjects can weaken the imperial systems in many ways.

Progressively, the periphery tends to appropriate and reelaborate the ideology, technology, military organization, and administration system of the empire to the point where the real and symbolic sources of imperial power are reduplicated in every province. Such redundancy can cause the pacific or violent splits, usually at times of political crisis at the core of the imperial society. In other cases, internal contradictions and factionalism in the imperial capital or its hinterland can trigger deep transformations, in which the subjects lose their original identity and loyalty to the empire. This is particularly typical in commoner groups who find themselves impoverished and disenfranchised by a voracious nobility or imperial bureaucracy. Yet other imperial societies find their end when they are absorbed by another larger empire, which either grew in one of their former provinces or beyond the frontiers. In situations like this the provinces usually fail to assist the metropolis with a calculated passivity or even by actually assisting the new invaders to defeat their former masters, as was the case with Tenochtitlan, where the imperial capital was defeated by a few Europeans assisted by tens of thousands of former imperial subjects. The process can then start again in a new empire with a highly dominant, waxing imperial city.

---

[13] Gregory A. Johnson, "Aspects of Regional Analysis in Archaeology," *Annual Review of Anthropology* 6 (1977), 479–508.

27

Conclusion: the meanings of early cities

NORMAN YOFFEE

At 4000 BCE Mesopotamian settlements were hardly a ripple on the alluvial plain of southern Iraq or in the foothills of the Taurus Mountains to the north in Syria. At 3000 BCE and thereafter a traveler on the roads or by boat in the rivers of Mesopotamia would have seen massive urban places surrounded by walls, with temples built on raised platforms, palaces, ceremonial precincts, and houses densely packed in neighborhoods. There were also gardens and orchards in the cities, and fields stretched beyond the city walls, flanked by canals and ditches. Our traveler would have been awed by the sight of an early Mesopotamian city, and the same can be said about a visitor to any of the early cities discussed in this volume. To the list of variables that "define" early cities[1] must be added one more: cities must be awesome.

Cities transformed the physical landscape of Mesopotamia, and they transformed the lives of Mesopotamians, citizens whose activities were routinized by streets, neighborhoods, plazas, work areas, ceremonial areas, temple and palatial complexes, and by the need for some, but not all, citizens to commute to outlying fields to cultivate crops and tend to animals. Mesopotamian cities were normally independent, fighting with neighbors over good land and water and access to transportation and trade routes, and were the central places in city-states, which consisted of several towns, villages, and farmsteads. There were rulers and ruled, local neighborhoods with community councils. People in the hinterlands came to cities for festivals, to submit required goods, and to receive materials produced by urban workshops. Elite Mesopotamians owned estates in the countryside and even houses in other cities.

Mesopotamian cities were very large, some of them over several hundreds of hectares in size and with several tens of thousands of inhabitants.

---

[1] See Chapter 1, this volume.

Since archaeologists are reverse architects, painstakingly destroying buildings in order to understand how they were built and what was left in them,
they work with surgical care. Thus, only small fractions of Mesopotamian
cities have been excavated, perhaps a good thing since techniques of excavation improve with time, and understanding of urban life grows as interpretations are refined and as material increases and analyses are sharpened.

But do Mesopotamian scholars know Mesopotamian cities if they know
Mesopotamia only? Today Mesopotamian cities are doubly ruined. First,
mudbrick, the basic building material in Mesopotamia, doesn't last and must
be constantly renewed or replaced. Cities rose as structures were leveled,
and new buildings were erected on the foundations of older ones. When
these early cities were abandoned, as they all eventually were, their remains
stood on the plain as large hills, occasionally with modern constructions
surrounding them or new settlements perched on them.

Then, as archaeologists have sorted through the layers of cities, destroying the remains of cities through meters of debris, they replicate the
activities of the past. Ancient cities themselves were scenes of ruin, constantly crumbling, being rebuilt, and they contained many sites of
abandonment.

Large-scale horizontal exposures of Mesopotamian cities are nearly
impossible due to the size of the cities and the mountains of stratified
remains in them. If only fragments of the Mesopotamian past survive, can
comparative studies contribute to the understanding of urban life in Mesopotamia? And can studies of Mesopotamian economics and politics, attested
in tens of thousands of cuneiform texts, which are found in the ruins of
cities, aid in the understanding of other early cities?

It is no surprise that the study of early cities, in Mesopotamia and
elsewhere, is in a beginning stage. Excavating a city is the hardest thing an
archaeologist can do. By definition cities are areally large and stratigraphi-
cally complex. Although Teotihuacan[2] can be mapped in a way that fills
Mesopotamian archaeologists with wonder and envy, only a small part of
Teotihuacan or any early city is or will ever be known. Can comparative
studies help us understand what early cities are like without essentializing the
concept of "early cities" or denying their distinctive qualities and histories?

The chapters in this volume highlight certain characteristic features of
early cities and how people lived in them. Thus, we trace the unmistakable

---

[2] See Sarah C. Clayton, this volume, Chapter 13.

and key importance of ceremonial events, procession ways, and sacred areas in cities, of information technologies, of transformations of urban land-scapes, and how cities transformed their countrysides and their economies, and not least of how new forms of power relations and inequalities of all sorts were invented in early cities. Although most of the chapters are quite detailed, much that archaeologists know about early cities cannot be depicted in this volume. We have not explored in detail urban topographies, the nature of class and social relations in neighborhoods, the forms of households and houses, agricultural practices and water systems, sanitation, the incidence of disease and morbidity, and the smaller and larger social and political changes over time, and the reasons for the collapse and abandon-ment of cities (although the persistence of some early cities, for example, Rome, Jerusalem, and Baghdad[3] are considered), and much else.[4]

This volume does provide hard-earned observations on important prin-ciples of organization in cities, and chapters compare the structures and functions of these principles across time and space. The comparisons are limited to the cities chosen for examination. The choices are imposed by the editor, whose purview is necessarily constrained, in part by cities where good information exists. Whereas some of the comparisons within the sections are traditional, others are meant to be provocative. Comparison, it hardly needs to be said, also implies contrast. By comparison one can ascertain how early cities differ and thus ask questions and structure research into why this is so. This volume is avowedly experimental; it seeks to know if we can compare cities and on what basis these comparisons are meaningful. It does not pretend to be the last word on the subject; indeed, it is practically the first attempt at comparing early cities on a global scale.

Scholars are normally well-advised – and so advise their students – to limit their research: to ask questions that can be explored with good data and to leave few loose ends that other scholars (such as reviewers) might say should have been considered. It is obvious that this volume about early cities and the comparative method does not exhaust our subject of comparing early cities. Those expecting a conclusion that is a "grand narrative" will be disappointed.[5] In the next section, I interrupt this

[3] See Nicola Terrenato, this volume, Chapter 25; Ann E. Killebrew, this volume, Chapter 20; and Françoise Micheau, this volume, Chapter 19.
[4] But see section in Chapter 21 on Cahokia on "Why was it abandoned?" For notes on collapse and persistence, see further in this chapter.
[5] Similarly, Penelope J. Cornfield, "Conclusion: Cities in Time," in Peter Clark (ed.), Cities in World History (Oxford: Oxford University Press, 2013), pp. 828–45.

synthesis, such as it is, with a meditation on the meaning of early cities in the present. I return in the final section of this chapter to our goal of comparing early cities without trivializing their distinct evolutionary trajectories and dismissing their characteristic institutions as epiphenomenal or uninteresting.

The meaning of early cities in the present

In the 2004 Olympics in Athens, the opening pageant included a dramatic display of the evolution of Greek history.[6] The show began with a gigantic "Cycladic figurine," at least 30 meters tall and made of plastic and other perishable material. "Real" Cycladic figurines, which date to the late part of the third millennium and early second millennium BCE, have been found in the Cyclades and other Aegean islands and are about 45 centimeters tall. They are light-colored, stylized representations in marble (mainly) of nude women, often with arms crossed at the waist, and have a flat geometric quality that reminds onlookers of Picasso's cubist figures. They became in the 1930s a focal point for the construction of Greek identity, promoted to replace in part Byzantine grandeur and the memory of Constantinople. The fame and affect of the figurines, embodying light, clarity of form, and even small scale served as a concise aesthetic concerning Greekness.

In the next scene at the pageant a centaur examines the beauty of the huge figurine, which then bursts open to reveal a Classical Greek torso. Finally, in the next scenes the torso is beheld by an actual human agent, a hero in a loincloth, who then jumps in a boat that travels center-stage. The implication is that the torso represents the birth of sculpture, mathematics, and logic, which the Classical Greeks delivered to the rest of the world. These scenes depict the unbroken line from the humble fishermen of the Aegean through Classical Greece (and especially Athens, where the pageant took place) to the present.

I owe the images I have described and their interpretation to a Greek archaeologist, Despina Margomenou, who is also interested in what the Olympic pageant leaves out of Greek history: the prehistory of northern

---

[6] I've developed some of this section, which I had been intending to use in this chapter, in a series of lectures, including an Astor Lecture at the University of Oxford. The bulk of that lecture now appears as Norman Yoffee, "The Earliest Cities and the Evolution of History," in Elizabeth Frood and Angela McDonald (eds.), *Decorum and Experience: Essays in Ancient Culture for John Baines* (Oxford: Griffith Institute, 2013), pp. 299–304.

Greece (Margomenou's field area), the Roman rule of Greece, and the period of Ottoman Turkish hegemony.[7]

Many of the cities in this volume loom important in the modern world today because they instantiate the images that form historical imaginations. Indeed, Susan Sontag wrote about history in terms of imagination and memory:

> What is called collective memory is not a remembering but a stipulating: that this is important, and this is a story about how it happened, with the pictures that lock the story in our minds. Ideologies create substantiating archives of images, representative images of significance and trigger predictable thoughts and feelings.[8]

These "collective memories" include what Johan Huizinga meant by his definition of history as "the way people render account of the past to themselves."[9]

In Mesopotamia, Uruk is the first city whose character we know in considerable detail.[10] Around 3200 BCE several tens of thousands of people lived in Uruk; it was the scene of extreme social stratification, high art, temple complexes, and writing. Although the evolution of cities in Mesopotamia also took place in the north, and just as early as in the south, the south was the heartland of high Mesopotamian culture. The evolution of Uruk and other southern cities was explosive, at least in archaeological terms. A few hundred years before Uruk there were only modest villages dotting the countryside. When the first cities (among them Uruk) appeared in southern Mesopotamia[11] at the end of the fourth millennium BCE, the countryside was effectively depopulated and villages were restructured as hinterlands of cities.

Cities became the locations of strangers, nodal points for military protection, homes of the most important shrines, as well as other things.[12] The

---

[7] See also Yannis Hamilakis, *The Nation and its Ruins: Antiquity, Archaeology and National Imagination in Greece* (Oxford: Oxford University Press, 2007).

[8] Susan Sontag, *Regarding the Pain of Others* (New York: Farrar, Straus and Giroux, 2003), p. 8.

[9] Johan Huizinga, "A Definition of the Concept of History," in Raymond Klibansky and H. J. Paton (eds.), *Philosophy and History: Essays Presented to Ernst Cassirer* (New York: Harper & Row, 1963), p. 8.

[10] Nissen, this volume, Chapter 6; and Emberling, this volume, Chapter 12.

[11] See Emberling, this volume, Chapter 12, for the development of northern Mesopotamian cities.

[12] As I have expressed it in Norman Yoffee, *Myths of the Archaic State: Evolution of the Earliest Cities, States, and Civilization* (Cambridge: Cambridge University Press, 2005). See Baines, this volume, Chapter 2.

state, that is, the administrative machinery of government in cities along with an ideology and its accompanying rituals, ceremonies, and materials was created in the evolution of cities. Cities, rulers, slaves, and inequality were not only natural but also timeless in the creation of this ideology.

After they were first excavated in the nineteenth century CE, the very name of Babylon and the glories of Assyria[13] have served as the images of historical greatness of modern Iraq. One remembers the many images of Saddam Hussein dressed as a Mesopotamian king.[14] The northern part of Iraq, now under Kurdish administration, is the scene of an international brigade of archaeologists who are investigating (among other things) the Assyrian Empire, which was "Mesopotamian," but also hostile to the Babylonians in the south. The meaning of Assyria for Kurds as opponents of southern Iraq is clear.

In modern India, culture wars (sometimes bloody ones) are waged over the meaning of Harappan/Indus Civilization cities.[15] According to certain parties, the original Aryans can be traced to the cities of Mohenjo Daro and Harappa (and others that are in modern India). This claim, of course, intends to cast Indian Muslims as invaders in the original and timeless Hindu homeland.

Teotihuacan,[16] like Uruk and other Mesopotamian cities, grew explosively from modest village predecessors and became the dominant, primate city in its region. In the 2010 celebrations of the 200th anniversary of Mexico's independence and the 100th year of the Mexican revolution, Teotihuacan, as well as Tenochtitlan, the Aztec capital,[17] were depicted as the roots of the modern nation.

In Guatemala, at the site of Tikal,[18] there is a fire pit near the base of the great Northern pyramid. It is a modern installation where modern Maya commemorate their historic connection to the Maya cities of the past.[19]

I can cite many other instances of how ancient cities form the historical memories and understandings of modern peoples and governments. But it is perhaps less obvious that these "memories" are not unbroken – in fact they are not memories at all. Uruk, Mohenjo Daro, Tikal, Yinxu,[20] Cahokia,[21] and

[13] Adelheid Otto, this volume, Chapter 23.
[14] Yoffee, "The Earliest Cities and the Evolution of History," p. 302.
[15] Carla M. Sinopoli, this volume, Chapter 15.
[16] Clayton, this volume, Chapter 13.
[17] Gerardo Gutiérrez, this volume, Chapter 24.
[18] Thomas G. Garrison and Stephen Houston, this volume, Chapter 3.
[19] Danny Law, this volume, Chapter 8.
[20] Wang Haicheng, this volume, Chapter 7.
[21] Timothy R. Pauketat, Susan M. Alt, and Jeffery D. Kruchten, this volume, Chapter 21.

other cities were unknown (or nearly so) to modern local people. They were discovered by archaeologists, and so archaeologists have been and continue to be the midwives in the formation of collective memories. They have furnished the images in which history is told and contested.

The fragility of early cities

In this section I return to the "social drama"[22] that existed in early cities. In Chapter 25, on Rome, by Terrenato and in Chapter 26, Terrenato and colleagues discuss the contrast among imperial cities. In Rome, conquered peoples were drawn into the orbit of Rome, and many people became Roman citizens. In the Neo-Assyrian case,[23] conquered people, such as the "Ten Lost Tribes" of Israel, who did not pay their tribute to the Assyrians, were deported in the tens of thousands to various parts of the Assyrian Empire. These workers built the new capitals of Neo-Assyrian kings and worked in the latifundia of Assyrian high officials and generals. There was little attempt to integrate these deportees into Assyrian society. Indeed, Assyrian rituals of state were embedded in the inner recesses of palaces and temples, increasingly remote from the people of Assyria, both Assyrians and others. As Assyrian kings were progressively concerned with becoming the center of Mesopotamian culture, for example by importing all manner of texts from repositories in Babylonia, they distanced themselves further from the overwhelmingly non-literate population in both cities and the countryside. Consequently, when Assyria was conquered by its enemies, and its capitals and other cities were destroyed, there was no reason for those in the countryside to rebuild Assyria, either physically or ideologically.

Many of the cities discussed in this volume were "fragile" in spite of the indisputably great power of kings and their courts. In China in the second millennium BCE, great cities emerged. Erlitou encompassed more than 300 hectares in area, flourished from c. 1900–1500, and had around 30,000 inhabitants.[24] Even larger was the subsequent city of Zhengzhou, 25 square kilometers with perhaps 100,000 inhabitants, in the time 1600–1400 BCE. In both cities there are palace compounds, craft workshops, elite cemeteries.

---

[22] Yoffee, this volume, Chapter 1.
[23] Otto, this volume, Chapter 23.
[24] The data are from Liu Li and Chen Xingcan, *The Archaeology of China: From the Late Paleolithic to the Early Bronze Age* (Cambridge: Cambridge University Press, 2012).

Finally, the last capital of second millennium BCE China, Yinxu, spread over more than 30 square kilometers and according to its excavator had a population of more than 100,000. Much is known about Yinxu,[25] since there have been large-scale excavations in several precincts, especially in craft workshop areas and in various cemeteries, including royal precincts in them. Also, as Wang makes clear, the oracle bone inscriptions document the power of a series of kings, c. 1275–1050 BCE.

The growth and extent of these early cities, the appearance of palaces and highly stratified workshop areas and cemeteries, and the vast extent of the walled cities (especially visible at Zhengzhou) have led archaeologists and historians to depict that enormous power of the kings and cities (and as capitals of states). Whereas this is not wrong, it does not follow that the power of the kings was uncontested or that such power led to the stability of the governments and the cities. Indeed, the short lives of the cities, and the records of the late Shang king at Yinxu, which show continuous campaigns of kings to control the hinterlands, indicate that the political structure of second millennium cities in China was highly unstable.

Can we pursue this scenario of instability in early cities in China by surveying other cities discussed in this volume? For those who read popular accounts of the Spanish Conquest of ancient Inka and Aztecs,[26] it may come as a surprise that both empires were riven by cleavage planes and that Native allies of the Spanish joined in the conquest of both empires. Gutiérrez[27] documents the growth of Tenochtitlan and the vast tribute exacted by the urban center on its hinterland that depleted the countryside. Tenochtitlan itself was the scene of intensive agriculture in chinampas and the large-scale construction of canals and bridges. Causeways marked the procession routes to the ceremonial center to which people streamed and tribute flowed. In the "collapse" of the empire, Native armies from conquered provinces allied with Spanish conquistadors to sack the city. Like Yinxu, Tenochtitlan was spectacular but short-lived. It was founded in 1325 CE and fell in 1521.

A roughly similar story accounts for the fall of Cuzco and the Inka Empire. Established in 1438 CE Native armies joined the Spanish to demolish

---

[25] Wang, this volume, Chapter 7.
[26] For example, Jared Diamond, *Guns, Germs, and Steel: The Fates of Human Societies* (New York: W. W. Norton & Company, 1999); and Jared Diamond, *Collapse: How Societies Choose to Fail or Succeed* (New York: Viking, 2005).
[27] Gutiérrez, this volume, Chapter 24.

Tawantinsuyu.[28] As Urton shows[29] the Inka rulers meticulously recorded the flow of people and goods in their empire. These "integrated" populations, however, quickly turned into Native armies that helped swiftly bring down the massively centralized and powerful but ultimately fragile political structure of the Inka state.

Cahokia was another city whose duration was brief, from the "big bang" of about 1050 to its virtual abandonment 200 years later.[30] Cahokia was a city in terms of its areal size, large population, and central place in its hinterland and wide influence in its region. Its ceremonial significance is undoubted. However, what kind of a city was it? Following Pauketat and others, Cahokia did not have a king or central government with specialized bureaucratic managers. Rather, leaders owed their power to their place in a kinship and ceremonial system. One is tempted to infer that Cahokia, home to various immigrant populations, did not develop state-like institutions and that attempts to integrate its diverse populations by traditional means didn't work. Although there are echoes of Cahokian rituals in later Native populations in the Cahokian sphere of influence, it seems that the actual memory of Cahokia did not survive. Might this suggest that Cahokia was a project that failed in the memories of later generations? In the "Chaco phenomenon" of the American Southwest, the great pilgrimage site that appeared as a "big bang" in the late ninth century CE and was abandoned in the early twelfth century, *was* remembered in modern Puebloan oral histories, but as a place cursed by the gods for the hubris of centralization.[31]

In Mesopotamia Nissen[32] discusses the development of the city from a modest place at the end of the fifth millennium BCE to the metropolis in which writing was invented at about 3200 BCE. Although Nissen does not continue the story, he has written elsewhere[33] that immediately succeeding

---

[28] David Cahill, "Advanced Andeans and Backward Europeans: Structure and Agency in the Collapse of the Inca Empire," in Patricia McAnany and Norman Yoffee (eds.), *Questioning Collapse: Human Resilience, Ecological Vulnerability, and the Aftermath of Empire* (Cambridge: Cambridge University Press, 2010), pp. 207–38.

[29] Gary Urton, this volume, Chapter 9.

[30] Pauketat, Alt, and Kruchten, this volume, Chapter 21. The phrase "big bang" is Pauketat's.

[31] Steve Lekson, *A History of the Ancient Southwest* (Santa Fe, NM: School of Advanced Research Press, 2008), p. 200.

[32] Nissen, this volume, Chapter 6.

[33] Hans J. Nissen, *The Early History of the Ancient Near East* (Chicago: The University of Chicago Press, 1988); Mario Liverani, *Uruk: The First City* (Chicago: The University of Chicago Press, 2006); and M. van Ess (ed.), *Uruk, 5000 Jahre Megacity* (Petersburg: Michael Imhof Verlag, 2013).

the phase in which the ceremonial precinct of Eanna flourished, the area was violently destroyed. Uruk became one city among many in the early third millennium BCE that struggled for independence and hegemony.

This story repeats for other Mesopotamian cities. In the middle of the third millennium BCE the city of Kish was supremely powerful in central Mesopotamia. There were palaces, ziggurats, royal cemeteries, and massive buildings that lined a presumed processional route in one major part of the site. A bare century later Kish was conquered by Sargon of Akkad, and it became a provincial outpost to other centers of power for the next 2,500 years. Otto[34] discusses the enormous constructions but rapid abandonments of several capital cities in the Neo-Assyrian period of north Mesopotamia.[35]

In a recent essay, Patricia McAnany and co-authors have studied the fragility in Maya cities[36] and their "collapse."[37] In particular they note that the royal courts in Maya cities in the southern Lowlands in the Late Classic period (c. ninth and tenth centuries CE) were abandoned, after which, in one to three generations, the sustaining populations migrated to other Maya cities, especially to the north, where new forms of less hierarchical political systems were invented. The authors focus not on factors of overcentralization or overpopulation in Maya cities, nor on increased warfare between cities in the Late Classic period, but on the "dynamics of diaspora." In fact there was a "staggering range of variation" in how the Maya cities were "de-peopled" and an equally "complex, multi-causal, multi-phased process of collapse." Although in some Maya regions the Late Classic was a period of climate change, in other regions there is little evidence of drought, deforestation, soil depletion, or overpopulation. McAnany and her colleagues suggest there was a "cascading effect" of local populations migrating from the collapsing Maya cities. If the royal courts could no longer command resources from tropical farmers in urban islands of low-density populations, each city with its focus on large-scale ceremonial constructions, including procession ways and ritual complexes, became increasingly fragile. The

---

[34] Otto, this volume, Chapter 23.

[35] Further reflections on the collapse of these cities in Norman Yoffee, "The Collapses of Ancient Mesopotamian States and Civilizations," in Norman Yoffee and George L. Cowgill (eds.), *The Collapse of Ancient States and Civilizations* (Cambridge: Cambridge University Press, 2005), pp. 44–68.

[36] Houston and Garrison, this volume, Chapter 3.

[37] Patricia McAnany, Jeremy A. Sabloff, Maxime Lamoreux St-Hilaire; and Gyles Iannone, "Leaving Classic Maya Cities," in Geoff Emberling (ed.), *Counternarratives: Agency and the Long-term in Archaeology and History* (Cambridge: Cambridge University Press, *forthcoming*).

remaining sustaining population in each city-state chose to migrate to areas more resilient to environmental changes. The demands of a political system, with its interlocking system of fractious alliances between royal courts and recondite royal rituals, grew increasingly remote from the concerns of farmers and merchants.

This scenario of collapse as emigration from unsustainable courts may suggest similar choices that were made by the people in Harappan/Indus cities. Although the evidence of "royal courts" is not so apparent as in Maya cities,[38] some cities (or at least Mohenjo Daro) had large centralized ceremonial precincts and required substantial agricultural support for the elites of the densely packed urban complex. In Angkor, another region of low-density urbanism, as in the Maya area, and characterized by an enormous array of ceremonial structures and with complex water systems,[39] exacerbation of the delicate political and environmental system may have led the sustaining population to abandon support of the religious and political elites. Can this scenario be extended to the city of Tiwanaku with its large-scale ceremonial constructions that were ultimately unsustainable when encountering environmental stress?[40]

Guy Middleton has refreshed the truism that "nothing lasts forever"[41] and argues that, "ancient polities were fragile entities."[42] This is particularly true of ancient cities. Their very size and complexity have led archaeologists to believe that early cities were "integrated" by rulers and by religious cosmologies, which were also ideologies of the state. Our survey of early cities in this volume questions the notion that such integration implies that everything was going well and that collapse occurred only when something bad happened, usually because of climate change (which scenario is clearly influenced by modern concerns with environmental degradation). Although archaeologists tend to talk about the "evolution of social complexity," as if complexity were the same as cooperation and integration, our examination of early cities shows that attempts at integration, which were really struggles for establishing control over the several social parts of a city and society, were the prelude to and often the cause of disintegration.

---

[38] Sinopoli, this volume, Chapter 15.

[39] Miriam T. Stark, this volume, Chapter 4.

[40] Janusek, this volume, Chapter 11.

[41] Guy Middleton, "Nothing Lasts Forever: Environmental Discourses on the Collapse of Past Societies," *Journal of Archaeological Research* 20 (2012), 257–307.

[42] Middleton, "Nothing Lasts Forever," p. 286.

The nature of fragility is highlighted by the appearance of the cities of Jerusalem, classical cities, and Baghdad. These cities were grounded in new kinds of continuities and were characterized by new kinds of overarching ideologies. These ideologies were not simply part of political systems and often were opposed to domestic politics. New kinds of elites, who did not owe their status to transient leaders, royal courts, and centralized bureaucracies and armies but to transcendental systems of values and beliefs, made these cities very different than the earliest cities. One might also ascribe the lack of extreme centralization in some of the cities portrayed in this volume, notably the Greek cities[43] and Jenne-Jeno,[44] and, perhaps in Harappan times, as a factor in the longer duration of these cities.

In the earliest cities, complexity was an irony; that is, these cities were products – with many variations – of the goal of reducing complexity, of making complexity into simplicity.[45] And thereby lay their fragility. Perhaps we should be studying not the "evolution of complexity" at all, but the "evolution of fragility."[46]

---

[43] Ian Morris and Alex R. Knodell, this volume, Chapter 16.

[44] Roderick J. McIntosh, this volume, Chapter 17.

[45] As James Scott has put it, making societies "legible" and so controlled by rulers: James Scott, *Seeing Like a State: How Certain Schemes to Improve the Human Condition Have Failed* (New Haven, CT: Yale University Press, 1999).

[46] And, of course, the exceptions to fragility.

Index

Printed in the USA
CPSIA information can be obtained
at www.ICGtesting.com
CBHW070237091224
18674CB00004B/74